HARMONY
OF THE
GOSPELS

HARMONY
OF THE
GOSPELS

STEVEN L. COX
KENDELL H. EASLEY

NASHVILLE, TENNESSEE

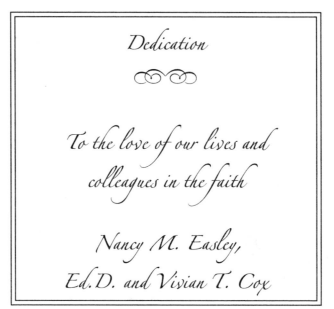

Dedication

To the love of our lives and colleagues in the faith

Nancy M. Easley, Ed.D. and Vivian T. Cox

HCSB Harmony of the Gospels
Copyright © 2007 by Holman Bible Publishers
Nashville, Tennessee. All Rights Reserved.

Holman Christian Standard Bible®
Copyright © 1999, 2000, 2002, 2003
by Holman Bible Publishers.

ISBN: 978-0-80549-444-0

Printed in the United States of America
1 2 3 4 5 6 10 09 08 07
R

Preface

The pattern of Gospel harmonization we have followed in the *HCSB Harmony of the Gospels* was begun by John A. Broadus in the nineteenth century and culminated in *A Harmony of the Gospels*, published in 1893. Broadus was aided with this volume by his protégé, A. T. Robertson. Over the next thirty years Robertson revised the Broadus harmony and published that revision in 1922 with George H. Doran Company and Harper & Brothers under the title *A Harmony of the Gospels for Students of the Life of Christ Based on the Broadus Harmony in the Revised Version*.

Both Broadus and Robertson brought their minds and their hearts to the study of the Gospels. Lifelong immersion in the Gospels had a transforming effect on both men. When Broadus died in March 1895, Rabbi Moses of Louisville paid him a remarkable tribute, saying that with Broadus's death, "The glory of Louisville has departed."

> Before I became familiar with Dr. Broadus, I knew Christianity only as a creed which seemed absolutely incomprehensible to me. I judged it mainly from the untold, unmerited misery, the agony of ages which Christian rulers and nations had entailed upon poor Israel under the impulse given by Christian priests and teachers. But when I learned to know and revere in Broadus a Christian, my conception of Christianity and my attitude toward it underwent a complete change. Broadus was the precious fruit by which I learned to judge of the tree of Christianity. . . . He greeted the most ordinary persons with gracious cordiality and utmost respect. Ah, it was his delight to honor and love men, and to inspire them with self-respect and moral courage. The central warmth of his great heart diffused itself as a genial influence in glance and smile, in clasp and word, on his family, his friends, his disciples. Broadus was an ideal American gentleman. He was perhaps the most amiable and lovable Southerner of his time." (*Life and Letters of John Albert Broadus* edited by A. T. Robertson [Philadelphia: American Baptist Publication Society, 1901, pp. 438-439].)

When the editors of B & H Publishing Group approached us about the opportunity to provide a twenty-first century update of this preeminent Baptist harmony, using the Holman Christian Standard Bible, we were both humbled and honored. We have followed the pericope numbering of Robertson's 1922 edition. As far as we know, this is the only Gospel harmony to include notes in the format now familiar in a variety of study Bibles. When we organized the task of writing the study notes, we assigned different Gospels to different writers. We have respected their individual conclusions and therefore, perhaps ironically, the reader will note that their comments occasionally conflict with each other. The same can be said for the writers of the essays. There is no claim to consensus among the writers of this Harmony. The result is, we believe, harmonious. For all of us, Scripture is the only infallible and inspired Word, so when we have disagreements with each other, this is a matter of scholarly divergence.

The editors are humbled to stand in the tradition of Broadus and Robertson. By no means do we believe ourselves worthy of the task, not because of their greatness but because of the supremacy of the subject, our Lord Jesus Christ. We are delighted to offer to the Christian community what we believe is the first Gospel harmony of the twenty-first century.

Soli Deo Gloria
Steven L. Cox, Mid-America Baptist Theological Seminary
Kendell H. Easley, Union University
October 1, 2006

Contributors

Daniel L. Akin, President, Southeastern Baptist Theological Seminary, Wake Forest, NC

Darrell Bock, Research Professor of New Testament Studies, Professor of Spiritual Development and Culture, Dallas Theological Seminary, Dallas, TX

James Bryant, Vice President for Academic Affairs , The Criswell College, Dallas, TX

Chad Brand, Associate Professor of Christian Theology (SBTS) Coordinator, Dept. of Bible and Theology Boyce College of The Southern Baptist Theological Seminary, Louisville, KY

Shawn Buice, Associate Professor of New Testament and Greek, Mid-America Theological Seminary, Schenectady, NY

Darrell Cornett, Assistant Professor and Chair, Department of Church History, Mid-America Baptist Theological Seminary, Germantown, TN

Steven L. Cox, Associate Professor of New Testament and Greek, Mid-America Baptist Theological Seminary, Germantown, TN

Stephen D. C. Corts, Associate Director, Starlight Ministries, Greer, SC

Gerald Cowen, Senior Professor of New Testament and Greek/Dean of Southeastern College of Southeastern Baptist Theological Seminary, Wake Forest, NC

David S. Dockery, President, Union University, Jackson, TN

Charles Draper, Associate Professor of Biblical Studies, Boyce College of The Southern Baptist Theological Seminary, Louisville, KY

Sidney D. Dyer, Associate Professor of Greek and New Testament, Greenville Presbyterian Theological Seminary, Taylors, SC

Kendell H. Easley, Director, Master of Christian Studies Program, Union University, Germantown, TN

Nancy M. Easley, Associate Professor, Education Director of Graduate Studies in Education, Union University, Germantown, TN

Dale Ellenburg, Academic Vice President and Professor of NT and Greek, Mid-America Baptist Theological Seminary, Germantown, TN

James Flanagan, President and Professor of New Testament and Greek, Luther Rice Seminar and Bible College, Lithonia, GA

Norman L. Geisler, President, Southern Evangelical Seminary, Matthews, NC

Gary R. Habermas, Distinguished Professor and Chair, Department of Philosophy and Theology, Liberty University, Lynchburg, VA

Harold W. Hoehner, Distinguished Professor of New Testament, Dallas Theological Seminary, Dallas, TX

R. Kirk Kirkpatrick, Associate Professor of Old Testament and Hebrew, Mid-America Baptist Theological Seminary, Germantown, TN

Andreas Köstenberger, Professor of NT and Greek Director of Ph.D. and Th.M. Studies, Southeastern Baptist Theological Seminary, Wake Forest, NC

Steve W. Lemke, Provost, New Orleans Baptist Theological Seminary, New Orleans, LA

Stanley May, Associate Professor of Missions and Chair, Department of Missions, Mid-America Baptist Theological Seminary, Germantown, TN

Richard Melick, Professor of New Testament Studies and Th.M. Program Director, Golden Gate Baptist Theological Seminary, Mill Valley, CA

H. David Philipps, Professor of Old Testament and Hebrew, Luther Rice Seminary and Bible College, Lithonia, GA

John B. Polhill, Buchanan Harrison Professor of New Testament Interpretation, The Southern Baptist Theological Seminary, Louisville, KY

Stanley E. Porter, President and Dean, Professor of New Testament, McMaster Divinity College, Hamilton, ON, Canada

Charles Quarles, Vice President for Integration of Faith and Learning, Associate Professor of Religion, and Chair, Division of Religious Studies, Louisiana College, Pineville, LA

David G. Shackelford, Professor of New Testament and Greek, Mid-America Baptist Theological Seminary, Germantown, TN

Michael R. Spradlin, President, Mid-America Baptist Theological Seminary, Germantown, TN

Robert Stewart, Assistant Professor of Philosophy and Theology, New Orleans Baptist Theological Seminary, New Orleans, LA

Mark E. Taylor, Assistant Professor of New Testament, Southwestern Baptist Theological Seminary, Fort Worth, TX

William F. Warren, Director, Center for New Testament Textual Studies and Professor of New Testament and Greek, New Orleans Baptist Theological Seminary, New Orleans, LA

Joel Williams, Associate Professor of Biblical Studies, Columbia International University, Columbia, SC

Contents

Preface v
Contributors vi
Introduction to the Holman CSB xi
Major Divisions of the Harmony xvii
Analytical Outline of the Harmony xviii
Table for Finding any Passage in the Harmony xxx

INTRODUCTORY ARTICLES

Is Harmonization Honest? 1
   Dale Ellenburg

A History of Harmonies: Major Steps 5
   Shawn Buice

Why There Are Four Gospels. 9
   Rick Melick

A Pastoral Use of Harmonies. 14
   Stephen D. C. Corts

The Academic Use of Gospel Harmonies 18
   Steve W. Lemke

HARMONY

A Harmony of the Gospels. 23

ISSUES IN GOSPEL HARMONIZATION

Textual Issues in the Gospels 231
   Bill Warren

The Geographical Setting of the Gospels. 236
   Sidney D. Dyer

The Religious Milieu in the Gospels 240
   Mark E. Taylor

Jewish Sects of the New Testament Era 245
   Steven L. Cox

The Gospels in the Light of Qumran and the Dead Sea Scrolls. .249
   Michael R. Spradlin

The Synoptic Problem/Question 253
   Daniel L. Akin

Critical Methodologies: Source Criticism, Form Criticism, Redaction Criticism 257
   Gerald Cowen

A Brief History of Hermeneutical Methods Used in the Quest of the Historical Jesus 261
Robert Stewart

Harmonization in the Patristic Period 267
Daryl Cornett

Christology in the Gospels 271
David G. Shackelford

A Chronology of the Life of Christ 275
Harold W. Hoehner

The Two Genealogies of Jesus Christ in Matthew and Luke 282
Stanley E. Porter

The Time of Jesus' Birth 287
John B. Polhill

The Language Jesus Spoke 292
Rick Melick

The Apostles: Four Lists 296
David G. Shackelford

Sermon on the Mount 299
Charles Quarles

Women in the Gospels 303
Nancy M. Easley

The Kingdom of God 308
David S. Dockery

Hell and Heaven 312
David S. Dockery

Demons in the Gospels 315
David G. Shackelford

The Arrest and Trials of Jesus 319
Darrell Bock

The Day, Hour, and Year of Jesus' Crucifixion 322
Brad Arnett and James Flanagan

The Amount of Time Between the Crucifixion and the Resurrection of Christ 327
R. Kirk Kilpatrick

The Resurrection of Jesus Christ 331
Norman L. Geisler

The Resurrection Appearances of Jesus 337
Gary R. Habermas

Messianic Prophecies Fulfilled in the Gospels. 341
  Craig Marlowe

Missiological Concepts in the Gospels 345
  Stan May

A List of the Parables of Jesus in the Gospels 348
  Steven L. Cox

A List of the Miracles of Jesus in the Gospels. 350
  Steven L. Cox

Old Testament Quotations in New Testament 352
  H. David Philipps

SELECTED BIBLIOGRAPHY. **357**

MAPS
     I.   Jesus Birth and Early Childhood
    II.   John the Baptizer
   III.   Galilee in the Time of Jesus
    IV.   The Ministry of Jesus Around the Sea of Galilee
     V.   Jesus' Journeys from Galilee to Judea
    VI.   The Ministry of Jesus Beyond Galilee
   VII.   Jesus in Judea and Jerusalem
  VIII.   The Passion Week in Jerusalem

Introduction to the
Holman Christian Standard Bible®

The Bible is God's revelation to man. It is the only book that gives us accurate information about God, man's need, and God's provision for that need. It provides us with guidance for life and tells us how to receive eternal life. The Bible can do these things because it is God's inspired Word, inerrant in the original manuscripts.

The Bible describes God's dealings with the ancient Jewish people and the early Christian church. It tells us about the great gift of God's Son, Jesus Christ, who fulfilled Jewish prophecies of the Messiah. It tells us about the salvation He accomplished through His death on the cross, His triumph over death in the resurrection, and His promised return to earth. It is the only book that gives us reliable information about the future, about what will happen to us when we die, and about where history is headed.

Bible translation is both a science and an art. It is a bridge that brings God's Word from the ancient world to the world today. In dependence on God to accomplish this sacred task, Holman Bible Publishers presents the Holman Christian Standard Bible, a new English translation of God's Word.

Textual base of the Holman CSB®

The textual base for the New Testament [NT] is the Nestle-Aland *Novum Testamentum Graece,* 27th edition, and the United Bible Societies' *Greek New Testament,* 4th corrected edition. The text for the Old Testament [OT] is the *Biblia Hebraica Stuttgartensia,* 5th edition. At times, however, the translators have followed an alternative manuscript tradition, disagreeing with the editors of these texts about the original reading.

Where there are significant differences among Hebrew [Hb] and Aramaic [Aram] manuscripts of the OT or among Greek [Gk] manuscripts of the NT, the translators have followed what they believe is the original reading and have indicated the main alternative(s) in footnotes. In a few places in the NT, large square brackets indicate texts that the translation team and most biblical scholars today believe were not part of the original text. However, these texts have been retained in brackets in the Holman CSB because of their undeniable antiquity and their value for tradition and the history of NT interpretation in the church. The Holman CSB uses traditional verse divisions found in most Protestant Bibles.

Goals of this translation

The goals of this translation are:
- to provide English-speaking people across the world with an accurate, readable Bible in contemporary English
- to equip serious Bible students with an accurate translation for personal study, private devotions, and memorization
- to give those who love God's Word a text that has numerous reader helps, is visually attractive on the page, and is appealing when heard
- to affirm the authority of Scripture as God's Word and to champion its absolute truth against social or cultural agendas that would compromise its accuracy

The name, Holman Christian Standard Bible, captures these goals: *Holman* Bible Publishers presents a new *Bible* translation, for *Christian* and English-speaking communities, which will be a *standard* in Bible translations for years to come.

Why is there a need for another English translation of the Bible?

There are several good reasons why Holman Bible publishers invested its resources in a modern language translation of the Bible:

1. Each generation needs a fresh translation of the Bible in its own language.

The Bible is the world's most important book, confronting each individual and each culture with issues that affect life, both now and forever. Since each new generation must be introduced to God's Word in its own language, there will always be a need for new translations such as the Holman Christian Standard Bible. The majority of Bible translations on the market today are revisions of translations from previous generations. The Holman CSB is a new translation for today's generation.

2. English, one of the world's greatest languages, is rapidly changing, and Bible translations must keep in step with those changes.

English is the first truly global language in history. It is the language of education, business, medicine, travel, research, and the Internet. More than 1.3 billion people around the world speak or read English as a primary or secondary language. The Holman CSB seeks to serve many of those people with a translation they can easily use and understand.

English is also the world's most rapidly changing language. The Holman CSB seeks to reflect recent changes in English by using modern punctuation, formatting, and vocabulary, while avoiding slang, regionalisms, or changes made specifically for the sake of political or social agendas. Modern linguistic and semantic advances have been incorporated into the Holman CSB, including modern grammar.

3. Rapid advances in biblical research provide new data for Bible translators.

This has been called the "information age," a term that accurately describes the field of biblical research. Never before in history has there been as much information about the Bible as there is today—from archaeological discoveries to analysis of ancient manuscripts to years of study and statistical research on individual Bible books. Translations made as recently as 10 or 20 years ago do not reflect many of these advances in biblical research. The translators have taken into consideration as much of this new data as possible.

4. Advances in computer technology have opened a new door for Bible translation.

The Holman CSB has used computer technology and telecommunications in its creation perhaps more than any Bible translation in history. Electronic mail was used daily and sometimes hourly for communication and transmission of manuscripts. An advanced Bible software program, Accordance®, was used to create and revise the translation at each step in its production. A developmental copy of the translation itself was used within Accordance to facilitate cross-checking during the translation process—something never done before with a Bible translation.

Translation Philosophy of the Holman CSB

Most discussions of Bible translations speak of two opposite approaches: formal equivalence and dynamic equivalence. Although this terminology is meaningful, Bible translations cannot be neatly sorted into these two categories any more than people can be neatly sorted into two categories according to height or weight. Holman Bible Publishers is convinced there is room for another category of translation philosophies that capitalizes on the strengths of the other two.

1. Formal Equivalence:

Often called "word-for-word" (or "literal") translation, the principle of formal equivalence seeks as nearly as possible to preserve the structure of the original language. It seeks to represent each word of the translated text with an exact equivalent word in the translation so that the reader can see word for word what the original human author wrote. The merits of this approach include its consistency with the conviction that the Holy Spirit did inspire the very words of Scripture in the original manuscripts. It also provides the English Bible student some access to the structure of the text in the original language. Formal equivalence can achieve accuracy to the degree that English has an exact equivalent for each word and that the grammatical patterns of the original language can be reproduced in understandable English. However, it can sometimes result in awkward, if not incomprehensible, English or in a misunderstanding of the author's intent. The literal rendering of ancient idioms is especially difficult.

2. Dynamic or Functional Equivalence:

Often called "thought-for-thought" translation, the principle of dynamic equivalence rejects a s misguided the desire to preserve the structure of the original language. It proceeds by distinguishing the meaning of a text from its form and then translating the meaning so that it makes the same impact on modern readers that the ancient text made on its original readers. Strengths of this approach include a high degree of clarity and readability, especially in places where the original is difficult to render word for word. It also acknowledges that accurate and effective translation requires interpretation. However, the meaning of a text cannot always be neatly separated from its form, nor can it always be precisely determined. A biblical author may have intended multiple meanings. In striving for readability, dynamic equivalence also sometimes overlooks some of the less prominent elements of meaning. Furthermore, lack of formal correspondence to the original makes it difficult to verify accuracy and thus can affect the usefulness of the translation for in-depth Bible study.

3. Optimal Equivalence:

In practice, translations are seldom if ever purely formal or dynamic but favor one theory of Bible translation or the other to varying degrees. Optimal equivalence as a translation philosophy recognizes that form cannot be neatly separated from meaning and should not be changed (for example, nouns to verbs or third person "they" to second person "you") unless comprehension demands it. The primary goal of translation is to convey the sense of the original with as much clarity as the original text and the translation language permit. Optimal equivalence appreciates the goals of formal equivalence but also recognizes its limitations.

Optimal equivalence starts with an exhaustive analysis of the text at every level (word, phrase, clause, sentence, discourse) in the original language to determine its original meaning and intention (or purpose). Then relying on the latest and best language tools and experts, the nearest corresponding semantic and linguistic equivalents are used to convey as much of the information and intention of the original text with as much clarity and readability as possible. This process assures the maximum transfer of both the words and thoughts contained in the original.

The Holman CSB uses optimal equivalence as its translation philosophy. When a literal translation meets these criteria, it is used. When clarity and readability demand an idiomatic translation, the reader can still access the form of the original text by means of a footnote with the abbreviation "Lit."

The gender language policy in Bible translation

Some people today ignore the Bible's teachings on distinctive roles of men and women in family and church and have an agenda to eliminate those distinctions in every arena of life. These people have begun a program to engineer the removal of a perceived male bias in the English language. The targets of this program have been such traditional linguistic practices as the generic use of "man" or "men," as well as "he," "him," and "his."

A group of Bible scholars, translators, and other evangelical leaders met in 1997 to respond to this issue as it affects Bible translation. This group produced the "Guidelines for Translation of Gender-Related Language in Scripture" (adopted May 27, 1997 and revised Sept. 9, 1997). The Holman Christian Standard Bible was produced in accordance with these guidelines.

The goal of the translators has not been to promote a cultural ideology but to faithfully translate the Bible. While the Holman CSB avoids using "man" or "he" unnecessarily, the translation does not restructure sentences to avoid them when they are in the text. For example, the translators have not changed "him" to "you" or to "them," neither have they avoided other masculine words such as "father" or "son" by translating them in generic terms such as "parent" or "child."

History of the Holman Christian Standard Bible

After several years of preliminary development, Holman Bible Publishers, the oldest Bible publisher in America, assembled an international, interdenominational team of 100 scholars, editors, stylists, and proofreaders, all of whom were committed to biblical inerrancy. Outside consultants and reviewers contributed valuable suggestions from their areas of expertise. An executive team then edited, polished, and reviewed the final manuscripts.

Traditional features found in the Holman CSB

In keeping with a long line of Bible publications, the Holman Christian Standard Bible has retained a number of features found in traditional Bibles:

1. Traditional theological vocabulary (such as *justification, sanctification, redemption,* etc.) has been retained since such terms have no translation equivalent that adequately communicates their exact meaning.
2. Traditional spellings of names and places found in most Bibles have been used to make the Holman CSB compatible with most Bible study tools.
3. Some editions of the Holman CSB will print the words of Christ in red letters to help readers easily locate the spoken words of the Lord Jesus Christ.
4. Nouns and personal pronouns that clearly refer to any person of the Trinity are capitalized.
5. Descriptive headings, printed above each section of Scripture, help readers quickly identify the contents of that section.
6. Small lower corner brackets: ⌞ ⌟ indicate words supplied for clarity by the translators (but see below, under Substitution of words in sentences, for supplied words that are not bracketed).
7. Two common forms of punctuation are used in the Holman CSB to help with clarity and ease of reading: em dashes (a long dash —) are used to indicate sudden breaks in thought or to help clarify long or difficult sentences. Parentheses are used infrequently to indicate words that are parenthetical in the original languages.

How certain names and terms are translated

The names of God

The Holman Christian Standard Bible OT consistently translates the Hebrew names for God as follows:

Holman CSB English:	Hebrew original:
God	*Elohim*
LORD	*YHWH (Yahweh)*
Lord	*Adonai*
Lord GOD	*Adonai Yahweh*
LORD of Hosts	*Yahweh Sabaoth*
God Almighty	*El Shaddai*

However, the Holman CSB OT uses Yahweh, the personal name of God in Hebrew, when a biblical text emphasizes Yahweh as a name: "His name is Yahweh" (Ps 68:4). Yahweh is used more often in the Holman CSB than in most Bible translations because the word LORD in English is a title of God and does not accurately convey to modern readers the emphasis on God's name in the original Hebrew.

The uses of Christ and Messiah

The Holman CSB translates the Greek word *Christos* ("anointed one") as either "Christ" or "Messiah" based on its use in different NT contexts. Where the NT emphasizes *Christos* as a name of our Lord or has a Gentile context, "Christ" is used (Eph 1:1 "Paul, an apostle of Christ Jesus…"). Where the NT *Christos* has a Jewish context, the title "Messiah" is used (Eph 1:12 "…we who had already put our hope in the Messiah"). The first use of "Messiah" in each chapter is also marked with a bullet referring readers to the Bullet Note at the back of most editions.

Place-names

In the original text of the Bible, particularly in the OT, a number of well-known places have names different from the ones familiar to contemporary readers. For example, "the Euphrates" often appears in the original text simply as "the River." In cases like this, the Holman Christian Standard Bible uses the modern name, "the Euphrates River," in the text without a footnote or lower corner brackets.

Substitution of words in sentences

A literal translation of the biblical text sometimes violates standard rules of English grammar, such as the agreement of subject and verb or person and number. In order to conform to standard usage, the Holman CSB has often made these kinds of grammatical constructions agree in English without footnotes or lower corner brackets.

In addition, the Greek or Hebrew texts sometimes seem redundant or ambiguous by repeating nouns where modern writing substitutes pronouns or by using pronouns where we would supply nouns for clarity and good style. When a literal translation of the original would make the English unclear, the Holman CSB sometimes changes a pronoun to its corresponding noun or a noun to its corresponding pronoun without a footnote or lower corner brackets. For example, Jn 1:42 reads: "And he brought Simon to Jesus . . ." The original Greek of this sentence reads: "And he brought him to Jesus."

Special Formatting Features

The Holman Christian Standard Bible has several distinctive formatting features:

1. OT passages quoted in the NT are set in boldface type. OT quotes consisting of two or more lines are block indented.
2. In dialogue, a new paragraph is used for each new speaker as in most modern publications.
3. Many passages, such as 1 Co 13, have been formatted as dynamic prose (separate block-indented lines like poetry) for ease in reading and comprehension. Special block-indented formatting has also been used extensively in both the OT and NT to increase readability and clarity in lists, series, genealogies and other parallel or repetitive texts.
4. Almost every Bible breaks lines in poetry using automatic typesetting programs with the result that words are haphazardly turned over to the next line. In the Holman CSB, special attention has been given to break every line in poetry and dynamic prose so that awkward or unsightly word wraps are avoided and complete units of thought turn over to the next line. The result is a Bible page that is much more readable and pleasing to the eye.
5. Certain foreign, geographical, cultural, or ancient words are preceded by a superscripted bullet (•*Abba*) at their first occurrence in each chapter. These words are listed in alphabetical order at the back of the

Bible under the heading **Holman CSB Bullet Notes**. A few important or frequently misunderstood words (•slaves) are marked with a bullet more than one time per chapter.

6. Italics are used in the text for a transliteration of Greek and Hebrew words (*"Hosanna!"* in Jn 12:13) and in footnotes for direct quotations from the biblical text and for words in the original languages (the footnote at Jn 1:1 reads: "The *Word* (Gk *logos*) is a title for Jesus…").

7. Since the majority of English readers do not need to have numbers and fractions spelled out in the text, the Holman CSB uses a similar style to that of modern newspapers in using Arabic numerals for the numbers 10 and above and in fractions, except in a small number of cases, such as when a number begins a sentence.

Footnotes

Footnotes are used to show readers how the original biblical language has been understood in the Holman Christian Standard Bible.

NT Textual Footnotes

NT textual notes indicate significant differences among Greek manuscripts (mss) and are normally indicated in one of three ways:

Other mss read _____
Other mss add _____
Other mss omit _____

In the NT, some textual footnotes that use the word "add" or "omit" also have square brackets before and after the corresponding verses in the biblical text (see the discussion above in the paragraph entitled "Textual base of the Holman CSB"). Examples of this use of square brackets are Mk 16:9-20, Jn 5:3-4, and Jn 7:53–8:11.

OT Textual Footnotes

OT textual notes show important differences among Hebrew manuscripts and among ancient OT versions, such as the Septuagint and the Vulgate. See the list of abbreviations on page xiii for a list of other ancient versions used.

Some OT textual notes (like NT textual notes) give only an alternate textual reading. However, other OT textual notes also give the support for the reading chosen by the editors as well as for the alternate textual reading. For example, the Holman CSB text of Ps 12:7 reads:

You will protect us[a] from this generation forever.

The textual footnote for this verse reads:

[a]**12:7** Some Hb mss, LXX; other Hb mss read him

The textual note in this example means that there are two different readings found in the Hebrew manuscripts: some manuscripts read *us* and others read *him*. The Holman CSB translators chose the reading *us*, which is also found in the Septuagint (LXX), and placed the other Hebrew reading *him* in the footnote.

Two other OT textual notes are:

Alt Hb tradition reads _____	a variation given by scribes in the Hebrew manuscript Tradition (known as *Kethiv/Qere* readings)
Hb uncertain	when it is uncertain what the original Hebrew text was

Other Kinds of Footnotes

Lit _____	a more literal rendering in English of the Hebrew, Aramaic, or Greek text
Or _____	an alternate or less likely English translation of the same Hebrew, Aramaic, or Greek text
=	an abbreviation for " it means" or "it is equivalent to"
Hb, Aram, Gk	the actual Hebrew, Aramaic, or Greek word is given using English letters
Hb obscure	the existing Hebrew text is especially difficult to translate
emend(ed) to _____	the original Hebrew text is so difficult to translate that competent scholars have conjectured or inferred a restoration of the original text based on the context, probable root meanings of the words, and uses incomparative languages

In some editions of the Holman Christian Standard Bible, additional footnotes clarify the meaning of certain biblical texts or explain biblical history, persons, customs, places, activities, and measurements. Cross-references are given for parallel passages or passages with similar wording, and in the NT, for passages quoted from the OT.

Commonly Used Abbreviations in the Holman CSB

A.D.	in the year of our Lord
alt	alternate
a.m.	from midnight until noon
Aq	Aquila
Aram	Aramaic
B.C.	before Christ
c.	circa
chap	chapter
DSS	Dead Sea Scrolls
Eng	English
Gk	Greek
Hb	Hebrew
Lat	Latin
Lit	Literally
LXX	Septuagint—an ancient translation of the Old Testament into Greek
MT	Masoretic Text
NT	New Testament
ms(s)	manuscript(s)
OT	Old Testament
p.m.	from noon until midnight
pl	plural
Ps(s)	psalm(s)
Sam	Samaritan Pentateuch
sg	singular
syn.	synonym
Sym	Symmachus
Syr	Syriac
Tg	Targum
Theod	Theodotian
v., vv.	verse, verses
Vg	Vulgate—an ancient translation of the Bible into Latin
vol(s).	volume(s)

Major Divisions of the Harmony

PART I: THE SOURCES OF THE GOSPELS 23

             Section 1

PART II   THE INCARNATION OF THE SON OF GOD 24

             Section 2

PART III: THE GENEALOGIES OF JESUS IN MATTHEW AND LUKE 26

             Section 3

PART IV: THE BIRTH AND CHILDHOOD OF JOHN THE BAPTIST
             AND JESUS 28

             Section 4–19

PART V: THE BEGINNING OF JOHN THE BAPTIST'S MINISTRY 39

             Sections 20–23

PART VI: THE BEGINNING OF CHRIST'S PUBLIC MINISTRY 43

             Sections 24–36

PART VII: THE GREAT GALILEAN MINISTRY 54

             Sections 37–71

PART VIII: THE SPECIAL TRAINING OF THE TWELVE IN DISTRICTS
             AROUND GALILEE 97

             Sections 72–95

PART IX: THE LATER JUDEAN MINISTRY 121

             Sections 96–111

PART X: THE LATER PEREAN MINISTRY 137

             Sections 112–127

PART XI: THE LAST PUBLIC MINISTRY IN JERUSALEM 155

             Sections 128a–138

PART XII: IN THE SHADOW WITH JESUS 171

             Sections 139–152

PART XIII: THE ARREST, TRIAL, CRUCIFIXION, AND BURIAL OF JESUS 193

             Sections 153–168

PART XIV: THE RESURRECTION, APPEARANCES, AND
             ASCENSION OF JESUS 216

             Sections 169–184

Analytical Outline of the Harmony

PART I: THE SOURCES OF THE GOSPELS
Section
1 Luke Explains His Purpose and His Method of Research and Writing 23
   Luke 1:1-4

PART II: THE INCARNATION OF THE SON OF GOD
Section
2 Prologue to John's Gospel 24
   John 1:1-18

PART III: THE GENEALOGIES OF JESUS IN MATTHEW AND LUKE
Section
3 Apparently Joseph's Genealogy in Matthew and Mary's in Luke 26
   Matthew 1:1-17; Luke 3:23b-38

**PART IV: THE BIRTH AND CHILDHOOD OF JOHN THE BAPTIST AND JESUS
      (SECTIONS 4-19)**
Section
4 Gabriel Predicts John's Birth 28
   Luke 1:5-25

5 Gabriel Predicts Jesus' Birth 29
   Luke 1:26-38

6 Mary's Visit to Elizabeth 30
   Luke 1:39-45

7 Mary's Praise 30
   Luke 1:46-56

8 The Birth and Naming of John 31
   Luke 1:57-80

9 The Nativity of the Messiah 32
   Matthew 1:18-25

10 The Birth of Jesus 33
   Luke 2:1-7

11 The Shepherds and the Angels 33
   Luke 2:8-20

12 The Circumcision of Jesus 34
   Luke 2:21

13 The Presentation of Jesus 34
   Luke 2:22-38

14 Wise Men Seek the King 35
   Matthew 2:1-12

Section

15   The Flight to Egypt and the Massacre of the Innocents 36
       Matthew 2:13-18

16   The Holy Family in Nazareth 37
       Matthew 2:19-23; Luke 2:39

17   Jesus' Childhood in Nazareth 37
       Luke 2:40

18   In His Father's House 37
       Luke 2:41-50

19   The Eighteen Years at Nazareth 38
       Luke 2:51-52

PART V: THE BEGINNING OF JOHN THE BAPTIST'S MINISTRY (SECTIONS 20-23)
Section

20   The Beginning of the Gospel 39
       Mark 1:1; Luke 3:1-2

21   The Messiah's Herald 39
       Matthew 3:1-6; Mark 1:2-6; Luke 3:3-6

22   John's Preaching 41
       Matthew 3:7-10; Luke 3:7-14

23   John's Expectation of the Messiah 42
       Matthew 3:11-12 ; Mark 1:7-8 ; Luke 3:15-18

PART VI: THE BEGINNING OF CHRIST'S PUBLIC MINISTRY (SECTIONS 24-36)
Section

24   The Baptism of Jesus 43
       Matthew 3:13-17; Mark 1:9-11; Luke 3:21-23a

25   The Temptations of Jesus 44
       Matthew 4:1-11; Mark 1:12-13; Luke 4:1-13

26   John the Baptist's Testimony 46
       John 1:19-28

27   The Lamb of God 46
       John 1:29-34

28   Jesus' First Disciples 47
       John 1:35-51

29   Jesus' First Sign: Turning Water into Wine 48
       John 2:1-11

30   Jesus at Capernaum 48
       John 2:12

31   Jesus' First Cleansing of the Temple Complex 48
       John 2:13-22

Section

32   Jesus and Nicodemus 49
      John 2:23–3:21

33   Jesus and John the Baptist 50
      John 3:22-36

34   Jesus' Reasons for Leaving Judea 51
      Matthew 4:12; Mark 1:14; Luke 3:19-20; 4:14a; John 4:1-4

35   Jesus and the Samaritan Woman 51
      John 4:5-42

36   Jesus Welcomed in Galilee. 53
      John 4:43-45

PART VII: THE GREAT GALILEAN MINISTRY (SECTIONS 37-71)

Section

37   Summary of Jesus' Teaching in Galilee. 54
      Matthew 4:17; Mark 1:14-15; Luke 4:14-15

38   Jesus' Second Sign: Healing an Official's Son. 54
      John 4:46-54

39   Rejection at Nazareth 55
      Luke 4:16-31

40   Jesus Makes Capernaum His Home 55
      Matthew 4:13-16

41   Jesus Calls Four Fishermen 56
      Matthew 4:18-22; Mark 1:16-20; Luke 5:1-11

42   Driving Out an Unclean Spirit 57
      Mark 1:21-28; Luke 4:31-37

43   Healings at Capernaum 57
      Matthew 8:14-17; Mark 1:29-34; Luke 4:38-41

44   Preaching in Galilee. 58
      Matthew 4:23-25; Mark 1:35-39; Luke 4:42-44

45   Cleansing a Leper. 59
      Matthew 8:2-4; Mark 1:40-45; Luke 5:12-16

46   The Son of Man Forgives and Heals 60
      Matthew 9:1-8; Mark 2:1-12; Luke 5:17-26

47   The Call of Matthew. 61
      Matthew 9:9-13; Mark 2:13-17; Luke 5:27-32

48   A Question About Fasting 62
      Matthew 9:14-17; Mark 2:18-22; Luke 5:33-39

49   Jesus' Third Sign: Healing the Sick 63
      John 5:1-47

Section
50   Lord of the Sabbath 64
      Matthew 12:1-8; Mark 2:23-28; Luke 6:1-5

51   The Man with the Paralyzed Hand...............................65
      Matthew 12:9-14; Mark 3:1-6; Luke 6:6-11

52   The Servant of the Lord 66
      Matthew 12:15-21; Mark 3:7-12

53   The 12 Apostles 67
      Mark 3:13-19; Luke 6:12-16

54   The Sermon on the Mount 67
      Matthew 5:1-2; Luke 6:17-19

      1.   *The Beatitudes and Woes*..............................68
           Matthew 5:3-12; Luke 6:20-26

      2.   *Jesus' Standards of Righteousness*...................69
           Matthew 5:13-20

      3.   *Jesus' Ethical Teachings* 69
           Matthew 5:21-48; Luke 6:27-30,32-36

      4.   *Authentic Righteousness* 71
           Matthew 6:1-18

      5.   *Single-hearted Devotion to God* 72
           Matthew 6:19-34

      6.   *Judging Others* 72
           Matthew 7:1-6; Luke 6:37-42

      7.   *Prayer and the Golden Rule* 73
           Matthew 7:7-12; Luke 6:31

      8.   *The Conclusion of the Sermon*.........................73
           Matthew 7:13–8:1; Luke 6:43-49

55   A Centurion's Faith 74
      Matthew 8:5-13; Luke 7:1-10

56   Jesus Raises a Widow's Son to Life............................75
      Luke 7:11-17

57   In Praise of John the Baptist.................................76
      Matthew 11:2-19; Luke 7:18-35

58   An Unresponsive Generation 78
      Matthew 11:20-30

59   Much Forgiveness, Much Love 78
      Luke 7:36-50

60   Many Women Support Christ's Work..............................79
      Luke 8:1-3

Section

61   A House Divided 79
      Matthew 12:22-37; Mark 3:20-30

62   Demand for a Sign 80
      Matthew 12:38-45

63   True Relationships 81
      Matthew 12:46-50; Mark 3:31-35; Luke 8:19-21

64   Jesus' First Group of Parables 81
      Matthew 13:1-3a; Mark 4:1-2; Luke 8:4

      1.   *To the Crowds by the Sea.* 82
           (a)   Parable of the Sower 82
                 Matthew 13:3b-23; Mark 4:3-25; Luke 8:5-18

           (b)   Parable of the Growing Seed 84
                 Mark 4:26-29

           (c)   Parable of the Wheat and the Weeds 85
                 Matthew 13:24-30

           (d)   Parable of the Mustard Seed 85
                 Matthew 13:31-32; Mark 4:30-32

           (e)   Parable of the Yeast and Many Such Parables 85
                 Matthew 13:33-35; Mark 4:33-34

      2.   *To the Disciples in the House* 86
           (a)   Jesus Interprets the Parable of the Weeds and Wheat 86
                 Matthew 13:36-43

           (b)   The Parable of the Hidden Treasure. 86
                 Matthew 13:44

           (c)   The Parable of the Pearl of Great Price 86
                 Matthew 13:45-46

           (d)   The Parable of the Net 86
                 Matthew 13:47-50

           (e)   The Storehouse of Truth 86
                 Matthew 13:51-53

65   Wind and Wave Obey the Master. 87
      Matthew 8:18-19,23-27; Mark 4:35-41; Luke 8:22-25

66   Demons Driven Out by the Master. 87
      Matthew 8:28-34; Mark 5:1-20; Luke 8:26-39

67   A Girl Restored and a Woman Healed 89
      Matthew 9:18-26; Mark 5:21-43; Luke 8:40-56

68   Healing the Blind and Driving Out a Demon. 91
      Matthew 9:27-34

Section

69 Rejection at Nazareth 92
Matthew 13:54-58; Mark 6:1-6a

70 Jesus Sends the 12 Out by Twos. 92
Matthew 9:35–11:1; Mark 6:6b-13; Luke 9:1-6

71 John the Baptist Beheaded 95
Matthew 14:1-12; Mark 6:14-29; Luke 9:7-9

PART VIII: THE SPECIAL TRAINING OF THE TWELVE IN DISTRICTS AROUND GALILEE (SECTIONS 72-95)

Section

72 Feeding 5,000 97
Matthew 14:13-21; Mark 6:30-44; Luke 9:10-17; John 6:1-13

73 Jesus Sends the Disciples On 99
Matthew 14:22-23; Mark 6:45-46; John 6:14-15

74 Walking on the Water 99
Matthew 14:24-33; Mark 6:47-52; John 6:16-21

75 Miraculous Healings. 100
Matthew 14:34-36; Mark 6:53-56

76 The Bread of Life 101
John 6:22-71

77 The Tradition of the Elders. 102
Matthew 15:1-20; Mark 7:1-23; John 7:1

78 A Gentile Mother's Faith 105
Matthew 15:21-28; Mark 7:24-30

79 Jesus Does Everything Well; Feeds 4,000 106
Matthew 15:29-38; Mark 7:31–8:9

80 The Sign of Jonah. 107
Matthew 15:39–16:4; Mark 8:10-12

81 The Yeast of the Pharisees and the Sadducees 108
Matthew 16:5-12; Mark 8:13-26

82 Peter's Confession of the Messiah 109
Matthew 16:13-20; Mark 8:27-30; Luke 9:18-21

83 Jesus Foretells His Death and Resurrection 110
Matthew 16:21-26; Mark 8:31-37; Luke 9:22-25

84 Public Commitment to the Son of Man 111
Matthew 16:27-28; Mark 8:34–9:1; Luke 9:26-27

85 The Transfiguration 112
Matthew 17:1-8; Mark 9:2-8; Luke 9:28-36a

86 The Disciples' Puzzlement Concerning Elijah and the Resurrection. 113
Matthew 17:9-13; Mark 9:9-13; Luke 9:36b

Section
  87   The Power of Faith over a Demon 114
        Matthew 17:14-21; Mark 9:14-29; Luke 9:37-43a

  88   Jesus' Second Prediction of His Death. 115
        Matthew 17:22-23; Mark 9:30-32; Luke 9:43b-45

  89   Paying the Temple Tax 116
        Matthew 17:24-27

  90   Who Is the Greatest? 116
        Matthew 18:1-5; Mark 9:33-37; Luke 9:46-48

  91   Warnings from Jesus. 117
        Matthew 18:6-14; Mark 9:38-50; Luke 9:49-50

  92   Restoration and Forgiveness. 118
        Matthew 18:15-35

  93   Following Jesus 119
        Matthew 8:18-22; Luke 9:57-62

  94   The Unbelief of Jesus' Brothers. 120
        John 7:2-9

  95   The Journey to Jerusalem. 120
        Luke 9:51-56; John 7:10

PART IX: THE LATER JUDEAN MINISTRY (SECTIONS 96-111)

Section
  96   Jesus at the Festival of Tabernacles 121
        John 7:11-52

  97   An Adulteress Forgiven 122
        John 7:53–8:11

  98   The Light of the World. 122
        John 8:12-20

  99   Jesus Predicts His Departure 123
        John 8:21-59

  100   The Sixth Sign: Healing a Man Born Blind. 124
        John 9:1-41

  101   The Ideal Shepherd. 125
        John 10:1-21

  102   Sending Out the Seventy 126
        Luke 10:1-24

  103   The Parable of the Good Samaritan 127
        Luke 10:25-37

  104   Mary and Martha 128
        Luke 10:38-42

Section

105   The Model Prayer...128
       Luke 11:1-13

106   A House Divided 129
       Luke 11:14-36

107   Religious Hypocrisy Denounced 130
       Luke 11:37-54

108   Jesus Warns about Covetousness and Worldly Anxieties.........132
       Luke 12:1-59

109   Repent or Perish...134
       Luke 13:1-9

110   Healing a Daughter of Abraham and a Repetition of the Parables of the
       Mustard Seed and of the Yeast 135
       Luke 13:10-21

111   Jesus at the Feast of Dedication; Renewed Efforts to Stone Him 135
       John 10:22-39

PART X: THE LATER PEREAN MINISTRY (SECTIONS 112-127)

Section

112   Many Beyond the Jordan Believe in Jesus......................137
       John 10:40-42

113   The Narrow Way...137
       Luke 13:22-35

114   A Sabbath Controversy..138
       Luke 14:1-24

115   The Cost of Following Jesus 139
       Luke 14:25-35

116   The Parables of the Lost Sheep, the Lost Coin, and the Lost Son 139
       Luke 15:1-32

117   Three Parables of Stewardship................................141
       Luke 16:1–17:10

118   The Seventh Sign: Jesus Raises Lazarus from Death............143
       John 11:1-44

119   The Plot to Kill Jesus 144
       John 11:45-54

120   Jesus Begins His Last Journey to Jerusalem 144
       Luke 17:11-37

121   Two Parables on Prayer 145
       Luke 18:1-14

122   The Question of Divorce 146
       Matthew 19:1-12; Mark 10:1-12

Section

123   Jesus Blesses the Children 147
      Matthew 19:13-15; Mark 10:13-16; Luke 18:15-17

124   Possessions and the Kingdom 148
      Matthew 19:16–20:16; Mark 10:17-31; Luke 18:18-30

125   Jesus' Third Prediction of His Death and Resurrection 151
      Matthew 20:17-28; Mark 10:32-45; Luke 18:31-34

126   Two Blind Men Healed 152
      Matthew 20:29-34; Mark 10:46-52; Luke 18:35-43

127   Jesus Visits Zacchaeus, Tells the Parable of the 10 Minas, and Departs for Jerusalem .153
      Luke 19:1-28

PART XI: THE LAST PUBLIC MINISTRY IN JERUSALEM (SECTIONS 128-139)

Section

128a Jesus Arrives at Bethany 155
      John 11:55–12:1,9-11

128b The Triumphal Entry 155
      Matthew 21:1-11,14-17; Mark 11:1-11; Luke 19:29-44; John 12:12-19

129   The Barren Fig Tree and the Cleansing of the Temple 158
      Matthew 21:18-19,12-13; Mark 11:12-18; Luke 19:45-48

130   Jesus Predicts His Crucifixion 159
      John 12:20-50

131   The Barren Fig Tree Withered 160
      Matthew 21:19b-22; Mark 11:19-26; Luke 21:37-38

132   Messiah's Authority Challenged 161
      Matthew 21:23–22:14; Mark 11:27–12:12; Luke 20:1-19

133   God and Caesar 164
      Matthew 22:15-22; Mark 12:13-17; Luke 20:20-26

134   The Sadducees and the Resurrection 165
      Matthew 22:23-33; Mark 12:18-27; Luke 20:27-40

135   The Primary Commandments 166
      Matthew 22:34-40; Mark 12:28-34

136   The Question about the Messiah 167
      Matthew 22:41-46; Mark 12:35-37; Luke 20:41-44

137   Religious Hypocrites Denounced 168
      Matthew 23:1-39; Mark 12:38-40; Luke 20:45-47

138   The Widow's Gift 170
      Mark 12:41-44; Luke 21:1-4

PART XII: IN THE SHADOW WITH JESUS (SECTIONS 139-152)

Section

139   Jesus' Great Eschatological Discourse. 171
Matthew 24–25; Mark 13:1-37; Luke 21:5-36

140   The Plot to Kill Jesus 178
Matthew 26:1-5; Mark 14:1-2; Luke 22:1-2

141   The Anointing at Bethany. 179
Matthew 26:6-13; Mark 14:3-9; John 12:2-8

142   Judas Bargains with the Chief Priests 180
Matthew 26:14-16; Mark 14:10-11; Luke 22:3-6

143   Betrayal at the Passover 180
Matthew 26:17-19; Mark 14:12-16; Luke 22:7-13

144   Jesus Shares the Passover Meal with the Twelve. 181
Matthew 26:20; Mark 14:17; Luke 22:14-16,24-30

145   Jesus Washes His Disciples' Feet. 181
John 13:1-20

146   Jesus' Betrayal Predicted 182
Matthew 26:21-25; Mark 14:18-21; Luke 22:21-23; John 13:21-30

147   The New Commandment 183
Matthew 26:31-35; Mark 14:27-31; Luke 22:31-38; John 13:31-38

148   The First Lord's Supper 185
Matthew 26:26-29; Mark 14:22-25; Luke 22:17-20; 1 Corinthians 11:23-26

149   Jesus' Farewell Discourse in the Upper Room. 186
John 14:1-31

150   Jesus' Farewill Discourse on the Way to Gethsemane. 187
John 15–16

151   Jesus' Intercessory Prayer 189
John 17:1-26

152   The Prayer in the Garden 191
Matthew 26:30,36-46; Mark 14:26,32-42; Luke 22:39-46; John 18:1

PART XIII: THE ARREST, TRIAL, CRUCIFIXION, AND BURIAL OF JESUS (SECTIONS 153-168)

Section

153   The Judas Kiss 193
Matthew 26:47-56; Mark 14:43-52; Luke 22:47-53; John 18:2-11

154   Jesus Arrested and Taken to Annas. 195
John 18:12-14,19-23

155   Jesus Faces Caiaphas and the Sanhedrin 196
Matthew 26:57,59-68; Mark 14:53,55-65; Luke 22:54a,63-65; John 18:24

Section
156   Peter Denies His Lord 197
       Matthew 26:58,69-75; Mark 14:54,66-72; Luke 22:54b-62; John 18:15-18,25-27

157   The Chief Priest and Elders Move to Put Jesus to Death 199
        Matthew 27:1; Mark 15:1a; Luke 22:66-71

158   Judas Hangs Himself 200
       Matthew 27:3-10; Acts 1:18-19

159   Jesus Faces Pilate 200
       Matthew 27:2,11-14; Mark 15:1b-5; Luke 23:1-5; John 18:28-38

160   Jesus Faces Herod Antipas 203
       Luke 23:6-12

161   Jesus Faces Pilate a Second Time. 203
       Matthew 27:15-26; Mark 15:6-15; Luke 23:13-25; John 18:39–19:16a

162   Mocked by the Military 207
       Matthew 27:27-30; Mark 15:16-19

163   The Way to the Cross 207
       Matthew 27:31-34; Mark 15:20-23; Luke 23:26-33a; John 19:16b-17

164   The Crucifixion. 208
       Matthew 27:35-44; Mark 15:24-32; Luke 23:33b-34,38,35-37, ; John 19:18b,23-24,
       39-43   19-22,25-27

165   The Death of Jesus 211
       Matthew 27:45-50; Mark 15:33-37; Luke 23:44-45a,46; John 19:28-30

166   Events that Accompanied the Death of Jesus. 212
       Matthew 27:51-56; Mark 15:38-41; Luke 23:45, 47-49

167   Jesus' Burial 213
       Matthew 27:57-60; Mark 15:42-46; Luke 23:50-54; John 19:31-42

168   The Closely Guarded Tomb 215
       Matthew 27:61-66; Mark 15:47; Luke 23:55-56

PART XIV: THE RESURRECTION, APPEARANCES, AND ASCENSION OF JESUS (SECTIONS 169-184)

Section
169   The Women Prepare to Visit Jesus' Tomb 216
       Matthew 28:1; Mark 16:1

170   An Angel of the Lord Rolls Back the Stone. 216
       Matthew 28:2-4

171   Early Sunday Morning 216
       Matthew 28:5-8; Mark 16:2-8; Luke 24:1-8; John 20:1

172   The Empty Tomb 218
       Luke 24:9-12; John 20:2-10

Section

173   Mary Magdalene Sees the Risen Lord 218
Mark 16:9-11; John 20:11-18

174   Jesus Appears to the Other Women 219
Matthew 28:9-10

175   The Soldiers Are Bribed to Lie. 219
Matthew 28:11-15

176   The Emmaus Disciples. 220
Mark 16:12-13; Luke 24:13-32

177   Jesus Appears to Simon Peter. 221
Luke 24:33-35; 1 Corinthians 15:5a

178   The Reality of the Risen Jesus 221
Mark 16:14; Luke 24:36-43; John 20:19-25

179   Jesus Appears to Thomas and the Other Disciples. 222
John 20:26-31; 1 Corinthians 15:5b

180   Jesus' Third Appearance to the Disciples. 223
John 21:1-25

181   Jesus Appears to 500 in Galilee and Gives the Great Commission 224
Matthew 28:16-20; Mark 16:15-18; 1 Corinthians 15:6

182   Jesus Appears to James. 225
1 Corinthians 15:7

183   Jesus Appears to His Disciples in Jerusalem 225
Luke 24:44-49; Acts 1:3-8

184   Jesus' Last Appearance and His Ascension 226
Mark 16:19-20; Luke 24:50-53; Acts 1:9-12

Scripture Index for the Harmony

Matthew

Chapter	Verse(s)	Section	Page	Chapter	Verse(s)	Section	Page
1	1-17	3	26	9	14-17	48	62
1	18-25	9	32	9	18-26	67	89
2	1-12	14	35	9	27-34	68	91
2	13-18	15	36	9	35–11:1	70	92
2	19-23	16	37	11	2-19	57	76
3	1-6	21	39	11	20-30	58	78
3	7-10	22	41	12	1-8	50	64
3	11-12	23	42	12	9-14	51	65
3	13-17	24	43	12	15-21	52	66
4	1-11	25	44	12	22-37	61	79
4	12	34	51	12	38-45	62	80
4	13-16	40	55	12	46-50	63	81
4	17	37	54	13	1-3a	64	81
4	18-22	41	56	13	3b-23	64	82
4	23-25	44	58	13	24-30	64	85
5	1-2	54	67	13	31-32	64	85
5	3-12	54	68	13	33-35	64	85
5	13-20	54	69	13	36-43	64	86
5	21-48	54	69	13	44	64	86
6	1-18	54	71	13	45-46	64	86
6	19-34	54	72	13	47-50	64	86
7	1-6	54	72	13	51-53	64	86
7	7-12	54	73	13	54-58	69	92
7	13–8:1	54	73	14	1-12	71	95
8	2-4	45	59	14	13-21	72	97
8	5-13	55	74	14	22-23	73	99
8	14-17	43	57	14	24-33	74	99
8	18-19, 23-27	65	87	14	34-36	75	100
				15	1-20	77	102
8	19-22	93	119	15	21-28	78	105
8	28-34	66	87	15	29-38	79	106
9	1-8	46	60	15	39-16:4	80	107
9	9-13	47	61				

Matthew (cont.)

Chapter	Verse(s)	Section	Page
16	5-12	81	108
16	13-20	82	109
16	21-26	83	110
16	27-28	84	111
17	1-8	85	112
17	9-13	86	113
17	14-21	87	114
17	22-23	88	115
17	24-27	89	116
18	1-5	90	116
18	6-14	91	117
18	15-35	92	118
19	1-12	122	146
19	13-15	123	147
19	16–20:16	124	148
20	17-28	125	151
20	29-34	126	152
21	1-11, 14-17	128b	155
21	18-19, 12-13	129	158
21	19b-22	131	160
21	23–22:14	132	161
22	15-22	133	164
22	23-33	134	165
22	34-40	135	166
22	41-46	136	167
23	1-39	137	168
24 and 25	—	139	171

Chapter	Verse(s)	Section	Page
26	1-5	140	178
26	6-13	141	179
26	14-16	142	180
26	17-19	143	180
26	20	144	181
26	21-25	146	182
26	26-29	148	185
26	30, 36-46	152	191
26	31-35	147	184
26	47-56	153	193
26	57,59-68	155	196
26	58,69-75	156	197
27	1	157	199
27	2,11-14	159	200
27	3-10	158	200
27	15-26	161	203
27	27-30	162	207
27	31-34	163	207
27	35-44	164	208
27	45-50	165	211
27	51-56	166	212
27	57-60	167	213
27	61-66	168	215
28	1	169	216
28	5-8	171	216
28	9-10	174	219
28	11-15	175	219
28	16-20	181	224
28	2-4	170	216

Mark

Chapter	Verse(s)	Section	Page	Chapter	Verse(s)	Section	Page
1	1	20	39	6	53-56	75	100
1	2-6	21	39	7	1-23	77	102
1	7-8	23	42	7	24-30	78	105
1	9-11	24	43	7	31–8:9	79	106
1	12-13	25	44	8	10-12	80	107
1	14	34	51	8	13-26	81	108
1	14-15	37	54	8	27-30	82	109
1	16-20	41	56	8	31-37	83	110
1	21-28	42	57	8	34–9:1	84	111
1	29-34	43	57	9	2-8	85	112
1	35-39	44	58	9	9-13	86	113
1	40-45	45	59	9	14-29	87	114
2	1-12	46	60	9	30-32	88	115
2	13-17	47	61	9	33-37	90	116
2	18-22	48	62	9	38-50	91	117
2	23-28	50	64	10	1-12	122	146
3	1-6	51	65	10	13-16	123	147
3	7-12	52	66	10	17-31	124	148
3	13-19	53	67	10	32-45	125	151
3	20-30	61	79	10	46-52	126	152
3	31-35	63	81	11	1-11	128b	155
4	1-2	64	81	11	12-18	129	158
4	3-25	64	82	11	19-26	131	160
4	26-29	64	84	11	27–12:12	132	161
4	30-32	64	85	12	13-17	133	164
4	33-34	64	85	12	18-27	134	165
4	35-41	65	87	12	28-34	135	166
5	1-20	66	87	12	35-37	136	167
5	21-43	67	89	12	38-40	137	168
6	1-6a	69	92	12	41-44	138	170
6	6b-13	70	92	13	1-37	139	171
6	14-29	71	95	14	1-2	140	178
6	30-44	72	97	14	3-9	141	179
6	45-46	73	99	14	10-11	142	180
6	47-52	74	99	14	12-16	143	180

Mark (cont.)

Chapter	Verse(s)	Section	Page
14	17	144	181
14	18-21	146	182
14	22-25	148	185
14	26, 32-42	152	191
14	27-31	147	184
14	43-52	153	193
14	53,55-65	155	196
14	54,66-72	156	197
15	1a	157	199
15	1b-5	159	200
15	6-15	161	203
15	16-19	162	207
15	20-23	163	207

Chapter	Verse(s)	Section	Page
15	24-32	164	208
15	33-37	165	211
15	38-41	166	212
15	42-46	167	213
15	47	168	215
16	1	169	216
16	2-8	171	216
16	9-11	173	218
16	12,13	176	220
16	14	178	221
16	15-18	181	224
16	19-20	184	226

Luke

Chapter	Verse(s)	Section	Page
1	1-4	1	23
1	5-25	4	28
1	26-38	5	29
1	39-45	6	30
1	46-56	7	30
1	57-80	8	31
2	1-7	10	33
2	8-20	11	33
2	21	12	34
2	22-38	13	34
2	39	16	37
2	40	17	37
2	41-50	18	37
2	51-52	19	38
3	1-2	20	39
3	3-6	21	39
3	7-14	22	41
3	15-18	23	42

Chapter	Verse(s)	Section	Page
3	19-20	34	51
3	21-23	24	43
3	23-38b	3	26
4	1-13	25	44
4	14a	34	51
4	14-15	37	54
4	16-31	39	55
4	31-37	42	57
4	38-41	43	57
4	42-44	44	58
5	1-11	41	56
5	12-16	45	59
5	17-26	46	60
5	27-32	47	61
5	33-39	48	62
6	1-5	50	64
6	6-11	51	65
6	12-16	53	67

Luke (cont.)

Chapter	Verse(s)	Section	Page	Chapter	Verse(s)	Section	Page
6	17-19	54	67	11	14-36	106	129
6	20-26	54	68	11	37-54	107	130
6	27-30, 32-36	54	70	12		108	132
				13	1-9	109	134
6	31	54	73	13	10-21	110	135
6	37-42	54	72	13	22-35	113	137
7	1-10	55	74	14	1-24	114	138
7	11-17	56	75	14	25-35	115	139
7	18-35	57	76	15	1-32	116	139
7	36-50	59	78	16	1–17:10	117	141
8	1-3	60	79	17	11-37	120	144
8	4	64	81	18	1-14	121	145
8	5-18	64	82	18	15-17	123	147
8	19-21	63	81	18	18-30	124	148
8	22-25	65	87	18	31-34	125	151
8	26-39	66	87	18	35-43	126	152
8	40-56	67	89	19	1-28	127	153
9	1-6	70	92	19	29-44	128b	155
9	7-9	71	95	19	45-48	129	158
9	10-17	72	97	20	1-19	132	161
9	18-21	82	109	20	20-26	133	164
9	22-25	83	110	20	27-40	134	165
9	26-27	84	111	20	41-44	136	167
9	28-36	85	112	20	45-47	137	168
9	36b	86	113	21	1-4	138	170
9	37-43	87	114	21	37-38	131	160
9	43b-45	88	115	21	5-36	139	171
9	46-48	90	116	22	1-2	140	178
9	49-50	91	117	22	3-6	142	180
9	51-56	95	120	22	7-13	143	180
9	57-62	93	119	22	14-16, 24-30	144	181
10	1-24	102	126				
10	25-37	103	127	22	17-20	148	185
10	38-42	104	128	22	21-23	146	182
11	1-13	105	128	22	31-38	147	184

Luke (cont.)

Chapter	Verse(s)	Section	Page
22	39-46	152	191
22	47-53	153	193
22	54a,63-65	155	196
22	54b-62	156	197
22	66-71	157	199
23	1-5	159	200
23	13-25	161	203
23	26-33a	163	207
23	33b-34, 38, 35-37, 39-43,	164	208

Chapter	Verse(s)	Section	Page
23	44-45a,46	165	211
23	45b, 47-49	166	212
23	50-54	167	213
23	55-56	168	215
24	1-8	171	216
24	9-12	172	218
24	13-32	176	220
24	33-35	177	221
24	36-43	178	221
24	44-49	183	225
24	50-53	184	226

John

Chapter	Verse(s)	Section	Page
1	1-18	2	24
1	19-28	26	46
1	29-34	27	46
1	35-51	28	47
2	1-11	29	48
2	12	30	48
2	13-22	31	48
2	23–3:21	32	49
3	22-36	33	50
4	1-4	34	51
4	5-42	35	51
4	43-45	36	53
4	46-54	38	54
5	1-47	49	63
6	1-13	72	97
6	14-15	73	99
6	16-21	74	99
6	22-71	76	101

Chapter	Verse(s)	Section	Page
7	1	77	102
7	2-9	94	120
7	10	95	120
7	11-52	96	121
7	53–8:11	97	122
8	12-20	98	122
8	21-59	99	123
9	1-41	100	124
10	1-21	101	125
10	22-39	111	135
10	40-42	112	137
11	1-44	118	143
11	45-54	119	144
11	55–12:1, 9-11	128a	155
12	12-19	128b	155
12	2-8	141	179
12	20-50	130	159

John (cont.)

Chapter	Verse(s)	Section	Page	Chapter	Verse(s)	Section	Page
13	1-20	145	181	18	39–19:16a	161	203
13	21-30	146	182	19	16b-17	163	207
13	31-38	147	183	19	18b, 23-24, 19-22, 25-27	164	208
14	—	149	186				
15–16	—	150	187				
17	—	151	189	19	28-30	165	211
18	1	152	191	19	31-42	167	213
18	12-14,19,23	154	195	20	1	171	216
18	15-18,25-27	156	197	20	2-10	172	218
				20	11-18	173	218
18	2-12	153	193	20	19-25	178	221
18	24	155	196	20	26-31	179	222
18	28-38	159	200	21	—	84	223

In addition to the Gospels the following Scripture is also used in the Harmony:

Acts 1:3-8 in section 183, page 225
Acts 1:9-12 in section 184, page 226
Acts 1:18-19 in section 158, page 200
1 Corinthians 15:5a in section 177, page 221
1 Corinthians 15:5b in section 179, page 222
1 Corinthians 15:6 in section 181, page 224

Is Harmonization Honest?

Dale Ellenburg

The most popular biography ever written is the account of Jesus' life contained in the four Gospels. For twenty centuries this story has inspired, challenged, and convicted mankind. The story never grows old, and it is today as inspiring as when it was first recorded by Matthew, Mark, Luke, and John. What is more, the accounts of the life of Jesus in the Gospels have not only survived, but they have thrived in spite of being subjected to unprecedented criticisms.

So it is not surprising that Gospel harmonies have long been a popular way of studying the life of Jesus. In fact, the practice of paralleling the similar texts of the four Gospels goes back to the second century when Tatian composed a harmony in the Syriac language. That effort was soon followed by Ammonius of Alexandria, who was first to arrange the text of the four Gospels in four parallel columns. Many refinements were made through the centuries, and Gospel harmonies remain an accepted tool for studying the words and works of our Lord. Two of the more popular harmonies used in recent years are Robertson's *A Harmony of the Gospels* and Robert Thomas & Stanley Gundry *An NIV Harmony of the Gospels.*

Why the Question?

Given the prominence and popularity of this methodology for studying the Gospels, the question regarding the "honesty" of harmonization may seem odd. Perhaps the better way to pose the question is, "Is Gospel harmonization legitimate?" But the question needs to be asked for several reasons. First, the devotees of modern criticisms (e.g., source, form, and redaction criticisms) no longer accept the validity of an enterprise such as this. They maintain that we cannot reconcile the seemingly impossible contradictions found within the four Gospels. But, as we shall see, some degree of harmonization must take place if we are to reconstruct any historical event.

Further, the question needs to be posed because it provides a natural context in which to define our terms. A Gospel harmony, like the one you hold in your hands, is the end product of the work of many Bible students who care deeply about Jesus' life. But behind the end product lie specific principles involved in the process of harmonization. This latter term refers to the procedure of seeking reasonable explanations for seeming discrepancies between parallel accounts of Scripture. When using a harmony, the reader quickly notes that the Gospel accounts are similar, but they are far from identical. Jesus' words are sometimes different from one Gospel to another. Differences in grammar or construction are common, synonymous expressions may appear in parallel Gospels, stylistic differences are obvious when comparing one story with another, and the chronologies are almost impossible to reconcile in some places. What reasonable ways do we account for these divergences?

Answering the Critics

It must be admitted that Gospel harmonies have always been embraced more by conservative students of Scripture than by those who do not hold a high view of inspiration. Until the rise of nineteenth-century higher criticism, there was not much dispute concerning the value of studying the Gospels in parallel fashion. Opposition from the higher critical perspective tends to be consistent with the presuppositions that lie behind the respective criticism itself. For example, form critical scholars maintain that the early church took fragmented, oral traditions about Jesus and "formed" the Gospels, elaborating and embellishing at many points, in a way that met the spiritual needs of the respective communities. Or, a redaction critic would argue that a writer/editor, not so much a community, was responsible for the documents we know as Matthew, Mark, Luke, and John. But that writer/editor did what the form critics said the community did—they molded the traditions in a way that reflected their own understanding of Jesus and His life. Then, of course, there were the demythologizers, who, with their complete anti-supernatural bias, insisted that any account of a miraculous act or claim on the part of Jesus must be expunged from the accounts.

We do not need here to repeat the well-documented presuppositions and conclusions of higher criticism.[1] But these few statements suffice to demonstrate why higher critics hold that harmonization is implausible. While these critical scholars emphasize the discrepancies between the Gospel accounts, more conservative scholars seek to show that there are valid explanations for many of the "impossible contradictions." I will be the first to sound an alarm against the kind of uncritical conservatism that led Osiander, in the sixth century, to suggest that Jairus' daughter was actually raised from the dead twice just so he could "harmonize" a seeming discrepancy.

A two-pronged answer can be offered to higher critics who reject *prima facie* the testimony of the Gospels. First, why does the burden of proof fall on the Bible believer? The Gospels claim to be based on eyewitness accounts of the life of Jesus, so until they are demonstrated to be incorrect or false (which, by the way, has never been done), why not trust them? Is it not disingenuous to suggest, as many critics do, that we can trust the Gospels to reconstruct a community of faith but we cannot trust them to reconstruct the Person upon whom that faith is based?

Another way that we can answer some of the objections of the critics and still be legitimate in our harmonizing efforts is to stress that the text should never be divorced from the author's intention. In this way, we can go a long way in suggesting that one of the most common areas of dispute, that is, the chronology of the Gospel accounts, is really not a problem at all. It is critical that we understand the nature, or genre, of the Gospels. They are not objective biographies written by disinterested or dispassionate men. They are theological biographies—accurate, reliable, but heavily laden with presuppositions—as are all biographies. The purpose of each Gospel writer was to present the facts about Jesus with the intention of showing Him to be the fulfillment of the Old Testament Messianic promises, the Son of Man, the Savior of the world, yes, even God Himself. So it should not seem inappropriate if their first concern was not chronology. Thomas Lea's comment is right on track: "The Gospel writers did not intend to provide a complete historical harmony of Jesus' life. Sometimes the writers arranged their material topically, and this makes it difficult to relate the chronology of events in one Gospel to that of another."[2]

An illustration from daily experience might help. Let us imagine that an automobile accident has taken place. Three people witnessed the accident. If we question the witnesses, they will each relate different details that stand out in their memory. We might even receive some minor disagreements in chronology. But just because one remembers a detail or a sequence that is different from the others, we do not discount all the witnesses. We know at that point that a bit of simple historical reconstruction can probably remove the apparent conflicts.

So, harmonization is a natural tendency of the human mind to resolve discord by drawing contrasting elements into a balanced composition. In music, it is not only useful but also necessary to blend separate tones into a chord. Otherwise, what we have is an unharmonious sound. In biblical studies, we merge two or more accounts into a composite version, perhaps within a larger

---

1. For a fuller discussion, see Ray Summers, "Contemporary Approaches in New Testament Studies," in vol. 8, *General Articles, Matthew-Mark*, of *Broadman Bible Commentary* (Nashville: Broadman, 1969), 48-58.
2. Thomas D. Lea, *The New Testament: Its Background and Message* (Nashville: Broadman & Holman, 1996), 86.

framework, thus preserving characteristic elements from each and giving a plausible account about how these diverse elements are related. Our conviction is that what we have in the trustworthy accounts of the four Gospels is not disharmony but convergence.

Harmony versus Synopsis

Although we have come to use the terms in a rather interchangeable fashion, "harmonies" and "synopses" are really not the same. Technically, a harmony refers to a literary work that has interwoven two or more sections of Scripture into a continuous narrative. In this way, the editors weave together the first four books of the NT into one continuous narrative. Scholars have long recognized four types of harmonizing: radical, synthetic, sequential and parallel. **Radical** harmonizing suppresses variant details in one text by replacing them with preferred wording drawn from another version. Radical harmonizing tends to produce a uniform official version of a saying or story in separate Gospels. A **synthetic** harmony expands a text by adding details from one account to another to produce a conflated version that is not identical with any one source. **Sequential** harmonizing preserves two or more versions of the same material as separate incidents in the same narrative. This produces repetitions of sayings and stories that literary critics call "doublets." This volume is an example of a **parallel** harmony, which presents two or more versions of the same account side by side in a synopsis for easy comparison. This type of Gospel harmony highlights both the similarities and the differences of the versions of a pericope and is a basic tool of modern Gospel scholarship.

A "synopsis," much like a parallel harmony, refers to works that set forth similar texts or accounts in parallel format, usually in a column arrangement. The United Bible Society has produced a valuable tool of this type and appropriately named it *Synopsis of the Four Gospels*. The key difference between a synopsis and a parallel harmony is that the "harmony" only lists a given text once, whereas a "synopsis" may list it several times without the editors making a judgment as to where they think it best fits in the flow of the Gospels.

What Reasonable Explanations Do We Seek to Explain Divergences?

Given the unparalleled scrutiny with which the Gospels have been examined, it must be admitted that there is remarkable similarity between them. After all, if the accounts contained verbatim literary parallel, the critics would cry foul on the charge of unscrupulous copying! Inevitably, however, critics point out the dissimilarities. We need to understand that those dissimilarities have been answered with viable explanations that have as much merit as the criticisms leveled against them. A full discussion of reasonable scholarly options for explaining the divergences we find in the Gospels is not possible here, but a sample list of options may be helpful.[3]

We have already cited one of the most common examples of divergent material in the Gospels—chronological differences. For example, did Jesus curse the fig tree before or after He cleansed the temple (cp. Mt 21:12-19 and Mk 11:12-14,20-24)? A close examination of Mark's account shows that Christ made two trips to the temple. Mark 11:11 says He entered the temple area on Sunday, but no mention is made of proclamations against the Jews and the temple. Verse 12 describes the events of the next day when the fig tree was cursed and the temple was cleansed. Matthew's account simply telescopes these two days into one. Such summarizing of events is certainly acceptable on the part of a historian.

---

3. For an excellent treatment see Craig Blomberg, *The Historical Reliability of the Gospels* (Downer's Grove, IL: InterVarsity, 1987), 113–52.

Another kind of divergence we find in the Gospels can be attributed to each evangelist's theological intent. One example we can note here is the perplexing issue of differences in Jesus' genealogy as presented by Matthew and Luke. Skeptics of all ages have asserted the impossibility of reconciling the differences in the two lists. But several possibilities do exist, the most plausible of which is to recognize that they differ because they are supposed to. Matthew may well have been giving us the real descent of Jesus' earthly father Joseph, while Luke's intent was to record Mary's descent.[4] The difference is one of intent, and we have already noted that the Gospels are theological biographies that reflect the objectives of each author.

Then, we also recognize that sometimes we find one writer paraphrasing what another writer treated in more detail. One example of this practice can be seen in the difficult words of Jesus in Luke 14:26. When Matthew records this statement, in 10:37, he seems to "tone down" the harshness of the statement. What is at stake here is whether we have the *ipsissima verba* (the actual words of Jesus) or the *ipsissima vox* (the essential voice). There is no question that historians often record the voice of a character without due diligence to his very words at some points. Matthew's record is a fair interpretation of Jesus' words in Luke—either way, allegiance to Jesus must take precedence over even family relations. Under this category we could also place another example of divergence—the matter of omissions. Gospel writers simply chose to include some material and leave out other material that is contained in another Gospel. We cannot know the reasons why, but even the most unsympathetic critic will admit to the writer's prerogative to select his own material for his own purposes. Luke's shorter version of Matthew's longer Sermon on the Mount is a case in point.[5]

Historical-contextual consideration is another way we can answer seemingly impossible divergences. In Matthew 10:5-6 Jesus commanded His disciples to go only to the house of Israel, not to the Gentiles. Later, in the Great Commission, He sends them to all the nations. Elaborate attempts have been made to solve this supposed conundrum, but once we see that Jesus and the disciples (unlike Paul) preached almost exclusively to the Jews, they turned their attention to the world at large. In reality, taking into account the historical context, there is no contradiction in Jesus' words at all.

Conclusion

Far from being a dishonest or disingenuous enterprise, harmonization is an effective way to study the records of Jesus' life. While allowing us to enjoy each Evangelist's unique voice, the process also allows us to hear all the parts in concert. One way that happens is when one Gospel fills in missing details from another. Also, the four accounts remind us of the historical importance of Christianity. Jesus said and did many things, and the presence of not one "official," stagnant record of His life, but four unique yet similar accounts argues for the historical validity of His life. Historians typically seek to harmonize apparent conflicts in any story, and the application of this discipline to the Gospels in no way impugns their historical integrity.

---

4. A. T. Robertson's *Harmony of the Gospels for Students of the Life of Christ: Based on the Broadus Harmony in the Revised Version* (New York, Evanston, and London: Harper and Row, 1922) contains a good discussion of the possibilities.

5. I am aware that some scholars do not accept this view concerning the differences between the two versions, but it is *one* plausible explanation.

A History of Harmonies: Major Steps

Shawn Buice

One unresolved issue in New Testament scholarship at the beginning of the twenty-first century is commonly known as the Synoptic Problem.[1] Because it is unresolved, research continues unabated as new generations of scholars are introduced to and challenged by the difficulties of determining the exact nature of the relationship between the first three canonical Gospels: Matthew, Mark, and Luke.

Vital to this quest is a careful analysis of the text of the Gospels themselves, comparing the similarities and differences of the parallel accounts of the life and teachings of Jesus. To facilitate this study, scholars through the centuries utilized various methods to examine and analyze the Gospel records. Scholars most commonly chose to use harmonies and synopses to integrate the Gospel accounts.

Definitions

The two major formats adopted and widely used today for synoptic Gospel research are called the *harmony* and the *synopsis*. Harmonies and synopses are distinctive types of work with a similar goal. Scholars use the different formats to compile material from the Gospels into one account. However, some argue about which type of work should be called a "harmony" and which type should be called a "synopsis." There are those, for example, who would prefer to use the one word, harmony, to describe both types of works.[2] Yet, careful consideration shows that the works are unique.

Harmonies were an effort by early scholars to compile the material from the Gospels into one account. The word *harmony* was used for centuries to describe a work that sought to incorporate all the material from the Gospels into a single flowing narrative.[3] One of the advantages of this format was that it allowed the reader to follow the events of the life of Jesus as they unfolded.

The word *synopsis,* on the other hand, was used to describe a work that placed each Gospel record in parallel columns so that the reader could see the related accounts of the life of Jesus. A significant advantage of this format was that the reader could more easily compare and contrast the respective accounts of the life of Jesus with parallel material from the other Gospels. This greatly facilitated the study of the Gospels by allowing one to take note of both the similarities and differences in similar events from each Gospel. Although this format was not fully developed and widely used until the eighteenth century, today it is the more popular of the two styles for synoptic Gospel research.

While other formats also developed, the harmony and the synopsis remain two popular forms scholars use to study the life of Jesus. Both forms are beneficial to the scholar, the pastor, and the student. Today, however, although some continue to maintain the distinction between these particular formats, the words *harmony* and *synopsis* are commonly used almost synonymously.[4]

---

1. Simply stated, this problem seeks to understand the relationship among the canonical Gospels, specifically the first three: Matthew, Mark, and Luke. For a more detailed discussion of the synoptic problem, see the article in this volume by Daniel Akin.

2. Harvey K. McArthur, *The Quest through the Centuries: The Search for the Historical Jesus* (Philadelphia: Fortress, 1966), 89.

3. An early example of this type of format was Tatian's *Diatessaron*. More will be said about this work later. A modern example is Kermit Zarley's *The Gospels Interwoven* (Wheaton: Victor, 1987). A more recent example is George W. Knight's *A Simplified Harmony of the Gospels* (Nashville: Broadman & Holman, 2001). Knight's harmony makes use of the recently completed Holman Christian Standard Bible®.

4. Besides the present work, see Robert L. Thomas and Stanley N. Gundry, *A Harmony of the Gospels* (New York: HarperCollins,

Early Precursors

Modern harmonies are not a recent development. In fact, they trace their roots to the middle of the second century. One of the earliest known attempts to produce a work that combined all the material from the Gospels and placed them into a single narrative was the *Diatessaron* compiled by Tatian around AD 160. According to Robert Stein, Tatian sought "to produce a single comprehensive text."[5] Stein noted that Tatian's work reduced the number of verses in the four Gospels from 3,780 to 2,769 without excluding any event or teaching from the life of Jesus.[6]

The forerunner of the modern synopsis appeared in the early part of the third century. Ammonius of Alexandria developed a system that enabled an individual to compare parallel accounts of the life of Jesus. He used the full text of Matthew's Gospel "and then copied alongside what he regarded to be the parallel portions of the other gospels [sic]."[7] A drawback to the work of Ammonius was that the material in the other three Gospels that had no parallel in the Gospel of Matthew was simply left out.

No other notable advances beyond the work of Tatian and Ammonius were made during this early period. Other harmonies were produced in this era, but, as Stephen Patterson explained, "no new gospel [sic] harmony seems to have appeared before the 15th century."[8] One reason for this was the influence of Tatian's *Diatessaron*. In fact, most of the works from this period in history followed the single narrative structure. P. Feine commented that "from Augustine until J. Clericus' *Harmonia evangelica*, . . . the material of the Gospels was treated preponderantly from the view-point of the interwoven narrative."[9] This perspective changed, however, beginning in the sixteenth century.

The Sixteenth through the Eighteenth Centuries

A study of the history of harmonies beginning with the sixteenth century reveals an amazing phenomenon: there is a significant increase in the production of harmonies. In fact, Harvey McArthur noted "a dramatic contrast between the paucity of harmonies in the preceding centuries and their proliferation in the sixteenth century."[10] The increase was such that this period "produced more harmonies than the combined fourteen centuries that preceded it!"[11]

Two questions arise at this point: why were so many harmonies produced during this era, and what advances were made to the existing formats? In response to the first question, one factor that certainly had an impact on the rise of harmonies during the sixteenth century was the invention of the printing press. The printing press greatly facilitated the production of books. Yet, this factor alone cannot account for the significant increase in the number of harmonies produced.

A second contributing factor was a renewed interest in the study of the Gospels themselves. In response to the question of what advances were made, the major advance to the format of harmonies produced during the sixteenth century was the development of the parallel column structure. Part of the impetus for the creation of this format, like the increase in the number of harmonies, can be traced to the rise of biblical criticism. In response to the assertions of more critical scholars,

---

1978) that uses the word "harmony" in its title but follows a parallel column format in presenting the text of the Gospels.

5. Robert Stein, *The Synoptic Problem* (Grand Rapids: Baker, 1988), 16.

6. Ibid.

7. Thomas and Gundry, *Harmony*, 269.

8. David Noel Freedman, Gary A. Herion, David F. Graf, and John David Pleins, *The Anchor Bible Dictionary*, volume 3 (New York: Doubleday, 1992), s.v., "Harmony of Gospels," by Stephen J. Patterson.

9. Schaff, Philip, *The New Schaff-Herzog Encyclopedia of Religious Knowledge*, editor-in-chief, Samuel Macauley Jackson, vol. 5 (Grand Rapids: Christian Classics Ethereal Library, 1910), s.v. "Harmony of the Gospels," by P. Feine.

10. McArthur, 86.

11. Ibid.

this new format sought to emphasize the trustworthiness of the Gospels by illustrating similarities among the various accounts of the life of Jesus.

Content, format, and text critical apparatus distinguish Johann Jacob Griesbach's parallel harmony of 1776 as the most notable. His, however, was not the first to use the parallel column style. While it is difficult to determine with certainty who created the first synopsis, several precursors to Griesbach's existed. For example, as early as 1565 Charles du Moulin opted for the same arrangement in his *Collatio et Unio Quatuor Evangelistarum Domini Nostri Jesu Christi*.[12] The parallel format also appeared in 1569 in the *Chronologia* of Gerhard Mercator.[13] The harmony most closely related to the work of Griesbach was produced in 1699 by Joannes Clericus. Clericus divided each page of his harmony into four columns.[14] When a particular Gospel lacked similar material, the column at that point was simply left blank.

It was this format, rather than the single narrative format, that Griesbach utilized for his synopsis. Griesbach himself explained, "I freely admit—and I wish to draw the readers' attention to this—that a 'harmonia' in the literal sense of the word is not the aim in this book."[15] Griesbach desired that the student see the parallel accounts from the Gospels so that "the individuality of each Evangelist, his style and vocabulary, his basic idea and structure, his method and sources, could all be made more visible."[16] One notable difference of Griesbach's original synopsis from its predecessors is that he excluded the material from John's Gospel. Otherwise, Griesbach's synopsis set a new standard for harmony formats that was followed for centuries. In fact, as one studies the history of harmonies, the significant influence that Griesbach's work had on subsequent generations is apparent.

Nineteenth Century to the Present

The nineteenth and twentieth centuries provided notable advances in harmony construction. One significant breakthrough in synopsis construction came in the late 1800s. W. G. Rushbrooke's *Synopticon* appeared in 1880, and Greeven claimed that the arrival of this work "must be termed a spectacular event in the history of the synopsis."[17] The reason this synopsis garnered such high praise was due to the fact that Rushbrooke became the first to compile a synopsis based on Marcan priority.

Thirteen years after Rushbrooke's synopsis appeared, John Broadus produced his harmony. Broadus's harmony deviated from previous harmonies by using divisions for the Gospel accounts based on historical considerations.[18] According to Robert Thomas and Stanley Gundry, "previous practice had been to divide [Christ's life] according to the feasts."[19]

Due to space considerations, only two other contributions will be mentioned. First, the work of Kurt Aland cannot be overlooked. His *Synopsis of the Four Gospels*[20] is perhaps the standard for an in-depth study of the Gospels. Robert Thomas and Stanley Gundry noted that "for the serious

---

12. McArthur, 89.
13. Ibid.
14. Heinrich Greeven, *The Gospel Synopsis from 1776 to the Present Day* (Cambridge: Cambridge University Press, 1978), 24.
15. J. J. Griesbach, quoted in Greeven, 27.
16. Ibid.
17. Ibid., 36.
18. A. T. Robertson, *A Harmony of the Gospels for Students of the Life of Christ* (New York: Harper & Row, 1922), vii. Robertson's work was a revision of Broadus' harmony. Further, the format chosen for this present harmony is a modified form of Robertson's.
19. Thomas and Gundry, 272.
20. Kurt Aland, *Synopsis of the Four Gospels*, 9th ed. (Stuttgart, Germany: German Bible Society, 1989).

student who uses Greek, Aland's work is indispensable for a comparative study of the Gospels."[21] One important feature of Aland's work is that it incorporates the full text of John's Gospel.

A second valuable contribution to synopsis construction in the twentieth century, also utilizing the Greek text, is John Orchard's *A Synopsis of the Four Gospels.*[22] Orchard explained that his synopsis "is the very first in the two-hundred year history of modern synopses to set out the Four Gospels according to the principle that Luke is the mean between Matthew and Mark."[23] In other words, Orchard's synopsis challenged the predominance of the theory of Marcan priority. Orchard believed that Matthew's Gospel was first, Luke's Gospel was second, and that Mark's came third. His work, therefore, illustrated the so-called two-Gospel hypothesis.

This brief historical sketch highlighted the major advances in harmony construction. Modern harmonies have a history that originated in the middle of the second century. While other harmonies could have been included, these were selected because of the specific contributions they made to synoptic Gospel formats.

Conclusion

The study of the history of harmonies is also a study of the Synoptic Problem. Changes made to the formats of harmonies reflect the thinking of scholars during specific time periods about the relationship of the Gospels to one another. A historical perspective of the advances in harmony construction reveals the advances scholars made in not only making the full story of the life of Christ more accessible but also revealing the significant relationship between the different Gospel accounts.

---

21. Thomas and Gundry, 270.
22. John Bernard Orchard, *A Synopsis of the Four Gospels* (Edinburgh: T. & T. Clark, 1983).
23. Orchard, xiv.

Why There Are Four Gospels

Rick Melick

Even the most casual reader of the NT notices four Gospels. Since there is only one Gospel message, and Jesus is the only Way to God, do we really need four Gospels? At a deeper level, scholars have differing opinions as to both the provenance of each Gospel and the perspectives of their authors.

Christians have always accepted four Gospels. It seems as soon as they were read, each of them was accepted as genuine and valuable to the church. The earliest collections of Christian books include the four Gospels of the NT. Among the church fathers before AD 200, only Polycarp (AD 150) includes only two (Matthew and John). Justin Martyr (AD 140) and Irenaeus (AD 170) include all four, as do the extant lists of accepted books. These include the Old Syriac (end of second century), Old Latin (before AD 200), the Muratorian Canon (AD 170), and Codex Barococcio (AD 206). The early church classified them among their *homolegoumena*, accepted books.

The case for the four Gospels strengthens in light of the spurious gospels the church did not accept. The church knew of many other "Gospels" written by non-apostles and heretical groups, such as the famous Gospel of Thomas. Consistently the church recognized the inferiority of these writings when compared with the four canonical Gospels.

The acceptance of four Gospels raises two questions: why are they so alike, and why are they so different? Regarding similarity, only approximately 8% of the Gospel of Mark is not found in Matthew or Luke. Approximately 30% of Matthew is unique to Matthew, and about 50% of Luke is unique. John contains almost entirely unique material. The three Synoptic Gospels share many of the same events recorded in the Gospels. Regarding the differences, each Gospel has a significant amount of unique material (from 8% to 90%). To be more precise, the actual words and details of the common events differ significantly. The church always acknowledged the need for four Gospels even with such similarity and such diversity.

Reasons for Four Gospels

The NT did not emerge in a vacuum, nor did its writers confer on the nature and number of the books to comprise it. Each of the four Gospels arose because of unique needs in the emerging church. It seems the Holy Spirit inspired four different Gospels for at least four reasons.

The Missionary/Evangelistic Advance of the Church

The early church grew spontaneously. Sometimes growth came in response to events like persecution (Ac 8:1,4; 11:19-20). Other times church leaders intentionally took the gospel to new areas (Ac 13:1ff). Historically, churches arose in Palestine, Samaria, Africa, Syria, modern Turkey, and Europe before any Gospel was written. Most of the Epistles, written primarily to these young churches, preceded the writing of the Gospels. The story of Jesus was transmitted orally until the Spirit inspired various writers to preserve it. The advance of the gospel called for preservation of the life and work of its Founder.

The Apostolic Memories Preserved

The early church rightly revered the apostles as the leaders of Christianity. The earliest explanation of the writing of the Gospels supports that. Papias, a church father (AD 110) explained that Matthew wrote first and that Mark wrote Peter's recollections. Similarly, the early church accepted Luke because of his association with the Apostle Paul, and John was revered as the last surviving apostle. Matthew, Peter (Mark), and John wrote their experiences, interpreting them for generations of Christians who would not have traveled with Jesus. It was important that each of the apostles, including Paul, record their understanding for the church's faith.

Connecting Interculturally

In the rapid spread of the gospel, the early missionaries encountered new ideas, foreign gods, and cultural patterns far different from Judaism. The cultural differences followed national and ethnic lines encountering local gods and sub-Christian practices. The cultures of the first century were quite diverse and much of the NT addresses these issues.

Some cultures were better prepared to understand the message of Jesus than others. Those who could not needed their own explanation of Jesus' life and work. The Great Commission calls for people of all perspectives to be able to connect with Jesus. The Holy Spirit inspired four accounts, each different in secondary emphases, but each one presenting the basic message of faith in Jesus. The secondary issues will become more apparent in the following discussion. It should suffice now to note that under the guidance of the Holy Spirit the various writers acknowledged that not all people value the same cultural qualities. Thus four Gospels present Jesus with enough diversity that even cultures quite foreign to Jewish faith are able to understand the message of redemption.

Theological Distinctives Emerge

Each of the Gospel writers presents a theological explanation of Jesus' life and death that complements the others. Often people overstress the theological differences and postulate from them a diverse Christianity. Nothing could be further from the truth. Yet each writer does present personal nuances and theological emphases. Collectively the four provide a broad understanding of the truth. The writers drew from their personal recollections and encounters as they spread the gospel.

The distinctive elements of each Gospel emerge when the Gospels are studied in layers. At the most basic layer, the Gospel writers describe the historical accounts of what Jesus said and did. As historians they reproduced these events with accuracy and integrity. Second, they wrote from their own perspectives. Each writer demonstrates variety in the manner in which the stories are told. This extends at times to the words chosen, which build the emphasis the writer remembered from each story. Finally, needs in the churches account for differences in presentation. The Gospel documents are applications of the events and perspectives to a particular cultural and ideological group. The separate Gospels enable various people of the world to identify with the story of Jesus. The unity of accounts produced confidence that the story was true.

The Gospel writers were in large part task theologians. They believed their message and sought to present it relevantly. At the same time, they defended it by presenting corrective and instructive information about Jesus' life. The four together weave a magnificent composite picture of Jesus' life, presented with sensitivity to diverse cultures. This may be seen by comparing the Synoptic Gospels.

The Distinctive Contributions of the Gospels

Matthew

Matthew is at once the most Jewish and the most universal of the Gospels. His Gospel is noteworthy in its use of the OT, containing more direct quotes and allusions than any of the others. At the same time it is the only Gospel to include the word "church" and it explains that the Great Commission includes everyone. It is written to people who are sympathetic to Jewish life. Yet it must explain how and why Christians have taken the message to non-Jewish cultures.

The writer carefully weaves his way through the minefield of accepting the Jewish religion that brought the world the Messiah, yet rejecting the narrow understanding of the Jews who rejected Him. The masterful way this occurs in his Gospel may be observed in the themes Matthew presents about Jesus and His predictions about the future of Christianity. Matthew is critical of Jewish life. Jesus confronted Jewish religious practices (6:5; 23:32-33) and Jewish intolerance of Christians (10:17; 23:34). The Jewish establishment will be judged (11:20-24; 22:8). Yet he affirms Jewish interpretations of the OT (5:21-33) and the validity of the Law (5:17-18).

Matthew balances particularism and universalism. He supports "kingdom theology," a distinctively Jewish expectation (4:23; 9:35; 24:14), using the word kingdom more than any other Gospel writer. Yet he includes global acknowledgement of the Jewish Messiah in the visit of the magi (2:1-12). He mentions the word "church" as though it were an established institution (16:19; 18:18). Further, while affirming the necessity of the kingdom, Matthew recalls Jesus' words about the worldwide impact of Jesus' ministry (8:11-12; 24:14; 28:19).

Matthew appears to be written in a setting that required explanation of Jesus as both Jewish and Christian. The Gospel is thoroughly Jewish in orientation. It is, simultaneously, thoroughly Christian in perspective. It maintains this balance by a Messianic theology that brings both theological and ethical tensions. Matthew and his readers are likely in a Jewish Messianic community, where there is both appreciation for Jewish heritage, hopes, and distinctives, and criticism for Jewish blindness, failures, and opposition to the spread of the Gospel.

Mark

Mark is the least Jewish and most Roman in perspective. This is evidenced by the specifically Roman characteristics of the book. Mark's presentation includes the relationship Jesus had to authority: He is both under authority and in authority. It includes short, quick events as the core of the book. The action orientation fits the Roman mentality well. Mark begins with Jesus as an adult and ready for ministry. The Roman world had little place for genealogy. Mark translates some Aramaic phrases, presumably because they are foreign to the readers, and he alone includes Latin phrases.

Somewhat like Matthew, Mark also guides the reader through cultural tensions in his presentation of Jesus. Jesus is the Jewish Christ, yet it is the Roman centurion who provides the ultimate validation of Jesus as Son of God (16:39). For Mark, Jesus is less the storyteller and teacher, and more the activist. His power over the difficulties people face provides a needed understanding of His person.

Mark's presentation of Jesus differs from Matthew's and Luke's. It is written to connect with a non-Jewish audience so that they can identify with the gospel message.

Luke

Luke's presentation acknowledges the universal appeal of Jesus, the perfect human. His presentation stresses the logical extension of Jesus' work beyond its Jewish packaging to the whole world. Clearly Jesus envisioned a universal movement of faith. Jesus' ministry extended to outcasts, women, and non-Jews (1:53; 2:32; 3:12; 9:51-56). Theologically Luke gives great emphasis to the Holy Spirit. He attributes the work of Jesus and His apostles to God through the impulse of the Holy Spirit leading them into the world.

Beyond these characteristics, Luke writes with sensitivity to the questions Gentiles might ask. First, how do Christians relate to the Roman government? Luke writes that, although their founder was a condemned Roman criminal and their movement was not sanctioned by Rome, Christians were no threat to the government. Second, how does Christianity relate to Judaism? Luke carefully demonstrates that Christianity was the fulfillment of Judaism that, once fulfilled, could indeed embrace the people of the world.

Third, how did Jesus relate to Jewish leaders? Luke explains that, although Christians are not accepted into synagogues and into the inner circles of Judaism, it was the Jews who failed to embrace the role as those through whom God would bless all nations. Christians exemplify God's heart for all people. Fourth, did God really expect that Christians would be His way of reaching the world? Luke attributes the spread of the gospel to God through the Holy Spirit. This is no afterthought. Christianity was the plan of God from the beginning.

Luke's presentation is to demonstrate to non-Jews that the gospel was applicable to everyone in the world.

John

The Gospel of John enjoys almost unanimous acclaim as "the universal Gospel." It, perhaps more than the others, is the Gospel most people can readily understand. The message is alive and simple. The Greek of the Gospel can be read by beginning Greek students, and yet the most sophisticated thinkers ponder the depth of its thought. Interpreters have debated its audience, including Greek, Gnostic, Alexandrian, and Rabbinic readers. Such scholarly latitudes reinforce the universal applicability of the Gospel of John.

Although utilizing the simplest of Greek language in writing, John carefully constructed his portrayal of Jesus. Clearly the purpose of writing is John 20:30-31. John crafts his writing to demonstrate that "the Christ is Jesus, the Son of God" (the most likely translation, which also suggests a Jewish context). He carries his readers to that point by an extended presentation of Jesus' public ministry, often called The Book of Signs (1–12), followed by an intimate conversation of one night in The Book of Discourse (13–17). The former consists of the interrelationships of seven miracles, called signs, with discourses that surround them. The signs have symbolic value pointing to One greater than signs who walked among them. The message conveyed comes in a thoroughly Jewish context, but often includes specific words capable of larger interpretation. These include knowledge, faith, and truth. The second section prepared the 12 disciples for Jesus' departure, providing timeless principles of how to remain faithful during His physical absence.

The most prominent theme is faith. John used the word for faith 98 times, more than any other writer. He used only its verbal form, "believing," never the noun "faith." The Gospel plots the development of genuine faith from a mere fascination with Jesus to a deeply personal, almost mystical relationship. Christian faith includes correct thought (theology) and life commitment.

Many believe John is the last book written in the NT canon. John put Jesus' life in historical and theological perspective reflecting on perhaps 60 years developing Christianity after the resurrection.

The Gospel presents trust in Jesus in a way that none can escape its significance, regardless of cultural or religious orientation.

Conclusion

One Message Four Ways

Anyone who reads the Gospels realizes that they tell the same story. The long passion narratives in each of the four Gospels reveal the central point: Jesus died in God's plan as the Savior of the world. Both the structure of the presentation of His life and the events recorded in His death reinforce that message.

Evangelistic Priorities

The reason for four Gospels has been suggested. First, the expansion of the church required a multi-cultural presentation of Jesus. Whether for evangelistic or apologetic reasons—and the church needed both—people with different cultural and religious backgrounds needed a way to connect with the Savior of the world. Without violating any of the historical elements of Jesus' life, each writer drew upon apostolic recollections and applied them skillfully to present a master picture of Jesus. From its earliest days the church has consistently affirmed that the four present an adequate picture of the Savior: no other Gospel is needed.

A Pastoral Use of Harmonies

Stephen D. C. Corts

One of the grand excellencies of the Gospels is the form they take: they are, more or less, historic biographies that render Jesus as He was in His earthly ministry.[1] A second, following close upon the first, is the fact that they come in a variety. Their narratives render for us four "portraits" of the one Christ.[2] Or, perhaps better, they yield four carefully crafted *montages*. Under the direction of the Spirit, each Gospel helps us to "see" the most important aspects of Jesus' person and work. Done in local color, absent any automatism and surrealism, the Gospels are carefully crafted, limited editions of Jesus the Christ.

These Gospels have always had a special place in the life of the believer, the local church, and hence in the work of the pastor. Jesus is the very center of the biblical story and the Christian faith. The Gospels are our primary sources of information about Him—His birth, life, teachings, death, and resurrection. They are critical to the leading pastoral tasks of maintaining vocational integrity, preaching Christ, and evangelizing a world in need of Him.

Because of the import of the Gospels and their diversity, a harmony of the Gospels is a required resource in a pastor's library. Such a harmony, if wisely used, can be an effective, multi-purpose ministry tool. The individual emphases that give each Gospel its distinctive qualities are made plain in a harmony. They give the pastor vital help as an under-shepherd of Christ, a preacher of the Gospels, and an ambassador to the lost.

The Harmonies and the Pastor's Calling

As under-shepherds called to be an example of Christ for the believers we serve, it seems obvious that the most critical aspect of the pastor's work is to know and reflect the life and ministry of Christ personally. "Be conscientious about yourself and your teaching" (1 Tm 4:16) is Paul's counsel to Timothy. Spiritual self-care comes first before teaching! Of course, all believers should aspire to a deeper knowledge of Christ in order to properly follow Him. But this is particularly true for the pastor—a man who must be able to live with integrity, saying to Christ's church: "Be imitators of me, as I also am of Christ" (1 Co 11:1). How is this to be done? For a start, it is accomplished by regular exposure to the Great Shepherd portrayed in the Gospels. C. S. Lewis, once calling for "real appreciation" of art, suggested an apt analogy for exposing our lives to Christ:

> We must use our eyes. We must look, and go on looking, till we have certainly seen exactly what is there. We sit down before the picture in order to have something done to us, not that we may do things with it. The first demand any work of art makes upon us is surrender. Look. Listen. Receive. Get yourself out of the way.[3]

It does every pastor unspeakable good to take a respite from speaking of and for Christ in order to surrender to Him afresh by watching Him. In this way we open ourselves to having something done to us by Christ rather than doing more of what we already do so well: doing for Him. In such times of quiet abandon, we are corrected and humbled. We see just how perfectly He orders His

---

1. Beyond this simple description, I will leave the question of the proper genre of the Gospels to others, *cedo maiori*.
2. See Richard Burridge, *Four Gospels, One Jesus?* (London: SPCK, 1994) for a profitable development of this idea of multiple portraits.
3. C. S. Lewis, *An Experiment in Criticism* (Cambridge: Cambridge University Press, 1961), 18–19.

life. We witness how His shepherding of people and His love for His Father are kept in effective balance, the latter nurturing the former.

A harmony of the Gospels is perfectly suited for such an endeavor. Time and study invested in exploring its broad, stereoscopic view of Jesus accomplishes something that does not come easily in ministry. It gets us out of the way. It reminds us of the portentous reality that we are called to love, feed, guard, and guide the sheep under our care like Christ did and still does. What is more, such a view reminds us that the sheep are His by costly sacrifice and not ours.

The Harmonies and Preaching

If maintaining integrity of calling is first in importance among the pastor's labors, preaching is surely second. Christ made preaching central—He literally preached His way to Calvary (see Mk 1:38). Paul felt himself compelled to preach as a high priority (see 1 Co 9:16-17). He made certain to underscore it for Timothy with his epigrammatic charge: "Proclaim the message; persist in it whether convenient or not" (2 Tm 4:2).

Preaching from the Gospels will be an important aspect of any pastor's work given their consequence for the spiritual health of the church. The pastor who makes certain that he knows the person and work of the Christ well in order to imitate Him will naturally give the flock under his care the same opportunity! Without question the Gospels had, as part of their original purpose, the training of new Christians in the essential story of Christ. They also serve to encourage established believers to seek deeper levels of faithfulness to Christ. Indeed, the Gospels function in no small way as training manuals for new believers, continuing education texts for maturing ones, and necessary teaching material for preachers.

Like all faithful preaching, preaching from the Gospels will deal directly with the explanation of a particular text and the application of it to the life situations of its hearers. This means that it will be concerned with sound exegesis and creative application throughout. There are two primary ways that harmonies can render aid in this vital endeavor.

First, a harmony of the Gospels can be used to establish the broader context for a Gospel pericope. Grappling with the ideas found in and about the main text are critical for the enterprise, of course. But part of the process of correctly teaching the Gospels also includes considering parallel texts. In this way, the larger fields of meaning are respected and reflected in the sermon itself.[4] When these parallels are duly considered, they have the effect of gathering the revealed light on a particular word or deed so as to make it better understood and more easily applied. Thus, a sermon constructed from one Gospel is enriched by materials from others.

Second, a harmony can give practical help in breaking out of what Haddon W. Robinson aptly describes as "sermon block."[5] Because so much of the Gospel accounts are committed to the coming of Christ, His death and resurrection,[6] pastoral preaching at Christmas, Palm Sunday, Good Friday, and Resurrection Sunday is easily done from them. Preparations for such days are easier in the first

---

4. Gordon Fee and Douglas Stuart show how this can be done. They suggest a two-fold way of thinking about gospel texts: horizontally and vertically. To think horizontally, one considers corresponding passages from other Gospels in order to better understand what is being said generally and what is being emphasized specifically. To think vertically is to consider the innate duality in the historical context of the Gospels: that of Jesus and then of the writer and his intended readers. Pastoral use of the harmonies in preaching comes primarily in the former: in the act of thinking horizontally. See Gordon D. Fee and Douglas Stuart, *How to Read the Bible for All Its Worth,* 3rd ed. (Grand Rapids: Zondervan, 2003), 135–143.
5. See Haddon W. Robinson, "Busting Out of Sermon Block," in *Making a Difference in Preaching* eds. Haddon W. Robinson and Scott M. Gibson (Grand Rapids: Baker, 1999), 96–106.
6. At minimum, a fourth of each of the four Gospels is committed to describing the eight-day period that begins with Palm Sunday and ends with Resurrection Day.

three years or so of ministry in one place. After that, it progressively becomes more of a creative challenge.

The harmonies can help the bleary preacher hurtling into yet another Christmas season to avoid the haunting sense that he is saying the same old thing in the same old ways to the same old people! Often whenever a harmony identifies an event or teaching as fleshed out by multiple texts, the additional information or particular emphases can yield a composite or comparative view that leads the preacher to discover and then render a well-known truth in its deeper implications or to reshape it with fresh insight.

With this said, it is important to offer a caveat. The best use of a harmony of the Gospels is not to construct and preach a synthesis of Gospel parallels. Many committed to expository preaching struggle at this point. Desiring to be faithful to all the information given in the Gospels as they address a particular teaching or event, expositors can be tempted to preach from multiple texts instead of the one initially chosen. Such an attempt can be done, of course. John Calvin, in the later years of his ministry, intentionally preached through all the Gospels in harmony—a worthy endeavor if the preacher and people have the capacity for such an extended treatment. The rest of us will probably do better to avoid preaching with any kind of synthesis as a goal. Besides, to do so runs the risk of blurring the distinct emphases of the individual Gospels. If this is done, we lose touch with the original intent of their authors. We fail to correctly teach the word of truth.[7]

The Harmony and Evangelism and Missions

Like Paul's protégé Timothy, today's faithful under-shepherd will be careful to do the work of an evangelist (2 Tm 4:5). Like any good worker seeking to "present yourself approved," you will select your tools carefully to secure the greatest effect for the cause of the kingdom. Chief among the pastor's evangelistic provisions are the Gospels themselves. Though this should be obvious, it is not for everyone, for whatever reason. Robert Sloan reminds us that

> It is no accident that the Gospels were given very early in Christian history titles (the Gospel according to Matthew, the Gospel according to Mark, etc.), [that] reflect the assumption of a singular Christian message (the gospel) with its focus upon certain central events, namely the death and resurrection of Jesus for our salvation.[8]

Similarly, Richard Melick urges that given the evangelistic nature of the Gospels, "while most of the material must be handled as historical record, one must always ask how the event presented functions to call men and women to Jesus as the saving Christ."[9] Today, the Gospels reverberate with the same call—they are evangelistic materials ready to be used in the Asian village, in the African bush, and the streets of Hometown, USA.

How might a harmony of the Gospels assist in evangelistic endeavors? The answer is simple: by helping us to identify the distinct emphases and themes that differentiate the Gospels and thereby equipping us to connect more effectively with the missionary opportunities God gives.

Consider how each evangelist calls persons to Christ in his own Spirit-inspired way. Each Gospel represents a deliberate, nuanced evangelistic effort focused on a particular community in need of

---

7. Of course, this is not to say that a preacher cannot or should not incorporate pertinent information or perspectives from other Gospels along the way. Rather, that the preacher must always beware of the very real danger of constructing by synthesis a new gospel of his own out of the four God has already provided.

8. Robert B. Sloan, "Canonical Theology of the New Testament," *Foundations for Biblical Interpretation*, David S. Dockery, et al., eds. (Nashville: Broadman and Holman Publishers, 1994), 576.

9. Richard R. Melick, Jr., "Literary Criticism of the New Testament," *Foundations for Biblical Interpretation*, David S. Dockery, et al., eds. (Nashville: Broadman and Holman, 1994), 437.

hearing and understanding the saving story of Jesus. Matthew proffers Christ as God's promised answer to those in need of hope. Mark presents Christ as powerful in His weakness for those broken by their weaknesses. Luke gives us Christ as Savior for all the world of men, regardless of wealth, race, or place. John portrays Christ as the Giver of life and purpose. Thus, each human author works strategically as he writes to show the ultimate relevance of Christ in the lives of the people he is engaging.

The Gospels themselves thus suggest one pastoral strategy for their effective use in evangelism: identifying the deep human needs and concerns that exist in the current evangelistic field of opportunity and engaging them with the gospel of Jesus. With knowledge of the lost and knowledge of the individual Gospels, the pastor-evangelist can select the most appropriate Gospel to use in a particular setting for preaching or evangelism. Indeed, knowing his audience as hopeless or powerless, class sensitive or purposeless, and having a sense of those audiences and emphases of the original evangelists make the pastor a worthy partner with the Holy Spirit in evangelism. What is more, such knowledge can open the flood gates of evangelistic creativity and confidence.

Conclusion

The life and labors of the pastor are unlike any other life and work. Few, if any, callings or professions make the variety of demands on one solitary person as does the pastorate. The pastor is called upon to be preacher, evangelist, counselor, theologian, visionary leader, caregiver, defender of the faith, ever-present friend, and helper of all.[10] Any tool that lifts his gaze, lightens his load, and enhances his effectiveness is always welcome. A harmony of the Gospels does precisely this in ways that can be surprising. Its careful use can revive the pallid minister and refresh his ministry. Indeed, it is worthy of his steady employment if only for fresh encounters with the Great Shepherd of God who is also the great *Agnus Dei.*

---

10. Richard Mayhue identifies no fewer than seventeen "primary" activities of the pastor in the Scripture! See Richard L. Mayhue, "Rediscovering Pastoral Ministry," *Rediscovering Pastoral Ministry: Shaping Contemporary Ministry With Biblical Mandates,* ed. John MacArthur, Jr. (Dallas: Word, 1995), 14–15.

The Academic Use of Gospel Harmonies

Steve W. Lemke

A harmony of the Gospels in the broader sense includes any account that attempts to construct a chronological account of the life of Jesus. Many scholars have written a "Life of Jesus" that collates the Gospel accounts into a single chronological narrative. In the narrower sense, however, a harmony of the Gospels depicts the chronology of Jesus' life by printing the accounts of each event from at least the three Synoptic Gospels (and usually John as well) in parallel columns.

Harmonies of the Gospels have been developed and used by academicians to achieve a variety of purposes. While harmonies of the Gospels have been written by scholars from across the theological spectrum, conservative scholars have particularly given attention to Gospel harmonies. It is incumbent on those who hold a high view of biblical inspiration to offer a defense of the truthfulness and accuracy of Scripture. Harmonies of the Gospels have been developed or utilized for at least the following purposes: to articulate a coherent chronological account of the life of Christ, to illustrate the process of biblical inspiration, to support the canonicity of the four Gospels, to address the "Synoptic Problem," to achieve a more accurate rendering of the original text of Scripture, to defend the historicity of the Christian faith, and to garner hermeneutical and exegetical insights.

Collating a Coherent Chronological Account of the Life of Jesus

The primary reason that Gospel harmonies have been developed (especially by conservative scholars) is to articulate a coherent chronological account of the life of Christ. Luke described his own purpose in writing his Gospel as setting the events of the life and ministry of Christ in "orderly sequence" (see Lk 1:1-3: Ac 1:1-3). Since the gospel of Jesus Christ is based so directly on the virgin birth, life, ministry, sacrificial death, and resurrection of Jesus Christ, an orderly account of the life and ministry of Christ offered by Gospel harmonies is of fundamental value to the Christian faith.

Providing Insights into the Process of Biblical Inspiration

Examining the four Gospels carefully in developing a Gospel harmony affords insights by Bible-believing scholars about the process of biblical inspiration. If God had chosen to reveal the Gospels in the same mechanical dictation process that He communicated the Ten Commandments to Moses, why would there be four Gospels? One perfect God-inspired Gospel would seem to be sufficient. It would appear obvious, then, that it pleased God to inspire the Gospels by working in and through key eyewitnesses of Jesus' life and resurrection, with the human authors writing the Gospels under the superintendence of the divine Author. This concursive process is precisely how the process of inspiration was described by Peter—"moved by the Holy Spirit, men spoke from God" (2Pt 1:21). The plenary verbal view of inspiration holds that God worked through human beings under the superintendence of the Holy Spirit to communicate precisely the message that God intended. The mystery of inspiration is that the diversity of language and perspective of the human authors of Scripture was so superintended by the Holy Spirit such that every word perfectly communicated the message and purpose of the divine Author of Scripture. By providing four Gospels, God doubled the usual scriptural requirement of two witnesses (Dt 17:6; 19:15;

Mt 18:16; 2 Co 13:1; 1 Tm 5:19; Heb 10:28; Rv 11:3) at the crucial point of bearing witness to the incarnation and resurrection of His Son.

The uniqueness of each Gospel and yet the common unifying message of the Gospels is seen nowhere more clearly than in a Gospel harmony. By setting each of the four accounts side by side, one can see how the Gospel writers communicated essentially the same message through their own unique language and perspective. The few harmonies that assumed a dictation theory of inspiration struggled to develop a coherent account because they refused to recognize the authenticity of complementary or divergent accounts describing the same event. For example, when Jesus is described as healing one blind man while leaving Jericho in Mark 10:46-52 and two blind men in the parallel account in Matthew 20:29-30, one with a dictation theory of inspiration must assume that these are two different events since they vary in detail. However, since both events are parallel in every other way (they occurred while Jesus was leaving Jericho, it involved healing the blind, and the dialogue between Jesus and the blind person is the same), it appears more likely that these are two parallel accounts that merely differ in detail. Mark focuses on the one blind man Bartimaeus, while Matthew mentions another blind person who was present but does not mention Bartimaeus by name. These minor differences of detail are not errors or contradictions but are simply incidental differences that arise from the specific memory and purpose of each Gospel writer. Mark did not say that there were not two men healed at that time—perhaps Jesus healed many blind persons that day. Mark simply focused on the personal reaction of one of the two blind men, rather than referring to both men in his account. The Gospel writers did not attempt to describe each event in Jesus' life exhaustively or in intricate detail, but they had larger spiritual purposes in mind (Jn 20:30-31). These parallel passages in the Gospel harmonies provide scholars with insights about how Gospel writers experienced the process of inspiration.

Offering Evidence for the Canonicity of the Four Gospels

The earliest Gospel harmonies provide some of the best evidence for the canonicity of the four Gospels. The name that Tatian and Ammonius gave their harmonies of the Gospels, *Diatessaron* ("through the four"), bears witness that the second- and third-century church recognized only the four canonical Gospels as authentic. The early Gospel harmonies provide proof that the early church never accorded the status of Holy Writ to apocryphal accounts such as the gospel of Thomas or the gospel of Peter.

Addressing the Synoptic Question

Scholars have also used Gospel harmonies to address the synoptic question—why Matthew, Mark, and Luke are so similar at many points, and yet different at other points. A number of proposals have been offered to answer the synoptic question, especially within the discipline of source criticism. Most early interpreters assumed that Matthew was the first Gospel to be written, and that it provided the basic outline and wording for the other Gospel writers. Later, the majority of the scholarly community became convinced of Markan priority—that Mark provided the basic outline used by the other Gospels. However, there remained other pericopes in Matthew and Luke, sometimes called the *Logia* ("sayings"), which had similarly worded accounts about some of Jesus' teachings. Some scholars proposed that the Gospel writers used other sources such as a hypothetical document Q (*Quelle*) as the source for these common accounts. Others proposed that the similarities and differences in the Synoptic Gospels arose from the access the Gospel writers had to brief accounts of the life of Jesus written on papyrus fragments and circulated in the early church before the first full Gospel was written. At any rate, the parallel presentation of the Gospel narratives afforded by a Gospel harmony provides the basic rubric for comparison as source critics address the synoptic question.

Discerning the Original Text of the New Testament

Another scholarly use of Gospel harmonies relates to textual criticism—ascertaining the original text of Scripture. It was no accident that J. A. Bengel, one of the pioneers of NT textual criticism, authored one of the prominent Gospel harmonies of his day. Textual critics study the parallel passages in a Gospel harmony to discern if some ancient manuscripts attempted to force an artificial harmonization on divergent NT texts that describe the same event. For example, in Matthew 4:1-11, the order of the temptations was first turning stones to bread, then jumping off the temple, and finally Satan offering Jesus the kingdoms of the world. In Luke 4:1-13, however, the order of temptations is the bread, the kingdoms, and the temple. A few manuscripts transposed Luke 4:5-8 to follow Luke 4:9-12, to make the Lukan account parallel the Matthean account.[1] Truth, however, should not be defended with deception or falsehood. It is better to ascertain the original text of Scripture and live with ambiguity in interpretation than to change the Word of God as God revealed it. Gospel harmonies are useful tools for scholars to identify these false harmonies in the text and to certify the original text of Scripture.

Defending the Historicity of the Christian Faith

The truthfulness of the foundational historical events of Christianity is more essential to the Christian faith than is the historicity of any other world religion's documents. The Apostle Paul was willing to acknowledge that if Jesus' resurrection were not indeed a historical fact, Christian faith and preaching are in vain (Rm 1:14-19). However, some modern critical scholars (such as those in the Jesus Seminar) have challenged the historicity of virtually every event in the NT, including the resurrection. As evidence for their claims, these scholars point to the divergence in details among parallel Gospel accounts describing the same event, such as the resurrection accounts (Mt 28:1-20; Mark 15:47–16:20; Lk 24:1-53; Jn 20:1-29). In Matthew's account, when Mary Magdalene and Mary go to the tomb, they see one shining angel. In Mark's Gospel, Mary Magdalene, Mary, and Salome see a young man at the tomb, and Mary Magdalene has another encounter later with the risen Christ in the garden. In the Gospel of Luke, Mary Magdalene, Mary, Joanna, and other women encounter two men in dazzling clothes at the tomb. In John's account, only Mary Magdalene is mentioned by name, and while nothing is mentioned about her seeing anyone on the first visit to the tomb, it is noted that she saw two angels at a subsequent visit.

How are these divergent accounts to be harmonized? Actually, these minor divergences in detail offer stronger evidence for the truthfulness of these recollections than for their error. Minor differences in recollection or description are common among eyewitnesses, and we do not demand perfect accuracy and detail in normal speech. Conservative scholars have used Gospel harmonies as a tool in attempting to do apologetics—to "always be ready to give a defense to anyone who asks you for a reason for the hope that is in you" (1Pt 3:15), particularly in defending the historicity of biblical events.

---

1. Bruce M. Metzger, *The Early Versions of the New Testament: Their Origin, Transmission, and Limitations* (Oxford: Clarendon Press, 1977), 114.

Offering Hermeneutical and Exegetical Insights

One of the most fruitful uses of Gospel harmonies is to assist exegetes to interpret Scripture more effectively. Clearly, setting the Gospel accounts side by side enriches the interpreter's understanding of these accounts as they supplement and complement each other by filling in details omitted in one account.

As various higher critical methodologies came to prominence in the late nineteenth and early twentieth centuries, the parallel presentation afforded by Gospel harmonies provided the foundational data for comparison between Gospel accounts. Advocates of form and source criticism, however, tended to atomize each Gospel pericope into a self-contained unit with little relationship to the material around it. In their view, the Gospel writers contributed little of their own material; they merely cut and pasted the accounts from earlier documents and oral traditions.

More recently, however, canonical criticism and redaction criticism have served as correctives to higher criticism. Canonical criticism restored the emphasis on the need to interpret each verse of Scripture in light of the whole canon of Scripture. In redaction criticism, the biblical authors are seen as authors who shaped the Gospels to meet their own unique perspective to the Gospels. The biblical authors edited (redacted) the previously existing material, shaping it and contributing their own standpoint. Redaction criticism can offer interesting hermeneutical insights. For example, redaction critic Heinz Joachim Held brought out the unique emphasis of Matthew in the parallel accounts of Jesus healing Simon Peter's mother-in-law (Mt 8:14-17; Mk 1:29-31; Lk 4:38-39). Held noted the following differences in the Matthean account: 1) only Jesus is mentioned entering the house, 2) no one tells Jesus about the woman's sickness, 3) some of the things mentioned in the other accounts that Jesus did to treat the woman is shortened to His touching her, 4) Jesus is the only subject of the verbs in the account, and 5) the woman serves "them" in the other accounts but "Him" in the Matthean account. Held proposed that Matthew's abbreviated and Christocentric account was to strip away nonessential details to focus on Jesus.[2] The Gospel harmonies thus offer a fruitful tool for interpreters in comparing the Gospel accounts to determine the unique contribution of each author.

---

2. Heinz Joachim Held, "Matthew as Interpreter of the Miracle Stories," in *Tradition and Interpretation in Matthew,* ed. Günther Bornkamm, Gerhard Barth, and Heinz Joachim Held (Philadelphia: Westminster, 1963), 169–171.

A HARMONY OF THE GOSPELS

PART I

THE SOURCES OF THE GOSPELS

Sec. 1   Luke Explains His Purpose and His Method of Research and Writing

Luke 1:1-4

[1]Many have undertaken to compile a narrative about the events that have been fulfilled[a] among us, [2] just as the original eyewitnesses and servants of the word handed them down to us. [3] It also seemed good to me, since I have carefully investigated everything from the very first, to write to you in an orderly sequence, most honorable Theophilus, [4] so that you may know the certainty of the things about which you have been instructed.[b]

[a]**1:1** Or *events that have been accomplished*, or *events most surely believed*   [b]**1:4** Or *informed*

Lk 1:1 *that have been fulfilled:* This phrase tells about what God has done through Jesus to fulfill His plan (see Lk 24:43-47).
Lk 1:2 *original eyewitnesses:* This verse refers to the preaching of the original oral tradition that circulated about Him before there were Gospels. These traditions were rooted in the preaching ministry of those who had been with Him.
Lk 1:3 *orderly sequence:* Since we know that Luke rearranged some events in his Gospel to be topical as opposed to chronological (see Lk 4:16-30 and parallels in Mark and Matthew), this orderly sequence has more to do with a general arrangement and order as opposed to meaning in temporal sequence.
Lk 1:4 *may know:* This is more than an intellectual knowledge, but the word has the idea of giving assurance in this context.

PART II

THE INCARNATION OF THE SON OF GOD

Sec. 2   Prologue to John's Gospel

John 1:1-18

¹ In the beginning was the Word,ᵃ
and the Word was with God,
and the Word was God.
² He was with God in the beginning.
³ All things were created through Him,
and apart from Him not one thing was created
that has been created.
⁴ Life was in Him,ᵇ
and that life was the light of men.
⁵ That light shines in the darkness,
yet the darkness did not overcomeᶜ it.

⁶ There was a man named John
who was sent from God.
⁷ He came as a witness
to testify about the light,
so that all might believe through him.ᵈ
⁸ He was not the light,
but he came to testify about the light.
⁹ The true light, who gives light to everyone,
was coming into the world.ᵉ

¹⁰ He was in the world,
and the world was created through Him,
yet the •world did not recognize Him.
¹¹ He came to His own,ᶠ
and His own peopleᶠ did not receive Him.
¹² But to all who did receive Him,
He gave them the right to beᵍ children of God,
to those who believe in His name,

ᵃ**1:1** The *Word* (Gk *Logos*) is a title for Jesus as the communication and the revealer of God the Father; Jn 1:14,18; Rv 19:13.
ᵇ**1:3-4** Other punctuation is possible: . . . *not one thing was created. What was created in Him was life*   ᶜ**1:5** Or *grasp,* or *comprehend,* or *overtake*; Jn 12:35   ᵈ**1:7** Or *through it* (the light)   ᵉ**1:9** Or *The true light who comes into the world gives light to everyone,* or *The true light enlightens everyone coming into the world.*   ᶠ**1:11** The same Gk adjective is used twice in this verse: the first refers to all that Jesus owned as Creator (*to His own*); the second refers to the Jews (*His own people*).   ᵍ**1:12** Or *become*

Jn 1:1-18 In the prologue John presents Jesus as the eternal, preexistent Word-become-flesh (1:1,14) and as the one-of-a-kind Son of the Father who is Himself God (1:1,18). God's revelation and redemption in Jesus is shown to culminate God's salvation history which previously included His giving the Law through Moses (1:17), His dwelling among His people in the Tabernacle (1:14), and the sending of John the Baptist (1:6-8,15). The prologue also introduces many of the major themes developed later in the Gospel, including Jesus as life, light, and truth; believers as God's children; and the world's rejection of Jesus.
Jn 1:1 *In the beginning:* The opening of the Gospel reminds the reader of Genesis 1:1, and indicates that in the incarnation of the Word or Logos (1:14) there is a recreation taking place. *the Word was God:* In this context, the notion of God is concrete and definite.
Jn 1:3 *All things were created through Him:* The Word was God's agent in the creation process.
Jn 1:5 *darkness did not overcome it:* An alternative translation is that the darkness did not understand it.
Jn 1:6 *John:* This section introduces John as sent by God but as witness to the one still to come, depicted as light.
Jn 1:10 *the world did not recognize Him:* As in the opening of Genesis, when the first humans did not recognize and follow God's commands, the Word though involved in creation was not recognized by this creation.
Jn 1:12 *children of God:* Those who accept and receive the Word are given the right to be called God's children, and recognized as adopted by God into His family. *to those who believe in His name:* The provision of adoption as children is predicated upon putting faith or trust in the Word.

John 1:1-18 (cont.)

¹³ who were born,
  not of blood,ᵃ
  or of the will of the flesh,
  or of the will of man,ᵇ
  but of God.

¹⁴ The Word became fleshᶜ
  and took up residenceᵈ among us.
  We observed His glory,
  the glory as the •One and Only Sonᵉ from the Father,
  full of grace and truth.

¹⁵ (John testified concerning Him and exclaimed,
  "This was the One of whom I said,
  'The One coming after me has surpassed me,
  because He existed before me.'")

¹⁶ Indeed, we have all received grace after grace
  from His fullness,

¹⁷ for although the law was given through Moses,
  grace and truth came through Jesus Christ.

¹⁸ No one has ever seen God.ᶠ
  The One and Only Sonᵍ —
  the One who is at the Father's sideʰ —
  He has revealed Him.

ᵃ**1:13** Lit *bloods*; the pl form of *blood* occurs only here in the NT. It may refer either to lineal descent (that is, blood from one's father and mother) or to the OT sacrificial system (that is, the various blood sacrifices). Neither is the basis for birth into the family of God.   ᵇ**1:13** Or *not of human lineage, or of human capacity, or of human volition*   ᶜ**1:14** The eternally existent Word (vv. 1-2) took on full humanity, but without sin; Heb 4:15.   ᵈ**1:14** Lit *and tabernacled*, or *and dwelt in a tent*; this word occurs only here in John. A related word, referring to the Festival of Tabernacles, occurs only in 7:2; Ex 40:34-38.   ᵉ**1:14** *Son* is implied from the reference to the Father and from Gk usage.   ᶠ**1:18** Since God is an infinite being, no one can see Him in His absolute essential nature; Ex 33:18-23.   ᵍ**1:18** Other mss read *God*   ʰ**1:18** Lit *is in the bosom of the Father*

Jn 1:13 *born . . . of God:* This indicates the second birth, by which those born the first time by human means (blood, flesh, human will) are born the second time of God.

Jn 1:14 *The Word became flesh:* The incarnation of the Word in fleshly form took place at the time of the birth of Jesus Christ. *We observed His glory:* The true glory of the divine Word was evident to those who had believed in Him.

Jn 1:15 *John testified:* The testimony of John in evidence of Jesus was that He was the one that he had been expecting and he recognized that He had surpassed him, not least because of His preexistence.

Jn 1:17 *law . . . grace and truth:* Law is associated with the Mosaic order, but grace and truth are associated with Jesus Christ.

Jn 1:18 *No one has ever seen God:* God did not appear directly to humans in the OT. In Jesus Christ God had become visible because He had appeared in human form. *The One and Only Son:* Jesus Christ was the one and only Son that God ever had, and He is positioned at God's side in collaborative action.

PART III

THE GENEALOGIES OF JESUS IN MATTHEW AND LUKE

Sec. 3 Apparently Joseph's Genealogy in Matthew and Mary's in Luke

Matthew 1:1-17	Luke 3:23b-38
[1] The historical record[a] of Jesus Christ, the Son of David, the Son of Abraham:	and was thought to be[a] the
	son of Joseph, ⌊son⌋[b] of Heli,
[2] Abraham fathered[b] Isaac,	[24] ⌊son⌋ of Matthat, ⌊son⌋ of Levi,
Isaac fathered Jacob,	⌊son⌋ of Melchi, ⌊son⌋ of Jannai,
Jacob fathered Judah and his brothers,	⌊son⌋ of Joseph, [25] ⌊son⌋ of Mattathias,
[3] Judah fathered Perez and Zerah by Tamar,	⌊son⌋ of Amos, ⌊son⌋ of Nahum,
Perez fathered Hezron,	⌊son⌋ of Esli, ⌊son⌋ of Naggai,
Hezron fathered Aram,	[26] ⌊son⌋ of Maath, ⌊son⌋ of Mattathias,
[4] Aram fathered Amminadab,	⌊son⌋ of Semein, ⌊son⌋ of Josech,
Amminadab fathered Nahshon,	⌊son⌋ of Joda, [27] ⌊son⌋ of Joanan,
Nahshon fathered Salmon,	⌊son⌋ of Rhesa, ⌊son⌋ of Zerubbabel,
[5] Salmon fathered Boaz by Rahab,	⌊son⌋ of Shealtiel, ⌊son⌋ of Neri,
Boaz fathered Obed by Ruth,	[28] ⌊son⌋ of Melchi, ⌊son⌋ of Addi,
Obed fathered Jesse,	⌊son⌋ of Cosam, ⌊son⌋ of Elmadam,
[6] and Jesse fathered King David.	⌊son⌋ of Er, [29] ⌊son⌋ of Joshua,
	⌊son⌋ of Eliezer, ⌊son⌋ of Jorim,
Then[c] David fathered Solomon by Uriah's wife,	⌊son⌋ of Matthat, ⌊son⌋ of Levi,
[7] Solomon fathered Rehoboam,	[30] ⌊son⌋ of Simeon, ⌊son⌋ of Judah,
Rehoboam fathered Abijah,	⌊son⌋ of Joseph, ⌊son⌋ of Jonam,
Abijah fathered Asa,[d]	⌊son⌋ of Eliakim, [31] ⌊son⌋ of Melea,
[8] Asa[d] fathered Jehoshaphat,	⌊son⌋ of Menna, ⌊son⌋ of Mattatha,
Jehoshaphat fathered Joram,[e]	⌊son⌋ of Nathan, ⌊son⌋ of David,
Joram fathered Uzziah,	[32] ⌊son⌋ of Jesse, ⌊son⌋ of Obed,
[9] Uzziah fathered Jotham,	⌊son⌋ of Boaz, ⌊son⌋ of Salmon,[c]
Jotham fathered Ahaz,	⌊son⌋ of Nahshon, [33] ⌊son⌋ of Amminadab,
Ahaz fathered Hezekiah,	⌊son⌋ of Ram,[d] ⌊son⌋ of Hezron,
[10] Hezekiah fathered Manasseh,	⌊son⌋ of Perez, ⌊son⌋ of Judah,
Manasseh fathered Amon,[f]	[34] ⌊son⌋ of Jacob, ⌊son⌋ of Isaac,
Amon[f] fathered Josiah,	⌊son⌋ of Abraham, ⌊son⌋ of Terah,
[11] and Josiah fathered Jechoniah and his brothers at the time of the exile to Babylon.	⌊son⌋ of Nahor, [35] ⌊son⌋ of Serug,
	⌊son⌋ of Reu, ⌊son⌋ of Peleg,
	⌊son⌋ of Eber, ⌊son⌋ of Shelah,

a1:1 Or *The book of the genealogy* **b1:2** In vv. 2-16 either a son, as here, or a later descendant, as in v. 8 **c1:6** Other mss add *King* **d1:7,8** Other mss read *Asaph* **e1:8** = Jehoram **f1:10** Other mss read *Amos*

a3:23 People did not know about His virgin birth; Lk 1:26-38; Mt 1:18-25 **b3:23** The relationship in some cases may be more distant than a son. **c3:32** Other mss read *Sala* **d3:33** Other mss read *Amminadab, son of Aram, son of Joram*; other mss read *Amminadab, son of Admin, son of Arni*

Mt 1:1 *Jesus Christ:* Jesus means "Yahweh saves;" For "Christ," see note on Mark 1:1. *Son of David, the Son of Abraham:* Since Matthew presents Jesus as King of the Jews, the genealogy here is Joseph's genealogy. Legal requirements for one to be recognized as the Messiah required first, that He be a Jew.

Mt 1:2 *fathered:* Does not necessarily mean immediate parentage but rather direct descent.

Mt. 1:3 *Tamar:* Note that Matthew includes five women in this genealogy (Tamar; Rahab and Ruth, v. 5; Uriah's wife, v. 6; and Mary, v. 16).

Lk 3:23-38 *son of Joseph . . . ⌊son of⌋ God:* This genealogy goes beyond that of Matthew, past Abraham to Adam as the Son of God. The point in going back to Adam is to make it clear that Jesus came for all humanity, not just for Israel, another point Luke and Acts highlight in their account. The differences between Matthew and Luke are much discussed (for example, Luke has Nathan as a descendant of David and Matthew has Solomon). We do not know the exact reason for these differences. Some have suggested one line is that of Mary and another is Joseph; however, neither list names Mary explicitly.

Matthew 1:1-17 (cont.)   Luke 3:23b-38 (cont.)

¹² Then after the exile to Babylon
Jechoniah fathered Shealtiel,
Shealtiel fathered Zerubbabel,
¹³ Zerubbabel fathered Abiud,
Abiud fathered Eliakim,
Eliakim fathered Azor,
¹⁴ Azor fathered Zadok,
Zadok fathered Achim,
Achim fathered Eliud,
¹⁵ Eliud fathered Eleazar,
Eleazar fathered Matthan,
Matthan fathered Jacob,
¹⁶ and Jacob fathered Joseph the husband of Mary,
who gave birth to[a] Jesus who is called
the •Messiah.

¹⁷ So all the generations from Abraham to David
were 14 generations; and from David until the exile
to Babylon, 14 generations; and from the exile to
Babylon until the Messiah, 14 generations.

[a]**1:16** Lit *Mary, from whom was born*

³⁶ ⌊son⌋ of Cainan, ⌊son⌋ of Arphaxad,
⌊son⌋ of Shem, ⌊son⌋ of Noah,
⌊son⌋ of Lamech, ³⁷ ⌊son⌋ of Methuselah,
⌊son⌋ of Enoch, ⌊son⌋ of Jared,
⌊son⌋ of Mahalaleel, ⌊son⌋ of Cainan,
³⁸ ⌊son⌋ of Enos, ⌊son⌋ of Seth,
⌊son⌋ of Adam, ⌊son⌋ of God.

Mt 1:16 *gave birth:* The Greek makes clear that Joseph had no part in the conception of the Messiah.
Mt 1:17 *generations:* This genealogy contains three distinct divisions: Abraham to David (2-6a), David to the Babylonian captivity (6b-11), and the Babylonian captivity to Jesus the Messiah (12-16).

PART IV

THE BIRTH AND CHILDHOOD OF JOHN THE BAPTIST AND JESUS

Sections 4–19. These sections include the annunciations, the birth, infancy, and the child-hood of both John and Jesus.

Sec. 4   Gabriel Predicts John's Birth

Luke 1:5-25

⁵ In the days of King •Herod of Judea, there was a priest of Abijah's division[a] named Zechariah. His wife was from the daughters of Aaron, and her name was Elizabeth. ⁶ Both were righteous in God's sight, living without blame according to all the commands and requirements of the Lord. ⁷ But they had no children[b] because Elizabeth could not conceive,[c] and both of them were well along in years.[d]

⁸ When his division was on duty and he was serving as priest before God, ⁹ it happened that he was chosen by lot, according to the custom of the priesthood, to enter the sanctuary of the Lord and burn incense. ¹⁰ At the hour of incense the whole assembly of the people was praying outside. ¹¹ An angel of the Lord appeared to him, standing to the right of the altar of incense. ¹² When Zechariah saw him, he was startled and overcome with fear.[e] ¹³ But the angel said to him:

> Do not be afraid, Zechariah,
> because your prayer has been heard.
> Your wife Elizabeth will bear you a son,
> and you will name him John.
> ¹⁴ There will be joy and delight for you,
> and many will rejoice at his birth.
> ¹⁵ For he will be great in the sight of the Lord
> and will never drink wine or beer.
> He will be filled with the Holy Spirit
> while still in his mother's womb.
> ¹⁶ He will turn many of the sons of Israel
> to the Lord their God.
> ¹⁷ And he will go before Him
> in the spirit and power of Elijah,
> to turn the hearts of fathers
> to their children,
> and the disobedient
> to the understanding of the righteous,
> to make ready for the Lord a prepared people.

¹⁸ "How can I know this?" Zechariah asked the angel. "For I am an old man, and my wife is well along in years."[f]

[a]**1:5** One of the 24 divisions of priests appointed by David for temple service; 1 Ch 24:10   [b]**1:7** Lit *child*   [c]**1:7** Lit *Elizabeth was sterile* or *barren*   [d]**1:7** Lit *in their days*   [e]**1:12** Lit *and fear fell on him*   [f]**1:18** Lit *in her days*

Lk 1:6 *righteous:* This description of John's parents is a way of highlighting that they were pious and righteous, walking in obedience to the Law.

Lk 1:9 *by lot:* The opportunity to offer the sacrifice on behalf of Israel in either the morning or afternoon came only once in a lifetime to a priest and was determined by the casting of lots.

Lk 1:12 *fear:* This emotion often appears when a supernatural figure is met.

Lk 1:13 *your prayer:* Verse 18 suggests that Zechariah had given up praying for a child. So the answered prayer is likely his prayer for the nation that accompanied the sacrifice.

Lk 1:15 *great in the sight of the Lord:* This description is in contrast to 1:32 where Jesus is simply called "great." In Luke 1–2, Jesus and John are set next to each other and compared, but Jesus is always placed in the superior position.

Lk 1:16 *will turn:* One of John's key roles was to reconcile Israelites to God and to each other (Mal 3:1). Properly relating to God impacts how we relate to others.

Luke 1:5-25 (cont.)

19 The angel answered him, "I am Gabriel, who stands in the presence of God, and I was sent to speak to you and tell you this good news. 20 Now listen! You will become silent and unable to speak until the day these things take place, because you did not believe my words, which will be fulfilled in their proper time."

21 Meanwhile, the people were waiting for Zechariah, amazed that he stayed so long in the sanctuary. 22 When he did come out, he could not speak to them. Then they realized that he had seen a vision in the sanctuary. He kept making signs to them and remained speechless. 23 When the days of his ministry were completed, he went back home.

24 After these days his wife Elizabeth conceived and kept herself in seclusion for five months. She said, 25 "The Lord has done this for me. He has looked with favor in these days to take away my disgrace among the people."

Lk 1:19 *Gabriel:* He is one of two angels given a name in the Bible. Michael is the other.

Lk 1:20 *silent:* This temporary judgment allowed Zechariah to reflect on the fact that what God says will take place; something he learned by verse 63.

Lk 1:25 *disgrace:* To be childless in Judaism was often viewed as a disgrace or a sign of possible judgment (Lv 20:20-21; Jr 22:30). This explanation was already ruled out by verse 6, but that does not mean that Elizabeth did not feel a sense of shame for her barrenness.

Sec. 5   Gabriel Predicts Jesus' Birth

Luke 1:26-38

26 In the sixth month, the angel Gabriel was sent by God to a town in Galilee called Nazareth, 27 to a virgin •engaged to a man named Joseph, of the house of David. The virgin's name was Mary. 28 And ⌊the angel⌋ came to her and said, "Rejoice, favored woman! The Lord is with you."a 29 But she was deeply troubled by this statement, wondering what kind of greeting this could be. 30 Then the angel told her:

Do not be afraid, Mary,
for you have found favor with God.
31 Now listen:
You will conceive and give birth to a son,
and you will call His name Jesus.
32 He will be great
and will be called the Son of the Most High,
and the Lord God will give Him
the throne of His father David.
33 He will reign over the house of Jacob forever,
and His kingdom will have no end.

34 Mary asked the angel, "How can this be, since I have not been intimate with a man?"b
35 The angel replied to her:

"The Holy Spirit will come upon you,
and the power of the Most High will overshadow you.
Therefore the holy One to be born
will be called the Son of God.

a1:28 Other mss add *blessed are you among women*   b1:34 Lit *since I do not know a man*

Lk 1:28 *favored woman:* This expression announces that Mary is the beneficiary of a gracious act of God.

Lk 1:32 *Son of the Most High*: This title, in contrast to John as prophet, is Luke's first note that Jesus will be unique in His relationship to God. This announcement is made like other announcements of the birth of other significant figures (Gn 16:7; Jdg 13:5; Is 7:14). *David:* Jesus will have human roots in the house of David, the royal line of Israel which shows His humanity and qualifies Him to be Messiah.

Lk 1:35 *The Holy Spirit will come upon you:* Here is Luke's declaration that God had a direct role in Jesus' conception. We are not told exactly how this took place, only that despite Mary's lack of sexual experience, she would conceive through the work of the Holy Spirit. This divine conception and virgin birth was another sign that Jesus was unique. *holy:* Holy simply means set apart, usually for a sacred task. Jesus was set apart from before His birth.

Luke 1:26-38 (cont.)

36 And consider your relative Elizabeth—even she has conceived a son in her old age, and this is the sixth month for her who was called childless. 37 For nothing will be impossible with God."

38 "I am the Lord's •slave,"a said Mary. "May it be done to me according to your word." Then the angel left her.

a1:38 Lit *Look, the Lord's slave*

Lk 1:37 *nothing will be impossible with God:* This is the lesson Mary is to gain from this experience.

Lk 1:38 *May it be done to me:* Mary has the exemplary attitude of God's servant, despite what this will cost her in reputation for those who do not appreciate what really happened.

Sec. 6   Mary's Visit to Elizabeth

Luke 1:39-45

39 In those days Mary set out and hurried to a town in the hill country of Judah 40 where she entered Zechariah's house and greeted Elizabeth. 41 When Elizabeth heard Mary's greeting, the baby leaped inside her,a and Elizabeth was filled with the Holy Spirit. 42 Then she exclaimed with a loud cry:

> You are the most blessed of women,
> and your child will be blessed!b

43 How could this happen to me, that the mother of my Lord should come to me? 44 For you see, when the sound of your greeting reached my ears, the baby leaped for joy inside me!c 45 She who has believed is blessed because what was spoken to her by the Lord will be fulfilled!"

a1:41 Lit *leaped in her abdomen* or *womb* **b1:42** Lit *and the fruit of your abdomen* (or *womb*) *is blessed* **c1:44** Lit *in my abdomen* or *womb*

Lk 1:41 *the baby leaped:* Even before they were born, John was testifying to Jesus as verse 15 predicted about His being filled with the Spirit from the womb, and verse 44 explains.

Lk 1:42 *blessed:* This term used twice in the verse means to be happy. In this case, it is because of God's gracious act on her behalf.

Lk 1:43 *How could this happen:* Elizabeth feels it an honor to be included in these events. She did nothing to earn this right.

Sec. 7   Mary's Praise

Luke 1:46-56

46 And Mary said:

> My soul proclaims the greatness ofa the Lord,
> 47 and my spirit has rejoiced in God my Savior,
> 48 because He has looked with favor
> on the humble condition of His slave.
> Surely, from now on all generations
> will call me blessed,
> 49 because the Mighty One
> has done great things for me,
> and His name is holy.

a1:46 Or *soul magnifies*

Lk 1:46 *proclaims the greatness of the Lord:* Mary utters a praise Psalm here, known as the *Magnificat,* a title that comes for the opening words of this psalm in the Latin version. A praise psalm is one where God is to be praised and the reason for that praise is given in what is said. Personal reasons appear in verses 46-49, while in verses 50-56 corporate reasons applying to certain types of people are noted. The major reason for the praise in this second section is that God is honoring His covenant.

Lk 1:48 *from now on:* Mary declares that things will be different from this point on because the Lord has come. This expression is one Luke likes (Lk 5:10; 12:52; 22:18,69; Ac 18:6). *blessed:* Mary is blessed not because of what she has done, but because of what she has experienced. Her attitude of joy in response to God's grace is exemplary.

Luke 1:46-56 (cont.)

50 His mercy is from generation to generation
   on those who fear Him.
51 He has done a mighty deed with His arm;
   He has scattered the proud
   because of the thoughts of their hearts;
52 He has toppled the mighty from their thrones
   and exalted the lowly.
53 He has satisfied the hungry with good things
   and sent the rich away empty.
54 He has helped His servant Israel,
   mindful of His mercy,ᵃ
55 just as He spoke to our ancestors,
   to Abraham and his descendantsᵇ forever.

56 And Mary stayed with her about three months; then she returned to her home.

ᵃ**1:54** Because He remembered His mercy; see Ps 98:3   ᵇ**1:55** Or *offspring*; lit *seed*

Lk 1:52-53 *mighty . . . lowly . . . hungry . . . rich:* These contrasts introduce themes Luke will present throughout his Gospel. God's message is for everyone, but it excludes those who think they are high and mighty on their own.
Lk 1:54 *mercy:* This is probably a reference to covenant loyalty that God has given to Israel, since the promise to Abraham is mentioned.

Sec. 8   The Birth and Naming of John

Luke 1:57-80

57 Now the time had come for Elizabeth to give birth, and she had a son. 58 Then her neighbors and relatives heard that the Lord had shown her His great mercy,ᵃ and they rejoiced with her.
59 When they came to circumcise the child on the eighth day, they were going to name him Zechariah, after his father. 60 But his mother responded, "No! He will be called John."
61 Then they said to her, "None of your relatives has that name." 62 So they motioned to his father to find out what he wanted him to be called. 63 He asked for a writing tablet and wrote:

> **HIS NAME IS JOHN**

And they were all amazed. 64 Immediately his mouth was opened and his tongue ⌊set free⌋, and he began to speak, praising God. 65 Fear came on all those who lived around them, and all these things were being talked about throughout the hill country of Judea. 66 All who heard about ⌊him⌋ took ⌊it⌋ to heart, saying, "What then will this child become?" For, indeed, the Lord's hand was with him.
67 Then his father Zechariah was filled with the Holy Spirit and prophesied:

68 Praise the Lord, the God of Israel,
   because He has visited
   and provided redemption for His people.
69 He has raised up a •horn of salvationᵇ for us
   in the house of His servant David,

ᵃ**1:58** Lit *the Lord magnified His mercy with her*   ᵇ**1:69** A strong Savior

Lk 1:63 *writing tablet*: In the ancient world this would have been something with wax on it.
Lk 1:64 *his mouth was opened:* As soon as Zechariah gave evidence he had learned the lesson that God's word would come to pass and should be followed, his temporary judgment came to an end.
Lk 1:67 *prophesied:* In Luke and Acts, the filling of the Spirit often led to prophecy, which in this context is the ability to praise God and declare what He is doing. The praise psalm that follows is called the *Benedictus,* after its opening words in the Latin version.
Lk 1:68 *visited:* The reason for the praise is that God has come to redeem His people. The idea of the visit will reappear in verse 78 showing that God's visit is tied to the coming of Jesus as Messiah, who is likened to the morning dawn that ends the night.
Lk 1:69 *horn of salvation . . . David:* Yet another allusion to Jesus being the fulfillment of promises made to the house of David about one to come and redeem God's people. A horn was a metaphor for power. Jesus has a power that is related to salvation.

Luke 1:57-80 (cont.)

70 just as He spoke by the mouth
   of His holy prophets in ancient times;
71 salvation from our enemies
   and from the clutches[a] of those who hate us.
72 He has dealt mercifully with our fathers
   and remembered His holy covenant—
73 the oath that He swore to our father Abraham.
   He has given us the privilege,
74 since we have been rescued
   from our enemies' clutches,[b]
   to serve Him without fear
75 in holiness and righteousness
   in His presence all our days.
76 And child, you will be called
   a prophet of the Most High,
   for you will go before the Lord
   to prepare His ways,
77 to give His people knowledge of salvation
   through the forgiveness of their sins.
78 Because of our God's merciful compassion,
   the Dawn from on high will visit us
79 to shine on those who live in darkness
   and the shadow of death,
   to guide our feet into the way of peace.

80 The child grew up and became spiritually strong, and he was in the wilderness until the day of his public appearance to Israel.

a1:71 Lit *the hand*   **b1:74** Lit *from the hand of enemies*

Lk 1:73 *Abraham:* What is taking place is a fulfillment of promises made to Abraham long ago, the first of which appears in Genesis 12:1-3.
Lk 1:74-75 *serve Him without fear in holiness and righteousness:* This is Zechariah's life desire, to faithfully serve God in a context where he has been rescued from his enemies. Luke shows that the key enemies are not other people, such as the Romans, but the devil and sin for which one needs forgiveness (v. 77) in order to find peace (v. 79).
Lk 1:76 *prophet:* John is a prophet of God called upon to give God's people a knowledge about salvation as found through the forgiveness of sin, something that will come through the One to come, the Morning Light that is Messiah (vv. 77-79).
Lk 1:78 *Dawn:* Jesus is compared to the morning light, an image from the OT (Is 11:1-10; Jr 23:5; 33:15; Zch 3:8; 6:12).
Lk 1:79 *peace:* The mission of Messiah is about giving people peace before God as He leads them from death to life.

Sec. 9   The Nativity of the Messiah

Matthew 1:18-25

18 The birth of Jesus Christ came about this way: After His mother Mary had been •engaged to Joseph, it was discovered before they came together that she was pregnant by the Holy Spirit. 19 So her husband Joseph, being a righteous man, and not wanting to disgrace her publicly, decided to divorce her secretly.

20 But after he had considered these things, an angel of the Lord suddenly appeared to him in a dream, saying, "Joseph, son of David, don't be afraid to take Mary as your wife, because what has been conceived in her is by the Holy Spirit. 21 She will give birth to a son, and you are to name Him Jesus,[a] because He will save His people from their sins."

a1:21 *Jesus* is the Gk form of the Hb name "Joshua," which = "The Lord saves" or "Yahweh saves."

Mt 1:18 *engaged:* There were three stages to a Jewish marriage: the arrangement, the engagement or betrothal, and the consummation. See the *Holman Illustrated Bible Dictionary,* "Marriage." *pregnant by the Holy Spirit:* Literally, "found in the womb." Three times in verses 18-25 Matthew emphasizes that Mary was a virgin and that this child was conceived by the Holy Spirit (vv. 18,20,25).
Mt 1:19 *divorce her secretly:* Joseph had several options open to him: take her to the priest and embarrass her publicly, have her stoned (Dt 22:23), or end the engagement privately with a bill of divorcement. He had decided on the latter until the angel instructed him otherwise.

Matthew 1:18-25 (cont.)

22 Now all this took place to fulfill what was spoken by the Lord through the prophet:

23 **See, the virgin will become pregnant**
   and give birth to a son,
   and they will name Him Immanuel,ᵃ

which is translated "God is with us."
   24 When Joseph got up from sleeping, he did as the Lord's angel had commanded him. He married her 25 but did not know her intimately until she gave birth to a son.ᵇ And he named Him Jesus.

ᵃ1:23 Is 7:14   **ᵇ1:25** Other mss read *to her firstborn son*

Mt 1:22 *to fulfill:* An important phrase in Matthew's Gospel, Matthew's desire was to show that Jesus fulfilled the OT promises about Messiah.

Sec. 10   The Birth of Jesus

Luke 2:1-7

1In those days a decree went out from Caesar Augustusᵃ that the whole empireᵇ should be registered. 2 This first registration took place whileᶜ Quirinius was governing Syria. 3 So everyone went to be registered, each to his own town.
   4 And Joseph also went up from the town of Nazareth in Galilee, to Judea, to the city of David, which is called Bethlehem, because he was of the house and family line of David, 5 to be registered along with Mary, who was •engaged to himᵈ and was pregnant. 6 While they were there, the time came for her to give birth. 7 Then she gave birth to her firstborn Son, and she wrapped Him snugly in cloth and laid Him in a feeding trough—because there was no room for them at the inn.

ᵃ2:1 Emperor who ruled the Roman Empire 27 B.C.–A.D. 14; also known as Octavian, he established the peaceful era known as the *Pax Romana*; Caesar was a title of Roman emperors.   **ᵇ2:1** Or *the whole inhabited world*   **ᶜ2:2** Or *This registration was the first while,* or *This registration was before*   **ᵈ2:5** Other mss read *was his engaged wife*

Lk 2:2 *registration:* This census is much discussed. Josephus mentions one in AD 6 that is too late to refer to Jesus' birth. It could be that this registration is one taken before that of Quirinius (see marginal note in translation) or it may be that this registration took some time and was completed under Quirinius and so became associated with his name.

Sec. 11   The Shepherds and the Angels

Luke 2:8-20

8 In the same region, shepherds were staying out in the fields and keeping watch at night over their flock. 9 Then an angel of the Lord stood beforeᵃ them, and the glory of the Lord shone around them, and they were terrified.ᵇ 10 But the angel said to them, "Don't be afraid, for look, I proclaim to you good news of great joy that will be for all the people: 11 today a Savior, who is •Messiah the Lord, was born for you in the city of David. 12 This will be the sign for you: you will find a baby wrapped snugly in cloth and lying in a feeding trough."
   13 Suddenly there was a multitude of the heavenly host with the angel, praising God and saying:

14 Glory to God in the highest heaven,
      and peace on earth to people He favors!ᶜ ᵈ

ᵃ2:9 Or *Lord appeared to*   **ᵇ2:9** Lit *they feared a great fear*   **ᶜ2:14** Other mss read *earth good will to people*   **ᵈ2:14** Or *earth to men of good will*

Lk 2:11 *Savior . . . Messiah . . . Lord:* These are three key titles of Jesus. He is deliverer, Messiah, and the One who has authority over salvation and the earth.
Lk 2:14 *people He favors:* This expression refers to God's chosen people, not to all people.

Luke 2:8-20 (cont.)

¹⁵ When the angels had left them and returned to heaven, the shepherds said to one another, "Let's go straight to Bethlehem and see what has happened, which the Lord has made known to us."
¹⁶ They hurried off and found both Mary and Joseph, and the baby who was lying in the feeding trough. ¹⁷ After seeing ⌊them⌋, they reported the message they were told about this child, ¹⁸ and all who heard it were amazed at what the shepherds said to them. ¹⁹ But Mary was treasuring up all these things[a] in her heart and meditating on them. ²⁰ The shepherds returned, glorifying and praising God for all they had seen and heard, just as they had been told.

ª2:19 Lit *these words*

Lk 2:20 *just as they had been told:* These words underscore the theme of Luke 1–2. God's word comes to pass.

Sec. 12   The Circumcision of Jesus

Luke 2:21

²¹ When the eight days were completed for His circumcision, He was named Jesus—the name given by the angel before He was conceived.[a]

ª2:21 Or *conceived in the womb*

Sec. 13   The Presentation of Jesus

Luke 2:22-38

²² And when the days of their purification according to the law of Moses were finished, they brought Him up to Jerusalem to present Him to the Lord ²³ (just as it is written in the law of the Lord: **Every firstborn male[a] will be dedicated[b] to the Lord[c]**) ²⁴ and to offer a sacrifice (according to what is stated in the law of the Lord: **a pair of turtledoves or two young pigeons[d]**).
²⁵ There was a man in Jerusalem whose name was Simeon. This man was righteous and devout, looking forward to Israel's consolation,[e] and the Holy Spirit was on him. ²⁶ It had been revealed to him by the Holy Spirit that he would not see death before he saw the Lord's Messiah. ²⁷ Guided by the Spirit, he entered[f] the •temple complex. When the parents brought in the child Jesus to perform for Him what was customary under the law, ²⁸ Simeon took Him up in his arms, praised God, and said:

²⁹ Now, Master,
You can dismiss Your •slave in peace,
as You promised.
³⁰ For my eyes have seen Your salvation.
³¹ You have prepared ⌊it⌋
in the presence of all peoples—
³² a light for revelation to the Gentiles[g]
and glory to Your people Israel.

ª2:23 Lit *"Every male that opens a womb* **b2:23** Lit *be called holy* **c2:23** Ex 13:2,12 **d2:24** Lv 5:11; 12:8 **e2:25** The coming of the Messiah with His salvation for the nation; Is 40:1; 61:2; Lk 2:26,30 **f2:27** Lit *And in the Spirit, he came into* **g2:32** Or *the nations*

Lk 2:22 *days of their purification:* Mary would need ceremonial purification according to the Law because she had given birth (Lv 12:2-4). More uncertain is why Joseph is included. It may well be he helped with the birth and thus also needed purification. They also brought Jesus to the temple to dedicate Him as a firstborn Son to the Lord.
Lk 2:29 *Now, Master:* This praise psalm is called the *Nunc Dimittis,* after the first words of the passage in the Latin version. God has completed His word to Simeon that he would see the Messiah, so he praises God and is ready to die.
Lk 2:32 *light:* Jesus is called a light for two reasons: as a source of revelation for the way of salvation to Gentiles, and because He is the glory of the people of Israel. The image is from Isaiah 9:1.

Luke 2:22-38 (cont.)

33 His father and mother[a] were amazed at what was being said about Him. 34 Then Simeon blessed them and told His mother Mary: "Indeed, this child is destined to cause the fall and rise of many in Israel and to be a sign that will be opposed[b] — 35 and a sword will pierce your own soul—that the thoughts[c] of many hearts may be revealed."

36 There was also a prophetess, Anna, a daughter of Phanuel, of the tribe of Asher. She was well along in years,[d] having lived with her husband seven years after her marriage,[e] 37 and was a widow for 84 years.[f] She did not leave the temple complex, serving God night and day with fastings and prayers. 38 At that very moment,[g] she came up and began to thank God and to speak about Him to all who were looking forward to the redemption of Jerusalem.[h]

a2:33 Other mss read *But Joseph and His mother* **b2:34** Or *spoken against* **c2:35** Or *schemes* **d2:36** Lit *in many days* **e2:36** Lit *years from her virginity* **f2:37** Or *she was a widow until the age of 84* **g2:38** Lit *very hour* **h2:38** Other mss read *in Jerusalem*

Lk 2:34 *fall and rise:* Jesus also will divide Israel as Simeon predicted, while the prophet also noted the pain Jesus' rejection will bring to Mary.

Lk 2:38 *redemption of Jerusalem:* As a good Jewish prophetess, Anna looked forward to God completing His promise of redemption for Israel. In Jesus, she saw and declared this fulfillment. Luke placed women and men next to each other in ministry, as here with Simeon and then Anna.

Sec. 14   Wise Men Seek the King

Matthew 2:1-12

1 After Jesus was born in Bethlehem of Judea in the days of King •Herod, •wise men from the east arrived unexpectedly in Jerusalem, 2 saying, "Where is He who has been born King of the Jews? For we saw His star in the east[a] and have come to worship Him."[b]

3 When King Herod heard this, he was deeply disturbed, and all Jerusalem with him. 4 So he assembled all the •chief priests and •scribes of the people and asked them where the •Messiah would be born.

5 "In Bethlehem of Judea," they told him, "because this is what was written by the prophet:

6 **And you, Bethlehem,** in the land of Judah,
are by no means **least among the leaders of Judah:**
because out of you will come a leader
who will shepherd My people Israel."[c]

7 Then Herod secretly summoned the wise men and asked them the exact time the star appeared. 8 He sent them to Bethlehem and said, "Go and search carefully for the child. When you find Him, report back to me so that I too can go and worship Him."[d]

a2:2 Or *star at its rising* **b2:2** Or *to pay Him homage* **c2:6** Mc 5:2 **d2:8** Or *and pay Him homage*

Mt 2:2 *born King:* Matthew alone records the visit of the magi or wise men. Only here is the question asked, "Where is He who is born King of the Jews?" This is not surprising since Matthew's portrait of Jesus is as the King of the Jews.

Mt 2:3 *he was deeply disturbed:* Herod was so wicked and ruthless that he had three of his own sons and a wife put to death in a jealous rage. Though 70 years of age, he could not bear the thought of anyone usurping him as ruler of the Jews.

Mt 2:4 *chief priests:* A group of Jewish temple officers that included the high priest, captain of the temple, temple overseers, and treasurers. *scribes:* A professional group in Judaism that copied the Law of Moses and interpreted it, especially in legal cases.

Mt 2:5 *the prophet:* Here is an indisputable direct fulfillment of Micah 5:2.

Mt 2:7 *asked them:* If the answer given by the wise men had been recorded, we would have known more accurately the date of Jesus' birth.

Mt 2:8 *worship Him:* His ultimate purpose was made clear by what he actually did in verse 16.

Matthew 2:1-12 (cont.)

[9] After hearing the king, they went on their way. And there it was—the star they had seen in the east![a] It led them until it came and stopped above the place where the child was. [10] When they saw the star, they were overjoyed beyond measure. [11] Entering the house, they saw the child with Mary His mother, and falling to their knees, they worshiped Him.[b] Then they opened their treasures and presented Him with gifts: gold, frankincense, and myrrh. [12] And being warned in a dream not to go back to Herod, they returned to their own country by another route.

[a]2:9 Or *star . . . at its rising*   **[b]2:11** Or *they paid Him homage*

Mt 2:9 *led them:* The star was not a natural heavenly body as it was able to stand directly over the house where Jesus and His family now lived.

Mt 2:11 *child:* The wise men did not find an infant, but a "child," a different word in Greek. Also, they found Him in a house, not in a stable. This happened several months after Jesus was born. *gold, frankincense, and myrrh:* Then, as now, gold was the most precious of metals and the universal symbol of material value and wealth. Frankincense and myrrh were fragrant spices and perfumes equally appropriate for such adoration and worship.

Sec. 15   The Flight to Egypt and the Massacre of the Innocents

Matthew 2:13-18

[13] After they were gone, an angel of the Lord suddenly appeared to Joseph in a dream, saying, "Get up! Take the child and His mother, flee to Egypt, and stay there until I tell you. For Herod is about to search for the child to destroy Him." [14] So he got up, took the child and His mother during the night, and escaped to Egypt. [15] He stayed there until Herod's death, so that what was spoken by the Lord through the prophet might be fulfilled: **Out of Egypt I called My Son.**[a]

[16] Then Herod, when he saw that he had been outwitted by the wise men, flew into a rage. He gave orders to massacre all the male children in and around Bethlehem who were two years[b] old and under, in keeping with the time he had learned from the wise men. [17] Then what was spoken through Jeremiah the prophet was fulfilled:

[18] **A voice was heard in Ramah,**
weeping,[c] **and great mourning,**
Rachel weeping for her children;
and she refused to be consoled,
because they were no more.[d]

[a]2:15 Hs 11:1   **[b]2:16** Lit *were from two years*   **[c]2:18** Other mss read *Ramah, lamentation, and weeping,*   **[d]2:18** Jr 31:15

Mt 2:15 *Out of Egypt I called My Son:* Matthew quotes Hosea 11:1 to show that this was in fulfillment of God's purpose to call His Son out of Egypt.

Mt 2:16 *outwitted:* Literally, he was "deluded" or "deceived." *massacre all the male children:* Herod did not know how old Jesus was, but he took no chances and included all the little boys in Bethlehem two years old and under. *two years old:* Herod's time reference implies the wise men told him they had seen the star less than two years before this visit.

Mt 2:17 *spoken through Jeremiah the prophet:* In its original context, Jeremiah 31:15 depicted the lament of mothers in Israel bewailing their sons who were led into exile. The passage is now used to describe the mothers in first-century Israel in anguish over the babies Herod massacred.

Sec. 16   The Holy Family in Nazareth

Matthew 2:19-23   Luke 2:39

[19] After Herod died, an angel of the Lord suddenly appeared in a dream to Joseph in Egypt, [20] saying, "Get up! Take the child and His mother and go to the land of Israel, because those who sought the child's life are dead." [21] So he got up, took the child and His mother, and entered the land of Israel. [22] But when he heard that Archelaus[a] was ruling over Judea in place of his father Herod, he was afraid to go there. And being warned in a dream, he withdrew to the region of Galilee. [23] Then he went and settled in a town called Nazareth to fulfill what was spoken through the prophets, that He will be called a •Nazarene.

[39] When they had completed everything according to the law of the Lord, they returned to Galilee, to their own town of Nazareth.

[a]2:22 A son of Herod the Great who ruled a portion of his father's kingdom 4 B.C.–A.D. 6

Mt 2:19 *Herod died:* We now know that Herod the Great died in 4 BC. Dionysius Exiguus, the sixth century monk, did not know that when he established the first Christian calendar. Based on Herod's calculations in verse 6, Jesus must have been born sometime between 6 BC and 4 BC. We do not know how long Herod lived after Jesus was taken to Egypt.

Mt 2:22 *Archelaus:* A son of Herod the Great who ruled a portion of his father's kingdom from about 4 BC to AD 6. He followed in his father's footsteps and ruthlessly murdered many Jews himself. Any Jew living in his jurisdiction would be in danger.

Mt 2:23 *Nazarene:* Growing up in Nazareth was an aspect of the Messiah's humble beginning.

Sec. 17   Jesus' Childhood in Nazareth

Luke 2:40

[40] The boy grew up and became strong, filled with wisdom, and God's grace was on Him.

Lk 2:40 *grew up:* Highlights the humanity of Jesus, who grew up like any child.

Sec. 18   In His Father's House

Luke 2:41-50

[41] Every year His parents traveled to Jerusalem for the •Passover Festival. [42] When He was 12 years old, they went up according to the custom of the festival. [43] After those days were over, as they were returning, the boy Jesus stayed behind in Jerusalem, but His parents[a] did not know it. [44] Assuming He was in the traveling party, they went a day's journey. Then they began looking for Him among their relatives and friends. [45] When they did not find Him, they returned to Jerusalem to search for Him. [46] After three days, they found Him in the temple complex sitting among the teachers, listening to them and asking them questions. [47] And all those who heard Him were astounded at His understanding and His answers. [48] When His parents saw Him, they were astonished, and His mother said to Him, "Son, why have You treated us like this? Your father and I have been anxiously searching for You."

[49] "Why were you searching for Me?" He asked them. "Didn't you know that I had to be in My Father's house?"[b] [50] But they did not understand what He said to them.

[a]2:43 Other mss read *but Joseph and His mother*   [b]2:49 Or *be involved in My Father's interests* (or *things*), or *be among My Father's people*

Lk 2:49 *had to be in My Father's house:* Jesus shows His self-understanding of His calling here as a young boy. His priority will be ministering in the manner God has called Him to do. Engaging in teaching about God will be central to this calling as the entire context of this scene shows.

Sec. 19   The Eighteen Years at Nazareth

Luke 2:51-52

[51] Then He went down with them and came to Nazareth and was obedient to them. His mother kept all these things in her heart. [52] And Jesus increased in wisdom and stature, and in favor with God and with people.

Lk 2:51 *kept all these things:* This note may suggest Mary was a source for what Luke related here. At the least it shows how these events made a deep impression on her. As Matthew 1–2 is told from Joseph's perspective, so Luke 1–2 is told from Mary's point of view.

PART V

THE BEGINNING OF JOHN THE BAPTIST'S MINISTRY

Sec. 20   The Beginning of the Gospel

Mark 1:1	Luke 3:1-2
¹The beginning of the gospel of Jesus Christ, the Son of God.	¹ In the fifteenth year of the reign of Tiberius Caesar,ᵃ while Pontius •Pilate was governor of Judea, •Herod was tetrarchᵇ of Galilee, his brother Philip tetrarch of the region of Itureaᶜ and Trachonitis,ᶜ and Lysanias tetrarch of Abilene,ᵈ ² during the high priesthood of Annas and Caiaphas, God's word came to John the son of Zechariah in the wilderness. ᵃ**3:1** Emperor who ruled the Roman Empire A.D. 14–37 ᵇ**3:1** Or *ruler* ᶜ**3:1** A small province northeast of Galilee ᵈ**3:1** A small Syrian province

Mk 1:1 *the gospel:* The gospel was the message of good news about Jesus and about the salvation that comes to those who believe in Him (Rm 1:1-6,16-17). Mark uses "gospel" in a similar way for the message about Jesus (1:1) that brings life and entrance into the kingdom of God to those who repent and believe (1:14-15; 8:35). *Christ:* The introduction reveals two major themes of Mark's Gospel. Jesus is the Christ, the King of God's people, and the Son of God. The title "Christ" represents the Greek equivalent for the Hebrew word translated "Messiah" (see Jn 1:41; 4:25). See the *Holman Illustrated Bible Dictionary,* "Christ." *the Son of God:* Also a messianic name. As a messianic title, "Son of God" is distinctive in that it expresses the close relationship between the anointed king and God Himself. See the *Holman Illustrated Bible Dictionary,* "Son of God."

Sec. 21   The Messiah's Herald

Matthew 3:1-6	Mark 1:2-6	Luke 3:3-6
¹In those days John the Baptist came, preaching in the Wilderness of Judea	² As it is written in Isaiah the prophet:ᵃ ᵃ**1:2** Other mss read *in the prophets*	³ He went into all the vicinity of the Jordan, preaching a baptism of repentanceᵃ for the forgiveness of sins, ⁴ as it is written in the book of the words of the prophet Isaiah: ᵃ**3:3** Or *baptism based on repentance*

Mt 3:1 *In those days* refers to the days of Jesus' life and serves as a transition between Matthew 2 and 3. *John:* A common name in the NT. John the Baptist (Mt 3:1), the son of Zechariah and forerunner of Christ, beheaded by order of Herod Antipas (Mt 3:4, 13,14; 14:2-4,8,10; Lk 1:13,60,63). See the *Holman Illustrated Bible Dictionary,* "John." *Baptist:* Literally, "Baptizer." It was an epitaph given to him because baptizing was such an important part of his ministry.

Mk 1:2 *Isaiah the prophet:* Mark regarded the promise of future salvation emphasized throughout the latter part of Isaiah to be the most important context for understanding the unfolding events in his Gospel. The Scripture citation that follows in Mark 1:2b-3 is a composite quotation from Exodus 23:20, Isaiah 40:3, and Malachi 3:1. The application of a Yahweh text to Jesus demonstrates Mark's conviction that Jesus was divine.

Lk 3:3 *a baptism of repentance:* Repentance is one of Luke's favorite terms for how to respond to the message of salvation, whether John the Baptist prepares for it or Jesus and the apostles proclaim it (Lk 24:47; Ac 2:37-38; 26:20). Those who participated in John's baptism were saying they had turned to God in preparation for the coming of His salvation. Christian baptism is different. It depicts the cleansing of God and the coming into new life that takes place when one turns to God in faith (Rm 6:1-11; 1 Pt 3:21, where the text is clear that baptism does not save but pictures what God has done in Christ and within the believer).

Matthew 3:1-6 (cont.)	Mark 1:2-6 (cont.)	Luke 3:3-6 (cont.)

2 and saying, "Repent, because the kingdom of heaven has come near!" 3 For he is the one spoken of through the prophet Isaiah, who said:

A voice of one crying out
   in the wilderness:
Prepare the way
   for the Lord;
   make His paths straight![a]

4 John himself had a camel-hair garment with a leather belt around his waist, and his food was locusts and wild honey. 5 Then ⌊people from⌋ Jerusalem, all Judea, and all the vicinity of the Jordan were flocking to him, 6 and they were baptized by him in the Jordan River as they confessed their sins.

a3:3 Is 40:3

Look, I am sending
My messenger ahead
of You,
who will prepare Your way.[a]

3 **A voice of one crying out**
   in the wilderness:
Prepare the way
   for the Lord;
   make His paths straight![b]

4 John came baptizing[c] in the wilderness and preaching a baptism of repentance[d] for the forgiveness of sins. 5 The whole Judean countryside and all the people of Jerusalem were flocking to him, and they were baptized by him in the Jordan River as they confessed their sins. 6 John wore a camel-hair garment with a leather belt around his waist and ate locusts and wild honey.

a1:2 Other mss add *before You*
b1:2-3 Is 40:3; Mal 3:1   **c1:4** Or *John the Baptist came*, or *John the Baptizer came*
d1:4 Or *a baptism based on repentance*

A voice of one crying out
   in the wilderness:
Prepare the way
   for the Lord;
   make His paths straight!
5 **Every valley will be filled,**
   and every mountain and hill
   will be made low;[a]
the crooked will become
   straight,
   the rough ways smooth,
6 **and everyone**[b] **will see**
   the salvation of God.[c]

a3:5 Lit *be humbled*   **b3:6** Lit *all flesh*
c3:4-6 Is 40:3-5

Mt 3:2 *Repent***:** Means much more than being sorry. The Greek (*metanoite*) signifies a change in both mental attitude and conduct. John's bold declaration that Jews, just like Gentiles, needed to repent infuriated the Jewish authorities. *kingdom of heaven:* Matthew uses this phrase thirty-two times, and is the only Gospel writer who uses it at all. Mark, Luke, and John use "the kingdom of God." *has come near:* The appearance of Jesus signaled God's interruption into human history of His power in a dramatic way.

Mt 3:4 *camel-hair . . . leather belt . . . locusts and wild honey:* His diet was consistent with that of desert dwellers of the day. His clothing was the garb of the original Elijah (2 Kg 1:8), rough cloth woven from the hair of camels, in accordance with Zechariah 13:4.

Mt 3:6 *baptized:* Literally, "were being baptized," stressing the repetition as person after person came to him. "Baptize" is from *baptizō*, the most common meaning being "to immerse." There were three types of baptism at this time. Jewish proselyte baptism was the final requirement for a Gentile becoming a Jew. He had to make an offering at the temple in Jerusalem, be circumcised, and finally be baptized. Jewish baptism symbolized the washing away of the filthiness of the Gentile flesh. John the Baptist's baptism symbolized repentance according to Matthew 3:2. Jesus was not a Gentile converting to Judaism. He certainly was not a sinner repenting of His sins. His baptism has to have a different meaning from both Jewish baptism and John's baptism. Acts 19:1-5 makes clear that there is a difference between John's baptism and Jesus' baptism. Paul tells us in Romans 6:4 that Jesus' baptism symbolized His coming death, burial, and resurrection. *confessed their sins:* Baptism carries its proper significance only when one confesses sin and turns to Christ in faith (Ac 2:38).

Lk 3:6 *everyone will see the salvation of God:* Only Luke lengthens the citation of Isaiah 40:3 to include 40:4-5 in describing John the Baptist. This allows another point to be highlighted. When that salvation does come, it will be visible in the entire world.

Sec. 22   John's Preaching

Matthew 3:7-10   Luke 3:7-14

7 When he saw many of the •Pharisees and •Sadducees coming to the place of his baptism,ᵃ he said to them, "Brood of vipers! Who warned you to flee from the coming wrath? 8 Therefore produce fruit consistent withᵇ repentance. 9 And don't presume to say to yourselves, 'We have Abraham as our father.' For I tell you that God is able to raise up children for Abraham from these stones! 10 Even now the ax is ready to strike the root of the trees! Therefore every tree that doesn't produce good fruit will be cut down and thrown into the fire.

ᵃ**3:7** Lit *to his baptism*   ᵇ**3:8** Lit *fruit worthy of*

7 He then said to the crowds who came out to be baptized by him, "Brood of vipers! Who warned you to flee from the coming wrath? 8 Therefore produce fruit consistent with repentance. And don't start saying to yourselves, 'We have Abraham as our father,' for I tell you that God is able to raise up children for Abraham from these stones! 9 Even now the ax is ready to strikeᵃ the root of the trees! Therefore every tree that doesn't produce good fruit will be cut down and thrown into the fire."

10 "What then should we do?" the crowds were asking him.

11 He replied to them, "The one who has two shirtsᵇ must share with someone who has none, and the one who has food must do the same."

12 Tax collectors also came to be baptized, and they asked him, "Teacher, what should we do?"

13 He told them, "Don't collect any more than what you have been authorized."

14 Some soldiers also questioned him: "What should we do?"

He said to them, "Don't take money from anyone by force or false accusation; be satisfied with your wages."

ᵃ**3:9** Lit *the ax lies at*   ᵇ**3:11** Lit *tunics*

Mt 3:7 *Pharisees and Sadducees:* Two of the three distinct Jewish sects that had developed in Judaism—the other being the Essenes. *Pharisee* means "separated ones," and members of the sect diligently tried to live up to their name. They were noted for strict observance of rites and ceremonies of the written law and for insistence on the validity of their own oral traditions concerning the law. *Sadducee* means "the righteous." They believed only in the Pentateuch as divinely inspired and would believe no doctrine that could not be derived from the five books of Moses. Hence, they rejected angels and the resurrection of the dead. *Brood of vipers:* Jesus used the same language on much the same people (12:34; 23:33). *Vipers* were small but very poisonous snakes. Broods of snakes were common in that desert area.

Mt 3:8 *produce fruit:* John's boldness was stunning—he identified as unworthy the very ones who posed as religious leaders of the Jewish people.

Mt 3:9 *Abraham . . . father:* They believed being Abraham's descendants made them spiritually secure.

Mt 3:10 *cut down and thrown into the fire:* Repentance without fruit is worthless and vain.

Lk 3:7 *crowds:* In Matthew 3:7, this remark is made to the Pharisees and Sadducees. Luke presents it as something said to the entire crowd, which included these Jewish leaders. Matthew is highlighting these leaders for criticism by John.

Lk 3:10 *What then should we do?:* This question gives John's application to his teaching. It and the responses in verses 10-14 are details about John's preaching only Luke gives to us. Note how repentance before God shows itself in how others are treated.

Sec. 23   John's Expectation of the Messiah

Matthew 3:11-12	Mark 1:7-8	Luke 3:15-18

11 "I baptize you with[a] water for repentance,[b] but the One who is coming after me is more powerful than I. I am not worthy to remove his[c] His sandals. He Himself will baptize you with[a] the Holy Spirit and fire. 12 His winnowing shovel[d] is in His hand, and He will clear His threshing floor and gather His wheat into the barn. But the chaff He will burn up with fire that never goes out."

[a]**3:11** Or *in*   [b]**3:11** Baptism was the means by which repentance was expressed publicly.   [c]**3:11** Or *to carry*   [d]**3:12** A wooden farm implement used to toss threshed grain into the wind so the lighter chaff would blow away and separate from the heavier grain

7 He was preaching: "Someone more powerful than I will come after me. I am not worthy to stoop down and untie the strap of His sandals. 8 I have baptized you with[a] water, but He will baptize you with[a] the Holy Spirit."

[a]**1:8** Or *in*

15 Now the people were waiting expectantly, and all of them were debating in their minds[a] whether John might be the •Messiah. 16 John answered them all, "I baptize you with[b] water, but One is coming who is more powerful than I. I am not worthy to untie the strap of His sandals. He will baptize you with[a] the Holy Spirit and fire. 17 His winnowing shovel[c] is in His hand to clear His threshing floor and gather the wheat into His barn, but the chaff He will burn up with a fire that never goes out." 18 Then, along with many other exhortations, he proclaimed good news to the people.

[a]**3:15** Or *hearts*   [b]**3:16** Or *in*   [c]**3:17** A wooden farm implement used to toss threshed grain into the wind so the lighter chaff would blow away and separate from the heavier grain

Mt 3:11 *for repentance:* Baptism is an outward expression of repentance. *with the Holy Spirit:* Baptism "with/in the Holy Spirit" appears six other times in the New Testament. Five of these texts refer to this very saying of John (Mk 1:8; Lk 3:16; Jn 1:33; Ac 1:5; 11:16). The Holy Spirit indwells all believers and joins them into the body of Christ. Some interpreters recognize Jesus as the baptizer and the Holy Spirit the element they are baptized in. *fire:* In both the preceding and following verses (10,12), John clearly uses fire to represent judgment and punishment.

Mk 1:7 *to stoop down and untie the strap of His sandals:* A disciple was expected to do any service for his teacher that a slave would do for his master, except for untying his sandals. Such a task was so demeaning that it was beneath the dignity of a disciple. John regarded himself as less worthy than a slave in comparison to Jesus.

Lk 3:15 *Messiah:* This is yet another detail only Luke gives us. John's remark about the coming One, which Matthew, Mark, and Luke share, comes in the context of speculation about John being the Messiah. His reply is that it is not him but the One who baptizes with the Spirit and brings a purging judgment, which is the point of the allusion to fire (Is 4:4-5), is the Messiah. The initial fulfillment of this promise is seen in Acts 2.

Part VI

THE BEGINNING OF CHRIST'S PUBLIC MINISTRY

Sec. 24 The Baptism of Jesus

Matthew 3:13-17

[13] Then Jesus came from Galilee to John at the Jordan, to be baptized by him. [14] But John tried to stop Him, saying, "I need to be baptized by You, and yet You come to me?"

[15] Jesus answered him, "Allow it for now, because this is the way for us to fulfill all righteousness." Then he allowed Him ⌊to be baptized⌋.

[16] After Jesus was baptized, He went up immediately from the water. The heavens suddenly opened for Him,[a] and He saw the Spirit of God descending like a dove and coming down on Him. [17] And there came a voice from heaven:

> This is My beloved Son.
> I take delight in Him!

[a]**3:16** Other mss omit *for Him*

Mark 1:9-11

[9] In those days Jesus came from Nazareth in Galilee and was baptized in the Jordan by John.

[10] As soon as He came up out of the water, He saw the heavens being torn open and the Spirit descending to Him like a dove. [11] And a voice came from heaven:

> You are My beloved Son;
> I take delight in You![a]

[a]**1:11** Or *In You I am well pleased*

Luke 3:21-23a

[21] When all the people were baptized, Jesus also was baptized. As He was praying, heaven opened, [22] and the Holy Spirit descended on Him in a physical appearance like a dove. And a voice came from heaven:

> You are My beloved Son.
> I take delight in You!

[23] As He began ⌊His ministry⌋, Jesus was about 30 years old

Mt 3:13 ***Then:*** We are not told the exact time to which the *then* refers, but the last time we saw Jesus in Matthew was in chapter 2, when He was a child in Galilee. ***to be baptized:*** Jesus did not need to repent or to "formally assume" His role as Messiah, but to inaugurate His public ministry and identify with the sinners He came to save.

Mt 3:15 ***to fulfill all righteousness:*** To complete everything that was necessary to be obedient to God. In so doing, Jesus identified with and endorsed John's ministry.

Mt 3:16 ***descending like a dove:*** Lk 3:22 clarifies that the Spirit came in "physical appearance like a dove." The dove is a symbol of the Holy Spirit.

Mk 1:9 ***from Nazareth in Galilee:*** In contrast to the many people who went out from Jerusalem and Judea to receive baptism from John (Mk 1:5), Jesus came from Nazareth in Galilee. See the *Holman Illustrated Bible Dictionary,* "Nazareth."

Mk 1:10 ***being torn open:*** At the beginning of Mark's Gospel, the heavens are torn open and a voice from heaven declares that Jesus is the Son of God (1:10-11). ***Spirit descending:*** The Spirit's descent in the form of a dove was probably reminiscent of the Spirit's brooding over creation in Genesis 1. The Spirit's descent on Jesus in this form indicates that Jesus bears the power of new creation.

Lk 3:22 ***beloved Son . . . delight:*** This saying combines background from two passages: Psalm 2:7 and Isaiah 42:1. Jesus is affirmed by God to His Son. These sayings in Matthew, Mark, and Luke are exactly the same except that Matthew (3:17) says, "This" is my beloved Son, not "You." A second time in Matthew (17:5), God the Father speaks from heaven acknowledging that Jesus is His Son.

Sec. 25　The Temptations of Jesus

Matthew 4:1-11	Mark 1:12-13	Luke 4:1-13

[1]Then Jesus was led up by the Spirit into the wilderness to be tempted by the Devil. [2] After He had fasted 40 days and 40 nights, He was hungry. [3] Then the tempter approached Him and said, "If You are the Son of God, tell these stones to become bread."

[4] But He answered, "It is written:

**Man must not live
on bread alone
but on every word
that comes
from the mouth of God."[a]**

[5] Then the Devil took Him to the holy city,[b] had Him stand on the pinnacle of the temple, [6] and said to Him, "If You are the Son of God, throw Yourself down. For it is written:

[a]**4:4** Dt 8:3　[b]**4:5** Jerusalem

[12] Immediately the Spirit drove Him into the wilderness. [13] He was in the wilderness 40 days, being tempted by Satan. He was with the wild animals, and the angels began to serve Him.

[1]Then Jesus returned from the Jordan, full of the Holy Spirit, and was led by the Spirit in the wilderness [2] for 40 days to be tempted by the Devil. He ate nothing during those days, and when they were over,[a] He was hungry. [3] The Devil said to Him, "If You are the Son of God, tell this stone to become bread."

[4] But Jesus answered him, "It is written: **Man must not live on bread alone."[b] [c]**

[5] So he took Him up[d] and showed Him all the kingdoms of the world in a moment of time. [6] The Devil said to Him, "I will give You their splendor and all this authority, because it has been given over to me, and I can give it to anyone I want. [7] If You, then, will worship me,[e] all will be Yours."

[8] And Jesus answered him,[f] "It is written:

[a]**4:2** Lit *were completed*　[b]**4:4** Other mss add *but on every word of God*　[c]**4:4** Dt 8:3　[d]**4:5** Other mss read *So the Devil took Him up on a high mountain*　[e]**4:7** Lit *will fall down before me*　[f]**4:8** Other mss add *"Get behind Me, Satan!*

Mt 4:1 *Then:* Indicates that the events described here occurred immediately after the baptism account in chapter 3. *to be tempted:* The Greek *peirazō* is a morally neutral word that can mean "to test" or "to tempt." Since the Devil is doing the tempting, it must be understood as "entice to evil." *the Devil:* "Devil" in Greek means *accuser,* as does "Satan" in Hebrew (v. 10).

Mt 4:2 *40 days and 40 nights:* Jesus spent forty days in the wilderness just as Moses spent forty days on Mount Sinai, where he received the Law. Elijah also spent 40 days and nights at Mount Horeb (1 Kg 19:8).

Mt 4:3 *If You are the Son of God:* This (as in v. 6) is a first class conditional clause in Greek and could be read, "*Since* you are the Son of God."

Mt 4:4 *It is written:* Jesus answered each temptation of the Devil with Scripture from Deuteronomy, establishing a link with the wilderness experiences of the Israelites.

Mt 4:5 *holy city:* Jerusalem. *pinnacle:* This may have been the roof that extended out over Herod's portico, with a drop of over 400 feet to the floor of the Kidron Valley.

Mt 4:6 Perhaps in quoting from Psalm 91 the Devil thought he could "back Jesus into a corner" since He claimed to live by the Word of God.

Mk 1:12 *Immediately:* Sometimes the word serves to indicate that one action took place shortly after another. At other times it is simply a stylistic feature that focuses attention on a particular event. In such cases, it can mean something similar to "Look at this!"

Mk 1:13 *with the wild animals:* The temptation demonstrates Jesus' divine authority over Satan, the animal kingdom, and heavenly beings. Jesus' peaceful coexistence with wild beasts shows that Jesus' ministry began the fulfillment of Isaiah 11:1-9.

Lk 4:1-13 The order of these temptations differs in Matthew and Luke. Matthew has the temple temptation second, while Luke has it last. Luke has the kingdoms temptation second, while Matthew has it last. This shows that sometimes chronological order is not the point for a Gospel writer. It is likely Luke made the change to highlight the temple temptation. Careful reading of Matthew shows that he dismisses Satan after his third temptation, a dismissal Luke lacks.

Lk 4:4 *on bread alone:* Matthew's account adds "but on every word that comes from the mouth of God."

Matthew 4:1-11 (cont.)   Luke 4:1-13 (cont.)

**He will give His angels orders
  concerning you, and
they will support you with their hands
so that you will not strike
your foot against a stone."ᵃ**

⁷ Jesus told him, "It is also written: **Do not test the Lord your God."ᵇ**

⁸ Again, the Devil took Him to a very high mountain and showed Him all the kingdoms of the world and their splendor. ⁹ And he said to Him, "I will give You all these things if You will fall down and worship me."ᶜ

¹⁰ Then Jesus told him, "Go away,ᵈ Satan! For it is written:

**Worship the Lord your God,
and serve only Him."ᵉ**

¹¹ Then the Devil left Him, and immediately angels came and began to serve Him.

ᵃ**4:6** Ps 91:11-12   ᵇ**4:7** Dt 6:16   ᶜ**4:9** Or *and pay me homage*
ᵈ**4:10** Other mss read *Get behind Me*   ᵉ**4:10** Dt 6:13

**Worship the Lord your God,
and serve Him only."ᵃ**

⁹ So he took Him to Jerusalem, had Him stand on the pinnacle of the temple, and said to Him, "If You are the Son of God, throw Yourself down from here. ¹⁰ For it is written:

**He will give His angels orders
  concerning you,
to protect you,ᵇ ¹¹ and
they will support you with their hands,
so that you will not strike
your foot against a stone."ᶜ**

¹² And Jesus answered him, "It is said: **Do not test the Lord your God."ᵈ**
¹³ After the Devil had finished every temptation, he departed from Him for a time.

ᵃ**4:8** Dt 6:13   ᵇ**4:10** Ps 91:11   ᶜ**4:11** Ps 91:12   ᵈ**4:12** Dt 6:16

Mt 4:8 *showed Him all the kingdoms of the world:* Because no *high mountain* anywhere could literally afford this kind of view, this was probably some visionary experience.

Mt 4:10 For a third time, Jesus quoted from Deuteronomy and challenged Satan that only the Lord God is worthy of worship.

Lk 4:6 *it has been given over to me:* Satan appeals to Jesus with a half truth here. He does have authority over the earth in terms of influence, but that authority is not as total as Satan suggests here, making his remark a half lie.

Lk 4:8 *and serve Him only:* Jesus shows His complete allegiance to God here.

Lk 4:12 *Do not test the Lord your God:* Jesus will not presume on God's protection by forcing God to act on His behalf.

Sec. 26   John the Baptist's Testimony

John 1:19-28

[19] This is John's testimony when the •Jews from Jerusalem sent priests and Levites to ask him, "Who are you?"

[20] He did not refuse to answer, but he declared: "I am not the •Messiah."

[21] "What then?" they asked him. "Are you Elijah?"

"I am not," he said.

"Are you the Prophet?"[a]

"No," he answered.

[22] "Who are you, then?" they asked. "We need to give an answer to those who sent us. What can you tell us about yourself?"

[23] He said, "I am a **voice of one crying out in the wilderness: Make straight the way of the Lord**[b] —just as Isaiah the prophet said."

[24] Now they had been sent from the •Pharisees. [25] So they asked him, "Why then do you baptize if you aren't the Messiah, or Elijah, or the Prophet?"

[26] "I baptize with[c] water," John answered them. "Someone stands among you, but you don't know ⌊Him⌋. [27] He is the One coming after me,[d] whose sandal strap I'm not worthy to untie."

[28] All this happened in Bethany[e] across the Jordan,[f] where John was baptizing.

[a]**1:21** Probably = the Prophet in Dt 18:15   [b]**1:23** Is 40:3   [c]**1:26** Or *in*   [d]**1:27** Other mss add *who came before me*   [e]**1:28** Other mss read *in Bethabara*   [f]**1:28** Another Bethany, near Jerusalem, was the home of Lazarus, Martha, and Mary; Jn 11:1.

Jn 1:19–2:11 Presents the first week of Jesus' ministry: Day 1: the Baptist's witness concerning Jesus (1:19-28); Day 2: the Baptist's encounter with Jesus (1:29-34); Day 3: the Baptist's referral of two of his disciples to Jesus (1:35-39); Day 4: Andrew's introduction of his brother Peter to Jesus (1:40-42); Day 5: the recruitment of Philip and Nathanael (1:43-51); and Day 7: the wedding at Cana (2:1-11). During this early stage of Jesus' ministry, He is hailed by the Baptist as "God's lamb" (1:29,36), is followed by His first disciples, and performs His first "sign," turning water into wine at the wedding at Cana (2:11).

Jn 1:19 *Who are you?:* This question was first asked of John the Baptist, not Jesus. He indicated that he was not the Messiah.

Jn 1:21 *Are you Elijah?... Are you the Prophet?:* The prophet mentioned is probably the prophet of Deuteronomy 18:15. John denied being either.

Jn 1:24-27 John's baptism was strictly one of water, as opposed to the baptism of the one he anticipated. This One was superior to John in every way.

Jn 1:28 *Bethany:* This reference locates John's baptism as taking place on the other side of the Jordan at a place called Bethany, now unknown (this is not the same place as where Jesus raised Lazarus (Jn 11). Some think it may be the region of Batanea, or Bashan.

Sec. 27   The Lamb of God

John 1:29-34

[29] The next day John saw Jesus coming toward him and said, "Here is the Lamb of God, who takes away the sin of the world! [30] This is the One I told you about: 'After me comes a man who has surpassed me, because He existed before me.' [31] I didn't know Him, but I came baptizing with[a] water so He might be revealed to Israel."

[32] And John testified, "I watched the Spirit descending from heaven like a dove, and He rested on Him. [33] I didn't know Him, but He[b] who sent me to baptize with[a] water told me, 'The One you see the Spirit descending and resting on—He is the One who baptizes with[a] the Holy Spirit.' [34] I have seen and testified that He is the Son of God!"[c]

[a]**1:31,33** Or *in*   [b]**1:33** *He* refers to God the Father, who gave John a sign to help him identify the Messiah. Vv. 32-34 indicate that John did not know that Jesus was the Messiah until the Spirit descended upon Him at His baptism.   [c]**1:34** Other mss read *is the Chosen One of God*

Jn 1:29 *Lamb of God:* Jesus is the passover lamb sacrificed for the people. This is the first reference to this theme in John, carried forward in such passages as 2:13-25; 6:1-14,22-71; 11:47–12:8; 13:1–17:26; 19:3-42.

Sec. 28   Jesus' First Disciples

John 1:35-51

[35] Again the next day, John was standing with two of his disciples. [36] When he saw Jesus passing by, he said, "Look! The Lamb of God!"

[37] The two disciples heard him say this and followed Jesus. [38] When Jesus turned and noticed them following Him, He asked them, "What are you looking for?"

They said to Him, "•Rabbi" (which means "Teacher"), "where are You staying?"

[39] "Come and you'll see," He replied. So they went and saw where He was staying, and they stayed with Him that day. It was about 10 in the morning.[a]

[40] Andrew, Simon Peter's brother, was one of the two who heard John and followed Him. [41] He first found his own brother Simon and told him, "We have found the Messiah!"[b] (which means "Anointed One"), [42] and he brought ⌊Simon⌋ to Jesus.

When Jesus saw him, He said, "You are Simon, son of John.[c] You will be called •Cephas" (which means "Rock").

[43] The next day He[d] decided to leave for Galilee. Jesus found Philip and told him, "Follow Me!"

[44] Now Philip was from Bethsaida, the hometown of Andrew and Peter. [45] Philip found Nathanael[e] and told him, "We have found the One Moses wrote about in the Law (and so did the prophets): Jesus the son of Joseph, from Nazareth!"

[46] "Can anything good come out of Nazareth?" Nathanael asked him.

"Come and see," Philip answered.

[47] Then Jesus saw Nathanael coming toward Him and said about him, "Here is a true Israelite; no deceit is in him."

[48] "How do you know me?" Nathanael asked.

"Before Philip called you, when you were under the fig tree, I saw you," Jesus answered.

[49] "Rabbi," Nathanael replied, "You are the Son of God! You are the King of Israel!"

[50] Jesus responded to him, "Do you believe ⌊only⌋ because I told you I saw you under the fig tree? You[f] will see greater things than this." [51] Then He said, "•I assure you: You[g] will see heaven opened and the angels of God ascending and descending on the •Son of Man."

[a]**1:39** Lit *about the tenth hour.* Various methods of reckoning time were used in the ancient world. John probably used a different method from the other 3 Gospels. If John used the same method of time reckoning as the other 3 Gospels, the translation would be: *It was about four in the afternoon.*   [b]**1:41** In the NT, the word Messiah translates the Gk word *Christos* ("Anointed One"), except here and in Jn 4:25 where it translates *Messias.*   [c]**1:42** Other mss read *Simon, son of Jonah*   [d]**1:43** Or *he,* referring either to Simon Peter (vv. 41-42) or Andrew (vv. 40-41)   [e]**1:45** Probably the Bartholomew of the other Gospels and Acts   [f]**1:50** *You* (sg in Gk) refers to Nathanael.   [g]**1:51** *You* is pl in Gk and refers to Nathanael and the other disciples.

Jn 1:37 *The two disciples . . . followed Jesus:* The events surrounding the beginning of Jesus' ministry compelled people to follow Him to find out more about Him.

Jn 1:38 *Rabbi:* Jesus was called a teacher from the outset of His ministry. A number of features of Jesus' ministry resembled the itinerant teachers of the day. He had followers who listened to His teaching and He drew crowds in the various cities He visited.

Jn 1:41 *We have found the Messiah:* Andrew made the first explicit affirmation of Jesus as the Messiah in John. John's Gospel was not written in Judea, so the author translated the term Messiah as "Anointed One."

Jn 1:43 *Galilee:* All of Jesus' events in John so far had occurred near Bethany, but now He went to Galilee, His home area.

Jn 1:48 Jesus attests to Nathanael that he had seen him before he had arrived. This relatively unspectacular event elicited a response that Jesus is the Son of God and the King of Israel, revealing that royal messianic expectations were prevalent during this time.

Jn 1:51 *You will see heaven opened:* Jesus closed His affirmation to Nathanael with an apocalyptic image of the open heaven, with communication taking place between God and humans by means of the angels.

Sec. 29   Jesus' First Sign: Turning Water into Wine

John 2:1-11

¹On the third day a wedding took place in Cana of Galilee. Jesus' mother was there, and ² Jesus and His disciples were invited to the wedding as well. ³ When the wine ran out, Jesus' mother told Him, "They don't have any wine."

⁴ "What has this concern of yours to do with Me,ᵃ •woman?" Jesus asked. "My hourᵇ has not yet come."

⁵ "Do whatever He tells you," His mother told the servants.

⁶ Now six stone water jars had been set there for Jewish purification. Each contained 20 or 30 gallons.ᶜ

⁷ "Fill the jars with water," Jesus told them. So they filled them to the brim. ⁸ Then He said to them, "Now draw some out and take it to the chief servant."ᵈ And they did.

⁹ When the chief servant tasted the water (after it had become wine), he did not know where it came from—though the servants who had drawn the water knew. He called the groom ¹⁰ and told him, "Everyone sets out the fine wine first, then, after people have drunk freely, the inferior. But you have kept the fine wine until now."

¹¹ Jesus performed this first signᵉ in Cana of Galilee. He displayed His glory, and His disciples believed in Him.

ᵃ**2:4** Or *You and I see things differently*; lit *What to Me and to you*; Mt 8:29; Mk 1:24; 5:7; Lk 8:28   ᵇ**2:4** The time of His sacrificial death and exaltation; Jn 7:30; 8:20; 12:23,27; 13:1; 17:1   ᶜ**2:6** Lit *2 or 3 measures*   ᵈ**2:8** Lit *ruler of the table*; perhaps *master of the feast*, or *headwaiter*   ᵉ**2:11** Lit *this beginning of the signs*; Jn 4:54; 20:30. Seven miraculous signs occur in John's Gospel and are so noted in the headings.

Jn 2:4 *What has this concern of yours to do with Me, woman?:* It would have been a socially awkward and embarrassing moment for the groom and bride to have run out of wine. Jesus' mother suspected He could do something about the situation. However, He did not appear to be as interested as she was. Repeatedly in John, Jesus said that His time had not yet come (2:4; 7:6,8,30; 8:20). Jesus chose not to reveal Himself openly to Israel (though He did perform numerous messianic signs; see note at 2:11).

Jn 2:11 The reference to Jesus' turning of water into wine at the wedding at Cana as the "first sign in Cana of Galilee" leads the reader to expect more "signs" in the following chapters. The corresponding reference in 4:54 is to Jesus' healing of the royal official's son again while at Cana, "the second sign Jesus performed after He came from Judea to Galilee." Beyond this, "signs" of Jesus include the (non-miraculous, but prophetic-style) temple clearing (2:13-22; one of Jesus' Judean signs; see 2:23; 3:2); His healing of a lame man (5:1-15); the feeding of the multitudes (6:1-15); the healing of the man born blind (9); and the raising of Lazarus (11).

Sec. 30   Jesus at Capernaum

John 2:12

¹² After this, He went down to Capernaum, together with His mother, His brothers, and His disciples, and they stayed there only a few days.

Sec. 31   Jesus' First Cleansing of the Temple Complex

John 2:13-22

¹³ The Jewish •Passover was near, so Jesus went up to Jerusalem. ¹⁴ In the •temple complex He found people selling oxen, sheep, and doves, and ⌊He also found⌋ the money changers sitting there. ¹⁵ After making a whip out of cords, He drove everyone out of the temple complex with their sheep and oxen. He also poured out the money changers' coins and overturned the tables. ¹⁶ He told those who were selling doves, "Get these things out of here! Stop turning My Father's house into a marketplace!"ᵃ

ᵃ**2:16** Lit *a house of business*

Jn 2:13-22 The first major confrontation with the Jewish leaders in John's Gospel took place at the occasion of Jesus' clearing of the Jerusalem temple at the Jewish Passover. (The Synoptic Gospels record a later temple clearing, just prior to the crucifixion; see Mk 11:15-19 and parallels.) The action prophetically foreshadowed Jesus' crucifixion and resurrection.

John 2:13-22 (cont.)

¹⁷ And His disciples remembered that it is written: **Zeal for Your house will consume Me.**ᵃ

¹⁸ So the •Jews replied to Him, "What sign ⌊of authority⌋ will You show us for doing these things?"

¹⁹ Jesus answered, "Destroy this sanctuary, and I will raise it up in three days."

²⁰ Therefore the Jews said, "This sanctuary took 46 years to build, and will You raise it up in three days?"

²¹ But He was speaking about the sanctuary of His body. ²² So when He was raised from the dead, His disciples remembered that He had said this. And they believed the Scripture and the statement Jesus had made.

ᵃ2:17 Ps 69:9

Jn 2:13 These are the first references to a Jewish festival in John's Gospel and the first reference to the Jewish Passover. Later, John refers to two more Passovers at 6:4 (Jesus in Galilee) and 11:55; 12:1 (Jesus' final Passover in Jerusalem). Beyond this, Matthew 12:1 and parallels may refer to another Passover not recorded in John. If so, Jesus' ministry may have included four Passovers and extended over about 3 ½ years.

Sec. 32   Jesus and Nicodemus

John 2:23–3:21

²³ While He was in Jerusalem at the Passover Festival, many trusted in His name when they saw the signs He was doing. ²⁴ Jesus, however, would not entrust Himself to them, since He knew them all ²⁵ and because He did not need anyone to testify about man; for He Himself knew what was in man.

¹There was a man from the •Pharisees named Nicodemus, a ruler of the Jews. ² This man came to Him at night and said, "•Rabbi, we know that You have come from God as a teacher, for no one could perform these signs You do unless God were with him."

³ Jesus replied, "•I assure you: Unless someone is born again,ᵃ he cannot see the kingdom of God."

⁴ "But how can anyone be born when he is old?" Nicodemus asked Him. "Can he enter his mother's womb a second time and be born?"

⁵ Jesus answered, "I assure you: Unless someone is born of water and the Spirit,ᵇ he cannot enter the kingdom of God. ⁶ Whatever is born of the flesh is flesh, and whatever is born of the Spirit is spirit. ⁷ Do not be amazed that I told you that youᶜ must be born again. ⁸ The windᵈ blows where it pleases, and you hear its sound, but you don't know where it comes from or where it is going. So it is with everyone born of the Spirit."

⁹ "How can these things be?" asked Nicodemus.

¹⁰ "Are you a teacherᵉ of Israel and don't know these things?" Jesus replied. ¹¹ "I assure you: We speak what We know and We testify to what We have seen, but youᶠ do not accept Our testimony.ᵍ

ᵃ3:3 The same Gk word can mean *again* or *from above* (also in v. 7).   ᵇ3:5 Or *spirit*, or *wind*; the Gk word pneuma can mean *wind, spirit,* or *Spirit*, each of which occurs in this context.   ᶜ3:7 The pronoun is pl in Gk.   ᵈ3:8 The Gk word pneuma can mean *wind, spirit,* or *Spirit,* each of which occurs in this context.   ᵉ3:10 Or *the teacher*   ᶠ3:11 The word *you* in Gk is pl here and throughout v. 12.   ᵍ3:11 The pl forms (*We, Our*) refer to Jesus and His authority to speak for the Father.

Jn 2:23–4:42 Here is a study in contrasts. A respected member of the Sanhedrin differs sharply from a Samaritan woman with a sinful past and present. In both cases, Jesus penetrated to the heart of the matter, confronting Nicodemus with his need of regeneration and the Samaritan with her sin.

Jn 3:1 *Nicodemus, a ruler of the Jews:* Nicodemus was both a Pharisee, the most well-known sect of Judaism of the time, and a member of the ruling council. Some time later, Nicodemus defended Christ before his peers (Jn 7:51) who were unaware that one of their number might have believed in Him (v. 48). The reference to Nicodemus' initial coming at night (3:2) makes all the more significant his standing up to his fellow Pharisees (Jn 7:45-52) and his later public participation in Jesus' burial (Jn 19:39-41). Nicodemus' contribution was enough aloes and spices to prepare a king for burial, and so he did.

Jn 3:2 *no one could perform these signs You do unless God were with him:* There seems to be a recognition on Nicodemus' part that Jesus had done spectacular things, although only the first sign has been done (see 2:1-12). Jesus' teaching also had no doubt indicated that He was God's messenger and hence merited the name Rabbi.

Jn 3:3 *born again:* The word translated "again" can be translated as "from above" as well. Jesus introduced the theme of the kingdom of God, which in John's Gospel seems to have arrived by the coming of Jesus in flesh.

Jn 3:5 *water and the Spirit:* There has been much discussion of what water and Spirit refer to, but probably they indicate that a human being (born of natural means, water) must also be born spiritually or of the Spirit in order to enter the kingdom of God (see v. 6).

John 2:23–3:21 (cont.)

[12] If I have told you about things that happen on earth and you don't believe, how will you believe if I tell you about things of heaven? [13] No one has ascended into heaven except the One who descended from heaven—the •Son of Man.[a] [14] Just as Moses lifted up the snake in the wilderness, so the Son of Man must be lifted up, [15] so that everyone who believes in Him will[b] have eternal life.

[16] "For God loved the world in this way: He gave His •One and Only Son, so that everyone who believes in Him will not perish but have eternal life. [17] For God did not send His Son into the world that He might condemn the world, but that the world might be saved through Him. [18] Anyone who believes in Him is not condemned, but anyone who does not believe is already condemned, because he has not believed in the name of the One and Only Son of God.

[19] "This, then, is the judgment: the light has come into the world, and people loved darkness rather than the light because their deeds were evil. [20] For everyone who practices wicked things hates the light and avoids it,[c] so that his deeds may not be exposed. [21] But anyone who lives by[d] the truth comes to the light, so that his works may be shown to be accomplished by God."[e]

[a]**3:13** Other mss add *who is in heaven*   [b]**3:15** Other mss add *not perish, but*   [c]**3:20** Lit *and does not come to the light*   [d]**3:21** Lit *who does*
[e]**3:21** It is possible that Jesus' words end at v. 15. Ancient Gk did not have quotation marks.

Jn 3:14 This is the first of three "lifted up" sayings in John's Gospel (the second and third are found in 8:28 and 12:32). All three sayings speak of the future "lifting up" of the Son of Man in typical Johannine double entendre.
Jn 3:15 *so that everyone who believes in Him will have eternal life:* This may mark the end of Jesus' discussion with Nicodemus.
Jn 3:16 *For God loved the world in this way:* The HCSB translates this correctly, with the words "in this way," indicating how God loved the world. *One and Only Son:* The term for "one and only," traditionally translated "only begotten," indicates uniqueness of status. Jesus is affirmed as God's unique Son.
Jn 3:19 The tendency of human beings is to love darkness rather than light, although light has come into the world.

Sec. 33   Jesus and John the Baptist

John 3:22-36

[22] After this, Jesus and His disciples went to the Judean countryside, where He spent time with them and baptized. [23] John also was baptizing in Aenon near Salim, because there was plenty of water there. People were coming and being baptized, [24] since John had not yet been thrown into prison.

[25] Then a dispute arose between John's disciples and a •Jew[a] about purification. [26] So they came to John and told him, "Rabbi, the One you testified about, and who was with you across the Jordan, is baptizing—and everyone is flocking to Him."

[27] John responded, "No one can receive a single thing unless it's given to him from heaven. [28] You yourselves can testify that I said, 'I am not the •Messiah, but I've been sent ahead of Him.' [29] He who has the bride is the groom. But the groom's friend, who stands by and listens for him, rejoices greatly[b] at the groom's voice. So this joy of mine is complete. [30] He must increase, but I must decrease."

[31] The One who comes from above is above all. The one who is from the earth is earthly and speaks in earthly terms.[c] The One who comes from heaven is above all. [32] He testifies to what He has seen and heard, yet no one accepts His testimony. [33] The one who has accepted His testimony has affirmed that God is true. [34] For God sent Him, and He speaks God's words, since He[d] gives the Spirit without measure. [35] The Father loves the Son and has given all things into His Hands. [36] The one who believes in the Son has eternal life, but the one who refuses to believe in the Son will not see life; instead, the wrath of God remains on him.

[a]**3:25** Other mss read *and the Jews*   [b]**3:29** Lit *with joy rejoices*   [c]**3:31** Or *of earthly things*   [d]**3:34** Other mss read *since God*

Jn 3:25 Jesus' and John's disciples were close by in Judea, and this proximity raised questions in the minds of John's disciples. A dispute with a Jew over purification created jealousy when John's disciples saw Jesus drawing a larger crowd.
Jn 3:28 *I am not the Messiah, but I've been sent ahead of Him:* John reaffirmed what he said earlier regarding his not being the Messiah but that he was the one sent as a forerunner. He compares himself to the groom's friend who shares in the groom's joy (v. 29).
Jn 3:30 *He must increase, but I must decrease:* John recognized the limitations of his ministry and that his transitional role made it inevitable that Jesus will increase in influence, scope and importance, while he must decrease.
Jn 3:33-36 There is an implied Trinitarian notion expressed here.

Sec. 34   Jesus' Reasons for Leaving Judea

John 4:1-4

[1]When Jesus[a] knew that the •Pharisees heard He was making and baptizing more disciples than John [2] (though Jesus Himself was not baptizing, but His disciples were), [3] He left Judea and went again to Galilee. [4] He had to travel through Samaria,

[a]**4:1** Other mss read *the Lord*

Luke 3:19-20

[19] But Herod the tetrarch, being rebuked by him about Herodias, his brother's wife, and about all the evil things Herod had done, [20] added this to everything else—he locked John up in prison.

Matthew 4:12	Mark 1:14	Luke 4:14a
[12] When He heard that John had been arrested, He withdrew into Galilee.	[14] After John was arrested, Jesus went to Galilee, preaching the good news[a] [b] of God:[c]	[14] Then Jesus returned to Galilee in the power of the Spirit,
	[a]**1:14** Other mss add *of the kingdom* [b]**1:14** Or *gospel* [c]**1:14** Either *from God* or *about God*	

Mt 4:12 *John had been arrested:* Herod Antipas had thrown him into a dungeon near the Dead Sea. John's fate is described in Matthew 11.
Jn 4:1 *He [Jesus] was making and baptizing more disciples than John:* Baptism was equated with being a follower of Jesus from the start, modeled after the baptism of John.
Jn 4:3 *went again to Galilee:* Galilee was Jesus' home. John's Gospel indicates that Jesus made a number of trips between Galilee and Jerusalem, especially around feast times.
Jn 4:4 *He had to travel through Samaria:* Much less is known of the Samaritans than of the Jews of the times. We do know that there was tension between them, stemming from the fact that the Jews were seen as the ones who had gone into exile, while the Samaritans were the descendants of those who had remained and intermarried with the conquerors. As a result, there were social, cultural and religious tensions with the Samaritans.

Sec. 35   Jesus and the Samaritan Woman

John 4:5-42

[5] so He came to a town of Samaria called Sychar near the property[a] that Jacob had given his son Joseph. [6] Jacob's well was there, and Jesus, worn out from His journey, sat down at the well. It was about six in the evening.[b]
[7] A woman of Samaria came to draw water.
"Give Me a drink," Jesus said to her, [8] for His disciples had gone into town to buy food.
[9] "How is it that You, a Jew, ask for a drink from me, a •Samaritan woman?" she asked Him. For Jews do not associate with[c] Samaritans.[d]
[10] Jesus answered, "If you knew the gift of God, and who is saying to you, 'Give Me a drink,' you would ask Him, and He would give you living water."

[a]**4:5** Lit *piece of land* [b]**4:6** Lit *the sixth hour*; see note at Jn 1:39; an alternate time reckoning would be *noon* [c]**4:9** Or *do not share vessels with* [d]**4:9** Other mss omit *For Jews do not associate with Samaritans.*

Jn 4:7 *A woman of Samaria came to draw water:* Drawing water was considered woman's work.
Jn 4:9 Contact between Samaritans and Jews was often tense, and it was thought inappropriate for a man to talk to a woman (see v. 27).
Jn 4:10-11 The woman interpreted Jesus' words about giving him a drink literally, so she was surprised that He asked for her to draw him water. She was intrigued by the notion of "living water," however, and wished to know more.

John 4:5-42 (cont.)

[11] "Sir," said the woman, "You don't even have a bucket, and the well is deep. So where do You get this 'living water'? [12] You aren't greater than our father Jacob, are You? He gave us the well and drank from it himself, as did his sons and livestock."

[13] Jesus said, "Everyone who drinks from this water will get thirsty again. [14] But whoever drinks from the water that I will give him will never get thirsty again—ever! In fact, the water I will give him will become a well[a] of water springing up within him for eternal life."

[15] "Sir," the woman said to Him, "give me this water so I won't get thirsty and come here to draw water."

[16] "Go call your husband," He told her, "and come back here."

[17] "I don't have a husband," she answered.

"You have correctly said, 'I don't have a husband,'" Jesus said. [18] "For you've had five husbands, and the man you now have is not your husband. What you have said is true."

[19] "Sir," the woman replied, "I see that You are a prophet. [20] Our fathers worshiped on this mountain,[b] yet you ⌊Jews⌋ say that the place to worship is in Jerusalem."

[21] Jesus told her, "Believe Me, •woman, an hour is coming when you will worship the Father neither on this mountain nor in Jerusalem. [22] You Samaritans[c] worship what you do not know. We worship what we do know, because salvation is from the Jews. [23] But an hour is coming, and is now here, when the true worshipers will worship the Father in spirit and truth. Yes, the Father wants such people to worship Him. [24] God is spirit, and those who worship Him must worship in spirit and truth."

[25] The woman said to Him, "I know that •Messiah[d] is coming" (who is called Christ). "When He comes, He will explain everything to us."

[26] "I am ⌊He⌋," Jesus told her, "the One speaking to you."

[27] Just then His disciples arrived, and they were amazed that He was talking with a woman. Yet no one said, "What do You want?" or "Why are You talking with her?"

[28] Then the woman left her water jar, went into town, and told the men, [29] "Come, see a man who told me everything I ever did! Could this be the Messiah?" [30] They left the town and made their way to Him.

[31] In the meantime the disciples kept urging Him, "•Rabbi, eat something."

[32] But He said, "I have food to eat that you don't know about."

[33] The disciples said to one another, "Could someone have brought Him something to eat?"

[34] "My food is to do the will of Him who sent Me and to finish His work," Jesus told them. [35] "Don't you say, 'There are still four more months, then comes the harvest'? Listen ⌊to what⌋ I'm telling you: Open[e] your eyes and look at the fields, for they are ready[f] for harvest. [36] The reaper is already receiving pay and gathering fruit for eternal life, so the sower and reaper can rejoice together. [37] For in this case the saying is true: 'One sows and another reaps.' [38] I sent you to reap what you didn't labor for; others have labored, and you have benefited from[g] their labor."

[39] Now many Samaritans from that town believed in Him because of what the woman said[h] when she testified, "He told me everything I ever did." [40] Therefore, when the Samaritans came to Him, they asked Him to stay with them, and He stayed there two days. [41] Many more believed because of what He said.[i] [42] And they told the woman, "We no longer believe because of what you said, for we have heard for ourselves and know that this really is the Savior of the world."[j]

---

[a]4:14 Or *spring* [b]4:20 Mount Gerizim, where there had been a Samaritan temple that rivaled Jerusalem's [c]4:22 *Samaritans* is implied since the Gk verb and pronoun are pl. [d]4:25 In the NT, the word Messiah translates the Gk word *Christos* ("Anointed One"), except here and in Jn 1:41 where it translates *Messias*. [e]4:35 Lit *Raise* [f]4:35 Lit *white* [g]4:38 Lit *you have entered into* [h]4:39 Lit *because of the woman's word* [i]4:41 Lit *because of His word* [j]4:42 Other mss add *the Messiah*

Jn 4:19 *I see that You are a prophet:* Jesus' knowledge of the woman's past and present lifestyle impressed the woman.

Jn 4:21-24 Jesus clarified that salvation comes by way of the Jews, that is, He as the source of eternal life is a Jew. As a result of His coming all people will worship God in spirit and in truth, and not in any particular location.

Jn 4:26 *I am ⌊He⌋:* Jesus makes an explicit claim to being the Messiah.

Jn 4:34 It is not only the Samaritan woman who interprets Jesus literally. When Jesus says that He had food to eat (v. 32), the disciples speculated that someone may have brought Him food (v. 33).

Jn 4:40 The Samaritans were more receptive of Jesus than the Jews in Jerusalem, so He stayed for two days at their invitation.

Sec. 36   Jesus Welcomed in Galilee

John 4:43-45

[43] After two days He left there for Galilee. [44] Jesus Himself testified that a prophet has no honor in his own country. [45] When they entered Galilee, the Galileans welcomed Him because they had seen everything He did in Jerusalem during the festival. For they also had gone to the festival.

Jn 4:43-54 The healing of the royal official's son completes the "Cana cycle" in John's Gospel, which spans from 2:1 to 4:54 and begins and ends with a "sign" performed by Jesus in Cana of Galilee (2:11; 4:54, Sec. 38). The present "sign" is a rare instance of a long-distance healing performed by Jesus. The story resembles that of the Gentile centurion in Matthew 8:5-13 and Luke 7:2-10, but this is not the same incident.

Jn 4:44 *Jesus Himself testified that a prophet has no honor in his own country:* After Jesus was welcomed in Samaria, He returned to His own country, Galilee, where He was not as well received.

PART VII

THE GREAT GALILEAN MINISTRY

Sec. 37   Summary of Jesus' Teaching in Galilee

Matthew 4:17	Mark 1:14-15	Luke 4:14-15
17 From then on Jesus began to preach, "Repent, because the kingdom of heaven has come near!"	14 After John was arrested, Jesus went to Galilee, preaching the good news[a] [b] of God:[c] 15 "The time is fulfilled, and the kingdom of God has come near. Repent and believe in the good news!" [a]1:14 Other mss add *of the kingdom* [b]1:14 Or *gospel* [c]1:14 Either *from God* or *about God*	14 Then Jesus returned to Galilee in the power of the Spirit, and news about Him spread throughout the entire vicinity. 15 He was teaching in their •synagogues, being acclaimed[a] by everyone. [a]4:15 Or *glorified*

Mt 4:17 *began to preach:* That is, in Galilee, for He had already been preaching elsewhere.

Mk 1:15 *the kingdom of God:* Both a present and a future reality. At times, Mark presents the kingdom of God as a future reality that will come with power (9:1; 14:25; 15:43). In a similar way, Jesus teaches about the Son of Man's coming in great power and glory, at which time the wicked will be judged and the elect gathered together (8:38; 13:26-27; 14:62). In His private teaching, however, Jesus teaches about a form of the kingdom that is a secret, a mystery able to be understood only by His followers (4:10-12).

Lk 4:14 *in the power of the Spirit:* An emphasis unique to Luke's introduction of the Galilean ministry.

Sec. 38   Jesus' Second Sign: Healing an Official's Son

John 4:46-54

46 Then He went again to Cana of Galilee, where He had turned the water into wine. There was a certain royal official whose son was ill at Capernaum. 47 When this man heard that Jesus had come from Judea into Galilee, he went to Him and pleaded with Him to come down and heal his son, for he was about to die.

48 Jesus told him, "Unless you ⌊people⌋ see signs and wonders, you will not believe."

49 "Sir," the official said to Him, "come down before my boy dies!"

50 "Go," Jesus told him, "your son will live." The man believed what[a] Jesus said to him and departed.

51 While he was still going down, his •slaves met him saying that his boy was alive. 52 He asked them at what time he got better. "Yesterday at seven in the morning[b] the fever left him," they answered. 53 The father realized this was the very hour at which Jesus had told him, "Your son will live." Then he himself believed, along with his whole household.

54 This therefore was the second sign Jesus performed after He came from Judea to Galilee.

[a]4:50 Lit *the word*   [b]4:52 Or *seven in the evening;* lit *at the seventh hour;* see note at Jn 1:39; an alt time reckoning would be *at one in the afternoon*

Jn 4:53 *Then he himself believed:* The initial belief of the man was simply in what Jesus had said to him. Now he had genuine faith, once he realized that exactly what Jesus had said had come true, and his son had been healed at the very hour when Jesus had spoken.

Sec. 39   Rejection at Nazareth

Luke 4:16-31

16 He came to Nazareth, where He had been brought up. As usual, He entered the synagogue on the Sabbath day and stood up to read. 17 The scroll of the prophet Isaiah was given to Him, and unrolling the scroll, He found the place where it was written:

18 **The Spirit of the Lord is on Me,**
because He has anointed Me
to preach good news to the poor.
He has sent Mea
to proclaim freedomb **to the captives**
and recovery of sight to the blind,
to set free the oppressed,
19 **to proclaim the year of the Lord's favor.**c d

20 He then rolled up the scroll, gave it back to the attendant, and sat down. And the eyes of everyone in the synagogue were fixed on Him. 21 He began by saying to them, "Today as you listen, this Scripture has been fulfilled."

22 They were all speaking well of Hime and were amazed by the gracious words that came from His mouth, yet they said, "Isn't this Joseph's son?"

23 Then He said to them, "No doubt you will quote this proverbf to Me: 'Doctor, heal yourself. ⌊So⌋ all we've heard that took place in Capernaum, do here in Your hometown also.'"

24 He also said, "•I assure you: No prophet is accepted in his hometown. 25 But I say to you, there were certainly many widows in Israel in Elijah's days, when the sky was shut up for three years and six months while a great famine came over all the land. 26 Yet Elijah was not sent to any of them—but to a widow at Zarephath in Sidon. 27 And in the prophet Elisha's time, there were many in Israel who had serious skin diseases, yet not one of them was healedg —only Naaman the Syrian."

28 When they heard this, everyone in the synagogue was enraged. 29 They got up, drove Him out of town, and brought Him to the edgeh of the hill that their town was built on, intending to hurl Him over the cliff. 30 But He passed right through the crowd and went on His way.

31 Then He went down to Capernaum, a town in Galilee, and was teaching them on the Sabbath.

a**4:18** Other mss add *to heal the brokenhearted,*   b**4:18** Or *release,* or *forgiveness*   c**4:19** The time of messianic grace   d**4:18-19** Is 61:1-2
e**4:22** Or *They were testifying against Him*   f**4:23** Or *parable*   g**4:27** Lit *cleansed*   h**4:29** Lit *brow*

Lk 4:17 *Isaiah:* Only Luke has the detail that Jesus read from Isaiah 61:1-2 and 58:6.
Lk 4:21 *Today . . . this Scripture has been fulfilled:* Jesus declared that He was the fulfillment of Isaiah's prophecy that He just read.
Lk 4:25-27 *Elijah . . . Elisha:* The mention of these two prophets caused the crowd to be angry. Jesus said that the prophets healed Gentiles because of Israel's unbelief. Jesus was warning them that rejecting Him was like the unfaithfulness of one of the worst periods in Israel's history.

Sec. 40   Jesus Makes Capernaum His Home

Matthew 4:13-16

13 He left Nazareth behind and went to live in Capernaum by the sea, in the region of Zebulun and Naphtali. 14 This was to fulfill what was spoken through the prophet Isaiah:

15 **Land of Zebulun and land of Naphtali,**
along the sea road, beyond the Jordan,
Galilee of the Gentiles!

Mt 4:13 *left Nazareth . . . Capernaum:* He went first to Nazareth, his home, but was rejected (Lk 4:16-31). Capernaum was larger and more significant, lying on the northwest shore of the Sea of Galilee.

Matthew 4:13–16 (cont.)

16 The people who live in darkness
   have seen a great light,
   and for those living in the shadowland of death,
   light has dawned.ᵃ ᵇ

ᵃ**4:16** Lit *dawned on them*   ᵇ**4:15-16** Is 9:1-2

Mt 4:15 *Zebulun . . . Naphtali:* Israelite territories that generally corresponded with regions of Galilee. Matthew quotes Isaiah 9:1-2 and applies the words about the delivery from Assyria to the Messiah.

Sec. 41   Jesus Calls Four Fishermen

Matthew 4:18-22	Mark 1:16-20	Luke 5:1-11
18 As He was walking along the Sea of Galilee, He saw two brothers, Simon, who was called Peter, and his brother Andrew. They were casting a net into the sea, since they were fishermen. 19 "Follow Me," He told them, "and I will make you fish forᵃ people!" 20 Immediately they left their nets and followed Him. 21 Going on from there, He saw two other brothers, James the son of Zebedee, and his brother John. They were in a boat with Zebedee their father, mending their nets, and He called them. 22 Immediately they left the boat and their father and followed Him. ᵃ**4:19** Lit *you fishers of*	16 As He was passing along by the Sea of Galilee, He saw Simon and Andrew, Simon's brother. They were casting a net into the sea, since they were fishermen. 17 "Follow Me," Jesus told them, "and I will make you fish forᵃ people!" 18 Immediately they left their nets and followed Him. 19 Going on a little farther, He saw James the son of Zebedee and his brother John. They were in their boat mending their nets. 20 Immediately He called them, and they left their father Zebedee in the boat with the hired men and followed Him. ᵃ**1:17** Lit *you to become fishers of*	1 As the crowd was pressing in on Jesus to hear God's word, He was standing by Lake Gennesaret.ᵃ 2 He saw two boats at the edge of the lake;ᵇ the fishermen had left them and were washing their nets. 3 He got into one of the boats, which belonged to Simon, and asked him to put out a little from the land. Then He sat down and was teaching the crowds from the boat. 4 When He had finished speaking, He said to Simon, "Put out into deep water and let downᶜ your nets for a catch." 5 "Master," Simon replied, "we've worked hard all night long and caught nothing! But at Your word, I'll let down the nets."ᵈ

6 When they did this, they caught a great number of fish, and their netsᵈ began to tear. 7 So they signaled to their partners in the other boat to come and help them; they came and filled both boats so full that they began to sink.

8 When Simon Peter saw this, he fell at Jesus' knees and said, "Go away from me, because I'm a sinful man, Lord!" 9 For he and all those with him were amazedᵉ at the catch of fish they took, 10 and so were James and John, Zebedee's sons, who were Simon's partners.

"Don't be afraid," Jesus told Simon. "From now on you will be catching people!" 11 Then they brought the boats to land, left everything, and followed Him.

ᵃ**5:1** = Sea of Galilee   ᵇ**5:2** Lit *boats standing by the lake*   ᶜ**5:4** Lit *and you* (Gk pl) *let down*   ᵈ**5:5,6** Other mss read *net* (Gk sg)   ᵉ**5:9** Lit *For amazement had seized him and all those with him*

Mt 4:18-22 The first of twelve disciples are called here. There are two sets of brothers. All were commercial fishermen.

Mt 4:19 *fish for people:* Andrew and Simon had already become disciples of Jesus (Jn 1:35-42), but now they are called to leave their business (fishermen) to follow Jesus.

Mt 4:21 *James the son of Zebedee, and his brother John:* These also had already become disciples of Jesus. *mending their nets:* Getting them ready to use.

Mk 1:18 *followed Him:* In Mark's Gospel, "to follow" sometimes means literally to walk behind someone who is taking the lead (3:7; 5:24; 14:13). At other times it bears the meaning of accompanying Jesus as a disciple (for example 1:18; 2:14-15; 8:34; 10:21,28; 15:41).

Lk 5:1-11 This account provides additional details to the parallel accounts in Matthew and Mark.

Lk 5:5 *all night long:* At the best time to catch fish, nothing was caught. Nonetheless at Jesus' word, Peter will cast the nets.

Lk 5:8 *I'm a sinful man:* The miracle showed Jesus to be a holy man. Peter thought he could not be in Jesus' presence as a result, because he knew he was a sinner. Jesus replied that Peter is precisely the kind of man He will call and use to draw others to the truth.

Sec. 42   Driving Out an Unclean Spirit

Mark 1:21-28	Luke 4:31-37
21 Then they went into Capernaum, and right away He entered the •synagogue on the Sabbath and began to teach. 22 They were astonished at His teaching because, unlike the •scribes, He was teaching them as one having authority. 23 Just then a man with an •unclean spirit was in their synagogue. He cried out,a 24 "What do You have to do with us,b Jesus—Nazarene? Have You come to destroy us? I know who You are—the Holy One of God!" 25 But Jesus rebuked him and said, "Be quiet,c and come out of him!" 26 And the unclean spirit convulsed him, shouted with a loud voice, and came out of him. 27 Then they were all amazed, so they began to argue with one another, saying, "What is this? A new teaching with authority!d He commands even the unclean spirits, and they obey Him." 28 News about Him then spread throughout the entire vicinity of Galilee.	31 Then He went down to Capernaum, a town in Galilee, and was teaching them on the Sabbath. 32 They were astonished at His teaching because His message had authority. 33 In the synagogue there was a man with an •unclean demonic spirit who cried out with a loud voice, 34 "Leave us alone!a What do You have to do with us,b Jesus—•Nazarene? Have You come to destroy us? I know who You are—the Holy One of God!" 35 But Jesus rebuked him and said, "Be quiet and come out of him!" And throwing him down before them, the demon came out of him without hurting him at all. 36 Amazement came over them all, and ⌊they⌋ kept saying to one another, "What is this message? For He commands the unclean spirits with authority and power, and they come out!" 37 And news about Him began to go out to every place in the vicinity.

a1:23 Other mss add to the beginning of v. 24: *"Leave us alone."*   b1:24 Lit *What to us and to You*   c1:25 Or *Be muzzled*   d1:27 Other mss read *What is this? What is this new teaching? For with authority*

a4:34 Or *Ha!*, or *Ah!*   b4:34 Lit *What to us and to You*

Mk 1:21 *the synagogue on the Sabbath:* A synagogue served primarily as a location for the reading and teaching of the Law of Moses, but it could also function as a place for prayer, for the education of children, and for community events. During Jesus' time, every significant Jewish community in Galilee had a synagogue.

Mk 1:23 *an unclean spirit:* Mark uses "unclean spirit" interchangeably with "demon," employing both terms with about the same frequency. These spirit beings take control of people for the purpose of destroying them through sickness or self-inflicted wounds (5:2-13; 9:17-27).

Lk 4:32 *authority:* This remark is slightly different than the parallel in Mark. What Mark says explicitly, Luke presents implicitly.

Lk 4:34 *Holy One:* The demons knew that Jesus was uniquely set apart by God. Jesus, however, silenced them because He didn't want testimony from demons.

Sec. 43   Healings at Capernaum

Matthew 8:14-17	Mark 1:29-34	Luke 4:38-41
14 When Jesus went into Peter's house, He saw his mother-in-law lying in bed with a fever. 15 So He touched her hand, and the fever left her. Then she got up and began to serve Him.	29 As soon as they left the synagogue, they went into Simon and Andrew's house with James and John. 30 Simon's mother-in-law was lying in bed with a fever, and they told Him about her at once. 31 So He went to her, took her by the hand, and raised her up. The fever left her,a and she began to serve them.	38 After He left the synagogue, He entered Simon's house. Simon's mother-in-law was suffering from a high fever, and they asked Him about her. 39 So He stood over her and rebuked the fever, and it left her. She got up immediately and began to serve them.

a1:31 Other mss add *at once*

Mt 8:14 *mother-in-law:* Peter was married (1 Co 9:5), and perhaps his mother-in-law lived with her daughter and Peter.

Lk 4:39 *rebuked:* The fever is almost treated like a hostile force.

Matthew 8:14-17 (cont.)	Mark 1:29-34 (cont.)	Luke 4:38-41 (cont.)
16 When evening came, they brought to Him many who were demon-possessed. He drove out the spirits with a word and healed all who were sick, 17 so that what was spoken through the prophet Isaiah might be fulfilled: **He Himself took our weaknesses and carried our diseases.**ᵃ	32 When evening came, after the sun had set, they began bringing to Him all those who were sick and those who were demon-possessed. 33 The whole town was assembled at the door, 34 and He healed many who were sick with various diseases and drove out many demons. But He would not permit the demons to speak, because they knew Him.	40 When the sun was setting, all those who had anyone sick with various diseases brought them to Him. As He laid His hands on each one of them, He would heal them. 41 Also, demons were coming out of many, shouting and saying, "You are the Son of God!" But He rebuked them and would not allow them to speak, because they knew He was the •Messiah.

ᵃ**8:17** Is 53:4

Mt 8:17 Matthew quotes Isaiah 53:4 to provide the scriptural context for Christ's ministry. The emphasis here is not on Jesus' death but on what He fulfilled in His life.
Lk 4:41 *Son of God . . . Messiah:* This extended explanatory remark is only in Luke.

Sec. 44   Preaching in Galilee

Matthew 4:23-25	Mark 1:35-39	Luke 4:42-44
	35 Very early in the morning, while it was still dark, He got up, went out, and made His way to a deserted place. And He was praying there. 36 Simon and his companions went searching for Him. 37 They found Him and said, "Everyone's looking for You!" 38 And He said to them, "Let's go on to the neighboring villages so that I may preach there too. This is why I have come." 39 So He went into all of Galilee, preaching in their synagogues and driving out demons.	42 When it was day, He went out and made His way to a deserted place. But the crowds were searching for Him. They came to Him and tried to keep Him from leaving them. 43 But He said to them, "I must proclaim the good news about the kingdom of God to the other towns also, because I was sent for this purpose." 44 And He was preaching in the synagogues of Galilee.ᵃ ᵃ**4:44** Other mss read *Judea*
23 Jesus was going all over Galilee, teaching in their •synagogues, preaching the good news of the kingdom, and healing everyᵃ disease and sickness among the people. 24 Then the news about Him spread throughout Syria. So they brought to Him all those who were afflicted, those suffering from various diseases and intense pains, the demon-possessed, the epileptics, and the paralytics. And He healed them. 25 Large crowds followed Him from Galilee, •Decapolis, Jerusalem, Judea, and beyond the Jordan. ᵃ**4:23** Or *every kind of*		

Lk 4:43 *I must proclaim:* The use of the term *must* indicates a divine necessity that guides Jesus' mission. He must preach the "kingdom of God."

Sec. 45   Cleansing a Leper

Matthew 8:2-4	Mark 1:40-45	Luke 5:12-16

2 Right away a man with a serious skin disease came up and knelt before Him, saying, "Lord, if You are willing, You can make me •clean."[a]

3 Reaching out His hand He touched him, saying, "I am willing; be made clean." Immediately his disease was healed.[b]

4 Then Jesus told him, "See that you don't tell anyone; but go, show yourself to the priest, and offer the gift that Moses prescribed, as a testimony to them."

[a]**8:2** In these vv., *clean* includes healing, ceremonial purification, return to fellowship with people, and worship in the temple; Lv 14:1-32.   [b]**8:3** Lit *cleansed*

40 Then a man with a serious skin disease came to Him and, on his knees,[a] begged Him: "If You are willing, You can make me •clean."[b]

41 Moved with compassion, Jesus reached out His hand and touched him. "I am willing," He told him. "Be made clean." 42 Immediately the disease left him, and he was healed.[c] 43 Then He sternly warned him and sent him away at once, 44 telling him, "See that you say nothing to anyone; but go and show yourself to the priest, and offer what Moses prescribed for your cleansing, as a testimony to them." 45 Yet he went out and began to proclaim it widely and to spread the news, with the result that Jesus could no longer enter a town openly. But He was out in deserted places, and they would come to Him from everywhere.

[a]**1:40** Other mss omit *on his knees*   [b]**1:40** In these vv., *clean* includes healing, ceremonial purification, return to fellowship with people, and worship in the temple; Lv 14:1-32.   [c]**1:42** Lit *made clean*

12 While He was in one of the towns, a man was there who had a serious skin disease all over him. He saw Jesus, fell facedown, and begged Him: "Lord, if You are willing, You can make me •clean."[a]

13 Reaching out His hand, He touched him, saying, "I am willing; be made clean," and immediately the disease left him. 14 Then He ordered him to tell no one: "But go and show yourself to the priest, and offer what Moses prescribed for your cleansing as a testimony to them."

15 But the news[b] about Him spread even more, and large crowds would come together to hear Him and to be healed of their sicknesses. 16 Yet He often withdrew to deserted places and prayed.

[a]**5:12** In these verses, *clean* includes healing, ceremonial purification, return to fellowship with people, and worship in the temple; Lv 14:1-32.   [b]**5:15** Lit *the word*

Mt 8:2 *skin disease:* The Greek word is *lepros,* the basis for our word leprosy. Two separate diseases are called leprosy in the Bible: 1) true leprosy, the kind known today that is virtually extinct due to medical advances, 2) white leprosy, a skin disease described in its various forms in Leviticus 13. When Jesus touched the diseased man, Jewish law declared Him unclean. But Jesus is Lord even over the law and His touch meant cleansing for the man.

Mt 8:4 *See that you don't tell anyone; but go, show yourself to the priest:* Jesus did not want the adulation of crowds who only wanted a miracle worker, but commanded the man to fulfill the laws of cleansing according to Leviticus 14.

Mk 1:43 *He sternly warned him:* Jesus' stern warning to the healed man stands in contrast to His previous response of compassion. Apparently Jesus sensed that the man was likely to disregard His command, which happened according to verse 45. Jesus' harsh warning, therefore, was an attempt to impress upon the man the seriousness of the following command.

Lk 5:12-16 This event begins a series of five controversies in Luke, reported in 5:12–6:11 that also occur in Mark 2:1–3:6. Matthew spread them across chapters 8–12.

Lk 5:13 *clean:* The miracle pictures a deeper reality. Jesus is able to make people clean physically and spiritually.

Sec. 46   The Son of Man Forgives and Heals

Matthew 9:1-8	Mark 2:1-12	Luke 5:17-26

¹So He got into a boat, crossed over, and came to His own town.

² Just then some men[a] brought to Him a paralytic lying on a mat.

Seeing their faith, Jesus told the paralytic, "Have courage, son, your sins are forgiven." ³ At this, some of the •scribes said among themselves, "He's blaspheming!" ⁴ But perceiving their thoughts, Jesus said, "Why are you thinking evil things in your hearts?[b] ⁵ For which is easier: to say, 'Your sins are forgiven,' or to say, 'Get up and walk'? ⁶ But so you may know that the •Son of Man has authority on earth to forgive sins"—then He told the paralytic, "Get up, pick up your mat, and go home." ⁷ And he got up and went home. ⁸ When the crowds saw this, they were awestruck[c][d] and gave glory to God who had given such authority to men.

[a]**9:2** Lit *then they*   [b]**9:4** Or *minds*
[c]**9:8** Other mss read *amazed*   [d]**9:8** Lit *afraid*

---

¹When He entered Capernaum again after some days, it was reported that He was at home. ² So many people gathered together that there was no more room, not even in the doorway, and He was speaking the message to them. ³ Then they came to Him bringing a paralytic, carried by four men. ⁴ Since they were not able to bring him to[a] Jesus because of the crowd, they removed the roof above where He was. And when they had broken through, they lowered the mat on which the paralytic was lying. ⁵ Seeing their faith, Jesus told the paralytic, "Son, your sins are forgiven." ⁶ But some of the •scribes were sitting there, thinking to themselves:[b] ⁷ "Why does He speak like this? He's blaspheming! Who can forgive sins but God alone?" ⁸ Right away Jesus understood in His spirit that they were thinking like this within themselves and said to them, "Why are you thinking these things in your hearts?[c] ⁹ Which is easier: to say to the paralytic, 'Your sins are forgiven,' or to say, 'Get up, pick up your mat, and walk'? ¹⁰ But so you may know that the •Son of Man has authority on earth to forgive sins," He told the paralytic, ¹¹ "I tell you: get up, pick up your mat, and go home." ¹² Immediately he got up, picked up the mat, and went out in front of everyone. As a result, they were all astounded and gave glory to God, saying, "We have never seen anything like this!"

[a]**2:4** Other mss read *able to get near*
[b]**2:6** Or *thinking in their hearts*
[c]**2:8** Or *minds*

---

¹⁷ On one of those days while He was teaching, •Pharisees and teachers of the law were sitting there who had come from every village of Galilee and Judea, and also from Jerusalem. And the Lord's power to heal was in Him. ¹⁸ Just then some men came, carrying on a mat a man who was paralyzed. They tried to bring him in and set him down before Him. ¹⁹ Since they could not find a way to bring him in because of the crowd, they went up on the roof and lowered him on the mat through the roof tiles into the middle of the crowd before Jesus. ²⁰ Seeing their faith He said, "Friend,[a] your sins are forgiven you." ²¹ Then the •scribes and the Pharisees began to think: "Who is this man who speaks blasphemies? Who can forgive sins but God alone?" ²² But perceiving their thoughts, Jesus replied to them, "Why are you thinking this in your hearts?[b] ²³ Which is easier: to say, 'Your sins are forgiven you,' or to say, 'Get up and walk'? ²⁴ But so you may know that the •Son of Man has authority on earth to forgive sins"—He told the paralyzed man, "I tell you: get up, pick up your mat, and go home." ²⁵ Immediately he got up before them, picked up what he had been lying on, and went home glorifying God. ²⁶ Then everyone was astounded, and they were giving glory to God. And they were filled with awe and said, "We have seen incredible things today!"

[a]**5:20** Lit *Man*   [b]**5:22** Or *minds*

Mt 9:1 *His own town:* Capernaum.
Mt 9:6 *Son of Man has authority on earth to forgive sins:* Because Jews regarded disease as the punishment of sin, their own principles argued that the healing of the infirmity implied the ability to forgive sins.
Mk 2:1-12 "Son of Man" was Jesus' favorite self-designation and alludes to Daniel 7:13-14. The title portrays Jesus as a king of heavenly origin who will reign over a universal and eternal kingdom.
Mk 2:7 *He's blaspheming:* Blasphemy is arrogantly disrespectful speech against God; speech that insults Him, or diminishes His uniqueness, or demeans His majesty.
Mk 2:9 *Which is easier:* Jesus is arguing in terms of external proof before a skeptical audience. To declare someone healed is more difficult in the sense that it is open to immediate verification. Everyone can see at once if the miraculous cure has taken place. To declare someone forgiven is easier in the sense that outside observers have no way of knowing for certain if the forgiveness is real.

Sec. 47   The Call of Matthew

Matthew 9:9-13	Mark 2:13-17	Luke 5:27-32

Mark 2:13-17

[13] Then Jesus went out again beside the sea. The whole crowd was coming to Him, and He taught them. [14] Then, moving on, He saw Levi the son of Alphaeus sitting at the tax office, and He said to him, "Follow Me!" So he got up and followed Him.

Matthew 9:9-13

[9] As Jesus went on from there, He saw a man named Matthew sitting at the tax office, and He said to him, "Follow Me!" So he got up and followed Him.

[10] While He was reclining at the table in the house, many tax collectors and sinners came as guests to eat[a] with Jesus and His disciples. [11] When the •Pharisees saw this, they asked His disciples, "Why does your Teacher eat with tax collectors and sinners?"

Mark (cont.)

[15] While He was reclining at the table in Levi's house, many tax collectors and sinners were also guests[a] with Jesus and His disciples, because there were many who were following Him. [16] When the scribes of the •Pharisees[b] saw that He was eating with sinners and tax collectors, they asked His disciples, "Why does He eat[c] with tax collectors and sinners?"

Luke 5:27-32

[27] After this, Jesus went out and saw a tax collector named Levi sitting at the tax office, and He said to him, "Follow Me!" [28] So, leaving everything behind, he got up and began to follow Him.

[29] Then Levi hosted a grand banquet for Him at his house. Now there was a large crowd of tax collectors and others who were guests[a] with them. [30] But the Pharisees and their scribes were complaining to His disciples, "Why do you eat and drink with tax collectors and sinners?"

[12] But when He heard this, He said, "Those who are well don't need a doctor, but the sick do. [13] Go and learn what this means: **I desire mercy and not sacrifice.**[b] For I didn't come to call the righteous, but sinners."[c]

[17] When Jesus heard this, He told them, "Those who are well don't need a doctor, but the sick ⌊do need one⌋. I didn't come to call the righteous, but sinners."

[31] Jesus replied to them, "The healthy don't need a doctor, but the sick do. [32] I have not come to call the righteous, but sinners to repentance."

[a]9:10 Lit *came, they were reclining* (at the table); at important meals the custom was to recline on a mat at a low table and lean on the left elbow.   **[b]9:13** Hs 6:6   **[c]9:13** Other mss add *to repentance*

[a]2:15 Lit *reclining* (at the table); at important meals the custom was to recline on a mat at a low table and lean on the left elbow.   **[b]2:16** Other mss read *scribes and Pharisees*   **[c]2:16** Other mss add *and drink*

[a]5:29 Lit *were reclining* (at the table); at important meals the custom was to recline on a mat at a low table and lean on the left elbow.

Mt 9:9 *Matthew:* A tax collector or *publican,* serving Rome against his own people.

Mt 9:13 *I desire mercy and not sacrifice:* Love and sympathy are of higher value than ceremonial rules.

Mk 2:14 *Levi the son of Alphaeus:* In the parallel account in Matthew 9:9, the tax collector called by Jesus is identified as Matthew. Apparently "Levi" and "Matthew" were two different names for the same person.

Mk 2:17 *righteous:* This refers to the "self-righteous" who failed to see their own need for repentance and salvation.

Lk 5:27 *Follow Me:* This call to Levi, a hated tax collector, as the following event makes clear, indicates that anyone who responds can receive the benefits Jesus offers. Levi chose to follow Jesus and let others know about Him.

Lk 5:30 *eat and drink with tax collectors and sinners:* This complaint by the Pharisees and scribes shows a fundamental difference between Jesus and the Jewish leadership. Jesus' view is that sinners are to be engaged and interacted with, because the kingdom is for sinners who recognize their need. Luke liked meal scenes (9:12-17; 10:38-42; 11:37-54; 14:1-24; 22:7-8; 24:29-32,41-43).

Lk 5:32 *to repentance:* Only Luke has this detail with this saying. Luke often refers to repentance as a proper response to God (Lk 3:3,8; 13:1-5; 15:7,10; 16:30; 24:47; Ac 2:38; 26:18-20).

Sec. 48   A Question About Fasting

Matthew 9:14-17	Mark 2:18-22	Luke 5:33-39

14 Then John's disciples came to Him, saying, "Why do we and the Pharisees fast often, but Your disciples do not fast?"

15 Jesus said to them, "Can the wedding guests[a] be sad while the groom is with them? The time[b] will come when the groom will be taken away from them, and then they will fast. **16** No one patches an old garment with unshrunk cloth, because the patch pulls away from the garment and makes the tear worse. **17** And no one puts[c] new wine into old wineskins. Otherwise, the skins burst, the wine spills out, and the skins are ruined. But they put new wine into fresh wineskins, and both are preserved."

a9:15 Lit *the sons of the bridal chamber*
b9:15 Lit *days*   **c9:17** Lit *And they do not put*

18 Now John's disciples and the Pharisees[a] were fasting. People came and asked Him, "Why do John's disciples and the Pharisees' disciples fast, but Your disciples do not fast?"
19 Jesus said to them, "The wedding guests[b] cannot fast while the groom is with them, can they? As long as they have the groom with them, they cannot fast. **20** But the time[c] will come when the groom is taken away from them, and then they will fast in that day.
21 No one sews a patch of unshrunk cloth on an old garment. Otherwise, the new patch pulls away from the old cloth, and a worse tear is made. **22** And no one puts new wine into old wineskins. Otherwise, the wine will burst the skins, and the wine is lost as well as the skins.[d] But new wine is for fresh wineskins."

a2:18 Other mss read *the disciples of John and of the Pharisees*   **b2:19** Lit *The sons of the bridal chamber*   **c2:20** Lit *the days*   **d2:22** Other mss read *the wine spills out and the skins will be ruined*

33 Then they said to Him, "John's disciples fast often and say prayers, and those of the Pharisees do the same, but Yours eat and drink."[a]

34 Jesus said to them, "You can't make the wedding guests[b] fast while the groom is with them, can you? **35** But the time[c] will come when the groom will be taken away from them—then they will fast in those days."
36 He also told them a parable: "No one tears a patch from a new garment and puts it on an old garment. Otherwise, not only will he tear the new, but also the piece from the new garment will not match the old. **37** And no one puts new wine into old wineskins. Otherwise, the new wine will burst the skins, it will spill, and the skins will be ruined. **38** But new wine should be put into fresh wineskins.[d] **39** And no one, after drinking old wine, wants new, because he says, 'The old is better.'"[e]

a5:33 Other mss read *"Why do John's . . . drink?"* (as a question)   **b5:34** Or *the friends of the groom*; lit *sons of the bridal chamber*   **c5:35** Lit *days*   **d5:38** Other mss add *And so both are preserved.*   **e5:39** Other mss read *is good*

Mt 9:14 By this time John the Baptist was probably in prison. His disciples came to Jesus with a problem. They themselves fasted often, but Jesus' disciples did not. Why not?

Mt 9:15 The Lord answered with an illustration. He was the bridegroom and His disciples were the wedding guests. As long as He was with them, there was no reason to fast as a sign of mourning.

Mt 9:16-17 *old garment with unshrunk cloth . . . new wine into old wineskins:* The new revelation of grace cannot be held within old Judaism.

Mk 2:22 *new wine into old wineskins:* Although a leather wineskin was initially soft and flexible, it would become brittle with age and could, therefore, easily burst under the pressure of new, fermenting wine. Attempts to constrain the teaching and ministry of Jesus within the existing traditions of the scribes and Pharisees simply will not work.

Lk 5:35 *groom will be taken away:* The first indication in Luke that He will be taken away. He compares His ministry to a wedding time that does not need to be a time of fasting.

Lk 5:36,37,39 *patch . . . wine . . . old wine:* These three illustrations make the point that what Jesus does is new and cannot be mixed with the old practices of Judaism. The first two are paralleled in Matthew and Mark. However, the last is unique to Luke. If someone likes the old wine, then they will not even try the new. Jesus applied this illustration to the Jewish leadership.

Sec. 49   Jesus' Third Sign: Healing the Sick

John 5:1-47

¹After this, a Jewish festival took place, and Jesus went up to Jerusalem. ² By the Sheep Gate in Jerusalem there is a pool, called Bethesdaª in Hebrew, which has five colonnades.ᵇ ³ Within these lay a multitude of the sick—blind, lame, and paralyzed [—waiting for the moving of the water, ⁴ because an angel would go down into the pool from time to time and stir up the water. Then the first one who got in after the water was stirred up recovered from whatever ailment he had].ᶜ

⁵ One man was there who had been sick for 38 years. ⁶ When Jesus saw him lying there and knew he had already been there a long time, He said to him, "Do you want to get well?"

⁷ "Sir," the sick man answered, "I don't have a man to put me into the pool when the water is stirred up, but while I'm coming, someone goes down ahead of me."

⁸ "Get up," Jesus told him, "pick up your mat and walk!" ⁹ Instantly the man got well, picked up his mat, and started to walk.

Now that day was the Sabbath, ¹⁰ so the •Jews said to the man who had been healed, "This is the Sabbath! It's illegal for you to pick up your mat."

¹¹ He replied, "The man who made me well told me, 'Pick up your mat and walk.'"

¹² "Who is this man who told you, 'Pick up ⌊your mat⌋ and walk'?" they asked. ¹³ But the man who was cured did not know who it was, because Jesus had slipped away into the crowd that was there.ᵈ

¹⁴ After this, Jesus found him in the •temple complex and said to him, "See, you are well. Do not sin anymore, so that something worse doesn't happen to you." ¹⁵ The man went and reported to the Jews that it was Jesus who had made him well.

¹⁶ Therefore, the Jews began persecuting Jesusᵉ because He was doing these things on the Sabbath. ¹⁷ But Jesus responded to them, "My Father is still working, and I am working also." ¹⁸ This is why the Jews began trying all the more to kill Him: not only was He breaking the Sabbath, but He was even calling God His own Father, making Himself equal with God.

¹⁹ Then Jesus replied, "•I assure you: The Son is not able to do anything on His own, but only what He sees the Father doing. For whatever the Fatherᶠ does, the Son also does these things in the same way. ²⁰ For the Father loves the Son and shows Him everything He is doing, and He will show Him greater works than these so that you will be amazed. ²¹ And just as the Father raises the dead and gives them life, so the Son also gives life to anyone He wants to. ²² The Father, in fact, judges no one but has given all judgment to the Son, ²³ so that all people will honor the Son just as they honor the Father. Anyone who does not honor the Son does not honor the Father who sent Him.

²⁴ "I assure you: Anyone who hears My word and believes Him who sent Me has eternal life and will not come under judgment but has passed from death to life.

²⁵ "I assure you: An hour is coming, and is now here, when the dead will hear the voice of the Son of God, and those who hear will live. ²⁶ For just as the Father has life in Himself, so also He has granted to the Son to have life in Himself. ²⁷ And He has granted Him the right to pass judgment, because He is the •Son of Man. ²⁸ Do not be amazed at this, because a time is coming when all who are in the graves will hear His voice ²⁹ and come out—those who have done good things, to the resurrection of life, but those who have done wicked things, to the resurrection of judgment.

ª**5:2** Other mss read *Bethzatha*; other mss read *Bethsaida*   ᵇ**5:2** Rows of columns supporting a roof   ᶜ**5:3-4** Other mss omit bracketed text   ᵈ**5:13** Lit *slipped away, there being a crowd in that place*   ᵉ**5:16** Other mss add *and trying to kill Him*   ᶠ**5:19** Lit *whatever that One*

Jn 5:1-47 The "festival cycle" in John's Gospel spans from 5:1 to 10:42. This cycle, characterized by escalating conflict between Jesus and the Jewish authorities, begins with yet another "sign," Jesus' healing of a lame man at an unnamed feast in Jerusalem. The fact that the healing took place on a Sabbath provokes a major controversy.

Jn 5:2-3 The pool of Bethesda was a place where the blind, lame and paralyzed were placed, in the hope that they would be healed.

Jn 5:5-7 One man had been sick for 38 years, but he did not have any person, such as a relative, to help him into the water when it was stirred. Some manuscripts include verses 3b-4, which explain that there was belief that an angel would come and stir the water, and then the first person into the water was healed.

Jn 5:14 Jesus found the healed man later in the temple and tells him not to sin any more. The implication is not that all illness is caused by sin, but that in this case the man may have been ill as a result of his sin.

Jn 5:19-23 Jesus defined His relationship with the Father. On the one hand, Jesus says that He is subordinate to the Father, in that He does not do anything on His own (see v. 30). On the other hand, the Son is given responsibilities and duties that go beyond the actions of the Father, such as judgment of humanity (see v. 27).

Jn 5:28-29 Jesus speaks of the resurrection of the dead at the end of time, at which event the good are rewarded and the wicked are punished. The good are those who have believed God.

John 5:1-47 (cont.)

30 "I can do nothing on My own. I judge only as I hear, and My judgment is righteous, because I do not seek My own will, but the will of Him who sent Me.
31 "If I testify about Myself, My testimony is not valid.[a] 32 There is Another who testifies about Me, and I know that the testimony He gives about Me is valid.[b] 33 You have sent ⌊messengers⌋ to John, and he has testified to the truth. 34 I don't receive man's testimony, but I say these things so that you may be saved. 35 John[c] was a burning and shining lamp, and for a time you were willing to enjoy his light.

36 "But I have a greater testimony than John's because of the works that the Father has given Me to accomplish. These very works I am doing testify about Me that the Father has sent Me. 37 The Father who sent Me has Himself testified about Me. You have not heard His voice at any time, and you haven't seen His form. 38 You don't have His word living in you, because you don't believe the One He sent. 39 You pore over[d] the Scriptures because you think you have eternal life in them, yet they testify about Me. 40 And you are not willing to come to Me so that you may have life.

41 "I do not accept glory from men, 42 but I know you—that you have no love for God within you. 43 I have come in My Father's name, yet you don't accept Me. If someone else comes in his own name, you will accept him. 44 How can you believe? While accepting glory from one another, you don't seek the glory that comes from the only God. 45 Do not think that I will accuse you to the Father. Your accuser is Moses, on whom you have set your hope. 46 For if you believed Moses, you would believe Me, because he wrote about Me. 47 But if you don't believe his writings, how will you believe My words?"

a5:31 Or *not true* **b5:32** Or *true* **c5:35** Lit *That man* **d5:39** In Gk this could be a command: *Pore over . . .*

Jn 5:31-47 In this section, Jesus speaks of several witnesses who bear testimony concerning Him: John the Baptist (5:32-36; compare 1:7-8,1519,32-34; 3:26); His own works (5:36; compare 10:25,32,37-38; 15:24); God the Father (5:37-38; 8:18); and the Scriptures (5:39), particularly those written by Moses (5:45-47). Elsewhere in this Gospel, reference is also made to the witness of Jesus Himself (3:11,32; 8:14,18; 18:37), the Spirit (14-16, especially15:26), the disciples (for example, 15:27), and the fourth evangelist (19:35; 21:24).
Jn 5:31 *If I testify about Myself, My testimony is not valid:* Jesus notes that there are validations of His testimony that go beyond simply his own self-witness.
Jn 5:32-47 Witnesses to Jesus include the father (vv. 32,37), John the Baptist (vv. 33,35), the works that Jesus is doing (v. 36), and Moses (v. 46).

Sec. 50   Lord of the Sabbath

Matthew 12:1-8	Mark 2:23-28	Luke 6:1-5
1At that time Jesus passed through the grainfields on the Sabbath. His disciples were hungry and began to pick and eat some heads of grain. 2 But when the •Pharisees saw it, they said to Him, "Look, Your disciples are doing what is not lawful to do on the Sabbath!" 3 He said to them, "Haven't you read what David did when he and those who were with him were hungry— 4 how he entered the house of God, and they ate[a] the •sacred bread, which is not lawful for him or for those with him to eat, but only for the priests?	23 On the Sabbath He was going through the grainfields, and His disciples began to make their way picking some heads of grain. 24 The Pharisees said to Him, "Look, why are they doing what is not lawful on the Sabbath?" 25 He said to them, "Have you never read what David and those who were with him did when he was in need and hungry— 26 how he entered the house of God in the time of Abiathar the high priest and ate the •sacred bread— which is not lawful for anyone to eat except the priests—and also gave some to his companions?"	1On a Sabbath,[a] He passed through the grainfields. His disciples were picking heads of grain, rubbing them in their hands, and eating them. 2 But some of the •Pharisees said, "Why are you doing what is not lawful on the Sabbath?" 3 Jesus answered them, "Haven't you read what David and those who were with him did when he was hungry— 4 how he entered the house of God, and took and ate the •sacred bread, which is not lawful for any but the priests to eat? He even gave some to those who were with him."

a12:4 Other mss read *he ate*

a 6:1 Other mss read *a second-first Sabbath;* perhaps a special Sabbath

Mt 12:2 *what is not lawful to do on the Sabbath:* The accusations of the Pharisees stemmed from oral tradition. Jesus was not bound by oral laws about the Sabbath.
Mt 12:3 *what David did:* When Ahimelech the high priest gave David the consecrated bread (1 Sm 21:6).

Matthew 12:1-8 (cont.)	Mark 2:23-28 (cont.)	Luke 6:1-5 (cont.)
[5] Or haven't you read in the Law[a] that on Sabbath days the priests in the temple violate the Sabbath and are innocent? [6] But I tell you that something greater than the temple is here! [7] If you had known what this means: **I desire mercy and not sacrifice**,[b] you would not have condemned the innocent. [8] For the •Son of Man is Lord of the Sabbath." [a]**12:5** The Torah (the Pentateuch) [b]**12:7** Hs 6:6	[27] Then He told them, "The Sabbath was made for[a] man and not man for[a] the Sabbath. [28] Therefore the Son of Man is Lord even of the Sabbath." [a]**2:27** Or *because of*	[5] Then He told them, "The •Son of Man is Lord of the Sabbath."

Mt 12:5 Jesus' second justification for the disciples' action (v. 1) appeals to Numbers 28:9-10, requiring priests to offer sacrifices on the Sabbath day.

Mt 12:6 *something greater than the temple is here:* The kingdom of God, present in the Person of the King.

Mt 12:8 *Son of Man is Lord of the Sabbath:* One is woefully wrong who thinks he can honor the Sabbath but rejects its Lord.

Mk 2:23-28 OT texts identified Yahweh as the Lord of the Sabbath (Ex 20:10; Dt 5:14). The self-designation is thus an assertion of Jesus' deity.

Mk 2:26 *the sacred bread:* Jesus was referring to the twelve loaves of bread that were set on a table in the holy place of the tabernacle as an offering to the Lord. Every Sabbath twelve fresh loaves were given to the Lord, and the old ones were removed and given to the priests to eat (Lv 24:5-9; see Ex 25:30; Nm 4:7).

Lk 6:5 *Lord of the Sabbath:* The key reason Jesus gives for His activity is that He has authority over the Sabbath, an important claim since the Sabbath was instituted by God.

Sec. 51   The Man with the Paralyzed Hand

Matthew 12:9-14	Mark 3:1-6	Luke 6:6-11
[9] Moving on from there, He entered their •synagogue. [10] There He saw a man who had a paralyzed hand. And in order to accuse Him they asked Him, "Is it lawful to heal on the Sabbath?" [11] But He said to them, "What man among you, if he had a sheep[a] that fell into a pit on the Sabbath, wouldn't take hold of it and lift it out? [12] A man is worth far more than a sheep, so it is lawful to do what is good on the Sabbath." [a]**12:11** Or *had one sheep*	[1]Now He entered the •synagogue again, and a man was there who had a paralyzed hand. [2] In order to accuse Him, they were watching Him closely to see whether He would heal him on the Sabbath. [3] He told the man with the paralyzed hand, "Stand before us."[a] [4] Then He said to them, "Is it lawful on the Sabbath to do what is good or to do what is evil, to save life or to kill?" But they were silent. [a]**3:3** Lit *Rise up in the middle*	[6] On another Sabbath He entered the •synagogue and was teaching. A man was there whose right hand was paralyzed. [7] The •scribes and Pharisees were watching Him closely, to see if He would heal on the Sabbath, so that they could find a charge against Him. [8] But He knew their thoughts and told the man with the paralyzed hand, "Get up and stand here."[a] So he got up and stood there. [9] Then Jesus said to them, "I ask you: is it lawful on the Sabbath to do what is good or to do what is evil, to save life or to destroy it?" [a]**6:8** Lit *stand in the middle*

Matthew 12:9-14 (cont.)	Mark 3:1-6 (cont.)	Luke 6:6-11 (cont.)
13 Then He told the man, "Stretch out your hand." So he stretched it out, and it was restored, as good as the other. 14 But the Pharisees went out and plotted against Him, how they might destroy Him.	5 After looking around at them with anger and sorrow at the hardness of their hearts, He told the man, "Stretch out your hand." So he stretched it out, and his hand was restored. 6 Immediately the •Pharisees went out and started plotting with the •Herodians against Him, how they might destroy Him.	10 After looking around at them all, He told him, "Stretch out your hand." He did so, and his hand was restored.a 11 They, however, were filled with rage and started discussing with one another what they might do to Jesus. a6:10 Other mss add *as sound as the other*

Mk 3:6 *the Herodians:* Influential people who were also political supporters of the Herod family of rulers and consequently of the Roman Empire, under whose authority they ruled.

Sec. 52   The Servant of the Lord

Matthew 12:15-21	Mark 3:7-12
15 When Jesus became aware of this, He withdrew from there. Huge crowdsa followed Him, and He healed them all.	7 Jesus departed with His disciples to the sea, and a great multitude followed from Galilee, Judea, 8 Jerusalem, Idumea, beyond the Jordan, and around Tyre and Sidon. The great multitude came to Him because they heard about everything He was doing. 9 Then He told His disciples to have a small boat ready for Him, so the crowd would not crush Him. 10 Since He had healed many, all who had diseases were pressing toward Him to touch Him. 11 Whenever the •unclean spirits saw Him, those possessed fell down before Him and cried out, "You are the Son of God!" 12 And He would strongly warn them not to make Him known.
16 He warned them not to make Him known, 17 so that what was spoken through the prophet Isaiah might be fulfilled:	

18 **Here is My Servant whom I have chosen,**
   My beloved in whom My soul delights;
   I will put My Spirit on Him,
   and He will proclaim justice to the nations.
19 **He will not argue or shout,**
   and no one will hear His voice in the streets.
20 **He will not break a bruised reed,**
   and He will not put out a smoldering wick,
   until He has led justice to victory.b
21 **The nations will put their hope in His name.c**

a**12:15** Other mss read *Many*   b**12:20** Or *until He has successfully put forth justice*   c**12:18-21** Is 42:1-4

Mt 12:18-21 These verses contain Isaiah 42:1-4 as interpreted by Matthew. It is not a word-for-word reproduction but the result of profound theological reflection. Isaiah 42:1-4 is the first of four prophecies regarding "the Servant of the Lord." (See also Is 49:1-9; 50:4-9; 52:13–53:12.)

Sec. 53   The 12 Apostles

Mark 3:13-19 | Luke 6:12-16

13 Then He went up the mountain and summoned those He wanted, and they came to Him. 14 He also appointed 12—He also named them apostles[a] —to be with Him, to send them out to preach, 15 and to have authority to[b] drive out demons.
16 He appointed the Twelve:[c]

To Simon, He gave the name Peter;
17 and to James the son of Zebedee,
and to his brother John,
He gave the name "Boanerges"
(that is, "Sons of Thunder");
18 Andrew;
Philip and Bartholomew;
Matthew and Thomas;
James the son of Alphaeus,
and Thaddaeus;
Simon the Zealot,[d]
19 and Judas Iscariot,[e]
who also betrayed Him.

12 During those days He went out to the mountain to pray and spent all night in prayer to God. 13 When daylight came, He summoned His disciples, and He chose 12 of them—He also named them apostles:

14 Simon, whom He also named Peter,
and Andrew his brother;
James and John;
Philip and Bartholomew;
15 Matthew and Thomas;
James the son of Alphaeus,
and Simon called the Zealot;
16 Judas the son of James,
and Judas Iscariot, who became a traitor.

[a]**3:14** Other mss omit *He also named them apostles* [b]**3:15** Other mss add *heal diseases, and to* [c]**3:16** Other mss omit *He appointed the Twelve* [d]**3:18** Lit *the Cananaean* [e]**3:19** *Iscariot* probably = "a man of Kerioth," a town in Judea.

Mk 3:13-19 Jesus probably chose twelve disciples to correspond with the number of the tribes of Israel. This implied Jesus' intention to create a new, spiritual Israel.
Mk 3:17 *Boanerges:* Mark translated the name as meaning "Sons of Thunder," which seems to characterize the brothers as hot-tempered, prone to outbursts of anger (see Mk 9:38; Lk 9:54).

Sec. 54   The Sermon on the Mount

Matthew 5:1-2 | Luke 6:17-19

1When He saw the crowds, He went up on the mountain, and after He sat down, His disciples came to Him. 2 Then[a] He began to teach them, saying:

[a]**5:2** Lit *Then opening His mouth*

17 After coming down with them, He stood on a level place with a large crowd of His disciples and a great multitude of people from all Judea and Jerusalem and from the seacoast of Tyre and Sidon. 18 They came to hear Him and to be healed of their diseases; and those tormented by •unclean spirits were made well. 19 The whole crowd was trying to touch Him, because power was coming out from Him and healing them all.

Mt 5–7 The Sermon on the Mount. More has been written on it than on any other biblical passage. The sermon contains both the Beatitudes (the "blessed") and the Lord's Prayer. Interpretation of the Sermon has been a matter of intense debate and discussion.

1. The Beatitudes and Woes

<table>
<tr><td align="center">Matthew 5:3-12</td><td align="center">Luke 6:20-26</td></tr>
</table>

Matthew 5:3-12

3 "The poor in spirit are blessed,
for the kingdom of heaven is theirs.
4 Those who mourn are blessed,
for they will be comforted.
5 The gentle are blessed,
for they will inherit the earth.
6 Those who hunger
and thirst for righteousness are blessed,
for they will be filled.
7 The merciful are blessed,
for they will be shown mercy.
8 The pure in heart are blessed,
for they will see God.
9 The peacemakers are blessed,
for they will be called sons of God.
10 Those who are persecuted
for righteousness are blessed,
for the kingdom of heaven is theirs.

11 "You are blessed when they insult and persecute you and falsely say every kind of evil against you because of Me. 12 Be glad and rejoice, because your reward is great in heaven. For that is how they persecuted the prophets who were before you.

Luke 6:20-26

20 Then looking up at[a] His disciples, He said:

"Blessed are you who are poor,
because the kingdom of God is yours.
21 Blessed are you who are hungry now,
because you will be filled.
Blessed are you who weep now,
because you will laugh.
22 Blessed are you when people hate you,
when they exclude you, insult you,
and slander your name as evil,
because of the Son of Man.

23 "Rejoice in that day and leap for joy! Take note— your reward is great in heaven, because this is the way their ancestors used to treat the prophets.

24 "But woe to you who are rich,
because you have received your comfort.
25 Woe to you who are full now,
because you will be hungry.
Woe to you[b] who are laughing now,
because you will mourn and weep.
26 Woe to you[b]
when all people speak well of you,
because this is the way their ancestors
used to treat the false prophets.

[a]6:20 Lit *Then lifting up His eyes to*   [b]6:25,26 Other mss omit *to you*

Mt 5:3 *poor in spirit:* A heart condition of realizing spiritual bankruptcy and need of grace. ***blessed:*** The Greek is *makarios*. It speaks of a happiness and contentment of heart, a peace and joy in knowing someone is doing God's will.
Mt 5:4 *mourn:* Not just sadness but godly sorrow for personal and social sins.
Mt 5:5 *gentle:* Humble, meek—power under control.
Mt 5:7 *merciful:* Includes the characteristics of being generous, forgiving, and compassionate.
Mt 5:11 An expansion of verse 10 that amplifies and personalizes the truth that God will reward those who suffer for His sake.
Lk 6:20 Luke's version of the Beatitudes is more concise than Matthew's, speaking to the poor, hungry, those who weep, and those who are hated because of the Son of Man. The Beatitudes encourage those who respond to Jesus and suffer for it.
Lk 6:23 *used to treat the prophets:* Rejecting God's way has been a pattern. God's prophets suffered for bringing God's message.
Lk 6:24 *woe:* A warning of judgment for those who do not respond properly to Jesus. They include the rich, the satisfied, and the popular who will not go God's way. These verses stand in contrast to the Beatitudes and are only in Luke.

2. Jesus' Standards of Righteousness

Matthew 5:13-20

¹³ "You are the salt of the earth. But if the salt should lose its taste, how can it be made salty? It's no longer good for anything but to be thrown out and trampled on by men.

¹⁴ "You are the light of the world. A city situated on a hill cannot be hidden. ¹⁵ No one lights a lamp and puts it under a basket,ᵃ but rather on a lampstand, and it gives light for all who are in the house. ¹⁶ In the same way, let your light shineᵇ before men, so that they may see your good works and give glory to your Father in heaven.

¹⁷ "Don't assume that I came to destroy the Law or the Prophets. I did not come to destroy but to fulfill. ¹⁸ For •I assure you: Until heaven and earth pass away, not the smallest letterᶜ or one stroke of a letter will pass from the law until all things are accomplished. ¹⁹ Therefore, whoever breaks one of the least of these commands and teaches people to do so will be called least in the kingdom of heaven. But whoever practices and teaches ⌊these commands⌋ will be called great in the kingdom of heaven. ²⁰ For I tell you, unless your righteousness surpasses that of the •scribes and •Pharisees, you will never enter the kingdom of heaven.

ᵃ**5:15** A large basket used to measure grain   ᵇ**5:16** Or *way, your light must shine*   ᶜ**5:18** Or *not one iota; iota* is the *smallest letter* of the Gk alphabet.

Mt 5:13-14 *salt of the earth . . . light of the world:* Two metaphors describing Jesus' true followers. Salt speaks of influence in a decaying world; light speaks of the outward testimony of good works that point to God.
Mt 5:17 *destroy . . . fulfill:* Jesus executed the law perfectly in His life, endured its curse for lawbreakers by dying on the cross, and fulfilled the prophecies concerning Messiah. *I assure you:* Used by Jesus to testify to the certainty and importance of His words; in the Synoptics it is literally *Amen, I say to you.* In John it is *Amen, amen, I say to you.*

3. Jesus' Ethical Teachings

Matthew 5:21-48

²¹ "You have heard that it was said to our ancestors,ᵃ **Do not murder,**ᵇ and whoever murders will be subject to judgment. ²² But I tell you, everyone who is angry with his brotherᶜ will be subject to judgment. And whoever says to his brother, 'Fool!'ᵈ will be subject to the •Sanhedrin. But whoever says, 'You moron!' will be subject to •hellfire.ᵉ ²³ So if you are offering your gift on the altar, and there you remember that your brother has something against you, ²⁴ leave your gift there in front of the altar. First go and be reconciled with your brother, and then come and offer your gift. ²⁵ Reach a settlement quickly with your adversary while you're on the way with him, or your adversary will hand you over to the judge, the judge toᶠ the officer, and you will be thrown into prison. ²⁶ I assure you: You will never get out of there until you have paid the last penny!ᵍ

²⁷ "You have heard that it was said, **Do not commit adultery.**ʰ ²⁸ But I tell you, everyone who looks at a woman to lust for her has already committed adultery with her in his heart. ²⁹ If your right eye •causes you to sin, gouge it out and throw it away. For it is better that you lose one of the parts of your body than for your whole body to be thrown into hell. ³⁰ And if your right hand causes you to sin, cut it off and throw it away. For it is better that you lose one of the parts of your body than for your whole body to go into hell!

³¹ "It was also said, **Whoever divorces his wife must give her a written notice of divorce.**ⁱ ³² But I tell you, everyone who divorces his wife, except in a case of sexual immorality,ʲ causes her to commit adultery. And whoever marries a divorced woman commits adultery.

ᵃ**5:21** Lit *to the ancients*   ᵇ**5:21** Ex 20:13; Dt 5:17   ᶜ**5:22** Other mss add *without a cause*   ᵈ**5:22** Lit *Raca,* an Aram term of abuse similar to "airhead"   ᵉ**5:22** Lit *the gehenna of fire*   ᶠ**5:25** Other mss read *judge will hand you over to*   ᵍ**5:26** Lit *quadrans,* the smallest and least valuable Roman coin, worth ¹/₆₄ of a daily wage   ʰ**5:27** Ex 20:14; Dt 5:18   ⁱ**5:31** Dt 24:1   ʲ**5:32** Gk *porneia* = fornication, or possibly a violation of Jewish marriage laws

Mt 5:21 *You have heard that it was said:* Jesus used this phrase (repeated in vv. 27,31,33,38,43) to compare the outward practice of the law with heart attitudes of true followers. *Do not murder:* Involves more than just the act of killing; rather, anger in the heart must be checked.
Mt 5:22 *hellfire:* Greek *gehenna;* Aramaic for Valley of Hinnom south of Jerusalem. It was formerly a place of human sacrifice and in NT times a place where garbage burned perpetually.
Mt 5:29-30 *right eye . . . right hand:* In antiquity both would be considered more valuable. Self-mutilation was not Christ's intent, since it is possible to be blind or crippled and still lust. Rather, Jesus' language is hyperbolic. He commanded drastic measures to avoid temptations to sexual sin.
Mt 5:27 *Do not commit adultery:* Jesus addressed the lust in the heart that leads to adultery.

Matthew 5:21-48 (cont.)

[33] "Again, you have heard that it was said to our ancestors,[a] **You must not break your oath, but you must keep your oaths to the Lord.**[b] [34] But I tell you, don't take an oath at all: either by heaven, because it is God's throne; [35] or by the earth, because it is His footstool; or by Jerusalem, because it is the city of the great King. [36] Neither should you swear by your head, because you cannot make a single hair white or black. [37] But let your word 'yes' be 'yes,' and your 'no' be 'no.'[c] Anything more than this is from the evil one.

[38] "You have heard that it was said, **An eye for an eye** and **a tooth for a tooth.**[d] [39] But I tell you, don't resist[e] an evildoer. On the contrary, if anyone slaps you on your right cheek, turn the other to him also. [40] As for the one who wants to sue you and take away your shirt,[f] let him have your coat[g] as well. [41] And if anyone forces[h] you to go one mile, go with him two. [42] Give to the one who asks you, and don't turn away from the one who wants to borrow from you.

[43] "You have heard that it was said, **Love your neighbor**[i] and hate your enemy. [44] But I tell you, love your enemies[j] and pray for those who[k] persecute you, [45] so that you may be[l] sons of your Father in heaven. For He causes His sun to rise on the evil and the good, and sends rain on the righteous and the unrighteous. [46] For if you love those who love you, what reward will you have? Don't even the tax collectors do the same? [47] And if you greet only your brothers, what are you doing out of the ordinary?[m] Don't even the Gentiles[n] do the same?

[48] Be perfect, therefore, as your heavenly Father is perfect.

Luke 6:27-30,32-36

[27] "But I say to you who listen: Love your enemies, do what is good to those who hate you, [28] bless those who curse you, pray for those who mistreat you. [29] If anyone hits you on the cheek, offer the other also. And if anyone takes away your coat, don't hold back your shirt either. [30] Give to everyone who asks from you, and from one who takes away your things, don't ask for them back.

[32] If you love those who love you, what credit is that to you? Even sinners love those who love them. [33] If you do what is good to those who are good to you, what credit is that to you? Even sinners do that. [34] And if you lend to those from whom you expect to receive, what credit is that to you? Even sinners lend to sinners to be repaid in full. [35] But love your enemies, do what is good, and lend, expecting nothing in return. Then your reward will be great, and you will be sons of the Most High. For He is gracious to the ungrateful and evil. [36] Be merciful, just as your Father also is merciful.

[a]**5:33** Lit *to the ancients* [b]**5:33** Lv 19:12; Nm 30:2; Dt 23:21 [c]**5:37** Say what you mean and mean what you say [d]**5:38** Ex 21:24; Lv 24:20; Dt 19:21 [e]**5:39** Or *don't set yourself against*, or *don't retaliate against* [f]**5:40** Lit *tunic* = inner garment [g]**5:40** Lit *robe*, or *garment* = outer garment [h]**5:41** Roman soldiers could require people to carry loads for them. [i]**5:43** Lv 19:18 [j]**5:44** Other mss add *bless those who curse you, do good to those who hate you*, [k]**5:44** Other mss add *mistreat you and* [l]**5:45** Or *may become*, or *may show yourselves to be* [m]**5:47** Lit *doing more*, or *doing that is superior* [n]**5:47** Other mss read *tax collectors*

Mt 5:39 *slaps you on your right cheek:* Implies a backhanded strike (an insult) from a right-handed person. To turn the other meant not responding to the insult.

Mt 5:41 *forces you to go one mile:* Roman soldiers could require a Jew to carry his belongings for one mile, but no more. Jesus encouraged going the second mile.

Mt 5:46 *tax collectors:* Despised by the Jews, because they worked for Rome in collecting tribute and were often corrupt in that they overcharged and "pocketed" the excess.

Lk 6:27 *Love your enemies:* One of the most famous parts of Jesus' sermon. Luke's version of Matthew's Sermon on the Mount is a condensed version highlighting this call to love one's enemies and pray for them.

Lk 6:32 *Even sinners:* The disciples' standard of love is to be greater than that of sinners who love only those who reciprocate that love.

Lk 6:35 *sons of the Most High:* This kind of love mimics the kind of love God has. To love this way is to show oneself as a child of God.

Lk 6:36 *Be merciful, just as your Father:* The example is always God. He shows mercy, so should His children.

4. Authentic Righteousness

Matthew 6:1-18

¹"Be careful not to practice your righteousnessª in front of people, to be seen by them. Otherwise, you will have no reward from your Father in heaven. ² So whenever you give to the poor, don't sound a trumpet before you, as the hypocrites do in the •synagogues and on the streets, to be applauded by people. •I assure you: They've got their reward! ³ But when you give to the poor, don't let your left hand know what your right hand is doing, ⁴ so that your giving may be in secret. And your Father who sees in secret will reward you.ᵇ

⁵ "Whenever you pray, you must not be like the hypocrites, because they love to pray standing in the synagogues and on the street corners to be seen by people. I assure you: They've got their reward! ⁶ But when you pray, go into your private room, shut your door, and pray to your Father who is in secret. And your Father who sees in secret will reward you.ᶜ ⁷ When you pray, don't babble like the idolaters,ᵈ since they imagine they'll be heard for their many words. ⁸ Don't be like them, because your Father knows the things you need before you ask Him.

⁹ "Therefore, you should pray like this:

Our Father in heaven,
Your name be honored as holy.
¹⁰ Your kingdom come.
Your will be done
on earth as it is in heaven.
¹¹ Give us today our daily bread.ᵉ
¹² And forgive us our debts,
as we also have forgiven our debtors.
¹³ And do not bring us intoᶠ temptation,
but deliver us from the evil one.ᵍ
[For Yours is the kingdom and the power
and the glory forever. •Amen.]ʰ

¹⁴ "For if you forgive people their wrongdoing,ⁱ your heavenly Father will forgive you as well. ¹⁵ But if you don't forgive people,ʲ your Father will not forgive your wrongdoing.ⁱ

¹⁶ "Whenever you fast, don't be sad-faced like the hypocrites. For they make their faces unattractiveᵏ so their fasting is obvious to people. I assure you: They've got their reward! ¹⁷ But when you fast, put oil on your head, and wash your face, ¹⁸ so that you don't show your fasting to people but to your Father who is in secret. And your Father who sees in secret will reward you.ᶜ

ª**6:1** Other mss read *charitable giving*   ᵇ**6:4** Other mss read *will Himself reward you openly*   ᶜ**6:6,18** Other mss add *openly*   ᵈ**6:7** Or *Gentiles,* or *nations,* or *heathen,* or *pagans*   ᵉ**6:11** Or *our necessary bread,* or *our bread for tomorrow*   ᶠ**6:13** Or *do not cause us to come into*   ᵍ**6:13** Or *from evil*   ʰ**6:13** Other mss omit bracketed text   ⁱ**6:14,15** Or *trespasses*   ʲ**6:15** Other mss add *their wrongdoing*   ᵏ**6:16** Or *unrecognizable,* or *disfigured*

Mt 6:6 *go into your private room, shut your door:* Jesus was not forbidding public, corporate prayer, but rather the practice of praying merely to appear righteous before others.

Mt 6:7 *don't babble like the idolaters:* In pagan religions of the day, worshipers prayed on and on because they believed that the longer and the louder they prayed, the greater was their chance of receiving what they desired.

Mt 6:9 *pray like this:* This prayer should not be mindlessly repeated lest we violate Jesus' very admonition. This is really a *model prayer,* a pattern for our prayers.

Mt 6:9-10 *Your name . . . Your Kingdom . . . Your will:* The aim and purpose for our prayers must always be that God will be glorified and His will done.

Mt 6:13 *do not bring us into temptation:* Literally, "do not cause us to be tempted." It cannot be a request that God not tempt us, for God cannot be tempted and He tempts no one (Jms 1:13). It is a petition for protection from the snares of Satan and all evil forces.

Mt 6:15 *your Father will not forgive your wrongdoing:* One who has experienced God's forgiveness is willing to forgive others.

Mt 6:16 Fasting had become a ritual to gain merit with God and attention before men. Many Pharisees fasted twice a week (Lk 18:12).

5. Single-hearted Devotion to God

Matthew 6:19-34

19 "Don't collect for yourselves treasures[a] on earth, where moth and rust destroy and where thieves break in and steal. 20 But collect for yourselves treasures in heaven, where neither moth nor rust destroys, and where thieves don't break in and steal. 21 For where your treasure is, there your heart will be also.

22 "The eye is the lamp of the body. If your eye is good, your whole body will be full of light. 23 But if your eye is bad, your whole body will be full of darkness. So if the light within you is darkness—how deep is that darkness!

24 "No one can be a •slave of two masters, since either he will hate one and love the other, or be devoted to one and despise the other. You cannot be slaves of God and of money.

25 "This is why I tell you: Don't worry about your life, what you will eat or what you will drink; or about your body, what you will wear. Isn't life more than food and the body more than clothing? 26 Look at the birds of the sky: they don't sow or reap or gather into barns, yet your heavenly Father feeds them. Aren't you worth more than they? 27 Can any of you add a single •cubit to his height[b] by worrying? 28 And why do you worry about clothes? Learn how the wildflowers of the field grow: they don't labor or spin thread. 29 Yet I tell you that not even Solomon in all his splendor was adorned like one of these! 30 If that's how God clothes the grass of the field, which is here today and thrown into the furnace tomorrow, won't He do much more for you—you of little faith? 31 So don't worry, saying, 'What will we eat?' or 'What will we drink?' or 'What will we wear?' 32 For the idolaters[c] eagerly seek all these things, and your heavenly Father knows that you need them. 33 But seek first the kingdom of God[d] and His righteousness, and all these things will be provided for you. 34 Therefore don't worry about tomorrow, because tomorrow will worry about itself. Each day has enough trouble of its own.

[a]**6:19** Or *valuables* [b]**6:27** Or *add one moment to his life-span* [c]**6:32** Or *Gentiles,* or *nations,* or *heathen,* or *pagans* [d]**6:33** Other mss omit *of God*

Mt 6:20 *treasures in heaven:* To lay up treasures in heaven means to work for God, investing in His kingdom, and serving others.
Mt 6:24 *money:* Not inherently evil, but often misused so that it is a means of evil (see 1 Tm 6:6-10,17-19).
Mt 6:27 *cubit:* About 18 inches. All the worry in the world won't add an inch to our height or a minute to our life.
Mt 6:34 *tomorrow will worry about itself:* Let tomorrow's concerns be reserved for tomorrow. Our concern each day should be whether or not we are obeying the command of verse 33.

6. Judging Others

Matthew 7:1-6	Luke 6:37-42
1"Do not judge, so that you won't be judged. 2 For with the judgment you use,[a] you will be judged, and with the measure you use,[b] it will be measured to you.	37 "Do not judge, and you will not be judged. Do not condemn, and you will not be condemned. Forgive, and you will be forgiven. 38 Give, and it will be given to you; a good measure—pressed down, shaken together, and running over—will be poured into your lap. For with the measure you use,[a] it will be measured back to you."
[a]**7:2** Lit *you judge* [b]**7:2** Lit *you measure*	39 He also told them a parable: "Can the blind guide the blind? Won't they both fall into a pit? 40 A disciple is not above his teacher, but everyone who is fully trained will be like his teacher.
	[a]**6:38** Lit *you measure*

Mt 7:1 *Do not judge:* Jesus directed against being judgmental and condemning in our attitudes, like the self-righteousness of the Pharisees.

Matthew 7:1-6 (cont.)	Luke 6:37-42 (cont.)

³ Why do you look at the speck in your brother's eye but don't notice the log in your own eye? ⁴ Or how can you say to your brother, 'Let me take the speck out of your eye,' and look, there's a log in your eye? ⁵ Hypocrite! First take the log out of your eye, and then you will see clearly to take the speck out of your brother's eye. ⁶ Don't give what is holy to dogs or toss your pearls before pigs, or they will trample them with their feet, turn, and tear you to pieces.

⁴¹ "Why do you look at the speck in your brother's eye, but don't notice the log in your own eye? ⁴² Or how can you say to your brother, 'Brother, let me take out the speck that is in your eye,' when you yourself don't see the log in your own eye? Hypocrite! First take the log out of your eye, and then you will see clearly to take out the speck in your brother's eye.

Mt 7:6 Do not present holy things to those who cannot appreciate them. The people to whom dogs and pigs refer do not respect the truth of God.

Lk 6:42 *First take the log out of your eye:* We see clearly the sins of others and fail to perceive our own sins. Being aware of our own sins will put others' sins in a different light.

7. Prayer and the Golden Rule

Matthew 7:7-12

⁷ "Keep asking,ᵃ and it will be given to you. Keep searching,ᵇ and you will find. Keep knocking,ᶜ and the doorᵈ will be opened to you. ⁸ For everyone who asks receives, and the one who searches finds, and to the one who knocks, the doorᵉ will be opened. ⁹ What man among you, if his son asks him for bread, will give him a stone? ¹⁰ Or if he asks for a fish, will give him a snake? ¹¹ If you then, who are evil, know how to give good gifts to your children, how much more will your Father in heaven give good things to those who ask Him! ¹² Therefore, whatever you want others to do for you, do also the same for them—this is the Law and the Prophets.ᶠ

Luke 6:31

³¹ Just as you want others to do for you, do the same for them.

ᵃ**7:7** Or *Ask* ᵇ**7:7** Or *Search* ᶜ**7:7** Or *Knock* ᵈ**7:7** Lit *and it* ᵉ**7:8** Lit *knocks, it* ᶠ**7:12** When capitalized, *the Law and the Prophets* = the OT

Mt 7:7 *Keep asking . . . searching . . . knocking:* The verb tenses are present, emphasizing that we should be persistent in our praying (see Lk 11:5-8; 18:1-5).

8. The Conclusion of the Sermon

Matthew 7:13–8:1

¹³ "Enter through the narrow gate. For the gate is wide and the road is broad that leads to destruction, and there are many who go through it. ¹⁴ How narrow is the gate and difficult the road that leads to life, and few find it.

¹⁵ "Beware of false prophets who come to you in sheep's clothing but inwardly are ravaging wolves. ¹⁶ You'll recognize them by their fruit. Are grapes gathered from thornbushes or figs from thistles? ¹⁷ In the same way, every good tree produces good fruit, but a bad tree produces bad fruit.

Mt 7:13 *narrow gate:* The narrowness implies the self-denial and difficulty of the Christian life.

Mt 7:15 *false prophets:* False teachers may appear in religious garb, but they will be known by their doctrine or practice ("their fruit," v. 16).

Matthew 7:13–8:1 (cont.)

Luke 6:43-49

18 A good tree can't produce bad fruit; neither can a bad tree produce good fruit. 19 Every tree that doesn't produce good fruit is cut down and thrown into the fire. 20 So you'll recognize them by their fruit.

21 "Not everyone who says to Me, 'Lord, Lord!' will enter the kingdom of heaven, but ⌊only⌋ the one who does the will of My Father in heaven. 22 On that day many will say to Me, 'Lord, Lord, didn't we prophesy in Your name, drive out demons in Your name, and do many miracles in Your name?' 23 Then I will announce to them, 'I never knew you! **Depart from Me, you lawbreakers!**'ᵃ ᵇ

24 "Therefore, everyone who hears these words of Mine and acts on them will be like a sensible man who built his house on the rock. 25 The rain fell, the rivers rose, and the winds blew and pounded that house. Yet it didn't collapse, because its foundation was on the rock. 26 But everyone who hears these words of Mine and doesn't act on them will be like a foolish man who built his house on the sand. 27 The rain fell, the rivers rose, the winds blew and pounded that house, and it collapsed. And its collapse was great!"

28 When Jesus had finished this sermon,ᶜ the crowds were astonished at His teaching, 29 because He was teaching them like one who had authority, and not like their •scribes.

1When He came down from the mountain, large crowds followed Him.

ᵃ**7:23** Lit *you who work lawlessness*   ᵇ**7:23** Ps 6:8   ᶜ**7:28** Lit *had ended these words*

43 "A good tree doesn't produce bad fruit; on the other hand, a bad tree doesn't produce good fruit. 44 For each tree is known by its own fruit. Figs aren't gathered from thornbushes, or grapes picked from a bramble bush. 45 A good man produces good out of the good storeroom of his heart. An evil man produces evil out of the evil storeroom, for his mouth speaks from the overflow of the heart.

46 "Why do you call Me 'Lord, Lord,' and don't do the things I say? 47 I will show you what someone is like who comes to Me, hears My words, and acts on them: 48 He is like a man building a house, who dug deepᵃ and laid the foundation on the rock. When the flood came, the river crashed against that house and couldn't shake it, because it was well built. 49 But the one who hears and does not act is like a man who built a house on the ground without a foundation. The river crashed against it, and immediately it collapsed. And the destruction of that house was great!"

ᵃ**6:48** Lit *dug and went deep*

Mt 7:21 *Not everyone . . . will enter the kingdom:* Outward religious effort and talk (note v. 22) do not insure that one is a kingdom citizen. The question is whether one has been cleansed inwardly (v. 17).

Mt 7:24-27 This parable pictures a sandy riverbed that could be dry in summer. A house built on such a foundation would be swept away when the heavy rains brought down the mountain flood, while the house built on rock above the torrent would be safe.

Mt 7:29 *not like their scribes:* The scribes quoted the rabbis before them and rarely expressed an idea without support by some predecessor. Jesus spoke as His own authority.

Lk 6:48-49 *like a man . . . like a man:* This passage is also built on a contrast. Jesus calls on His listeners to respond and obey His words. The difference is between a wise builder and a foolish one. The wise builder's house survives the trying weather, while the foolish man's house cannot withstand bad weather. Jesus leaves the choice to the listener as to the kind of builder he will be.

Sec. 55   A Centurion's Faith

Matthew 8:5-13

Luke 7:1-10

5 When He entered Capernaum, a •centurion came to Him, pleading with Him, 6 "Lord, my servant is lying at home paralyzed, in terrible agony!"

1When He had concluded all His sayings in the hearing of the people, He entered Capernaum. 2 A •centurion's •slave, who was highly valued by him,

Lk 7:1-10 Note the difference between Matthew's version and Luke. Luke has emissaries sent on the centurion's behalf, while Matthew appears to have the centurion speak with Jesus directly. It may well be that Matthew, as he often does, condenses and simplifies the event. In the ancient world, if someone sent a representative, it was as good as if they were present and speaking, much like a press secretary can speak for the President. This likely explains the difference.

Matthew 8:5-13 (cont.)   Luke 7:1-10 (cont.)

was sick and about to die. ³ When the centurion heard about Jesus, he sent some Jewish elders to Him, requesting Him to come and save the life of his slave. ⁴ When they reached Jesus, they pleaded with Him earnestly, saying, "He is worthy for You to grant this, ⁵ because he loves our nation and has built us a •synagogue." ⁶ Jesus went with them, and when He was not far fromª the house, the centurion sent friends to tell Him, "Lord, don't trouble Yourself, since I am not worthy to have You come under my roof. ⁷ That is why I didn't even consider myself worthy to come to You. But say the word, and my servant will be cured.ᵇ

⁷ "I will come and heal him," He told him.

⁸ "Lord," the centurion replied, "I am not worthy to have You come under my roof. But only say the word, and my servant will be cured.

⁹ For I too am a man under authority, having soldiers under my command.ª I say to this one, 'Go!' and he goes; and to another, 'Come!' and he comes; and to my •slave, 'Do this!' and he does it."

⁸ For I too am a man placed under authority, having soldiers under my command.ᶜ I say to this one, 'Go!' and he goes; and to another, 'Come!' and he comes; and to my slave, 'Do this!' and he does it."

¹⁰ Hearing this, Jesus was amazed and said to those following Him, "•I assure you: I have not found anyone in Israel with so great a faith! ¹¹ I tell you that many will come from east and west, and recline at the table with Abraham, Isaac, and Jacob in the kingdom of heaven. ¹² But the sons of the kingdom will be thrown into the outer darkness. In that place there will be weeping and gnashing of teeth." ¹³ Then Jesus told the centurion, "Go. As you have believed, let it be done for you." And his servant was cured that very moment.ᵇ

⁹ Jesus heard this and was amazed at him, and turning to the crowd following Him, He said, "I tell you, I have not found so great a faith even in Israel!" ¹⁰ When those who had been sent returned to the house, they found the slave in good health.

ª7:6 Lit *and He already was not far from*   ᵇ7:7 Other mss read *and let my servant be cured*   ᶜ7:8 Lit *under me*

ª8:9 Lit *under me*   ᵇ8:13 Or *that hour*; lit *very hour*

Mt 8:8 *I am not worthy:* The man twice called Jesus Lord, affirming Christ's lordship and expressing belief that Jesus was indeed God and consequently had the power to heal his servant.

Mt 8:12 *sons of the kingdom:* Those within Judaism. The centurion's faith showed that many Gentiles will be included in the kingdom, while many Jews will not be.

Lk 7:2 *centurion:* This soldier had authority over one hundred others.

Lk 7:9 *Jesus . . . was amazed:* Jesus marveled at a faith that understood the power of Jesus' word and His authority to heal even from a distance. *so great a faith even in Israel:* Jesus openly commended the action of another. Several points about faith are made: the soldier is humble, understands and is responsive to Jesus' authority, and shows that great faith can exist outside of Israel. Luke was laying groundwork for his emphasis on salvation being offered to all in the book of Acts.

Sec. 56   Jesus Raises a Widow's Son to Life

Luke 7:11-17

¹¹ Soon afterward He was on His way to a town called Nain. His disciples and a large crowd were traveling with Him. ¹² Just as He neared the gate of the town, a dead man was being carried out. He was his mother's only son, and she was a widow. A large crowd from the city was also with her. ¹³ When the Lord saw her, He had compassion on her and said, "Don't cry." ¹⁴ Then He came up and touched the open coffin,ª and the pallbearers stopped. And He said, "Young man, I tell you, get up!"

ª7:14 Or *the bier*

Luke 7:11-17 (cont.)

15 The dead man sat up and began to speak, and Jesus gave him to his mother. 16 Then feara came over everyone, and they glorified God, saying, "A great prophet has risen among us," and "God has visitedb His people." 17 This report about Him went throughout Judea and all the vicinity.

a**7:16** Or *awe*   b**7:16** Or *come to help*

Lk 7:15 *The dead man sat up:* This miracle is only in Luke.

Lk 7:16 *A great prophet has risen:* Nain is approximately two miles north of Shunem where Elisha raised the son of a widow from death. The people who witnessed Jesus' miracle were reminded of the prophets Elijah and Elisha.

Sec. 57   In Praise of John the Baptist

Matthew 11:2-19	Luke 7:18-35

2 When John heard in prison what the •Messiah was doing, he sent ⌊a message⌋ by his disciples 3 and asked Him, "Are You the One who is to come, or should we expect someone else?"

4 Jesus replied to them, "Go and report to John what you hear and see: 5 the blind see, the lame walk, those with skin diseases are healed,a the deaf hear, the dead are raised, and the poor are told the good news. 6 And if anyone is not offended because of Me, he is blessed."

7 As these men went away, Jesus began to speak to the crowds about John: "What did you go out into the wilderness to see? A reed swaying in the wind? 8 What then did you go out to see? A man dressed in soft clothes? Look, those who wear soft clothes are in kings' palaces. 9 But what did you go out to see? A prophet? Yes, I tell you, and far more than a prophet. 10 This is the one it is written about:

a**11:5** Lit *cleansed*

18 Then John's disciples told him about all these things. So John summoned two of his disciples 19 and sent them to the Lord, asking, "Are You the One who is to come, or should we look for someone else?" 20 When the men reached Him, they said, "John the Baptist sent us to ask You, 'Are You the One who is to come, or should we look for someone else?'" 21 At that time Jesus healed many people of diseases, plagues, and evil spirits, and He granted sight to many blind people. 22 He replied to them, "Go and report to John the things you have seen and heard: The blind receive their sight, the lame walk, those with skin diseases are healed,a the deaf hear, the dead are raised, and the poor are told the good news. 23 And anyone who is not offended because of Me is blessed." 24 After John's messengers left, He began to speak to the crowds about John: "What did you go out into the wilderness to see? A reed swaying in the wind? 25 What then did you go out to see? A man dressed in soft robes? Look, those who are splendidly dressedb and live in luxury are in royal palaces. 26 What then did you go out to see? A prophet? Yes, I tell you, and far more than a prophet. 27 This is the one it is written about:

a**7:22** Lit *cleansed*   b**7:25** Or *who have glorious robes*

Mt 11:2 *in prison:* Herod Antipas had imprisoned John in the fortress of Machaerus east of the Dead Sea.

Mt 11:3 *Are You the One who is to come:* John had been in prison long enough to become depressed and doubtful, and, besides, Jesus had done nothing to get him out of Machaerus. John longed for reassurance.

Mt 11:7 *Jesus began to speak to the crowds about John:* Jesus was concerned that John be remembered for his faithful life. He occupied the role of a prophet and fulfilled Malachi 3:1; 4:5.

Lk 7:19 *One who is to come:* Refers to the Messiah who comes to bring salvation. Jesus' style of not wielding coercive power had raised the question anew among John and his followers.

Lk 7:22 *Go and report:* Jesus did not answer with a direct yes or a no. He replied using language from passages in Isaiah describing what will happen when God comes to save His people in the era of salvation (Is 26:19; 29:18-19; 35:5-6; 61:1). So the answer is yes.

Lk 7:23 *anyone who is not offended because of Me is blessed:* Jesus underscored that the issue in salvation is response to Him and His teaching. Put positively, blessing comes to the one who embraces Jesus.

Lk 7:26 *far more than a prophet:* John the Baptist had a high place in God's program because he was a prophet who pointed the way to the arrival of salvation. He is "more than a prophet," because of the special time he announced. The citation from Malachi 3:1 underlines the point. John prepared the way for the Lord's salvation.

Matthew 11:2-19 (cont.)   Luke 7:18-35 (cont.)

Look, I am sending My messenger
 ahead of You;[a]
he will prepare Your way before You.[b]

Look, I am sending My messenger
 ahead of You;[a]
he will prepare Your way before You.[b]

[11] "•I assure you: Among those born of women no one greater than John the Baptist has appeared,[c] but the least in the kingdom of heaven is greater than he. [12] From the days of John the Baptist until now, the kingdom of heaven has been suffering violence,[d] and the violent have been seizing it by force. [13] For all the prophets and the Law prophesied until John; [14] if you're willing to accept it, he is the Elijah who is to come. [15] Anyone who has ears[e] should listen!

[28] I tell you, among those born of women no one is greater than John,[c] but the least in the kingdom of God is greater than he."

[29] (And when all the people, including the tax collectors, heard this, they acknowledged God's way of righteousness,[d] because they had been baptized with John's baptism. [30] But since the •Pharisees and experts in the law had not been baptized by him, they rejected the plan of God for themselves.)

[16] "To what should I compare this generation? It's like children sitting in the marketplaces who call out to each other:

[31] "To what then should I compare the people of this generation, and what are they like? [32] They are like children sitting in the marketplace and calling to each other:

[17] We played the flute for you,
   but you didn't dance;
   we sang a lament,
   but you didn't mourn!'[f]

  We played the flute for you,
   but you didn't dance;
   we sang a lament,
   but you didn't weep!

[18] For John did not come eating or drinking, and they say, 'He has a demon!' [19] The •Son of Man came eating and drinking, and they say, 'Look, a glutton and a drunkard, a friend of tax collectors and sinners!' Yet wisdom is vindicated[g] by her deeds."[h]

[33] For John the Baptist did not come eating bread or drinking wine, and you say, 'He has a demon!' [34] The •Son of Man has come eating and drinking, and you say, 'Look, a glutton and a drunkard, a friend of tax collectors and sinners!' [35] Yet wisdom is vindicated[e] by all her children."

[a]**11:10** Lit *messenger before Your face*   [b]**11:10** Mal 3:1   [c]**11:11** Lit *arisen*   [d]**11:12** Or *has been forcefully advancing*   [e]**11:15** Other mss add *to hear*   [f]**11:17** Or *beat your breasts*   [g]**11:19** Or *declared right*   [h]**11:19** Other mss read *children*

[a]**7:27** Lit *messenger before Your face*   [b]**7:27** Mal 3:1   [c]**7:28** Other mss read *women is not a greater prophet than John the Baptist*   [d]**7:29** Lit *they justified God*   [e]**7:35** Or *wisdom is declared right*

Lk 7:28 *least in the kingdom . . . is greater than he:* Jesus contrasted the greatness of the new era to the old one John represented. John was the greatest person of the old era, spanning the creation up to that time. However, the least or lowest in the new era is greater than the greatest of the old era.

Lk 7:32 *like children:* The religious leaders reaction to John and Jesus' very different styles remind Jesus of children playing in the market place. For whether God's messenger came in a pious, ascetic manner, as John did, or came in an engaging manner that fellowshipped with all types of people, those who watched them were not happy.

Sec. 58   An Unresponsive Generation

Matthew 11:20-30

20 Then He proceeded to denounce the towns where most of His miracles were done, because they did not repent: 21 "Woe to you, Chorazin! Woe to you, Bethsaida! For if the miracles that were done in you had been done in Tyre and Sidon, they would have repented in sackcloth and ashes long ago! 22 But I tell you, it will be more tolerable for Tyre and Sidon on the day of judgment than for you. 23 And you, Capernaum, will you be exalted to heaven? You will go down to •Hades. For if the miracles that were done in you had been done in Sodom, it would have remained until today. 24 But I tell you, it will be more tolerable for the land of Sodom on the day of judgment than for you."

25 At that time Jesus said, "I praise[a] You, Father, Lord of heaven and earth, because You have hidden these things from the wise and learned and revealed them to infants. 26 Yes, Father, because this was Your good pleasure.[b] 27 All things have been entrusted to Me by My Father. No one knows[c] the Son except the Father, and no one knows the Father except the Son and anyone to whom the Son desires[d] to reveal Him.

28 "Come to Me, all of you who are weary and burdened, and I will give you rest. 29 All of you, take up My yoke and learn from Me, because I am gentle and humble in heart, and you will find rest for yourselves. 30 For My yoke is easy and My burden is light."

[a]11:25 Or *thank*   [b]11:26 Lit *was well-pleasing in Your sight*   [c]11:27 Or *knows exactly*   [d]11:27 Or *wills*, or *chooses*

Mt 11:21-23 *Chorazin . . . Bethsaida . . . Capernaum:* No cities were ever more privileged. The Son of God walked their streets, taught in their midst, and performed most of His miracles (v. 20) before their watching eyes. Yet they had stubbornly refused to repent. **Hades** Greek for the place of the dead, corresponding to the Hebrew *Sheol*.
Mt 11:27 *All things have been entrusted to Me by My Father:* Jesus assured them that He was moving irresistibly toward eventual glorious triumph.
Mt 11:29 *take up My yoke and learn from Me:* A yoke was part of the animal harness used to pull a cart or plow. A student was often spoken of as being under the yoke of his teacher.

Sec. 59   Much Forgiveness, Much Love

Luke 7:36-50

36 Then one of the Pharisees invited Him to eat with him. He entered the Pharisee's house and reclined at the table. 37 And a woman in the town who was a sinner found out that Jesus was reclining at the table in the Pharisee's house. She brought an alabaster jar of fragrant oil 38 and stood behind Him at His feet, weeping, and began to wash His feet with her tears. She wiped His feet with the hair of her head, kissing them and anointing them with the fragrant oil.

39 When the Pharisee who had invited Him saw this, he said to himself, "This man, if He were a prophet, would know who and what kind of woman this is who is touching Him—she's a sinner!"

40 Jesus replied to him, "Simon, I have something to say to you."

"Teacher," he said, "say it."

41 "A creditor had two debtors. One owed 500 •denarii, and the other 50. 42 Since they could not pay it back, he graciously forgave them both. So, which of them will love him more?"

Lk 7:36-50 Told only in Luke. The other anointing of Jesus in Matthew, Mark, and John take place in the last week and the one who anoints Jesus is not a sinful woman. The woman here is unnamed. She is not Mary Magdalene, who is introduced as a new figure in 8:1-3.
Lk 7:37 *alabaster jar:* This is therefore precious perfume (some refer to it as a prostitute's perfume) and probably very expensive. The woman was showing both great nerve and sacrifice in honoring Jesus this way.
Lk 7:39 *if He were a prophet:* In Greek, the wording here reflects the fact that Simon did not think Jesus is a prophet because He allowed this sinful woman to approach Him this way.
Lk 7:42 *which of them will love him more?* In this question is the parable's lesson. The one who has been forgiven the most, will love more. A sinner who understands the depth of sin and is forgiven will love more than a person who thinks they are inherently righteous. The lesson is that those who appreciate what Jesus has done, love Him with a great love and respond in a way that honors Him.

Luke 7:36-50 (cont.)

43 Simon answered, "I suppose the one he forgave more."

"You have judged correctly," He told him. 44 Turning to the woman, He said to Simon, "Do you see this woman? I entered your house; you gave Me no water for My feet, but she, with her tears, has washed My feet and wiped them with her hair. 45 You gave Me no kiss, but she hasn't stopped kissing My feet since I came in. 46 You didn't anoint My head with olive oil, but she has anointed My feet with fragrant oil. 47 Therefore I tell you, her many sins have been forgiven; that's whyᵃ she loved much. But the one who is forgiven little, loves little." 48 Then He said to her, "Your sins are forgiven."

49 Those who were at the table with Him began to say among themselves, "Who is this man who even forgives sins?"

50 And He said to the woman, "Your faith has saved you. Go in peace."

ᵃ7:47 Her love shows that she has been forgiven

Lk 7:49 *Who is this man who even forgives sins?:* Like Luke 5:21, Jesus' remarks about forgiving raises questions.

Sec. 60   Many Women Support Christ's Work

Luke 8:1-3

1Soon afterward He was traveling from one town and village to another, preaching and telling the good news of the kingdom of God. The Twelve were with Him, 2 and also some women who had been healed of evil spirits and sicknesses: Mary, called •Magdalene (seven demons had come out of her); 3 Joanna the wife of Chuza, •Herod's steward; Susanna; and many others who were supporting them from their possessions.

Lk 8:1-3 This account is unique to Luke. It shows women of every social stratum contributed to His ministry.

Sec. 61   A House Divided

Matthew 12:22-37	Mark 3:20-30
	20 Then He went home, and the crowd gathered again so that they were not even able to eat.ᵃ 21 When His family heard this, they set out to restrain Him, because they said, "He's out of His mind."
22 Then a demon-possessed man who was blind and unable to speak was brought to Him. He healed him, so that the manᵃ could both speak and see. 23 And all the crowds were astounded and said, "Perhaps this is the Son of David!"	
24 When the Pharisees heard this, they said, "The man drives out demons only by •Beelzebul, the ruler of the demons."	22 The •scribes who had come down from Jerusalem said, "He has •Beelzebul in Him!" and, "He drives out demons by the ruler of the demons!"
ᵃ12:22 Lit *mute*	ᵃ3:20 Lit *eat bread*, or *eat a meal*

Mt 12:23 *Perhaps this is the Son of David:* In the Greek this is really a question: "Is this *really* the Son of David?" It seemed too good to be true.

Mk 3:21 *they set out to restrain Him:* Jesus' family wanted to force Him away from all the public attention He was receiving. Reports concerning the commotion surrounding Jesus caused them to worry about Jesus' sanity and undoubtedly also about the family's reputation.

Mk 3:22 *Beelzebul:* The scribes are using "Beelzebul" as an alternative name for Satan, the ruler of the demons (Mk 3:22-23). The term "Beelzebul" probably originated as a name for the Canaanite god Baal, meaning "lord of the household." This same name may stand behind the reference to Baal-zebub, the god of Ekron, mentioned in 2 Kings 1:2-6, since the name Baal-zebub (meaning "lord of the flies") appears to be a deliberate distortion of the real name, a distortion intended to ridicule the pagan god.

Matthew 12:22-37 (cont.)

Mark 3:19-30 (cont.)

25 Knowing their thoughts, He told them: "Every kingdom divided against itself is headed for destruction, and no city or house divided against itself will stand. 26 If Satan drives out Satan, he is divided against himself. How then will his kingdom stand? 27 And if I drive out demons by Beelzebul, who is it your sons drive them out by? For this reason they will be your judges. 28 If I drive out demons by the Spirit of God, then the kingdom of God has come to you. 29 How can someone enter a strong man's house and steal his possessions unless he first ties up the strong man? Then he can rob his house. 30 Anyone who is not with Me is against Me, and anyone who does not gather with Me scatters. 31 Because of this, I tell you, people will be forgiven every sin and blasphemy, but the blasphemy against[a] the Spirit will not be forgiven.[b] 32 Whoever speaks a word against the Son of Man, it will be forgiven him. But whoever speaks against the Holy Spirit, it will not be forgiven him, either in this age or in the one to come.

33 "Either make the tree good and its fruit good, or make the tree bad[c] and its fruit bad; for a tree is known by its fruit. 34 Brood of vipers! How can you speak good things when you are evil? For the mouth speaks from the overflow of the heart. 35 A good man produces good things from his storeroom of good,[d] and an evil man produces evil things from his storeroom of evil. 36 I tell you that on the day of judgment people will have to account for every careless word they speak.[e] 37 For by your words you will be acquitted, and by your words you will be condemned."

[a]12:31 Or *of* [b]12:31 Other mss add *people* [c]12:33 Lit *rotten*, or *decayed* [d]12:35 Other mss read *from the storehouse of his heart* [e]12:36 Lit *will speak*

23 So He summoned them and spoke to them in parables: "How can Satan drive out Satan? 24 If a kingdom is divided against itself, that kingdom cannot stand. 25 If a house is divided against itself, that house cannot stand. 26 And if Satan rebels against himself and is divided, he cannot stand but is finished![a]

27 "On the other hand, no one can enter a strong man's house and rob his possessions unless he first ties up the strong man. Then he will rob his house. 28 •I assure you: People will be forgiven for all sins[b] and whatever blasphemies they may blaspheme. 29 But whoever blasphemes against the Holy Spirit never has forgiveness, but is guilty of an eternal sin"[c] — 30 because they were saying, "He has an unclean spirit."

[a]3:26 Lit *but he has an end*   [b]3:28 Lit *All things will be forgiven the sons of men*   [c]3:29 Other mss read *is subject to eternal judgment*

Mt 12:25-27 The charge that Jesus was in league with Beelzebul was absurd (vv. 25,26) and inconsistent (v. 27). *who is it your sons drive them out by?* Some Jews professed to perform exorcisms. Whether they really did so does not affect Christ's argument.

Mt 12:31 *blasphemy against the Spirit will not be forgiven:* This warning was directed at Jewish leaders who attributed to Satan the work of the Spirit through Jesus (v. 26). This is a case of calling something that is clearly good, evil.

Mt 12:34 *Brood of vipers:* John the Baptist used these same words on the Pharisees and Sadducees in Matthew 3:7.

Mk 3:29 *an eternal sin:* The preceding phrase "never has forgiveness" helps to define what Jesus means by an eternal sin. It is a rejection of God's truth that is so serious and so final that it has eternal consequences. Jesus' words should function as a warning to those who persist in deliberate and stubborn rejection. They should not serve as a cause for fear and doubt among those who have a tender conscience about their sin.

Sec. 62   Demand for a Sign

Matthew 12:38-45

38 Then some of the •scribes and Pharisees said to Him, "Teacher, we want to see a sign from You."

39 But He answered them, "An evil and adulterous generation demands a sign, but no sign will be given to it except the sign of the prophet Jonah. 40 For as Jonah was in the belly of the huge fish three days and three nights, so the Son of Man will be in the heart of the earth three days and three nights. 41 The men of Nineveh will stand up at the judgment with this generation and condemn it, because they repented at Jonah's procla-

Matthew 12:38-45 (cont.)

mation; and look—something greater than Jonah is here! 42 The queen of the south will rise up at the judgment with this generation and condemn it, because she came from the ends of the earth to hear the wisdom of Solomon; and look—something greater than Solomon is here!

43 "When an •unclean[a] spirit comes out of a man, it roams through waterless places looking for rest but doesn't find any. 44 Then it says, 'I'll go back to my house that I came from.' And returning, it arrives, it finds ⌊the house⌋ vacant, swept, and put in order. 45 Then off it goes and brings with it seven other spirits more evil than itself, and they enter and settle down there. As a result, that man's last condition is worse than the first. That's how it will also be with this evil generation."

[a]12:43 Morally or ceremonially impure

Mt 12:42 *queen of the south:* The Queen of Sheba whose kingdom is identified with Abyssinia.
Mt 12:43 *waterless places:* The Jews believed evil spirits wandered in deserts when not possessing persons.

Sec. 63   True Relationships

Matthew 12:46-50	Mark 3:31-35	Luke 8:19-21
46 He was still speaking to the crowds when suddenly His mother and brothers were standing outside wanting to speak to Him. 47 Someone told Him, "Look, Your mother and Your brothers are standing outside, wanting to speak to You."[a]	31 Then His mother and His brothers came, and standing outside, they sent ⌊word⌋ to Him and called Him. 32 A crowd was sitting around Him and told Him, "Look, Your mother, Your brothers, and Your sisters[a] are outside asking for You."	19 Then His mother and brothers came to Him, but they could not meet with Him because of the crowd. 20 He was told, "Your mother and Your brothers are standing outside, wanting to see You."
48 But He replied to the one who told Him, "Who is My mother and who are My brothers?" 49 And stretching out His hand toward His disciples, He said, "Here are My mother and My brothers! 50 For whoever does the will of My Father in heaven, that person is My brother and sister and mother."	33 He replied to them, "Who are My mother and My brothers?" 34 And looking about at those who were sitting in a circle around Him, He said, "Here are My mother and My brothers! 35 Whoever does the will of God is My brother and sister and mother."	21 But He replied to them, "My mother and My brothers are those who hear and do the word of God."
[a]12:47 Other mss omit this v.	**[a]3:32** Other mss omit *and Your sisters*	

Mt 12:47 *Your brothers:* Brothers of Jesus, younger sons of Joseph and Mary. This statement counters the doctrine of the perpetual virginity of Mary.
Mk 3:31-35 Although some groups venerate Jesus' physical family, Jesus Himself more highly valued His spiritual family which consisted of those who do the will of God.

Sec. 64   Jesus' First Group of Parables

Matthew 13:1-3a	Mark 4:1-2	Luke 8:4
1 On that day Jesus went out of the house and was sitting by the sea. 2 Such large crowds gathered around Him that He got into a boat and sat down, while the whole crowd stood on the shore. 3 Then He told them many things in parables, saying:	1 Again He began to teach by the sea, and a very large crowd gathered around Him. So He got into a boat on the sea and sat down, while the whole crowd was on the shore facing the sea. 2 He taught them many things in parables, and in His teaching He said to them:	4 As a large crowd was gathering, and people were flocking to Him from every town, He said in a parable:

1. To the Crowds by the Sea

(a) Parable of the Sower

Matthew 13:3b-23	Mark 4:3-25	Luke 8:5-18

"Consider the sower who went out to sow. 4 As he was sowing, some seeds fell along the path, and the birds came and ate them up. 5 Others fell on rocky ground, where there wasn't much soil, and they sprang up quickly since the soil wasn't deep. 6 But when the sun came up they were scorched, and since they had no root, they withered. 7 Others fell among thorns, and the thorns came up and choked them. 8 Still others fell on good ground and produced a crop: some 100, some 60, and some 30 times ⌊what was sown⌋. 9 Anyone who has ears[a] should listen!"

10 Then the disciples came up and asked Him, "Why do You speak to them in parables?"

11 He answered them, "Because the secrets[b] of the kingdom of heaven have been given for you to know, but it has not been given to them. 12 For whoever has, ⌊more⌋ will be given to him, and he will have more than enough. But whoever does not have, even what he has will be taken away from him. 13 For this reason I speak to them in parables, because looking they do not see, and hearing they do not listen or understand. 14 Isaiah's prophecy is fulfilled in them, which says:

a13:9 Other mss add *to hear*   **b13:11** The Gk word *mysteria* does not mean "mysteries" in the Eng sense; it means what we can know only by divine revelation.

3 "Listen! Consider the sower who went out to sow. 4 As he sowed, this occurred: Some seed fell along the path, and the birds came and ate it up. 5 Other seed fell on rocky ground where it didn't have much soil, and it sprang up right away, since it didn't have deep soil. 6 When the sun came up, it was scorched, and since it didn't have a root, it withered. 7 Other seed fell among thorns, and the thorns came up and choked it, and it didn't produce a crop. 8 Still others fell on good ground and produced a crop that increased 30, 60, and 100 times ⌊what was sown⌋." 9 Then He said, "Anyone who has ears to hear should listen!"

10 When He was alone with the Twelve, those who were around Him asked Him about the parables. 11 He answered them, "The secret[a] of the kingdom of God has been given to you, but to those outside, everything comes in parables 12 so that

a4:11 The Gk word *mysterion* does not mean "mystery" in the Eng sense; it means what we can know only by divine revelation.

5 "A sower went out to sow his seed. As he was sowing, some fell along the path; it was trampled on, and the birds of the sky ate it up. 6 Other seed fell on the rock; when it sprang up, it withered, since it lacked moisture.

7 Other seed fell among thorns; the thorns sprang up with it and choked it. 8 Still other seed fell on good ground; when it sprang up, it produced a crop: 100 times ⌊what was sown⌋." As He said this, He called out, "Anyone who has ears to hear should listen!" 9 Then His disciples asked Him, "What does this parable mean?" 10 So He said, "The secrets[a] of the kingdom of God have been given for you to know, but to the rest it is in parables, so that

a8:10 The Gk word *mysteria* does not mean "mysteries" in the Eng sense; it means what we can know only by divine revelation.

Mt 13:5 *rocky:* A thin layer of earth over the underlying rock.

Mt 13:9 Those with spiritual capacity ("ears") should ponder this parable and apply its lesson.

Mt 13:11 *secrets:* Literally, *mysterion*, which gives us our word "mystery." The Greek word means "revealed secret"—that which is knowable only by divine revelation.

Mk 4:3-9; 13-20 Only one of the four types of soil represents a hearer who is a genuine disciple of Jesus. Jesus insisted that true discipleship resulted in life transformation and involved the production of the "fruit" of good character and behavior. The sixty and one-hundred-fold crops were remarkable in this era of primitive agriculture.

Mk 4:3 *Listen:* Jesus' teaching in Mark 4 contains repeated commands to "listen" or "hear" (4:3,9,23,24). Mark included two lengthy teaching sections: the parables discourse (4:1-34) in which Jesus commanded the crowd to listen and the eschatological discourse (13:1-37) in which He commanded the disciples to watch (13:5,9,23,33).

Matthew 13:3-23 (cont.)   Mark 4:3-25 (cont.)   Luke 8:5-18 (cont.)

	they may look and look, yet not perceive; they may listen and listen, yet not understand; otherwise, they might turn back— and be forgiven.''a b	Looking they may not see, and hearing they may not understand.a

**You will listen and listen,
yet never understand;
and you will look and look,
yet never perceive.** 15 **For this people's heart
   has grown callous;
their ears are hard
   of hearing,
and they have shut
   their eyes;
otherwise they might see
   with their eyes
and hear with their ears,
understand
   with their hearts
and turn back—
and I would cure them.**a

16 "But your eyes are blessed because they do see, and your ears because they do hear! 17 For •I assure you: Many prophets and righteous people longed to see the things you see yet didn't see them; to hear the things you hear yet didn't hear them.

18 "You, then, listen to the parable of the sower: 19 When anyone hears the wordb about the kingdom and doesn't understand it, the evil one comes and snatches away what was sown in his heart. This is the one sown along the path. 20 And the one sown on rocky ground— this is one who hears the word and immediately receives it with joy.

a**13:14-15** Is 6:9-10   b**13:19** Gk *logos* = *word*, or *message*, or *saying*, or *thing*

13 Then He said to them: "Don't you understand this parable? How then will you understand any of the parables? 14 The sower sows the word. 15 Thesec are the ones along the path where the word is sown: when they hear, immediately Satan comes and takes away the word sown in them.d 16 And these aree the ones sown on rocky ground: when they hear the word, immediately they receive it with joy.

a**4:12** Other mss read *and their sins be forgiven them*   b**4:12** Is 6:9-10   c**4:15** Some people   d**4:15** Other mss read *in their hearts*   e**4:16** Other mss read *are like*

11 "This is the meaning of the parable:b The seed is the word of God. 12 The seeds along the path are those who have heard. Then the Devil comes and takes away the word from their hearts, so that they may not believe and be saved. 13 And the seeds on the rock are those who, when they hear, welcome the word with joy.

a**8:10** Is 6:9   b**8:11** Lit *But this is the parable:*

Mt 13:14-15 Isaiah 6:9-10 is fulfilled in the conduct of the Pharisees.

Mt 13:18 *You, then, listen:* Jesus had explained that He did not expect the hard of heart to understand His parables, but He was concerned that His disciples "get it."

Mk 4:10-12 These verses are perplexing since they appear to teach that Jesus taught in parables in order to prevent His audience from understanding His teaching. The words "so that" introduce a paraphrase of Is 6:9-10 and are equivalent to "in order that it might be fulfilled" as Matthew later interpreted them (see Mt 13:14).

Mk 4:13 *Don't you understand:* The first of a number of instances in Mark in which the twelve are criticized for lack of understanding. The dullness of the disciples is an important Markan theme. They struggle to understand Jesus' identity and the extent of His power to care for them (4:35-41; 6:45-52; 8:14-21). Even after they recognize that Jesus is the Messiah (8:29), they have difficulty grasping His path of suffering and what it will cost to follow Him (8:31-33; 9:30-34; 10:32-41).

Lk 8:11-15 Three of the four seeds have a tragic outcome, not reaching the goal for which the seed was planted. The three bad kinds of soil highlight obstacles that prevent the word from bearing fruit.

Matthew 13:3-23 (cont.)	Mark 4:3-25 (cont.)	Luke 8:5-18 (cont.)
21 Yet he has no root in himself, but is short-lived. When pressure or persecution comes because of the word, immediately he stumbles. 22 Now the one sown among the thorns—this is one who hears the word, but the worries of this age and the seduction[a] of wealth choke the word, and it becomes unfruitful. 23 But the one sown on the good ground—this is one who hears and understands the word, who does bear fruit and yields: some 100, some 60, some 30 times ⌊what was sown⌋."	17 But they have no root in themselves; they are short-lived. When pressure or persecution comes because of the word, they immediately stumble. 18 Others are sown among thorns; these are the ones who hear the word, 19 but the worries of this age, the seduction[a] of wealth, and the desires for other things enter in and choke the word, and it becomes unfruitful. 20 But the ones sown on good ground are those who hear the word, welcome it, and produce a crop: 30, 60, and 100 times ⌊what was sown⌋."	Having no root, these believe for a while and depart in a time of testing. 14 As for the seed that fell among thorns, these are the ones who, when they have heard, go on their way and are choked with worries, riches, and pleasures of life, and produce no mature fruit. 15 But the seed in the good ground—these are the ones who,[a] having heard the word with an honest and good heart, hold on to it and by enduring, bear fruit.

a13:22 Or *pleasure*, or *deceitfulness*

21 He also said to them, "Is a lamp brought in to be put under a basket or under a bed? Isn't it to be put on a lampstand? 22 For nothing is concealed except to be revealed, and nothing hidden except to come to light. 23 If anyone has ears to hear, he should listen!" 24 Then He said to them, "Pay attention to what you hear. By the measure you use,[b] it will be measured and added to you. 25 For to the one who has, it will be given, and from the one who does not have, even what he has will be taken away."

a4:19 Or *pleasure*, or *deceitfulness*
b4:24 Lit *you measure*

16 "No one, after lighting a lamp, covers it with a basket or puts it under a bed, but puts it on a lampstand so that those who come in may see its light. 17 For nothing is concealed that won't be revealed, and nothing hidden that won't be made known and come to light. 18 Therefore, take care how you listen. For whoever has, more will be given to him; and whoever does not have, even what he thinks he has will be taken away from him."

a8:15 Or *these are the kind who*

Mt 13:21 A sober reminder that even the most enthusiastic outward response to the gospel offers no guarantee that one is a true disciple.

Lk 8:18 *take care how you listen:* To the one who responds, more is given. The danger of the non-listener is that he is self-deceived. He thinks he hears, but he doesn't.

(b) Parable of the Growing Seed

Mark 4:26-29

26 "The kingdom of God is like this," He said. "A man scatters seed on the ground; 27 he sleeps and rises—night and day, and the seed sprouts and grows—he doesn't know how. 28 The soil produces a crop by itself—first the blade, then the head, and then the ripe grain on the head. 29 But as soon as the crop is ready, he sends for the sickle, because the harvest has come."

Mk 4:28 *by itself:* Only Mark included this parable of the seed that grows without human care or attention. The soil by itself produces a crop. In a similar way, the kingdom of God inevitably grows, not on account of human effort, but because it is the work of God.

(c) Parable of the Wheat and the Weeds

Matthew 13:24-30

24 He presented another parable to them: "The kingdom of heaven may be compared to a man who sowed good seed in his field. 25 But while people were sleeping, his enemy came, sowed weeds[a] among the wheat, and left. 26 When the plants sprouted and produced grain, then the weeds also appeared. 27 The landowner's •slaves came to him and said, 'Master, didn't you sow good seed in your field? Then where did the weeds come from?'

28 "'An enemy did this!' he told them.

"'So, do you want us to go and gather them up?' the slaves asked him.

29 "'No,' he said. 'When you gather up the weeds, you might also uproot the wheat with them. 30 Let both grow together until the harvest. At harvest time I'll tell the reapers: Gather the weeds first and tie them in bundles to burn them, but store the wheat in my barn.'"

[a]**13:25** Or *darnel,* a weed similar in appearance to wheat in the early stages

Mt 13:25 *weeds:* Or *darnel,* a weed similar in appearance to wheat in the early stages. Those who have responded to the good news and those who have not live together in the world.

(d) Parable of the Mustard Seed

Matthew 13:31-32	Mark 4:30-32
31 He presented another parable to them: "The kingdom of heaven is like a mustard seed that a man took and sowed in his field. 32 It's the smallest of all the seeds, but when grown, it's taller than the vegetables and becomes a tree, so that the birds of the sky come and nest in its branches."	30 And He said: "How can we illustrate the kingdom of God, or what parable can we use to describe it? 31 It's like a mustard seed that, when sown in the soil, is smaller than all the seeds on the ground. 32 And when sown, it comes up and grows taller than all the vegetables, and produces large branches, so that the birds of the sky can nest in its shade."

Mt 13:31-32 The third parable of the chapter teaches that God's kingdom has come in Christ but, like a mustard seed, it begins as something small and humble.

Mk 4:31 *a mustard seed:* The small size of the mustard seed was proverbial, especially in comparison to the size of seeds for all the other garden plants (see Mt 17:20; Lk 17:6). The kingdom of God will grow. Its final manifestation will be surprisingly out of proportion in comparison to its small beginning in the ministry of Jesus among His followers.

(e) Parable of the Yeast and Many Such Parables

Matthew 13:33-35	Mark 4:33-34
33 He told them another parable: "The kingdom of heaven is like yeast that a woman took and mixed into 50 pounds[a] of flour until it spread through all of it."[b] 34 Jesus told the crowds all these things in parables, and He would not speak anything to them without a parable, 35 so that what was spoken through the prophet might be fulfilled:	33 He would speak the word to them with many parables like these, as they were able to understand. 34 And He did not speak to them without a parable. Privately, however, He would explain everything to His own disciples.

    I will open My mouth in parables;
    I will declare things kept secret
    from the foundation of the world.[c]

[a]**13:33** Lit *3 sata*; about 40 quarts [b]**13:33** Or *until all of it was leavened* [c]**13:35** Ps 78:2

Mt 13:35 *prophet:* Asaph, also called a "seer" or "prophet" in 2 Chronicles 29:30.

2. *To the Disciples in the House*

(a) Jesus Interprets the Parable of the Weeds and Wheat

Matthew 13:36-43

36 Then He dismissed the crowds and went into the house. His disciples approached Him and said, "Explain the parable of the weeds in the field to us."

37 He replied: "The One who sows the good seed is the •Son of Man; 38 the field is the world; and the good seed—these are the sons of the kingdom. The weeds are the sons of the evil one, 39 and the enemy who sowed them is the Devil. The harvest is the end of the age, and the harvesters are angels. 40 Therefore just as the weeds are gathered and burned in the fire, so it will be at the end of the age. 41 The Son of Man will send out His angels, and they will gather from His kingdom everything that causes sin[a] and those guilty of lawlessness.[b] 42 They will throw them into the blazing furnace where there will be weeping and gnashing of teeth. 43 Then the righteous will shine like the sun in their Father's kingdom. Anyone who has ears[c] should listen!

[a]**13:41** Or *stumbling*   [b]**13:41** Or *those who do lawlessness*   [c]**13:43** Other mss add *to hear*

(b) The Parable of the Hidden Treasure

Matthew 13:44

44 "The kingdom of heaven is like treasure, buried in a field, that a man found and reburied. Then in his joy he goes and sells everything he has and buys that field.

Mt 13:44-46 The kingdom is a treasure so inestimably precious that one who obtains it is willing to surrender anything that could interfere with having it. See Paul's testimony in Philippians 3:8-9.

(c) The Parable of the Pearl of Great Price

Matthew 13:45-46

45 "Again, the kingdom of heaven is like a merchant in search of fine pearls. 46 When he found one priceless[a] pearl, he went and sold everything he had, and bought it.

[a]**13:46** Or *very precious*

(d) The Parable of the Net

Matthew 13:47-50

47 "Again, the kingdom of heaven is like a large net thrown into the sea. It collected every kind ⌊of fish⌋, 48 and when it was full, they dragged it ashore, sat down, and gathered the good ⌊fish⌋ into containers, but threw out the worthless ones. 49 So it will be at the end of the age. The angels will go out, separate the evil people from the righteous, 50 and throw them into the blazing furnace. In that place there will be weeping and gnashing of teeth.

(e) The Storehouse of Truth

Matthew 13:51-53

51 "Have you understood all these things?"[a]

"Yes," they told Him.

52 "Therefore," He said to them, "every student of Scripture[b] instructed in the kingdom of heaven is like a landowner who brings out of his storeroom what is new and what is old." 53 When Jesus had finished these parables, He left there.

[a]**13:51** Other mss add *Jesus asked them*   [b]**13:52** Or *every scribe*

Sec. 65   Wind and Wave Obey the Master

| Matthew 8:18-19,23-27 | Mark 4:35-41 | Luke 8:22-25 |

18 When Jesus saw large crowds[a] around Him, He gave the order to go to the other side ⌊of the sea⌋.[b] 19 A •scribe approached Him and said, "Teacher, I will follow You wherever You go!"

23 As He got into the[c] boat, His disciples followed Him. 24 Suddenly, a violent storm arose on the sea, so that the boat was being swamped by the waves. But He was sleeping. 25 So the disciples came and woke Him up, saying, "Lord, save ⌊us⌋! We're going to die!"

26 But He said to them, "Why are you fearful, you of little faith?" Then He got up and rebuked the winds and the sea. And there was a great calm.

27 The men were amazed and asked, "What kind of man is this?—even the winds and the sea obey Him!"

a8:18 Other mss read *saw a crowd*
b8:18 Sea of Galilee   **c8:23** Other mss read *to a*

35 On that day, when evening had come, He told them, "Let's cross over to the other side ⌊of the sea⌋." 36 So they left the crowd and took Him along since He was ⌊already⌋ in the boat. And other boats were with Him. 37 A fierce windstorm arose, and the waves were breaking over the boat, so that the boat was already being swamped. 38 But He was in the stern, sleeping on the cushion. So they woke Him up and said to Him, "Teacher! Don't you care that we're going to die?"

39 He got up, rebuked the wind, and said to the sea, "Silence! Be still!" The wind ceased, and there was a great calm. 40 Then He said to them, "Why are you fearful? Do you still have no faith?"

41 And they were terrified and asked one another, "Who then is this? Even the wind and the sea obey Him!"

22 One day He and His disciples got into a boat, and He told them, "Let's cross over to the other side of the lake." So they set out, 23 and as they were sailing He fell asleep. Then a fierce windstorm came down on the lake; they were being swamped and were in danger.

24 They came and woke Him up, saying, "Master, Master, we're going to die!" Then He got up and rebuked the wind and the raging waves. So they ceased, and there was a calm. 25 He said to them, "Where is your faith?"

They were fearful and amazed, asking one another, "Who can this be?[a] He commands even the winds and the waves, and they obey Him!"

a8:25 Lit *Who then is this?*

Mk 4:35-41 The OT taught that only God could control the wind and waves (Ps 65:7; 89:9; 107:23-32). Jesus' miracle is unique since He did not appeal to God to still the storm but did so by the power of His own command.

Sec. 66   Demons Driven Out by the Master

| Matthew 8:28-34 | Mark 5:1-20 | Luke 8:26-39 |

28 When He had come to the other side, to the region of the Gadarenes,[a] two demon-possessed men met Him as they came out of the tombs. They were so violent that no one could pass that way.

a8:28 Other mss read *Gergesenes*

1 Then they came to the other side of the sea, to the region of the Gerasenes.[a] 2 As soon as He got out of the boat, a man with an •unclean spirit came out of the tombs and met Him. 3 He lived in the tombs.

a5:1 Other mss read *Gadarenes*; other mss read *Gergesenes*

26 Then they sailed to the region of the Gerasenes,[a] which is opposite Galilee. 27 When He got out on land, a demon-possessed man from the town met Him. For a long time he had worn no clothes and did not stay in a house but in the tombs.

a8:26 Other mss read *the Gadarenes*

Mt 8:28 *Gadarenes:* See note on Mark 5:1.
Mk 5:1 *the region of the Gerasenes:* Some confusion exists over the exact location of this demon-possessed man's healing. The oldest manuscripts of Mark locate the event in the region of the Gerasenes (see Lk 8:26), while later manuscripts place it in the region of the Gadarenes (see Mt 8:28) or the Gergesenes. Mark seems to have located the healing near a little-known town named Gerasa on the eastern shore of the Sea of Galilee, which corresponds to the modern site known as Kersa. Matthew 8:28 uses the region of the Gadarenes for the location, pointing to the more well-known city of Gadara, which was about six miles southeast of the Sea of Galilee. The main idea is that by crossing over the Sea of Galilee Jesus has now entered into Gentile territory.
Lk 8:26-39 This event takes place in a Gentile area (because of the pigs). Jesus' power works in that context as well as among the Jews.

Matthew 8:28-34 (cont.)	Mark 5:1-20 (cont.)	Luke 8:26-39
	No one was able to restrain him anymore—even with chains—⁴ because he often had been bound with shackles and chains, but had snapped off the chains and smashed the shackles. No one was strong enough to subdue him. ⁵ And always, night and day, he was crying out among the tombs and in the mountains and cutting himself with stones.	
²⁹ Suddenly they shouted, "What do You have to do with us,ᵃ ᵇ Son of God? Have You come here to torment us before the time?"	⁶ When he saw Jesus from a distance, he ran and knelt down before Him. ⁷ And he cried out with a loud voice, "What do You have to do with me,ᵃ Jesus, Son of the Most High God? I begᵇ You before God, don't torment me!" ⁸ For He had told him, "Come out of the man, you unclean spirit!"	²⁸ When he saw Jesus, he cried out, fell down before Him, and said in a loud voice, "What do You have to do with me,ᵃ Jesus, You Son of the Most High God? I beg You, don't torment me!" ²⁹ For He had commanded the •unclean spirit to come out of the man. Many times it had seized him, and though he was guarded, bound by chains and shackles, he would snap the restraints and be driven by the demon into deserted places.
	⁹ "What is your name?" He asked him. "My name is Legion,"ᶜ he answered Him, "because we are many." ¹⁰ And he kept begging Him not to send them out of the region.	³⁰ "What is your name?" Jesus asked him. "Legion," he said—because many demons had entered him. ³¹ And they begged Him not to banish them to the •abyss.
³⁰ Now a long way off from them, a large herd of pigs was feeding. ³¹ "If You drive us out," the demons begged Him, "send us into the herd of pigs." ³² "Go!" He told them. So when they had come out, they entered the pigs. And suddenly the whole herd rushed down the steep bank into the sea and perished in the water. ³³ Then the men who tended them fled. They went into the city and reported everything—especially what had happened to those who were demon-possessed. ³⁴ At that, the whole town went out to meet Jesus.	¹¹ Now a large herd of pigs was there, feeding on the hillside. ¹² The demonsᵈ begged Him, "Send us to the pigs, so we may enter them." ¹³ And He gave them permission. Then the unclean spirits came out and entered the pigs, and the herd of about 2,000 rushed down the steep bank into the sea and drowned there. ¹⁴ The men who tended themᵉ ran off and reported it in the town and the countryside, and people went to see what had	³² A large herd of pigs was there, feeding on the hillside. The demons begged Him to permit them to enter the pigs, and He gave them permission. ³³ The demons came out of the man and entered the pigs, and the herd rushed down the steep bank into the lake and drowned. ³⁴ When the men who tended them saw what had happened, they ran off and reported it in the town and in the countryside. ³⁵ Then people went out to see what had

ᵃ8:29 Other mss add *Jesus* ᵇ8:29 Lit *What to us and to You*

ᵃ5:7 Lit *What to me and to You* ᵇ5:7 Or *adjure* ᶜ5:9 A Roman legion contained up to 6,000 soldiers; here *legion* indicates a large number. ᵈ5:12 Other mss read *All the demons* ᵉ5:14 Other mss read *tended the pigs*

ᵃ8:28 Lit *What to me and to You*

Mt 8:31 *demons begged Him:* Demons must obey His Word, and His one word "Go!" expelled them.
Mk 5:9 *Legion:* The name given by the demon-possessed man was a military term used for the largest unit of troops in the Roman army. In the first century AD, a legion at full strength consisted of approximately 6,000 soldiers.

Matthew 8:28-34 (cont.)	Mark 5:1-20 (cont.)	Luke 8:26-39 (cont.)
	happened. [15] They came to Jesus and saw the man who had been demon-possessed by the legion, sitting there, dressed and in his right mind; and they were afraid. [16] The eyewitnesses described to them what had happened to the demon-possessed man and ⌊told⌋ about the pigs. [17] Then they began to beg Him to leave their region.	happened. They came to Jesus and found the man the demons had departed from, sitting at Jesus' feet, dressed and in his right mind. And they were afraid. [36] Meanwhile, the eyewitnesses reported to them how the demon-possessed man was delivered. [37] Then all the people of the Gerasene region[a] asked Him to leave them, because they were gripped by great fear. So getting into the boat, He returned.
When they saw Him, they begged Him to leave their region.	[18] As He was getting into the boat, the man who had been demon-possessed kept begging Him to be with Him. [19] But He would not let him; instead, He told him, "Go back home to your own people, and report to them how much the Lord has done for you and how He has had mercy on you." [20] So he went out and began to proclaim in the •Decapolis how much Jesus had done for him, and they were all amazed.	[38] The man from whom the demons had departed kept begging Him to be with Him. But He sent him away and said, [39] "Go back to your home, and tell all that God has done for you." And off he went, proclaiming throughout the town all that Jesus had done for him. **a8:37** Other mss read *the Gadarenes*

Mt 8:34 *they begged Him to leave their region:* Mark 5:14-15 indicates that the townspeople were frightened at Jesus and His unusual power.

Sec. 67   A Girl Restored and a Woman Healed

Matthew 9:18-26	Mark 5:21-43	Luke 8:40-56
	[21] When Jesus had crossed over again by boat to the other side, a large crowd gathered around Him while He was by the sea. [22] One of the •synagogue leaders, named Jairus, came, and when he saw Jesus, he fell at His feet [23] and kept begging Him, "My little daughter is at death's door.[a] Come and lay Your hands on her so she can get well and live."	[40] When Jesus returned, the crowd welcomed Him, for they were all expecting Him. [41] Just then, a man named Jairus came. He was a leader of the •synagogue. He fell down at Jesus' feet and pleaded with Him to come to his house, [42] because he had an only daughter about 12 years old, and she was at death's door.[a]
[18] As He was telling them these things, suddenly one of the leaders[a] came and knelt down before Him, saying, "My daughter is near death,[b] but come and lay Your hand on her, and she will live." [19] So Jesus and His disciples got up and followed him. **a9:18** A leader of a synagogue; Mk 5:22 **b9:18** Lit *daughter has now come to the end*	[24] So Jesus went with him, and a large crowd was following and pressing against Him. **a5:23** Lit *My little daughter has it finally*; = to be at the end of life	While He was going, the crowds were nearly crushing Him. **a8:42** Lit *she was dying*

Lk 8:44 *touched the tassel:* The woman sought with her weak but real faith to get help from Jesus without anyone knowing about it.

Matthew 9:18-26 (cont.)

20 Just then, a woman who had suffered from bleeding for 12 years approached from behind and touched the •tassel on His robe, 21 for she said to herself, "If I can just touch His robe, I'll be made well!"[a]

22 But Jesus turned and saw her. "Have courage, daughter," He said. "Your faith has made you well."[b] And the woman was made well from that moment.[c]

23 When Jesus came to the leader's house, He saw the flute players and a crowd lamenting loudly.

[a]**9:21** Or *be delivered* [b]**9:22** Or *has saved you* [c]**9:22** Lit *hour*

Mark 5:21-43 (cont.)

25 A woman suffering from bleeding for 12 years 26 had endured much under many doctors. She had spent everything she had and was not helped at all. On the contrary, she became worse. 27 Having heard about Jesus, she came behind Him in the crowd and touched His robe. 28 For she said, "If I can just touch His robes, I'll be made well!" 29 Instantly her flow of blood ceased, and she sensed in her body that she was cured of her affliction.

30 At once Jesus realized in Himself that power had gone out from Him. He turned around in the crowd and said, "Who touched My robes?"

31 His disciples said to Him, "You see the crowd pressing against You, and You say, 'Who touched Me?' "

32 So He was looking around to see who had done this. 33 Then the woman, knowing what had happened to her, came with fear and trembling, fell down before Him, and told Him the whole truth. 34 "Daughter," He said to her, "your faith has made you well.[a] Go in peace and be free[b] from your affliction."

35 While He was still speaking, people came from the synagogue leader's house and said, "Your daughter is dead. Why bother the Teacher anymore?"

36 But when Jesus overheard what was said, He told the synagogue leader, "Don't be afraid. Only believe." 37 He did not let anyone accompany Him except Peter, James, and John, James' brother. 38 They came to the leader's house, and He saw a commotion—people weeping and wailing loudly. 39 He went in and said to them, "Why are you making a commotion and weeping? The child is not dead but asleep."

[a]**5:34** Or *has saved you* [b]**5:34** Lit *healthy*

Luke 8:40-56 (cont.)

43 A woman suffering from bleeding for 12 years, who had spent all she had on doctors[a] yet could not be healed by any,

44 approached from behind and touched the •tassel of His robe. Instantly her bleeding stopped.

45 "Who touched Me?" Jesus asked.

When they all denied it, Peter[b] said, "Master, the crowds are hemming You in and pressing against You."[c]

46 "Someone did touch Me," said Jesus. "I know that power has gone out from Me." 47 When the woman saw that she was discovered,[d] she came trembling and fell down before Him. In the presence of all the people, she declared the reason she had touched Him and how she was instantly cured.

48 "Daughter," He said to her, "your faith has made you well.[e] Go in peace."

49 While He was still speaking, someone came from the synagogue leader's ⌊house⌋, saying, "Your daughter is dead. Don't bother the Teacher anymore."

50 When Jesus heard it, He answered him, "Don't be afraid. Only believe, and she will be made well." 51 After He came to the house, He let no one enter with Him except Peter, John, James, and the child's father and mother. 52 Everyone was crying and mourning for her. But He said, "Stop crying, for she is not dead but asleep."

[a]**8:43** Other mss omit *who had spent all she had on doctors* [b]**8:45** Other mss add *and those with him* [c]**8:45** Other mss add *and You say, 'Who touched Me?'* [d]**8:47** Lit *she had not escaped notice* [e]**8:48** Or *has saved you*

Mt 9:23 ***a crowd lamenting loudly:*** Hired musicians assisted at funeral lamentations in which all the relations and friends joined.

Mk 5:30 ***Jesus realized in Himself that power had gone out:*** This healing is unique in that it appears to have occurred apart from any conscious decision on the part of Jesus (see Mk 6:56). God knows all about this woman and honored her faith through the power at work in Jesus.

Matthew 9:18-26 (cont.)	Mark 5:21-43 (cont.)	Luke 8:40-56 (cont.)
	40 They started laughing at Him, but He put them all outside. He took the child's father, mother, and those who were with Him, and entered the place where the child was. 41 Then He took the child by the hand and said to her, *"Talitha koum!"*[a] (which is translated, "Little girl, I say to you, get up!"). 42 Immediately the girl got up and began to walk. (She was 12 years old.) At this they were utterly astounded. 43 Then He gave them strict orders that no one should know about this and said that she should be given something to eat.	53 They started laughing at Him, because they knew she was dead.
24 "Leave," He said, "because the girl isn't dead, but sleeping." And they started laughing at Him. 25 But when the crowd had been put outside, He went in and took her by the hand, and the girl got up.		54 So He[a] took her by the hand and called out, "Child, get up!" 55 Her spirit returned, and she got up at once. Then He gave orders that she be given something to eat.
26 And this news spread throughout that whole area.		56 Her parents were astounded, but He instructed them to tell no one what had happened.
	a5:41 An Aram expression	**a8:54** Other mss add *having put them all outside*

Mt 9:24 *because the girl isn't dead, but sleeping:* Likely a euphemism for death. Jesus used the same metaphor with regard to Lazarus in John 11:11.

Lk 8:50 *Only believe:* Jairus also must have his faith strengthened, so both miracles focus on the importance of faith and show how it can grow.

Lk 8:56 *instructed them to tell no one:* This instruction seems strange at first glance. Those present knew the girl had died so it would be obvious what took place. The point seems to be that Jesus did not want excessive publicity of this event. The worry was that people would focus on His miracles and not the more important reality that they pointed to. Jesus is not so much a miracle worker, but one who brings salvation.

Sec. 68   Healing the Blind and Driving Out a Demon

Matthew 9:27-34

27 As Jesus went on from there, two blind men followed Him, shouting, "Have mercy on us, Son of David!"

28 When He entered the house, the blind men approached Him, and Jesus said to them, "Do you believe that I can do this?"

"Yes, Lord," they answered Him.

29 Then He touched their eyes, saying, "Let it be done for you according to your faith!" 30 And their eyes were opened. Then Jesus warned them sternly, "Be sure that no one finds out!"[a] 31 But they went out and spread the news about Him throughout that whole area.

32 Just as they were going out, a demon-possessed man who was unable to speak was brought to Him. 33 When the demon had been driven out, the man[b] spoke. And the crowds were amazed, saying, "Nothing like this has ever been seen in Israel!"

34 But the Pharisees said, "He drives out demons by the ruler of the demons!"

a9:30 Lit *no one knows*   **b9:33** Lit *the man who was unable to speak*

Mt 9:27 In addressing Jesus as Son of David, they recognized Him as the long-awaited Messiah and rightful King of Israel.

Mt 9:30 *Be sure that no one finds out:* The people were as yet unrepentant. They did not see that He must die for their sins.

Sec. 69   Rejection at Nazareth

Matthew 13:54-58   Mark 6:1-6a

54 He went to His hometown and began to teach them in their •synagogue, so that they were astonished and said, "How did this wisdom and these miracles come to Him? 55 Isn't this the carpenter's son? Isn't His mother called Mary, and His brothers James, Joseph,[a] Simon, and Judas? 56 And His sisters, aren't they all with us? So where does He get all these things?" 57 And they were offended by Him.

But Jesus said to them, "A prophet is not without honor except in his hometown and in his household." 58 And He did not do many miracles there because of their unbelief.

[a]13:55 Other mss read *Joses*; Mk 6:3

1He went away from there and came to His hometown, and His disciples followed Him. 2 When the Sabbath came, He began to teach in the •synagogue, and many who heard Him were astonished. "Where did this man get these things?" they said. "What is this wisdom given to Him, and how are these miracles performed by His hands? 3 Isn't this the carpenter, the son of Mary, and the brother of James, Joses, Judas, and Simon? And aren't His sisters here with us?" So they were offended by Him.

4 Then Jesus said to them, "A prophet is not without honor except in his hometown, among his relatives, and in his household." 5 So He was not able to do any miracles[a] there, except that He laid His hands on a few sick people and healed them. 6 And He was amazed at their unbelief.

[a]6:5 Lit *miracle*

Mk 6:1 *His hometown:* Luke more clearly identifies Nazareth as Jesus' hometown (Lk 4:16,23-24). In 6:1, Mark only refers to Jesus' hometown, although earlier in his narrative he reported that Jesus was from Nazareth (Mk 1:9,24).

Mk 6:3 *the carpenter:* In Matthew's account, the people from Jesus' hometown identify Him as a carpenter's son (Mt 13:55). Probably both Jesus and Joseph were carpenters, since one of the responsibilities of a father was to teach his son a trade. The disbelief of Nazareth stands in stark contrast to the faith of Jairus and the woman in the preceding text.

Sec. 70   Jesus Sends the 12 Out by Twos

Matthew 9:35–11:1   Mark 6:6b-13   Luke 9:1-6

35 Then Jesus went to all the towns and villages, teaching in their •synagogues, preaching the good news of the kingdom, and healing every[a] disease and every sickness.[b] 36 When He saw the crowds, He felt compassion for them, because they were weary and worn out, like sheep without a shepherd. 37 Then He said to His disciples, "The harvest is abundant, but the workers are few. 38 Therefore, pray to the Lord of the harvest to send out workers into His harvest."

1 Summoning His 12 disciples, He gave them authority over •unclean[c] spirits, to drive them out and to heal every[a] disease and sickness. 2 These are the names of the 12 apostles:

[a]9:35; 10:1 Or *every kind of* [b]9:35 Other mss add *among the people* [c]10:1 Morally or ceremonially impure

Now He was going around the villages in a circuit, teaching.

7 He summoned the Twelve and began to send them out in pairs and gave them authority over •unclean spirits.

1 Summoning the Twelve, He gave them power and authority over all the demons, and ⌊power⌋ to heal[a] diseases.

[a]9:1 In this passage, different Gk words are translated as *heal*. In Eng, "to heal" or "to cure" are synonyms with little distinction in meaning. Technically, we do not heal or cure diseases. People are healed or cured from diseases.

Matthew 9:35–11:1 (cont.)	Mark 6:6b-13 (cont.)	Luke 9:1-6 (cont.)
First, Simon, who is called Peter, and Andrew his brother; James the son of Zebedee, and John his brother; [3] Philip and Bartholomew;[a] Thomas and Matthew the tax collector; James the son of Alphaeus, and Thaddaeus;[b] [4] Simon the Zealot,[c] and Judas Iscariot,[d] who also betrayed Him.		
[5] Jesus sent out these 12 after giving them instructions: "Don't take the road leading to other nations, and don't enter any •Samaritan town. [6] Instead, go to the lost sheep of the house of Israel. [7] As you go, announce this: 'The kingdom of heaven has come near.' [8] Heal the sick, raise the dead, cleanse those with skin diseases, drive out demons. You have received free of charge; give free of charge. [9] Don't take along gold, silver, or copper for your money-belts. [10] Don't take a traveling bag for the road, or an extra shirt, sandals, or a walking stick, for the worker is worthy of his food.	[8] He instructed them to take nothing for the road except a walking stick: no bread, no traveling bag, no money in their belts. [9] They were to wear sandals, but not put on an extra shirt.	[2] Then He sent them to proclaim the kingdom of God and to heal the sick. [3] "Take nothing for the road," He told them, "no walking stick, no traveling bag, no bread, no money; and don't take an extra shirt.
[11] "When you enter any town or village, find out who is worthy, and stay there until you leave. [12] Greet a household when you enter it, [13] and if the household is worthy, let your peace be on it. But if it is unworthy, let your peace return to you. [14] If anyone will not welcome you or listen to your words, shake the dust off your feet when you	[10] Then He said to them, "Whenever you enter a house, stay there until you leave that place. [11] If any place does not welcome you and people refuse to listen to you, when you leave there, shake the dust off your feet as a testimony against them."[a]	[4] Whatever house you enter, stay there and leave from there. [5] If they do not welcome you, when you leave that town, shake off the dust from your feet as a testimony against them."

[a]**10:3** Probably the Nathanael of Jn 1:45-51 [b]**10:3** Other mss read *and Lebbaeus, whose surname was Thaddaeus* [c]**10:4** Lit *the Cananaean* [d]**10:4** *Iscariot* probably = "a man of Kerioth," a town in Judea.

[a]**6:11** Other mss add *I assure you, it will be more tolerable for Sodom or Gomorrah on judgment day than for that town.*

Mt 10:3-4 *Bartholomew* is likely the Nathanael. *Thaddaeus* is Judas, not Iscariot, the brother of James (Jn 14:22). *Simon the Zealot* may have belonged to an extremist party of that day called the Zealots who advocated the overthrow of Roman rule over Palestine.

Mt 10:5 *don't enter any Samaritan town:* They were to give the Jews the first opportunity to repent. Later Jesus ordered them to make disciples from all the Gentiles (Mt 28:19).

Mt 10:9-11 Jesus later instructed them quite differently regarding what they were to take and where they were to go (Lk 22:36). This campaign, however, was brief and intense, so they should travel light.

Lk 9:2 *to proclaim . . . to heal:* The twelve are to preach the kingdom and to heal. In other words, their message is to be supported by the care of their ministry. Word and deed go together to make the witness to the gospel.

Matthew 9:35–11:1 (cont.)

leave that house or town. [15] •I assure you: It will be more tolerable on the day of judgment for the land of Sodom and Gomorrah than for that town.

[16] "Look, I'm sending you out like sheep among wolves. Therefore be as shrewd as serpents and as harmless as doves. [17] Because people will hand you over to sanhedrins[a] and flog you in their •synagogues, beware of them. [18] You will even be brought before governors and kings because of Me, to bear witness to them and to the nations. [19] But when they hand you over, don't worry about how or what you should speak. For you will be given what to say at that hour, [20] because you are not speaking, but the Spirit of your Father is speaking through you.

[21] "Brother will betray brother to death, and a father his child. Children will even rise up against their parents and have them put to death. [22] You will be hated by everyone because of My name. But the one who endures to the end will be delivered.[b] [23] When they persecute you in one town, escape to another. For I assure you: You will not have covered the towns of Israel before the •Son of Man comes. [24] A disciple[c] is not above his teacher, or a •slave above his master. [25] It is enough for a disciple to become like his teacher and a slave like his master. If they called the head of the house '•Beelzebul,' how much more the members of his household!

[26] "Therefore, don't be afraid of them, since there is nothing covered that won't be uncovered, and nothing hidden that won't be made known. [27] What I tell you in the dark, speak in the light. What you hear in a whisper,[d] proclaim on the housetops. [28] Don't fear those who kill the body but are not able to kill the soul; rather, fear Him who is able to destroy both soul and body in •hell. [29] Aren't two sparrows sold for a penny?[e] Yet not one of them falls to the ground without your Father's consent.[f] [30] But even the hairs of your head have all been counted. [31] Don't be afraid therefore; you are worth more than many sparrows.

[32] "Therefore, everyone who will acknowledge Me before men, I will also acknowledge him before My Father in heaven. [33] But whoever denies Me before men, I will also deny him before My Father in heaven. [34] Don't assume that I came to bring peace on the earth. I did not come to bring peace, but a sword. [35] For I came to turn

> **a man against his father,**
> **a daughter against her mother,**
> **a daughter-in-law against her mother-in-law;**
> [36] **and a man's enemies will be**
> **the members of his household.[g]**

[37] The person who loves father or mother more than Me is not worthy of Me; the person who loves son or daughter more than Me is not worthy of Me. [38] And whoever doesn't take up his cross and follow[h] Me is not worthy of Me. [39] Anyone finding[i] his life will lose it, and anyone losing[j] his life because of Me will find it.

[a]**10:17** Local Jewish courts or local councils   [b]**10:22** Or *saved*   [c]**10:24** Or *student*   [d]**10:27** Lit *in the ear*   [e]**10:29** Gk *assarion*, a small copper coin   [f]**10:29** Lit *ground apart from your Father*   [g]**10:35-36** Mc 7:6   [h]**10:38** Lit *follow after*   [i]**10:39** Or *The one who finds*   [j]**10:39** Or *and the one who loses*

Mt 10:15 *more tolerable . . . Sodom and Gomorrah:* Men and women who scorn the gospel face a worse fate than the ancient cities destroyed in Genesis 19.

Mt 10:16 *shrewd . . . harmless:* Shrewd is literally "prudent, wise;" harmless is "innocent, guileless." Their wise, innocent behavior would comfort the sheep and give the wolves no cause for accusation.

Mt 10:17 *sanhedrins:* Local Jewish courts or local councils held in city synagogues.

Mt 10:19 *when they hand you over:* This prophecy was abundantly fulfilled as noted in Acts.

Mt 10:22 *the one who endures to the end will be delivered:* Endurance does not produce or protect salvation, but endurance is *evidence* of salvation, that a person is a child of God.

Mt 10:23 *before the Son of Man comes:* The reference may be to the transfiguration, the coming of the Holy Spirit at Pentecost, the fall of Jerusalem in AD 70, or the Second Coming.

Mt 10:25 *Beelzebul:* A term of slander, variously interpreted "lord of flies," "lord of dung," or "ruler of demons." (2 Kg 1:2; Mk 3:22).

Mt 10:34 *I did not come to bring peace, but a sword:* Jesus does give peace with God. But His mission did not involve peace with the world and its values. Those who share the triumph of the cross will also know the "offense of the cross."

Mt 10:39 *finding his life . . . losing his life:* Earthly life is only temporary, and the person who rejects Jesus in this life forfeits the eternal life that he cannot lose.

Matthew 9:35–11:1 (cont.)	Mark 6:6b-13 (cont.)	Luke 9:1-6 (cont.)
⁴⁰ "The one who welcomes you welcomes Me, and the one who welcomes Me welcomes Him who sent Me. ⁴¹ Anyone whoᵃ welcomes a prophet because he is a prophetᵇ will receive a prophet's reward. And anyone whoᶜ welcomes a righteous person because he's righteousᵈ will receive a righteous person's reward. ⁴² And whoever gives just a cup of cold water to one of these little ones because he is a discipleᵉ —I assure you: He will never lose his reward!"		
¹ When Jesus had finished giving orders to His 12 disciples, He moved on from there to teach and preach in their towns.	¹² So they went out and preached that people should repent. ¹³ And they were driving out many demons, anointing many sick people with olive oil, and healing.	⁶So they went out and traveled from village to village, proclaiming the good news and healing everywhere.

ᵃ**10:41** Or *The one who*   ᵇ**10:41** Lit *prophet in the name of a prophet*   ᶜ**10:41** Or *And the one who*   ᵈ**10:41** Lit *person in the name of a righteous person*   ᵉ**10:42** Lit *little ones in the name of a disciple*

Sec. 71   John the Baptist Beheaded

Matthew 14:1-12	Mark 6:14-29	Luke 9:7-9
¹At that time •Herod the tetrarch heard the report about Jesus. ² "This is John the Baptist!" he told his servants. "He has been raised from the dead, and that's why supernatural powers are at work in him."	¹⁴ King •Herod heard of this, because Jesus' name had become well known. Someᵃ said, "John the Baptist has been raised from the dead, and that's why supernatural powers are at work in him." ¹⁵ But others said, "He's Elijah." Still others said, "He's a prophetᵇ —like one of the prophets."	⁷ •Herod the tetrarch heard about everything that was going on. He was perplexed, because some said that John had been raised from the dead, ⁸ some that Elijah had appeared, and others that one of the ancient prophets had risen. ⁹ "I beheaded John," Herod said, "but who is this I hear such things about?" And he wanted to see Him.
³ For Herod had arrested John, chainedᵃ him, and put him in prison on account of Herodias, his brother Philip's wife,	¹⁶ When Herod heard of it, he said, "John, the one I beheaded, has been raised!" ¹⁷ For Herod himself had given orders to arrest John and to chain him in prison on account of Herodias, his brother Philip's wife, whom he had married.	

ᵃ**14:3** Or *bound*

ᵃ**6:14** Other mss read *He*   ᵇ**6:15** Lit *Others said, "A prophet*

Mt 14:3 *Herodias:* Daughter of Aristobulus, granddaughter of Herod the Great. She divorced Antipas' half brother Philip (probably not the same individual as Philip the tetrarch) to marry Antipas himself, in violation of Leviticus 18:16.

Lk 9:7 *perplexed:* Herod could not decide which view of Jesus was right. Was He John the Baptist raised, Elijah, or one of the ancient prophets? The parallel in Matthew 14:2 has him settle on John the Baptist raised, which probably means the spirit of John is seen to be alive in Jesus.

Matthew 14:1-12 (cont.)   Mark 6:14-29 (cont.)

4 since John had been telling him, "It's not lawful for you to have her!" 5 Though he wanted to kill him, he feared the crowd, since they regarded him as a prophet.

18 John had been telling Herod, "It is not lawful for you to have your brother's wife!" 19 So Herodias held a grudge against him and wanted to kill him. But she could not, 20 because Herod was in awe ofª John and was protecting him, knowing he was a righteous and holy man. When Herod heard him he would be very disturbed,ᵇ yet would hear him gladly.

6 But when Herod's birthday celebration came, Herodias' daughter danced before themª and pleased Herod. 7 So he promised with an oath to give her whatever she might ask. 8 And prompted by her mother, she answered, "Give me John the Baptist's head here on a platter!" 9 Although the king regretted it, he commanded that it be granted because of his oaths and his guests. 10 So he sent orders and had John beheaded in the prison. 11 His head was brought on a platter and given to the girl, who carried it to her mother. 12 Then his disciples came, removed the corpse,ᵇ buried it, and went and reported to Jesus.

21 Now an opportune time came on his birthday, when Herod gave a banquet for his nobles, military commanders, and the leading men of Galilee. 22 When Herodias' own daughterᶜ came in and danced, she pleased Herod and his guests. The king said to the girl, "Ask me whatever you want, and I'll give it to you." 23 So he swore oaths to her: "Whatever you ask me I will give you, up to half my kingdom."

24 Then she went out and said to her mother, "What should I ask for?"

"John the Baptist's head!" she said.

25 Immediately she hurried to the king and said, "I want you to give me John the Baptist's head on a platter—right now!"

26 Though the king was deeply distressed, because of his oaths and the guestsᵈ he did not want to refuse her. 27 The king immediately sent for an executioner and commanded him to bring John's head. So he went and beheaded him in prison, 28 brought his head on a platter, and gave it to the girl. Then the girl gave it to her mother. 29 When his disciplesᵉ heard about it, they came and removed his corpse and placed it in a tomb.

ª**14:6** Lit *danced in the middle*   ᵇ**14:12** Other mss read *body*

ª**6:20** Or *Herod feared*   ᵇ**6:20** Other mss read *When he heard him, he did many things*   ᶜ**6:22** Other mss read *When his daughter Herodias*   ᵈ**6:26** Lit *and those reclining at the table*   ᵉ**6:29** John's disciples

Mt 14:6 *Herodias' daughter:* Salome. She learned from her mother, for she later married her uncle Philip the tetrarch.

PART VIII

THE SPECIAL TRAINING OF THE TWELVE
IN DISTRICTS AROUND GALILEE

Sec. 72   Feeding 5,000

Matthew 14:13-21	Mark 6:30-44	Luke 9:10-17	John 6:1-13

13 When Jesus heard about it, He withdrew from there by boat to a remote place to be alone.

When the crowds heard this, they followed Him on foot from the towns. 14 As He stepped ashore,a He saw a huge crowd, felt compassion for them, and healed their sick.

a14:14 Lit Coming out (of the boat)

30 The apostles gathered around Jesus and reported to Him all that they had done and taught. 31 He said to them, "Come away by yourselves to a remote place and rest a while." For many people were coming and going, and they did not even have time to eat. 32 So they went away in the boat by themselves to a remote place, 33 but many saw them leaving and recognized them. People ran there by land from all the towns and arrived ahead of them.a 34 So as He stepped ashore, He saw a huge crowd and had compassion on them, because they were like sheep without a shepherd. Then He began to teach them many things.

a6:33 Other mss add and gathered around Him

10 When the apostles returned, they reported to Jesus all that they had done. He took them along and withdrew privately to aa town called Bethsaida.

11 When the crowds found out, they followed Him. He welcomed them, spoke to them about the kingdom of God, and curedb those who needed healing.

a9:10 Other mss add deserted place near a   b9:11 Or healed; in this passage, different Gk words are translated as heal. In Eng, "to heal" or "to cure" are synonyms with little distinction in meaning. Technically, we do not heal or cure diseases. People are healed or cured from diseases.

1After this, Jesus crossed the Sea of Galilee (or Tiberias). 2 And a huge crowd was following Him because they saw the signs that He was performing on the sick. 3 So Jesus went up a mountain and sat down there with His disciples.

Mt 14:13 *remote place:* The wilderness or unpopulated area east of Galilee.

Mk 6:34,39 The description of the people as "sheep without a shepherd" recalls numerous OT indictments against Israel's leaders and the promises that God Himself would shepherd His people (Ezk 34). Jesus acts as the divine Shepherd (Ezk 34:11-16) and the Davidic servant (Ezk 34:23-24). As a faithful shepherd, Jesus causes His sheep to recline in green pastures and prepares food for them so that they will not be in want (Ps 23:1-2,5).

Jn 6:1-71 The feeding of 5,000 constitutes yet another of Jesus' messianic "signs," placing Jesus in the line of God's provision of manna to Israel in the wilderness through Moses (see 6:30-31). In response to the people's challenge to perform a sign greater than Moses' signs and wonders at the exodus, Jesus claimed to be the "bread of life" that provides spiritual nourishment for all those who believe in Him and "eat His flesh" and "drink His blood." This statement proved too difficult even for many of Jesus' disciples, who stopped following Jesus at this watershed in His ministry (6:60-66). The Twelve, however, through Peter as their spokesman, reaffirmed their allegiance to Jesus.

Matthew 14:13-21 (cont.)	Mark 6:30-44 (cont.)	Luke 9:10-17 (cont.)	John 6:1-13 (cont.)
15 When evening came, the disciples approached Him and said, "This place is a wilderness, and it is already late.a Send the crowds away so they can go into the villages and buy food for themselves." 16 "They don't need to go away," Jesus told them. "You give them something to eat."	35 When it was already late, His disciples approached Him and said, "This place is a wilderness, and it is already late! 36 Send them away, so they can go into the surrounding countryside and villages to buy themselves something to eat." 37 "You give them something to eat," He responded. They said to Him, "Should we go and buy 200 •denarii worth of bread and give them something to eat?" 38 And He asked them, "How many loaves do you have? Go look."	12 Late in the day,a the Twelve approached and said to Him, "Send the crowd away, so they can go into the surrounding villages and countryside to find food and lodging, because we are in a deserted place here." 13 "You give them something to eat," He told them.	4 Now the •Passover, a Jewish festival, was near. 5 Therefore, when Jesus looked up and noticed a huge crowd coming toward Him, He asked Philip, "Where will we buy bread so these people can eat?" 6 He asked this to test him, for He Himself knew what He was going to do. 7 Philip answered, "Two hundred •denarii worth of bread wouldn't be enough for each of them to have a little." 8 One of His disciples, Andrew, Simon Peter's brother, said to Him,
17 "But we only have five loaves and two fish here," they said to Him.	When they found out they said, "Five, and two fish."	"We have no more than five loaves and two fish," they said, "unless we go and buy food for all these people." 14 (For about 5,000 men were there.)	9 "There's a boy here who has five barley loaves and two fish—but what are they for so many?"
18 "Bring them here to Me," He said. 19 Then He commanded the crowds to sit downb on the grass. He took the five loaves and the two fish, and looking up to heaven, He blessed them. He broke the loaves and gave them to the disciples, and the disciples ⌊gave them⌋ to the crowds.	39 Then He instructed them to have all the people sit downa in groups on the green grass. 40 So they sat down in ranks of hundreds and fifties. 41 Then He took the five loaves and the two fish, and looking up to heaven, He blessed and broke the loaves. He kept giving them to His disciples to set before the people. He also divided the two fish among them all.	Then He told His disciples, "Have them sit downb in groups of about 50 each." 15 They did so, and had them all sit down. 16 Then He took the five loaves and the two fish, and looking up to heaven, He blessed and broke them. He kept giving them to the disciples to set before the crowd.	10 Then Jesus said, "Have the people sit down." There was plenty of grass in that place, so they sat down. The men numbered about 5,000. 11 Then Jesus took the loaves, and after giving thanks He distributed them to those who were seated—so also with the fish, as much as they wanted.
a14:15 Lit *and the time* (for the evening meal) *has already passed* b14:19 Lit *to recline*	a6:39 Lit *people recline*	a9:12 Lit *When the day began to decline* b9:14 Lit *them recline*	

Mt 14:15-21 The miracle of the feeding of five thousand is the only one of Jesus' mighty acts recorded in all four Gospels.

Mt 14:19 *loaves and . . . fish:* Not a "loaf" in the English sense, but a flat, round, pancake-like piece of bread, and small, pickled fish similar to a sardine.

Mt 14:21 *5,000 men, besides women and children:* The total crowd size could have been as much as 20,000!

Mk 6:37 *200 denarii:* The denarius (the standard silver coin in Jesus' time) served as an appropriate daily wage for a laborer (Mt 20:2). In other words, the disciples estimated that it would take an average worker more than half a year to earn enough money to feed the crowd. As a faithful shepherd, Jesus causes His sheep to recline in green pastures and prepares food for them so that they will not be in want (Ps 23:1-2,5).

Lk 9:16 *He kept giving them to the disciples:* The miracle of the multiplication of the loaves and fishes pictures Jesus' ability to provide basic needs in abundance and evokes the image of the messianic banquet, where Messiah sits in fellowship with His people.

Matthew 14:13-21 (cont.)	Mark 6:30-44 (cont.)	Luke 9:10-17 (cont.)	John 6:1-13 (cont.)
20 Everyone ate and was filled. Then they picked up 12 baskets full of leftover pieces! 21 Now those who ate were about 5,000 men, besides women and children.	42 Everyone ate and was filled. 43 Then they picked up 12 baskets full of pieces of bread and fish. 44 Now those who ate the loaves were 5,000 men.	17 Everyone ate and was filled. Then they picked upa 12 baskets of leftover pieces. a9:17 Lit *Then were picked up by them*	12 When they were full, He told His disciples, "Collect the leftovers so that nothing is wasted." 13 So they collected them and filled 12 baskets with the pieces from the five barley loaves that were left over by those who had eaten.

Sec. 73   Jesus Sends the Disciples On

Matthew 14:22-23	Mark 6:45-46	John 6:14-15
22 Immediately Hea made the disciples get into the boat and go ahead of Him to the other side, while He dismissed the crowds. 23 After dismissing the crowds, He went up on the mountain by Himself to pray. When evening came, He was there alone. a14:22 Other mss read *Jesus*	45 Immediately He made His disciples get into the boat and go ahead of Him to the other side, to Bethsaida, while He dismissed the crowd. 46 After He said good-bye to them, He went away to the mountain to pray.	14 When the people saw the signa He had done, they said, "This really is the Prophet who was to come into the world!" 15 Therefore, when Jesus knew that they were about to come and take Him by force to make Him king, He withdrew againb to the mountain by Himself. a6:14 Other mss read *signs* b6:15 A previous withdrawal is mentioned in Mk 6:31-32, an event that occurred just before the feeding of the 5,000.

Sec. 74   Walking on the Water

Matthew 14:24-33	Mark 6:47-52	John 6:16-21
24 But the boat was already over a milea from land,b battered by the waves, because the wind was against them. 25 Around three in the morning,c He came toward them walking on the sea. a14:24 Lit *already many stadia; 1 stadion = 600 feet* b14:24 Other mss read *already in the middle of the sea* c14:25 Lit *fourth watch of the night = 3 to 6 a.m.*	47 When evening came, the boat was in the middle of the sea, and He was alone on the land. 48 He saw them being battered as they rowed,a because the wind was against them. Around three in the morningb He came toward them walking on the sea and wanted to pass by them. a6:48 Or *them struggling as they rowed* b6:48 Lit *Around the fourth watch of the night = 3 to 6 a.m.*	16 When evening came, His disciples went down to the sea 17 got into a boat, and started across the sea to Capernaum. Darkness had already set in, but Jesus had not yet come to them. 18 Then a high wind arose, and the sea began to churn.

Mt 14:24 *over a mile:* Literally, *already many stadia; 1 stadion* = 600 feet.

Mk 6:45-52 Jesus' walking upon the water recalls the description of Yahweh in Job 9:8 and thus demonstrates Jesus' identity as God.

Mk 6:48 *Around three in the morning:* Literally Mark says "around the fourth watch of the night." Here Mark follows the Roman custom of dividing the night (the time between 6:00 P.M. and 6:00 A.M.) into four equal periods or "watches," so-called because each period represented the time during which someone would be responsible for watching, that is, standing guard. Therefore, the fourth watch of the night was from 3:00 A.M. to 6:00 A.M. *wanted to pass by them:* The background for making sense of Jesus' desire to pass by the disciples is in the language used for God's revelation of His glory to Moses (Ex 33:17–34:8). After Moses asks to see God's glory, the Lord places him in the cleft of the rock and protects his life by covering him with His hand while His glory "is passing by" (Ex 33:18-22; see 1 Kg 19:11-13). Jesus' desire to pass by His disciples, therefore, does not indicate that He wanted to go beyond them to reach another location but rather that He wanted to reveal His glory to them.

Matthew 14:24-33 (cont.)	Mark 6:47-52 (cont.)	John 6:16-21 (cont.)
26 When the disciples saw Him walking on the sea, they were terrified. "It's a ghost!" they said, and cried out in fear. 27 Immediately Jesus spoke to them. "Have courage! It is I. Don't be afraid." 28 "Lord, if it's You," Peter answered Him, "command me to come to You on the water." 29 "Come!" He said. And climbing out of the boat, Peter started walking on the water and came toward Jesus. 30 But when he saw the strength of the wind,ᵃ he was afraid. And beginning to sink he cried out, "Lord, save me!" 31 Immediately Jesus reached out His hand, caught hold of him, and said to him, "You of little faith, why did you doubt?" 32 When they got into the boat, the wind ceased. 33 Then those in the boat worshiped Him and said, "Truly You are the Son of God!" ᵃ14:30 Other mss read *saw the wind*	49 When they saw Him walking on the sea, they thought it was a ghost and cried out; 50 for they all saw Him and were terrified. Immediately He spoke with them and said, "Have courage! It is I. Don't be afraid." 51 Then He got into the boat with them, and the wind ceased. They were completely astounded,ᵃ 52 because they had not understood about the loaves. Instead, their hearts were hardened. ᵃ6:51 Lit *were astounded in themselves*	19 After they had rowed about three or four miles,ᵃ they saw Jesus walking on the sea. He was coming near the boat, and they were afraid. 20 But He said to them, "It is I.ᵇ Don't be afraid!" 21 Then they were willing to take Him on board, and at once the boat was at the shore where they were heading. ᵃ6:19 Lit *25 or 30 stadia*; 1 *stadion* = 600 feet ᵇ6:20 Lit *I am*

Mt 14:26 *ghost:* Greek *phantasma,* which refers to an apparition or a creature of the imagination. It is the word from which we derive *phantom.*

Mt 14:32 Perhaps the most spectacular and miraculous part of this episode was accomplished without Jesus saying a word or raising a hand. The moment He and Peter *got into the boat* with the other disciples, *the wind ceased.*

Mt 14:33 *You are the Son of God:* Satan and an evil spirit (4:3 and 8:29) had applied this title to Jesus, but this is the first time a man confesses it.

Sec. 75   Miraculous Healings

Matthew 14:34-36	Mark 6:53-56
34 Once they crossed over, they came to land at Gennesaret. 35 When the men of that place recognized Him, they alertedᵃ the whole vicinity and brought to Him all who were sick. 36 They were begging Him that they might only touch the •tassel on His robe. And as many as touched it were made perfectly well. ᵃ14:35 Lit *sent into*	53 When they had crossed over, they came to land at Gennesaret and beached the boat. 54 As they got out of the boat, people immediately recognized Him. 55 They hurried throughout that vicinity and began to carry the sick on mats to wherever they heard He was. 56 Wherever He would go, into villages, towns, or the country, they laid the sick in the marketplaces and begged Him that they might touch just the •tassel of His robe. And everyone who touched it was made well.

Mk 6:56 *the tassel of His robe:* In Numbers 15:37-41, the Lord commanded the men of Israel to wear tassels on the corners of their garments (see Dt 22:12). The tassels were to serve as a reminder for them to obey God's commandments and to set themselves apart as holy, belonging to God. Some of the sick believed that they would become well if they touched one of the tassels on Jesus' garment. Apparently God saw their faith and granted them healing through the power residing in Jesus (see Mk 5:28)

Sec. 76   The Bread of Life

John 6:22-71

22 The next day, the crowd that had stayed on the other side of the sea knew there had been only one boat.[a] ⌊They also knew⌋ that Jesus had not boarded the boat with His disciples, but that His disciples had gone off alone. 23 Some boats from Tiberias came near the place where they ate the bread after the Lord gave thanks. 24 When the crowd saw that neither Jesus nor His disciples were there, they got into the boats and went to Capernaum looking for Jesus.

25 When they found Him on the other side of the sea, they said to Him, "•Rabbi, when did You get here?"

26 Jesus answered, "•I assure you: You are looking for Me, not because you saw the signs, but because you ate the loaves and were filled. 27 Don't work for the food that perishes but for the food that lasts for eternal life, which the •Son of Man will give you, because God the Father has set His seal of approval on Him."

28 "What can we do to perform the works of God?" they asked.

29 Jesus replied, "This is the work of God: that you believe in the One He has sent."

30 "What sign then are You going to do so we may see and believe You?" they asked. "What are You going to perform? 31 Our fathers ate the manna in the wilderness, just as it is written: **He gave them bread from heaven to eat.**"[b] [c]

32 Jesus said to them, "I assure you: Moses didn't give you the bread from heaven, but My Father gives you the real bread from heaven. 33 For the bread of God is the One who comes down from heaven and gives life to the world."

34 Then they said, "Sir, give us this bread always!"

35 "I am the bread of life," Jesus told them. "No one who comes to Me will ever be hungry, and no one who believes in Me will ever be thirsty again. 36 But as I told you, you've seen Me,[d] and yet you do not believe. 37 Everyone the Father gives Me will come to Me, and the one who comes to Me I will never cast out. 38 For I have come down from heaven, not to do My will, but the will of Him who sent Me. 39 This is the will of Him who sent Me: that I should lose none of those He has given Me but should raise them up on the last day. 40 For this is the will of My Father: that everyone who sees the Son and believes in Him may have eternal life, and I will raise him up on the last day."

41 Therefore the •Jews started complaining about Him, because He said, "I am the bread that came down from heaven." 42 They were saying, "Isn't this Jesus the son of Joseph, whose father and mother we know? How can He now say, 'I have come down from heaven'?"

43 Jesus answered them, "Stop complaining among yourselves. 44 No one can come to Me unless the Father who sent Me draws[e] him, and I will raise him up on the last day. 45 It is written in the Prophets: **And they will all be taught by God.**[f] Everyone who has listened to and learned from the Father comes to Me— 46 not that anyone has seen the Father except the One who is from God. He has seen the Father.

47 "I assure you: Anyone who believes[g] has eternal life. 48 I am the bread of life. 49 Your fathers ate the manna in the wilderness, and they died. 50 This is the bread that comes down from heaven so that anyone may eat of it and not die. 51 I am the living bread that came down from heaven. If anyone eats of this bread he will live forever. The bread that I will give for the life of the world is My flesh."

52 At that, the Jews argued among themselves, "How can this man give us His flesh to eat?"

53 So Jesus said to them, "I assure you: Unless you eat the flesh of the Son of Man and drink His blood, you do not have life in yourselves. 54 Anyone who eats My flesh and drinks My blood has eternal life, and I will raise him up on the last day, 55 because My flesh is real food and My blood is real drink. 56 The one who eats My flesh and drinks My blood lives in Me, and I in him. 57 Just as the living Father sent Me and I live because of the Father, so the one who feeds on Me will live because of Me. 58 This is the bread that came down from heaven; it is not like the manna[h] your fathers ate—and they died. The one who eats this bread will live forever."

a6:22 Other mss add *into which His disciples had entered*   **b6:31** Bread miraculously provided by God for the Israelites   **c6:31** Ex 16:4; Ps 78:24   **d6:36** Other mss omit *Me*   **e6:44** Or *brings*, or *leads*; see the use of this Gk verb in Jn 12:32; 21:6; Ac 16:19; Jms 2:6.   **f6:45** Is 54:13   **g6:47** Other mss add *in Me*   **h6:58** Other mss omit *the manna*

John 6:35,48,51 Jesus' claim of being "the bread of life" constitutes the first of seven "I am sayings" recorded in this Gospel. Subsequent sayings include Jesus' self-reference as "the light of the world" (8:12; 9:5); as "the door of the sheep" (10:7,9) and as the "good shepherd" (10:11,14); as "the resurrection and the life" (11:25); as "the way, the truth, and the life" (14:6); and as "the true vine" (15:1). Apart from these sayings where "I am" is followed by a predicate nominative, there are also several absolute statements where Jesus refers to Himself as "I am" (e.g., 6:20; 8:24,28,58; 18:5) in keeping with the reference to God as "I AM" in Exodus 3:14 and the book of Isaiah.

John 6:22-71 (cont.)

59 He said these things while teaching in the •synagogue in Capernaum.

60 Therefore, when many of His disciples heard this, they said, "This teaching is hard! Who can accept[a] it?"

61 Jesus, knowing in Himself that His disciples were complaining about this, asked them, "Does this offend you? 62 Then what if you were to observe the Son of Man ascending to where He was before? 63 The Spirit is the One who gives life. The flesh doesn't help at all. The words that I have spoken to you are spirit and are life. 64 But there are some among you who don't believe." (For Jesus knew from the beginning those who would not[b] believe and the one who would betray Him.) 65 He said, "This is why I told you that no one can come to Me unless it is granted to him by the Father."

66 From that moment many of His disciples turned back and no longer accompanied Him. 67 Therefore Jesus said to the Twelve, "You don't want to go away too, do you?"

68 Simon Peter answered, "Lord, who will we go to? You have the words of eternal life. 69 We have come to believe and know that You are the Holy One of God!"[c]

70 Jesus replied to them, "Didn't I choose you, the Twelve? Yet one of you is the Devil!" 71 He was referring to Judas, Simon Iscariot's son,[d] [e] one of the Twelve, because he was going to betray Him.

a6:60 Lit *hear*   **b6:64** Other mss omit *not*   **c6:69** Other mss read *You are the Messiah, the Son of the Living God*   **d6:71** Other mss read *Judas Iscariot, Simon's son*   **e6:71** Lit *Judas, of Simon Iscariot*

Sec. 77   The Tradition of the Elders

Matthew 15:1-20	Mark 7:1-23	John 7:1
1 Then •Pharisees and •scribes came from Jerusalem to Jesus and asked,	1 The •Pharisees and some of the •scribes who had come from Jerusalem gathered around Him. 2 They observed that some of His disciples were eating their bread with •unclean—that is, unwashed—hands. 3 (For the Pharisees, in fact all the Jews, will not eat unless they wash their hands ritually, keeping the tradition of the elders. 4 When they come from the marketplace, they do not eat unless they have washed.	1 After this, Jesus traveled in Galilee, since He did not want to travel in Judea because the •Jews were trying to kill Him.
2 "Why do Your disciples break the tradition of the elders? For they don't wash their hands when they eat!"[a]		

a15:2 Lit *eat bread* – eat a meal

Mt 15:2 *wash their hands when they eat:* Hand washing before meals is not a requirement of the OT, but the rabbis made it a mark of righteousness. This matter was magnified at great length in the oral teaching. The washing (*niptontai*) of the hands called for minute regulations.

Mt 15:3 *God's commandment . . . tradition:* The Lord Jesus reminded His critics that *they* transgressed *God's commandment,* not simply the *tradition* of the elders. The law commanded men to *honor* (v. 4) their parents, including supporting them financially if necessary.

Mk 7:1-16 Mark explaining Jewish practices to his readers is a good indication that he was originally writing for a predominantly Gentile church. The washings that Mark described were ritual purification rites, not for good hygiene.

Mk 7:2 *with unclean–that is, unwashed–hands:* The word "unclean" in this context means ritually impure or ceremonially defiled and not properly set apart as holy to the Lord (see Ac 10:14,28; 11:8; Rm 14:14). Therefore, the problem was not that the disciples had dirty hands but that they did not follow the Pharisees' teaching concerning the ceremonial washing of the hands before eating, as many other Jews did.

Mk 7:3 *the tradition of the elders:* Mark was referring to the oral law, the traditional rules and interpretations passed on by important teachers that helped to define the proper application of the written Law of Moses. The Pharisees sought to follow this oral law with great care. A ceremonial washing of the hands was a requirement in the written Law only for the priests involved in service at the tabernacle (Ex 30:18-21; 40:30-31). The Pharisees' oral law extended this responsibility to everyone, apparently on the theory that every Jew should live as a priest and every Jewish home should be a place of worship. This tradition was later codified in the Mishnah.

Matthew 15:1-20 (cont.)

Mark 7:1-23 (cont.)

3 He answered them, "And why do you break God's commandment because of your tradition? 4 For God said:a

**Honor your father and your mother;b and,
The one who speaks evil of father or mother
must be put to death.c**

5 But you say, 'Whoever tells his father or mother, "Whatever benefit you might have received from me is a gift ⌊committed to the temple⌋'— 6 he does not have to honor his father.'d In this way, you have revoked God's worde because of your tradition. 7 Hypocrites! Isaiah prophesied correctly about you when he said:

8 **These peoplef honor Me with their lips,
but their heart is far from Me.**
9 **They worship Me in vain,
teaching as doctrines the commands of men."g**

10 Summoning the crowd, He told them, "Listen and understand:

a**15:4** Other mss read *commanded, saying*   b**15:4** Ex 20:12; Dt 5:16   c**15:4** Ex 21:17; Lv 20:9   d**15:6** Other mss read *then he does not have to honor his father or mother*   e**15:6** Other mss read *commandment*   f**15:8** Other mss add *draws near to Me with their mouths, and*   g**15:8-9** Is 29:13 LXX

And there are many other customs they have received and keep, like the washing of cups, jugs, copper utensils, and dining couches.a) 5 Then the Pharisees and the scribes asked Him, "Why don't Your disciples live according to the tradition of the elders, instead of eating bread with ritually uncleanb hands?"

6 He answered them, "Isaiah prophesied correctly about you hypocrites, as it is written:

**These people honor Me with their lips,
but their heart is far from Me.**
7 **They worship Me in vain,
teaching as doctrines the commands of men.c**

8 Disregarding the command of God, you keep the tradition of men."d 9 He also said to them, "You completely invalidate God's command in order to maintaine your tradition! 10 For Moses said:

**Honor your father and your mother;f and
Whoever speaks evil of father or mother
must be put to death.g**

11 But you say, 'If a man tells his father or mother: Whatever benefit you might have received from me is Corban'" (that is, a gift ⌊committed to the temple⌋), 12 "you no longer let him do anything for his father or mother. 13 You revoke God's word by your tradition that you have handed down. And you do many other similar things." 14 Summoning the crowd again, He told them, "Listen to Me, all of you, and understand: 15 Nothing that goes into a person from outside can defile him, but the things that come out of a person are what defile him. 16 If anyone has ears to hear, he should listen!"h

a**7:4** Other mss omit *and dining couches*   b**7:5** Other mss read *with unwashed*   c**7:6-7** Is 29:13   d**7:8** Other mss add *The washing of jugs, and cups, and many other similar things you practice.*   e**7:9** Other mss read *to establish*   f**7:10** Ex 20:12; Dt 5:16   g**7:10** Ex 21:17; Lv 20:9   h**7:16** Other mss omit this verse

Mt 15:5 *gift committed to the temple:* They had devised a tradition by which to avoid their responsibility. When asked for help by *father or mother,* all they had to do was recite words such as, "Any money which I have and which could be used to support you has been dedicated *to the temple,* and therefore I cannot give it to you." By reciting this formula, they were free from financial responsibility to their parents.

Mk 7:11 *Corban:* This loan word from Hebrew was a technical term for a gift or offering reserved for God and therefore no longer available for ordinary use (see Lv 1:2). The scribes of Jesus' day considered such a dedication as a binding vow, one that could not be broken even if it resulted in harm to one's parents.

Mk 7:15 *defile:* Jesus is explaining what makes a person unclean and therefore unacceptable in the presence of God. Unwashed hands do not defile food or the one who eats it. Instead, what makes fellowship with God impossible is the moral pollution that begins in the heart.

Matthew 15:1-20 (cont.)   Mark 7:1-23 (cont.)

[11] It's not what goes into the mouth that defiles a man, but what comes out of the mouth, this defiles a man."

[12] Then the disciples came up and told Him, "Do You know that the Pharisees took offense when they heard this statement?"

[13] He replied, "Every plant that My heavenly Father didn't plant will be uprooted. [14] Leave them alone! They are blind guides.[a] And if the blind guide the blind, both will fall into a pit."

[15] Then Peter replied to Him, "Explain this parable to us."

[16] "Are even you still lacking in understanding?" He[b] asked. [17] "Don't you realize[c] that whatever goes into the mouth passes into the stomach and is eliminated?[d] [18] But what comes out of the mouth comes from the heart, and this defiles a man. [19] For from the heart come evil thoughts, murders, adulteries, sexual immoralities, thefts, false testimonies, blasphemies. [20] These are the things that defile a man, but eating with unwashed hands does not defile a man."

[17] When He went into the house away from the crowd, the disciples asked Him about the parable. [18] And He said to them, "Are you also as lacking in understanding? Don't you realize that nothing going into a man from the outside can defile him? [19] For it doesn't go into his heart but into the stomach and is eliminated."[a] (As a result, He made all foods •clean.[b]) [20] Then He said, "What comes out of a person—that defiles him. [21] For from within, out of people's hearts, come evil thoughts, sexual immoralities, thefts, murders, [22] adulteries, greed, evil actions, deceit, lewdness, stinginess,[c] blasphemy, pride, and foolishness. [23] All these evil things come from within and defile a person."

a15:14 Other mss add *for the blind* **b15:16** Other mss read *Jesus* **c15:17** Other mss add *yet* **d15:17** Lit *and goes out into the toilet*

a7:19 Lit *goes out into the toilet* **b7:19** Other mss read *is eliminated, making all foods clean."* **c7:22** Lit *evil eye*

Mt 15:11 *defiles a man:* Here the great Lawgiver paved the way for the abrogation of the whole system of ceremonial defilement. He said that the food His disciples ate with unwashed hands did not defile them. The hypocrisy of the scribes and Pharisees was what truly defiled.

Mt 15:14 *fall into a pit:* Unprotected wells, quarries, and holes were common in Palestine.

Mt 15:15 *parable:* The disciples were undoubtedly confused by this complete reversal of all they had been taught about clean and unclean foods. It was like a *parable* to them.

Mk 7:17-23 Mark's parenthetical commentary on Jesus' teaching offers a good model for deriving principles from biblical teaching in order to apply it in new settings. When Jesus taught that "nothing that goes into a person from outside can defile him," He referred particularly to food eaten with ritually unclean hands. Mark recognized that the general principle also had implications for the question of whether or not keeping OT dietary laws was obligatory for believers, an important question for the early church. Although some critics argue that the Gospel writers invented sayings of Jesus that had no basis in actual history, the fact that the Gospels do not address key issues for the early church (like whether circumcision is obligatory for Gentiles believers) shows that they did not feel free to create such material. This text does address an important issue in the early church, but it does so only indirectly. Had Mark felt free to create material from his own imagination, he could have easily composed a "saying of Jesus" that more directly related to the church's pressing question. This confirms that Mark records actual history.

Mk 7:19 *He made all foods clean:* This parenthetical statement represents Mark's own interpretive comment on the implications of Jesus' teaching in 7:15,18-19 that people cannot defile themselves by what they put into their bodies from the outside. Mark saw this teaching as relevant to the question of how followers of Jesus should respond to the food laws contained in the Law of Moses (Lv 11,17). The early church struggled with this question, especially when Gentiles began to respond to the message of the gospel (Ac 10:1–11:18; 15:1-29; Rm 14:13-23; Gl 2:11-14).

Sec. 78   A Gentile Mother's Faith

Matthew 15:21-28	Mark 7:24-30

21 When Jesus left there, He withdrew to the area of Tyre and Sidon. 22 Just then a Canaanite woman from that region came and kept crying out,a "Have mercy on me, Lord, Son of David! My daughter is cruelly tormented by a demon."

23 Yet He did not say a word to her. So His disciples approached Him and urged Him, "Send her away because she cries out after us."b

24 He replied, "I was sent only to the lost sheep of the house of Israel."

25 But she came, knelt before Him, and said, "Lord, help me!"

26 He answered, "It isn't right to take the children's bread and throw it to their dogs."

27 "Yes, Lord," she said, "yet even the dogs eat the crumbs that fall from their masters' table!"

28 Then Jesus replied to her, "•Woman, your faith is great. Let it be done for you as you want." And from that momentc her daughter was cured.

24 He got up and departed from there to the region of Tyre and Sidon.a He entered a house and did not want anyone to know it, but He could not escape notice. 25 Instead, immediately after hearing about Him, a woman whose little daughter had an unclean spirit came and fell at His feet. 26 Now the woman was Greek, a Syrophoenician by birth, and she kept asking Him to drive the demon out of her daughter.

27 He said to her, "Allow the children to be satisfied first, because it isn't right to take the children's bread and throw it to the dogs."

28 But she replied to Him, "Lord, even the dogs under the table eat the children's crumbs."

29 Then He told her, "Because of this reply, you may go. The demon has gone out of your daughter." 30 When she went back to her home, she found her child lying on the bed, and the demon was gone.

a**15:22** Other mss read *and cried out to Him*   b**15:23** Lit *she is yelling behind us* or *after us*   c**15:28** Lit *hour*

a**7:24** Other mss omit *and Sidon*

Mt 15:22 *Canaanite woman:* The woman is called a Syrophoenician by Mark (7:26). *Canaan* means "lowland country" and originally included the whole coast of Palestine from Sidon to Gaza. Matthew pointed to the woman's ancestry in identifying her as "a Canaanite woman" (Mt 15:22). This designation heightens the irony, since it portrays her as a descendent of Israel's ancient enemies coming to Israel's Messiah for help. ***Son of David:*** A Gentile had no right to approach Him on that basis. That is why He did not answer her at first.

Mt 15:24 *lost sheep of the house of Israel:* The personal ministry of Christ, like that of the apostles (see 10:5-6), was first offered to the Jews.

Mt 15:25 Dropping the title *Son of David,* she worshiped Him, saying, *"Lord, help me!"* If she could not come to Him as a Jew to her Messiah, she would come as a servant to her Master.

Mt 15:27 *dogs:* Greek *kunaria,* our word *canine.* The word is for "little, domesticated dog," such as would be common under the dinner table.

Mk 7:24-30 Jesus' words to the woman in verse 27 seem unduly harsh. Jews sometimes referred to Gentiles as "dogs" and many suspect that Jesus was issuing a similar insult. However, Jesus used a diminutive form ("pet dog") which is not used elsewhere in a pejorative sense. The diminutive form functions as a term of endearment in a household illustration. A person loves a household pet and desires to meet its needs, but he cannot prioritize the needs of his pet above those of his own children. Similarly, Jesus had a covenant obligation to prioritize the spiritual needs of Israel. The word "first" shows that Jesus did not intend to neglect the spiritual needs of the Gentiles. He would address their needs after giving proper attention to the Jewish people. She acknowledges the priority of Israel but believes that just a leftover crumb of attention from Jesus is sufficient to meet her need. In response to her words, Jesus heals her daughter.

Mk 7:26 *Greek:* In this context, "Greek" is equivalent to the term "Gentile," that is, someone who is not Jewish (see Rm 1:16; 2:9-10; 3:9; 10:12; 1 Co 1:22-24; 12:13; Gl 3:28). The woman was not Greek in her ethnic origin, since Mark immediately describes her nationality as Syrophoenician. Phoenicia was the coastal area of the Roman province of Syria, along the Mediterranean Sea north of the land of Israel.

Sec. 79   Jesus Does Everything Well; Feeds 4,000

Matthew 15:29-38	Mark 7:31–8:9

29 Moving on from there, Jesus passed along the Sea of Galilee. He went up on a mountain and sat there,

31 Again, leaving the region of Tyre, He went by way of Sidon to the Sea of Galilee, through[a] the region of the •Decapolis. **32** They brought to Him a deaf man who also had a speech difficulty, and begged Jesus to lay His hand on him. **33** So He took him away from the crowd privately. After putting His fingers in the man's ears and spitting, He touched his tongue. **34** Then, looking up to heaven, He sighed deeply and said to him, *"Ephphatha!"*[b]

30 and large crowds came to Him, having with them the lame, the blind, the deformed, those unable to speak, and many others. They put them at His feet, and He healed them. **31** So the crowd was amazed when they saw those unable to speak talking, the deformed restored, the lame walking, and the blind seeing. And they gave glory to the God of Israel.

(that is, "Be opened!"). **35** Immediately his ears were opened, his speech difficulty was removed,[c] and he began to speak clearly. **36** Then He ordered them to tell no one, but the more He would order them, the more they would proclaim it.

32 Now Jesus summoned His disciples and said, "I have compassion on the crowd, because they've already stayed with Me three days and have nothing to eat. I don't want to send them away hungry; otherwise they might collapse on the way."

37 They were extremely astonished and said, "He has done everything well! He even makes deaf people hear, and people unable to speak, talk!"

1 In those days there was again a large crowd, and they had nothing to eat. He summoned the disciples and said to them, **2** "I have compassion on the crowd, because they've already stayed with Me three days and have nothing to eat. **3** If I send them home hungry,[d] they will collapse on the way, and some of them have come a long distance."

33 The disciples said to Him, "Where could we get enough bread in this desolate place to fill such a crowd?"

34 "How many loaves do you have?" Jesus asked them.

"Seven," they said, "and a few small fish."

4 His disciples answered Him, "Where can anyone get enough bread here in this desolate place to fill these people?"

5 "How many loaves do you have?" He asked them.

"Seven," they said. **6** Then He commanded the crowd to sit down on the ground. Taking the seven loaves, He gave thanks, broke the ⌊loaves⌋, and kept on giving ⌊them⌋ to His disciples to set before ⌊the people⌋. So they served the ⌊loaves⌋ to the crowd. **7** They also had a few small fish, and when He had blessed them, He said these were to be served as well.

35 After commanding the crowd to sit down on the ground, **36** He took the seven loaves and the fish, and He gave thanks, broke them, and kept on giving them to the disciples, and the disciples ⌊gave them⌋ to the crowds.

a7:31 Or *into*   **b7:34** An Aram expression   **c7:35** Lit *opened, the bond of his tongue was untied*   **d8:3** Or *fasting*

Mt 15:32-38 Critics claim that the feeding of the 4,000 was merely an adaptation of the previous miracle of feeding 5,000. A careful examination of the records shows that this accusation is ungrounded: the ethnic makeup of the crowd was different, the number of people and the baskets left over are different, and the place is not the same. In Matthew 16:5-12 Jesus Himself shows that they are two different events.

Mk 7:31-37 Jesus' travel through Decapolis may indicate that Jesus focused His ministry primarily on Gentiles during this time, thus fulfilling the intention that He expressed in Mark 7:27. The healing of the deaf man marks Jesus' fulfillment of Isaiah 35:5, a passage which, according to first-century Jewish belief, related to the reign of the Messiah.

Mk 7:34 *Ephphatha:* The command *ephphatha* means "be opened" or "be released" in Aramaic, which was probably the everyday language of Jesus. Aramaic words turn up at various places in Mark's narrative: *Boanerges* (3:17); *talitha koum* (5:41); *ephphatha* (7:34); *hosanna* (11:9-10); *Abba* (14:36); *Eloi, Eloi lema sabachthani* (15:34). Mark translates all of these words for his Greek-speaking audience, with the exception of the word *hosanna* (11:9-10).

Mk 8:1 *In those days:* The last location mentioned in the narrative is "the region of the Decapolis" (Mk 7:31), a largely Gentile territory on the southeast side of the Sea of Galilee. The phrase "in those days" indicates that Jesus is still ministering in that same area. Mark's Gospel includes two similar miracles in which Jesus feeds a large crowd (6:31-44; 8:1-9). The most significant difference between the two events is that the first one takes place in a predominantly Jewish area, while the second occurs in a predominantly Gentile area.

Matthew 15:29-38 (cont.)	Mark 7:31–8:9 (cont.)
37 They all ate and were filled. Then they collected the leftover pieces—seven large baskets full. 38 Now those who ate were 4,000 men, besides women and children.	8 They ate and were filled. Then they collected seven large baskets of leftover pieces. 9 About 4,000 ⌊men⌋ were there.

Sec. 80   The Sign of Jonah

Matthew 15:39–16:4	Mark 8:10-12
39 After dismissing the crowds, He got into the boat and went to the region of Magadan.a 1 The •Pharisees and •Sadducees approached, and as a test, asked Him to show them a sign from heaven. 2 He answered them: "When evening comes you say, 'It will be good weather because the sky is red.' 3 And in the morning, 'Today will be stormy because the sky is red and threatening.' Youb know how to read the appearance of the sky, but you can't read the signs of the times.c 4 An evil and adulterous generation demands a sign, but no sign will be given to it except the sign ofd Jonah." Then He left them and went away.	10 and immediately got into the boat with His disciples and went to the district of Dalmanutha.a 11 The •Pharisees came out and began to argue with Him, demanding of Him a sign from heaven to test Him. 12 But sighing deeply in His spirit, He said, "Why does this generation demand a sign? •I assure you: No sign will be given to this generation!"
a**15:39** Other mss read *Magdala* b**16:3** Other mss read *Hypocrites! You* c**16:2-3** Other mss omit *When* (v. 2) through end of v. 3 d**16:4** Other mss add *the prophet*	a**8:10** Probably on the western shore of the Sea of Galilee

Mt 16:1 *show them a sign:* This was the fourth time the religious leaders had asked for a sign (Mt 12:38; Jn 2:12; 6:30). Miracles do not convince people of sin or give a desire for salvation, but they do offer confirmation where there is genuine faith.

Mt 16:2-3 When they saw a *red* sky in the *evening,* they forecasted *good weather* for the next day. They also knew that a *red, threatening* sky *in the morning* meant storms for that day. They had expertise in interpreting the appearance of the sky, but they could not interpret *the signs of the times.*

Mt 16:4 *sign of Jonah:* Jesus had mentioned the sign of Jonah before (see Mt 12:38-45). It spoke of the Lord's crucifixion, burial, and resurrection, which were a sign to Israel that He was their Messiah.

Mk 8:11 *a sign:* The Pharisees are demanding a visible demonstration from God that will compel them to believe in Jesus' divine authority. In Mark's Gospel, the desire for a sign has negative connotations, since it reveals a stubborn refusal to believe (Mk 8:11-12; see also 1 Co 1:21-23) or a dangerous openness to deception (Mk 13:4-5,22; see also 2 Th 2:9-10).

Sec. 81   The Yeast of the Pharisees and the Sadducees

Matthew 16:5-12   Mark 8:13-26

⁵ The disciples reached the other shore,ᵃ and they had forgotten to take bread.

⁶ Then Jesus told them, "Watch out and beware of the yeastᵇ of the Pharisees and Sadducees."

⁷ And they discussed among themselves, "We didn't bring any bread."

⁸ Aware of this, Jesus said, "You of little faith! Why are you discussing among yourselves that you do not have bread? ⁹ Don't you understand yet? Don't you remember the five loaves for the 5,000 and how many baskets you collected? ¹⁰ Or the seven loaves for the 4,000 and how many large baskets you collected? ¹¹ Why is it you don't understand that when I told you, 'Beware of the yeast of the Pharisees and Sadducees,' it wasn't about bread?" ¹² Then they understood that He did not tell them to beware of the yeast in bread, but of the teaching of the Pharisees and Sadducees.

ᵃ16:5 Lit *disciples went to the other side*   ᵇ16:6 Or *leaven*

¹³ Then He left them, got on board ⌊the boat⌋ again, and went to the other side.

¹⁴ They had forgotten to take bread and had only one loaf with them in the boat. ¹⁵ Then He commanded them: "Watch out! Beware of the yeast of the Pharisees and the yeast of •Herod."

¹⁶ They were discussing among themselves that they did not have any bread. ¹⁷ Aware of this, He said to them, "Why are you discussing that you do not have any bread? Don't you yet understand or comprehend? Is your heart hardened? ¹⁸ **Do you have eyes, and not see, and do you have ears, and not hear?**ᵃ And do you not remember? ¹⁹ When I broke the five loaves for the 5,000, how many baskets full of pieces of bread did you collect?"

"Twelve," they told Him.

²⁰ "When I broke the seven loaves for the 4,000, how many large baskets full of pieces of bread did you collect?"

"Seven," they said.

²¹ And He said to them, "Don't you understand yet?"

²² Then they came to Bethsaida. They brought a blind man to Him and begged Him to touch him. ²³ He took the blind man by the hand and brought him out of the village. Spitting on his eyes and laying His hands on him, He asked him, "Do you see anything?"

²⁴ He looked up and said, "I see people—they look to me like trees walking."

²⁵ Again Jesus placed His hands on the man's eyes, and he saw distinctly. He was cured and could see everything clearly. ²⁶ Then He sent him home, saying, "Don't even go into the village."ᵇ

ᵃ8:18 Jr 5:21; Ezk 12:2   ᵇ8:26 Other mss add *or tell anyone in the village*

Mt 16:7 *We didn't bring any bread:* The disciples totally missed the point of Jesus' warning against the "leaven" of the Pharisees' and Sadducees' corrupt religion.

Mk 8:15 *the yeast of the Pharisees and the yeast of Herod:* As a metaphor, yeast symbolizes something small that has the power to permeate and to spread its influence throughout, often negatively (see 1 Co 5:6; Gl 5:9). Matthew's Gospel is more explicit in identifying this yeast as false teaching (Mt 16:12), while Mark's Gospel leaves Jesus' reference to yeast as an unexplained riddle, one that is misunderstood by the disciples (Mk 8:15-16). Luke records a similar warning by Jesus but on a different occasion to a broader audience (Lk 12:1). Luke's Gospel equates the yeast of the Pharisees with hypocrisy.

Mk 8:22-26 The miracles in 7:31-36 and 22-26 are closely connected. Both miracles function as fulfillments of Isaiah 35:5. In both miracles, Jesus applied spit to the person that He healed. The miracles serve as brackets for the question in 8:18, "Do you have eyes and not see, and do you have ears and not hear?" The question refers to spiritual sight and spiritual understanding. Thus these two healing miracles portray Jesus' ability to open spiritual eyes and ears and to give people the ability to understand spiritual truths. Jesus performed literal and historical miracles, but these miracles provided pictures of spiritual realities. This probably explains why Jesus healed the blind man gradually rather than instantaneously. He wanted to show that spiritual enlightenment is often a gradual process.

Mk 8:25 *Again Jesus placed His hands on the man's eyes:* This miracle story is unique in the Gospels in that the miracle requires a second touch by Jesus to bring about a complete restoration for the blind man. Jesus begins by healing the man's blindness, and then after placing His hands on his eyes again He gives clear sight to the man. The placement of this story in the flow of Mark's narrative is important because Jesus has just finished accusing His disciples of spiritual blindness (8:18) and in the next scene He will rebuke them for their inadequate perception of His identity (8:29-33). The healing of the blind man in two stages creates the expectation that Jesus is able to heal both blindness and inadequate perception, whether physical or spiritual.

Sec. 82   Peter's Confession of the Messiah

Matthew 16:13-20	Mark 8:27-30	Luke 9:18-21

13 When Jesus came to the region of Caesarea Philippi,[a] He asked His disciples, "Who do people say that the •Son of Man is?"[b]

14 And they said, "Some say John the Baptist; others, Elijah; still others, Jeremiah or one of the prophets."

15 "But you," He asked them, "who do you say that I am?"

16 Simon Peter answered, "You are the •Messiah, the Son of the living God!"

17 And Jesus responded, "Simon son of Jonah,[c] you are blessed because flesh and blood did not reveal this to you, but My Father in heaven. 18 And I also say to you that you are Peter,[d] and on this rock[e] I will build My church, and the forces[f] of •Hades will not overpower it. 19 I will give you the keys of the kingdom of heaven, and whatever you bind on earth is already bound[g] in heaven, and whatever you loose on earth is already loosed[h] in heaven."

[a]**16:13** A town north of Galilee at the base of Mount Hermon   [b]**16:13** Other mss read *that I, the Son of Man, am*   [c]**16:17** Or *son of John*   [d]**16:18** *Peter* (Gk *Petros*) = a specific stone or rock   [e]**16:18** *Rock* (Gk *petra*) = a rocky crag or bedrock   [f]**16:18** Lit *gates*   [g]**16:19** Or *earth will be bound*   [h]**16:19** Or *earth will be loosed*

27 Jesus went out with His disciples to the villages of Caesarea Philippi. And on the road He asked His disciples, "Who do people say that I am?"

28 They answered Him, "John the Baptist; others, Elijah; still others, one of the prophets."

29 "But you," He asked them again, "who do you say that I am?"

Peter answered Him, "You are the •Messiah!"

18 While He was praying in private and His disciples were with Him, He asked them, "Who do the crowds say that I am?"

19 They answered, "John the Baptist; others, Elijah; still others, that one of the ancient prophets has come back."[a]

20 "But you," He asked them, "who do you say that I am?"

Peter answered, "God's •Messiah!"

[a]**9:19** Lit *has risen*

Mt 16:13-26 In this event Jesus uses the word "church" for the first time. To become a baptized member of a New Testament Church today the penitent believer must make the same confession of faith that Peter made. Paul adds to that confession in Romans 10:9 a confession that Jesus is Lord and that we believe He died and rose again.

Mt 16:13 *Caesarea Philippi:* A town north of Galilee at the base of Mount Hermon. Philip the tetrarch changed its name from Paneas to Caesarea. Philippi was added to distinguish it from the better-known Caesarea on the coast of Samaria.

Mt 16:18 *you are Peter . . . on this rock:* Jesus used a play on words. *Peter* is from *petros,* which means a stone or loose rock; *rock* is *petra,* a rock mass such as a rocky ledge. So what Jesus really said was " . . . *you are Peter* (stone)*, and on this rock* (massive ledge) *I will build My church.*"

Mt 16:19 *keys of the kingdom:* Keys speak of access or entrance. We see Peter first using the keys on the Day of Pentecost. They were not given to him exclusively, but as a representative of all the disciples. Note that in Matthew 18:18 the same promise is given to them all.

Lk 9:20 *God's Messiah:* This event is told in more detail in Matthew; however, the key element of the event, Peter's confession of Jesus to be the Christ, that is, the Messiah sent by God, is in Matthew, Mark, and Luke. It is on the basis of this belief that Jesus can bless, but as the next events also show, Jesus has much to teach the disciples about what being Messiah means, both in terms of suffering and His exalted status.

Matthew 16:13-20 (cont.)	Mark 8:27-30 (cont.)	Luke 9:18-21 (cont.)
20 And He gave the disciples orders to tell no one that He wasᵃ the Messiah.	30 And He strictly warned them to tell no one about Him.	21 But He strictly warned and instructed them to tell this to no one,

ᵃ**16:20** Other mss add *Jesus*

Mk 8:30 *He strictly warned them to tell no one:* Peter's answer was true; Jesus is the Messiah. Yet Jesus prevented any public declaration of this truth, presumably because of popular misconceptions concerning the nature and mission of the Messiah. In the following verses, Peter shows his own inability to understand appropriately what it means for Jesus to be the Messiah, since he refuses to accept Jesus' teaching concerning His future suffering (8:31-33). If Jesus' own disciples misunderstood, the potential for misunderstanding was even greater in a wider audience. In Mark 9:9, Jesus indicates that the time for the disciples' secrecy would be over at the resurrection, since at that point Jesus' destiny in the cross would be able to clarify His identity as the Messiah.

Sec. 83   Jesus Foretells His Death and Resurrection

Matthew 16:21-26	Mark 8:31-37	Luke 9:22-25
21 From then on Jesus began to point out to His disciples that He must go to Jerusalem and suffer many things from the elders, •chief priests, and •scribes, be killed, and be raised the third day. 22 Then Peter took Him aside and began to rebuke Him, "Oh no,ᵃ Lord! This will never happen to You!" 23 But He turned and told Peter, "Get behind Me, Satan! You are an offense to Me because you're not thinking about God's concerns,ᵇ but man's."	31 Then He began to teach them that the •Son of Man must suffer many things and be rejected by the elders, the •chief priests, and the •scribes, be killed, and rise after three days. 32 He was openly talking about this. So Peter took Him aside and began to rebuke Him. 33 But turning around and looking at His disciples, He rebuked Peter and said, "Get behind Me, Satan, because you're not thinking about God's concerns,ᵃ but man's!"	22 saying, "The •Son of Man must suffer many things and be rejected by the elders, •chief priests, and •scribes, be killed, and be raised the third day."

ᵃ**16:22** Lit *Mercy to You = May God have mercy on You*   ᵇ**16:23** Lit *about the things of God*

ᵃ**8:33** Lit *about the things of God*

Mt 16:23 *Get behind Me, Satan:* Satan is a transliteration from *Satana.* Peter was playing the part of an "adversary" in attempting to turn Jesus aside from obedience to God's will.

Mk 8:31-33 Jesus' prediction goes beyond the information that was available in OT Messianic prophecies and demonstrates his prophetic ability.

Mk 8:31 *the Son of Man:* The most frequently used messianic title in Mark's Gospel is "Son of Man," although in Mark the title only occurs in the sayings of Jesus. Jesus seems to have preferred this title to other possibilities, since when others called Him "the Messiah" or "the Son of God" He identified Himself as "the Son of Man" in His reply to them (8:29-31; 14:61-62; see also 13:21-26). Apparently Jesus maintained this preference because the regular use of a more explicit messianic title would have created expectations that did not match Jesus' own understanding of His mission.

Mk 8:34-38 Mark's Gospel knows nothing of the distinction between believers and disciples. The demands of discipleship described here are for all followers of Jesus without exception. "Take up his cross" does not refer to evangelism, experiencing hardship, or wearing the sign of the cross. It refers to preparation for a martyr's death. True disciples are willing to give their lives literally for the Son of Man.

Lk 9:22 *Son of Man must suffer many things:* This is the first of six predictions of the Passion in Luke (9:44; 12:49-50; 13:33; 17:25; 18:31-33; plus looking back, 24:7,46-47). It combines three major ideas. The Son of Man, although He is the exalted figure of Daniel 7, still must suffer according to the divine plan. This was something Jews did not anticipate about Messiah, expecting Him to be a victorious and powerful figure. This path was a part of the divine necessity about the One sent (Lk 24:44-47). The key time frame for the suffering is three days, probably counted inclusively as it turned out, so Friday is the first day and Sunday is the third.

Lk 9:23 *cross daily:* Only Luke has the detail of the need to take up the cross daily. The need to constantly deny oneself is basic to following in the path Jesus sets, because it may well include suffering.

Matthew 16:21-26 (cont.)	Mark 8:31-37 (cont.)	Luke 9:22-25 (cont.)
²⁴ Then Jesus said to His disciples, "If anyone wants to come with Me, he must deny himself, take up his cross, and follow Me. ²⁵ For whoever wants to save his •life will lose it, but whoever loses his life because of Me will find it. ²⁶ What will it benefit a man if he gains the whole world yet loses his life? Or what will a man give in exchange for his life?	³⁴ Summoning the crowd along with His disciples, He said to them, "If anyone wants to be My follower, he must deny himself, take up his cross, and follow Me. ³⁵ For whoever wants to save his •life will lose it, but whoever loses his life because of Me and the gospel will save it. ³⁶ For what does it benefit a man to gain the whole world yet lose his life? ³⁷ What can a man give in exchange for his life?	²³ Then He said to ⌊them⌋ all, "If anyone wants to come with[a] Me, he must deny himself, take up his cross daily,[b] and follow Me. ²⁴ For whoever wants to save his •life will lose it, but whoever loses his life because of Me will save it. ²⁵ What is a man benefited if he gains the whole world, yet loses or forfeits himself?

[a]9:23 Lit *come after*   **[b]9:23** Other mss omit *daily*

Mk 8:34 *take up his cross:* Crucifixion on a cross was a brutal form of execution, a public event intended to deter others from opposing the ruling authorities. As part of the punishment, the condemned man carried his own cross beam out to the place of execution. There the outstretched arms of the prisoner were tied or nailed to the cross beam, and the beam, along with the prisoner's body, was raised up and fastened to an upright post already implanted in the ground. Jesus calls on His followers to take up the cross, that is, to accept the position of one already condemned to death, already prepared to die at any moment for His sake.

Mk 8:35 *life:* In Mark 8:35-37, Jesus uses the word "life" with a double meaning, for physical existence in the present age and for eternal existence in the age to come. If you cling to your present life at any cost, you will lose out on the more valuable life of the age to come. If you willingly give up your devotion to this present life and all that might be gained from it for the sake of Jesus, you will discover that you have preserved an unending life with God along with its eternal rewards. This eternal life is more valuable than anything in this present world, and only a foolish person would let it slip away.

Lk 9:24 *Save . . . will lose . . . loses . . . will save:* Jesus develops contrast here. In the denial of self that is a part of discipleship, one really gains life by losing the selfishness of life and going Jesus' way. So to lose one's life to Jesus is to gain real life (Jn 10:10).

Sec. 84   Public Commitment to the Son of Man

Matthew 16:27-28	Mark 8:34–9:1	Luke 9:26-27
²⁷ For the Son of Man is going to come with His angels in the glory of His Father, and then He will reward each according to what he has done. ²⁸ •I assure you: There are some standing here who will not taste death until they see the Son of Man coming in His kingdom."	³⁸ For whoever is ashamed of Me and of My words in this adulterous and sinful generation, the Son of Man will also be ashamed of him when He comes in the glory of His Father with the holy angels." ¹ Then He said to them, "•I assure you: There are some standing here who will not taste death until they see the kingdom of God come in power."	²⁶ For whoever is ashamed of Me and My words, the Son of Man will be ashamed of him when He comes in His glory and that of the Father and the holy angels. ²⁷ I tell you the truth: there are some standing here who will not taste death until they see the kingdom of God."

Mk 8:38 *whoever is ashamed:* In a similar statement recorded in Matthew's Gospel, Jesus promises to confess before His Father those who confess Him and deny before His Father those who deny Him (Mt 10:32-33). In Mark 8:38, Jesus' words about being ashamed are comparable to this language of confession and denial. Those who are ashamed of Jesus deny any relationship with Him. They refuse to confess or publicly declare any loyalty to Him. In turn, Jesus will repudiate them and refuse to acknowledge any relationship with them when He comes in the glory of His Father.

Mk 9:1 *until they see the kingdom:* Some object that Jesus' prediction failed since His hearers died before His expected return. The fulfillment of Jesus' promise in Mark 9:1 seems to come in the next passage, at the transfiguration of Jesus (9:2-8). Some of those who were standing there, namely Peter, James, and John, have a "taste" of the coming kingdom when they see Jesus in His glory.

Sec. 85   The Transfiguration

Matthew 17:1-8	Mark 9:2-8	Luke 9:28-36a

1 After six days Jesus took Peter, James, and his brother John and led them up on a high mountain by themselves. **2** He was transformed[a] in front of them, and His face shone like the sun. Even His clothes became as white as the light. **3** Suddenly, Moses and Elijah appeared to them, talking with Him.

2 After six days Jesus took Peter, James, and John and led them up on a high mountain by themselves to be alone. He was transformed[a] in front of them, **3** and His clothes became dazzling—extremely white as no launderer on earth could whiten them. **4** Elijah appeared to them with Moses, and they were talking with Jesus.

28 About eight days after these words, He took along Peter, John, and James and went up on the mountain to pray. **29** As He was praying, the appearance of His face changed, and His clothes became dazzling white. **30** Suddenly, two men were talking with Him— Moses and Elijah. **31** They appeared in glory and were speaking of His death,[a] which He was about to accomplish in Jerusalem. **32** Peter and those with him were in a deep sleep,[b] and when they became fully awake, they saw His glory and the two men who were standing with Him. **33** As the two men were departing from Him,

4 Then Peter said to Jesus, "Lord, it's good for us to be here! If You want, I will make[b] three •tabernacles here: one for You, one for Moses, and one for Elijah."

5 Then Peter said to Jesus, "•Rabbi, it's good for us to be here! Let us make three •tabernacles: one for You, one for Moses, and one for Elijah"— **6** because he did not know what he should say, since they were terrified.

Peter said to Jesus, "Master, it's good for us to be here! Let us make three •tabernacles: one for You, one for Moses, and one for Elijah"— not knowing what he said.

[a]**17:2** Or *transfigured* [b]**17:4** Other mss read *wish, let's make*

[a]**9:2** Or *transfigured*

[a]**9:31** Or *departure*; Gk *exodus* [b]**9:32** Lit *were weighed down with sleep*

Mt 17:1 *high mountain:* Tradition names Mt. Tabor as the scene of the Transfiguration, but that is debatable because the summit of Tabor was occupied by a fortress. It was more likely Mt. Hermon, a snow-capped mountain near Caesarea Philippi.

Mt 17:2 *transformed:* Our word *metamorphosis* comes from the Greek word used here. The scene was a preview of what the Lord Jesus will be like when He comes back to establish His visible kingdom.

Mt 17:4 *tabernacles:* "Booths," shelters formed from branches of trees such as the people customarily made for the Feast of Tabernacles.

Mt 17:5 *voice:* A voice from heaven spoke to Jesus on two other occasions (see Mt 3:17 and Jn 12:28). The words spoken here are the same as at His baptism, with the addition of *Listen to Him!*

Mk 9:2 *After six days:* No other time reference in Mark's Gospel (outside of the passion narrative in chapters 14–16) is so precise as this one. The effect is to link the transfiguration account in Mark 9:2-8 with Jesus' prediction in 9:1. The phrase "after six days" in both Matthew and Mark may also be a deliberate echo of Exodus 24:16, where Moses goes up Mount Sinai after six days in response to the voice of God speaking to him from out of the cloud that had overshadowed the mountain (Mt 17:1; Mk 9:1). Instead of "after six days," Luke's Gospel has "about eight days after," which was probably an equivalent expression to "about a week later" (Lk 9:28).

Mk 9:2-12 Both the dazzling light and the cloud are reminiscent of OT theophanies, visible manifestations of God's presence. The words "This is My beloved Son" are reminiscent of Psalm 2 and thus probably depict the inauguration of Jesus' reign. The statement supports seeing the transfiguration as a fulfillment of Jesus' promise in Mark 9:1.

Lk 9:29 *His face changed:* This scene involves Jesus' giving some of the disciples a glimpse of His glory and receiving a commendation from a heavenly voice that shows He is God's unique Son. The voice repeats what was said at Jesus' baptism by John the Baptist with one addition, the call to listen to Him (Dt 18:15).

Lk 9:33 *three tabernacles:* Peter's response to the scene is a desire to celebrate in a manner that honors Jesus as an equal to Moses and Elijah, a compliment to be sure, but not quite a correct assessment. Tabernacles celebrated God's deliverance of the nation under Moses, and Elijah represents either the prophets or the promise of God's coming one. The heavenly voice makes it clear that Jesus is unique and that the disciples need to listen carefully to His teaching.

Matthew 17:1-8 (cont.)	Mark 9:2-8 (cont.)	Luke 9:28-36a (cont.)
5 While he was still speaking, suddenly a bright cloud covered[a] them, and a voice from the cloud said:	7 A cloud appeared, overshadowing them, and a voice came from the cloud:	34 While he was saying this, a cloud appeared and overshadowed them. They became afraid as they entered the cloud. 35 Then a voice came from the cloud, saying:
This is My beloved Son. I take delight in Him. Listen to Him!	This is My beloved Son; listen to Him!	This is My Son, the Chosen One;[a] listen to Him!
6 When the disciples heard it, they fell facedown and were terrified. 7 Then Jesus came up, touched them, and said, "Get up; don't be afraid." 8 When they looked up they saw no one except Him[b] — Jesus alone.	8 Then suddenly, looking around, they no longer saw anyone with them except Jesus alone.	36 After the voice had spoken, only Jesus was found.

[a]**17:5** Or *enveloped*; Ex 40:34-35
[b]**17:8** Other mss omit *Him*

[a]**9:35** Other mss read *the Beloved*

Sec. 86   The Disciples' Puzzlement Concerning Elijah and the Resurrection

Matthew 17:9-13	Mark 9:9-13	Luke 9:36b
9 As they were coming down from the mountain, Jesus commanded them, "Don't tell anyone about the vision until the •Son of Man is raised[a] from the dead." 10 So the disciples questioned Him, "Why then do the •scribes say that Elijah must come first?" 11 "Elijah is coming[b] and will restore everything," He replied.[c] 12 "But I tell you: Elijah has already come, and they didn't recognize him. On the contrary, they did whatever they pleased to him. In the same way the Son of Man is going to suffer at their hands."[d] 13 Then the disciples understood that He spoke to them about John the Baptist.	9 As they were coming down from the mountain, He ordered them to tell no one what they had seen until the •Son of Man had risen from the dead. 10 They kept this word to themselves, discussing what "rising from the dead" meant. 11 Then they began to question Him, "Why do the •scribes say that Elijah must come first?" 12 "Elijah does come first and restores everything," He replied. "How then is it written about the Son of Man that He must suffer many things and be treated with contempt? 13 But I tell you that Elijah really has come, and they did whatever they pleased to him, just as it is written about him."	They kept silent, and in those days told no one what they had seen.

[a]**17:9** Other mss read *Man has risen*
[b]**17:11** Other mss add *first*   [c]**17:11** Other mss read *Jesus said to them*   [d]**17:12** Lit *suffer by them*

Mt 17:9 *Don't tell anyone about the vision:* They would not be able to understand completely what all this meant until after the resurrection.
Mk 9:12 *Elijah does come:* Here Jesus alludes to Malachi 4:5-6, where God promises to send Elijah before the Day of the Lord, in order that he might restore the hearts of fathers to their children and the hearts of children to their fathers. However, this work of restoration by Elijah and the predicted suffering of the Messiah stand in tension with one another and call for further reflection.

Sec. 87   The Power of Faith over a Demon

Matthew 17:14-21	Mark 9:14-29	Luke 9:37-43a

14 When they reached the crowd, a man approached and knelt down before Him. **15** "Lord," he said, "have mercy on my son, because he has seizures[a] and suffers severely. He often falls into the fire and often into the water. **16** I brought him to Your disciples, but they couldn't heal him."

14 When they came to the disciples, they saw a large crowd around them and scribes disputing with them. **15** All of a sudden, when the whole crowd saw Him, they were amazed[a] and ran to greet Him. **16** Then He asked them, "What are you arguing with them about?"
17 Out of the crowd, one man answered Him, "Teacher, I brought my son to You. He has a spirit that makes him unable to speak. **18** Wherever it seizes him, it throws him down, and he foams at the mouth, grinds his teeth, and becomes rigid. So I asked Your disciples to drive it out, but they couldn't."

37 The next day, when they came down from the mountain, a large crowd met Him. **38** Just then a man from the crowd cried out, "Teacher, I beg You to look at my son, because he's my only ⌊child⌋. **39** Often a spirit seizes him; suddenly he shrieks, and it throws him into convulsions until he foams at the mouth;[a] wounding[b] him, it hardly ever leaves him. **40** I begged Your disciples to drive it out, but they couldn't."

17 Jesus replied, "You unbelieving and rebellious[b] generation! How long will I be with you? How long must I put up with you? Bring him here to Me."

19 He replied to them, "You unbelieving generation! How long will I be with you? How long must I put up with you? Bring him to Me."
20 So they brought him to Him. When the spirit saw Him, it immediately convulsed the boy. He fell to the ground and rolled around, foaming at the mouth. **21** "How long has this been happening to him?" Jesus asked his father.
"From childhood," he said. **22** "And many times it has thrown him into fire or water to destroy him. But if You can do anything, have compassion on us and help us."

41 Jesus replied, "You unbelieving and rebellious[c] generation! How long will I be with you and put up with you? Bring your son here."
42 As the boy was still approaching, the demon knocked him down and threw him into severe convulsions. But Jesus rebuked the •unclean spirit, cured the boy, and gave him back to his father. **43** And they were all astonished at the greatness of God.

[a]**17:15** Lit *he is moonstruck*; thought to be a form of epilepsy [b]**17:17** Or *corrupt*, or *perverted*, or *twisted*; Dt 32:5

[a]**9:15** Or *surprised*

[a]**9:39** Lit *convulsions with foam* [b]**9:39** Or *bruising*, or *mauling* [c]**9:41** Or *corrupt*, or *perverted*, or *twisted*; Dt 32:5

Mt 17:15 *seizures and suffers severely:* Literally "moonstruck," a common term used for epilepsy. Mark described him as a mute, who often fell to the ground foaming at the mouth and grinding his teeth. While these conditions can have a physical cause, this boy was under the control of a demon.

Mk 9:14-29 Some interpreters argue that the symptoms of the demon-possessed man were caused by epilepsy rather than a spiritual condition and that Jesus and the disciples' lack of medical knowledge prompted them to misattribute the malady to demonic activity. However, certain symptoms like the suicidal tendencies and shrieking of the demon during the exorcism do not directly relate to epilepsy. Rather than Jesus and the disciples misunderstanding the event because of a pre-scientific worldview, it is more likely that moderns misunderstand the event because of their anti-supernatural bias.

Mk 9:24 *Help my unbelief:* Faith and unbelief are not mutually exclusive categories in Mark's Gospel (see 4:40). The father of the possessed boy experiences both attitudes at the same time. Those who trust in Jesus may also struggle with doubt during a time of crisis. To this man's credit, he is at least aware of his unbelief and asks for help to overcome it.

Lk 9:41 *unbelieving and rebellious generation:* Jesus rebuked the failure of the disciples to perform this exorcism while He was away. Nonetheless He graciously performed the miracle.

Matthew 17:14-21 (cont.)   Mark 9:14-29 (cont.)

23 Then Jesus said to him, " 'If You can?'ᵃ ᵇ Everything is possible to the one who believes."
24 Immediately the father of the boy cried out, "I do believe! Help my unbelief."
25 When Jesus saw that a crowd was rapidly coming together, He rebuked the •unclean spirit, saying to it, "You mute and deaf spirit,ᶜ I command you: come out of him and never enter him again!"

18 Then Jesus rebuked the demon,ᵃ and itᵇ came out of him, and from that momentᶜ the boy was healed.
19 Then the disciples approached Jesus privately and said, "Why couldn't we drive it out?"
20 "Because of your little faith," Heᵈ told them. "For •I assure you: If you have faith the size ofᵉ a mustard seed, you will tell this mountain, 'Move from here to there,' and it will move. Nothing will be impossible for you. [21 However, this kind does not come out except by prayer and fasting.]"ᶠ

26 Then it came out, shrieking and convulsing himᵈ violently. The boy became like a corpse, so that many said, "He's dead." 27 But Jesus, taking him by the hand, raised him, and he stood up.
28 After He went into a house, His disciples asked Him privately, "Why couldn't we drive it out?"
29 And He told them, "This kind can come out by nothing but prayer [and fasting]."ᵉ

ᵃ**17:18** Lit *rebuked him* or *it*   ᵇ**17:18** Lit *the demon*   ᶜ**17:18** Lit *hour*
ᵈ**17:20** Other mss read *your unbelief," Jesus*   ᵉ**17:20** Lit *faith like*
ᶠ**17:21** Other mss omit bracketed text; Mk 9:29

ᵃ**9:23** Other mss add *believe*   ᵇ**9:23** Jesus appears to quote the father's words in v. 22 and then comment on them.   ᶜ**9:25** A spirit that caused the boy to be deaf and unable to speak   ᵈ**9:26** Other mss omit *him*   ᵉ**9:29** Other mss omit bracketed text

Mt 17:20 *the size of a mustard seed:* A mustard seed was proverbial for something very small.
Mk 9:29 *prayer:* Mark's Gospel portrays Jesus as regularly finding time for prayer either early in the morning or late in the evening (1:35; 6:46; 14:32-39). Therefore, according to the example left by Jesus, the spiritual authority for dealing with a powerful unclean spirit comes from a life pattern of prayer and dependence on God, not from a specific prayer spoken at the moment of conflict (which, after all, Jesus did not do in this case)

Sec. 88   Jesus' Second Prediction of His Death

Matthew 17:22-23   Mark 9:30-32   Luke 9:43b-45

22 As they were meetingᵃ in Galilee, Jesus told them, "The Son of Man is about to be betrayed into the hands of men. 23 They will kill Him, and on the third day He will be raised up." And they were deeply distressed.

30 Then they left that place and made their way through Galilee, but He did not want anyone to know it. 31 For He was teaching His disciples and telling them, "The Son of Man is being betrayedᵃ into the hands of men. They will kill Him, and after He is killed, He will rise three days later." 32 But they did not understand this statement, and they were afraid to ask Him.

While everyone was amazed at all the things He was doing, He told His disciples, 44 "Let these words sink in:ᵃ the Son of Man is about to be betrayed into the hands of men."
45 But they did not understand this statement; it was concealed from them so that they could not grasp it, and they were afraid to ask Him about it.ᵇ

ᵃ**17:22** Other mss read *were staying*

ᵃ**9:31** Or *handed over*

ᵃ**9:44** Lit *Put these words in your ears*
ᵇ**9:45** Lit *about this statement*

Mk 9:30-32 The disciples' fear was due to Jesus' rebuke of Peter following the first prediction of His death in Mark 8:31-33. This second prediction explicitly mentioned Jesus' betrayal by Judas. The details of the prediction exceed the abilities of mere human prognostication and exhibit Jesus' prophetic power.
Lk 9:45 *did not understand:* When Jesus made this second prediction, Luke notes the disciples' inability to understand. This probably does not mean that they did not understand the sentence but that they did not understand how Jesus could possibly be betrayed and how that belonged in God's plan. The fact that they were afraid to ask Him means they understood what Jesus said, just not how it really would or could work.

Sec. 89   Paying the Temple Tax

Matthew 17:24-27

²⁴ When they came to Capernaum, those who collected the double-drachma tax[a] approached Peter and said, "Doesn't your Teacher pay the double-drachma tax?"

²⁵ "Yes," he said.

When he went into the house, Jesus spoke to him first,[b] "What do you think, Simon? Who do earthly kings collect tariffs or taxes from? From their sons or from strangers?"[c]

²⁶ "From strangers," he said.[d]

"Then the sons are free," Jesus told him. ²⁷ "But, so we won't offend them, go to the sea, cast in a fishhook, and take the first fish that you catch. When you open its mouth you'll find a coin.[e] Take it and give it to them for Me and you."

a17:24 Jewish men paid this tax to support the temple; Ex 30:11-16. A double-drachma could purchase 2 sheep.   **b17:25** Lit *Jesus anticipated him by saying*   **c17:25** Or *foreigners*   **d17:26** Other mss read *Peter said to Him*   **e17:27** Gk *stater*, worth 2 double-drachmas

Mt 17:24 *double-drachma tax:* Jewish men paid this tax to support the temple (Ex 30:11-16). A double-drachma could purchase two sheep.

Mt 17:27 Rather than cause needless offense, Jesus agreed to pay the tax. This miracle is often overlooked: of all the fish in the sea Jesus knew exactly which one had a coin in its mouth!

Sec. 90   Who Is the Greatest?

Matthew 18:1-5	Mark 9:33-37	Luke 9:46-48
¹ At that time[a] the disciples came to Jesus and said, "Who is greatest in the kingdom of heaven?"	³³ Then they came to Capernaum. When He was in the house, He asked them, "What were you arguing about on the way?" ³⁴ But they were silent, because on the way they had been arguing with one another about who was the greatest. ³⁵ Sitting down, He called the Twelve and said to them, "If anyone wants to be first, he must be last of all and servant of all." ³⁶ Then He took a child, had him stand among them, and taking him in His arms, He said to them,	⁴⁶ Then an argument started among them about who would be the greatest of them.
² Then He called a child to Him and had him stand among them. ³ "•I assure you," He said, "unless you are converted[b] and become like children, you will never enter the kingdom of heaven. ⁴ Therefore, whoever humbles himself like this child—this one is the greatest in the kingdom of heaven. ⁵ And whoever welcomes[c] one child like this in My name welcomes Me.	³⁷ "Whoever welcomes[a] one little child such as this in My name welcomes Me. And whoever welcomes Me does not welcome Me, but Him who sent Me."	⁴⁷ But Jesus, knowing the thoughts of their hearts, took a little child and had him stand next to Him. ⁴⁸ He told them, "Whoever welcomes[a] this little child in My name welcomes Me. And whoever welcomes Me welcomes Him who sent Me. For whoever is least among you—this one is great."
a18:1 Lit *hour* **b18:3** Or *are turned around* **c18:5** Or *receives*	**a9:37** Or *Whoever receives*	**a9:48** Or *receives*, throughout the verse

Mt 18:3 *converted:* Or "turned around." Jesus charged them to turn from their sinful ambition and jealousy exhibited in verse 1.

Lk 9:46 *an argument:* While Jesus was discussing His coming suffering, the disciples argued over who was number one among them, showing their lack of understanding.

Lk 9:47 *child:* A child in the ancient world had no real status, so to use a child as an example of the humility one must have was a powerful illustration. To welcome a child was to welcome someone with no status, and yet Jesus gave that child a status equal to His own. In this way, the least are to be seen as great.

Sec. 91   Warnings from Jesus

Matthew 18:6-14	Mark 9:38-50	Luke 9:49-50

Mark 9:38-50

³⁸ John said to Him, "Teacher, we saw someone^a driving out demons in Your name, and we tried to stop him because he wasn't following us." ³⁹ "Don't stop him," said Jesus, "because there is no one who will perform a miracle in My name who can soon afterward speak evil of Me. ⁴⁰ For whoever is not against us is for us. ⁴¹ And whoever gives you a cup of water to drink because of My name,^b since you belong to the •Messiah—I assure you: He will never lose his reward.

Luke 9:49-50

⁴⁹ John responded, "Master, we saw someone driving out demons in Your name, and we tried to stop him because he does not follow us." ⁵⁰ "Don't stop him," Jesus told him, "because whoever is not against you is for you."^a

^a**9:50** Other mss read *against us is for us*

Matthew 18:6-14

⁶ "But whoever •causes the downfall of one of these little ones who believe in Me—it would be better for him if a heavy millstone^a were hung around his neck and he were drowned in the depths of the sea! ⁷ Woe to the world because of offenses.^b For offenses must come, but woe to that man by whom the offense comes. ⁸ If your hand or your foot causes your downfall, cut it off and throw it away. It is better for you to enter life maimed or lame, than to have two hands or two feet and be thrown into the eternal fire. ⁹ And if your eye causes your downfall, gouge it out and throw it away. It is better for you to enter life with one eye, rather than to have two eyes and be thrown into •hellfire!^c

Mark 9:42

⁴² "But whoever •causes the downfall of one of these little ones who believe in Me—it would be better for him if a heavy millstone^c were hung around his neck and he were thrown into the sea. ⁴³ And if your hand causes your downfall, cut it off. It is better for you to enter life maimed than to have two hands and go to •hell—the unquenchable fire, [⁴⁴ where

^a**9:38** Other mss add *who didn't go along with us* ^b**9:41** Lit *drink in the name;* = Messiah ^c**9:42** A millstone turned by a donkey

^a**18:6** A millstone turned by a donkey ^b**18:7** Or *causes of stumbling* ^c**18:9** Lit *gehenna of fire*

Mt 18:6 *causes the downfall:* The Greek word is *skandalizō* and refers to a cause for offense or stumbling.

Mt 18:8-9 This is Christ's way of saying that anything, however dear, must be sacrificed if it is a hindrance to salvation (5:29).

Mk 9:39-41 At first glance, the statement in v. 40 seems to conflict with Matthew 12:30 and Luke 11:23. However, the situations are quite different. Although Mark's text relates to someone who recognized and respected Jesus' authority over demonic spirits, Matthew and Luke's texts deal with opponents of Jesus who attributed his exorcisms to the power of Satan.

Mk 9:42 *a heavy millstone:* A more literal translation for this phrase would be "a donkey-driven millstone." Some millstones (flat stones used for grinding grain into flour) were small enough to be moved by hand. Others, such as the one mentioned in this verse, were so large and heavy that they required the strength of a donkey to be turned around. Jesus' words respond to His disciples' uncompassionate rejection of the man mentioned in vv. 38-39. Believers should embrace new believers and offer them guidance rather than rejecting them and possibly causing their spiritual downfall.

Mk 9:43 *hell:* The word for hell in this verse (Gehenna) comes from the Hebrew name for the Valley of Hinnom, a valley south of Jerusalem. During the reigns of Ahaz and Manasseh, this valley served as a place for offering child sacrifices to the god Molech (2 Kg 16:3; 21:6; Jr 7:31; 32:35). Because of this abomination, the reforming king Josiah defiled the valley, putting an end to child sacrifice (2 Kg 23:10). Thereafter, the valley became a place for burning garbage. Eventually Gehenna came to be a symbolic name for hell, the place where God judges the wicked with an unquenchable fire.

Lk 9:50 *Don't stop him:* Again the disciples needed instruction. They were to regard those who work in Jesus' name as a part of them. Their role as the Twelve was not one in which they were to be the only ministers for Jesus.

Matthew 18:6-14 (cont.)

Mark 9:38-50 (cont.)

10 "See that you don't look down on one of these little ones, because I tell you that in heaven their angels continually view the face of My Father in heaven. [11 For the •Son of Man has come to save the lost.]ᵃ

**Their worm does not die,
and the fire is not quenched.**]ᵃ ᵇ

45 And if your foot causes your downfall, cut it off. It is better for you to enter life lame than to have two feet and be thrown into hell— [the unquenchable fire, 46 where

**Their worm does not die,
and the fire is not quenched.**]ᵃ ᵇ

47 And if your eye causes your downfall, gouge it out. It is better for you to enter the kingdom of God with one eye than to have two eyes and be thrown into hell, 48 where

**Their worm does not die,
and the fire is not quenched.**ᵇ

49 For everyone will be salted with fire.ᶜ ᵈ 50 Salt is good, but if the salt should lose its flavor, how can you make it salty? Have salt among yourselves and be at peace with one another."

12 What do you think? If a man has 100 sheep, and one of them goes astray, won't he leave the 99 on the hillside and go and search for the stray? 13 And if he finds it, I assure you: He rejoices over that sheepᵇ more than over the 99 that did not go astray. 14 In the same way, it is not the will of your Father in heaven that one of these little ones perish.

ᵃ**9:44,46** Other mss omit bracketed text ᵇ**9:44,46,48** Is 66:24
ᶜ**9:49** Other mss add *and every sacrifice will be salted with salt*
ᵈ**9:49** Lv 2:16; Ezk 43:24

ᵃ**18:11** Other mss omit bracketed text ᵇ**18:13** Lit *over it*

Mt 18:10 *angels:* Probably guardian angels who serve mankind (see also Heb 1:14) and have access to the very presence of God.

Mt 18:14 *not the will of your Father . . . perish:* If they are important enough to have the attention of angels, the Lord Jesus, and God the Father, then clearly we should never despise them, no matter how lowly they might seem.

Mk 9:43-48 Jesus taught elsewhere that one's heart, rather than various limbs of his body, was the source of sin (Mk 3:5; 6:52; 7:6,21; 10:5). The call for amputation of the hand and foot and the removal of the eye is a clear example of hyperbole, an intentional exaggeration for the sake of making a point. The point is that one should be willing to take drastic action in order to conquer sin.

Mk 9:49 *salted with fire:* According to the OT, priests were to add salt to certain sacrifices before they offered them to the Lord (Lv 2:13; Ezk 43:24). In this verse, Jesus uses the picture of a sacrificial offering, except that He portrays the sacrifice as seasoned not with salt but with fire, probably as a metaphor for trials and persecution (see 1Pt 1:7; 4:12). Those who escape the fire of hell must realize that they will face the fire of trials and persecution as a part of being pure and acceptable sacrifices to God.

Sec. 92   Restoration and Forgiveness

Matthew 18:15-35

15 "If your brother sins against you,ᵃ go and rebuke him in private.ᵇ If he listens to you, you have won your brother. 16 But if he won't listen, take one or two more with you, so that **by the testimonyᶜ of two or three witnesses every fact may be established.**ᵈ 17 If he pays no attention to them, tell the church.ᵉ But if he

ᵃ**18:15** Other mss omit *against you* ᵇ**18:15** Lit *him between you and him alone* ᶜ**18:16** Lit *mouth* ᵈ**18:16** Dt 19:15 ᵉ**18:17** Or *congregation*

Mt 18:17 *the church:* Or "congregation." The early church was modeled in part after the Jewish synagogues. The question is: what church does Jesus have in mind? Is He speaking prophetically of the time of the Acts or is He affirming that the apostles constituted the first church?

Matthew 18:15-35 (cont.)

doesn't pay attention even to the church, let him be like an unbeliever[a] and a tax collector to you. [18] I assure you: Whatever you bind on earth is already bound[b] in heaven, and whatever you loose on earth is already loosed[c] in heaven. [19] Again, I assure you: If two of you on earth agree about any matter that you[d] pray for, it will be done for you[e] by My Father in heaven. [20] For where two or three are gathered together in My name, I am there among them."

[21] Then Peter came to Him and said, "Lord, how many times could my brother sin against me and I forgive him? As many as seven times?"

[22] "I tell you, not as many as seven," Jesus said to him, "but 70 times seven.[f] [23] For this reason, the kingdom of heaven can be compared to a king who wanted to settle accounts with his •slaves. [24] When he began to settle accounts, one who owed 10,000 talents[g] was brought before him. [25] Since he had no way to pay it back, his master commanded that he, his wife, his children, and everything he had be sold to pay the debt.

[26] "At this, the slave fell facedown before him and said, 'Be patient with me, and I will pay you everything!' [27] Then the master of that slave had compassion, released him, and forgave him the loan.

[28] "But that slave went out and found one of his fellow slaves who owed him 100 •denarii.[h] He grabbed him, started choking him, and said, 'Pay what you owe!'

[29] "At this, his fellow slave fell down[i] and began begging him, 'Be patient with me, and I will pay you back.' [30] But he wasn't willing. On the contrary, he went and threw him into prison until he could pay what was owed. [31] When the other slaves saw what had taken place, they were deeply distressed and went and reported to their master everything that had happened.

[32] "Then, after he had summoned him, his master said to him, 'You wicked slave! I forgave you all that debt because you begged me. [33] Shouldn't you also have had mercy on your fellow slave, as I had mercy on you?' [34] And his master got angry and handed him over to the jailers[j] until he could pay everything that was owed. [35] So My heavenly Father will also do to you if each of you does not forgive his brother[k] from his[l] heart."

[a]**18:17** Or *like a Gentile*   [b]**18:18** Or *earth will be bound*   [c]**18:18** Or *earth will be loosed*   [d]**18:19** Lit *they*   [e]**18:19** Lit *for them*   [f]**18:22** Or *but 77 times*   [g]**18:24** A huge sum of money that could never be repaid by a slave; a talent = 6,000 denarii   [h]**18:28** A small sum compared to 10,000 talents   [i]**18:29** Other mss add *at his feet*   [j]**18:34** Or *torturers*   [k]**18:35** Other mss add *his trespasses*   [l]**18:35** Lit *your*

Mt 18:18 *bind . . . loosed:* These words must be interpreted in light of what precedes. When an assembly, prayerfully and in obedience to the Word, binds disciplinary action upon a person, that action is honored *in heaven.*

Mt 18:21 *how many times:* The Rabbis ruled that no one should ask forgiveness more than three times. Peter's question shows that he had not yet grasped the spirit of Christian forgiveness. Jesus' answer in v. 22 means an indefinite number of times.

Mt 18:24 *10,000 talents:* A talent was 6,000 denarii. Ten thousand times that amount would be several million dollars, an enormous sum for any time.

Mt 18:35 The application of the parable is clear. God is the King and all of us, His servants, have contracted a great debt of sin that we are unable to pay. In wonderful grace and compassion, the Lord paid the debt and granted full and free forgiveness. Now all Christians should exhibit the same willingness to forgive one another.

Sec. 93   Following Jesus

Matthew 8:18-22	Luke 9:57-62
[18] When Jesus saw large crowds[a] around Him, He gave the order to go to the other side ⌊of the sea⌋.[b] [19] A •scribe approached Him and said, "Teacher, I will follow You wherever You go!" [20] Jesus told him, "Foxes have dens and birds of the sky have nests, but the Son of Man has no place to lay His head."	[57] As they were traveling on the road someone said to Him, "I will follow You wherever You go!" [58] Jesus told him, "Foxes have dens, and birds of the sky[a] have nests, but the Son of Man has no place to lay His head." [59] Then He said to another, "Follow Me."
[a]**8:18** Other mss read *saw a crowd* [b]**8:18** Sea of Galilee	[a]**9:58** Wild birds, as opposed to domestic birds "

Mt 8:20 *Son of Man:* A phrase used by Daniel 7:13, and was understood by the Jews to be the Messiah. During our Lord's life He alone applied this title to Himself (more than 80 times). Jesus did something unknown in Judaism at that time—He incorporated the idea of sovereignty and preexistence stressed by Daniel, with the Suffering Servant theme of Isaiah.

Matthew 8:19-22 (cont.)	Luke 9:57-62 (cont.)
21 "Lord," another of His disciples said, "first let me go bury my father."a 22 But Jesus told him, "Follow Me, and let the dead bury their own dead." **a8:21** Not necessarily meaning his father was already dead	"Lord," he said, "first let me go bury my father."a 60 But He told him, "Let the dead bury their own dead, but you go and spread the news of the kingdom of God." 61 Another also said, "I will follow You, Lord, but first let me go and say good-bye to those at my house." 62 But Jesus said to him, "No one who puts his hand to the plow and looks back is fit for the kingdom of God." **a9:59** Not necessarily meaning his father was already dead

Mt 8:22 *let the dead bury their own dead:* This enigmatic expression seems cold and heartless, but the man's father perhaps was old but still living. However interpreted, the statement stresses that following Jesus must take precedence over even family relationships.

Lk 9:57-62 These strong words by Jesus reinforce the priority that comes from being a disciple. Following Jesus is not a hobby. It reflects the highest commitment of life one can make.

Sec. 94   The Unbelief of Jesus' Brothers

John 7:2-9

2 The Jewish Festival of Tabernaclesa b was near, 3 so His brothers said to Him, "Leave here and go to Judea so Your disciples can see Your works that You are doing. 4 For no one does anything in secret while he's seeking public recognition. If You do these things, show Yourself to the world." 5 (For not even His brothers believed in Him.)

6 Jesus told them, "My time has not yet arrived, but your time is always at hand. 7 The world cannot hate you, but it does hate Me because I testify about it—that its deeds are evil. 8 Go up to the festival yourselves. I'm not going up to the festival yet,c because My time has not yet fully come." 9 After He had said these things, He stayed in Galilee.

a7:2 Or *Booths*   **b7:2** One of 3 great Jewish religious festivals, along with Passover and Pentecost; Ex 23:14; Dt 16:16   **c7:8** Other mss omit *yet*

Sec. 95   The Journey to Jerusalem

Luke 9:51-56	John 7:10
51 When the days were coming to a close for Him to be taken up,a He determinedb to journey to Jerusalem. 52 He sent messengers ahead of Him, and on the way they entered a village of the •Samaritans to make	10 After His brothers had gone up to the festival, then He also went up, not openly but secretly.

preparations for Him. 53 But they did not welcome Him, because He determined to journey to Jerusalem. 54 When the disciples James and John saw this, they said, "Lord, do You want us to call down fire from heaven to consume them?"c

55 But He turned and rebuked them,d 56 and they went to another village.

a9:51 His ascension   **b9:51** Lit *He stiffened His face to go;* Is 50:7   **c9:54** Other mss add *as Elijah also did*   **d9:55-56** Other mss add *and said, "You don't know what kind of spirit you belong to.* 56 *For the Son of Man did not come to destroy people's lives but to save them,"*

Lk 9:51-55 This unit begins a long section in Luke 9:52–19:44, where Jesus journeyed to Jerusalem and taught the disciples in preparation for His death and departure. Its organization is unique to Luke, although it develops themes in Mark's Gospel. Many sections unique to Luke appear in this unit, especially many of Jesus' parables. It highlights discipleship, that suffering will come with it, as it also details how the Jewish leadership became more opposed to Jesus despite His warnings to them, and His actions that showed God was with Him before them. This journey is not a straight line trip from Galilee to Jerusalem to meet His death, but a journey of divinely directed events that Jesus had to take.

Lk 9:54 *call down fire:* The disciples asked to exercise judgment like Elijah did. Jesus was simply silent and moved on. The disciples still had much to learn.

PART IX

THE LATER JUDEAN MINISTRY

Sec. 96   Jesus at the Festival of Tabernacles

John 7:11-52

¹¹ The Jews were looking for Him at the festival and saying, "Where is He?" ¹² And there was a lot of discussion about Him among the crowds. Some were saying, "He's a good man." Others were saying, "No, on the contrary, He's deceiving the people." ¹³ Still, nobody was talking publicly about Him because they feared the Jews.

¹⁴ When the festival was already half over, Jesus went up into the •temple complex and began to teach. ¹⁵ Then the Jews were amazed and said, "How does He know the Scriptures, since He hasn't been trained?"

¹⁶ Jesus answered them, "My teaching isn't Mine but is from the One who sent Me. ¹⁷ If anyone wants to do His will, he will understand whether the teaching is from God or if I am speaking on My own. ¹⁸ The one who speaks for himself seeks his own glory. But He who seeks the glory of the One who sent Him is true, and there is no unrighteousness in Him. ¹⁹ Didn't Moses give you the law? Yet none of you keeps the law! Why do you want to kill Me?"

²⁰ "You have a demon!" the crowd responded. "Who wants to kill You?"

²¹ "I did one work, and you are all amazed," Jesus answered. ²² "Consider this: Moses has given you circumcision—not that it comes from Moses but from the fathers—and you circumcise a man on the Sabbath. ²³ If a man receives circumcision on the Sabbath so that the law of Moses won't be broken, are you angry at Me because I made a man entirely well on the Sabbath? ²⁴ Stop judging according to outward appearances; rather judge according to righteous judgment."

²⁵ Some of the people of Jerusalem were saying, "Isn't this the man they want to kill? ²⁶ Yet, look! He's speaking publicly and they're saying nothing to Him. Can it be true that the authorities know He is the •Messiah? ²⁷ But we know where this man is from. When the Messiah comes, nobody will know where He is from."

²⁸ As He was teaching in the temple complex, Jesus cried out, "You know Me and you know where I am from. Yet I have not come on My own, but the One who sent Me is true. You don't know Him; ²⁹ I know Him because I am from Him, and He sent Me."

³⁰ Then they tried to seize Him. Yet no one laid a hand on Him because His hour[a] had not yet come. ³¹ However, many from the crowd believed in Him and said, "When the Messiah comes, He won't perform more signs than this man has done, will He?"

³² The •Pharisees heard the crowd muttering these things about Him, so the •chief priests and the Pharisees sent temple police to arrest Him.

³³ Then Jesus said, "I am only with you for a short time. Then I'm going to the One who sent Me. ³⁴ You will look for Me, but you will not find Me; and where I am, you cannot come."

³⁵ Then the Jews said to one another, "Where does He intend to go so we won't find Him? He doesn't intend to go to the Dispersion[b] among the Greeks and teach the Greeks, does He? ³⁶ What is this remark He made: 'You will look for Me, and you will not find Me; and where I am, you cannot come'?"

³⁷ On the last and most important day of the festival, Jesus stood up and cried out, "If anyone is thirsty, he should come to Me[c] and drink! ³⁸ The one who believes in Me, as the Scripture has said,[d] will have streams of living water flow from deep within him." ³⁹ He said this about the Spirit. Those who believed in Jesus were going to receive the Spirit, for the Spirit[e] had not yet been received,[f] [g] because Jesus had not yet been glorified.

⁴⁰ When some from the crowd heard these words, they said, "This really is the Prophet!"[h] ⁴¹ Others said, "This is the Messiah!" But some said, "Surely the Messiah doesn't come from Galilee, does He? ⁴² Doesn't the Scripture say that the Messiah comes from David's offspring[i] and from the town of Bethlehem, where David once lived?" ⁴³ So a division occurred among the crowd because of Him. ⁴⁴ Some of them wanted to seize Him, but no one laid hands on Him.

ᵃ**7:30** The time of His sacrificial death and exaltation; Jn 2:4; 8:20; 12:23,27; 13:1; 17:1   ᵇ**7:35** Jewish people scattered throughout Gentile lands who spoke Gk and were influenced by Gk culture   ᶜ**7:37** Other mss omit *to Me*   ᵈ**7:38** Jesus may have had several OT passages in mind; Is 58:11; Ezk 47:1-12; Zch 14:8   ᵉ**7:39** Other mss read *Holy Spirit*   ᶠ**7:39** Other mss read *had not yet been given*   ᵍ**7:39** Lit *the Spirit was not yet*; the word *received* is implied from the previous clause.   ʰ**7:40** Probably = the Prophet in Dt 18:15   ⁱ**7:42** Lit *seed*

John 7:11-52 (cont.)

45 Then the temple police came to the chief priests and Pharisees, who asked them, "Why haven't you brought Him?"

46 The police answered, "No man ever spoke like this!"a

47 Then the Pharisees responded to them: "Are you fooled too? 48 Have any of the rulers or Pharisees believed in Him? 49 But this crowd, which doesn't know the law, is accursed!"

50 Nicodemus—the one who came to Him previously, being one of them—said to them, 51 "Our law doesn't judge a man before it hears from him and knows what he's doing, does it?"

52 "You aren't from Galilee too, are you?" they replied. "Investigate and you will see that no prophet arises from Galilee."b

a7:46 Other mss read *like this man*   b7:52 Jonah and probably other prophets did come from Galilee; 2Kgs 14:25

Sec. 97   An Adulteress Forgiven

John 7:53–8:11

[53 So each one went to his house.

1 But Jesus went to the •Mount of Olives.

2 At dawn He went to the •temple complex again, and all the people were coming to Him. He sat down and began to teach them.

3 Then the •scribes and the •Pharisees brought a woman caught in adultery, making her stand in the center. 4 "Teacher," they said to Him, "this woman was caught in the act of committing adultery. 5 In the law Moses commanded us to stone such women. So what do You say?" 6 They asked this to trap Him, in order that they might have evidence to accuse Him.

Jesus stooped down and started writing on the ground with His finger. 7 When they persisted in questioning Him, He stood up and said to them, "The one without sin among you should be the first to throw a stone at her."

8 Then He stooped down again and continued writing on the ground. 9 When they heard this, they left one by one, starting with the older men. Only He was left, with the woman in the center. 10 When Jesus stood up, He said to her, "•Woman, where are they? Has no one condemned you?"

11 "No one, Lord,"a she answered.

"Neither do I condemn you," said Jesus. "Go, and from now on do not sin anymore."]b

a8:11 Or *Sir*; Jn 4:15,49; 5:7; 6:34; 9:36   b8:11 Other mss omit bracketed text

Jn 7:53–8:11 While the story of Jesus and the adulteress may well be authentic, there is considerable debate whether the account is part of John's original Gospel: (1) the account is absent from all of the oldest manuscripts of the Gospel of John; (2) where it does occur in later manuscripts, it is found at various places (after Jn 7:36,44,52; at the end of John's Gospel; or after Lk 21:38); (3) virtually every verse from 8:1-11 (except for 8:5) features words not elsewhere found in John's Gospel, and standard Johannine vocabulary is conspicuously absent; (4) the account appears to interrupt the narrative flow from 7:52 to 8:12, breaking the literary unit 7:1–8:59; and (5) the account is virtually unknown by any of the early church fathers prior to the fourth century. For this reason it may be best to view the story of Jesus and the adulterous woman as a possibly authentic but probably non-Johannine account.

Sec. 98   The Light of the World

John 8:12-20

12 Then Jesus spoke to them again: "I am the light of the world. Anyone who follows Me will never walk in the darkness but will have the light of life."

Jn 8:12 Jesus as "the light of the world" develops further the affirmation in the prologue that Jesus is "the light of men" and that "that light shines in the darkness" (1:4-5). On this basis, Jesus exhorted His hearers to put their trust in the light while they had Him with them, so that they might become "sons of light" (12:35-36). Jesus' concluding testimony was that He came into the world as light so that no one who believes in Him should stay in darkness (12:46). Yet, according to the evangelist, the verdict is this: light has come into the world, but people loved darkness rather than light, because their deeds were evil (3:19-21).

John 8:12-20 (cont.)

¹³ So the Pharisees said to Him, "You are testifying about Yourself. Your testimony is not valid."ᵃ

¹⁴ "Even if I testify about Myself," Jesus replied, "My testimony is valid,ᵇ because I know where I came from and where I'm going. But you don't know where I come from or where I'm going. ¹⁵ You judge by human standards.ᶜ I judge no one. ¹⁶ And if I do judge, My judgment is true, because I am not alone, but I and the Father who sent Me ⌊judge together⌋. ¹⁷ Even in your law it is written that the witness of two men is valid. ¹⁸ I am the One who testifies about Myself, and the Father who sent Me testifies about Me."

¹⁹ Then they asked Him, "Where is Your Father?"

"You know neither Me nor My Father," Jesus answered. "If you knew Me, you would also know My Father." ²⁰ He spoke these words by the treasury,ᵈ while teaching in the temple complex. But no one seized Him, because His hourᵉ had not come.

ᵃ**8:13** The law of Moses required at least 2 witnesses to make a claim legally valid (v. 17).   ᵇ**8:14** Or *true*   ᶜ**8:15** Lit *You judge according to the flesh*   ᵈ**8:20** A place for offerings to be given, perhaps in the court of women   ᵉ**8:20** The time of His sacrificial death and exaltation; Jn 2:4; 7:30; 12:23,27; 13:1; 17:1

Sec. 99   Jesus Predicts His Departure

John 8:21-59

²¹ Then He said to them again, "I'm going away; you will look for Me, and you will die in your sin. Where I'm going, you cannot come."

²² So the •Jews said again, "He won't kill Himself, will He, since He says, 'Where I'm going, you cannot come'?"

²³ "You are from below," He told them, "I am from above. You are of this world; I am not of this •world. ²⁴ Therefore I told you that you will die in your sins. For if you do not believe that I am ⌊He⌋,ᵃ you will die in your sins."

²⁵ "Who are You?" they questioned.

"Precisely what I've been telling you from the very beginning," Jesus told them. ²⁶ "I have many things to say and to judge about you, but the One who sent Me is true, and what I have heard from Him—these things I tell the world."

²⁷ They did not know He was speaking to them about the Father. ²⁸ So Jesus said to them, "When you lift up the •Son of Man, then you will know that I am ⌊He⌋, and that I do nothing on My own. But just as the Father taught Me, I say these things. ²⁹ The One who sent Me is with Me. He has not left Me alone, because I always do what pleases Him."

³⁰ As He was saying these things, many believed in Him. ³¹ So Jesus said to the Jews who had believed Him, "If you continue in My word,ᵇ you really are My disciples. ³² You will know the truth, and the truth will set you free."

³³ "We are descendantsᶜ of Abraham," they answered Him, "and we have never been enslaved to anyone. How can You say, 'You will become free'?"

³⁴ Jesus responded, "•I assure you: Everyone who commits sin is a •slave of sin. ³⁵ A slave does not remain in the household forever, but a son does remain forever. ³⁶ Therefore if the Son sets you free, you really will be free. ³⁷ I know you are descendantsᶜ of Abraham, but you are trying to kill Me because My wordᵇ is not welcome among you. ³⁸ I speak what I have seen in the presence of the Father,ᵈ and therefore you do what you have heard from your father."

³⁹ "Our father is Abraham!" they replied.

"If you were Abraham's children," Jesus told them, "you would do what Abraham did. ⁴⁰ But now you are trying to kill Me, a man who has told you the truth that I heard from God. Abraham did not do this! ⁴¹ You're doing what your father does."

"We weren't born of sexual immorality," they said. "We have one Father—God."

⁴² Jesus said to them, "If God were your Father, you would love Me, because I came from God and I am here. For I didn't come on My own, but He sent Me. ⁴³ Why don't you understand what I say? Because you cannot listen toᵉ My word. ⁴⁴ You are of your father the Devil, and you want to carry out your father's desires. He was a murderer from the beginning and has not stood in the truth, because there is no truth in him. When

ᵃ**8:24** Jesus claimed to be deity, but the Pharisees didn't understand His meaning.   ᵇ**8:31,37** Or *My teaching*, or *My message*   ᶜ**8:33,37** Or *offspring*; lit *seed*; Jn 7:42   ᵈ**8:38** Other mss read *of My Father*   ᵉ**8:43** Or *cannot hear*

John 8:21-59 (cont.)

he tells a lie, he speaks from his own nature,ᵃ because he is a liar and the father of liars.ᵇ ⁴⁵ Yet because I tell the truth, you do not believe Me. ⁴⁶ Who among you can convict Me of sin? If I tell the truth, why don't you believe Me? ⁴⁷ The one who is from God listens to God's words. This is why you don't listen, because you are not from God."

⁴⁸ The Jews responded to Him, "Aren't we right in saying that You're a •Samaritan and have a demon?"

⁴⁹ "I do not have a demon," Jesus answered. "On the contrary, I honor My Father and you dishonor Me. ⁵⁰ I do not seek My glory; the One who seeks it also judges. ⁵¹ I assure you: If anyone keeps My word, he will never see death—ever!"

⁵² Then the Jews said, "Now we know You have a demon. Abraham died and so did the prophets. You say, 'If anyone keeps My word, he will never taste death—ever!' ⁵³ Are You greater than our father Abraham who died? Even the prophets died. Who do You pretend to be?"ᶜ

⁵⁴ "If I glorify Myself," Jesus answered, "My glory is nothing. My Father—you say about Him, 'He is our God'—He is the One who glorifies Me. ⁵⁵ You've never known Him, but I know Him. If I were to say I don't know Him, I would be a liar like you. But I do know Him, and I keep His word. ⁵⁶ Your father Abraham was overjoyed that he would see My day; he saw it and rejoiced."

⁵⁷ The Jews replied, "You aren't 50 years old yet, and You've seen Abraham?"ᵈ

⁵⁸ Jesus said to them, "I assure you: Before Abraham was, I am."ᵉ

⁵⁹ At that, they picked up stones to throw at Him. But Jesus was hiddenᶠ and went out of the temple complex.ᵍ

ᵃ**8:44** Lit *from his own things*   ᵇ**8:44** Lit *of it*   ᶜ**8:53** Lit *Who do You make Yourself?*   ᵈ**8:57** Other mss read *and Abraham has seen You?*
ᵉ**8:58** *I AM* is the name God gave Himself at the burning bush; Ex 3:13-14; see note at Jn 8:24.   ᶠ**8:59** Or *Jesus hid Himself*   ᵍ**8:59** Other mss add *and having gone through their midst, He passed by*

Sec. 100   The Sixth Sign: Healing a Man Born Blind

John 9:1-41

¹As He was passing by, He saw a man blind from birth. ² His disciples questioned Him: "•Rabbi, who sinned, this man or his parents, that he was born blind?"

³ "Neither this man nor his parents sinned," Jesus answered. "⌊This came about⌋ so that God's works might be displayed in him. ⁴ Weᵃ must do the works of Him who sent Meᵇ while it is day. Night is coming when no one can work. ⁵ As long as I am in the world, I am the light of the world."

⁶ After He said these things He spit on the ground, made some mud from the saliva, and spread the mud on his eyes. ⁷ "Go," He told him, "wash in the pool of Siloam" (which means "Sent"). So he left, washed, and came back seeing.

⁸ His neighbors and those who formerly had seen him as a beggar said, "Isn't this the man who sat begging?" ⁹ Some said, "He's the one." "No," others were saying, "but he looks like him."

He kept saying, "I'm the one!"

¹⁰ Therefore they asked him, "Then how were your eyes opened?"

¹¹ He answered, "The man called Jesus made mud, spread it on my eyes, and told me, 'Go to Siloam and wash.' So when I went and washed I received my sight."

¹² "Where is He?" they asked.

"I don't know," he said.

¹³ They brought the man who used to be blind to the •Pharisees. ¹⁴ The day that Jesus made the mud and opened his eyes was a Sabbath. ¹⁵ So again the Pharisees asked him how he received his sight.

"He put mud on my eyes," he told them. "I washed and I can see."

¹⁶ Therefore some of the Pharisees said, "This man is not from God, for He doesn't keep the Sabbath!" But others were saying, "How can a sinful man perform such signs?" And there was a division among them.

ᵃ**9:4** Other mss read *I*   ᵇ**9:4** Other mss read *sent us*

Jn 9:1-41 Jesus' claim of being "the light of the world" is promptly given expression in His sixth and penultimate "sign" recorded in this Gospel, healing the man born blind. The account of the healing in chapter 9 and the "Good Shepherd" discourse in chapter 10 form another unit, evident from the lack of transition between these two chapters. As in chapter 5, Jesus healed a man on a Sabbath and promptly suffered persecution from the Jewish leaders for making mud in the process of healing the blind man (9:6,13-16). In contrast to the sick man in chapter 5, however, who not only showed no faith but reported Jesus to the authorities, the formerly blind man showed a progression of faith and ended up falling down at Jesus' feet in worship (9:38). The Pharisees, for their part, were confirmed in their spiritual blindness (9:40-41).

John 9:1-41 (cont.)

17 Again they asked the blind man,[a] "What do you say about Him, since He opened your eyes?" "He's a prophet," he said.

18 The •Jews did not believe this about him—that he was blind and received sight—until they summoned the parents of the one who had received his sight.

19 They asked them, "Is this your son, ⌊the one⌋ you say was born blind? How then does he now see?"

20 "We know this is our son and that he was born blind," his parents answered. 21 "But we don't know how he now sees, and we don't know who opened his eyes. Ask him; he's of age. He will speak for himself."

22 His parents said these things because they were afraid of the Jews, since the Jews had already agreed that if anyone confessed Him as •Messiah, he would be banned from the •synagogue. 23 This is why his parents said, "He's of age; ask him."

24 So a second time they summoned the man who had been blind and told him, "Give glory to God.[b] We know that this man is a sinner!"

25 He answered, "Whether or not He's a sinner, I don't know. One thing I do know: I was blind, and now I can see!"

26 Then they asked him, "What did He do to you? How did He open your eyes?"

27 "I already told you," he said, "and you didn't listen. Why do you want to hear it again? You don't want to become His disciples too, do you?"

28 They ridiculed him: "You're that man's disciple, but we're Moses' disciples. 29 We know that God has spoken to Moses. But this man—we don't know where He's from!"

30 "This is an amazing thing," the man told them. "You don't know where He is from, yet He opened my eyes! 31 We know that God doesn't listen to sinners, but if anyone is God-fearing and does His will, He listens to him. 32 Throughout history[c] no one has ever heard of someone opening the eyes of a person born blind. 33 If this man were not from God, He wouldn't be able to do anything."

34 "You were born entirely in sin," they replied, "and are you trying to teach us?" Then they threw him out.[d]

35 When Jesus heard that they had thrown the man out, He found him and asked, "Do you believe in the •Son of Man?"[e]

36 "Who is He, Sir, that I may believe in Him?" he asked.

37 Jesus answered, "You have seen Him; in fact, He is the One speaking with you."

38 "I believe, Lord!" he said, and he worshiped Him.

39 Jesus said, "I came into this world for judgment, in order that those who do not see will see and those who do see will become blind."

40 Some of the Pharisees who were with Him heard these things and asked Him, "We aren't blind too, are we?"

41 "If you were blind," Jesus told them, "you wouldn't have sin.[f] But now that you say, 'We see'—your sin remains.

---

[a]**9:17** = the man who had been blind   [b]**9:24** *Give glory to God* was a solemn charge to tell the truth; Jos 7:19.   [c]**9:32** Lit *From the age*   [d]**9:34** = they banned him from the synagogue; v. 22   [e]**9:35** Other mss read *the Son of God*   [f]**9:41** To *have sin* is an idiom that refers to guilt caused by sin.

Sec. 101   The Ideal Shepherd

John 10:1-21

1"•I assure you: Anyone who doesn't enter the sheep pen by the door but climbs in some other way, is a thief and a robber. 2 The one who enters by the door is the shepherd of the sheep. 3 The doorkeeper opens it for him, and the sheep hear his voice. He calls his own sheep by name and leads them out. 4 When he has brought all his own outside, he goes ahead of them. The sheep follow him because they recognize his voice. 5 They will never follow a stranger; instead they will run away from him, because they don't recognize the voice of strangers."

Jn 10:1-42 In His "Good Shepherd" discourse, Jesus chastised the Jewish leaders for failing to give proper spiritual guidance to God's people Israel. By contrast, He is the "good Shepherd" who laid down His life for the sheep. Hence chapter 10 provides a commentary on the previous chapter that revealed the Jewish leaders' legal pettiness, rigidity, and hardening toward the purposes of God. Not only is Jesus the good shepherd, He is also the door through which those who believe in Him find entrance into abundant, eternal life (10:9-10). The following interchange, culminating in yet another attempt at stoning Jesus on account of blasphemy, took place at the Festival of Dedication (10:22-39). It is followed by a final reference to the Baptist, which closes out the "festival cycle" of chapter 5 through 10 and the entire section 1:19–10:42, which began with an account of the Baptist's ministry and witness to Jesus.

John 10:1-21 (cont.)

[6] Jesus gave them this illustration, but they did not understand what He was telling them.

[7] So Jesus said again, "I assure you: I am the door of the sheep. [8] All who came before Me[a] are thieves and robbers, but the sheep didn't listen to them. [9] I am the door. If anyone enters by Me, he will be saved and will come in and go out and find pasture. [10] A thief comes only to steal and to kill and to destroy. I have come so that they may have life and have it in abundance.

[11] "I am the good shepherd. The good shepherd lays down his life for the sheep. [12] The hired man, since he is not the shepherd and doesn't own the sheep, leaves them[b] and runs away when he sees a wolf coming. The wolf then snatches and scatters them. [13] ⌊This happens⌋ because he is a hired man and doesn't care about the sheep.

[14] "I am the good shepherd. I know My own sheep, and they know Me, [15] as the Father knows Me, and I know the Father. I lay down My life for the sheep. [16] But I have other sheep that are not of this fold; I must bring them also, and they will listen to My voice. Then there will be one flock, one shepherd. [17] This is why the Father loves Me, because I am laying down My life so I may take it up again. [18] No one takes it from Me, but I lay it down on My own. I have the right to lay it down, and I have the right to take it up again. I have received this command from My Father."

[19] Again a division took place among the Jews because of these words. [20] Many of them were saying, "He has a demon and He's crazy! Why do you listen to Him?" [21] Others were saying, "These aren't the words of someone demon-possessed. Can a demon open the eyes of the blind?"

[a]**10:8** Other mss omit *before Me*   [b]**10:12** Lit *leaves the sheep*

Sec. 102   Sending Out the Seventy

Luke 10:1-24

[1] After this, the Lord appointed 70[a] others, and He sent them ahead of Him in pairs to every town and place where He Himself was about to go. [2] He told them: "The harvest is abundant, but the workers are few. Therefore, pray to the Lord of the harvest to send out workers into His harvest. [3] Now go; I'm sending you out like lambs among wolves. [4] Don't carry a money-bag, traveling bag, or sandals; don't greet anyone along the road. [5] Whatever house you enter, first say, 'Peace to this household.' [6] If a son of peace[b] is there, your peace will rest on him; but if not, it will return to you. [7] Remain in the same house, eating and drinking what they offer, for the worker is worthy of his wages. Don't be moving from house to house. [8] When you enter any town, and they welcome you, eat the things set before you. [9] Heal the sick who are there, and tell them, 'The kingdom of God has come near you.' [10] When you enter any town, and they don't welcome you, go out into its streets and say, [11] 'We are wiping off ⌊as a witness⌋ against you even the dust of your town that clings to our feet. Know this for certain: the kingdom of God has come near.' [12] I tell you, on that day it will be more tolerable for Sodom than for that town.

[13] "Woe to you, Chorazin! Woe to you, Bethsaida! For if the miracles that were done in you had been done in Tyre and Sidon, they would have repented long ago, sitting in sackcloth and ashes! [14] But it will be more tolerable for Tyre and Sidon at the judgment than for you. [15] And you, Capernaum, will you be exalted to heaven? No, you will go down to •Hades! [16] Whoever listens to you listens to Me. Whoever rejects you rejects Me. And whoever rejects Me rejects the One who sent Me."

[a]**10:1** Other mss read 72   [b]**10:6** A peaceful person; one open to the message of the kingdom

Lk 10:1-12 Many of the instructions here repeat what was said in Luke 9:1-6. Luke is the only Gospel to note two such missions: the Twelve and the seventy.

Lk 10:2 *the Lord of the harvest:* Although Jesus sent out 70 here, He told them to pray for more help to bring in the "harvest" of those who would respond to His sowing of the seed of the word of the kingdom. Harvest imagery merely extends the seed and fruit picture of the parable of the sower of the seed in Luke 8.

Lk 10:9 *The kingdom of God has come near:* This message of the 70 meant that God's promised rule had shown up in the person of the Messiah Jesus. To reject Him is to reject the kingdom. To receive Him is to receive God's peace and be a child of the king.

Lk 10:12 *more tolerable for Sodom:* There is no judgment greater than the one that comes to one for rejecting God's kingdom and the Son who ministers in it.

Lk 10:13-16 This unit is unique to Luke and indicates the risk that towns have put themselves under by rejecting the message of the kingdom and the opportunity to experience God's blessing and salvation.

Luke 10:1-24 (cont.)

[17] The Seventy[a] returned with joy, saying, "Lord, even the demons submit to us in Your name."
[18] He said to them, "I watched Satan fall from heaven like a lightning flash. [19] Look, I have given you the authority to trample on snakes and scorpions and over all the power of the enemy; nothing will ever harm you. [20] However, don't rejoice that[b] the spirits submit to you, but rejoice that your names are written in heaven."
[21] In that same hour He[c] rejoiced in the Holy[d] Spirit and said, "I praise[e] You, Father, Lord of heaven and earth, because You have hidden these things from the wise and the learned and have revealed them to infants. Yes, Father, because this was Your good pleasure.[f] [22] All things have[g] been entrusted to Me by My Father. No one knows who the Son is except the Father, and who the Father is except the Son, and anyone to whom the Son desires[h] to reveal Him."
[23] Then turning to His disciples He said privately, "The eyes that see the things you see are blessed! [24] For I tell you that many prophets and kings wanted to see the things you see yet didn't see them; to hear the things you hear yet didn't hear them."

[a]**10:17** Other mss read *The Seventy-two*   [b]**10:20** Lit *don't rejoice in this, that*   [c]**10:21** Other mss read *Jesus*   [d]**10:21** Other mss omit *Holy*
[e]**10:21** Or *thank*, or *confess*   [f]**10:21** Lit *was well-pleasing in Your sight*   [g]**10:22** Other mss read *And turning to the disciples, He said, "Everything has*   [h]**10:22** Or *wills*, or *chooses*

Lk 10:18 *I watched Satan fall from heaven:* Jesus makes the point that the ministry He has sent out depicts the ultimate defeat of Satan. The authority these disciples had to cast out demons depicts this defeat.
Lk 10:20 *don't rejoice:* The real blessing, however, is not the power they have to heal and exorcize, but that they have an unbroken, eternal relationship to God that is recorded in heaven.
Lk 10:21 *You have hidden these things . . . and have revealed them:* Jesus praised God's plan that does not measure itself by human wisdom, standards, or status. God is sovereign and He has chosen to reveal it to the simplest of people, even infants.
Lk 10:22 *All things have been entrusted to Me:* Here the inextricable bond between Jesus and God is affirmed. The Son shares sovereignty with the Father and the right to reveal Himself to whomever He wills. No one knows the Father but the Son and the one to whom the Son reveals it. This verse sounds much like several sayings we meet in John's Gospel that stress the union of the Father and the Son.
Lk 10:23 *The eyes that see the things you see are blessed:* Jesus makes the point that Moses, David, and the prophets longed to see what the disciples are experiencing in Jesus.

Sec. 103   The Parable of the Good Samaritan

Luke 10:25-37

[25] Just then an expert in the law stood up to test Him, saying, "Teacher, what must I do to inherit eternal life?"
[26] "What is written in the law?" He asked him. "How do you read it?"
[27] He answered:

Love the Lord your God with all your heart, with all your soul, with all your strength, and with all your mind; and your neighbor as yourself.[a]

[28] "You've answered correctly," He told him. "Do this and you will live."
[29] But wanting to justify himself, he asked Jesus, "And who is my neighbor?"

[a]**10:27** Lv 19:18; Dt 6:5

Lk 10:25 *what must I do to inherit eternal life?:* This question asks in a Jewish expression what it takes to be saved. Jesus affirms the scribe's initial answer from Deuteronomy 6:5, which teaches that one is to obey God, that is, be responsive to Him, and that means letting Him into the life in a way that we are also compassionate to our neighbors and others around us. The parable of the good Samaritan illustrates that point. Luke 18:18-30 will develop this idea and show that to love God means to be responsive to the kingdom and Jesus, which gives one a heart to be the kind of person Jesus described in this parable.
Lk 10:29 *who is my neighbor?:* The question suggests that there are people who do not need to be regarded as a neighbor. Jesus rejects this by telling a parable where the example to be followed is a Samaritan, someone the questioner probably would have put in the "not a neighbor" category. Jews believed Samaritans were traitors to the faith by having married outside of Judaism when Israel fell to the Assyrians. Their mixed race was not respected by more pious Jews.

Luke 10:25-37 (cont.)

30 Jesus took up ⌊the question⌋ and said: "A man was going down from Jerusalem to Jericho and fell into the hands of robbers. They stripped him, beat him up, and fled, leaving him half dead. 31 A priest happened to be going down that road. When he saw him, he passed by on the other side. 32 In the same way, a Levite, when he arrived at the place and saw him, passed by on the other side. 33 But a •Samaritan on his journey came up to him, and when he saw ⌊the man⌋, he had compassion. 34 He went over to him and bandaged his wounds, pouring on oil and wine. Then he put him on his own animal, brought him to an inn, and took care of him. 35 The next daya he took out two •denarii, gave them to the innkeeper, and said, 'Take care of him. When I come back I'll reimburse you for whatever extra you spend.'

36 "Which of these three do you think proved to be a neighbor to the man who fell into the hands of the robbers?"

37 "The one who showed mercy to him," he said.

Then Jesus told him, "Go and do the same."

a**10:35** Other mss add *as he was leaving*

Lk 10:37 *The one who showed mercy . . . Go and do the same:* Jesus did not directly answer the question who is my neighbor. Rather He told the Jewish legal expert to be a neighbor by showing mercy. This is the first key point of the parable. The second is that neighbors can come in surprising places, as the Samaritan would be the last person this Jewish legal expert would view as a spiritual example. By picking a "non-neighbor" as the example of a neighbor, Jesus did in fact answer the original question. Neighbors can be anyone.

Sec. 104   Mary and Martha

Luke 10:38-42

38 While they were traveling, He entered a village, and a woman named Martha welcomed Him into her home.a 39 She had a sister named Mary, who also sat at the Lord'sb feet and was listening to what He said.c 40 But Martha was distracted by her many tasks, and she came up and asked, "Lord, don't You care that my sister has left me to serve alone? So tell her to give me a hand."d

41 The Lorde answered her, "Martha, Martha, you are worried and upset about many things, 42 but one thing is necessary. Mary has made the right choice,f and it will not be taken away from her."

a**10:38** Other mss omit *into her home*   b**10:39** Other mss read *at Jesus'*   c**10:39** Lit *to His word* or *message*   d**10:40** Or *tell her to help me*
e**10:41** Other mss read *Jesus*   f**10:42** Lit *has chosen the good part*

Lk 10:42 *right choice:* Martha was doing something good but wanted Jesus to make Mary do it as well. This Jesus refused to do. Mary had made a good choice to sit at Jesus' feet and Martha risked missing the benefit of meaningful time with Jesus by being distracted by "many things" that needed, in her view, to get done. Mary's right choice was that she kept the priority of sitting at Jesus' feet.

Sec. 105   The Model Prayer

Luke 11:1-13

1 He was praying in a certain place, and when He finished, one of His disciples said to Him, "Lord, teach us to pray, just as John also taught his disciples."

2 He said to them, "Whenever you pray, say:

Lk 11:1-4 Two versions of this prayer exist. One appears in the Sermon on the Mount in Matthew. Here there is a request for Jesus to give His disciples a prayer like John the Baptist did his disciples. Judaism had set liturgical prayers. Luke's version is the shorter and less well known of the two versions. The result is what is often called the Lord's Prayer because it came from Him, but it really is the disciples' prayer because it shows disciples how to pray for each other and depend on God for life's basic needs. There is one statement about God's uniqueness, two declarations about God's kingdom coming and His will being done, and three requests about daily bread, forgiveness, and protection from temptation. Luke likes to highlight prayer (3:21; 5:16; 6:12; 9:28-29; 11:1; 22:41; 23:34,46).

Luke 11:1-13 (cont.)

Father,[a]
Your name be honored as holy.
Your kingdom come.[b]
3 Give us each day our daily bread.[c]
4 And forgive us our sins,
for we ourselves also forgive everyone
in debt to us.[d]
And do not bring us into temptation."[e]

5 He also said to them: "Suppose one of you[f] has a friend and goes to him at midnight and says to him, 'Friend, lend me three loaves of bread, 6 because a friend of mine on a journey has come to me, and I don't have anything to offer him.'[g] 7 Then he will answer from inside and say, 'Don't bother me! The door is already locked, and my children and I have gone to bed. I can't get up to give you anything.' 8 I tell you, even though he won't get up and give him anything because he is his friend, yet because of his ⌊friend's⌋ persistence,[h] he will get up and give him as much as he needs.

9 "So I say to you, keep asking,[i] and it will be given to you. Keep searching,[j] and you will find. Keep knocking,[k] and the door will be opened to you. 10 For everyone who asks receives, and the one who searches finds, and to the one who knocks, the door will be opened. 11 What father among you, if his son[l] asks for a fish, will give him a snake instead of a fish? 12 Or if he asks for an egg, will give him a scorpion? 13 If you then, who are evil, know how to give good gifts to your children, how much more will the heavenly Father give[m] the Holy Spirit to those who ask Him?"

[a]11:2 Other mss read *Our Father in heaven*   [b]11:2 Other mss add *Your will be done on earth as it is in heaven*   [c]11:3 Or *our bread for tomorrow*   [d]11:4 Or *everyone who wrongs us*   [e]11:4 Other mss add *But deliver us from the evil one*   [f]11:5 Lit *Who of you*   [g]11:6 Lit *I have nothing to set before him*   [h]11:8 Or *annoying persistence*, or *shamelessness*   [i]11:9 Or *you, ask*   [j]11:9 Or *Search*   [k]11:9 Or *Knock*   [l]11:11 Other mss read *son asks for bread, would give him a stone? Or if he*   [m]11:13 Lit *the Father from heaven will give*

Lk 11:4 *debt:* Because sin has such devastating consequences, it is often described as a debt. The commitment to forgiveness shows an appreciation for God's forgiveness of our own great debt. What we receive, we also are willing to give.

Lk 11:5-13 The parable starting this unit is unique to Luke. It is a call to persistent prayer and ends with a note that God will give what is needed, in particular the direction of the Spirit, as v. 13 explains.

Lk 11:8 *persistence:* The Greek term here is difficult to summarize in an English word. In this context, it refers to a persistence that also is especially bold. The term summarizes the parable and sets up the following remarks about asking, searching, and knocking.

Lk 11:13 *how much more:* In Judaism, such how-much-more arguments were common. In this case, God is more likely to be responsive to the request for our needs than even sinful earthly fathers who know how to care for their children.

Sec. 106 A House Divided

Luke 11:14-36

14 Now He was driving out a demon that was mute.[a] When the demon came out, the man who had been mute, spoke, and the crowds were amazed. 15 But some of them said, "He drives out demons by •Beelzebul, the ruler of the demons!" 16 And others, as a test, were demanding of Him a sign from heaven.

17 Knowing their thoughts, He told them: "Every kingdom divided against itself is headed for destruction, and a house divided against itself falls. 18 If Satan also is divided against himself, how will his kingdom stand? For you say I drive out demons by Beelzebul. 19 And if I drive out demons by Beelzebul, who is it

[a]11:14 A demon that caused the man to be mute

Lk 11:15 *He drives out demons by Beelzebul:* In this vicious charge is hidden an important fact. The Jewish leadership could not deny that Jesus was performing acts of power that were not normal. What they tried to argue is that this power was from below, not above. Beelzebul is simply another name for the Devil.

Lk 11:19 *if I drive out demons by Beelzebul:* Jesus argued that if He uses a malevolent power to do good things, then Satan is fighting against himself which is not likely. In addition, if Jesus is doing such acts by Satan's power, then to whom would they attribute similar acts their own perform? These inconsistencies undercut the argument that the Devil is at work through Jesus and leads to only one alternative, namely that Jesus works through God's power.

Luke 11:14-36 (cont.)

your sons[a] drive them out by? For this reason they will be your judges. [20] If I drive out demons by the finger of God, then the kingdom of God has come to you. [21] When a strong man, fully armed, guards his estate, his possessions are secure.[b] [22] But when one stronger than he attacks and overpowers him, he takes from him all his weapons[c] he trusted in, and divides up his plunder. [23] Anyone who is not with Me is against Me, and anyone who does not gather with Me scatters.

[24] "When an •unclean spirit comes out of a man, it roams through waterless places looking for rest, and not finding rest, it then[d] says, 'I'll go back to my house where I came from.' [25] And returning, it finds ⌊the house⌋ swept and put in order. [26] Then it goes and brings seven other spirits more evil than itself, and they enter and settle down there. As a result, that man's last condition is worse than the first."

[27] As He was saying these things, a woman from the crowd raised her voice and said to Him, "The womb that bore You and the one who nursed You are blessed!"

[28] He said, "Even more, those who hear the word of God and keep it are blessed!"

[29] As the crowds were increasing, He began saying: "This generation is an evil generation. It demands a sign, but no sign will be given to it except the sign of Jonah.[e] [30] For just as Jonah became a sign to the people of Nineveh, so also the •Son of Man will be to this generation. [31] The queen of the south will rise up at the judgment with the men of this generation and condemn them, because she came from the ends of the earth to hear the wisdom of Solomon, and look—something greater than Solomon is here! [32] The men of Nineveh will rise up at the judgment with this generation and condemn it, because they repented at Jonah's proclamation, and look—something greater than Jonah is here!

[33] "No one lights a lamp and puts it in the cellar or under a basket,[f] but on a lampstand, so that those who come in may see its light. [34] Your eye is the lamp of the body. When your eye is good, your whole body is also full of light. But when it is bad, your body is also full of darkness. [35] Take care then, that the light in you is not darkness. [36] If therefore your whole body is full of light, with no part of it in darkness, the whole body will be full of light, as when a lamp shines its light on you."[g]

a11:19 Your exorcists   **b11:21** Lit *his possessions are in peace*   **c11:22** Gk *panoplia*, the armor and weapons of a foot soldier; Eph 6:11,13
d11:24 Other mss omit *then*   **e11:29** Other mss add *the prophet*   **f11:33** Other mss omit *or under a basket*   **g11:36** Or *shines on you with its rays*

Lk 11:20 *If I drive out demons by the finger of God:* Jesus presented the contrast. If God does His work, then the promised kingdom or rule of God has come. The implication is that they should be responsive to the coming of God's promise and authority. Jesus drives home the point with a parable that portrays Him as a stronger man who has overrun Satan's estate.

Lk 11:24 *unclean spirit . . . roams:* In Judaism, the belief was that a spirit was on the lookout for a place to dwell.

Lk 11:26 *man's last condition is worse:* This parable makes the point that if God blesses and that is ignored by leaving the house empty rather than receiving what God makes available, then the spirit that controlled the person will return with even more malevolent force, resulting in a worse situation. An unresponsive heart can become a hard heart is the warning.

Lk 11:28 *hear . . . and keep:* Once again Jesus emphasizes that obeying the word is what leads to blessing.

Lk 11:29-32 This event is also present in two versions. In Luke's version, the emphasis is focused on the preaching of the word as Jonah's and Solomon's sign. The point is to see the sign as the revelation of God's wisdom and judgment that leads to blessing if one repents. In Matthew, the sign is to respond to the three days in the fish, a focus on the death and resurrection of Jesus as key to that message.

Lk 11:31-32 *wisdom . . . proclamation:* The Queen of Sheba came to Solomon to hear his wisdom (1 Kg 10:1-3; 2 Ch 9:1-12), while Jonah went to preach a call of repentance. Jesus' message combines both into one and is a greater message because Jesus preaches the realization of promise.

Lk 11:34 *eye is the lamp of the body:* In the ancient world, it is not what goes in the eye that is key but what comes out of it, what it looks for. So the warning is to be careful about what comes or shines out from the core of our being. If it is light, it will shine.

Sec. 107   Religious Hypocrisy Denounced

Luke 11:37-54

[37] As He was speaking, a •Pharisee asked Him to dine with him. So He went in and reclined at the table. [38] When the Pharisee saw this, he was amazed that He did not first perform the ritual washing[a] before dinner. [39] But the Lord said to him: "Now you Pharisees •clean the outside of the cup and dish, but inside you are full of greed and evil. [40] Fools! Didn't He who made the outside make the inside too? [41] But give from what is within to the poor,[b] and then everything is clean for you.

a11:38 Lit *He did not first wash*   **b11:41** Or *But donate from the heart as charity*

Luke 11:37-54 (cont.)

[42] "But woe to you Pharisees! You give a tenth[a] of mint, rue, and every kind of herb, and you bypass[b] justice and love for God.[c] These things you should have done without neglecting the others.

[43] "Woe to you Pharisees! You love the front seat in the •synagogues and greetings in the marketplaces.

[44] "Woe to you![d] You are like unmarked graves; the people who walk over them don't know it."

[45] One of the experts in the law answered Him, "Teacher, when You say these things You insult us too."

[46] Then He said: "Woe also to you experts in the law! You load people with burdens that are hard to carry, yet you yourselves don't touch these burdens with one of your fingers.

[47] "Woe to you! You build monuments[e] to the prophets, and your fathers killed them. [48] Therefore you are witnesses that you approve[f] the deeds of your fathers, for they killed them, and you build their monuments.[g] [49] Because of this, the wisdom of God said, 'I will send them prophets and apostles, and some of them they will kill and persecute,' [50] so that this generation may be held responsible for the blood of all the prophets shed since the foundation of the world[h] — [51] from the blood of Abel to the blood of Zechariah, who perished between the altar and the sanctuary.

"Yes, I tell you, this generation will be held responsible.[i]

[52] "Woe to you experts in the law! You have taken away the key of knowledge! You didn't go in yourselves, and you hindered those who were going in."

[53] When He left there,[j] the •scribes and the Pharisees began to oppose Him fiercely and to cross-examine Him about many things; [54] they were lying in wait for Him to trap Him in something He said.[k]

[a]11:42 Or *a tithe* [b]11:42 Or *neglect* [c]11:42 Lit *the justice and the love of God* [d]11:44 Other mss read *you scribes and Pharisees, hypocrites!* [e]11:47 Or *graves* [f]11:48 Lit *witnesses and approve* [g]11:48 Other mss omit *their monuments* [h]11:50 Lit *so that the blood of all . . . world may be required of this generation,* [i]11:51 Lit *you, it will be required of this generation* [j]11:53 Other mss read *And as He was saying these things to them* [k]11:54 Other mss add *so that they might bring charges against Him*

Lk 11:37-54 This denunciation of Pharisees and Jewish religious experts, also known as scribes, is a variation of another condemnation that shows up in Matthew 23 of the Pharisees. It is likely Jesus said such things on multiple occasions to warn different sets of these leaders. The directness of Jesus here reflects Jewish and Middle Eastern practice of being very direct when it comes to the consideration of themes related to God. This is no meek and mild Jesus, because the consequences of the failure of the leadership was so devastating.

Lk 11:41 *give from what is within to the poor:* There is a comparison here that is vivid. Just as one consciously gives charity to those in need, so one should give attention to what is in the heart.

Lk 11:42 *give a tenth:* Pharisees took pride in the religious responsibility that they tithed (or gave a tenth of everything) to God. This even included the tedious process of tithing small bits of spice. That kind of attention should have been given also to justice and love.

Lk 11:44 *like unmarked graves:* In Judaism, contact with the dead left one unclean. This remark would have especially stung, as the Pharisees saw themselves as paragons of life, righteousness, and purity.

Lk 11:46 *don't touch these burdens:* It is hard to know here if Jesus means these scribes do not keep the rules they ask others to keep or do not offer help to others to keep such rules. Either way, Jesus' point is that there is no real engagement with these burdens.

Lk 11:47 *your fathers:* Jesus accused the leaders of honoring the death of the prophets whom their fathers murdered, washing their grave stones in support of their elimination, something they showed by continuing to do this with God's current prophets and apostles, leaving them accountable for rejecting the entire message of the entire row of prophets since Abel. For all that the prophets said pointed to what Jesus was doing.

Lk 11:52 *taken away the key of knowledge:* Jesus accused the leaders of doing the exact opposite of what they thought they were doing. Rather than being a key to knowledge, they actually prevented people from entering.

Sec. 108   Jesus Warns about Covetousness and Worldly Anxieties

Luke 12:1-59

[1] In these circumstances,[a] a crowd of many thousands came together, so that they were trampling on one another. He began to say to His disciples first: "Be on your guard against the yeast[b] of the •Pharisees, which is hypocrisy. [2] There is nothing covered that won't be uncovered, nothing hidden that won't be made known. [3] Therefore whatever you have said in the dark will be heard in the light, and what you have whispered in an ear in private rooms will be proclaimed on the housetops.

[4] "And I say to you, My friends, don't fear those who kill the body, and after that can do nothing more. [5] But I will show you the One to fear: Fear Him who has authority to throw ⌊people⌋ into •hell after death. Yes, I say to you, this is the One to fear! [6] Aren't five sparrows sold for two pennies?[c] Yet not one of them is forgotten in God's sight. [7] Indeed, the hairs of your head are all counted. Don't be afraid; you are worth more than many sparrows!

[8] "And I say to you, anyone who acknowledges Me before men, the •Son of Man will also acknowledge him before the angels of God, [9] but whoever denies Me before men will be denied before the angels of God. [10] Anyone who speaks a word against the Son of Man will be forgiven, but the one who blasphemes against the Holy Spirit will not be forgiven. [11] Whenever they bring you before •synagogues and rulers and authorities, don't worry about how you should defend yourselves or what you should say. [12] For the Holy Spirit will teach you at that very hour what must be said."

[13] Someone from the crowd said to Him, "Teacher, tell my brother to divide the inheritance with me."

[14] "Friend,"[d] He said to him, "who appointed Me a judge or arbitrator over you?" [15] He then told them, "Watch out and be on guard against all greed because one's life is not in the abundance of his possessions."

[16] Then He told them a parable: "A rich man's land was very productive. [17] He thought to himself, 'What should I do, since I don't have anywhere to store my crops? [18] I will do this,' he said. 'I'll tear down my barns and build bigger ones and store all my grain and my goods there. [19] Then I'll say to myself, "You[e] have many goods stored up for many years. Take it easy; eat, drink, and enjoy yourself."'

[20] "But God said to him, 'You fool! This very night your •life is demanded of you. And the things you have prepared—whose will they be?'

[21] "That's how it is with the one who stores up treasure for himself and is not rich toward God."

[22] Then He said to His disciples: "Therefore I tell you, don't worry about your life, what you will eat; or about the body, what you will wear. [23] For life is more than food and the body more than clothing. [24] Consider the ravens: they don't sow or reap; they don't have a storeroom or a barn; yet God feeds them. Aren't you worth much more than the birds? [25] Can any of you add a •cubit to his height[f] by worrying? [26] If then you're not able to do even a little thing, why worry about the rest?

[a]**12:1** Or *Meanwhile,* or *At this time,* or *During this period*   [b]**12:1** Or *leaven*   [c]**12:6** Lit *two assaria*; the *assarion* (sg) was a small copper coin   [d]**12:14** Lit *Man*   [e]**12:19** Lit *say to my soul, "Soul, you*   [f]**12:25** Or *add one moment to his life-span*

Lk 12:1 *yeast:* In some biblical contexts, yeast is a metaphor for a contagion that spoils a loaf of bread.

Lk 12:5 *Fear Him who has authority to throw people into hell:* Rather than court human popularity and reception, Jesus warned that one should be responsive to God as well as making the note that God can be trusted because He is aware of even the smallest details about the smallest creatures, and we are worth more than they are.

Lk 12:10 *blasphemes against the Holy Spirit:* The parallel in Mark 3:28-30 helps to explain this idea. Blasphemy against the Spirit is decisively rejecting the testimony and evidence the Spirit gives that God is working through Jesus. Just as the leaders thought in Mark 3 that Jesus was performing miracles through an unclean spirit. To speak against the Son of Man is something less, for it is to make a remark about Jesus at a given point, rather than to engage in an outright or ongoing rejection. So one act is forgivable, the other is not.

Lk 12:12 *the Holy Spirit will teach you:* Here Jesus promised those who will be persecuted that the Spirit will give them ability to speak on behalf of God.

Lk 12:13-21 This parable is unique to Luke. It is dominated by the first person pronoun, which shows the selfishness and self-focus of the rich person who is condemned here, not for being rich but for the selfish way in which his bountiful crop is used. The parable serves as a warning against greed.

Lk 12:20 *whose will they be:* The key question of the parable makes a few points. All the effort to build a self-focused life does him no good in eternity when God calls him to account. The one person who will not own what has been built up is the fool who incorrectly thought it was his all along. So the exhortation is to be rich toward God, perhaps even to give to God the same kind of attention this man gave to his possessions.

Lk 12:22-34 Once again a portion of a saying found in the Sermon on the Mount in Matthew shows up as a single teaching in Luke.

Lk 12:24-27 *ravens . . . wildflowers:* These two pictures of God's care to provide food (ravens) and clothing (wildflowers) show that God will care for us in the basic needs of life, so that we need not be anxious.

Luke 12:1-59 (cont.)

27 "Consider how the wildflowers grow: they don't labor or spin thread. Yet I tell you, not even Solomon in all his splendor was adorned like one of these! 28 If that's how God clothes the grass, which is in the field today and is thrown into the furnace tomorrow, how much more will He do for you—you of little faith? 29 Don't keep striving for what you should eat and what you should drink, and don't be anxious. 30 For the Gentile world eagerly seeks all these things, and your Father knows that you need them.

31 "But seek His kingdom, and these things will be provided for you. 32 Don't be afraid, little flock, because your Father delights to give you the kingdom. 33 Sell your possessions and give to the poor. Make money-bags for yourselves that won't grow old, an inexhaustible treasure in heaven, where no thief comes near and no moth destroys. 34 For where your treasure is, there your heart will be also.

35 "Be ready for service[a] and have your lamps lit. 36 You must be like people waiting for their master to return[b] from the wedding banquet so that when he comes and knocks, they can open ⌊the door⌋ for him at once. 37 Those •slaves the master will find alert when he comes will be blessed. •I assure you: He will get ready,[c] have them recline at the table, then come and serve them. 38 If he comes in the middle of the night, or even near dawn,[d] and finds them alert, those slaves are blessed. 39 But know this: if the homeowner had known at what hour the thief was coming, he would not have let his house be broken into. 40 You also be ready, because the Son of Man is coming at an hour that you do not expect."

41 "Lord," Peter asked, "are You telling this parable to us or to everyone?"

42 The Lord said: "Who then is the faithful and sensible manager his master will put in charge of his household servants to give them their allotted food at the proper time? 43 That •slave whose master finds him working when he comes will be rewarded. 44 I tell you the truth: he will put him in charge of all his possessions. 45 But if that slave says in his heart, 'My master is delaying his coming,' and starts to beat the male and female slaves, and to eat and drink and get drunk, 46 that slave's master will come on a day he does not expect him and at an hour he does not know. He will cut him to pieces[e] and assign him a place with the unbelievers.[f] 47 And that slave who knew his master's will and didn't prepare himself or do it[g] will be severely beaten. 48 But the one who did not know and did things deserving of blows will be beaten lightly. Much will be required of everyone who has been given much. And even more will be expected of the one who has been entrusted with more.[h]

49 "I came to bring fire on the earth, and how I wish it were already set ablaze! 50 But I have a baptism to be baptized with, and how it consumes Me until it is finished! 51 Do you think that I came here to give peace to the earth? No, I tell you, but rather division! 52 From now on, five in one household will be divided: three against two, and two against three.

[a]**12:35** Lit *Let your loins be girded*; an idiom for tying up loose outer clothing in preparation for action; Ex 12:11   [b]**12:36** Lit *master, when he should return*   [c]**12:37** Lit *will gird himself*   [d]**12:38** Lit *even in the second or third watch*   [e]**12:46** Lit *him in two*   [f]**12:46** Or *unfaithful, or untrustworthy*   [g]**12:47** Lit *or do toward his will*   [h]**12:48** Or *much*

Lk 12:30 *your Father knows that you need them:* The point of Jesus' remark is that God is aware of our needs.

Lk 12:31 *seek His kingdom:* Jesus' application is that the kind of attention we normally give to worrying about everyday matters is what we should give to seeking God's kingdom, while trusting in God's care.

Lk 12:33 *Sell . . . give to the poor:* This kind of trust also should lead to generosity toward those in need. One of the ways God meets needs is through the generosity of those who have enough to share. This kind of giving is what Jesus calls storing up real treasure, because it is pleasing to God.

Lk 12:35 *Be ready:* This idea, expressed twice in the passage, is a call to recognize that we are accountable to a master who will return. Blessing comes to the one the master finds doing what he commanded (vv. 38, 43). Especially important here is the note that the return and accountability could come at any time night or day, thus the need to always be ready.

Lk 12:43 *will be rewarded:* Rewards come to the one who is ready and obeys. Jesus did not answer Peter's question. He simply said whoever you are and whatever your role, be like this.

Lk 12:46 *cut him to pieces:* To the "servant" who does the exact opposite of what the master commands, meaning he did not serve at all as he should, there will only be judgment. There is no harsher penalty than the one symbolized by being cut to pieces, an indication that complete judgment is intended. This stands in contrast to the other punishments of a severe beating or a few lashes, which picture a kind of disciplining judgment that is short of rejection. Jesus teaches with an eye to some who think they belong to Him but really do not respond to Him at all.

Lk 12:49 *I came to bring fire:* In this remark, Jesus makes it clear that He will be a cause for division as He will generate a variety of responses. Something reinforced later in the passage with the mention of division in families. When Jesus came, He did bring division to many Jewish families.

Lk 12:50 *baptism to be baptized with:* This is a reference to Jesus' approaching death.

Luke 12:1-59 (cont.)

53 **They will be divided, father against son,**
son against father,
mother against daughter,
daughter against mother,
mother-in-law against her daughter-in-law,
and daughter-in-law against mother-in-law."ᵃ

54 He also said to the crowds: "When you see a cloud rising in the west, right away you say, 'A storm is coming,' and so it does. 55 And when the south wind is blowing, you say, 'It's going to be a scorcher!' and it is. 56 Hypocrites! You know how to interpret the appearance of the earth and the sky, but why don't you know how to interpret this time?

57 "Why don't you judge for yourselves what is right? 58 As you are going with your adversary to the ruler, make an effort to settle with him on the way. Then he won't drag you before the judge, the judge hand you over to the bailiff, and the bailiff throw you into prison. 59 I tell you, you will never get out of there until you have paid the last cent."ᵇ

ᵃ**12:53** Mc 7:6   ᵇ**12:59** Gk *lepton*, the smallest and least valuable copper coin in use

Lk 12:56 *Hypocrites:* Jesus chastises the crowd that sees the signs of approaching weather when clouds of moisture from the west (and the Mediterranean) point to a storm or winds from the desert south point to heat, but they cannot read the signs Jesus performs right before their eyes.

Lk 12:58 *settle with him on the way:* This event is distinct from the use of this imagery in the Sermon on the Mount. There it meant to get reconciled with another person who was an adversary, but in Luke's context with all the remarks about coming judgment, it points to settling accounts with God or else one will fully pay the debt. This shows that Jesus can use the same imagery to make different points in different contexts.

Sec. 109   Repent or Perish

Luke 13:1-9

1 At that time, some people came and reported to Him about the Galileans whose blood •Pilate had mixed with their sacrifices. 2 And Heᵃ responded to them, "Do you think that these Galileans were more sinful than all Galileans because they suffered these things? 3 No, I tell you; but unless you repent, you will all perish as well! 4 Or those 18 that the tower in Siloam fell on and killed—do you think they were more sinful than all the people who live in Jerusalem? 5 No, I tell you; but unless you repent, you will all perish as well!"

6 And He told this parable: "A man had a fig tree that was planted in his vineyard. He came looking for fruit on it and found none. 7 He told the vineyard worker, 'Listen, for three years I have come looking for fruit on this fig tree and haven't found any. Cut it down! Why should it even waste the soil?'

8 "But he replied to him, 'Sir,ᵇ leave it this year also, until I dig around it and fertilize it. 9 Perhaps it will bear fruit next year, but if not, you can cut it down.'"

ᵃ**13:2** Other mss read *Jesus*   ᵇ**13:8** Or *Lord*

Lk 13:3-5 *unless you repent:* This phrase, used twice in the passage argues that the question is not whether a humanly wrought death or a natural disaster is a sign of greater sin, the issue is to repent of sin, for sin leads to death. The issue then is not the timing of death or its cause, but the response to sin. This exhortation to repent is only recorded in Luke's Gospel.

Lk 13:9 *Perhaps it will bear fruit . . . but if not:* The fig tree pictures Israel that has failed to bear fruit even though it has had time to do so. The request is to give the tree another chance. If it fails, then it can be cut down. In the Greek this is expressed with the probability that failure is still likely.

Sec. 110   Healing a Daughter of Abraham and a Repetition of the Parables of the Mustard Seed and of the Yeast

Luke 13:10-21

¹⁰ As He was teaching in one of the •synagogues on the Sabbath, ¹¹ a woman was there who had been disabled by a spiritᵃ for over 18 years. She was bent over and could not straighten up at all.ᵇ ¹² When Jesus saw her, He called out to her,ᶜ "•Woman, you are free of your disability." ¹³ Then He laid His hands on her, and instantly she was restored and began to glorify God.

¹⁴ But the leader of the synagogue, indignant because Jesus had healed on the Sabbath, responded by telling the crowd, "There are six days when work should be done; therefore come on those days and be healed and not on the Sabbath day."

¹⁵ But the Lord answered him and said, "Hypocrites! Doesn't each one of you untie his ox or donkey from the feeding trough on the Sabbath and lead it to water? ¹⁶ Satan has bound this woman, a daughter of Abraham, for 18 years—shouldn't she be untied from this bondage on the Sabbath day?"

¹⁷ When He had said these things, all His adversaries were humiliated, but the whole crowd was rejoicing over all the glorious things He was doing.

¹⁸ He said therefore, "What is the kingdom of God like, and what can I compare it to? ¹⁹ It's like a mustard seed that a man took and sowed in his garden. It grew and became a tree, and the birds of the sky nested in its branches."

²⁰ Again He said, "What can I compare the kingdom of God to? ²¹ It's like yeast that a woman took and mixed into 50 poundsᵈ of flour until it spread through the entire mixture."ᵉ

ᵃ**13:11** Lit *had a spirit of disability*   ᵇ**13:11** Or *straighten up completely*   ᶜ**13:12** Or *He summoned her*   ᵈ**13:21** Lit *3 sata*; about 40 quarts   ᵉ**13:21** Or *until all of it was leavened*

Lk 13:10-17 This miracle is found only in Luke's Gospel.

Lk 13:15 *ox:* Jesus uses the example of rescuing their animals on the Sabbath as a justification for healing this woman.

Lk 13:16 *Satan has bound this woman, a daughter of Abraham:* Jesus underscored that it is appropriate on the Sabbath to heal one of Abraham's children and rescue her from Satan's grip.

Lk 13:18 *what can I compare it to:* Jesus compared the kingdom to a mustard seed where birds come to dwell and to yeast that spreads through flour. In both cases, the emphasis is on the growth of the kingdom. What starts out small becomes a place of shelter (mustard seed) and penetrates the whole of where it is placed (yeast). Ezekiel 17:22-23 may be the background for the reference to the birds' sheltered image, which points to what God planned to do through the restored house of David.

Sec. 111   Jesus at the Feast of Dedication; Renewed Efforts to Stone Him

John 10:22-39

²² Then the Festival of Dedicationᵃ took place in Jerusalem, and it was winter. ²³ Jesus was walking in the •temple complex in Solomon's Colonnade.ᵇ ²⁴ Then the •Jews surrounded Him and asked, "How long are You going to keep us in suspense?ᶜ If You are the •Messiah, tell us plainly."ᵈ

²⁵ "I did tell you and you don't believe," Jesus answered them. "The works that I do in My Father's name testify about Me. ²⁶ But you don't believe because you are not My sheep.ᵉ ²⁷ My sheep hear My voice, I know them, and they follow Me. ²⁸ I give them eternal life, and they will never perish—ever! No one will snatch them out of My hand. ²⁹ My Father, who has given them to Me, is greater than all. No one is able to snatch them out of the Father's hand. ³⁰ The Father and I are one."ᶠ

³¹ Again the Jews picked up rocks to stone Him.

³² Jesus replied, "I have shown you many good works from the Father. Which of these works are you stoning Me for?"

³³ "We aren't stoning You for a good work," the Jews answered, "but for blasphemy, because You—being a man—make Yourself God."

ᵃ**10:22** Or *Hanukkah*, also called *the Feast of Lights*; this festival commemorated the rededication of the temple in 164 B.C.   ᵇ**10:23** Rows of columns supporting a roof   ᶜ**10:24** Lit *How long are you taking away our life?*   ᵈ**10:24** Or *openly*, or *publicly*   ᵉ**10:26** Other mss add *just as I told you*   ᶠ**10:30** Lit *I and the Father—We are one.*

John 10:22-39 (cont.)

³⁴ Jesus answered them, "Isn't it written in your law,^a **I said, you are gods**?^b ³⁵ If He called those whom the word of God came to 'gods'—and the Scripture cannot be broken— ³⁶ do you say, 'You are blaspheming' to the One the Father set apart and sent into the world, because I said: I am the Son of God? ³⁷ If I am not doing My Father's works, don't believe Me. ³⁸ But if I am doing them and you don't believe Me, believe the works. This way you will know and understand^c that the Father is in Me and I in the Father." ³⁹ Then they were trying again to seize Him, yet He eluded their grasp.

^a**10:34** Other mss read *in the law*   ^b**10:34** Ps 82:6   ^c**10:38** Other mss read *know and believe*

PART X

THE LATER PEREAN MINISTRY

Sec. 112   Many Beyond the Jordan Believe in Jesus

John 10:40-42

⁴⁰ So He departed again across the Jordan to the place where John had been baptizing earlier, and He remained there. ⁴¹ Many came to Him and said, "John never did a sign, but everything John said about this man was true." ⁴² And many believed in Him there.

Sec. 113   The Narrow Way

Luke 13:22-35

²² He went through one town and village after another, teaching and making His way to Jerusalem. ²³ "Lord," someone asked Him, "are there few being saved?"ᵃ

He said to them, ²⁴ "Make every effort to enter through the narrow door, because I tell you, many will try to enter and won't be able ²⁵ once the homeowner gets up and shuts the door. Then you will standᵇ outside and knock on the door, saying, 'Lord, open up for us!' He will answer you, 'I don't know you or where you're from.' ²⁶ Then you will say,ᶜ 'We ate and drank in Your presence, and You taught in our streets!' ²⁷ But He will say, 'I tell you, I don't know you or where you're from. Get away from Me, all you workers of unrighteousness!' ²⁸ There will be weeping and gnashing of teeth in that place, when you see Abraham, Isaac, Jacob, and all the prophets in the kingdom of God but yourselves thrown out. ²⁹ They will come from east and west, from north and south, and recline at the table in the kingdom of God. ³⁰ Note this: some are last who will be first, and some are first who will be last."

³¹ At that time some •Pharisees came and told Him, "Go, get out of here! •Herod wants to kill You!"

³² He said to them, "Go tell that fox, 'Look! I'm driving out demons and performing healings today and tomorrow, and on the third dayᵈ I will complete My work.'ᵉ ³³ Yet I must travel today, tomorrow, and the next day, because it is not possible for a prophet to perish outside of Jerusalem!

³⁴ "Jerusalem, Jerusalem! The city who kills the prophets and stones those who are sent to her. How often I wanted to gather your children together, as a hen gathers her chicks under her wings, but you were not willing! ³⁵ See, your houseᶠ is abandoned to you. And I tell you, you will not see Me until the time comes when you say, **Blessed is He who comes in the name of the Lord!**"ᵍ

ᵃ**13:23** Or *are the saved few?* (in number); lit *are those being saved few?*   ᵇ**13:25** Lit *you will begin to stand*   ᶜ**13:26** Lit *you will begin to say*   ᵈ**13:32** Very shortly   ᵉ**13:32** Lit *I will be finished*   ᶠ**13:35** Probably the temple; Jr 12:7; 22:5   ᵍ**13:35** Ps 118:26

Lk 13:24 *narrow door:* Jesus warned that the saved may well be few, since the entryway is narrow, but that is not the real question. The issue is not will the saved be few but will the saved include you.

Lk 13:25 *open up for us:* This portion of the parable warns that there will come a time when it will be too late to respond.

Lk 13:26 *We ate and drank in Your presence:* This part of the parable stresses that it is not knowing about Jesus or even having seen Him that is important, but knowing Him and responding to Him.

Lk 13:28 *weeping and gnashing of teeth:* This is an image that points to final judgment.

Lk 13:29 *from east and west, from north and south:* The kingdom will have plenty of people from everywhere in it, but it may exclude some from Israel who thought they would be in.

Lk 13:33 *outside of Jerusalem:* Jesus takes the warning about Herod's plot and says if He must face death, He will. He knows He will die in Jerusalem and that Herod will play a role.

Lk 13:34 *Jerusalem, Jerusalem:* Jesus mourned for Jerusalem, who, as she did when she slew the prophets, rejected God's way. *as a hen:* Jesus spoke in the first person to highlight God's will—how He longed to protect Israel but she would not have any of it.

Lk 13:35 *your house is abandoned:* Jesus declared an exilic-like judgment on Israel, using the language of the abandoned house from the prophets (Jr 12:7; 22:5). *when you say:* The judgment will last until the nation recognizes Jesus. Jesus quoted from Psalm 118:26 to make the point.

Sec. 114   A Sabbath Controversy

Luke 14:1-24

[1] One Sabbath, when He went to eat[a] at the house of one of the leading •Pharisees, they were watching Him closely. [2] There in front of Him was a man whose body was swollen with fluid.[b] [3] In response, Jesus asked the law experts and the Pharisees, "Is it lawful to heal on the Sabbath or not?" [4] But they kept silent. He took the man, healed him, and sent him away. [5] And to them, He said, "Which of you whose son or ox falls into a well, will not immediately pull him out on the Sabbath day?" [6] To this they could find no answer.

[7] He told a parable to those who were invited, when He noticed how they would choose the best places for themselves: [8] "When you are invited by someone to a wedding banquet, don't recline at the best place, because a more distinguished person than you may have been invited by your host.[c] [9] The one who invited both of you may come and say to you, 'Give your place to this man,' and then in humiliation, you will proceed to take the lowest place.

[10] "But when you are invited, go and recline in the lowest place, so that when the one who invited you comes, he will say to you, 'Friend, move up higher.' You will then be honored in the presence of all the other guests. [11] For everyone who exalts himself will be humbled, and the one who humbles himself will be exalted."

[12] He also said to the one who had invited Him, "When you give a lunch or a dinner, don't invite your friends, your brothers, your relatives, or your rich neighbors, because they might invite you back, and you would be repaid. [13] On the contrary, when you host a banquet, invite those who are poor, maimed, lame, or blind. [14] And you will be blessed, because they cannot repay you; for you will be repaid at the resurrection of the righteous."

[15] When one of those who reclined at the table with Him heard these things, he said to Him, "The one who will eat bread in the kingdom of God is blessed!"

[16] Then He told him: "A man was giving a large banquet and invited many. [17] At the time of the banquet, he sent his •slave to tell those who were invited, 'Come, because everything is now ready.'

[18] "But without exception[d] they all began to make excuses. The first one said to him, 'I have bought a field, and I must go out and see it. I ask you to excuse me.'

[19] "Another said, 'I have bought five yoke of oxen, and I'm going to try them out. I ask you to excuse me.'

[20] "And another said, 'I just got married,[e] and therefore I'm unable to come.'

[21] "So the slave came back and reported these things to his master. Then in anger, the master of the house told his slave, 'Go out quickly into the streets and alleys of the city, and bring in here the poor, maimed, blind, and lame!'

[22] "'Master,' the slave said, 'what you ordered has been done, and there's still room.'

[23] "Then the master told the slave, 'Go out into the highways and lanes and make them come in, so that my house may be filled. [24] For I tell you, not one of those men who were invited will enjoy my banquet!'"

[a]**14:1** Lit *eat bread*; = eat a meal   [b]**14:2** Afflicted with dropsy or edema   [c]**14:8** Lit *by him*   [d]**14:18** Lit *And from one* (voice)   [e]**14:20** Lit *I have married a woman*

Lk 14:5 *ox:* This miracle replicates one in the last chapter and also serves as a "mirror" miracle after Jesus' warnings to see if Israel had learned anything. Tragically, her response had not changed.

Lk 14:9 *take the lowest place:* Jesus highlights how one should not seek places of honor, lest one more honorable comes. Rather take the lowest place and then you may be called up. There is no shame in honor given to one who does not seek it. Exaltation from God comes to the humble.

Lk 14:13 *invite those who are poor . . . blind:* Jesus teaches one should care for those who cannot care for themselves. True generosity is that given which does not expect a payback.

Lk 14:18 *all began to make excuses:* The background to this scene is important. In the ancient world, a person would have accepted an invitation long before the banquet so the food could be prepared for the right count. So these excuses at the last second are rude. We planned to attend but now something more important has taken place. God will fill the banquet table anyway, but those originally invited will miss out.

Sec. 115   The Cost of Following Jesus

Luke 14:25-35

25 Now great crowds were traveling with Him. So He turned and said to them: 26 "If anyone comes to Me and does not hate his own father and mother, wife and children, brothers and sisters—yes, and even his own life—he cannot be My disciple. 27 Whoever does not bear his own cross and come after Me cannot be My disciple.

28 "For which of you, wanting to build a tower, doesn't first sit down and calculate the cost to see if he has enough to complete it? 29 Otherwise, after he has laid the foundation and cannot finish it, all the onlookers will begin to make fun of him, 30 saying, 'This man started to build and wasn't able to finish.'

31 "Or what king, going to war against another king, will not first sit down and decide if he is able with 10,000 to oppose the one who comes against him with 20,000? 32 If not, while the other is still far off, he sends a delegation and asks for terms of peace. 33 In the same way, therefore, every one of you who does not say good-bye to[a] all his possessions cannot be My disciple.

34 "Now, salt is good, but if salt should lose its taste, how will it be made salty? 35 It isn't fit for the soil or for the manure pile; they throw it out. Anyone who has ears to hear should listen!"

[a]14:33 Or *does not renounce* or *leave*

Lk 14:26 *hate his own father and mother . . . his own life:* This saying says rhetorically that love for Jesus is the highest priority. It is not teaching hate for parents or for one's life, but that such devotion is of a lesser status than love and devotion to God and Jesus.

Lk 14:28 *tower:* This is the first of two short comparisons that are unique to Luke. The picture of the tower stresses that one should be aware that discipleship carries with it a cost.

Lk 14:31 *war:* The second image refers to being sure you are strong enough to overcome your opponent, and if not, be sure to get terms for peace.

Sec. 116   The Parables of the Lost Sheep, the Lost Coin, and the Lost Son

Luke 15:1-32

1 All the tax collectors and sinners were approaching to listen to Him. 2 And the •Pharisees and •scribes were complaining, "This man welcomes sinners and eats with them!"

3 So He told them this parable: 4 "What man among you, who has 100 sheep and loses one of them, does not leave the 99 in the open field[a] and go after the lost one until he finds it? 5 When he has found it, he joyfully puts it on his shoulders, 6 and coming home, he calls his friends and neighbors together, saying to them, 'Rejoice with me, because I have found my lost sheep!' 7 I tell you, in the same way, there will be more joy in heaven over one sinner who repents than over 99 righteous people who don't need repentance.

8 "Or what woman who has 10 silver coins,[b] if she loses one coin, does not light a lamp, sweep the house, and search carefully until she finds it? 9 When she finds it, she calls her women friends and neighbors together, saying, 'Rejoice with me, because I have found the silver coin I lost!' 10 I tell you, in the same way, there is joy in the presence of God's angels over one sinner who repents."

[a]15:4 Or *the wilderness*   [b]15:8 Gk 10 *drachmas*; a *drachma* was a silver coin = a •denarius.

Lk 15:1-7 This parable has a variation in Matthew 18, but the contexts are different.

Lk 15:2 *welcomes sinners:* The three parables of Luke 15 are a response to the complaints of the Pharisees. Jesus underscores the joy of finding something precious that has been lost. That is why He came to earth.

Lk 15:7 *joy in heaven:* This phrase explains the anticipated result of seeking the lost. Upon finding a lost sheep, that is, getting a response of repentance, heaven rejoices.

Lk 15:8 *silver coins:* Anyone who has lost something that they know is in the room understands this parable. The stress here is on the effort to find, the search. Note how the initiative is with the one seeking the lost.

Lk 15:10 *joy in the presence of God's angels:* As with the previous parable, this phrase explains the anticipated result of seeking the lost. Upon finding a lost sheep, that is, getting a response of repentance, heaven rejoices.

Luke 15:1-32 (cont.)

¹¹ He also said: "A man had two sons. ¹² The younger of them said to his father, 'Father, give me the share of the estate I have coming to me.' So he distributed the assetsᵃ to them. ¹³ Not many days later, the younger son gathered together all he had and traveled to a distant country, where he squandered his estate in foolish living. ¹⁴ After he had spent everything, a severe famine struck that country, and he had nothing.ᵇ ¹⁵ Then he went to work forᶜ one of the citizens of that country, who sent him into his fields to feed pigs. ¹⁶ He longed to eat his fill fromᵈ the carob podsᵉ the pigs were eating, but no one would give him any. ¹⁷ When he came to his senses,ᶠ he said, 'How many of my father's hired hands have more than enough food, and here I am dyingᵍ of hunger!ʰ ¹⁸ I'll get up, go to my father, and say to him, Father, I have sinned against heaven and in your sight. ¹⁹ I'm no longer worthy to be called your son. Make me like one of your hired hands.' ²⁰ So he got up and went to his father. But while the son was still a long way off, his father saw him and was filled with compassion. He ran, threw his arms around his neck,ⁱ and kissed him. ²¹ The son said to him, 'Father, I have sinned against heaven and in your sight. I'm no longer worthy to be called your son.'

²² "But the father told his •slaves, 'Quick! Bring out the best robe and put it on him; put a ring on his fingerʲ and sandals on his feet. ²³ Then bring the fattened calf and slaughter it, and let's celebrate with a feast, ²⁴ because this son of mine was dead and is alive again; he was lost and is found!' So they began to celebrate.

²⁵ "Now his older son was in the field; as he came near the house, he heard music and dancing. ²⁶ So he summoned one of the servants and asked what these things meant. ²⁷ 'Your brother is here,' he told him, 'and your father has slaughtered the fattened calf because he has him back safe and sound.'ᵏ

²⁸ "Then he became angry and didn't want to go in. So his father came out and pleaded with him. ²⁹ But he replied to his father, 'Look, I have been slaving many years for you, and I have never disobeyed your orders, yet you never gave me a young goat so I could celebrate with my friends. ³⁰ But when this son of yours came, who has devoured your assetsᵃ with prostitutes, you slaughtered the fattened calf for him.'

³¹ "'Son,'ˡ he said to him, 'you are always with me, and everything I have is yours. ³² But we had to celebrate and rejoice, because this brother of yours was dead and is alive again; he was lost and is found.'"

ᵃ15:12,30 Lit *livelihood*, or *living*   ᵇ15:14 Lit *and he began to be in need*   ᶜ15:15 Lit *went and joined with*   ᵈ15:16 Other mss read *to fill his stomach with*   ᵉ15:16 Seed casings of a tree used as food for cattle, pigs, and sometimes the poor   ᶠ15:17 Lit *to himself*   ᵍ15:17 The word *dying* is translated *lost* in vv. 4-9 and vv. 24,32.   ʰ15:17 Or *dying in the famine*; v. 14   ⁱ15:20 Lit *He ran, fell on his neck*   ʲ15:22 Lit *hand*   ᵏ15:27 Lit *him back healthy*   ˡ15:31 Or *Child*

Lk 15:11-32 This parable is often titled with relationship to the son, but it really stresses the response of the father to the lost son who returns. It elaborates the first two parables of Luke 15 and is unique to Luke. It is the parable of the forgiving father.

Lk 15:12 *give me the share of the estate:* In Jewish culture, this request would be an insult to the father, expressing a severance of the family bond. But the father allows it. This pictures God allowing us to go our own way, even if we choose the way of harm with its consequences.

Lk 15:15 *feed pigs:* In Judaism, there is hardly any job more humiliating than tending pigs, which were unclean animals, and it left one constantly unclean. This shows how bad things were for the son especially when the pigs were eating better than he was!

Lk 15:18 *Father, I have sinned against heaven and in your sight:* This is the confession of one who is truly repentant.

Lk 15:20 *threw his arms around his neck:* The father, always watching for the lost son, went out to meet him. The father's taking the initiative went counter to cultural expectations. A hearty welcome was offered before the son could ask for it. The father's running toward the son would have been viewed as undignified for a man of his age and position in life.

Lk 15:22 *best robe:* The father completely reinstated the son and had a celebration to rejoice (vv. 7,10) at the lost son's return.

Lk 15:24 *was dead and is alive . . . was lost and is found:* These two explanations in verses 24 and 32 summarize the point of the parable.

Lk 15:28 *became angry:* The older brother did not care for this forgiveness, a picture of the Pharisees and scribes noted in verse 2. He was told that everything that the younger son had was available to him. There is not room for jealousy. Rather there should be joy.

Lk 15:30-32 *this son of yours . . . this brother of yours:* These two phrases at the end of the parable distinguish the attitudes of the older brother and father. The brother does not even want to acknowledge a relationship to his returning brother. The father will not let him forget that the one returning is his brother. We are all related to each other as sinners who need the forgiveness of the Father.

Sec. 117   Three Parables of Stewardship

Luke 16:1–17:10

[1] He also said to the disciples: "There was a rich man who received an accusation that his manager was squandering his possessions. [2] So he called the manager in and asked, 'What is this I hear about you? Give an account of your management, because you can no longer be ⌊my⌋ manager.'

[3] "Then the manager said to himself, 'What should I do, since my master is taking the management away from me? I'm not strong enough to dig; I'm ashamed to beg. [4] I know what I'll do so that when I'm removed from management, people will welcome me into their homes.'

[5] "So he summoned each one of his master's debtors. 'How much do you owe my master?' he asked the first one.

[6] "'A hundred measures of oil,' he said.

"'Take your invoice,' he told him, 'sit down quickly, and write 50.'

[7] "Next he asked another, 'How much do you owe?'

"'A hundred measures of wheat,' he said.

"'Take your invoice,' he told him, 'and write 80.'

[8] "The master praised the unrighteous manager because he had acted astutely. For the sons of this age are more astute than the sons of light ⌊in dealing⌋ with their own people.[a] [9] And I tell you, make friends for yourselves by means of the unrighteous money so that when it fails,[b] they may welcome you into eternal dwellings. [10] Whoever is faithful in very little is also faithful in much, and whoever is unrighteous in very little is also unrighteous in much. [11] So if you have not been faithful with the unrighteous money, who will trust you with what is genuine? [12] And if you have not been faithful with what belongs to someone else, who will give you what is your own? [13] No household slave can be the •slave of two masters, since either he will hate one and love the other, or he will be devoted to one and despise the other. You can't be slaves to both God and money."

[14] The •Pharisees, who were lovers of money, were listening to all these things and scoffing at Him. [15] And He told them: "You are the ones who justify yourselves in the sight of others, but God knows your hearts. For what is highly admired by people is revolting in God's sight.

[16] "The Law and the Prophets were[c] until John; since then, the good news of the kingdom of God has been proclaimed, and everyone is strongly urged to enter it. [d] [17] But it is easier for heaven and earth to pass away than for one stroke of a letter in the law to drop out.

[18] "Everyone who divorces his wife and marries another woman commits adultery, and everyone who marries a woman divorced from her husband commits adultery.

[19] "There was a rich man who would dress in purple and fine linen, feasting lavishly every day. [20] But a poor man named Lazarus, covered with sores, was left at his gate. [21] He longed to be filled with what fell from the rich man's table, but instead the dogs would come and lick his sores. [22] One day the poor man died

---

[a]**16:8** Lit *own generation*   [b]**16:9** Other mss read *when you fail* or *pass away*   [c]**16:16** Perhaps *were proclaimed*, or *were in effect*
[d]**16:16** Or *everyone is forcing his way into it*

Lk 16:1-16 This is one of the most difficult of Jesus' parables. What is unclear is whether in verses 5-7 the steward takes a cut in his own commission to lower the rates of his master's clients or continues to cheat. Either way, the point is that Christians should be as resourceful (while being honest) with material things as this man was.

Lk 16:8 *more astute:* In this remark is the lesson. The call is for the sons of light, or Jesus' disciples to be more astute in their affairs. The details follow in the next verses.

Lk 16:9 *make friends . . . by means of the unrighteous money:* The call here is to be generous with our possessions, which God sees and honors when we come to the "eternal dwellings," that is, heaven.

Lk 16:12 *have not been faithful with what belongs to someone else:* How we are stewards of God's blessings is the point here. Why reward us with something of great value if we cannot handle something of lesser value.

Lk 16:16 *strongly urged to enter it:* There is an era break between the coming of John the Baptist and Jesus, who preaches the kingdom and urges all to respond.

Lk 16:17 *one stroke of a letter in the law to drop out:* God's law is the expression of His holy character and so does not change. Jesus came to fulfill God's law and to enable others to fulfill it.

Lk 16:18 *Everyone who divorces his wife:* This remark on marriage and divorce serves as an example that underscores Jesus' coming will maintain the ethical standards of the old era. It highlights that Jesus taught against divorce. Because it is an example as opposed to a full discussion, the treatment of Matthew 5:32 and 19:9 are more detailed treatments of the issue.

Lk 16:21 *lick his sores:* In Judaism, being hungry and having wild dogs lick your sores was a picture of true destitution.

Luke 16:1–17:10 (cont.)

and was carried away by the angels to Abraham's side.[a] The rich man also died and was buried. [23] And being in torment in •Hades, he looked up and saw Abraham a long way off, with Lazarus at his side. [24] 'Father Abraham!' he called out, 'Have mercy on me and send Lazarus to dip the tip of his finger in water and cool my tongue, because I am in agony in this flame!'

[25] "'Son,'[b] Abraham said, 'remember that during your life you received your good things, just as Lazarus received bad things, but now he is comforted here, while you are in agony. [26] Besides all this, a great chasm has been fixed between us and you, so that those who want to pass over from here to you cannot; neither can those from there cross over to us.'

[27] "'Father,' he said, 'then I beg you to send him to my father's house— [28] because I have five brothers—to warn them, so they won't also come to this place of torment.'

[29] "But Abraham said, 'They have Moses and the prophets; they should listen to them.'

[30] "'No, father Abraham,' he said. 'But if someone from the dead goes to them, they will repent.'

[31] "But he told him, 'If they don't listen to Moses and the prophets, they will not be persuaded if someone rises from the dead.'"

[1] He said to His disciples, "Offenses[c] will certainly come,[d] but woe to the one they come through! [2] It would be better for him if a millstone[e] were hung around his neck and he were thrown into the sea than for him to cause one of these little ones to •stumble. [3] Be on your guard. If your brother sins,[f] rebuke him, and if he repents, forgive him. [4] And if he sins against you seven times in a day, and comes back to you seven times, saying, 'I repent,' you must forgive him."

[5] The apostles said to the Lord, "Increase our faith."

[6] "If you have faith the size of[g] a mustard seed," the Lord said, "you can say to this mulberry tree, 'Be uprooted and planted in the sea,' and it will obey you.

[7] "Which one of you having a •slave tending sheep or plowing will say to him when he comes in from the field, 'Come at once and sit down to eat'? [8] Instead, will he not tell him, 'Prepare something for me to eat, get ready,[h] and serve me while I eat and drink; later you can eat and drink'? [9] Does he thank that slave because he did what was commanded?[i] [10] In the same way, when you have done all that you were commanded, you should say, 'We are good-for-nothing slaves; we've only done our duty.'"

[a]**16:22** Lit *to the fold of Abraham's robe*, or *to Abraham's bosom*; see Jn 13:23   [b]**16:25** Lit *Child*   [c]**17:1** Or *Traps*, or *Bait-sticks*, or *Causes of stumbling*, or *Causes of sin*   [d]**17:1** Lit *It is impossible for offenses not to come*   [e]**17:2** Large stone used for grinding grains into flour   [f]**17:3** Other mss add *against you*   [g]**17:6** Lit *faith like*   [h]**17:8** Lit *eat, tuck in your robe*, or *eat, gird yourself*   [i]**17:9** Other mss add *I don't think so*

Lk 16:22 *Abraham's side:* A Jewish way to speak of heaven.

Lk 16:24 *Father Abraham:* Heaven and hell are separated by a chasm that cannot be bridged. Hell is a destination with no exit. *Lazarus:* This is the only figure in a parable to be named and there is a reason. The fact that the rich man knew Lazarus' name means that he knew that Lazarus was outside his door and even could identify him, but the rich man did nothing for him. The rich man also continues to view Lazarus as someone who is only there to serve the rich man's needs. The rich man's heart is revealed as having learned nothing.

Lk 16:29 *They have Moses and the prophets:* That is, the Scriptures.

Lk 16:30 *they will repent:* The rich man thinks a message from beyond will help his brothers.

Lk 16:31 *If they don't listen to Moses and the prophets, they will not be persuaded if someone rises from the dead:* This reply argues that one who does not respond to Scripture will not respond when its promises (like the resurrection) are realized. One either responds to God's revelation or not. Miracles may well change nothing for such a person.

Lk 17:1 *Offenses:* This term in all likelihood refers to leading disciples into apostasy or some other kind of severe sin.

Lk 17:4 *sins against you seven times in a day:* This figure means that we should forgive and be forgiving. To ask seven times in one day is to ask constantly.

Lk 17:6 *faith the size of a mustard seed:* Since a mustard seed is a very small seed, the point is made about what even a small amount of faith can accomplish. It can accomplish unbelievable things.

Lk 17:10 *good-for-nothing slaves:* Verses 7-10 are unique to Luke. The point of this description is to make the point that a slave is to do one's duty for the master. In that sense, they have no rights. And so when they feed the master after a full day's work, it is only doing one's duty; what should be done.

Sec. 118   The Seventh Sign: Jesus Raises Lazarus from Death

John 11:1-44

[1] Now a man was sick, Lazarus, from Bethany, the village of Mary and her sister Martha. [2] Mary was the one who anointed the Lord with fragrant oil and wiped His feet with her hair, and it was her brother Lazarus who was sick. [3] So the sisters sent a message to Him: "Lord, the one You love is sick."

[4] When Jesus heard it, He said, "This sickness will not end in death but is for the glory of God, so that the Son of God may be glorified through it." [5] Now Jesus loved Martha, her sister, and Lazarus. [6] So when He heard that he was sick, He stayed two more days in the place where He was. [7] Then after that, He said to the disciples, "Let's go to Judea again."

[8] "•Rabbi," the disciples told Him, "just now the •Jews tried to stone You, and You're going there again?"

[9] "Aren't there 12 hours in a day?" Jesus answered. "If anyone walks during the day, he doesn't stumble, because he sees the light of this world. [10] If anyone walks during the night, he does stumble, because the light is not in him." [11] He said this, and then He told them, "Our friend Lazarus has fallen •asleep, but I'm on My way to wake him up."

[12] Then the disciples said to Him, "Lord, if he has fallen asleep, he will get well."

[13] Jesus, however, was speaking about his death, but they thought He was speaking about natural sleep. [14] So Jesus then told them plainly, "Lazarus has died. [15] I'm glad for you that I wasn't there so that you may believe. But let's go to him."

[16] Then Thomas (called "Twin") said to his fellow disciples, "Let's go so that we may die with Him."

[17] When Jesus arrived, He found that Lazarus had already been in the tomb four days. [18] Bethany was near Jerusalem (about two miles[a] away). [19] Many of the Jews had come to Martha and Mary to comfort them about their brother. [20] As soon as Martha heard that Jesus was coming, she went to meet Him. But Mary remained seated in the house.

[21] Then Martha said to Jesus, "Lord, if You had been here, my brother wouldn't have died. [22] Yet even now I know that whatever You ask from God, God will give You."

[23] "Your brother will rise again," Jesus told her.

[24] Martha said, "I know that he will rise again in the resurrection at the last day."

[25] Jesus said to her, "I am the resurrection and the life. The one who believes in Me, even if he dies, will live. [26] Everyone who lives and believes in Me will never die—ever. Do you believe this?"

[27] "Yes, Lord," she told Him, "I believe You are the •Messiah, the Son of God, who was to come into the world."

[28] Having said this, she went back and called her sister Mary, saying in private, "The Teacher is here and is calling for you."

[29] As soon as she heard this, she got up quickly and went to Him. [30] Jesus had not yet come into the village but was still in the place where Martha had met Him. [31] The Jews who were with her in the house consoling her saw that Mary got up quickly and went out. So they followed her, supposing that she was going to the tomb to cry there.

[32] When Mary came to where Jesus was and saw Him, she fell at His feet and told Him, "Lord, if You had been here, my brother would not have died!"

[33] When Jesus saw her crying, and the Jews who had come with her crying, He was angry[b] in His spirit and deeply moved. [34] "Where have you put him?" He asked.

"Lord," they told Him, "come and see."

[35] Jesus wept.

[36] So the Jews said, "See how He loved him!" [37] But some of them said, "Couldn't He who opened the blind man's eyes also have kept this man from dying?"

[38] Then Jesus, angry in Himself again, came to the tomb. It was a cave, and a stone was lying against it. [39] "Remove the stone," Jesus said.

[a]**11:18** Lit *15 stadia*; 1 *stadion* = 600 feet   [b]**11:33** The Gk word is very strong and probably indicates Jesus' anger against sin's tyranny and death.

Jn 11:1-57 The raising of Lazarus constitutes the seventh and climactic messianic "sign" of Jesus in this Gospel. This spectacular miracle (recorded only by John) anticipates Jesus' own resurrection and reveals Jesus as "the resurrection and the life" (11:25). Raising the dead is very rare in the OT (Elijah: 1 Kg 17:17-24; Elisha: 2 Kg 4:32-37; 13:21) and also in the Gospels (Jesus raising Jairus's daughter: Mk 5:22-24,38-42 and Jesus raising the widow's son at Nain: Lk 7:11-15). Raising Lazarus also serves as a final event triggering the Jewish leaders' resolve to have Jesus arrested and tried for blasphemy (11:45-57).

John 11:1-44 (cont.)

Martha, the dead man's sister, told Him, "Lord, he already stinks. It's been four days."
[40] Jesus said to her, "Didn't I tell you that if you believed you would see the glory of God?"
[41] So they removed the stone. Then Jesus raised His eyes and said, "Father, I thank You that You heard Me. [42] I know that You always hear Me, but because of the crowd standing here I said this, so they may believe You sent Me." [43] After He said this, He shouted with a loud voice, "Lazarus, come out!" [44] The dead man came out bound hand and foot with linen strips and with his face wrapped in a cloth. Jesus said to them, "Loose him and let him go."

Sec. 119   The Plot to Kill Jesus

John 11:45-54

[45] Therefore many of the Jews who came to Mary and saw what He did believed in Him. [46] But some of them went to the •Pharisees and told them what Jesus had done.
[47] So the •chief priests and the Pharisees convened the •Sanhedrin and said, "What are we going to do since this man does many signs? [48] If we let Him continue in this way, everyone will believe in Him! Then the Romans will come and remove both our place[a] and our nation."
[49] One of them, Caiaphas, who was high priest that year, said to them, "You know nothing at all! [50] You're not considering that it is to your[b] advantage that one man should die for the people rather than the whole nation perish." [51] He did not say this on his own, but being high priest that year he prophesied that Jesus was going to die for the nation, [52] and not for the nation only, but also to unite the scattered children of God. [53] So from that day on they plotted to kill Him. [54] Therefore Jesus no longer walked openly among the Jews but departed from there to the countryside near the wilderness, to a town called Ephraim. And He stayed there with the disciples.

[a]**11:48** The temple or possibly all of Jerusalem   [b]**11:50** Other mss read *to our*

Sec. 120   Jesus Begins His Last Journey to Jerusalem

Luke 17:11-37

[11] While traveling to Jerusalem, He passed between[a] Samaria and Galilee. [12] As He entered a village, 10 men with serious skin diseases met Him. They stood at a distance [13] and raised their voices, saying, "Jesus, Master, have mercy on us!"
[14] When He saw them, He told them, "Go and show yourselves to the priests." And while they were going, they were healed.[b]
[15] But one of them, seeing that he was healed, returned and, with a loud voice, gave glory to God. [16] He fell facedown at His feet, thanking Him. And he was a •Samaritan.
[17] Then Jesus said, "Were not 10 cleansed? Where are the nine? [18] Didn't any return[c] to give glory to God except this foreigner?" [19] And He told him, "Get up and go on your way. Your faith has made you well."[d]
[20] Being asked by the •Pharisees when the kingdom of God will come, He answered them, "The kingdom of God is not coming with something observable; [21] no one will say,[e] 'Look here!' or 'There!' For you see, the kingdom of God is among you."
[22] Then He told the disciples: "The days are coming when you will long to see one of the days of the •Son of Man, but you won't see it. [23] They will say to you, 'Look there!' or 'Look here!' Don't follow or run after them. [24] For as the lightning flashes from horizon to horizon and lights up the sky, so the Son of Man will be in His day. [25] But first He must suffer many things and be rejected by this generation.

[a]**17:11** Or *through the middle of* [b]**17:14** Lit *cleansed* [c]**17:18** Lit *Were they not found returning* [d]**17:19** Or *faith has saved you*
[e]**17:21** Lit *they will not say*

Lk 17:18 *except this foreigner:* Jesus notes that the only leper appreciative of his healing was a foreigner. This theme extends back to the faith of the centurion in Luke 8, another foreigner who responded in an exemplary way to Jesus.
Lk 17:20-37 This teaching on the coming kingdom is like material in Mark 13 and Matthew 24 but is uttered outside Jerusalem before Jesus' last week. So Luke has two speeches on the end, while Mark and Matthew have one. This speech deals with the coming of the Son of Man.
Lk 17:21 *the kingdom of God is among you:* Jesus teaches that the kingdom is already in the midst of the people. This refers to Jesus' presence and the promise He brings. In this remark Jesus looks at the beginning of the kingdom's coming, not its arrival in full.

Luke 17:11-37 (cont.)

26 "Just as it was in the days of Noah, so it will be in the days of the Son of Man: 27 people went on eating, drinking, marrying and giving in marriage until the day Noah boarded the ark, and the flood came and destroyed them all. 28 It will be the same as it was in the days of Lot: people went on eating, drinking, buying, selling, planting, building. 29 But on the day Lot left Sodom, fire and sulfur rained from heaven and destroyed them all. 30 It will be like that on the day the Son of Man is revealed. 31 On that day, a man on the housetop, whose belongings are in the house, must not come down to get them. Likewise the man who is in the field must not turn back. 32 Remember Lot's wife! 33 Whoever tries to make his •life secure[a] [b] will lose it, and whoever loses his life will preserve it. 34 I tell you, on that night two will be in one bed: one will be taken and the other will be left. 35 Two women will be grinding grain together: one will be taken and the other left. [36 Two will be in a field: one will be taken, and the other will be left.]"[c]

37 "Where, Lord?" they asked Him.

He said to them, "Where the corpse is, there also the vultures will be gathered."

[a]17:33 Other mss read *to save his life*   [b]17:33 Or *tries to retain his life*   [c]17:36 Other mss omit bracketed text

Lk 17:24 *For as the lightning flashes:* The arrival of the Son of Man, who signals the coming of the kingdom in judgment, will not come by people pointing out where it is coming, but quickly and visibly like a flash of lightning in the night.

Lk 17:25 *first He must suffer:* In a remark unique to Luke, Jesus points out that the Son of Man must suffer death before any of this can take place.

Lk 17:26-28 *Noah . . . Lot:* The coming of the Son of Man will be in the midst of life going on as normal. It will come suddenly like the flood came and the judgment on Sodom and Gomorrah happened. But this "coming" will involve a sudden separation of people.

Lk 17:37 *vultures:* This image is a picture of death. The return of the Son of Man means judgment for many.

Sec. 121   Two Parables on Prayer

Luke 18:1-14

1 He then told them a parable on the need for them to pray always and not become discouraged: 2 "There was a judge in one town who didn't fear God or respect man. 3 And a widow in that town kept coming to him, saying, 'Give me justice against my adversary.'

4 "For a while he was unwilling, but later he said to himself, 'Even though I don't fear God or respect man, 5 yet because this widow keeps pestering me,[a] I will give her justice, so she doesn't wear me out[b] by her persistent coming.'"

6 Then the Lord said, "Listen to what the unjust judge says. 7 Will not God grant justice to His elect who cry out to Him day and night? Will He delay ⌊to help⌋ them?[c] 8 I tell you that He will swiftly grant them justice. Nevertheless, when the •Son of Man comes, will He find that faith[d] on earth?"

9 He also told this parable to some who trusted in themselves that they were righteous and looked down on everyone else: 10 "Two men went up to the •temple complex to pray, one a •Pharisee and the other a tax collector. 11 The Pharisee took his stand[e] and was praying like this: 'God, I thank You that I'm not like other people[f] —greedy, unrighteous, adulterers, or even like this tax collector. 12 I fast twice a week; I give a tenth[g] of everything I get.'

[a]18:5 Lit *widow causes me trouble*   [b]18:5 Or *doesn't give me a black eye,* or *doesn't ruin my reputation*   [c]18:7 Or *Will He put up with them?*   [d]18:8 Or *faith,* or *that kind of faith,* or *any faith,* or *the faith,* or *faithfulness;* the faith that persists in prayer for God's vindication
[e]18:11 Or *Pharisee stood by himself*   [f]18:11 Or *like the rest of men*   [g]18:12 Or *give tithes*

Lk 18:3 *widow:* In the culture, a widow had little power and was very vulnerable.

Lk 18:5 *keeps pestering me:* The teaching about always praying is this point. Believers are to be diligent in prayer like this widow. It is especially focused on prayers related to God granting justice in the context of persecution as verses 7-8a suggest.

Lk 18:8 *will He find that faith on earth:* This remark is a clue that the return of the Son of Man may take some time, for there is a possibility that the faith of some will die out as they wait for Him to come. The remark is a call to remain faithful until He comes back.

Lk 18:11 *I thank You that I'm not like:* This prayer is a distorted version of a praise psalm. The Pharisee is really grateful that he is such a wonderful person. Note all the uses of the first person pronoun in his remarks.

Luke 18:1-14 (cont.)

[13] "But the tax collector, standing far off, would not even raise his eyes to heaven but kept striking his chest[a] and saying, 'God, turn Your wrath from me[b] —a sinner!' [14] I tell you, this one went down to his house justified rather than the other; because everyone who exalts himself will be humbled, but the one who humbles himself will be exalted."

[a]**18:13** Mourning   [b]**18:13** Lit *God, be propitious to me*; = May Your wrath be turned aside by the sacrifice

Lk 18:13 *turn Your wrath from me:* The contrast of the tax collector's attitude is obvious. Jesus commends the humility of the tax collector as verse 14 shows.

Sec. 122   The Question of Divorce

Matthew 19:1-12   Mark 10:1-12

Matthew 19:1-12	Mark 10:1-12
[1] When Jesus had finished this instruction, He departed from Galilee and went to the region of Judea across the Jordan. [2] Large crowds followed Him, and He healed them there. [3] Some •Pharisees approached Him to test Him. They asked, "Is it lawful for a man to divorce his wife on any grounds?"	[1] He set out from there and went to the region of Judea and across the Jordan. Then crowds converged on Him again and, as He usually did, He began teaching them once more. [2] Some •Pharisees approached Him to test Him. They asked, "Is it lawful for a man to divorce ⌊his⌋ wife?" [3] He replied to them, "What did Moses command you?" [4] They said, "Moses permitted us to write divorce papers and send her away." [5] But Jesus told them, "He wrote this command for you because of the hardness of your hearts. [6] But from the beginning of creation God[a] **made them male and female.**[b]
[4] "Haven't you read," He replied, "that He who created[a] them in the beginning **made them male and female,**[b] [5] and He also said:	
For this reason a man will leave his father and mother and be joined to his wife, and the two will become one flesh?[c]	[7] **For this reason a man will leave his father and mother [and be joined to his wife],**[c] [8] **and the two will become one flesh.**[d]
[6] So they are no longer two, but one flesh. Therefore what God has joined together, man must not separate."	So they are no longer two, but one flesh. [9] Therefore what God has joined together, man must not separate."

[a]**19:4** Other mss read *made* [b]**19:4** Gn 1:27; 5:2 [c]**19:5** Gn 2:24

[a]**10:6** Other mss omit *God* [b]**10:6** Gn 1:27; 5:2 [c]**10:7** Other mss omit bracketed text [d]**10:7-8** Gn 2:24

Mt 19:1 *He departed from Galilee:* So far as we know from the NT, this was the end of Jesus' ministry in Galilee; He would never return there until after His resurrection. *the region of Judea across the Jordan:* Apparently Jesus left Galilee to go to Judea by way of Perea as the Galileans often did to avoid Samaria. No part of Judea itself lies east of the Jordan.

Mt 19:3 There were two interpretations of the Mosaic divorce law in Jesus' time. Two of the most famous Jewish rabbis lived during the inter-biblical period (between the OT and NT). They interpreted Deuteronomy 24:1-4 differently. Rabbi Hillel focused on the phrase, ". . . but she becomes displeasing to him," meaning a man could seek a divorce for any and every cause. It was not "no fault" divorce, but "any fault" divorce. Rabbi Shammai focused on the phrase "he finds something improper about her." He interpreted this to mean a man could divorce his wife only if she had committed adultery. Jesus sided with Shammai.

Mk 10:3 *What did Moses command:* In Mark's account of this incident, Jesus asks about what Moses *commanded*, and the Pharisees respond by reporting what Moses *permitted* (10:4). They support their position by pointing to Deuteronomy 24:1-4, a passage that acknowledges the reality of divorce and seeks to limit its damaging consequences. Jesus responds by directing them back to the commands of God. God's command, His will for a husband and a wife, is to be joined together and to remain as one.

Matthew 19:1-12 (cont.)	Mark 10:1-12 (cont.)

7 "Why then," they asked Him, "did Moses command ⌊us⌋ to give divorce papers and to send her away?"

8 He told them, "Moses permitted you to divorce your wives because of the hardness of your hearts. But it was not like that from the beginning. 9 And I tell you, whoever divorces his wife, except for sexual immorality, and marries another, commits adultery."[a]

10 His disciples said to Him, "If the relationship of a man with his wife is like this, it's better not to marry!"

11 But He told them, "Not everyone can accept this saying, but only those it has been given to. 12 For there are eunuchs who were born that way from their mother's womb, there are eunuchs who were made by men, and there are eunuchs who have made themselves that way because of the kingdom of heaven. Let anyone accept this who can."

[a]**19:9** Other mss add *Also whoever marries a divorced woman commits adultery*; Mt 5:32

10 Now in the house the disciples questioned Him again about this matter.

11 And He said to them, "Whoever divorces his wife and marries another commits adultery against her. 12 Also, if she divorces her husband and marries another, she commits adultery."

Mt 19:7 *divorce papers:* Literally, "bill," from the Greek *biblios*. A man could simply give his wife a written statement, then put her out of the house (Dt 24:1-4).

Mt 19:8 Jesus agreed that *Moses* had *permitted* divorce, not as God's best for mankind, but because of Israel's backslidden condition.

Mt 19:9 *sexual immorality:* The Greek word is *porneia*, a general term for sexual immorality, including and especially adultery. The Lord stated with absolute authority that the past leniency on divorce was ungodly. He here "shuts the door" on such leniency and asserts that there is only one valid ground for divorce—sexual infidelity.

Mt 19:10-12 Since Jesus' command was stricter than Shammai's, even with the exception clause, the disciples thought it would be better not to marry. Jesus agreed and explained that God has designed some people not to marry. He then clarified that the ability to remain celibate was not the general rule; only those to whom special grace was given could forego marriage.

Mk 10:12 *if she divorces:* The balancing statement in verse 12 about the wife who divorces and marries again is unique to Mark's Gospel. It may represent Mark's own application of Jesus' teaching to his primarily Gentile audience, since Jewish law at the time of Jesus did not allow a wife to divorce her husband. Of course, Jesus Himself, aware of divorce practices in the broader Greco-Roman society, may have decided to expand His teaching to make it relevant beyond the customs of His own people.

Sec. 123   Jesus Blesses the Children

Matthew 19:13-15	Mark 10:13-16	Luke 18:15-17

13 Then children were brought to Him so He might put His hands on them and pray. But the disciples rebuked them. 14 Then Jesus said, "Leave the children alone, and don't try to keep them from coming to Me, because the kingdom of heaven is made up of people like this."[a]

[a]**19:14** Lit *heaven is of such ones*

13 Some people were bringing little children to Him so He might touch them, but His disciples rebuked them. 14 When Jesus saw it, He was indignant and said to them, "Let the little children come to Me. Don't stop them, for the kingdom of God belongs to such as these.

15 Some people were even bringing infants to Him so He might touch them, but when the disciples saw it, they rebuked them. 16 Jesus, however, invited them: "Let the little children come to Me, and don't stop them, because the kingdom of God belongs to such as these.

Mt 19:14 *kingdom of heaven is made up of people like this:* The verse does not teach that all children are saved but that all who come to Christ for salvation must do so with a childlike humility and dependence on Him.

Matthew 19:13-15 (cont.)	Mark 10:13-16 (cont.)	Luke 18:15-17 (cont.)
	15 •I assure you: Whoever does not welcomeᵃ the kingdom of God like a little child will never enter it."	17 •I assure you: Whoever does not welcome the kingdom of God like a little child will never enter it."
15 After putting His hands on them, He went on from there.	16 After taking them in His arms, He laid His hands on them and blessed them.	
	ᵃ**10:15** Or *not receive*	

Mk 10:15 *like a little child:* Earlier in Mark 9:36-37, Jesus used a child as an object lesson to show his disciples that true greatness involves accepting and serving children; that is, those who have no power, position, or wealth. In a similar way, Jesus uses the illustration of a child to show that entering into God's kingdom does not come by pursuing power and prestige but by humbly recognizing one's own helplessness before God.

Lk 18:17 *Whoever does not welcome the kingdom of God like a little child:* In the ancient world, the child was almost a nonperson. So Jesus' receiving children was significant. He turns it into a picture of spiritual truth when He says that one must come to the kingdom like a child, with trust and dependence.

Sec. 124   Possessions and the Kingdom

Matthew 19:16–20:16	Mark 10:17-31	Luke 18:18-30
16 Just then someone came up and asked Him, "Teacher, what good must I do to have eternal life?"	17 As He was setting out on a journey, a man ran up, knelt down before Him, and asked Him, "Good Teacher, what must I do to inherit eternal life?"	18 A ruler asked Him, "Good Teacher, what must I do to inherit eternal life?"
17 "Why do you ask Me about what is good?"ᵃ He said to him. "There is only One who is good.ᵇ If you want to enter into life, keep the commandments." 18 "Which ones?" he asked Him. Jesus answered,	18 "Why do you call Me good?" Jesus asked him. "No one is good but One—God. 19 You know the commandments:	19 "Why do you call Me good?" Jesus asked him. "No one is good but One—God. 20 You know the commandments:
Do not murder; do not commit adultery; do not steal; do not bear false witness; 19 honor your father and your mother; and love your neighbor as yourself.ᶜ	**Do not murder; do not commit adultery; do not steal; do not bear false witness; do not defraud; honor your father and mother."**ᵃ	**Do not commit adultery; do not murder; do not steal; do not bear false witness; honor your father and mother."**ᵃ
ᵃ**19:17** Other mss read *Why do you call Me good?* ᵇ**19:17** Other mss read *No one is good but One—God* ᶜ**19:18-19** Ex 20:12-16; Lv 19:18; Dt 5:16-20	ᵃ**10:19** Ex 20:12-16; Dt 5:16-20	ᵃ**18:20** Ex 20:12-16; Dt 5:16-20

Mt 19:17 *There is only One who is good:* The challenge to the young man was to recognize that if only God is good, was he ready to confess not only that Jesus was good, but also that He was God.

Mk 10:17-22 Verse 18 is not a denial of Jesus' personal goodness. The statement was intended to prompt the man to question his own goodness on which he relied for his salvation. Jesus changed the order of the commandments and rephrased one of the commandments probably in order to highlight the man's failure to fulfill God's law and to undermine his self-righteousness. By selling all that he had, the rich young man would learn to shift his dependence from himself to God. The young man apparently does not take the opportunity to rethink his perspective, since in Mark 10:20 he simply drops the offending word and addresses Jesus as "Teacher" rather than "Good Teacher."

Lk 18:18-23 Luke tells us this man is rich. The parallel in Matthew 19:22 tell us he is young.

Matthew 19:16–20:16 (cont.)	Mark 10:17-31 (cont.)	Luke 18:18-30 (cont.)
20 "I have kept all these,"a the young man told Him. "What do I still lack?" 21 "If you want to be perfect,"b Jesus said to him, "go, sell your belongings and give to the poor, and you will have treasure in heaven. Then come, follow Me." 22 When the young man heard that command, he went away grieving, because he had many possessions. 23 Then Jesus said to His disciples, "•I assure you: It will be hard for a rich person to enter the kingdom of heaven! 24 Again I tell you, it is easier for a camel to go through the eye of a needle than for a rich person to enter the kingdom of God." 25 When the disciples heard this, they were utterly astonished and asked, "Then who can be saved?" 26 But Jesus looked at them and said, "With men this is impossible, but with God all things are possible." 27 Then Peter responded to Him, "Look, we have left everything and followed You. So what will there be for us?"	20 He said to Him, "Teacher, I have kept all these from my youth." 21 Then, looking at him, Jesus loved him and said to him, "You lack one thing: Go, sell all you have and give to the poor, and you will have treasure in heaven. Then come,a follow Me." 22 But he was stunnedb at this demand, and he went away grieving, because he had many possessions. 23 Jesus looked around and said to His disciples, "How hard it is for those who have wealth to enter the kingdom of God!" 24 But the disciples were astonished at His words. Again Jesus said to them, "Children, how hard it isc to enter the kingdom of God! 25 It is easier for a camel to go through the eye of a needle than for a rich person to enter the kingdom of God." 26 So they were even more astonished, saying to one another, "Then who can be saved?" 27 Looking at them, Jesus said, "With men it is impossible, but not with God, because all things are possible with God." 28 Peter began to tell Him, "Look, we have left everything and followed You."	21 "I have kept all these from my youth," he said. 22 When Jesus heard this, He told him, "You still lack one thing: sell all that you have and distribute it to the poor, and you will have treasure in heaven. Then come, follow Me." 23 After he heard this, he became extremely sad, because he was very rich. 24 Seeing that he became sad,a Jesus said, "How hard it is for those who have wealth to enter the kingdom of God! 25 For it is easier for a camel to go through the eye of a needle than for a rich person to enter the kingdom of God." 26 Those who heard this asked, "Then who can be saved?" 27 He replied, "What is impossible with men is possible with God." 28 Then Peter said, "Look, we have left what we had and followed You."

a19:20 Other mss add *from my youth*
b19:21 Or *complete*

a10:21 Other mss add *taking up the cross, and*   b10:22 Or *he became gloomy*
c10:24 Other mss add *for those trusting in wealth*

a18:24 Other mss omit *he became sad*

Mt 19:21 *sell your belongings:* His willingness to obey this command would not "purchase" salvation but it would be evidence that he desired salvation above everything else. Jesus had to show the young man that his possessions were really his god.

Mk 10:19 *do not defraud:* In Mark's account, Jesus' summary of the second half of the ten commandments includes a command against defrauding others, which is probably an expansion and elaboration of the command against stealing. To defraud others means to cheat them or to withhold what rightfully belongs to them through deceitful actions such as the underpayment of employees (Jms 5:4) or the pursuit of unjust lawsuits (1 Co 6:7-8).

Mk 10:25 *the eye of a needle:* Jesus is referring to the small hole in a sewing needle. In other words, the chances of a rich man entering into the kingdom of God are worse than the chances of a large camel squeezing through such a small opening. The only hope for the wealthy is in the God who can do the impossible (10:27).

Lk 18:27 *is possible with God:* Jesus replies that God alone makes salvation possible.

Matthew 19:16–20:16 (cont.)	Mark 10:17-31 (cont.)	Luke 18:18-30 (cont.)
28 Jesus said to them, "I assure you: In the Messianic Age,a when the •Son of Man sits on His glorious throne, you who have followed Me will also sit on 12 thrones, judging the 12 tribes of Israel. 29 And everyone who has left houses, brothers or sisters, father or mother,b children, or fields because of My name will receive 100 times more and will inherit eternal life. 30 But many who are first will be last, and the last first.	29 "I assure you," Jesus said, "there is no one who has left house, brothers or sisters, mother or father,a children, or fields because of Me and the gospel, 30 who will not receive 100 times more, now at this time—houses, brothers and sisters, mothers and children, and fields, with persecutions—and eternal life in the age to come. 31 But many who are first will be last, and the last first."	29 So He said to them, "I assure you: There is no one who has left a house, wife or brothers, parents or children because of the kingdom of God, 30 who will not receive many times more at this time, and eternal life in the age to come."

a**10:29** Other mss add *or wife*

1 "For the kingdom of heaven is like a landowner who went out early in the morning to hire workers for his vineyard. 2 After agreeing with the workers on one •denarius for the day, he sent them into his vineyard. 3 When he went out about nine in the morning,c he saw others standing in the marketplace doing nothing. 4 To those men he said, 'You also go to my vineyard, and I'll give you whatever is right.' So off they went. 5 About noon and at three,d he went out again and did the same thing. 6 Then about fivee he went and found others standing around,f and said to them, 'Why have you been standing here all day doing nothing?'

7 "'Because no one hired us,' they said to him.

"'You also go to my vineyard,' he told them.g 8 When evening came, the owner of the vineyard told his foreman, 'Call the workers and give them their pay, starting with the last and ending with the first.'h

9 "When those who were hired about fivee came, they each received one denarius. 10 So when the first ones came, they assumed they would get more, but they also received a denarius each. 11 When they received it, they began to complain to the landowner: 12 'These last men put in one hour, and you made them equal to us who bore the burden of the day and the burning heat!'

13 "He replied to one of them, 'Friend, I'm doing you no wrong. Didn't you agree with me on a denarius? 14 Take what's yours and go. I want to give this last man the same as I gave you. 15 Don't I have the right to do what I want with my business?i Are you jealousj because I'm generous?'k

16 "So the last will be first, and the first last."l

a**19:28** Lit *the regeneration*   b**19:29** Other mss add *or wife*   c**20:3** Lit *about the third hour*   d**20:5** Lit *about the sixth hour and the ninth hour* e**20:6,9** Lit *about the eleventh hour*   f**20:6** Other mss add *doing nothing*   g**20:7** Other mss add *'and you'll get whatever is right.'*   h**20:8** Lit *starting from the last until the first*   i**20:15** Lit *with what is mine*   j**20:15** Lit *Is your eye evil*; an idiom for jealousy or stinginess   k**20:15** Lit *good*   l**20:16** Other mss add *For many are called, but few are chosen.*

Mt 19:28 *In the Messianic Age:* Literally, "the regeneration." The new birth of the world will be fulfilled when Jesus sits on His throne ot glory.

Mt 20:1-16 The parable of the landowner, found only in Matthew, serves to illustrate the truth of 19:30. It illustrates the reality that while all true disciples will be rewarded, the order of rewards will be determined by the spirit in which the disciple served.

Mt 20:15 *jealous:* The normal word for jealousy is not used, rather, an idiomatic phrase "Is your eye evil?" The complainer had a grudging eye while the landowner had a generous eye. The lesson in the verse is that God is sovereign. He can do as He pleases, and what He pleases will always be right, just, and fair.

Mk 10:30 *with persecutions:* Only Mark's Gospel includes the words "with persecutions" in this saying of Jesus (see Mt 19:29; Lk 18:29-30). For those who follow Jesus, the present time involves both reward and suffering. For other passages in Mark's Gospel on the subject of persecution, see 4:17; 8:34-38; 9:49; 10:38-40; 13:9-13.

Sec. 125   Jesus' Third Prediction of His Death and Resurrection

Matthew 20:17-28	Mark 10:32-45	Luke 18:31-34

¹⁷ While going up to Jerusalem, Jesus took the 12 disciples aside privately and said to them on the way:	³² They were on the road, going up to Jerusalem, and Jesus was walking ahead of them. They were astonished, but those who followed Him were afraid. Taking the Twelve aside again, He began to tell them the things that would happen to Him.	³¹ Then He took the Twelve aside and told them,

[17] While going up to Jerusalem, Jesus took the 12 disciples aside privately and said to them on the way:

[32] They were on the road, going up to Jerusalem, and Jesus was walking ahead of them. They were astonished, but those who followed Him were afraid. Taking the Twelve aside again, He began to tell them the things that would happen to Him.

[31] Then He took the Twelve aside and told them,

[18] "Listen! We are going up to Jerusalem. The •Son of Man will be handed over to the •chief priests and •scribes, and they will condemn Him to death. [19] Then they will hand Him over to the Gentiles to be mocked, flogged,[a] and crucified, and He will be resurrected[b] on the third day."

[33] "Listen! We are going up to Jerusalem. The •Son of Man will be handed over to the •chief priests and the •scribes, and they will condemn Him to death. Then they will hand Him over to the Gentiles, [34] and they will mock Him, spit on Him, flog[a] Him, and kill Him, and He will rise after three days."

"Listen! We are going up to Jerusalem. Everything that is written through the prophets about the Son of Man will be accomplished. [32] For He will be handed over to the Gentiles, and He will be mocked, insulted, spit on; [33] and after they flog Him, they will kill Him, and He will rise on the third day." [34] They understood none of these things. This saying[a] was hidden from them, and they did not grasp what was said.

a18:34 The meaning of the saying

[20] Then the mother of Zebedee's sons approached Him with her sons. She knelt down to ask Him for something. [21] "What do you want?" He asked her.

"Promise,"[c] she said to Him, "that these two sons of mine may sit, one on Your right and the other on Your left, in Your kingdom." [22] But Jesus answered, "You don't know what you're asking. Are you able to drink the cup[d] that I am about to drink?"[e]

"We are able," they said to Him.

[35] Then James and John, the sons of Zebedee, approached Him and said, "Teacher, we want You to do something for us if we ask You." [36] "What do you want Me to do for you?" He asked them. [37] They answered Him, "Allow us to sit at Your right and at Your left in Your glory." [38] But Jesus said to them, "You don't know what you're asking. Are you able to drink the cup I drink or to be baptized with the baptism I am baptized with?" [39] "We are able," they told Him.

a20:19 Or *scourged* **b20:19** Other mss read *will rise again* **c20:21** Lit *Say* **d20:22** Figurative language referring to His coming suffering; Mt 26:39; Jn 8:11 **e20:22** Other mss add *and (or) to be baptized with the baptism that I am baptized with?"*

a10:34 Or *scourge*

Mt 20:17 *going up to Jerusalem:* Apparently the Lord was leaving Perea for the trip to Jerusalem via Jericho (see v. 29).
Mt 20:18 *chief priests:* A group of Jewish temple officers that included the high priest, captain of the temple, temple overseers, and treasurers.
Mt 20:19 *crucified:* For the first time Jesus referred to the way He would die—crucifixion.
Mt 20:20 *mother of Zebedee's sons:* The mother of Zebedee's sons was Salome (Mt 27:56 and Mk 15: 40).
Mt 20:22 *You don't know what you're asking:* They do not yet understand the nature of Jesus' kingdom. He redirects their attention to His coming suffering. *cup:* A common Old Testament metaphor for suffering.
Mk 10:32-34 This third prediction of Jesus' death is even more explicit than the previous predictions.
Mk 10:37 *at Your right and at Your left:* The place of highest honor was at the right, while the place next in honor was at the left (see 2 Sm 16:6; 1 Kg 2:19; Ps 45:9; 110:1). Ironically, Mark uses almost the exact same phrase later in his Gospel to describe the two criminals who were crucified with Jesus, one on His right and one on His left (15:27). Therefore, Jesus was correct in stating that James and John did not know what they were requesting (10:38).
Lk18:32-33 *will be handed over . . . will rise:* Once again Jesus notes what the prophets taught about the Son of Man. In this passage Son of Man is a way to describe Jesus in His suffering and may well include the idea of the Son of Man also being the Suffering Servant of God (Is 52:13–53:12).

Matthew 20:17-28 (cont.)

Mark 10:32-45 (cont.)

23 He told them, "You will indeed drink My cup.ᵃ But to sit at My right and left is not Mine to give; instead, it belongs to those for whom it has been prepared by My Father." 24 When the 10 ⌊disciples⌋ heard this, they became indignant with the two brothers. 25 But Jesus called them over and said, "You know that the rulers of the Gentiles dominate them, and the men of high position exercise power over them. 26 It must not be like that among you. On the contrary, whoever wants to become great among you must be your servant, 27 and whoever wants to be first among you must be your •slave; 28 just as the Son of Man did not come to be served, but to serve, and to give His life—a ransom for many."

ᵃ20:23 Other mss add *and be baptized with the baptism that I am baptized with.*

Jesus said to them, "You will drink the cup I drink, and you will be baptized with the baptism I am baptized with. 40 But to sit at My right or left is not Mine to give; instead, it is for those it has been prepared for." 41 When the ⌊other⌋ 10 ⌊disciples⌋ heard this, they began to be indignant with James and John.

42 Jesus called them over and said to them, "You know that those who are regarded as rulers of the Gentiles dominate them, and their men of high positions exercise power over them. 43 But it must not be like that among you. On the contrary, whoever wants to become great among you must be your servant, 44 and whoever wants to be first among you must be a •slave to all. 45 For even the Son of Man did not come to be served, but to serve, and to give His life—a ransom for many."ᵃ

ᵃ10:45 Or *in the place of many*; Is 53:10-12

Mt 20:23 *not Mine to give:* Though equal in essence with the Father, Jesus willingly became functionally subordinate to Him while on earth.

Mt 20:28 *ransom:* The rich NT word *lutron*, signifying the price paid for a bond-slave who is then set free by the one who bought him. Christ redeems us from our slavery to sin.

Mk 10:39 Drinking from Jesus' cup and sharing Jesus' baptism meant that by doing so, James and John would share their Master's fate, for example, die at the hands of sinful people who rejected Jesus.

Mk 10:45 *ransom:* The word "ransom" means a payment given to buy freedom for those held in bondage, including, for example, prisoners of war, slaves, and debtors. In this verse, Jesus presents His death as a payment that brings about release for those who are held under spiritual bondage and slavery (see Mt 20:28; 1 Tm 2:6). This is the clearest reference to Jesus' death as a substitutionary atonement in the Gospel.

Sec. 126   Two Blind Men Healed

Matthew 20:29-34

Mark 10:46-52

Luke 18:35-43

29 As they were leaving Jericho, a large crowd followed Him.

30 There were two blind men sitting by the road. When they heard that Jesus was passing by, they cried out, "Lord, have mercy on us, Son of David!" 31 The crowd told them to keep quiet, but they cried out all the more, "Lord, have mercy on us, Son of David!"

46 They came to Jericho. And as He was leaving Jericho with His disciples and a large crowd, Bartimaeus (the son of Timaeus), a blind beggar, was sitting by the road. 47 When he heard that it was Jesus the •Nazarene, he began to cry out, "Son of David, Jesus, have mercy on me!" 48 Many people told him to keep quiet, but he was crying out all the more, "Have mercy on me, Son of David!"

35 As He drew near Jericho, a blind man was sitting by the road begging. 36 Hearing a crowd passing by, he inquired what this meant. 37 "Jesus the •Nazarene is passing by," they told him.

38 So he called out, "Jesus, Son of David, have mercy on me!" 39 Then those in front told him to keep quiet,ᵃ but he kept crying out all the more, "Son of David, have mercy on me!"

ᵃ18:39 Or *those in front rebuked him*

Mt 20:29 *Jericho:* Jericho was about seventeen miles northeast of Jerusalem. After its destruction by Joshua it was rebuilt in the days of Ahab.

Mt 20:30 *two blind men:* Mark (10:46) and Luke (18:35) mention only one blind man, Bartimaeus. That they mention only one does not mean there could not have been two, only that he may have been the more vocal or dominant.

Matthew 20:29-34 (cont.)	Mark 10:46-52 (cont.)	Luke 18:35-43 (cont.)
[32] Jesus stopped, called them, and said, "What do you want Me to do for you?" [33] "Lord," they said to Him, "open our eyes!" [34] Moved with compassion, Jesus touched their eyes. Immediately they could see, and they followed Him.	[49] Jesus stopped and said, "Call him." So they called the blind man and said to him, "Have courage! Get up; He's calling for you." [50] He threw off his coat, jumped up, and came to Jesus. [51] Then Jesus answered him, "What do you want Me to do for you?" *"Rabbouni,"*[a] the blind man told Him, "I want to see!" [52] "Go your way," Jesus told him. "Your faith has healed you." Immediately he could see and began to follow Him on the road.	[40] Jesus stopped and commanded that he be brought to Him. When he drew near, He asked him, [41] "What do you want Me to do for you?" "Lord," he said, "I want to see!" [42] "Receive your sight!" Jesus told him. "Your faith has healed you."[a] [43] Instantly he could see, and he began to follow Him, glorifying God. All the people, when they saw it, gave praise to God.
	[a]**10:51** Hb for *my teacher*; Jn 20:16	[a]**18:42** Or *has saved you*

Mk 10:47 *Son of David:* The name "Son of David" is a messianic title that highlights God's promises to David that He would establish David's royal line so that his house, kingdom, and throne would endure forever (2 Sm 7:12-16). To call Jesus the "Son of David," therefore, expresses the hope that Jesus would be the descendent of David through whom God will fulfill His promises and will restore the kingdom of David to Israel (see Mk 11:9-10). By healing the blind man, Jesus shows that He accepts the title of "Son of David," but later in the narrative Jesus also teaches that the Messiah is more than David's son, He is also David's Lord (Mk 12:35-37).

Mk 10:51 *Rabbouni:* This title also appears in John 20:16, where John translates the word for his readers as "Teacher." In Mark's Gospel, this intensified form does not seem to differ in any significant way from the more common title of "Rabbi" (see Mk 9:5; 11:21; 14:45).

Lk 18:42 *Your faith has healed you:* Jesus commends the exemplary faith of the man who is no longer blind.

Sec. 127   Jesus Visits Zacchaeus, Tells the Parable of the 10 Minas, and Departs for Jerusalem

Luke 19:1-28

[1] He entered Jericho and was passing through. [2] There was a man named Zacchaeus who was a chief tax collector, and he was rich. [3] He was trying to see who Jesus was, but he was not able because of the crowd, since he was a short man. [4] So running ahead, he climbed up a sycamore tree to see Jesus, since He was about to pass that way. [5] When Jesus came to the place, He looked up and said to him, "Zacchaeus, hurry and come down because today I must stay at your house."

[6] So he quickly came down and welcomed Him joyfully. [7] All who saw it began to complain, "He's gone to lodge with a sinful man!"

[8] But Zacchaeus stood there and said to the Lord, "Look, I'll give[a] half of my possessions to the poor, Lord! And if I have extorted anything from anyone, I'll pay[b] back four times as much!"

[a]**19:8** Or *I give*   [a]**19:8** Or *I pay*

Lk 19:7 *He's gone to lodge with a sinful man:* Once again there is complaint about Jesus being with sinners as was noted in Luke 5:28 and 15:1.

Lk 19:8 *pay back four times:* Zacchaeus, in confessing his faults and promising restitution, picked the maximum penalty of the law (see Ex 22:1). This expresses the repentance of Zacchaeus, something Jesus' remark about staying with him triggered.

Luke 19:1-28 (cont.)

[9] "Today salvation has come to this house," Jesus told him, "because he too is a son of Abraham. [10] For the •Son of Man has come to seek and to save the lost."[a]

[11] As they were listening to this, He went on to tell a parable because He was near Jerusalem, and they thought the kingdom of God was going to appear right away.

[12] Therefore He said: "A nobleman traveled to a far country to receive for himself authority to be king[b] and then return. [13] He called 10 of his •slaves, gave them 10 minas,[c] and told them, 'Engage in business until I come back.'

[14] "But his subjects hated him and sent a delegation after him, saying, 'We don't want this man to rule over us!'

[15] "At his return, having received the authority to be king,[b] he summoned those slaves he had given the money to, so he could find out how much they had made in business. [16] The first came forward and said, 'Master, your mina has earned 10 more minas.'

[17] "'Well done, good[d] slave!' he told him. 'Because you have been faithful in a very small matter, have authority over 10 towns.'

[18] "The second came and said, 'Master, your mina has made five minas.'

[19] "So he said to him, 'You will be over five towns.'

[20] "And another came and said, 'Master, here is your mina. I have kept it hidden away in a cloth [21] because I was afraid of you, for you're a tough man: you collect what you didn't deposit and reap what you didn't sow.'

[22] "He told him, 'I will judge you by what you have said,[e] you evil slave! ⌊If⌋ you knew I was a tough man, collecting what I didn't deposit and reaping what I didn't sow, [23] why didn't you put my money in the bank? And when I returned, I would have collected it with interest!' [24] So he said to those standing there, 'Take the mina away from him and give it to the one who has 10 minas.'

[25] "But they said to him, 'Master, he has 10 minas.'

[26] "'I tell you, that to everyone who has, more will be given; and from the one who does not have, even what he does have will be taken away. [27] But bring here these enemies of mine, who did not want me to rule over them, and slaughter[f] them in my presence.'"

[28] When He had said these things, He went on ahead, going up to Jerusalem.

[a]**19:10** Or *save what was lost*   [b]**19:12,15** Lit *to receive for himself a kingdom* or *sovereignty*   [c]**19:13** = Gk coin worth 100 drachmas or about 100 days' wages   [d]**19:17** Or *capable*   [e]**19:22** Lit *you out of your mouth*   [f]**19:27** Or *execute*

Lk 19:9 *salvation has come to this house:* Jesus affirms that Zacchaeus is saved and that he is a true child of Abraham.

Lk 19:10 *Son of Man has come to seek and to save the lost:* This kind of statement from Jesus about His call is known as a mission statement. It explains why Jesus spends time with sinners.

Lk 19:11-27 This parable is told to explain the accountability disciples and so-called disciples have until the Lord returns. The last servant has no relationship to the master and does not trust him at all, as he remarks in verse 21 "because I was afraid of you," which is why he ends up with nothing and faces judgment.

Lk 19:17 *have authority over 10 towns:* The faithfulness of the obedient slave is rewarded as it also will be with the slave who made five minas. This is a picture of God honoring faithfulness.

Lk 19:21 *you're a tough man: you collect what you didn't deposit:* A confession of the servant's lack of trust in the master, picturing someone associated with Jesus who does not know Him. Judas Iscariot is an example of such a person.

PART XI

THE LAST PUBLIC MINISTRY IN JERUSALEM

Sec. 128a   Jesus Arrives at Bethany

John 11:55–12:1,9-11

55 The Jewish •Passover was near, and many went up to Jerusalem from the country to purify[a] themselves before the Passover. 56 They were looking for Jesus and asking one another as they stood in the •temple complex: "What do you think? He won't come to the festival, will He?" 57 The chief priests and the Pharisees had given orders that if anyone knew where He was, he should report it so they could arrest Him.

1 Six days before the •Passover, Jesus came to Bethany where Lazarus[b] was, the one Jesus had raised from the dead.

9 Then a large crowd of the Jews learned He was there. They came not only because of Jesus, but also to see Lazarus the one He had raised from the dead. 10 Therefore the •chief priests decided to also kill Lazarus, 11 because he was the reason many of the Jews were deserting them[c] and believing in Jesus.

[a]11:55 The law of Moses required God's people to purify or cleanse themselves so they could celebrate the Passover. Jews often came to Jerusalem a week early to do this; Nm 9:4-11.   [b]12:1 Other mss read *Lazarus who died*   [c]12:11 Lit *going away*

12:1 The Passover was approaching (Jn 11:55), and Jesus returned to Bethany, where Lazarus had been raised.
12:10-11 Although Lazarus had been raised from the dead and had not raised himself, the hostility toward Jesus by the Jewish leaders was so intense that they decided that they wanted to kill Lazarus, since his coming back to life had prompted others to believe in Jesus.

Sec. 128b   The Triumphal Entry

Matthew 21:1-11,14-17	Mark 11:1-11	Luke 19:29-44	John 12:12-19
1 When they approached Jerusalem and came to Bethphage at the •Mount of Olives, Jesus then sent two disciples, 2 telling them, "Go into the village ahead of you. At once you will find a donkey tied there, and a colt with her. Untie them and bring them to Me. 3 If anyone says anything to you, you should say that the Lord needs them, and immediately he will send them."	1 When they approached Jerusalem, at Bethphage and Bethany near the •Mount of Olives, He sent two of His disciples 2 and told them, "Go into the village ahead of you. As soon as you enter it, you will find a young donkey tied there, on which no one has ever sat. Untie it and bring it here. 3 If anyone says to you, 'Why are you doing this?' say, 'The Lord needs it and will send it back here right away.'"	29 As He approached Bethphage and Bethany, at the place called the •Mount of Olives, He sent two of the disciples 30 and said, "Go into the village ahead of you. As you enter it, you will find a young donkey tied there, on which no one has ever sat. Untie it and bring it here. 31 If anyone asks you, 'Why are you untying it?' say this: 'The Lord needs it.'"	

Mt 21:1 *Bethphage:* Mentioned only here in the NT. It apparently lay on the eastern slope of the Mount of Olives.

Matthew 21:1-11,14-17 (cont.)	Mark 11:1-11 (cont.)	Luke 19:29-44 (cont.)	John 12:12-19 (cont.)
6 The disciples went and did just as Jesus directed them. **7** They brought the donkey and the colt; then they laid their robes on them, and He sat on them. **4** This took place so that what was spoken through the prophet might be fulfilled:	**4** So they went and found a young donkey outside in the street, tied by a door. They untied it, **5** and some of those standing there said to them, "What are you doing, untying the donkey?" **6** They answered them just as Jesus had said, so they let them go. **7** Then they brought the donkey to Jesus and threw their robes on it, and He sat on it.	**32** So those who were sent left and found it just as He had told them. **33** As they were untying the young donkey, its owners said to them, "Why are you untying the donkey?" **34** "The Lord needs it," they said. **35** Then they brought it to Jesus, and after throwing their robes on the donkey, they helped Jesus get on it.	**12** The next day, when the large crowd that had come to the festival heard that Jesus was coming to Jerusalem, **13** they took palm branches and went out to meet Him. They kept shouting: "•*Hosanna!* **Blessed is He who comes in the name of the Lord**ᵃ —the King of Israel!"
5 **Tell Daughter Zion, "See, your King is coming to you, gentle, and mounted on a donkey, even on a colt, the foal of a beast of burden."**ᵃ			**14** Jesus found a young donkey and sat on it, just as it is written: **15** **Fear no more, Daughter Zion; look! your King is coming, sitting on a donkey's colt.**ᵇ
8 A very large crowd spread their robes on the road; others were cutting branches from the trees and spreading them on the road. **9** Then the crowds who went ahead of Him and those who followed kept shouting:	**8** Many people spread their robes on the road, and others spread leafy branches cut from the fields.ᵃ **9** Then those who went ahead and those who followed kept shouting:	**36** As He was going along, they were spreading their robes on the road. **37** Now He came near the path down the Mount of Olives, and the whole crowd of the disciples began to praise God joyfully with a loud voice for all the miracles they had seen:	**16** His disciples did not understand these things at first. However, when Jesus was glorified, then they remembered that these things had been written about Him and that they had done these things to Him. **17** Meanwhile, the crowd, which had been with Him when He called Lazarus out of the tomb and raised him from the dead, continued to testify.ᶜ **18** This is also why the crowd met Him, because they heard He had done this sign.
•*Hosanna* to the Son of David! **Blessed is He who comes in the name of the Lord!**ᵇ *Hosanna* in the highest heaven!	•*Hosanna!* **Blessed is He who comes in the name of the Lord!**ᵇ **10** **Blessed is the coming kingdom of our father David!** *Hosanna* in the highest heaven!	**38** **Blessed is the King who comes in the name of the Lord.**ᵃ ᵇ Peace in heaven and glory in the highest heaven!	
ᵃ**21:5** Is 62:11; Zch 9:9 ᵇ**21:9** Ps 118:25-26	ᵃ**11:8** Other mss read *others were cutting leafy branches from the trees and spreading them on the road* ᵇ**11:9** Ps 118:26	ᵃ**19:38** The words *the King* are substituted for *He* in Ps 118:26. ᵇ**19:38** Ps 118:26	ᵃ**12:13** Ps 118:25-26 ᵇ**12:15** Zch 9:9 ᶜ**12:17** Other mss read *Meanwhile the crowd, which had been with Him, continued to testify that He had called Lazarus out of the tomb and raised him from the dead.*

Mt 21:5 The first line is from Isaiah 62:11; the rest is from Zechariah 9:9. *donkey:* This beast of burden was often ridden by rulers in times of peace.

Mt 21:7 *He sat on them:* Mark 11:7 and Luke 19:35 show that Jesus rode the colt.

Mt 21:9 Hosanna transliterates a Hebrew expression meaning "Save us now!" or "Please save us!" It had become an exclamation of praise used by Jews as a liturgical formula.

Mk 11:1-11 The spreading of robes and branches in the pathway of the colt parallels the royal dignity given Jehu in 2 Kings 9:13. The reference to the coming kingdom of father David recalls Messianic prophecies, particularly Isaiah 9:7.

Matthew 21:1-11,14-17 (cont.)	Mark 11:1-11 (cont.)	Luke 19:29-44 (cont.)	John 12:12-19 (cont.)
		39 Some of the •Pharisees from the crowd told Him, "Teacher, rebuke Your disciples." 40 He answered, "I tell you, if they were to keep silent, the stones would cry out!"	19 Then the •Pharisees said to one another, "You see? You've accomplished nothing. Look—the world has gone after Him!"
10 When He entered Jerusalem, the whole city was shaken, saying, "Who is this?" 11 And the crowds kept saying, "This is the prophet Jesus from Nazareth in Galilee!" 14 The blind and the lame came to Him in the temple complex, and He healed them. 15 When the •chief priests and the •scribes saw the wonders that He did and the children in the temple complex cheering, "*Hosanna to the Son of David!*" they were indignant 16 and said to Him, "Do You hear what these ⌊children⌋ are saying?"	11 And He went into Jerusalem and into the •temple complex. After looking around at everything, since it was already late, He went out to Bethany with the Twelve.	41 As He approached and saw the city, He wept over it, 42 saying, "If you knew this day what ⌊would bring⌋ peace—but now it is hidden from your eyes. 43 For the days will come on you when your enemies will build an embankment against you, surround you, and hem you in on every side. 44 They will crush you and your children within you to the ground, and they will not leave one stone on another in you, because you did not recognize the time of your visitation."	

Mt 21:16 By this appeal to Psalm 8:3 Jesus affirmed that God approved His actions. Children, together with the blind and the crippled, are now the recipients of God's grace

Lk 19:39 *rebuke Your disciples:* This verse and the next are unique to Luke. Jesus' entry was politically volatile in a city ruled by Rome and religiously volatile to the Jewish leaders.

Lk 19:40 *the stones would cry out:* The picture of creation speaking goes back to the image of Abel's blood crying out to God when he was slain by Cain. When creation needs to speak, the matter is of importance.

Lk 19:41-44 This passage is unique to Luke.

Lk 19:43 *days will come:* Jesus predicted the overthrow of Jerusalem after a siege in AD 70. The reason for the judgment comes in verse 44.

Lk 19:44 *you did not recognize the time of your visitation:* The reason for Israel's judgment is that the people missed the day of God's visit in the person of Messiah.

Matthew 21:1-11,14-17 (cont.)

"Yes," Jesus told them. "Have you never read:

**You have prepared[a] praise
from the mouths of children
and nursing infants**?"[b]

17 Then He left them, went out of the city to Bethany, and spent the night there.

ª21:16 Or *restored*   **ᵇ21:16** Ps 8:2

Sec. 129   The Barren Fig Tree and the Cleansing of the Temple

Matthew 21:18-19,12-13	Mark 11:12-18	Luke 19:45-48
18 Early in the morning, as He was returning to the city, He was hungry.	12 The next day when they came out from Bethany, He was hungry. 13 After seeing in the distance a fig tree with leaves, He went to find out if there was anything on it. When He came to it, He found nothing but leaves, because it was not the season for figs. 14 He said to it, "May no one ever eat fruit from you again!" And His disciples heard it.	
19 Seeing a lone fig tree by the road, He went up to it and found nothing on it except leaves. And He said to it, "May no fruit ever come from you again!" At once the fig tree withered.		
12 Jesus went into the •temple complex[a] and drove out all those buying and selling in the temple. He overturned the money changers' tables and the chairs of those selling doves.	15 They came to Jerusalem, and He went into the temple complex and began to throw out those buying and selling in the temple. He overturned the money changers' tables and the chairs of those selling doves, 16 and would not permit anyone to carry goods through the temple complex.	45 He went into the •temple complex and began to throw out those who were selling,[b]
ª21:12 Other mss add *of God*		**ª19:45** Other mss add *and buying in it*

Mt 21:12 *buying and selling:* Temple service required provisions to be made for what was needed to offer sacrifices, such as animals, doves, wood, and oil.

Mt 21:13 *den of thieves:* What should have been a solemn and sacred place had taken on the atmosphere of a market, with the temple authorities gloating over their profits.

Mk 11:12-14,20-21 The destruction of the fruitless fig tree warned about the coming destruction of Jerusalem. The fig tree was frequently associated with Israel in the Prophets (Jr 29:17; Hs 9:10, 16; Mc 7:1-6). Micah 7:1-6 compared the absence of early figs to the dearth of righteousness.

Mk 11:15-19 Although the temple was to be a house of prayer "for all nations," Jewish leaders had effectively excluded other nations from worship of the one true God. Jesus' drastic action was motivated by His compassion for sinners of every ethnicity.

Mk 11:15 *the money changers' tables:* According to Exodus 3:13-16, every adult Jewish male was required to pay a half-shekel tax to the temple each year, a tax that had to be paid in the currency "of the sanctuary." At the time of Jesus, the Tyrian shekel was the closest equivalent to the old Hebrew shekel and so was used for the temple tax. Money changers at the temple helped to exchange Tyrian coins for the more common Roman money, and the temple authorities permitted them to charge for this service.

Lk 19:45 *began the throw out those who were selling:* A direct challenge of the Jewish leadership, especially those who controlled the temple. It made the leaders nervous at two levels: 1) it raised questions about their authority and 2) if the temple became a place of civil instability, the Romans might move in.

Matthew 21:18-19,12-13 (cont.)	Mark 11:12-18 (cont.)	Luke 19:45-48 (cont.)
13 And He said to them, "It is written, **My house will be called a house of prayer.**[a] But you are making it **a den of thieves!**"[b] [a]**21:13** Is 56:7 [b]**21:13** Jr 7:11	17 Then He began to teach them: "Is it not written, **My house will be called a house of prayer for all nations**?[a] But you have made it **a den of thieves!**"[b] 18 Then the •chief priests and the •scribes heard it and started looking for a way to destroy Him. For they were afraid of Him, because the whole crowd was astonished by His teaching. [a]**11:17** Is 56:7 [b]**11:17** Jr 7:11	46 and He said, "It is written, **My house will be a house of prayer,** but you have made it **a den of thieves!**"[a] 47 Every day He was teaching in the temple complex. The •chief priests, the •scribes, and the leaders of the people were looking for a way to destroy Him, 48 but they could not find a way to do it, because all the people were captivated by what they heard.[b] [a]**19:46** Is 56:7; Jr 7:11 [b]**19:48** Lit *people hung on what they heard*

Mk 11:17 *for all nations:* Only Mark finishes the sentence from Isaiah with the phrase "for all nations." In this way, Mark's Gospel includes Jesus' concern for the Gentiles as part of His protest against business as usual in the temple.

Sec. 130   Jesus Predicts His Crucifixion

John 12:20-50

20 Now some Greeks were among those who went up to worship at the festival. 21 So they came to Philip, who was from Bethsaida in Galilee, and requested of him, "Sir, we want to see Jesus."

22 Philip went and told Andrew; then Andrew and Philip went and told Jesus. 23 Jesus replied to them, "The hour has come for the •Son of Man to be glorified.

24 "•I assure you: Unless a grain of wheat falls to the ground and dies, it remains by itself. But if it dies, it produces a large crop.[a] 25 The one who loves his life will lose it, and the one who hates his life in this world will keep it for eternal life. 26 If anyone serves Me, he must follow Me. Where I am, there My servant also will be. If anyone serves Me, the Father will honor him.

27 "Now My soul is troubled. What should I say—Father, save Me from this hour? But that is why I came to this hour. 28 Father, glorify Your name!"[b]

Then a voice came from heaven: "I have glorified it, and I will glorify it again!"

29 The crowd standing there heard it and said it was thunder. Others said that an angel had spoken to Him.

30 Jesus responded, "This voice came, not for Me, but for you. 31 Now is the judgment of this world. Now the ruler of this •world will be cast out. 32 As for Me, if I am lifted up[c] from the earth I will draw all ⌊people⌋ to Myself." 33 He said this to signify what kind of death He was about to die.

34 Then the crowd replied to Him, "We have heard from the law that the •Messiah will remain forever. So how can You say, 'The Son of Man must be lifted up'?[c] Who is this Son of Man?"

[a]**12:24** Lit *produces much fruit*   [b]**12:28** Other mss read *Your Son*   [c]**12:32,34** Or *exalted*

Jn 12:23 Jesus recognized that the time has come to be glorified. Previously He has denied that the time was right, but now He recognized that the events had come to fruition.

Jn 12:27-28 Jesus had a clear sense of the impending trouble and articulated His fear. On the one hand He wished to escape the pain, but on the other He realized that this is the purpose for His coming, to glorify God's name.

Jn 12:28 *Then a voice came from heaven:* A voice attested that God's name has been glorified and will be glorified again through the events that Jesus faces.

Jn 12:29 The crowd did not expect to hear this, and as a result did not understand the voice, confusing it with thunder or another supernatural phenomenon.

Jn 12:30 The voice was intended to bear witness to others, not Him, regarding God's purposes.

Jn 12:31 Jesus encapsulated the purpose of His impending death and resurrection.

Jn 12:34 The crowd expected a Messiah who would establish his eternal kingdom in the present. Jesus indicated that He anticipated being crucified, and the people did not understand.

John 12:20-50 (cont.)

35 Jesus answered, "The light will be with you only a little longer. Walk while you have the light so that darkness doesn't overtake you. The one who walks in darkness doesn't know where he's going. 36 While you have the light, believe in the light so that you may become sons of light." Jesus said this, then went away and hid from them.

37 Even though He had performed so many signs in their presence, they did not believe in Him. 38 But this was to fulfill the word of Isaiah the prophet, who said:a

Lord, who has believed our message?
And who has the arm of the Lord
been revealed to?b

39 This is why they were unable to believe, because Isaiah also said:

40 **He has blinded their eyes**
and hardened their hearts,
so that they would not see with their eyes
or understand with their hearts,
and be converted,
and I would heal them.c

41 Isaiah said these things becaused he saw His glory and spoke about Him.

42 Nevertheless, many did believe in Him even among the rulers, but because of the Pharisees they did not confess Him, so they would not be banned from the •synagogue. 43 For they loved praise from men more than praise from God.e

44 Then Jesus cried out, "The one who believes in Me believes not in Me, but in Him who sent Me. 45 And the one who sees Me sees Him who sent Me. 46 I have come as a light into the world, so that everyone who believes in Me would not remain in darkness. 47 If anyone hears My words and doesn't keep them, I do not judge him; for I did not come to judge the world but to save the world. 48 The one who rejects Me and doesn't accept My sayings has this as his judge:f the word I have spoken will judge him on the last day. 49 For I have not spoken on My own, but the Father Himself who sent Me has given Me a command as to what I should say and what I should speak. 50 I know that His command is eternal life. So the things that I speak, I speak just as the Father has told Me."

a**12:38** Lit *which he said*   b**12:38** Is 53:1   c**12:40** Is 6:10   d**12:41** Other mss read *when*   e**12:43** Lit *loved glory of men more than glory of God*; v. 41; Jn 5:41   f**12:48** Lit *has the one judging him*

Jn 12:35 Jesus offered the analogy of light to indicate that the time remaining for the people to realize the nature and purpose of His ministry was coming to a close.
Jn 12:37-38 Jesus had done a number of sign miracles in front of the crowds, but many still did not understand who Jesus was and respond in faith. The question of Isaiah 53:1 about who has believed the message anticipated the answer, "Not many have done so."
Jn 12:42 John clarified that some believed in Jesus despite the pressure from the Jewish leaders.

Sec. 131   The Barren Fig Tree Withered

Matthew 21:19b-22	Mark 11:19-26	Luke 21:37-38
At once the fig tree withered. 20 When the disciples saw it, they were amazed and said, "How did the fig tree wither so quickly?"	19 And whenever evening came, they would go out of the city. 20 Early in the morning, as they were passing by, they saw the fig tree withered from the roots up. 21 Then Peter remembered and said to Him, "•Rabbi, look! The fig tree that You cursed is withered."	37 During the day, He was teaching in the temple complex, but in the evening He would go out and spend the night on what is called the •Mount of Olives. 38 Then all the people would come early in the morning to hear Him in the temple complex.

Mt 21:21 Jesus' response to the disciples' question is reminiscent of His words in Matthew 17:20. In the earlier passage the emphasis was on the power of minimum faith, but here the emphasis is on the contrast between faith and doubt.
Mk 11:21 *The fig tree that You cursed:* The cursing of the fig tree represented the judgment soon to come to the religious leaders in Jerusalem. Like a fig tree with leaves but no fruit, they put on a show of honoring God, but their hearts were far from Him (see Mark 7:6).

Matthew 21:19b-22 (cont.)   Mark 11:19-26

²¹ Jesus answered them, "•I assure you: If you have faith and do not doubt, you will not only do what was done to the fig tree, but even if you tell this mountain, 'Be lifted up and thrown into the sea,' it will be done. ²² And if you believe, you will receive whatever you ask for in prayer."

²² Jesus replied to them, "Have faith in God. ²³ •I assure you: If anyone says to this mountain, 'Be lifted up and thrown into the sea,' and does not doubt in his heart, but believes that what he says will happen, it will be done for him. ²⁴ Therefore, I tell you, all the things you pray and ask for—believe that you have receivedᵃ them, and you will have them. ²⁵ And whenever you stand praying, if you have anything against anyone, forgive him, so that your Father in heaven will also forgive you your wrongdoing. [²⁶ But if you don't forgive, neither will your Father in heaven forgive your wrongdoing."]ᵇ ᶜ

ᵃ**11:24** Other mss read *you receive*; other mss read *you will receive* ᵇ**11:26** Other mss omit bracketed text ᶜ**11:26** These are the only uses of this word in Mk. It means "the violation of the Law" or "stepping over a boundary" or "departing from the path" or "trespass."

Sec. 132   Messiah's Authority Challenged

Matthew 21:23–22:14   Mark 11:27–12:12   Luke 20:1-19

²³ When He entered the temple complex, the chief priests and the elders of the people came up to Him as He was teaching and said, "By what authority are You doing these things? Who gave You this authority?"

²⁴ Jesus answered them, "I will also ask you one question, and if you answer it for Me, then I will tell you by what authority I do these things. ²⁵ Where did John's baptism come from? From heaven or from men?"

They began to argue among themselves, "If we say, 'From heaven,' He will say to us, 'Then why didn't you believe him?' ²⁶ But if we say, 'From men,' we're afraid of the crowd, because everyone thought John was a prophet." ²⁷ So they answered Jesus, "We don't know."

²⁷ They came again to Jerusalem. As He was walking in the temple complex, the chief priests, the scribes, and the elders came ²⁸ and asked Him, "By what authority are You doing these things? Who gave You this authority to do these things?"

²⁹ Jesus said to them, "I will ask you one question; then answer Me, and I will tell you by what authority I am doing these things. ³⁰ Was John's baptism from heaven or from men? Answer Me."

³¹ They began to argue among themselves: "If we say, 'From heaven,' He will say, 'Then why didn't you believe him?' ³² But if we say, 'From men' "—they were afraid of the crowd, because everyone thought that John was a genuine prophet. ³³ So they answered Jesus, "We don't know."

¹ One dayᵃ as He was teaching the people in the •temple complex and proclaiming the good news, the •chief priests and the •scribes, with the elders, came up ² and said to Him: "Tell us, by what authority are You doing these things? Who is it who gave You this authority?"

³ He answered them, "I will also ask you a question. Tell Me, ⁴ was the baptism of John from heaven or from men?"

⁵ They discussed it among themselves: "If we say, 'From heaven,' He will say, 'Why didn't you believe him?' ⁶ But if we say, 'From men,' all the people will stone us, because they are convinced that John was a prophet."

⁷ So they answered that they did not know its origin.ᵇ

ᵃ**20:1** Lit *It happened on one of the days* ᵇ**20:7** Or *know where it was from*

Mt 21:24 *John's baptism:* A reference to John's entire ministry.
Mk 11:27 *chief priests:* These included the current high priest as well as those who had served as high priest before him. Under the Romans, the chief priests showed leadership over the internal affairs of the Jews through their position on the Sanhedrin (Ac 4:5-6).
elders: The elders were lay members of the Sanhedrin. Unlike the chief priests the elders did not belong to priestly families.
Lk 20:1-8 This passage begins a series of controversies running through Luke 20.
Lk 20:2 *by what authority are You doing these things:* The Jewish leaders asked Jesus where He got the right to do the things He is doing. They had in mind the cleansing of the temple as well as the way He healed on the Sabbath, treated sinners, and handled the Law.
Lk 20:4 *was the baptism of John from heaven or from men?:* Jesus gave them a question back. They knew they were trapped as the next verses indicate, so they did not reply. The reader of the Gospels know the answer (Lk 3:1-20). It was from God. So also, by implication, is Jesus' work.

Matthew 21:23–22:14 (cont.)	Mark 11:27–12:12 (cont.)	Luke 20:1-19 (cont.)
And He said to them, "Neither will I tell you by what authority I do these things.	And Jesus said to them, "Neither will I tell you by what authority I do these things."	[8] And Jesus said to them, "Neither will I tell you by what authority I do these things."

And He said to them, "Neither will I tell you by what authority I do these things.

[28] "But what do you think? A man had two sons. He went to the first and said, 'My son, go, work in the vineyard today.'

[29] "He answered, 'I don't want to!' Yet later he changed his mind and went. [30] Then the man went to the other and said the same thing.

"'I will, sir,' he answered. But he didn't go.

[31] "Which of the two did his father's will?"

"The first," they said.

Jesus said to them, "I assure you: Tax collectors and prostitutes are entering the kingdom of God before you! [32] For John came to you in the way of righteousness,[a] and you didn't believe him. Tax collectors and prostitutes did believe him, but you, when you saw it, didn't even change your minds then and believe him.

[33] "Listen to another parable: There was a man, a landowner, who planted a vineyard, put a fence around it, dug a winepress in it, and built a watchtower. He leased it to tenant farmers and went away. [34] When the grape harvest[b] drew near, he sent his •slaves to the farmers to collect his fruit. [35] But the farmers took his slaves, beat one, killed another, and stoned a third. [36] Again, he sent other slaves, more than the first group, and they did the same to them.

[a]**21:32** John came preaching and practicing righteousness   [b]**21:34** Lit *the season of fruits*

Mark:
[1] Then He began to speak to them in parables: "A man planted a vineyard, put a fence around it, dug out a pit for a winepress, and built a watchtower. Then he leased it to tenant farmers and went away. [2] At harvest time he sent a slave to the farmers to collect some of the fruit of the vineyard from the farmers. [3] But they took him, beat him, and sent him away empty-handed. [4] Again he sent another slave to them, and they[a] hit him on the head and treated him shamefully.[b] [5] Then he sent another, and they killed that one. ⌊He⌋ also ⌊sent⌋ many others; they beat some and they killed some.

[a]**12:4** Other mss add *threw stones and*
[b]**12:4** Other mss add *and sent him off*

Luke:
[9] Then He began to tell the people this parable: "A man planted a vineyard, leased it to tenant farmers, and went away for a long time. [10] At harvest time he sent a •slave to the farmers so that they might give him some fruit from the vineyard. But the farmers beat him and sent him away empty-handed. [11] He sent yet another slave, but they beat that one too, treated him shamefully, and sent him away empty-handed. [12] And he sent yet a third, but they wounded this one too and threw him out.

Mt 21:28-32 The parable of the two sons is unique to Matthew.
Mt 21:32 *Tax collectors and prostitutes:* A combination used in the NT only here and in v. 32. According to Jewish opinion these two groups had no part in the coming world.
Mt 21:33-40 The parable has allegorical characteristics: the landowner is God; the vineyard is Israel; the tenants are Israel's rulers and leaders; the slaves (or messengers) are the prophets; the son is Jesus; the punishment (v. 43) is God's rejection of Israel; and the people to whom the vineyard will be given are Gentiles. See Isaiah 5:1-2.
Mk 12:1 *tenant farmers:* Large farms often belonged to absentee owners, who leased the land to tenant farmers. The tenant farmers did the actual planting, cultivating, and harvesting. The lease agreement identified what portion of the harvest went to the owner as rent.

Matthew 21:23–22:14 (cont.)	Mark 11:27–12:12 (cont.)	Luke 20:1-19 (cont.)

Matthew 21:23–22:14 (cont.)

37 Finally, he sent his son to them. 'They will respect my son,' he said.

38 "But when the tenant farmers saw the son, they said among themselves, 'This is the heir. Come, let's kill him and take his inheritance!' 39 So they seized him, threw him out of the vineyard, and killed him. 40 Therefore, when the owner of the vineyard comes, what will he do to those farmers?"

41 "He will completely destroy those terrible men," they told Him, "and lease his vineyard to other farmers who will give him his produce at the harvest."ᵃ

42 Jesus said to them, "Have you never read in the Scriptures:

> The stone that
> the builders rejected
> has become
> the cornerstone.ᵇ
> This came from the Lord
> and is wonderful
> in our eyes?ᶜ

43 Therefore I tell you, the kingdom of God will be taken away from you and given to a nation producing itsᵈ fruit. [44 Whoever falls on this stone will be broken to pieces; but whoever it falls on, it will grind him to powder!]"ᵉ

ᵃ**21:41** Lit *him the fruits in their seasons*
ᵇ**21:42** Lit *the head of the corner*   ᶜ**21:42** Ps 118:22-23   ᵈ**21:43** The word *its* refers back to *kingdom*.   ᵉ**21:44** Other mss omit this v.

Mark 11:27–12:12 (cont.)

6 "He still had one to send, a beloved son. Finally he sent him to them, saying, 'They will respect my son.'

7 "But those tenant farmers said among themselves, 'This is the heir. Come, let's kill him, and the inheritance will be ours!' 8 So they seized him, killed him, and threw him out of the vineyard.

9 "Therefore, what will the ownerᵃ of the vineyard do? He will come and destroy the farmers and give the vineyard to others.

10 Haven't you read this Scripture:

> The stone that
> the builders rejected
> has become the cornerstone.ᵇ
> 11 This came from the Lord
> and is wonderful in
> our eyes?"ᶜ

ᵃ**12:9** Or *lord*   ᵇ**12:10** Lit *the head of the corner*   ᶜ**12:10-11** Ps 118:22-23

Luke 20:1-19 (cont.)

13 "Then the owner of the vineyard said, 'What should I do? I will send my beloved son. Perhapsᵃ they will respect him.'

14 "But when the tenant farmers saw him, they discussed it among themselves and said, 'This is the heir. Let's kill him, so the inheritance will be ours!' 15 So they threw him out of the vineyard and killed him.

"Therefore, what will the owner of the vineyard do to them? 16 He will come and destroy those farmers and give the vineyard to others."

But when they heard this they said, "No—never!"

17 But He looked at them and said, "Then what is the meaning of this Scripture:ᵇ

> The stone that the builders
> rejected—
> this has become
> the cornerstone?ᶜ ᵈ

18 Everyone who falls on that stone will be broken to pieces, and if it falls on anyone, it will grind him to powder!"

ᵃ**20:13** Other mss add *when they see him*   ᵇ**20:17** Lit *What then is this that is written*   ᶜ**20:17** Lit *the head of the corner*   ᵈ**20:17** Ps 118:22

Mt 21:42 From Psalm 118:22, the stone originally represented the Jewish nation in captivity and then restored. Christ applied the metaphor to Himself: rejected by Jews, but the cornerstone of the church.

Mt 21:44 *grind him to powder:* The verb was used of winnowing out the chaff and then of grinding it to powder. This is the fate of those on whom this rejected stone falls.

Mk 12:10 *cornerstone:* The cornerstone was a squared stone, the first to be laid, and it established the overall location and direction for the rest of the construction. Jesus has become the decisive and foundational cornerstone for all of God's building plans.

Lk 20:14 *Let's kill him:* This remark shows the blindness of sin. To think that by killing the heir one might gain the property was silly.

Lk 20:16 *He will come and destroy those farmers and give the vineyard to others:* Here is the point of the parable. The leadership will be judged. The others include the Twelve who will lead God's people. Gentiles will also be blessed and have a place in the vineyard, which pictures God's promise as given to Israel.

Lk 20:17 *The stone that the builders rejected:* Jesus cited Psalm 118:22, which makes the point that the rejected one is lifted up by God. In the original setting of the psalm, this would have been Israel's king and the rejection would have been from the nations.

Matthew 21:23–22:14 (cont.)	Mark 11:27–12:12 (cont.)	Luke 20:1-19 (cont.)
[45] When the chief priests and the •Pharisees heard His parables, they knew He was speaking about them. [46] Although they were looking for a way to arrest Him, they feared the crowds, because they[a]	[12] Because they knew He had said this parable against them, they were looking for a way to arrest Him, but they were afraid of the crowd. So they left Him and went away.	[19] Then the scribes and the chief priests looked for a way to get their hands on Him that very hour, because they knew He had told this parable against them, but they feared the people.

regarded Him as a prophet.

[1] Once more Jesus spoke to them in parables: [2] "The kingdom of heaven may be compared to a king who gave a wedding banquet for his son. [3] He sent out his •slaves to summon those invited to the banquet, but they didn't want to come. [4] Again, he sent out other slaves, and said, 'Tell those who are invited: Look, I've prepared my dinner; my oxen and fattened cattle have been slaughtered, and everything is ready. Come to the wedding banquet.'

[5] "But they paid no attention and went away, one to his own farm, another to his business. [6] And the others seized his slaves, treated them outrageously and killed them. [7] The king[b] was enraged, so he sent out his troops, destroyed those murderers, and burned down their city.

[8] "Then he told his slaves, 'The banquet is ready, but those who were invited were not worthy. [9] Therefore, go to where the roads exit the city and invite everyone you find to the banquet.' [10] So those slaves went out on the roads and gathered everyone they found, both evil and good. The wedding banquet was filled with guests.[c] [11] But when the king came in to view the guests, he saw a man there who was not dressed for a wedding. [12] So he said to him, 'Friend, how did you get in here without wedding clothes?' The man was speechless.

[13] "Then the king told the attendants, 'Tie him up hand and foot,[d] and throw him into the outer darkness, where there will be weeping and gnashing of teeth.'

[14] "For many are invited, but few are chosen."

a21:46 The crowds   **b22:7** Other mss read *But when the (that) king heard about it he*   **c22:10** Lit *those reclining* (to eat)   **d22:13** Other mss add *take him away*

Mt 22:2-14 A parallel is found in Luke 14:15–24, though there are differences in structure and detail. Those listening were familiar with wedding feasts in general and had some idea of the magnificence of one that a king would prepare for his own son.
Mt 22:2 *wedding banquet:* The Greek word is plural and commonly referred not to just one aspect of the wedding but of all festivities involved.
Mt 22:11 Apparently the king in Jesus' story provided appropriate clothing for each guest. The proper wedding garment of a true believer is God-imputed righteousness, without which no one can enter the kingdom.
Mt 22:14 *invited . . . chosen:* All are called through the good news of the gospel; only those who respond to God's gracious invitation are chosen.
Mk 12:12 The Jewish leaders recognized that they were the tenants of the parable.

Sec. 133   God and Caesar

Matthew 22:15-22	Mark 12:13-17	Luke 20:20-26
[15] Then the •Pharisees went and plotted how to trap Him by what He said.[a] [16] They sent their disciples to Him, with the •Herodians. "Teacher," they said, "we know	[13] Then they sent some of the •Pharisees and the •Herodians to Him to trap Him by what He said.[a] [14] When they came, they said to	[20] They[a] watched closely and sent spies who pretended to be righteous,[b] so they could catch Him in what He said,[c] to hand Him
a22:15 Lit *trap Him in [a] word*	**a12:13** Lit *trap Him in (a) word*	**a20:20** The scribes and chief priests of v. 19 **b20:20** Or *upright*; that is, loyal to God's law **c20:20** Lit *catch Him in [a] word*

Mt 22:16 *Herodians:* Not members of Herod's family or Herod's soldiers, but partisans loyal to Herod's dynasty. That they were in collusion with their bitter rivals, the Pharisees, shows the animosity Jesus generated.
Mk 12:13-17 Since human beings bear the image of God, everything they have and are belongs to God.

Matthew 22:15-22 (cont.)	Mark 12:13-17 (cont.)	Luke 20:20-26 (cont.)
that You are truthful and teach truthfully the way of God. You defer to no one, for You don't show partiality.[a] ¹⁷ Tell us, therefore, what You think. Is it lawful to pay taxes to Caesar or not?" ¹⁸ But perceiving their malice, Jesus said, "Why are you testing Me, hypocrites? ¹⁹ Show Me the coin used for the tax." So they brought Him a •denarius. ²⁰ "Whose image and inscription is this?" He asked them. ²¹ "Caesar's," they said to Him. Then He said to them, "Therefore, give back to Caesar the things that are Caesar's, and to God the things that are God's." ²² When they heard this, they were amazed. So they left Him and went away.	Him, "Teacher, we know You are truthful and defer to no one, for You don't show partiality[a] but teach truthfully the way of God. Is it lawful to pay taxes to Caesar or not? ¹⁵ Should we pay, or should we not pay?" But knowing their hypocrisy, He said to them, "Why are you testing Me? Bring Me a •denarius to look at." ¹⁶ So they brought one. "Whose image and inscription is this?" He asked them. "Caesar's," they said. ¹⁷ Then Jesus told them, "Give back to Caesar the things that are Caesar's, and to God the things that are God's." And they were amazed at Him.	over to the governor's rule and authority. ²¹ They questioned Him, "Teacher, we know that You speak and teach correctly, and You don't show partiality,[a] but teach truthfully the way of God. ²² Is it lawful for us to pay taxes to Caesar or not?" ²³ But detecting their craftiness, He said to them,[b] ²⁴ "Show Me a •denarius. Whose image and inscription does it have?" "Caesar's," they said. ²⁵ "Well then," He told them, "give back to Caesar the things that are Caesar's and to God the things that are God's." ²⁶ They were not able to catch Him in what He said[c] in public,[d] and being amazed at His answer, they became silent.
a22:16 Lit *don't look on the face of men*; that is, on the outward appearance	**a12:14** Lit *don't look on the face of men*; that is, on the outward appearance	**a20:21** Lit *You don't receive a face* **b20:23** Other mss add *"Why are you testing Me?* **c20:26** Lit *catch Him in [a] word* **d20:26** Lit *in front of the people*

Mk 12:14 *taxes:* All provinces under direct Roman rule, such as Judea (but not Galilee), were required to take a census for taxation purposes. The census involved an enrollment of names and an assessment of property. The term that the Pharisees and Herodians used shows that they were asking about the census tax, one that was particularly despised.

Lk 20:22 *pay taxes to Caesar or not:* A trick question. If Jesus said to pay, then people will wonder if He is the Messiah who has come to free them from Rome, which was the expectation for many. If He said not to pay, then Jesus' enemies could present Him as one fomenting revolution.

Lk 20:25 *give back to Caesar . . . and to God:* Jesus' answer avoided the trap. Government has the right to exist and collect taxes and God is to be honored for His rule as well. The either-or question became a both-and.

Sec. 134 The Sadducees and the Resurrection

Matthew 22:23-33	Mark 12:18-27	Luke 20:27-40
²³ The same day some •Sadducees, who say there is no resurrection, came up to Him and questioned Him: ²⁴ "Teacher, Moses said, **if a man dies, having no children, his brother is to marry his wife and raise up offspring for his brother.**[a] ²⁵ Now there	¹⁸ Some •Sadducees, who say there is no resurrection, came to Him and questioned Him: ¹⁹ "Teacher, Moses wrote for us that **if a man's brother dies**, leaves his wife behind, and **leaves no child, his brother should take the wife and produce •offspring for his brother.**[a] ²⁰ There were	²⁷ Some of the •Sadducees, who say there is no resurrection, came up and questioned Him: ²⁸ "Teacher, Moses wrote for us that **if a man's brother** has a wife, and **dies childless, his brother should take the wife and produce •offspring for his brother.**[a] ²⁹ Now there were
a22:24 Dt 25:5	**a12:19** Gn 38:8; Dt 25:5	**a20:28** Dt 25:5

Mt 22:24 *his brother is to marry his wife:* The Sadducees cited the levirate law of Deuteronomy 25:5-6. The case was hypothetical, formulated to confound the Pharisees, who did believe in resurrection.

Mk 12:18-27 The Sadducees denied that a person had any continuing existence after death. Jesus defended the reality of the afterlife based on God's words to Moses from the burning bush. Jesus probably appealed to Exodus rather than later texts because the Sadducees valued the five books of Moses above all others.

Lk 20:27-40 An attempt to trip Jesus up theologically.

Matthew 22:23-33 (cont.)	Mark 12:18-27 (cont.)	Luke 20:27-40 (cont.)
were seven brothers among us. The first got married and died. Having no offspring, he left his wife to his brother. 26 The same happened to the second also, and the third, and so to all seven.[a] 27 Then last of all the woman died. 28 Therefore, in the resurrection, whose wife will she be of the seven? For they all had married her."[b] 29 Jesus answered them, "You are deceived, because you don't know the Scriptures or the power of God. 30 For in the resurrection they neither marry nor are given in marriage but are like[c] angels in heaven. 31 Now concerning the resurrection of the dead, haven't you read what was spoken to you by God: 32 **I am the God of Abraham and the God of Isaac and the God of Jacob**?[d] He[e] is not the God of the dead, but of the living." 33 And when the crowds heard this, they were astonished at His teaching.	seven brothers. The first took a wife, and dying, left no offspring. 21 The second also took her, and he died, leaving no offspring. And the third likewise. 22 So the seven[a] left no offspring. Last of all, the woman died too. 23 In the resurrection, when they rise,[b] whose wife will she be, since the seven had married her?"[c] 24 Jesus told them, "Are you not deceived because you don't know the Scriptures or the power of God? 25 For when they rise from the dead, they neither marry nor are given in marriage but are like angels in heaven. 26 Now concerning the dead being raised—haven't you read in the book of Moses, in the passage about the burning bush, how God spoke to him: **I am the God of Abraham and the God of Isaac and the God of Jacob**?[d] 27 He is not God of the dead but of the living. You are badly deceived."	seven brothers. The first took a wife and died without children. 30 Also the second[a] 31 and the third took her. In the same way, all seven died and left no children. 32 Finally, the woman died too. 33 Therefore, in the resurrection, whose wife will the woman be? For all seven had married her."[b] 34 Jesus told them, "The sons of this age marry and are given in marriage. 35 But those who are counted worthy to take part in that age and in the resurrection from the dead neither marry nor are given in marriage. 36 For they cannot die anymore, because they are like angels and are sons of God, since they are sons of the resurrection. 37 Moses even indicated ⌊in the passage⌋ about the burning bush that the dead are raised, where he calls the Lord **the God of Abraham and the God of Isaac and the God of Jacob.**[c] 38 He is not God of the dead but of the living, because all are living to[d] Him." 39 Some of the scribes answered, "Teacher, You have spoken well." 40 And they no longer dared to ask Him anything.
[a]**22:26** Lit *so until the seven* [b]**22:28** Lit *all had her* [c]**22:30** Other mss add *God's* [d]**22:32** Ex 3:6,15-16 [e]**22:32** Other mss read *God*	[a]**12:22** Other mss add *had taken her and* [b]**12:23** Other mss omit *when they rise* [c]**12:23** Lit *the seven had her as a wife* [d]**12:26** Ex 3:6,15-16	[a]**20:30** Other mss add *took her as wife, and he died without children* [b]**20:33** Lit *had her as wife* [c]**20:37** Ex 3:6,15 [d]**20:38** Or *with*

Mt 22:32 Jesus' exegetical argument was based on the emphatic present tense of the *I am* used in the passage from Exodus 3:14. After *Abraham* and *Isaac* and *Jacob* were long dead, the Lord was still as much their *God* as when they were alive.

Sec. 135   The Primary Commandments

Matthew 22:34-40	Mark 12:28-34
34 When the Pharisees heard that He had silenced the Sadducees, they came together in the same place. 35 And one of them, an expert in the law, asked a question to test Him: 36 "Teacher, which command in the law is the greatest?"[a] [a]**22:36** Lit *is great*	28 One of the •scribes approached. When he heard them debating and saw that Jesus answered them well, he asked Him, "Which command is the most important of all?"[a] [a]**12:28** Lit *Which commandment is first of all?*

Mt 22:35 *an expert in the law:* A learned and astute specialist on scriptural and rabbinical law.

Mt 22:40 *depend:* Translates a verb meaning "hang on." "Sum up" could also be used. These two commands contain everything Scripture said concerning God's will.

Mk 12:34 *not far from the kingdom of God:* Mark's Gospel portrays the scribe in a positive manner, detailing his acceptance of Jesus' teaching as well as Jesus' commendation of him. It is not a subtle criticism, implying some continuing lack in the scribe's thoughts about the commands of God.

Matthew 22:34-40 (cont.)	Mark 12:28-34 (cont.)

29 "This is the most important,"[a] Jesus answered:

37 He said to him, **"Love the Lord your God with all your heart, with all your soul, and with all your mind.**[a] **38** This is the greatest and most important[b] command. **39** The second is like it: **Love your neighbor as yourself.**[c] **40** All the Law and the Prophets depend[d] on these two commands."

Listen, Israel! The Lord our God, the Lord is One.[b] **30** **Love the Lord your God with all your heart, with all your soul, with all your mind, and with all your strength.**[c] [d]

31 "The second is: **Love your neighbor as yourself.**[e] There is no other command greater than these."

[a]**22:37** Dt 6:5 [b]**22:38** Lit *and first* [c]**22:39** Lv 19:18 [d]**22:40** Or *hang*

32 Then the scribe said to Him, "You are right, Teacher! You have correctly said that He is One, and there is no one else except Him. **33** And to love Him with all your heart, with all your understanding,[f] and with all your strength, and to love your neighbor as yourself, is far more ⌊important⌋ than all the burnt offerings and sacrifices."

34 When Jesus saw that he answered intelligently, He said to him, "You are not far from the kingdom of God." And no one dared to question Him any longer.

[a]**12:29** Other mss add *of all the commandments* [b]**12:29** Or *The Lord our God is one Lord.* [c]**12:30** Dt 6:4-5; Jos 22:5 [d]**12:30** Other mss add *This is the first commandment.* [e]**12:31** Lv 19:18 [f]**12:33** Other mss add *with all your soul*

Sec. 136   The Question about the Messiah

Matthew 22:41-46	Mark 12:35-37	Luke 20:41-44

41 While the Pharisees were together, Jesus questioned them, **42** "What do you think about the •Messiah? Whose Son is He?"

"David's," they told Him.

43 He asked them, "How is it then that David, inspired by the Spirit,[a] calls Him 'Lord':

44 **The Lord declared
    to my Lord,
    'Sit at My right hand
    until I put Your enemies
        under Your feet'?**[b] [c]

45 "If David calls Him 'Lord,' how then can the Messiah be his Son?" **46** No one was able to answer Him at all,[d] and from that day no one dared to question Him anymore.

[a]**22:43** Lit *David in Spirit* [b]**22:44** Other mss read *until I make Your enemies Your footstool* [c]**22:44** Ps 110:1 [d]**22:46** Lit *answer Him a word*

35 So Jesus asked this question as He taught in the •temple complex, "How can the scribes say that the •Messiah is the Son of David? **36** David himself says by the Holy Spirit:

**The Lord declared to
    my Lord,
    'Sit at My right hand
    until I put Your enemies
        under Your feet.'**[a]

37 David himself calls Him 'Lord'; how then can the Messiah be his Son?" And the large crowd was listening to Him with delight.

[a]**12:36** Ps 110:1

41 Then He said to them, "How can they say that the •Messiah is the Son of David? **42** For David himself says in the Book of Psalms:

**The Lord declared
    to my Lord,
    'Sit at My right hand
43   until I make Your enemies
        Your footstool.'**[a]

44 David calls Him 'Lord'; how then can the Messiah be his Son?"

[a]**20:42-43** Ps 110:1

Mt 22:45 Jesus' argument was this: by human descent Messiah is (you admit) the Son of David. But David spoke of Messiah as "Lord," a term no man would apply to his own human descendant. Therefore, Messiah must be more than human. As man He is the Son of David, as divine He is David's Lord.

Sec. 137   Religious Hypocrites Denounced

Matthew 23:1-39	Mark 12:38-40	Luke 20:45-47

¹ Then Jesus spoke to the crowds and to His disciples: ² "The •scribes and the •Pharisees are seated in the chair of Moses.ᵃ ³ Therefore do whatever they tell you and observe ⌊it⌋. But don't do what they do,ᵇ because they don't practice what they teach. ⁴ They tie up heavy loads that are hard to carryᶜ and put them on people's shoulders, but they themselves aren't willing to lift a fingerᵈ to move them. ⁵ They do everythingᵉ to be observed by others: They enlarge their phylacteriesᶠ and lengthen their •tassels.ᵍ ⁶ They love the place of honor at banquets, the front seats in the •synagogues, ⁷ greetings in the marketplaces, and to be called '•Rabbi' by people.

⁸ "But as for you, do not be called 'Rabbi,' because you have one Teacher,ʰ and you are all brothers. ⁹ Do not call anyone on earth your father, because you have one Father, who is in heaven. ¹⁰ And do not be called masters either, because you have one Master,ⁱ

³⁸ He also said in His teaching, "Beware of the scribes,

who want to go around in long robes, and who want greetings in the marketplaces, ³⁹ the front seats in the •synagogues, and the places of honor at banquets.

⁴⁵ While all the people were listening, He said to His disciples, ⁴⁶ "Beware of the scribes,

who want to go around in long robes and who love greetings in the marketplaces, the front seats in the •synagogues, and the places of honor at banquets.

ᵃ**23:2** Perhaps a special chair for teaching in synagogues, or a metaphorical phrase for teaching with Moses' authority   ᵇ**23:3** Lit *do according to their works*   ᶜ**23:4** Other mss omit *that are hard to carry*   ᵈ**23:4** Lit *lift with their finger*   ᵉ**23:5** Lit *do all their works*   ᶠ**23:5** Small leather boxes containing OT texts, worn by Jews on their arms and foreheads   ᵍ**23:5** Other mss add *on their robes*   ʰ**23:8** Other mss add *the Messiah*   ⁱ**23:10** Or *Teacher*

Mt 23:2 *seated in the chair of Moses:* The metaphor may point to a literal stone seat in front of the synagogue where the teacher (usually a scribe) sat. In any case Jesus' words reflected the Pharisees' claim that Moses could be understood only as they interpreted him.

Mt 23:4 *aren't willing to lift a finger:* The Pharisees made demands of others without helping them perform those duties.

Mt 23:5 *phylacteries . . . tassels:* Phylacteries consisted of four strips of parchment inscribed with texts (Ex 13:3–10,11–16; Dt 6:4–9; 11:13–21) and enclosed in a leather case. Adult Jews wore them bound to the left arm and the forehead. They also wore tassels with a "blue cord" on their garments as a reminder of the Lord's commands (Nm 15:37–41).

Mt 23:9 Jesus also forbad the designation *father* with reference to spiritual things. Certainly it is not wrong to call one's biological father by that title, but it is wrong to use it when addressing a spiritual leader.

Mk 12:38 *in long robes:* The priests wore long robes, which were special temple garments (see Ex 29:21,29; 31:10). The scribes wore long robes, probably in imitation of the priests, as a way to draw attention to themselves as religious leaders.

Mk 12:39 *the front seats in the synagogues:* A bench just in front of the chest containing the Scriptures, facing the congregation, was reserved for respected guests and learned scholars. The scribes enjoyed the prestige that came with these seats.

Lk 20:46 *Beware:* Jesus warned against the hypocrisy and pride of the scribes.

Matthew 23:1-39 (cont.)	Mark 12:38-40 (cont.)	Luke 20:45-47 (cont.)
the •Messiah. [11] The greatest among you will be your servant. [12] Whoever exalts himself will be humbled, and whoever humbles himself will be exalted. [13] "But woe to you, scribes and Pharisees, hypocrites! You lock up the kingdom of heaven from people. For you don't go in, and you don't allow those entering to go in. [[14] "Woe to you, scribes and Pharisees, hypocrites! You devour widows' houses and make long prayers just for show.[a] This is why you will receive a harsher punishment.][b]	[40] They devour widows' houses and say long prayers just for show. These will receive harsher punishment."	[47] They devour widows' houses and say long prayers just for show. These will receive greater punishment."[a] [a]20:47 Or *judgment*

[15] "Woe to you, scribes and Pharisees, hypocrites! You travel over land and sea to make one •proselyte, and when he becomes one, you make him twice as fit for •hell[c] as you are!

[16] "Woe to you, blind guides, who say, 'Whoever takes an oath by the sanctuary, it means nothing. But whoever takes an oath by the gold of the sanctuary is bound by his oath.'[d] [17] Blind fools![e] For which is greater, the gold or the sanctuary that sanctified the gold? [18] Also, 'Whoever takes an oath by the altar, it means nothing. But whoever takes an oath by the gift that is on it is bound by his oath.'[d] [19] Blind people![f] For which is greater, the gift or the altar that sanctifies the gift? [20] Therefore the one who takes an oath by the altar takes an oath by it and by everything on it. [21] The one who takes an oath by the sanctuary takes an oath by it and by Him who dwells in it. [22] And the one who takes an oath by heaven takes an oath by God's throne and by Him who sits on it.

[23] "Woe to you, scribes and Pharisees, hypocrites! You pay a tenth of[g] mint, dill, and cumin,[h] yet you have neglected the more important matters of the law—justice, mercy, and faith. These things should have been done without neglecting the others. [24] Blind guides! You strain out a gnat, yet gulp down a camel!

[25] "Woe to you, scribes and Pharisees, hypocrites! You •clean the outside of the cup and dish, but inside they are full of greed[i] and self-indulgence! [26] Blind Pharisee! First clean the inside of the cup,[j] so the outside of it[k] may also become clean.

[27] "Woe to you, scribes and Pharisees, hypocrites! You are like whitewashed tombs, which appear beautiful on the outside, but inside are full of dead men's bones and every impurity. [28] In the same way, on the outside you seem righteous to people, but inside you are full of hypocrisy and lawlessness.

[29] "Woe to you, scribes and Pharisees, hypocrites! You build the tombs of the prophets and decorate the monuments of the righteous, [30] and you say, 'If we had lived in the days of our fathers, we wouldn't have taken part with them in shedding the prophets' blood.'[l] [31] You therefore testify against yourselves that you are sons of those who murdered the prophets. [32] Fill up, then, the measure of your fathers' sins![m]

[a]23:14 Or *prayers with false motivation* [b]23:14 Other mss omit bracketed text [c]23:15 Lit *twice the son of gehenna* [d]23:16,18 Lit *is obligated* [e]23:17 Lit *Fools and blind* [f]23:19 Other mss read *Fools and blind* [g]23:23 Or *You tithe* [h]23:23 A plant whose seeds are used as a seasoning [i]23:25 Or *full of violence* [j]23:26 Other mss add *and dish* [k]23:26 Other mss read *of them* [l]23:30 Lit *have been partakers with them in the blood of the prophets* [m]23:32 Lit *the measure of your fathers*

Mt 23:13 *woe:* Or "alas" is the rendering of most translations. A more dramatic reading could be, "How terrible it will be." The eight woes in the following verses can be contrasted with the eight beatitudes in Matthew 5.

Mt 23:15 *twice as fit for hell:* Literally, "son of Gehenna," meaning one fitted and destined for Gehenna, worthy of the most severe judgment.

Mt 23:16 They would take an oath and use some sacred object to substantiate that oath—the gold in the temple, for example, or the gift on the altar. But they would not swear by the temple itself or the altar.

Mt 23:23 *mint, dill, and cumin: Mint* contains a pleasant-smelling oil (the Greek word means "sweet smelling"). *Dill* contains aromatic seeds which the Jews used for seasoning. *Cumin* is a plant of the carrot family. Jews cultivated it for its spicy seeds.

Mt 23:24 *strain out a gnat:* To touch a dead body involved ceremonial pollution, so to avoid the chance of a gnat having fallen into their drink Pharisees first strained it.

Mt 23:27 *whitewashed tombs:* The tombstones of the poor in the fields or the roadside were whitened with powdered lime dust. These were not the rock-hewn tombs of the wealthy.

Mt 23:31 *testify against yourselves:* They confessed themselves to be the children of murderers by descent; they would prove themselves to be so by their deeds.

Matthew 23:1-39 (cont.)

33 "Snakes! Brood of vipers! How can you escape being condemned to hell?ᵃ 34 This is why I am sending you prophets, sages, and scribes. Some of them you will kill and crucify, and some of them you will flog in your synagogues and hound from town to town. 35 So all the righteous blood shed on the earth will be charged to you,ᵇ from the blood of righteous Abel to the blood of Zechariah, son of Berechiah, whom you murdered between the sanctuary and the altar. 36 •I assure you: All these things will come on this generation!

37 "Jerusalem, Jerusalem! The city who kills the prophets and stones those who are sent to her. How often I wanted to gather your children together, as a hen gathers her chicksᶜ under her wings, yet you were not willing! 38 See, your house is left to you desolate. 39 For I tell you, you will never see Me again until you say, **Blessed is He who comes in the name of the Lord!**"ᵈ

ᵃ**23:33** Lit *escape from the judgment of gehenna*   ᵇ**23:35** Lit *will come on you*   ᶜ**23:37** Or *as a mother bird gathers her young*   ᵈ**23:39** Ps 118:26

Mt 23:33 *Brood of vipers:* The same expression used by John the Baptist in Matthew 3:7.
Mt 23:35 *Zechariah, son of Berechiah:* Many interpreters assume that the Zechariah here is the murdered prophet of 2 Chronicles 24:20–21, in which case Berechiah would be a mistaken reference to Jehoiada. But there is no reason the Zechariah mentioned here was not truly the son of Berechiah, that is, the prophet who wrote the next-to-last book of the OT (Zch 1:1).

Sec. 138   The Widow's Gift

Mark 12:41-44	Luke 21:1-4
41 Sitting across from the temple treasury, He watched how the crowd dropped money into the treasury. Many rich people were putting in large sums. 42 And a poor widow came and dropped in two tiny coins worth very little.ᵃ 43 Summoning His disciples, He said to them, "•I assure you: This poor widow has put in more than all those giving to the temple treasury. 44 For they all gave out of their surplus, but she out of her poverty has put in everything she possessed—all she had to live on."	1 He looked up and saw the rich dropping their offerings into the temple treasury. 2 He also saw a poor widow dropping in two tiny coins.ᵃ 3 "I tell you the truth," He said. "This poor widow has put in more than all of them. 4 For all these people have put in gifts out of their surplus, but she out of her poverty has put in all she had to live on."

ᵃ**12:42** Lit *dropped in two lepta, which is a quadrans*; the *lepton* was the smallest and least valuable Gk coin in use. The *quadrans*, 1/64 of a daily wage, was the smallest Roman coin.

ᵃ**21:2** Lit *two lepta*; the *lepton* was the smallest and least valuable Gk coin in use.

Mk 12:41 *the temple treasury:* Thirteen trumpet-shaped receptacles were placed along the wall of the Court of the Women within the temple complex for the purpose of collecting the temple tax as well as voluntary offerings.
Mk 12:42 *two tiny coins worth very little:* Literally, "two *lepta,* which is a *quadrans*." A lepton was a small copper coin, the least valuable piece of money in circulation. Mark clarified the value of two *lepta* by pointing out that together they were equal to one *quadrans,* the smallest Roman coin, worth 1/64 of a *denarius.*
Lk 21:3 *put in more than all:* Jesus commended her gift because it came out of her meager resources. Her sincerity and devotion was sacrificial and stood in contrast to scribes.

PART XII

IN THE SHADOW WITH JESUS

Sec. 139   Jesus' Great Eschatological Discourse

Matthew 24–25	Mark 13:1-37	Luke 21:5-36

[1] As Jesus left and was going out of the •temple complex, His disciples came up and called His attention to the temple buildings. [2] Then He replied to them,

"Don't you see all these things? •I assure you: Not one stone will be left here on another that will not be thrown down!"

[3] While He was sitting on the •Mount of Olives, the disciples approached Him privately and said, "Tell us, when will these things happen? And what is the sign of Your coming and of the end of the age?"

[1] As He was going out of the •temple complex, one of His disciples said to Him, "Teacher, look! What massive stones! What impressive buildings!"

[2] Jesus said to him, "Do you see these great buildings? Not one stone will be left here on another that will not be thrown down!"

[3] While He was sitting on the •Mount of Olives across from the temple complex, Peter, James, John, and Andrew asked Him privately, [4] "Tell us, when will these things happen? And what will be the sign when all these things are about to take place?"

[5] As some were talking about the •temple complex, how it was adorned with beautiful stones and gifts dedicated to God,[a] He said, [6] "These things that you see—the days will come when not one stone will be left on another that will not be thrown down!"

[7] "Teacher," they asked Him, "so when will these things be? And what will be the sign when these things are about to take place?"

[a]**21:5** Gifts given to the temple in fulfillment of vows to God

Mt 24:1 *temple buildings:* Herod began to rebuild the temple complex around 20 BC. It was still under renovation in Jesus' day. Some of the stones were white marble, and portions of the temple were gold plated.

Mt 24:2 *stone . . . thrown down:* This prediction came true during the Jewish-Roman War. The Roman army laid siege to Jerusalem and finally captured it after a long struggle. In AD 70 they completely destroyed the temple.

Mt 24:3 *Mount of Olives:* Thus this chapter and the next are called the "Olivet Discourse." *Your coming:* Translates the Greek *parousia,* meaning "presence, coming, arrival." This important word is used 24 times in the NT and includes the ideas surrounding the appearing of Jesus in glory at the end of human history. *the end of the age:* Used six times in the NT, five of which are in Matthew.

Mk 13:1-37 Jesus predicted two different events: the fall of Jerusalem that occurred in AD 70 and His own return. In general, readers can distinguish predictions of the two events by tracing the use of the demonstrative pronouns. The near demonstrative, "these," is connected to the events that would occur soon after Jesus' prophesy. The remote demonstrative, "those," is connected to events that would occur in the more distant future. Consequently, verses 5-13 relate primarily to first-century events. Verses 14-27 relate to the second coming. Verses 28-31 relate to first-century events, particularly the fall of Jerusalem. Verses 32-37 relate to the second coming.

Lk 21:5-6 Luke 21:5-36 is the second discourse about these events and Jesus' return in Luke. Luke 17:22-37 is the other.

Lk 21:6 *not one stone will be left on another:* Here Jesus predicted that the temple will be completely destroyed, fulfilled in AD 70.

Lk 21:7 *when will these things be . . . what will be the sign?:* One has to pay close attention to this question and the reply. The marking point for this question in Luke is the predicted destruction of the temple, which has implications in the disciples' view about the end. Jesus discussed both the destruction of the temple and the end here, but they are not the same event.

Matthew 24–25 (cont.)	Mark 13:1-37 (cont.)	Luke 21:5-36 (cont.)

4 Then Jesus replied to them: "Watch out that no one deceives you. **5** For many will come in My name, saying, 'I am the •Messiah,' and they will deceive many. **6** You are going to hear of wars and rumors of wars. See that you are not alarmed, because these things must take place, but the end is not yet. **7** For nation will rise up against nation, and kingdom against kingdom. There will be faminesᵃ and earthquakes in various places. **8** All these events are the beginning of birth pains.

9 "Then they will hand you over for persecution,ᵇ and they will kill you. You will be hated by all nations because of My name. **10** Then many will take offense, betray one another and hate one another.

ᵃ**24:7** Other mss add *epidemics*   ᵇ**24:9** Or *tribulation*, or *distress*

5 Then Jesus began by telling them: "Watch out that no one deceives you. **6** Many will come in My name, saying, 'I am He,' and they will deceive many. **7** When you hear of wars and rumors of wars, don't be alarmed; these things must take place, but the end is not yet. **8** For nation will rise up against nation, and kingdom against kingdom. There will be earthquakes in various places, and famines.ᵃ These are the beginning of birth pains.

9 "But you, be on your guard! They will hand you over to sanhedrins,ᵇ and you will be flogged in the •synagogues. You will stand before governors and kings because of Me, as a witness to them. **10** And the good newsᶜ must first be proclaimed to all nations. **11** So when they arrest you and hand you over, don't worry beforehand what you will say. On the contrary, whatever is given to you in that hour—say it. For it isn't you speaking, but the Holy Spirit. **12** Then brother will betray brother to death, and a father his child. Children will rise up against parents and put them to death. **13** And you will be hated by everyone because of My name.

ᵃ**13:8** Other mss add *and disturbances*
ᵇ**13:9** Local Jewish courts or local councils
ᶜ**13:10** Or *the gospel*

8 Then He said, "Watch out that you are not deceived. For many will come in My name, saying, 'I am He,' and, 'The time is near.' Don't follow them. **9** When you hear of wars and rebellions,ᵃ don't be alarmed. Indeed, these things must take place first, but the end won't come right away."

10 Then He told them: "Nation will be raised up against nation, and kingdom against kingdom. **11** There will be violent earthquakes, and famines and plagues in various places, and there will be terrifying sights and great signs from heaven. **12** But before all these things, they will lay their hands on you and persecute you. They will hand you over to the •synagogues and prisons, and you will be brought before kings and governors because of My name. **13** It will lead to an opportunity for you to witness.ᵇ **14** Therefore make up your mindsᶜ not to prepare your defense ahead of time, **15** for I will give you such wordsᵈ and a wisdom that none of your adversaries will be able to resist or contradict. **16** You will even be betrayed by parents, brothers, relatives, and friends. They will kill some of you. **17** You will be hated by everyone because of My name, **18** but not a hair of your head will be lost. **19** By your endurance gaineᵉ your •lives.

ᵃ**21:9** Or *insurrections*, or *revolutions*
ᵇ**21:13** Lit *lead to a testimony for you*
ᶜ**21:14** Lit *Therefore place* (determine) *in your hearts*   ᵈ**21:15** Lit *you a mouth*
ᵉ**21:19** Other mss read *endurance you will gain*

Mt 24:5 *many will come in My name:* Jesus warned that many would claim to be acting in His name and would deceive many people. Some messianic figures appeared before AD 70 and many have appeared since.

Mt 24:6 *wars and rumors of wars:* Not every disaster means the end of the age is at hand. False messiahs, wars and natural disasters, persecution and betrayal, false prophets, great evil, and apostasy are only the beginning of troubles to be expected by believers.

Mk 13:9 *sanhedrins:* "Sanhedrin" (singular) referred to the ruling council in Jerusalem, the highest Jewish court. However, other local Jewish councils existed beyond Jerusalem. Traditionally, a local council of 23 members was formed in any community with at least 120 Jewish men.

Mk 13:5 *Watch out:* Jesus' teaching on the future in Mark 13 includes repeated commands to watch out (13:5,23,33). In addition, a literal rendering of the phrase "be on your guard" in 13:9 would be "watch out." Mark included two long teaching sections, the parables discourse (4:1-34) and the eschatological discourse (13:1-37). The latter contains a commands to "watch;" the former contains commands to "listen" (4:3,9,23,24).

Lk 21:12 *But before all these things:* The most important time marker in the speech, found only in Luke's version. Jesus was saying that before the coming of people claiming to be Messiah and before the political and natural chaos, there will be persecution. This looks at the time when disciples will be brought before kings and governors and be given opportunity to witness. These events were fulfilled in part in Acts.

Lk 21:15 *I will give you such words:* Jesus promised to speak through them during these interrogations.

Lk 21:16 *will kill some of you.* Some will be martyred during such persecution.

Lk 21:18 *not a hair of your head will be lost:* Since Jesus had just said that some will die, this means that whatever happens, they will be preserved and be with God.

Matthew 24–25 (cont.) Mark 13:1-37 (cont.) Luke 21:5-36 (cont.)

[11] Many false prophets will rise up and deceive many. [12] Because lawlessness will multiply, the love of many will grow cold. [13] But the one who endures to the end will be delivered.[a] [14] This good news of the kingdom will be proclaimed in all the world[b] as a testimony to all nations. And then the end will come.

But the one who endures to the end will be delivered.[a]

[15] "So when you see **the abomination that causes desolation**,[c][d] spoken of by the prophet Daniel, standing in the holy place" (let the reader understand[e]), [16] "then those in Judea must flee to the mountains! [17] A man on the housetop[f] must not come down to get things out of his house. [18] And a man in the field must not go back to get his clothes. [19] Woe to pregnant women and nursing mothers in those days! [20] Pray that your escape may not be in winter or on a Sabbath. [21] For at that time there will be great tribulation, the kind that hasn't taken place from the beginning of the world until now and never will again! [22] Unless those days were limited, no one would[g] survive.[h] But those days will be limited because of the elect.

[14] "When you see the **abomination that causes desolation**[b] standing where it should not" (let the reader understand[c]), "then those in Judea must flee to the mountains! [15] A man on the housetop must not come down or go in to get anything out of his house. [16] And a man in the field must not go back to get his clothes. [17] Woe to pregnant women and nursing mothers in those days! [18] Pray it[d] won't happen in winter. [19] For those will be days of tribulation, the kind that hasn't been from the beginning of the world,[e] which God created, until now and never will be again! [20] Unless the Lord limited those days, no one would survive.[f] But He limited those days because of the elect, whom He chose.

[20] "When you see Jerusalem surrounded by armies, then recognize that its desolation has come near. [21] Then those in Judea must flee to the mountains! Those inside the city[a] must leave it, and those who are in the country must not enter it, [22] because these are days of vengeance to fulfill all the things that are written. [23] Woe to pregnant women and nursing mothers in those days,

for there will be great distress in the land[b] and wrath against this people. [24] They will fall by the edge of the sword and be led captive into all the nations, and Jerusalem will be trampled by the Gentiles[c] until the times of the Gentiles are fulfilled.

a24:13 Or *be saved* **b**24:14 Or *in all the inhabited earth* **c**24:15 Or *abomination of desolation,* or *desolating sacrilege* **d**24:15 Dn 9:27 **e**24:15 These are, most likely, Matthew's words to his readers. **f**24:17 Or *roof* **g**24:22 Lit *short, all flesh would not* **h**24:22 Or *be saved* or *delivered*

a13:13 Or *saved* **b**13:14 Dn 9:27 **c**13:14 These are, most likely, Mark's words to his readers. **d**13:18 Other mss read *pray that your escape* **e**13:19 Lit *creation* **f**13:20 Lit *days, all flesh would not survive*

a21:21 Lit *inside her* **b**21:23 Or *the earth* **c**21:24 Or *nations*

Mt 24:15 *the abomination that causes desolation:* A quotation from Daniel 9:27 and 12:11. Most interpreters believe this prophecy was fulfilled in 168 BC., when the Syrian ruler Antiochus sacrificed a pig on the altar in the Jerusalem temple. Jesus was probably referring to a second such abomination that He predicted would occur. Some interpreters think this was the appearance of Roman soldiers in the temple in AD 70.

Lk 21:20 *When you see Jerusalem surrounded by armies:* The destruction of Jerusalem will be a terrible time when people need to flee or stay away from Jerusalem. People in the city will suffer greatly.

Lk 21:24 *be led captive into all the nations:* The city will be overrun as will the nation. *Jerusalem will be trampled by the Gentiles until the times of the Gentiles are fulfilled:* Jesus predicted a long period of time here. The program of God will focus on Gentiles until these times are fulfilled.

Matthew 24–25 (cont.)	Mark 13:1-37 (cont.)	Luke 21:5-36 (cont.)
23 "If anyone tells you then, 'Look, here is the Messiah!' or, 'Over here!' do not believe it! 24 False messiahs[a] and false prophets will arise and perform great signs and wonders to lead astray, if possible, even the elect. 25 Take note: I have told you in advance. 26 So if they tell you, 'Look, He's in the wilderness!' don't go out; 'Look, He's in the inner rooms!' do not believe it. 27 For as the lightning comes from the east and flashes as far as the west, so will be the coming of the •Son of Man. 28 Wherever the carcass is, there the vultures[b] will gather.	21 "Then if anyone tells you, 'Look, here is the •Messiah! Look—there!' do not believe it! 22 For false messiahs[a] and false prophets will rise up and will perform signs and wonders to lead astray, if possible, the elect. 23 And you must watch! I have told you everything in advance.	
29 "Immediately after the tribulation of those days:	24 "But in those days, after that tribulation:	25 "Then there will be signs in the sun, moon, and stars; and there will be anguish on the earth among nations bewildered by the roaring sea and waves. 26 People will faint from fear and expectation of the things that are coming on the world, because the celestial powers will be shaken.
The sun will be darkened, and the moon will not shed its light; the stars will fall from the sky, and the celestial powers will be shaken.	The sun will be darkened, and the moon will not shed its light; 25 the stars will be falling from the sky, and the celestial powers will be shaken.	
30 "Then the sign of the Son of Man will appear in the sky, and then all the peoples of the earth[c] will mourn;[d] and they will see the Son of Man coming on the clouds of heaven with power and great glory. 31 He will send out His angels with a loud trumpet, and they will gather His elect from the four winds, from one end of the sky to the other.	26 Then they will see the •Son of Man coming in clouds with great power and glory. 27 He will send out the angels and gather His elect from the four winds, from the end of the earth to the end of the sky. [a]13:22 Or *false christs*	27 Then they will see the •Son of Man coming in a cloud with power and great glory.
[a]24:24 Or *False christs* [b]24:28 Or *eagles* [c]24:30 Or *all the tribes of the land* [d]24:30 Lit *will beat*; = beat their breasts		28 But when these things begin to take place, stand up and lift up your heads, because your •redemption is near!"

Mt 24:28 The *carcass* pictures the apostate world system in league with Satan against God and Christ. The *vultures* (or "eagles" as some translations render it) typify the judgments God will unleash in connection with the Messiah's appearing.

Mt 24:29 *sun . . . moon . . . stars:* With these words Jesus described His second coming and the spectacular signs that will occur when His return is near. Then the "sign of the Son of Man" will appear (v. 30). Some believe this sign is the appearance of Jesus Himself.

Mk 13:28 *the fig tree:* Most trees in Israel are evergreens, but the fig tree sheds its leaves for the winter and then sprouts them again in the spring. Therefore, sprouting fig leaves signaled that winter is past. Since Jesus was giving this parable just before Passover, nearby fig trees looked just as He described them, with tender branches and leaves.

Mk 13:30 *This generation:* Elsewhere Jesus used the phrase "this generation" as a metaphor for sinful people destined for judgment (see Mk 8:12,38; 9:19; Mt 11:16; 12:45; 16:4; 17:17; 23:36; Lk 7:31; 9:41; 11:29-32,50-51; 16:8; 17:25). One possible interpretation is that Jesus was warning His disciples that sinful and unbelieving people who oppose God and His messengers will be present up to the end of this age.

Lk 21:27 *Then they will see the Son of Man coming in a cloud with power:* Who are "they" who will see? Jesus is clearly talking past His disciples to discuss others. The imagery is from Daniel 7:9-14, where the Son of Man is given judgment authority.

Lk 21:28 *But when these things begin to take place, stand up and lift your heads:* The start of these events (which the disciples Jesus was first addressing would experience in AD 70), are the guarantee that they will all take place.

Matthew 24–25 (cont.) | Mark 13:1-37 (cont.) | Luke 21:5-36 (cont.)

32 "Now learn this parable from the fig tree: As soon as its branch becomes tender and sprouts leaves, you know that summer is near. 33 In the same way, when you see all these things, recognizea that Heb is near—at the door! 34 I assure you: This generation will certainly not pass away until all these things take place. 35 Heaven and earth will pass away, but My words will never pass away.

36 "Now concerning that day and hour no one knows—neither the angels in heaven, nor the Sonc — except the Father only. 37 As the days of Noah were, so the coming of the Son of Man will be. 38 For in those days before the flood they were eating and drinking, marrying and giving in marriage, until the day Noah boarded the ark. 39 They didn't knowd until the flood came and swept them all away. So this is the way the coming of the Son of Man will be: 40 Then two men will be in the field: one will be taken and one left. 41 Two women will be grinding at the mill: one will be taken and one left. 42 Therefore be alert, since you don't know what daye your Lord is coming.

a**24:33** Or *things, you know*   b**24:33** Or *it; = summer*   c**24:36** Other mss omit *nor the Son*   d**24:39** *They didn't know* the day and hour of the coming judgment   e**24:42** Other mss read *hour; = time*

28 "Learn this parable from the fig tree: As soon as its branch becomes tender and sprouts leaves, you know that summer is near. 29 In the same way, when you see these things happening, knowa that Heb is near—at the door! 30 •I assure you: This generation will certainly not pass away until all these things take place. 31 Heaven and earth will pass away, but My words will never pass away.

32 "Now concerning that day or hour no one knows—neither the angels in heaven nor the Son—except the Father.

33 Watch! Be alert!c For you don't know when the time is ⌊coming⌋. 34 It is like a man on a journey, who left his house, gave authority to his •slaves, gave each one his work, and commanded the doorkeeper to be alert. 35 Therefore be alert, since you don't know when the master of the house is coming—whether in the evening or at midnight or at the crowing of the rooster or early in the morning. 36 Otherwise, he might come suddenly and find you sleeping. 37 And what I say to you, I say to everyone: Be alert!"

a**13:29** Or *you know*   b**13:29** Or *it; = summer*   c**13:33** Other mss add *and pray*

29 Then He told them a parable: "Look at the fig tree, and all the trees. 30 As soon as they put out ⌊leaves⌋ you can see for yourselves and recognize that summer is already near. 31 In the same way, when you see these things happening, recognizea that the kingdom of God is near. 32 •I assure you: This generation will certainly not pass away until all things take place. 33 Heaven and earth will pass away, but My words will never pass away.

34 "Be on your guard, so that your minds are not dulledb from carousing,c drunkenness, and worries of life, or that day will come on you unexpectedly 35 like a trap. For it will come on all who live on the face of the whole earth. 36 But be alert at all times, praying that you may have strengthd to escape all these things that are going to take place and to stand before the Son of Man."

a**21:31** Or *you know*   b**21:34** Lit *your hearts are not weighed down*   c**21:34** Or *hangovers*   d**21:36** Other mss read *you may be counted worthy*

Mt 24:36 *no one knows:* No one but God knows the time of Christ's coming. As in the time of Noah, people will be going about their usual tasks and will be caught unprepared. Believers should be ready for this event at all times.

Mt 24:40-41 *one will be taken and one left:* In both analogies, one will be swept away by the flood of judgment and the other left to enjoy the blessings of Christ's reign.

Lk 21:32 *generation will certainly not pass away:* This is a difficult verse. It means one of two things. In the Bible, generation can refer to a kind of people, such as the "evil generation." This is known as an ethical force for the term. So Jesus may well be saying that this evil generation will not pass away until this all takes place, since the passage highlights judgment (vv. 34-35). Be assured judgment will come. Or the text may mean that once the events of the very end start, it will all take place within a generation.

Lk 21:33 *My words will never pass away:* Jesus assured them that what He told them will take place. This teaching and these events are more certain than the existence of the creation.

Lk 21:34-36 *Be on your guard . . . be alert:* The application is that they should always be ready, for the day could come at any time, even an unexpected one.

Lk 21:36 *to stand before the Son of Man:* The call to be faithful means the one who trusts Jesus and His work will stand approved before the Son of Man when He comes.

Matthew 24–25 (cont.)

⁴³ But know this: If the homeowner had known what timeª the thief was coming, he would have stayed alert and not let his house be broken into. ⁴⁴ This is why you also must be ready, because the Son of Man is coming at an hour you do not expect.

⁴⁵ "Who then is a faithful and sensible •slave, whom his master has put in charge of his household, to give them food at the proper time? ⁴⁶ That slave whose master finds him working when he comes will be rewarded. ⁴⁷ I assure you: He will put him in charge of all his possessions. ⁴⁸ But if that wicked slave says in his heart, 'My master is delayed,' ⁴⁹ and starts to beat his fellow slaves, and eats and drinks with drunkards, ⁵⁰ that slave's master will come on a day he does not expect and at an hour he does not know. ⁵¹ He will cut him to piecesᵇ and assign him a place with the hypocrites. In that place there will be weeping and gnashing of teeth.

¹ "Then the kingdom of heaven will be like 10 virginsᶜ who took their lamps and went out to meet the groom. ² Five of them were foolish and five were sensible. ³ When the foolish took their lamps, they didn't take olive oil with them. ⁴ But the sensible ones took oil in their flasks with their lamps. ⁵ Since the groom was delayed, they all became drowsy and fell asleep.

⁶ "In the middle of the night there was a shout: 'Here's the groom! Come out to meet him.'

⁷ "Then all those virgins got up and trimmed their lamps. ⁸ But the foolish ones said to the sensible ones, 'Give us some of your oil, because our lamps are going out.'

⁹ "The sensible ones answered, 'No, there won't be enough for us and for you. Go instead to those who sell, and buy oil for yourselves.'

¹⁰ "When they had gone to buy some, the groom arrived. Then those who were ready went in with him to the wedding banquet, and the door was shut.

¹¹ "Later the rest of the virgins also came and said, 'Master, master, open up for us!'

¹² "But he replied, '•I assure you: I do not know you!'

¹³ "Therefore be alert, because you don't know either the day or the hour.ᵈ

¹⁴ "For it is just like a man going on a journey. He called his own •slaves and turned over his possessions to them. ¹⁵ To one he gave five talents;ᵉ to another, two; and to another, one—to each according to his own ability. Then he went on a journey. Immediately ¹⁶ the man who had received five talents went, put them to work, and earned five more. ¹⁷ In the same way the man with two earned two more. ¹⁸ But the man who had received one talent went off, dug a hole in the ground, and hid his master's money.

¹⁹ "After a long time the master of those slaves came and settled accounts with them. ²⁰ The man who had received five talents approached, presented five more talents, and said, 'Master, you gave me five talents. Look, I've earned five more talents.'

²¹ "His master said to him, 'Well done, good and faithful slave! You were faithful over a few things; I will put you in charge of many things. Share your master's joy!'

²² "Then the man with two talents also approached. He said, 'Master, you gave me two talents. Look, I've earned two more talents.'

ª**24:43** Lit *watch*; a division of the night in ancient times   ᵇ**24:51** Lit *him in two*   ᶜ**25:1** Or *bridesmaids*   ᵈ**25:13** Other mss add *in which the Son of Man is coming.*   ᵉ**25:15** Worth a very large sum of money; a talent = 6,000 •denarii

---

Mt 25:1 *10 virgins:* In Jewish weddings, the groom went to the bride's home to escort her to his own home, where the ceremony took place. But the language of this parable suggests that the bride and her maidens were already at her future home. The groom had left the house, and the time of his return was not known.

Mt 25:2 *foolish . . . sensible:* Being uncertain about the groom's return, the wise maidens had gathered a reserve of oil for their lamps. The foolish maidens made no such provision.

Mt 25:7 *Give us some of your oil:* Readiness is commanded of us all, and each one must be personally prepared because we cannot do it for others.

Mt 25:10 *those who were ready went in:* A solemn warning against casual attitudes toward the groom's return. We must always be ready for Christ's return.

Mt 25:15 *five talents . . . two . . . one:* A talent was the largest measure of weight, used to measure precious metals such as gold or silver. While the master was away, they were expected to handle his possessions in a trustworthy manner.

Mt 25:19 *the master of those slaves came:* Represents the future return of Jesus.

Mt 25:20,22 *I've earned:* The slave with five talents was commended for doubling his master's money and was rewarded with greater responsibilities. The master's words to the second slave are almost the same as to the first slave because he had also doubled his talents. He was rewarded on the basis of what his master had entrusted to him.

Matthew 24–25 (cont.)

²³ "His master said to him, 'Well done, good and faithful slave! You were faithful over a few things; I will put you in charge of many things. Share your master's joy!'

²⁴ "Then the man who had received one talent also approached and said, 'Master, I know you. You're a difficult man, reaping where you haven't sown and gathering where you haven't scattered seed. ²⁵ So I was afraid and went off and hid your talent in the ground. Look, you have what is yours.'

²⁶ "But his master replied to him, 'You evil, lazy slave! If you knew that I reap where I haven't sown and gather where I haven't scattered, ²⁷ thenᵃ you should have deposited my money with the bankers. And when I returned I would have received my moneyᵇ back with interest.

²⁸ "'So take the talent from him and give it to the one who has 10 talents. ²⁹ For to everyone who has, more will be given, and he will have more than enough. But from the one who does not have, even what he has will be taken away from him. ³⁰ And throw this good-for-nothing •slave into the outer darkness. In that place there will be weeping and gnashing of teeth.'

³¹ "When the •Son of Man comes in His glory, and all the angelsᶜ with Him, then He will sit on the throne of His glory. ³² All the nationsᵈ will be gathered before Him, and He will separate them one from another, just as a shepherd separates the sheep from the goats. ³³ He will put the sheep on His right, and the goats on the left. ³⁴ Then the King will say to those on His right, 'Come, you who are blessed by My Father, inherit the kingdom prepared for you from the foundation of the world.

³⁵ For I was hungry
and you gave Me something to eat;
I was thirsty
and you gave Me something to drink;
I was a stranger and you took Me in;
³⁶ I was naked and you clothed Me;
I was sick and you took care of Me;
I was in prison and you visited Me.'

³⁷ "Then the righteous will answer Him, 'Lord, when did we see You hungry and feed You, or thirsty and give You something to drink? ³⁸ When did we see You a stranger and take You in, or without clothes and clothe You? ³⁹ When did we see You sick, or in prison, and visit You?'

⁴⁰ "And the King will answer them, 'I assure you: Whatever you did for one of the least of these brothers of Mine, you did for Me.' ⁴¹ Then He will also say to those on the left, 'Depart from Me, you who are cursed, into the eternal fire prepared for the Devil and his angels!

⁴² For I was hungry
and you gave Me nothing to eat;
I was thirsty
and you gave Me nothing to drink;

ᵃ**25:26-27** Or *So you knew . . . scattered? Then* (as a question)   ᵇ**25:27** Lit *received what is mine*   ᶜ**25:31** Other mss read *holy angels*
ᵈ**25:32** Or *the Gentiles*

Mt 25:25 *I was afraid . . . hid your talent:* The third slave thought his master was the kind of man who harvested what he did not plant. His primary attitude toward his master was fear.

Mt 25:27 *my money back with interest:* The master replied that if the slave had really believed he was a harsh, demanding person, he should have put the money in the bank at the safest level of risk. What we do with what God has entrusted to us determines whether we are judged faithful or unfaithful.

Mt 25:31 *all the angels:* Associated with the Son of Man in the judgment will be the angels. They are mentioned here not only because they enhance His glory but also because they are given a task to perform. They will gather the wicked before the judgment throne and cast them into the furnace of fire (Mt 13:41,42; 24:31; 2 Th 1:7,8; Rv 14:17-20).

Mt 25:32 *All the nations:* Those gathered before the throne are persons, individuals, without any regard to nationality; hence, "all the nations." What matters is whether one has during earthly life given evidence of faith in the Lord Jesus. *the sheep from the goats:* Though sheep and goats often intermingle during the day, when the shepherd calls the sheep, the goats do not respond. Sheep are those who trust in, that is, "follow" the Savior.

Mt 25:35-36,42-43 *hungry . . . thirsty . . . in prison:* All these conditions would happen to loyal disciples—hunger, thirst, imprisonment, deprivation of all sorts. Those who came to their aid and ministered to their needs would be considered as ministering to Christ Himself. Their deeds were the expression of their transformed natures as His disciples.

Matthew 24–25 (cont.)

43 I was a stranger
and you didn't take Me in;
I was naked
and you didn't clothe Me,
sick and in prison
and you didn't take care of Me.'

44 "Then they too will answer, 'Lord, when did we see You hungry, or thirsty, or a stranger, or without clothes, or sick, or in prison, and not help You?'

45 "Then He will answer them, 'I assure you: Whatever you did not do for one of the least of these, you did not do for Me either.'

46 "And they will go away into eternal punishment, but the righteous into eternal life."

Mt 25:46 *eternal punishment . . . eternal life:* The same One who taught eternal life taught eternal punishment. Since the same word for "eternal" is used to describe both, it is inconsistent to accept one without the other.

Sec. 140   The Plot to Kill Jesus

Matthew 26:1-5	Mark 14:1-2	Luke 22:1-2
1 When Jesus had finished saying all this, He told His disciples, 2 "You knowa that the •Passover takes place after two days, and the •Son of Man will be handed over to be crucified." 3 Then the •chief priestsb and the elders of the people assembled in the palace of the high priest, who was called Caiaphas, 4 and they conspired to arrest Jesus in a treacherous way and kill Him. 5 "Not during the festival," they said, "so there won't be rioting among the people."	1 After two days it was the •Passover and the Festival of •Unleavened Bread. The •chief priests and the •scribes were looking for a treacherous way to arrest and kill Him. 2 "Not during the festival," they said, "or there may be rioting among the people."	1 The Festival of •Unleavened Bread, which is called •Passover, was drawing near. 2 The •chief priests and the •scribes were looking for a way to put Him to death, because they were afraid of the people.

a**26:2** Or *Know* (as a command)
b**26:3** Other mss add *and the scribes*

Mt 26:5 *Not during the festival:* The plotters feared that among the thousands of Galileans attending the festivities, Jesus would have many friends and adherents, people who might make trouble for the authorities should they take action against Him.

Mk 14:1 *Festival of Unleavened Bread:* This followed directly after the Passover and lasted for seven days, it served as a reminder of the rapid departure from Egypt. Mark's verse carefully listed both festivals, although in practice the two were treated together as a single commemoration, with the result that either festival name could designate the entire eight days (Mk 14:12; Lk 22:1).

Lk 22:2 *because they were afraid of the people:* The attention Jesus was getting made seizing Him in public difficult. So there needed to be another way to get Him.

Sec. 141   The Anointing at Bethany

Matthew 26:6-13	Mark 14:3-9	John 12:2-8

Matthew 26:6-13

6 While Jesus was in Bethany at the house of Simon, a man who had a serious skin disease, 7 a woman approached Him with an alabaster jar of very expensive fragrant oil. She poured it on His head as He was reclining at the table. 8 When the disciples saw it, they were indignant. "Why this waste?" they asked. 9 "This might have been sold for a great deal and given to the poor."

10 But Jesus, aware of this, said to them, "Why are you bothering this woman? She has done a noble thing for Me. 11 You always have the poor with you, but you do not always have Me. 12 By pouring this fragrant oil on My body, she has prepared Me for burial. 13 •I assure you: Wherever this gospel is proclaimed in the whole world, what this woman has done will also be told in memory of her."

Mark 14:3-9

3 While He was in Bethany at the house of Simon who had a serious skin disease, as He was reclining at the table, a woman came with an alabaster jar of pure and expensive fragrant oil of nard. She broke the jar and poured it on His head. 4 But some were expressing indignation to one another: "Why has this fragrant oil been wasted? 5 For this oil might have been sold for more than 300 •denarii and given to the poor." And they began to scold her.

6 Then Jesus said, "Leave her alone. Why are you bothering her? She has done a noble thing for Me. 7 You always have the poor with you, and you can do what is good for them whenever you want, but you do not always have Me. 8 She has done what she could; she has anointed My body in advance for burial. 9 •I assure you: Wherever the gospel is proclaimed in the whole world, what this woman has done will also be told in memory of her."

John 12:2-8

2 So they gave a dinner for Him there; Martha was serving them, and Lazarus was one of those reclining at the table with Him. 3 Then Mary took a pound of fragrant oil—pure and expensive nard—anointed Jesus' feet, and wiped His feet with her hair. So the house was filled with the fragrance of the oil.

4 Then one of His disciples, Judas Iscariot (who was about to betray Him), said, 5 "Why wasn't this fragrant oil sold for 300 •denarii[a] and given to the poor?" 6 He didn't say this because he cared about the poor but because he was a thief. He was in charge of the money-bag and would steal part of what was put in it.

7 Jesus answered, "Leave her alone; she has kept it for the day of My burial. 8 For you always have the poor with you, but you do not always have Me."

[a]**12:5** This amount was about a year's wages for a common worker.

Mt 26:12 *she has prepared Me for burial:* It was customary to anoint the dead and lay the body in spices. Mary was impelled by her love of the Lord and desire to honor Him; but Jesus, about to die and be buried, declared the anointing a fit preparation.

Mk 14:3 *at the house of Simon:* According to Mark and Matthew, this anointing of Jesus took place at the house of Simon, a man with a serious skin disease (Mk 14:3; Mt 26:6). Luke 7:36-50 recorded a different incident in which a sinful woman anointed Jesus' feet at the house of Simon the Pharisee. Simon was such a common name at that time that it is unnecessary to explain how the same name could appear in these two similar stories. *pure and expensive fragrant oil of nard:* The woman's fragrant oil was made of nard, oil drawn from the root of the nard plant and imported from India (Jn 12:3).

Mk 14:7 *You always have the poor with you:* Jesus was not implying that care for the poor is unimportant. Instead He was insisting that the needs of the poor should not be a pretense for criticizing this woman who has seized an opportunity to give her best to Him.

Jn 12:2-3 Mary and Martha, along with Lazarus, were people of some means, since they gave a dinner for Jesus, at which Mary took expensive oil and anointed Jesus' feet. It was worth 300 denarii, about a year's wages for a worker.

Jn 12:6 Judas' comments about the value of the perfume were not because he was concerned about the poor but because he was the treasurer for the group and had just been deprived of further money to steal.

Jn 12:7-8 Jesus anticipated His death by interpreting Mary's actions as anointing His body for burial.

Sec. 142   Judas Bargains with the Chief Priests

Matthew 26:14-16	Mark 14:10-11	Luke 22:3-6
¹⁴ Then one of the Twelve—the man called Judas Iscariot—went to the chief priests ¹⁵ and said, "What are you willing to give me if I hand Him over to you?" So they weighed out 30 pieces of silver for him. ¹⁶ And from that time he started looking for a good opportunity to betray Him.	¹⁰ Then Judas Iscariot, one of the Twelve, went to the chief priests to hand Him over to them. ¹¹ And when they heard this, they were glad and promised to give him silver.ᵃ So he started looking for a good opportunity to betray Him.	³ Then Satan entered Judas, called Iscariot, who was numbered among the Twelve. ⁴ He went away and discussed with the chief priests and temple police how he could hand Him over to them. ⁵ They were glad and agreed to give him silver.ᵃ ⁶ So he accepted ⌊the offer⌋ and started looking for a good opportunity to betray Him to them when the crowd was not present.

ᵃ**14:11** Or *money*; in Mt 26:15 it is specified as 30 pieces of silver; see Zch 11:12-13

ᵃ**22:5** Or *money*; Mt 26:15 specifies 30 pieces of silver; Zch 11:12-13

Mt 26:15 *30 pieces of silver:* The pieces were silver shekels, temple money, and amounted to the price of a slave (Ex 21:32).
Lk 22:3 *Satan entered Judas:* Satan reappears directly in Luke for the first time since the temptation account. Of course, Satan has been battling Jesus through the presence of demons. Now Judas is influenced by Satan to give Jesus over to the Jewish authorities.

Sec. 143   Betrayal at the Passover

Matthew 26:17-19	Mark 14:12-16	Luke 22:7-13
¹⁷ On the first day of •Unleavened Bread the disciples came to Jesus and asked, "Where do You want us to prepare the Passover so You may eat it?" ¹⁸ "Go into the city to a certain man," He said, "and tell him, 'The Teacher says: My time is near; I am celebrating the Passover at your placeᵃ with My disciples.'" ¹⁹ So the disciples did as Jesus had directed them and prepared the Passover.	¹² On the first day of Unleavened Bread, when they sacrifice the Passover lamb, His disciples asked Him, "Where do You want us to go and prepare the Passover so You may eat it?" ¹³ So He sent two of His disciples and told them, "Go into the city, and a man carrying a water jug will meet you. Follow him. ¹⁴ Wherever he enters, tell the owner of the house, 'The Teacher says, "Where is the guest room for Me to eat the Passover with My disciples?"' ¹⁵ He will show you a large room upstairs, furnished and ready. Make the preparations for us there." ¹⁶ So the disciples went out, entered the city, and found it just as He had told them, and they prepared the Passover.	⁷ Then the Day of Unleavened Bread came when the Passover lamb had to be sacrificed. ⁸ Jesus sent Peter and John, saying, "Go and prepare the Passover meal for us, so we can eat it." ⁹ "Where do You want us to prepare it?" they asked Him. ¹⁰ "Listen," He said to them, "when you've entered the city, a man carrying a water jug will meet you. Follow him into the house he enters. ¹¹ Tell the owner of the house, 'The Teacher asks you, "Where is the guest room where I can eat the Passover with My disciples?"' ¹² Then he will show you a large, furnished room upstairs. Make the preparations there." ¹³ So they went and found it just as He had told them, and they prepared the Passover.

ᵃ**26:18** Lit *Passover with you*

Mt 26:17 *On the first day of Unleavened Bread:* Passover was a one-day feast, while the Feast of Unleavened Bread had evolved from a seven to an eight-day-long festival beginning the day before Passover, but in popular thinking the two holidays had come together.
Mk 14:13 *a man carrying a water jug:* At that time men normally carried water in skins while women carried water in jugs.
Lk 22:7 *Passover:* This feast day celebrated the Exodus and the deliverance of Israel described in the book of Exodus. Jesus instructed His disciples to prepare to celebrate this meal.

Sec. 144   Jesus Shares the Passover Meal with the Twelve

Matthew 26:20	Mark 14:17	Luke 22:14-16,24-30
²⁰ When evening came, He was reclining at the table with the Twelve. ²¹ While they were eating, He said, "I assure you: One of you will betray Me."	¹⁷ When evening came, He arrived with the Twelve.	¹⁴ When the hour came, He reclined at the table, and the apostles with Him. ¹⁵ Then He said to them, "I have fervently desired to eat this Passover with you before I suffer. ¹⁶ For I tell you, I will not eat it again[a] until it is fulfilled in the kingdom of God."

²⁴ Then a dispute also arose among them about who should be considered the greatest. ²⁵ But He said to them, "The kings of the Gentiles dominate them, and those who have authority over them are called[b] 'Benefactors.'[c] ²⁶ But it must not be like that among you. On the contrary, whoever is greatest among you must become like the youngest, and whoever leads, like the one serving. ²⁷ For who is greater, the one at the table or the one serving? Isn't it the one at the table? But I am among you as the One who serves. ²⁸ You are the ones who stood by Me in My trials. ²⁹ I bestow on you a kingdom, just as My Father bestowed one on Me, ³⁰ so that you may eat and drink at My table in My kingdom. And you will sit on thrones judging the 12 tribes of Israel.

[a]**22:16** Other mss omit *again*   [b]**22:25** Or *them call themselves*   [c]**22:25** Title of honor given to those who benefited the public good

Mt 26:20 *When evening came:* The lamb was slain "between two evenings," that is, between three and five in the afternoon (see Ex 12:6). The supper followed on the same night.

Lk 22:16 *I will not eat it again until it is fulfilled in the kingdom of God:* This is the last celebratory meal He will have until the kingdom of God comes in full.

Lk 22:26 *But it must not be like that among you:* Jesus contrasted the way greatness is defined in the world versus how His disciples should be great. Greatness must not be measured in normal cultural ways.

Lk 22:27 *I am among you as the One who serves:* This picture of service is one Jesus also followed.

Lk 22:29 *I bestow on you a kingdom, just as My Father bestowed one on Me:* Jesus announced to His faithful core that they will share in kingdom authority.

Sec. 145   Jesus Washes His Disciples' Feet

John 13:1-20

¹ Before the •Passover Festival, Jesus knew that His hour had come to depart from this world to the Father. Having loved His own who were in the world, He loved them to the end.[a]

² Now by the time of supper, the Devil had already put it into the heart of Judas, Simon Iscariot's son, to betray Him. ³ Jesus knew that the Father had given everything into His hands, that He had come from God, and that He was going back to God. ⁴ So He got up from supper, laid aside His robe, took a towel, and tied it around Himself. ⁵ Next, He poured water into a basin and began to wash His disciples' feet and to dry them with the towel tied around Him.

⁶ He came to Simon Peter, who asked Him, "Lord, are You going to wash my feet?"

⁷ Jesus answered him, "What I'm doing you don't understand now, but afterward you will know."

⁸ "You will never wash my feet—ever!" Peter said.

Jesus replied, "If I don't wash you, you have no part with Me."

⁹ Simon Peter said to Him, "Lord, not only my feet, but also my hands and my head."

[a]**13:1** *to the end = completely* or *always*

Jn 13:1 Jesus knew that His time had come to depart from this world, but although this event was upon Him, He intended to continue to demonstrate love for His followers.

Jn 13:2 Judas was not merely a malcontent or a thief. The Devil had already seized his heart.

Jn 13:7 The washing of the disciples' feet serves as a substitute in John for the last supper in the Synoptic Gospels. Jesus' action was one of complete humility and offering Himself on behalf of His followers.

John 13:1-20 (cont.)

[10] "One who has bathed," Jesus told him, "doesn't need to wash anything except his feet, but he is completely •clean. You are clean, but not all of you." [11] For He knew who would betray Him. This is why He said, "You are not all clean."

[12] When Jesus had washed their feet and put on His robe, He reclined[a] again and said to them, "Do you know what I have done for you? [13] You call Me Teacher and Lord. This is well said, for I am. [14] So if I, your Lord and Teacher, have washed your feet, you also ought to wash one another's feet. [15] For I have given you an example that you also should do just as I have done for you.

[16] "•I assure you: A •slave is not greater than his master,[b] and a messenger is not greater than the one who sent him. [17] If you know these things, you are blessed if you do them. [18] I'm not speaking about all of you; I know those I have chosen. But the Scripture must be fulfilled: **The one who eats My bread[c] has raised his heel against Me.**[d]

[19] "I am telling you now before it happens, so that when it does happen you will believe that I am ⌊He⌋. [20] I assure you: Whoever receives anyone I send receives Me, and the one who receives Me receives Him who sent Me."

a13:12 At important meals the custom was to recline on a mat at a low table and lean on the left elbow.　**b13:16** Or *lord*　**c13:18** Other mss read *eats bread with Me*　**d13:18** Ps 41:9

Jn 13:14-15 After washing His disciples' feet, Jesus told them that they should demonstrate humility and servanthood.
Jn 13:18 Jesus indicated through the quoting of Psalm 41:9 that He realized one of those in His closest circle would betray Him.

Sec. 146　Jesus' Betrayal Predicted

Matthew 26:21-25	Mark 14:18-21	Luke 22:21-23	John 13:21-30
[21] While they were eating, He said, "I assure you: One of you will betray Me."	[18] While they were reclining and eating, Jesus said, "I assure you: One of you will betray Me—one who is eating with Me!"	[21] But look, the hand of the one betraying Me is at the table with Me! [22] For the •Son of Man will go away as it has been determined, but woe to that man by whom He is betrayed!"	[21] When Jesus had said this, He was troubled in His spirit and testified, "I assure you: One of you will betray Me!"
[22] Deeply distressed, each one began to say to Him, "Surely not I, Lord?" [23] He replied, "The one who dipped his hand with Me in the bowl—he will betray Me. [24] The Son of Man will go just as it is written about Him,	[19] They began to be distressed and to say to Him one by one, "Surely not I?" [20] He said to them, "⌊It is⌋ one of the Twelve—the one who is dipping ⌊bread⌋ with Me in the bowl. [21] For the •Son of Man will go just as it is written about Him, but woe	[23] So they began to argue among themselves which of them it could be who was going to do this thing.	[22] The disciples started looking at one another—uncertain which one He was speaking about.

Mt 26:23 *dipped his hand with Me in the bowl:* Instead of plates being used, all helped themselves with their fingers from a common bowl (dish) as desired.
Mk 14:19 *Surely not I?:* A speaker could construct a question so as to communicate that "no" was the expected answer. Each disciple, presumably including Judas, used this construction in forming his question in hope that Jesus would answer, "No, you are not the betrayer."
Lk 22:22 *the Son of Man will go away as it has been determined:* These events were no surprise, for the plan of God was working itself out. *woe to that man:* The judgment that Judas will face.
Jn 13:21 The disciples had not understood what Jesus was saying, because they expressed surprise.

Matthew 26:21-25 (cont.)	Mark 14:18-21 (cont.)
but woe to that man by whom the Son of Man is betrayed! It would have been better for that man if he had not been born." 25 Then Judas, His betrayer, replied, "Surely not I, •Rabbi?" "You have said it," He told him.	to that man by whom the Son of Man is betrayed! It would have been better for that man if he had not been born."

John 13:21-30 (cont.)

23 One of His disciples, the one Jesus loved, was reclining close beside Jesus.a 24 Simon Peter motioned to him to find out who it was He was talking about. 25 So he leaned back against Jesus and asked Him, "Lord, who is it?"

26 Jesus replied, "He's the one I give the piece of bread to after I have dipped it." When He had dipped the bread, He gave it to Judas, Simon Iscariot's son.b 27 After ⌊Judas ate⌋ the piece of bread, Satan entered him. Therefore Jesus told him, "What you're doing, do quickly."

28 None of those reclining at the table knew why He told him this. 29 Since Judas kept the money-bag, some thought that Jesus was telling him, "Buy what we need for the festival," or that he should give something to the poor. 30 After receiving the piece of bread, he went out immediately. And it was night.

a**13:23** Lit *reclining at Jesus' breast*; that is, on His right; Jn 1:18   b**13:26** Other mss read *Judas Iscariot, Simon's son*

Mt 26:25 *You have said it:* In other words, "You are the traitor." John's Gospel noted that Judas left before the Lord's Supper was instituted.

Jn 13:23 The reference to the "disciple Jesus loved" as "reclining close beside Jesus" echoes the earlier description of Jesus as "the One who is at the Father's side" in 1:18. See also the back reference to 13:23 at 21:20, which identifies that disciple as present at the institution of the Last Supper and as the author of the Gospel.

Jn 13:26 The disciples still did not realize what had transpired (v. 28).

Sec. 147   The New Commandment

John 13:31-38

31 When he had gone out, Jesus said, "Now the •Son of Man is glorified, and God is glorified in Him. 32 If God is glorified in Him,a God will also glorify Him in Himself and will glorify Him at once.

33 "Children, I am with you a little while longer. You will look for Me, and just as I told the •Jews, 'Where I am going you cannot come,' so now I tell you.

34 "I give you a new command: love one another. Just as I have loved you, you must also love one another. 35 By this all people will know that you are My disciples, if you have love for one another."

36 "Lord," Simon Peter said to Him, "where are You going?"

Jesus answered, "Where I am going you cannot follow Me now, but you will follow later."

a**13:32** Other mss omit *If God is glorified in Him*

Jn 13:34-35 By the love His followers have for each other, people will recognize them as His followers.

Matthew 26:31-35	Mark 14:27-31	Luke 22:31-38	John 13:31-38 (cont.)

Matthew 26:31-35

31 Then Jesus said to them, "Tonight all of you will run away[a] because of Me, for it is written:

**I will strike
the shepherd,
and the sheep
of the flock
will be scattered.[b]**

32 But after I have been resurrected, I will go ahead of you to Galilee."
33 Peter told Him, "Even if everyone runs away because of You, I will never run away!"
34 "I assure you," Jesus said to him, "tonight, before the rooster crows, you will deny Me three times!"
35 "Even if I have to die with You," Peter told Him, "I will never deny You!" And all the disciples said the same thing.

[a]**26:31** Or •*stumble*   [a]**26:31** Zch 13:7

Mark 14:27-31

27 Then Jesus said to them, "All of you will run away,[a] [b] because it is written:

**I will strike
the shepherd,
and the sheep
will be scattered.[c]**

28 But after I have been resurrected, I will go ahead of you to Galilee."
29 Peter told Him, "Even if everyone runs away, I will certainly not!"
30 "I assure you," Jesus said to him, "today, this very night, before the rooster crows twice, you will deny Me three times!"
31 But he kept insisting, "If I have to die with You, I will never deny You!" And they all said the same thing.

[a]**14:27** Other mss add *because of Me this night*   [b]**14:27** Or •*stumble*   [c]**14:27** Zch 13:7

Luke 22:31-38

31 "Simon, Simon,[a] look out! Satan has asked to sift you[b] like wheat. 32 But I have prayed for you[c] that your faith may not fail. And you, when you have turned back, strengthen your brothers."
33 "Lord," he told Him, "I'm ready to go with You both to prison and to death!"
34 "I tell you, Peter," He said, "the rooster will not crow today until[d] you deny three times that you know Me!"

35 He also said to them, "When I sent you out without money-bag, traveling bag, or sandals, did you lack anything?"
"Not a thing," they said. 36 Then He said to them, "But now, whoever has a money-bag should take it, and also a traveling bag. And whoever doesn't have a sword should sell his robe and buy one. 37 For I tell you, what is written must be fulfilled in Me: **And He was counted among the outlaws.**[e] Yes, what is written about Me is coming to its fulfillment."
38 "Lord," they said, "look, here are two swords."
"Enough of that!"[f] He told them.

[a]**22:31** Other mss read *Then the Lord said, "Simon, Simon*   [b]**22:31** *you* (pl in Gk)   [c]**22:32** *you* (sg in Gk)   [d]**22:34** Other mss read *before*   [e]**22:37** Is 53:12   [f]**22:38** Or *It is enough!*

John 13:31-38 (cont.)

37 "Lord," Peter asked, "why can't I follow You now? I will lay down my life for You!"
38 Jesus replied, "Will you lay down your life for Me? I assure you: A rooster will not crow until you have denied Me three times.

Jn 13:37-38 Still not understanding what Jesus was saying, Peter rejected the notion of Jesus' departure and wanted to go with Him.

Sec. 148   The First Lord's Supper

Matthew 26:26-29	Mark 14:22-25	Luke 22:17-20	1 Corinthians 11:23-26
		¹⁷ Then He took a cup, and after giving thanks, He said, "Take this and share it among yourselves. ¹⁸ For I tell you, from now on I will not drink of the fruit of the vine until the kingdom of God comes."	²³ For I received from the Lord what I also passed on to you: on the night when He was betrayed, the Lord Jesus took bread, ²⁴ gave thanks, broke it, and said,
²⁶ As they were eating, Jesus took bread, blessed and broke it, gave it to the disciples, and said, "Take and eat it; this is My body." ²⁷ Then He took a cup, and after giving thanks, He gave it to them and said, "Drink from it, all of you. ²⁸ For this is My blood ⌊that establishes⌋ the covenant;ᵃ it is shed for many for the forgiveness of sins. ²⁹ But I tell you, from this moment I will not drink of this fruit of the vine until that day when I drink it in a new wayᵇ in My Father's kingdom with you."	²² As they were eating, He took bread, blessed and broke it, gave it to them, and said, "Take ⌊it⌋;ᵃ this is My body." ²³ Then He took a cup, and after giving thanks, He gave it to them, and so they all drank from it. ²⁴ He said to them, "This is My blood ⌊that establishes⌋ the covenant;ᵇ it is shed for many. ²⁵ I assure you: I will no longer drink of the fruit of the vine until that day when I drink it in a new wayᶜ in the kingdom of God."	¹⁹ And He took bread, gave thanks, broke it, gave it to them, and said, "This is My body, which is given for you. Do this in remembrance of Me." ²⁰ In the same way He also took the cup after supper and said, "This cup is the new covenant ⌊established by⌋ My blood; it is shed for you.ᵃ	"This is My body, which is for you. Do this in remembrance of Me." ²⁵ In the same way ⌊He⌋ also ⌊took⌋ the cup, after supper, and said, "This cup is the new covenant in My blood. Do this, as often as you drink it, in remembrance of Me." ²⁶ For as often as you eat this bread and drink the cup, you proclaim the Lord's death until He comes.
ᵃ26:28 Other mss read *new covenant* **ᵇ26:29** Or *drink new wine*; lit *drink it new*	**ᵃ14:22** Other mss add *eat;* **ᵇ14:24** Other mss read *the new covenant* **ᶜ14:25** Or *drink new wine*; lit *drink it new*	**ᵃ22:19-20** Other mss omit *which is given for you* (v. 19) through the end of v. 20	

Mt 26:26-27 Jesus at the end of a Passover meal established the Lord's Supper. Since the elements of the Passover were symbolic, it follows that the bread and wine Jesus used were symbols as well. The bread symbolizes His broken body. The wine represents His shed blood.

Mt 26:29 *I will not drink of this fruit of the vine until that day:* At this sad moment Jesus pointed them to a future reunion at the marriage supper of the Lamb.

Mk 14:24 Biblical covenants were often sealed with a sacrifice. Jesus' death is a sacrifice that seals the new covenant promised in Jeremiah 31:33-34. The new covenant involved not only forgiveness of sins but also the writing of God's law on the hearts of His people.

Lk 22:19 *This is My body, which is given for you:* Jesus transformed the imagery of the Passover into a remembrance about His death.

Lk 22:20 *This cup is the new covenant . . . My blood; it is shed for you:* Jesus appealed to the realization of the New Covenant (Jr 31:31-33; Ezk 36:24-26) that comes through His shed blood. Again, Jesus changed the imagery of the Passover and pointed to a deliverance tied to Him.

Sec. 149   Jesus' Farewell Discourse in the Upper Room

John 14:1-31

[1] "Your heart must not be troubled. Believe[a] in God; believe also in Me. [2] In My Father's house are many dwelling places;[b] if not, I would have told you. I am going away to prepare a place for you. [3] If I go away and prepare a place for you, I will come back and receive you to Myself, so that where I am you may be also. [4] You know the way ⌊to⌋ where I am going."[c]

[5] "Lord," Thomas said, "we don't know where You're going. How can we know the way?"

[6] Jesus told him, "I am the way, the truth, and the life. No one comes to the Father except through Me.

[7] "If you know Me, you will also know[d] My Father. From now on you do know Him and have seen Him."

[8] "Lord," said Philip, "show us the Father, and that's enough for us."

[9] Jesus said to him, "Have I been among you all this time without your knowing Me, Philip? The one who has seen Me has seen the Father. How can you say, 'Show us the Father'? [10] Don't you believe that I am in the Father and the Father is in Me? The words I speak to you I do not speak on My own. The Father who lives in Me does His works. [11] Believe Me that I am in the Father and the Father is in Me. Otherwise, believe[e] because of the works themselves.

[12] "•I assure you: The one who believes in Me will also do the works that I do. And he will do even greater works than these, because I am going to the Father. [13] Whatever you ask in My name, I will do it so that the Father may be glorified in the Son. [14] If you ask Me[f] anything in My name, I will do it.[g]

[15] "If you love Me, you will keep[h] My commands. [16] And I will ask the Father, and He will give you another •Counselor to be with you forever. [17] He is the Spirit of truth. The •world is unable to receive Him because it doesn't see Him or know Him. But you do know Him, because He remains with you and will be[i] in you. [18] I will not leave you as orphans; I am coming to you.

[19] "In a little while the world will see Me no longer, but you will see Me. Because I live, you will live too. [20] In that day you will know that I am in My Father, you are in Me, and I am in you. [21] The one who has My commands and keeps them is the one who loves Me. And the one who loves Me will be loved by My Father. I also will love him and will reveal Myself to him."

[22] Judas (not Iscariot) said to Him, "Lord, how is it You're going to reveal Yourself to us and not to the world?"

[23] Jesus answered, "If anyone loves Me, he will keep My word. My Father will love him, and We will come to him and make Our home with him. [24] The one who doesn't love Me will not keep My words. The word that you hear is not Mine but is from the Father who sent Me.

[25] "I have spoken these things to you while I remain with you. [26] But the Counselor, the Holy Spirit—the Father will send Him in My name—will teach you all things and remind you of everything I have told you.

[a]14:1 Or *You believe*   [b]14:2 The Vg used the Lat term *mansio*, a traveler's resting place. The Gk word is related to the verb *meno*, meaning *remain* or *stay*, which occurs 40 times in John.   [c]14:4 Other mss read this verse: *And you know where I am going, and you know the way*   [d]14:7 Other mss read *If you had known Me, you would have known*   [e]14:11 Other mss read *believe Me*   [f]14:14 Other mss omit *Me*   [g]14:14 Other mss omit all of v. 14   [h]14:15 Other mss read *If you love Me, keep* (as a command)   [i]14:17 Other mss read *and is*

Jn 14:2-3 Jesus' departure involved going to be with His Father. The analogy of a rich man's house is used for heaven.

Jn 14:6 An exclusive claim on the part of Jesus: He alone is able to provide access to God. He is the way everyone must follow. He is the truth (compare Jn 1:14,17; 5:33; 18:37; compare Jn 8:40,45-46), and all other conflicting claims are false. In His very essence, Jesus is truth and life, and He is the one and only way of salvation. This statement is offered in anticipation of Jesus' confrontation with Pilate.

Jn 14:10 Jesus defined His existence in terms of the Father's, and vice versa, such that the one is in the other. Here Jesus clarified the ontological commonality between the two functional persons, Father and Son.

Jn 14:12 Those who believe in Him will do even greater works than He did. The reason is that He will be with the Father, interceding on behalf of them.

Jn 14:15 The response to the love of Jesus is obedience to His commandments. The commandments referred to here no doubt include the command to love one another (13:34).

Jn 14:16 The other Counselor the Father will give is the way that John's Gospel refers to the Holy Spirit. He is given exclusively to those who recognize Him, and He will continue to teach them even after Jesus' departure (Jn 14:26).

John 14:1-31 (cont.)

27 "Peace I leave with you. My peace I give to you. I do not give to you as the world gives. Your heart must not be troubled or fearful. 28 You have heard Me tell you, 'I am going away and I am coming to you.' If you loved Me, you would have rejoiced that I am going to the Father, because the Father is greater than I. 29 I have told you now before it happens so that when it does happen you may believe. 30 I will not talk with you much longer, because the ruler of the world is coming. He has no power over Me.a 31 On the contrary, ⌊I am going away⌋b so that the world may know that I love the Father. Just as the Father commanded Me, so I do.
"Get up; let's leave this place."

a**14:30** Lit *He has nothing in Me*   b**14:31** Probably refers to the cross

Jn 14:28 Jesus' departure was necessary for a variety of reasons, including making it possible for Him to return. As a result, His disciples should rejoice that He is going to the Father.
Jn 14:31 The transition between 14:31 to 15:1 is at times viewed as a literary seam, that is, an indication that the present Gospel derived from different literary sources.

Sec. 150   Jesus' Farewill Discourse on the Way to Gethsemane

John 15–16

1 "I am the true vine, and My Father is the vineyard keeper. 2 Every branch in Me that does not produce fruit He removes, and He prunes every branch that produces fruit so that it will produce more fruit. 3 You are already •clean because of the word I have spoken to you. 4 Remain in Me, and I in you. Just as a branch is unable to produce fruit by itself unless it remains on the vine, so neither can you unless you remain in Me.
5 "I am the vine; you are the branches. The one who remains in Me and I in him produces much fruit, because you can do nothing without Me. 6 If anyone does not remain in Me, he is thrown aside like a branch and he withers. They gather them, throw them into the fire, and they are burned. 7 If you remain in Me and My words remain in you, ask whatever you want and it will be done for you. 8 My Father is glorified by this: that you produce much fruit and prove to bea My disciples.
9 "As the Father has loved Me, I have also loved you. Remain in My love. 10 If you keep My commands you will remain in My love, just as I have kept My Father's commands and remain in His love.
11 "I have spoken these things to you so that My joy may be in you and your joy may be complete. 12 This is My command: love one another as I have loved you. 13 No one has greater love than this, that someone would lay down his life for his friends. 14 You are My friends if you do what I command you. 15 I do not call you •slaves anymore, because a slave doesn't know what his masterb is doing. I have called you friends, because I have made known to you everything I have heard from My Father. 16 You did not choose Me, but I chose you. I appointed you that you should go out and produce fruit and that your fruit should remain, so that whatever you ask the Father in My name, He will give you. 17 This is what I command you: love one another.
18 "If the •world hates you, understand that it hated Me before it hated you. 19 If you were of the world, the world would love ⌊you as⌋ its own. However, because you are not of the world, but I have chosen you out of it, the world hates you. 20 Remember the word I spoke to you: 'A slave is not greater than his master.' If they persecuted Me, they will also persecute you. If they kept My word, they will also keep yours. 21 But they will do all these things to you on account of My name, because they don't know the One who sent Me. 22 If I had not come and spoken to them, they would not have sin.c Now they have no excuse for their sin. 23 The one

a**15:8** Or *and become*   b**15:15** Or *lord*   c**15:22** To *have sin* is an idiom that refers to guilt caused by sin.

Jn 15:1 *I am the true vine, and My Father is the vineyard keeper:* Those who are His followers are branches, but only those branches that produce fruit remain on the vine. Those that do not are removed or pruned. In fact, the only way for the branch to produce fruit is to remain on the vine.
Jn 15:12-17 Jesus returned to His command for His followers to love one another (Jn 13:34), by repeating it.
Jn 15:18 Jesus' followers can anticipate hatred from those around, since they hated Him before they hated them. This pattern of growing hatred has been demonstrated throughout John.
Jn 15:19 Being "of the world" means having and exemplifying the world's values. Jesus' disciples are meant to be "not of the world," since He has chosen them out of it. As a result, the world is going to hate them because they are traitors to it.
Jn 15:22 Jesus' coming gave clear guidelines on the right response to Him. Now no one has an excuse for sin, since He clarified what God expects of each one. Jesus' miracles were a means of showing what God expects and how poorly many responded.

John 15–16 (cont.)

who hates Me also hates My Father. [24] If I had not done the works among them that no one else has done, they would not have sin. Now they have seen and hated both Me and My Father. [25] But ⌊this happened⌋ so that the statement written in their law might be fulfilled: **They hated Me for no reason.**[a]

[26] "When the •Counselor comes, the One I will send to you from the Father—the Spirit of truth who proceeds from the Father—He will testify about Me. [27] You also will testify, because you have been with Me from the beginning.

[1]"I have told you these things to keep you from stumbling. [2] They will ban you from the •synagogues. In fact, a time is coming when anyone who kills you will think he is offering service to God. [3] They will do these things because they haven't known the Father or Me. [4] But I have told you these things so that when their time[b] comes you may remember I told them to you. I didn't tell you these things from the beginning, because I was with you.

[5] "But now I am going away to Him who sent Me, and not one of you asks Me, 'Where are You going?' [6] Yet, because I have spoken these things to you, sorrow has filled your heart. [7] Nevertheless, I am telling you the truth. It is for your benefit that I go away, because if I don't go away the •Counselor will not come to you. If I go, I will send Him to you. [8] When He comes, He will convict the world about sin, righteousness, and judgment: [9] about sin, because they do not believe in Me; [10] about righteousness, because I am going to the Father and you will no longer see Me; [11] and about judgment, because the ruler of this •world has been judged.

[12] "I still have many things to tell you, but you can't bear them now. [13] When the Spirit of truth comes, He will guide you into all the truth. For He will not speak on His own, but He will speak whatever He hears. He will also declare to you what is to come. [14] He will glorify Me, because He will take from what is Mine and declare it to you. [15] Everything the Father has is Mine. This is why I told you that He takes from what is Mine and will declare it to you.

[16] "A little while and you will no longer see Me; again a little while and you will see Me."[c]

[17] Therefore some of His disciples said to one another, "What is this He tells us: 'A little while and you will not see Me; again a little while and you will see Me'; and, 'because I am going to the Father'?" [18] They said, "What is this He is saying,[d] 'A little while'? We don't know what He's talking about!"

[19] Jesus knew they wanted to question Him, so He said to them, "Are you asking one another about what I said, 'A little while and you will not see Me; again a little while and you will see Me'?

[20] "•I assure you: You will weep and wail, but the world will rejoice. You will become sorrowful, but your sorrow will turn to joy. [21] When a woman is in labor she has pain because her time has come. But when she has given birth to a child, she no longer remembers the suffering because of the joy that a person has been born into the world. [22] So you also have sorrow[e] now. But I will see you again. Your hearts will rejoice, and no one will rob you of your joy. [23] In that day you will not ask Me anything.

[a]**15:25** Ps 69:4   [b]**16:4** Other mss read *when the time*   [c]**16:16** Other mss add *because I am going to the Father*   [d]**16:18** Other mss omit *He is saying*   [e]**16:22** Other mss read *will have sorrow*

Jn 15:25 Psalm 69:4 says that "they hated me for no reason," a statement Jesus applied to Himself regarding how humanity responded to Himself and His Father.

Jn 16:1 The purpose of Jesus' instruction is so that the disciples will remain faithful and not stumble. Throughout John some believed in Jesus only to fall away later. Jesus desired His followers to be as informed as they can be, in order to avoid falling away.

Jn 16:2 *They will ban you from the synagogues:* Christians were being banned from the synagogues by the time of the composition of John, but this banishment probably also took place much earlier.

Jn 16:13 A further function of the Spirit of truth is to lead Jesus' followers into the truth. What He instructs them in is not simply of His own volition but what He hears from God regarding both the present and the future.

Jn 16:16 *A little while and you will no longer see Me; again a little while and you will see Me:* Jesus anticipated both His death/resurrection and His return in glory. His disciples did not understand what He is saying (vv. 17-18).

Jn 16:20 Jesus' followers will go through a time of mourning and grief that is the prelude to rejoicing at the time of His return. He equated this with the pain and then joy that a pregnant woman experiences (v. 21).

Jn 16:23-24 Jesus offered His disciples an opportunity they had previously not exercised, the ability to ask for something in His name. Asking in Jesus' name is the opportunity to ask in line with Jesus' will and intention, especially in circumstances such as the disciples face.

John 15–16 (cont.)

"I assure you: Anything you ask the Father in My name, He will give you. ²⁴ Until now you have asked for nothing in My name. Ask and you will receive, so that your joy may be complete.

²⁵ "I have spoken these things to you in figures of speech. A time is coming when I will no longer speak to you in figures, but I will tell you plainly about the Father. ²⁶ In that day you will ask in My name. I am not telling you that I will make requests to the Father on your behalf. ²⁷ For the Father Himself loves you, because you have loved Me and have believed that I came from God.ᵃ ²⁸ I came from the Father and have come into the world. Again, I am leaving the world and going to the Father."

²⁹ "Ah!" His disciples said. "Now You're speaking plainly and not using any figurative language. ³⁰ Now we know that You know everything and don't need anyone to question You. By this we believe that You came from God."

³¹ Jesus responded to them, "Do you now believe? ³² Look: An hour is coming, and has come, when each of you will be scattered to his own home, and you will leave Me alone. Yet I am not alone, because the Father is with Me. ³³ I have told you these things so that in Me you may have peace. You will have suffering in this world. Be courageous! I have conquered the world."

ᵃ**16:27** Other mss read *from the Father*

Jn 16:25 *I have spoken these things to you in figures of speech:* Jesus assured them that there is a time when such symbolic language will not be necessary, and that He will be able to talk with them plainly about God the Father.
Jn 16:29 When Jesus said He was leaving the world and going to the Father (v. 28), His disciples responded with understanding because what He was saying seemed clear to them.
Jn 16:31 Jesus was astounded that on the basis of His simple statement that He was leaving, the disciples declared that they knew He was from God. This indicated to Him that they did not really understand what He had been talking about.

Sec. 151   Jesus' Intercessory Prayer

John 17:1-26

¹ Jesus spoke these things, looked up to heaven, and said:

Father,
the hour has come.
Glorify Your Son
so that the Son may glorify You,
² for You gave Him authority
over all flesh;ᵃ
so He may give eternal life
to all You have given Him.
³ This is eternal life:
that they may know You, the only true God,
and the One You have sent—Jesus Christ.
⁴ I have glorified You on the earth
by completing the work You gave Me to do.
⁵ Now, Father, glorify Me in Your presence
with that glory I had with You
before the world existed.

⁶ I have revealed Your name
to the men You gave Me from the world.
They were Yours, You gave them to Me,
and they have kept Your word.

ᵃ**17:2** Or *people*

Jn 17:2 As the mediator between God and humanity, Jesus has authority over the human realm, including giving eternal life.

John 17:1-26 (cont.)

7 Now they know that all things
   You have given to Me are from You,
8 because the words that You gave Me,
   I have given them.
   They have received them
   and have known for certain
   that I came from You.
   They have believed that You sent Me.
9 I pray[a] for them.
   I am not praying for the •world
   but for those You have given Me,
   because they are Yours.
10 Everything I have is Yours,
   and everything You have is Mine,
   and I have been glorified in them.
11 I am no longer in the world,
   but they are in the world,
   and I am coming to You.
   Holy Father,
   protect[b] them by Your name
   that You have given Me,
   so that they may be one as We are one.
12 While I was with them,
   I was protecting them by Your name
   that You have given Me.
   I guarded them and not one of them is lost,
   except the son of destruction,[c]
   so that the Scripture may be fulfilled.
13 Now I am coming to You,
   and I speak these things in the world
   so that they may have My joy completed in them.
14 I have given them Your word.
   The world hated them
   because they are not of the world,
   as I am not of the world.
15 I am not praying
   that You take them out of the world
   but that You protect them from the evil one.
16 They are not of the world,
   as I am not of the world.
17 Sanctify[d] them by the truth;
   Your word is truth.
18 As You sent Me into the world,
   I also have sent them into the world.
19 I sanctify Myself for them,
   so they also may be sanctified by the truth.

---

[a]**17:9** Lit *ask* (throughout this passage) [b]**17:11** Lit *keep* (throughout this passage) [c]**17:12** The one destined for destruction, loss, or perdition [d]**17:17** Set apart for special use

Jn 17:9 Jesus distinguishes between the world of unbelieving humanity and those entrusted to Him by God the Father. They are the ones He prays for.
Jn 17:11 He was in the process of departing from the world, but His followers were still in the world, and He asked God to protect them as a unified group.
Jn 17:12 Jesus offered assurance that none of His followers has been lost while He has been protecting them, except for the one who was forecast as destined for destruction.
Jn 17:14-15 The disciples had already been hated because they did not participate in the structures of the world, although they lived in the world.
Jn 17:16 Both the disciples and Jesus are not of the world, in the sense that they both live lives not defined by the values of the world.
Jn 17:17 *Your word is truth:* God's word is the basis of truth and is the means by which one is kept from sin (v. 19).

John 17:1-26 (cont.)

20 I pray not only for these,
    but also for those who believe in Me
    through their message.
21 May they all be one,
    as You, Father, are in Me and I am in You.
    May they also be one[a] in Us,
    so the world may believe You sent Me.
22 I have given them the glory You have given Me.
    May they be one as We are one.
23 I am in them and You are in Me.
    May they be made completely one,
    so the world may know You have sent Me
    and have loved them as You have loved Me.
24 Father,
    I desire those You have given Me
    to be with Me where I am.
    Then they will see My glory,
    which You have given Me
    because You loved Me before the world's foundation.
25 Righteous Father!
    The world has not known You.
    However, I have known You,
    and these have known that You sent Me.
26 I made Your name known to them
    and will make it known,
    so the love You have loved Me with
    may be in them and I may be in them.

[a]17:21 Other mss omit *one*

Jn 17:20 Jesus extended His prayer beyond His immediate disciples to any who believe in Him through hearing the message the disciples preach.
Jn 17:22 The glory of Jesus is also extended to those who believe in Him. Jesus emphasized the unity of His followers. (See v. 21).
Jn 17:26 Jesus closed this prayer by recognizing that, though the world did not recognize God the Father (v. 25), through His ministry He has revealed the character of God to them.

Sec. 152   The Prayer in the Garden

Matthew 26:30,36-46	Mark 14:26,32-42	Luke 22:39-46	John 18:1
30 After singing psalms,[a] they went out to the •Mount of Olives.	26 After singing psalms,[a] they went out to the •Mount of Olives.	39 He went out and made His way as usual to the •Mount of Olives, and the disciples followed Him. 40 When He reached the place, He told them,	1 After Jesus had said these things, He went out with His disciples across the Kidron Valley, where there was a garden, and He and His disciples went into it.
[a]26:30 Pss 113–118 were sung during and after the Passover meal.	[a]14:26 Pss 113–118 were sung during and after the Passover meal.		

Mk 14:26 *After singing psalms:* The singing of Psalms 113–118 was a traditional part of the Passover celebration, with the last three of these Psalms coming at the close of the meal. Therefore, Jesus probably sang Psalm 118 just before He went to Gethsemane. Psalm 118 describes how God guides the righteous through distress and the prospect of death.

Matthew 26:30,36-46 (cont.)   Mark 14:26,32-42 (cont.)   Luke 22:39-46 (cont.)

36 Then Jesus came with them to a place called Gethsemane,[a] and He told the disciples, "Sit here while I go over there and pray." 37 Taking along Peter and the two sons of Zebedee, He began to be sorrowful and deeply distressed. 38 Then He said to them, "My soul is swallowed up in sorrow[b] —to the point of death.[c] Remain here and stay awake with Me." 39 Going a little farther,[d] He fell facedown and prayed, "My Father! If it is possible, let this cup pass from Me. Yet not as I will, but as You will."

40 Then He came to the disciples and found them sleeping. He asked Peter, "So, couldn't you[e] stay awake with Me one hour? 41 Stay awake and pray, so that you won't enter into temptation. The spirit is willing, but the flesh is weak."

42 Again, a second time, He went away and prayed, "My Father, if this[f] cannot pass[g] unless I drink it, Your will be done." 43 And He came again and found them sleeping, because they could not keep their eyes open.[h]

44 After leaving them, He went away again and prayed a third time, saying the same thing once more. 45 Then He came to the disciples and said to them, "Are you still sleeping and resting?[i] Look, the time is near. The Son of Man is being betrayed into the hands of sinners. 46 Get up; let's go! See, My betrayer is near."

32 Then they came to a place named Gethsemane, and He told His disciples, "Sit here while I pray." 33 He took Peter, James, and John with Him, and He began to be deeply distressed and horrified. 34 Then He said to them, "My soul is swallowed up in sorrow[a] —to the point of death. Remain here and stay awake." 35 Then He went a little farther, fell to the ground, and began to pray that if it were possible, the hour might pass from Him. 36 And He said, "•Abba, Father! All things are possible for You. Take this cup away from Me. Nevertheless, not what I will, but what You will."

37 Then He came and found them sleeping. "Simon, are you sleeping?" He asked Peter. "Couldn't you stay awake one hour? 38 Stay awake and pray so that you won't enter into temptation. The spirit is willing, but the flesh is weak."

39 Once again He went away and prayed, saying the same thing. 40 And He came again and found them sleeping, because they could not keep their eyes open.[b] They did not know what to say to Him. 41 Then He came a third time and said to them, "Are you still sleeping and resting? Enough! The time has come. Look, the Son of Man is being betrayed into the hands of sinners. 42 Get up; let's go! See—My betrayer is near."

a14:34 Or *I am deeply grieved* b14:40 Lit *because their eyes were weighed down*

"Pray that you may not enter into temptation." 41 Then He withdrew from them about a stone's throw, knelt down, and began to pray, 42 "Father, if You are willing, take this cup away from Me—nevertheless, not My will, but Yours, be done." [43 Then an angel from heaven appeared to Him, strengthening Him. 44 Being in anguish, He prayed more fervently, and His sweat became like drops of blood falling to the ground.]a 45 When He got up from prayer and came to the disciples, He found them sleeping, exhausted from their grief.b 46 "Why are you sleeping?" He asked them. "Get up and pray, so that you won't enter into temptation."

a22:43-44 Other mss omit bracketed text b22:45 Lit *sleeping from grief*

a26:36 A garden east of Jerusalem at the base of the Mount of Olives; *Gethsemane* = olive oil press b26:38 Or *I am deeply grieved*, or *I am overwhelmed by sorrow*; Ps 42:6,11; 43:5 c26:38 Lit *unto death* d26:39 Other mss read *Drawing nearer* e26:40 *You* = all 3 disciples because the verb in Gk is pl f26:42 Other mss add *cup* g26:42 Other mss add *from Me* h26:43 Lit *because their eyes were weighed down* i26:45 Or *Sleep on now and take your rest.*

Mt 26:39 *let this cup pass from Me:* Jesus was saying in effect, "Father, if there is any other way by which sinners can be saved than by My going to the cross, reveal that way now! But in all of this, I want it known that I desire nothing contrary to Your will."

Mk 14:32 *Gethsemane:* Means "oil press," which suggests that the place Jesus went to pray was an olive grove, the normal location for an oil press. Both Luke and John mention this as a customary meeting place for Jesus and His disciples (Lk 22:39; Jn 18:2).

Mk 14:36 *Abba:* This Aramaic word was part of the everyday language of the home, a term for addressing one's father. Children, but also adult sons and daughters, used *Abba* in speaking to their fathers. *Abba* also appears in Romans 8:15 and Galatians 4:6, both again in the context of prayer. *cup:* A cup may symbolize the judgment and wrath of God (Ps 75:8; Is 51:17,22; Jr 25:15-17; 49:12; Ezk 23:31-35; Hab 2:16). Jesus viewed His death as redemptive and receiving the judgment of God for the sake of many others (Mk 10:45; 14:24).

Lk 22:40 *Pray that you may not enter into temptation:* Jesus warned the disciples that they will need to depend on God to respond properly to what is about to take place.

PART XIII

THE ARREST, TRIAL, CRUCIFIXION, AND BURIAL OF JESUS

Sec. 153   The Judas Kiss

Matthew 26:47-56	Mark 14:43-52	Luke 22:47-53	John 18:2-11
⁴⁷ While He was still speaking, Judas, one of the Twelve, suddenly arrived. A large mob, with swords and clubs, was with him from the chief priests and elders of the people.	⁴³ While He was still speaking, Judas, one of the Twelve, suddenly arrived. With him was a mob, with swords and clubs, from the chief priests, the scribes, and the elders.	⁴⁷ While He was still speaking, suddenly a mob was there, and one of the Twelve named Judas was leading them.	² Judas, who betrayed Him, also knew the place, because Jesus often met there with His disciples. ³ So Judas took a •company of soldiers and some temple police from the •chief priests and the •Pharisees and came there with lanterns, torches, and weapons. ⁴ Then Jesus, knowing everything that was about to happen to Him, went out and said to them, "Who is it you're looking for?" ⁵ "Jesus the •Nazarene," they answered. "I am He,"ᵃ Jesus told them. Judas, who betrayed Him, was also standing with them. ⁶ When He told them, "I am He," they stepped back and fell to the ground. ⁷ Then He asked them again, "Who is it you're looking for?" "Jesus the Nazarene," they said.

ᵃ**18:5** Lit *I am;* see note at Jn 8:58

Mt 26:47 *with swords:* In the hands of the soldiers. *clubs:* In the hands of the mob.

Jn 18:3 Judas led a group of soldiers and temple police to a familiar site where Jesus regularly met with His disciples outside the city.

Jn 18:4 Events about to transpire were all known to Jesus, so He took anticipatory action and went out to meet those coming to Him.

Jn 18:5 *I am He:* The reason that they did not recognize Him may be because of the physical or even spiritual darkness, or it may be that Jesus' appearance was not what they were expecting. Jesus' acknowledgment of His identity used the same phrase He used in 8:58, using the divine name (Ex 3:13-14).

Jn 18:6 This falling may simply be a reflex out of shock or surprise, but is more likely caused by the power of Jesus' invoking of God's name for Himself. In any case, the events were clearly going to happen as Jesus allowed and directed.

Matthew 26:47-56 (cont.)	Mark 14:43-52 (cont.)	Luke 22:47-53 (cont.)	John 18:2-11 (cont.)
			[8] "I told you I am ⌊He⌋," Jesus replied. "So if you're looking for Me, let these men go." [9] This was to fulfill the words He had said: "I have not lost one of those You have given Me."
[48] His betrayer had given them a sign: "The One I kiss, He's the One; arrest Him!" [49] So he went right up to Jesus and said, "Greetings, Rabbi!" and kissed Him.	[44] His betrayer had given them a signal. "The One I kiss," he said, "He's the One; arrest Him and take Him away under guard." [45] So when he came, he went right up to Him and said, "•Rabbi!"—and kissed Him.		
		He came near Jesus to kiss Him, [48] but Jesus said to him, "Judas, are you betraying the Son of Man with a kiss?"	
[50] "Friend," Jesus asked him, "why have you come?"[a] Then they came up, took hold of Jesus, and arrested Him. [51] At that moment one of those with Jesus reached out his hand and drew his sword. He struck the high priest's •slave and cut off his ear. [52] Then Jesus told him, "Put your sword back in its place because all who take up a sword will perish by a sword. [53] Or do you think that I cannot call on My Father, and He will provide Me at once with more than 12 legions[b] of angels? [54] How, then, would the Scriptures be fulfilled that say it must happen this way?"	[46] Then they took hold of Him and arrested Him. [47] And one of those who stood by drew his sword, struck the high priest's •slave, and cut off his ear.	[49] When those around Him saw what was going to happen, they asked, "Lord, should we strike with the sword?" [50] Then one of them struck the high priest's •slave and cut off his right ear. [51] But Jesus responded, "No more of this!"[a] And touching his ear, He healed him.	[10] Then Simon Peter, who had a sword, drew it, struck the high priest's •slave, and cut off his right ear. (The slave's name was Malchus.) [11] At that, Jesus said to Peter, "Sheathe your sword! Am I not to drink the cup the Father has given Me?"
		[a]**22:51** Lit *Permit as far as this*	
[a]**26:50** Or *Jesus told him, "do what you have come for."* (as a statement) [b]**26:53** A Roman legion contained up to 6,000 soldiers.			

Mt 26:49 *kissed Him:* A common method of salutation among close friends. A sign was needed to point Jesus out to the soldiers.

Mt 26:52 *all who take up a sword will perish by a sword:* The violent usually die violent deaths.

Mt 26:53 *12 legions:* A Roman legion contained up to 6,000 soldiers.

Lk 22:48 *are you betraying the Son of Man with a kiss?:* This remark must have been stunning. The Son of Man has judgment authority at the end, and that is who Judas betrayed.

Jn 18:10-11 Peter drew his sword and cut off the right ear of a servant named Malchus, but Jesus told him to put the sword away. Jesus wanted nothing to interrupt fulfillment of God's plan.

Lk 22:51 *No more of this:* Jesus stopped the effort by the disciples to defend Jesus and healed the ear of a priest's servant. The disciples misunderstood the remark about swords in v. 36.

Matthew 26:47-56 (cont.)   Mark 14:43-52 (cont.)   Luke 22:47-53 (cont.)

55 At that time Jesus said to the crowds, "Have you come out with swords and clubs, as if I were a criminal,ᵃ to capture Me? Every day I used to sit, teaching in the •temple complex, and you didn't arrest Me. 56 But all this has happened so that the prophetic Scripturesᵇ would be fulfilled." Then all the disciples deserted Him and ran away.	48 But Jesus said to them, "Have you come out with swords and clubs, as though I were a criminal,ᵃ to capture Me? 49 Every day I was among you, teaching in the •temple complex, and you didn't arrest Me. But the Scriptures must be fulfilled." 50 Then they all deserted Him and ran away. 51 Now a certain young man,ᵇ having a linen cloth wrapped around his naked body, was following Him. They caught hold of him, 52 but he left the linen cloth behind and ran away naked.	52 Then Jesus said to the chief priests, temple police, and the elders who had come for Him, "Have you come out with swords and clubs as if I were a criminal?ᵃ 53 Every day while I was with you in the •temple complex, you never laid a hand on Me. But this is your hour—and the dominion of darkness."

a26:55 Lit *as against a criminal*
b26:56 Or *the Scriptures of the prophets*

a14:48 Lit *as against a criminal*
b14:51 Perhaps John Mark who later wrote this Gospel

a22:52 Lit *as against a criminal*

Mk 14:51 *a certain young man:* Only Mark included this brief note. It serves to characterize the desertion of Jesus as a shameful and overwhelming defeat.
Lk 22:53 *this is your hour–and the dominion of darkness:* Another note that Satan was at work in these events.

Sec. 154   Jesus Arrested and Taken to Annas

John 18:12-14,19-23

¹² Then the company of soldiers, the commander, and the Jewish temple police arrested Jesus and tied Him   ¹³ First they led Him to Annas, for he was the father-in-law of Caiaphas, who was high priest that year. ¹⁴ Caiaphas was the one who had advised the •Jews that it was advantageous that one man should die for the people.
¹⁹ The high priest questioned Jesus about His disciples and about His teaching.
²⁰ "I have spoken openly to the world," Jesus answered him. "I have always taught in the •synagogue and in the •temple complex, where all the Jews congregate, and I haven't spoken anything in secret. ²¹ Why do you question Me? Question those who heard what I told them. Look, they know what I said."
²² When He had said these things, one of the temple police standing by slapped Jesus, saying, "Is this the way you answer the high priest?"
²³ "If I have spoken wrongly," Jesus answered him, "give evidenceᵃ about the wrong; but if rightly, why do you hit Me?"

a18:23 Or *him, testify*

Jn 18:13 Although Caiaphas was high priest (see 11:49-50), Annas his father-in-law had been high priest before and was still a powerful person in the Jewish hierarchy.
Jn 18:19 Jesus was interrogated by, Annas, about His followers and His teaching.
Jn 18:20-21 *I have spoken openly to the world:* Jesus stated candidly that He has spoken openly. This includes the fact that He had been plain and straightforward in His teaching. Many had heard what He said who could attest to what He said.
Jn 18:22-23 One of the temple police interpreted Jesus as being insolent with regard to the high priest. Jesus, however, challenged the Jewish leaders to provide evidence if He has said anything not correct.

Sec. 155   Jesus Faces Caiaphas and the Sanhedrin

Matthew 26:57,59-68	Mark 14:53,55-65	Luke 22:54a,63-65	John 18:24

57 Those who had arrested Jesus led Him away to Caiaphas the high priest, where the •scribes and the elders had convened.

59 The chief priests and the whole •Sanhedrin were looking for false testimony against Jesus so they could put Him to death. 60 But they could not find any, even though many false witnesses came forward.[a] Finally, two[b] who came forward 61 stated, "This man said, 'I can demolish God's sanctuary and rebuild it in three days.'"

62 The high priest then stood up and said to Him, "Don't You have an answer to what these men are testifying against You?" 63 But Jesus kept silent. Then the high priest said to Him, "By the living God I place You under oath: tell us if You are the •Messiah, the Son of God!"

[a]26:60 Other mss add *they found none*   [b]26:60 Other mss add *false witnesses*

53 They led Jesus away to the high priest, and all the chief priests, the elders, and the scribes convened. 55 The chief priests and the whole •Sanhedrin were looking for testimony against Jesus to put Him to death, but they could find none. 56 For many were giving false testimony against Him, but the testimonies did not agree. 57 Some stood up and were giving false testimony against Him, stating, 58 "We heard Him say, 'I will demolish this sanctuary made by ⌊human⌋ hands, and in three days I will build another not made by hands.'" 59 Yet their testimony did not agree even on this. 60 Then the high priest stood up before them all and questioned Jesus, "Don't You have an answer to what these men are testifying against You?" 61 But He kept silent and did not answer anything. Again the high priest questioned Him, "Are You the •Messiah, the Son of the Blessed One?"

54 They seized Him, led Him away, and brought Him into the high priest's house.

24 Then Annas sent Him bound to Caiaphas the high priest.

Mt 26:57 *led Him away to Caiaphas:* He was first examined by Annas, the former high priest, the father-in-law of Caiaphas, probably while the Sanhedrin was assembling in the darkness of night (Jn 18:13).

Mk 14:53 *the high priest:* At the time of Jesus, the high priest was also a governmental leader and a political representative for the nation. The Roman governor appointed the high priest (always from a select number of influential priestly families), and he could remove the high priest at any time.

Mk 14:61 *the Blessed One:* The high priest avoided any direct reference to God's name. Therefore, he ironically showed reverence for God's name at the same time that he condemned God's Son. He honored God with his lips while his heart was far from Him (Mk 7:6).

Matthew 26:57,59-68 (cont.)	Mark 14:53,55-65 (cont.)	Luke 22:54a,63-65 (cont.)

64 "You have said it,"a Jesus told him. "But I tell you, in the futureb you will see **the Son of Man seated at the right hand** of the Power and **coming on the clouds of heaven.**"c

65 Then the high priest tore his robes and said, "He has blasphemed! Why do we still need witnesses? Look, now you've heard the blasphemy! 66 What is your decision?"d

They answered, "He deserves death!" 67 Then they spit in His face and beat Him; others slapped Him 68 and said, "Prophesy to us, Messiah! Who hit You?"

a26:64 Or *That is true,* an affirmative oath; Mt 27:11; Mk 15:2 **b26:64** Lit *you, from now* **c26:64** Ps 110:1; Dn 7:13
d26:66 Lit *What does it seem to you?*

62 "I am," said Jesus, "and all of youa will see **the Son of Man seated at the right hand** of the Power and **coming with the clouds of heaven.**"b 63 Then the high priest tore his robes and said, "Why do we still need witnesses? 64 You have heard the blasphemy! What is your decision?"c

And they all condemned Him to be deserving of death. 65 Then some began to spit on Him, to blindfold Him, and to beat Him, saying, "Prophesy!" The temple police also took Him and slapped Him.

a14:62 Lit *and you* (pl in Gk)
b14:62 Ps 110:1; Dn 7:13
c14:64 Lit *How does it appear to you?*

63 The men who were holding Jesus started mocking and beating Him. 64 After blindfolding Him, they kepta asking, "Prophesy! Who hit You?" 65 And they were saying many other blasphemous things against Him.

a22:64 Other mss add *striking Him on the face and*

Mk 14:64 *the Son of Man seated at the right hand:* The background for Jesus' statement concerning the Son of Man is Daniel 7:13-14. The background for Jesus' statement about sitting at the right hand of power is in Psalm 110:1, where the one at God's right hand will receive the place of honor, ruling over all enemies and judging all nations.

Lk 22:64 *Prophesy! Who hit You?:* This mocking is a game to the soldiers. These remarks were blasphemous, a verbal insult against Jesus.

Sec. 156   Peter Denies His Lord

Matthew 26:58,69-75	Mark 14:54,66-72	Luke 22:54b-62	John 18:15-18,25-27

58 Meanwhile, Peter was following Him at a distance

right to the high priest's courtyard.a He went in

26:58 Or *high priest's palace*

54 Peter followed Him at a distance,

right into the high priest's courtyard.

Meanwhile Peter was following at a distance.

15 Meanwhile, Simon Peter was following Jesus, as was another disciple. That disciple was an acquaintance of the high priest; so he went with Jesus into the high priest's courtyard. 16 But Peter remained standing outside by the door. So the other disciple, the one known to the high priest,

Jn 18:15 John explained how so much was known of the interrogation and trial of Jesus.

Matthew 26:58,69-75 (cont.)	Mark 14:54,66-72 (cont.)	Luke 22:54b-62 (cont.)	John 18:15-18,25-27 (cont.)
			went out and spoke to the girl who was the door-keeper and brought Peter in.
and was sitting with the temple police[a] to see the outcome.[b] ⁶⁹ Now Peter was sitting outside in the courtyard. A servant approached him and she said,	He was sitting with the temple police,[a] warming himself by the fire.[b] ⁶⁶ While Peter was in the courtyard below, one of the high priest's servants came. ⁶⁷ When she saw Peter warming himself, she looked at him and	⁵⁵ They lit a fire in the middle of the courtyard and sat down together, and Peter sat among them. ⁵⁶ When a servant saw him sitting in the firelight, and looked closely at him, she said, "This man was with Him too."	¹⁷ Then the slave girl who was the doorkeeper said to Peter, "You aren't one of this man's disciples too, are you?"
"You were with Jesus the Galilean too." ⁷⁰ But he denied it in front of everyone: "I don't know what you're talking about!"	said, "You also were with that •Nazarene, Jesus." ⁶⁸ But he denied it: "I don't know or understand what you're talking about!" Then he went out to the entryway, and a rooster crowed.[c]	⁵⁷ But he denied it: "Woman, I don't know Him!"	"I am not!" he said. ¹⁸ Now the slaves and the temple police had made a charcoal fire, because it was cold. They were standing there warming themselves, and Peter was standing with them, warming himself.
⁷¹ When he had gone out to the gateway, another woman saw him and told those who were there, "This man was with Jesus the •Nazarene!" ⁷² And again he denied it with an oath, "I don't know the man!"	⁶⁹ When the servant saw him again she began to tell those standing nearby, "This man is one of them!" ⁷⁰ But again he denied it.	⁵⁸ After a little while, someone else saw him and said, "You're one of them too!" "Man, I am not!" Peter said.	²⁵ Now Simon Peter was standing and warming himself. They said to him, "You aren't one of His disciples too, are you?" He denied it and said, "I am not!"
⁷³ After a little while those standing there approached and said to Peter, "You certainly are one of them, since even your accent[c] gives you away."	After a little while those standing there said to Peter again, "You certainly are one of them, since you're also a Galilean!"[d]	⁵⁹ About an hour later, another kept insisting, "This man was certainly with Him, since he's also a Galilean."	²⁶ One of the high priest's slaves, a relative of the man whose ear Peter had cut off, said, "Didn't I see you with Him in the garden?"

[a]26:58 Or *the officers*, or *the servants* [b]26:58 Lit *end* [c]26:73 Or *speech*

[a]14:54 Or *the officers*; lit *the servants* [b]14:54 Lit *light* [c]14:68 Other mss omit *and a rooster crowed* [d]14:70 Other mss add *and your speech shows it*

Mt 26:73 *accent:* Galileans pronounced gutturals peculiarly and had a sort of lisp.

Lk 22:69 But from now on, the Son of Man will be seated at the right hand of the power of God: The reply combined imagery from Daniel 7:9-14 and Psalm 110:1. Jesus was claiming that God will bring Him to His side to share in His presence and rule. To Jewish ears, this was a brash claim. It raised the questions, Who is able to sit permanently at God's side? and What was Jesus claiming?

Jn 18:17 The slave girl keeping the door began the interrogation that leads to Peter's denial. The phrasing of the question in verse 17 and verse 25 was expected to elicit a negative response. Unfortunately, Peter obliged in both instances.

Matthew 26:58,69-75 (cont.)	Mark 14:54,66-72 (cont.)	Luke 22:54b-62 (cont.)	John 18:15-18,25-27 (cont.)
74 Then he started to curse[a] and to swear with an oath, "I do not know the man!"	71 Then he started to curse[a] and to swear with an oath, "I don't know this man you're talking about."	60 But Peter said, "Man, I don't know what you're talking about!"	27 Peter then denied it again.
Immediately a rooster crowed, 75 and Peter remembered the words Jesus had spoken, "Before the rooster crows, you will deny Me three times." And he went outside and wept bitterly.	72 Immediately a rooster crowed a second time, and Peter remembered when Jesus had spoken the word to him, "Before the rooster crows twice, you will deny Me three times." When he thought about it, he began to weep.[b]	Immediately, while he was still speaking, a rooster crowed. 61 Then the Lord turned and looked at Peter. So Peter remembered the word of the Lord, how He had said to him, "Before the rooster crows today, you will deny Me three times." 62 And he went outside and wept bitterly.	Immediately a rooster crowed.
[a]**26:74** To call down curses on himself if what he said weren't true	[a]**14:71** To call down curses on himself if what he said weren't true [b]**14:72** Or *he burst into tears*, or *he broke down*		

Mk 14:71 *he started to curse:* Peter sought to prove the truth of what he was saying by vowing to call down a curse on himself if he was lying (Ac 23:12,14,21).

Sec. 157   The Chief Priest and Elders Move to Put Jesus to Death

Matthew 27:1	Mark 15:1a	Luke 22:66-71
1 When daybreak came, all the •chief priests and the elders of the people plotted against Jesus to put Him to death.	1 As soon as it was morning, the •chief priests had a meeting with the elders, •scribes, and the whole •Sanhedrin.	66 When daylight came, the elders[a] of the people, both the chief priests and the scribes, convened and brought Him before their •Sanhedrin. 67 They said, "If You are the •Messiah, tell us." But He said to them, "If I do tell you, you will not believe. 68 And if I ask you, you will not answer. 69 But from now on, the Son of Man will be seated at the right hand of the Power of God." 70 They all asked, "Are You, then, the Son of God?" And He said to them, "You say that I am." 71 "Why do we need any more testimony," they said, "since we've heard it ourselves from His mouth?"
		[a]**22:66** Or *council of elders*

Mk 15:1 *had a meeting:* Mark conveyed the idea that the Sanhedrin met again in the morning after its initial examination during the night. The purpose for this morning meeting may have been to confirm the earlier decision (Lk 22:66-71) and to make preparations for turning Jesus over to Pilate on a political charge.

Lk 22:71 *Why do we need any more testimony?:* The priests now had what they needed. They were trying to gather information to take to Rome to get Jesus crucified as a "threat" to Caesar. The basis of Jesus' death, humanly speaking, came from His own testimony at His examination by the Jewish leadership. His claim to sit at God's right hand and come with power moved the process along. This gave them their evidence against Jesus.

Sec. 158   Judas Hangs Himself

Matthew 27:3-10   Acts 1:18-19

3 Then Judas, His betrayer, seeing that He had been condemned, was full of remorse and returned the 30 pieces of silver to the chief priests and elders. 4 "I have sinned by betraying innocent blood," he said.

"What's that to us?" they said. "See to it yourself!"

5 So he threw the silver into the sanctuary and departed. Then he went and hanged himself.

6 The chief priests took the silver and said, "It's not lawful to put it into the temple treasury,ᵃ since it is blood money."ᵇ 7 So they conferred together and bought the potter's field with it as a burial place for foreigners. 8 Therefore that field has been called "Blood Field" to this day. 9 Then what was spoken through the prophet Jeremiah was fulfilled:

They took the 30 pieces of silver, the price of Him whose price was set by the Israelites, 10 and they gave them for the potter's field, as the Lord directed me.ᶜ

18 Now this man acquired a field with his unrighteous wages; and falling headfirst, he burst open in the middle, and all his insides spilled out. 19 This became known to all the residents of Jerusalem, so that in their own language that field is called Hakeldama, that is, Field of Blood.

ᵃ**27:6** See Mk 7:11 where the same Gk word used here (*Corban*) means a gift (pledged to the temple).   ᵇ**27:6** Lit *the price of blood*
ᶜ**27:9-10** Jr 32:6-9; Zch 11:12-13

Mt 27:5 *threw the silver into the sanctuary:* Exactly where Judas threw the money is uncertain.
Mt 27:6 *It's not lawful . . . blood money:* The priests kept the letter of the law while being oblivious to its spirit. The temple officials refused to keep the money because it was impure, so they bought a field for use as a cemetery for foreigners (v. 7).
Mt 27:9 *what was spoken through the prophet Jeremiah:* The purchase of the "Potter's Field" fulfilled the prophecy of Zechariah 11:13. Jeremiah 18–19 also has to do with a potter's field; so it is possible that Jeremiah *spoke* the prophecy but that it was *written* by Zechariah later. Matthew reported much of what happened to Jesus on His crucifixion day as fulfillment of prophecy, demonstrating Him to be the Messiah.

Sec. 159   Jesus Faces Pilate

Matthew 27:2,11-14   Mark 15:1b-5   Luke 23:1-5   John 18:28-38

2 After tying Him up, they led Him away and handed Him over to •Pilate,ᵃ the governor.

ᵃ**27:2** Other mss read *Pontius Pilate*

After tying Jesus up, they led Him away and handed Him over to •Pilate.

1 Then their whole assembly rose up and brought Him before •Pilate.

28 Then they took Jesus from Caiaphas to the governor's •headquarters. It was early morning. They did not enter the headquarters themselves; otherwise they would be defiled and unable to eat the •Passover.

Jn 18:28 Caiaphas functioned as the duty officer to bring the captive Jesus to the Roman governor. In the light of the approaching Passover, and not having sufficient time to purify themselves from entering the home of a Gentile, the Jewish leaders would not enter the Roman headquarters.

Matthew 27:2,11-14 (cont.)	Mark 15:1b-5 (cont.)	Luke 23:1-5 (cont.)	John 18:28-38 (cont.)
		² They began to accuse Him, saying, "We found this man subverting our nation, opposing payment of taxes to Caesar, and saying that He Himself is the •Messiah, a King."	²⁹ Then •Pilate came out to them and said, "What charge do you bring against this man?" ³⁰ They answered him, "If this man weren't a criminal,^a we wouldn't have handed Him over to you." ³¹ So Pilate told them, "Take Him yourselves and judge Him according to your law." "It's not legal^b for us to put anyone to death," the Jews declared. ³² They said this so that Jesus' words might be fulfilled signifying what kind of death He was going to die. ³³ Then Pilate went back into the headquarters, summoned Jesus, and said to Him, "Are You the King of the Jews?"
¹¹ Now Jesus stood before the governor. "Are You the King of the Jews?" the governor asked Him. Jesus answered, "You have said it."^a	² So Pilate asked Him, "Are You the King of the Jews?" He answered him, "You have said it."^a	³ So Pilate asked Him, "Are You the King of the Jews?" He answered him, "You have said it."^a	³⁴ Jesus answered, "Are you asking this on your own, or have others told you about Me?"
^a**27:11** Or *That is true*, an affirmative oath; Mt 26:64; Mk 15:2	^a**15:2** Or *That is true*, an affirmative oath; Mt 26:64; 27:11	^a**23:3** Or *That is true*; an affirmative oath	³⁵ "I'm not a Jew, am I?" Pilate replied. "Your own nation and the chief priests handed You over to me. What have You done?"
			^a**18:30** Lit *an evil doer* ^b**18:31** According to Roman law

Mt 27:11 *Are You the King of the Jews?:* The council condemned Jesus for blasphemy for claiming to be God's Son (Mt 26:63-65); but before Pilate they changed their charge.

Mk 15:2 *the King of the Jews:* The use of the title "King" is rare in Mark's Gospel in comparison to the other Gospels. Perhaps Mark was trying to communicate that Jesus' perspective on what it meant for Him to be King was far different than those rejecting Him.

Lk 23:3 *You have said it:* Again Jesus answered the question about being King of the Jews with a qualified yes, but not meaning quite in the sense that the question was raised. Jesus was not a political threat to Rome.

Jn 18:29-31 Pilate suspected that the matter of Jesus was merely a matter of Jewish rivalry, and could be adequately judged by Jewish law.

Jn 18:32 Jesus had predicted that he would be lifted from the earth (12:32-33), referring to the Roman means of execution, crucifixion. The Jewish leaders fulfilled Jesus' words.

Jn 18:33 *Are You the King of the Jews?:* The most significant question for Pilate would be whether Jesus constituted a threat to Roman civil order. Such order could be threatened by rival kings, so he asked Jesus whether He considered Himself King of the Jews.

Jn 18:34 Jesus realized that the Jewish leaders had been prompting Pilate, so he asked whether Pilate had heard anything about Him on his own.

Matthew 27:2,11-14 (cont.)	Mark 15:1b-5 (cont.)	Luke 23:1-5 (cont.)	John 18:28-38 (cont.)
			36 "My kingdom is not of this •world," said Jesus. "If My kingdom were of this world, My servantsᵃ would fight, so that I wouldn't be handed over to the Jews. As it is, My kingdom does not have its origin here."ᵇ **37** "You are a king then?" Pilate asked. "You say that I'm a king," Jesus replied. "I was born for this, and I have come into the world for this: to testify to the truth. Everyone who is of the truth listens to My voice." **38** "What is truth?" said Pilate. After he had said this,
		4 Pilate then told the •chief priests and the crowds, "I find no grounds for charging this man."	he went out to the Jews again and told them, "I find no grounds for charging Him.
			ᵃ**18:36** Or *attendants*, or *helpers* ᵇ**18:36** Lit *My kingdom is not from here*
12 And while He was being accused by the chief priests and elders, He didn't answer. **13** Then Pilate said to Him, "Don't You hear how much they are testifying against You?" **14** But He didn't answer him on even one charge, so that the governor was greatly amazed.	**3** And the chief priests began to accuse Him of many things. **4** Then Pilate questioned Him again, "Are You not answering anything? Look how many things they are accusing You of!" **5** But Jesus still did not answer anything, so Pilate was amazed.		
		5 But they kept insisting, "He stirs up the people, teaching throughout all Judea, from Galilee where He started even to here."	

Mt 27:14 *the governor was greatly amazed:* That Jesus refused to answer such serious and life-threatening charges was astonishing. According to Luke 23:6-12, at this point Pilate sent Jesus to Herod.

Lk 23:4 *no grounds:* One of several times Jesus will be declared innocent.

Jn 18:36 *My kingdom is not of this world:* Jesus tacitly admitted that He was King of the Jews (v. 37), but He clarified that He was not a king such as the Jews or Romans were expecting.

Jn 18:37 Jesus' purpose as a king is the unusual one of testifying to the truth.

Jn 18:38 *What is truth?:* Reflecting on his immediate confusion over what to do with Jesus, the larger issues that a person such as a Roman governor faced, and the overwhelming human issues regarding existence, Pilate asked Jesus what truth is. Jesus had already answered this, as the reader knows, by stating that He is the way, the truth, and the life.

Sec. 160   Jesus Faces Herod Antipas

Luke 23:6-12

[6] When Pilate heard this,[a] he asked if the man was a Galilean. [7] Finding that He was under •Herod's jurisdiction, he sent Him to Herod, who was also in Jerusalem during those days. [8] Herod was very glad to see Jesus; for a long time he had wanted to see Him because he had heard about Him and was hoping to see some miracle[b] performed by Him. [9] So he kept asking Him questions, but Jesus did not answer him. [10] The chief priests and the •scribes stood by, vehemently accusing Him. [11] Then Herod, with his soldiers, treated Him with contempt, mocked Him, dressed Him in a brilliant robe, and sent Him back to Pilate. [12] That very day Herod and Pilate became friends.[c] Previously, they had been hostile toward each other.

[a]23:6 Other mss read *heard "Galilee"*   **[b]23:8** Or *sign*   **[c]23:12** Lit *friends with one another*

Lk 23:9 *Jesus did not answer:* Recalls the language of the Suffering Servant (Is 53:7).

Sec. 161   Jesus Faces Pilate a Second Time

Matthew 27:15-26	Mark 15:6-15	Luke 23:13-25	John 18:39–19:16a
[15] At the festival the governor's custom was to release to the crowd a prisoner they wanted. [16] At that time they had a notorious prisoner called Barabbas.[a]	[6] At the festival it was Pilate's custom to release for the people a prisoner they requested. [7] There was one named Barabbas, who was in prison with rebels who had committed murder during the rebellion. [8] The crowd came up and began to ask ⌊Pilate⌋ to do for them as was his custom.	[13] Pilate called together the chief priests, the leaders, and the people, [14] and said to them, "You have brought me this man as one who subverts the people. But in fact, after examining Him in your presence, I have found no grounds to charge this man with those things you accuse Him of. [15] Neither has Herod, because he sent Him back to us. Clearly, He has done nothing to deserve death. [16] Therefore	
[17] So when they had gathered together, Pilate said to them, "Who is it you want me to release for you—Barabbas,[a] or Jesus who is called •Messiah?" [18] For he knew they had handed Him over because of envy.	[9] So Pilate answered them, "Do you want me to release the King of the Jews for you?" [10] For he knew it was because of envy that the chief priests had handed Him over.		[39] You have a custom that I release one ⌊prisoner⌋ to you at the Passover. So, do you want me to release to you the King of the Jews?"

[a]27:16,17 Other mss read *Jesus Barabbas*

Lk 23:14 *no grounds:* Jesus' innocence is again declared.
Lk 23:15 *Neither has Herod:* Yet another declaration of innocence.
Jn 18:39-40 The custom of release of a prisoner is not known apart from the NT. It resulted in the release of someone who was actually in prison for the very thing that Jesus was being accused of, an insurrectionist.

Matthew 27:15-26 (cont.)	Mark 15:6-15 (cont.)	Luke 23:13-25 (cont.)	John 18:39–19:16a (cont.)
[19] While he was sitting on the judge's bench, his wife sent word to him, "Have nothing to do with that righteous man, for today I've suffered terribly in a dream because of Him!" [20] The chief priests and the elders, however, persuaded the crowds to ask for Barabbas and to execute Jesus. [21] The governor asked them, "Which of the two do you want me to release for you?" "Barabbas!" they answered.	[11] But the chief priests stirred up the crowd so that he would release Barabbas to them instead.	I will have Him whipped[a] and ⌊then⌋ release Him." [[17] For according to the festival he had to release someone to them.][b] [18] Then they all cried out together, "Take this man away! Release Barabbas to us!" [19] (He had been thrown into prison for a rebellion that had taken place in the city, and for murder.) **[a]23:16** Gk *paideuo*; to discipline or "teach a lesson"; 1 Kg 12:11,14 LXX; 2 Ch 10:11,14; perhaps a way of referring to the Roman scourging; Lat *flagellatio* **[b]23:17** Other mss omit bracketed text	[40] They shouted back, "Not this man, but Barabbas!" Now Barabbas was a revolutionary.[a] [1] Then •Pilate took Jesus and had Him flogged. [2] The soldiers also twisted together a crown of thorns, put it on His head, and threw a purple robe around Him. [3] And they repeatedly came up to Him and said, "Hail, King of the Jews!" and were slapping His face. [4] Pilate went outside again and said to them, "Look, I'm bringing Him outside to you to let you know I find no grounds for charging Him." [5] Then Jesus came out wearing the crown of thorns and the purple robe. Pilate said to them, "Here is the man!" **[a]18:40** Or *robber*; see Jn 10:1,8 for the same Gk word used here

Mt 27:20 *Barabbas:* Means "son of the father." Note the irony in the names: Jesus was the heavenly Son of a heavenly Father. They rejected the Son of God for a murderer.

Lk 23:16 *whipped:* Pilate hoped to punish Jesus as an attempt to dissuade them from seeking the death penalty, but this plan did not work out.

Jn 19:1-3 Pilate had Jesus punished according to what he thought was necessary—a scourging so that He would remember who was in authority. The fact that Jesus was dressed up and mocked as king of the Jews indicates the scorn the Romans had toward the Jews.

Matthew 27:15-26 (cont.)

²² Pilate asked them, "What should I do then with Jesus, who is called Messiah?"

They all answered, "Crucify Him!"ᵃ

²³ Then he said, "Why? What has He done wrong?"

But they kept shouting, "Crucify Him!" all the more.

ᵃ27:22 Lit *"Him—be crucified!"*

Mark 15:6-15 (cont.)

¹² Pilate asked them again, "Then what do you want me to do with the One you call the King of the Jews?"

¹³ Again they shouted, "Crucify Him!"

¹⁴ Then Pilate said to them, "Why? What has He done wrong?"

But they shouted, "Crucify Him!" all the more.

Luke 23:13-25 (cont.)

²⁰ Pilate, wanting to release Jesus, addressed them again, ²¹ but they kept shouting, "Crucify! Crucify Him!"

²² A third time he said to them, "Why? What has this man done wrong? I have found in Him no grounds for the death penalty. Therefore I will have Him whipped and ⌊then⌋ release Him."

John 18:39–19:16a (cont.)

⁶ When the •chief priests and the temple police saw Him, they shouted, "Crucify! Crucify!"

Pilate responded, "Take Him and crucify Him yourselves, for I find no grounds for charging Him."

⁷ "We have a law," the •Jews replied to him, "and according to that law He must die, because He made Himselfᵃ the Son of God."

⁸ When Pilate heard this statement, he was more afraid than ever. ⁹ He went back into the •headquarters and asked Jesus, "Where are You from?" But Jesus did not give him an answer. ¹⁰ So Pilate said to Him, "You're not talking to me? Don't You know that I have the authority to release You and the authority to crucify You?"

¹¹ "You would have no authority over Me at all," Jesus answered him, "if it hadn't been given you from above. This is why the one who handed Me over to you has the greater sin."ᵇ

ᵃ19:7 He claimed to be
ᵇ19:11 To *have sin* is an idiom that refers to guilt caused by sin.

Lk 23:22 *What has this man done wrong? . . . no grounds:* Yet another recognition that Jesus was innocent, but Pilate did not have the conviction to release Him.

Jn 19:6 *Crucify!:* After Pilate presented Jesus to the people assembled outside his headquarters, the chief priest and the temple police begin to shout for crucifixion. Pilate turned Jesus over to them, rather than having a local uprising on his hands.

Jn 19:7 The leaders may be referring to Leviticus 24:16, concerning blasphemy as involving the claim to being God.

Jn 19:8 Pilate became more fearful when he heard the specific charge against Jesus in terms of a claim to being the Son of God. The Caesar was sometimes designated as a son of God and celebrated in such language in places throughout the empire, especially in the East.

Jn 19:11 After Pilate told Jesus that he has authority over Him, Jesus told him that the only authority is from above. This brings to fulfillment a theme that Jesus spoke of several times in John, that His authority derives from God, who has all authority (see 5:27,30; 8:28; 12:49; 14:10).

Matthew 27:15-26 (cont.)   Mark 15:6-15 (cont.)   Luke 23:13-25 (cont.)   John 18:39–19:16a (cont.)

¹² From that moment Pilate made every effortᵃ to release Him. But the Jews shouted, "If you release this man, you are not Caesar's friend. Anyone who makes himself a king opposes Caesar!" ¹³ When Pilate heard these words, he brought Jesus outside. He sat down on the judge's bench in a place called the Stone Pavement (but in Hebrew *Gabbatha*). ¹⁴ It was the preparation day for the •Passover, and it was about six in the morning.ᵇ Then he told the Jews, "Here is your king!"

²⁴ When Pilate saw that he was getting nowhere,ᵃ but that a riot was starting instead, he took some water, washed his hands in front of the crowd, and said, "I am innocent of this man's blood.ᵇ See to it yourselves!"
²⁵ All the people answered, "His blood be on us and on our children!" ²⁶ Then he released Barabbas to them. But after having Jesus flogged,ᶜ he handed Him over to be crucified.

ᵃ**27:24** Lit *that it availed nothing*   ᵇ**27:24** Other mss read *this righteous man's blood*   ᶜ**27:26** Roman flogging was done with a whip made of leather strips embedded with pieces of bone or metal that brutally tore the flesh.

¹⁵ Then, willing to gratify the crowd, Pilate released Barabbas to them. And after having Jesus flogged,ᵃ he handed Him over to be crucified.

ᵃ**15:15** Roman flogging was done with a whip made of leather strips embedded with pieces of bone or metal that brutally tore the flesh.

²³ But they kept up the pressure, demanding with loud voices that He be crucified. And their voicesᵃ won out. ²⁴ So Pilate decided to grant their demand ²⁵ and released the one they were asking for, who had been thrown into prison for rebellion and murder. But he handed Jesus over to their will.

ᵃ**23:23** Other mss add *and those of the chief priests*

¹⁵ But they shouted, "Take Him away! Take Him away! Crucify Him!"
Pilate said to them, "Should I crucify your king?"
"We have no king but Caesar!" the chief priests answered.
¹⁶ So then, because of them, he handed Him over to be crucified.

ᵃ**19:12** Lit *Pilate was trying*   ᵇ**19:14** Lit *the sixth hour*; see note at Jn 1:39; an alternate time reckoning would be *about noon*

Mt 27:24 *washed his hands:* Hand washing was not a Roman custom. After living several years among the Jews he detested, Pilate picked up one of their own customs (Dt 21:6; Ps 26:6) and contemptuously used it before them.
Jn 19:12 The Jewish leaders played on typical Roman paranoia regarding stability in the Empire. They reminded Pilate that as Caesar's "friend" or emissary he was responsible for ensuring there were no rivals to Caesar.
Jn 19:14 The specific season and time are given. It was the time for preparation for the Passover, approximately noon.
Jn 19:15 *We have no king but Caesar:* A political and theological sell-out to Roman rule in order to secure their end of destroying Jesus. Earlier some Jews who had come to Jesus had asserted their independence by saying they had never been enslaved. Now they willingly embraced Caesar as their king.

Sec. 162   Mocked by the Military

Matthew 27:27-30

Mark 15:16-19

27 Then the governor's soldiers took Jesus into •headquarters and gathered the whole •company around Him. 28 They stripped Him and dressed Him in a scarlet robe. 29 They twisted together a crown of thorns, put it on His head, and placed a reed in His right hand. And they knelt down before Him and mocked Him: "Hail, King of the Jews!" 30 Then they spit on Him, took the reed, and kept hitting Him on the head.

16 Then the soldiers led Him away into the courtyard (that is, •headquarters) and called the whole •company together. 17 They dressed Him in a purple robe, twisted together a crown of thorns, and put it on Him. 18 And they began to salute Him, "Hail, King of the Jews!" 19 They kept hitting Him on the head with a reed and spitting on Him. Getting down on their knees, they were paying Him homage.

Mt 27:27 *headquarters:* The Latin word *Praetorium* was used by Greek writers for the residence of the Roman governor. It may also refer to military headquarters, the imperial court, or the emperor's guard.

Mt 27:28 *scarlet robe.* Probably the short red cloak worn by Roman military and civilian officials.

Mk 15:16 *the whole company:* A company (or cohort) was a Roman military unit of 600, although the number could vary. Mark may have only wanted to refer in a general way to all the soldiers on duty at their headquarters.

Mk 15:17 *a purple robe:* A purple robe was an expensive luxury, worn only by kings and the very wealthy. Just as a wreath of thorns was a cruel substitute for a crown, so also it is likely that some readily available cloak or material served as the pretended purple robe of a king. In other words, Mark narrated parts of this scene using the mocking words of the soldiers (Jn 19:2). Matthew's Gospel, by way of contrast, refers to a scarlet robe, apparently that of a Roman soldier (Mt 27:28).

Sec. 163   The Way to the Cross

Matthew 27:31-34

Mark 15:20-23

Luke 23:26-33a

John 19:16b-17

31 When they had mocked Him, they stripped Him of the robe, put His clothes on Him, and led Him away to crucify Him.

32 As they were going out, they found a Cyrenian man named Simon. They forced this man to carry His cross.

20 When they had mocked Him, they stripped Him of the purple robe, put His clothes on Him, and led Him out to crucify Him.

21 They forced a man coming in from the country, who was passing by, to carry Jesus' cross. He was Simon, a Cyrenian, the father of Alexander and Rufus.

26 As they led Him away, they seized Simon, a Cyrenian, who was coming in from the country, and laid the cross on him to carry behind Jesus. 27 A great multitude of the people followed Him, including women who were mourning and lamenting Him. 28 But turning to them, Jesus said, "Daughters of Jerusalem, do not weep for Me, but weep for yourselves and your children. 29 Look, the days are coming when

Therefore they took Jesus away.[a] 17 Carrying His own cross,

[a]**19:16** Other mss add *and led him out*

Mt 27:32 *They forced this man to carry His cross:* It was customary for the convicted criminal to bear his own cross as a testimony of guilt.

Mk 15:21 *a Cyrenian:* Simon was from Cyrene, a city on the African coast. He may have been a Jew of the Diaspora (one living outside the land of Israel) visiting Jerusalem for the Passover. Alexander and Rufus were possibly known by Mark's original readers. They could confirm Mark's account of Jesus' passion based on the testimony of their father.

Lk 23:28 *weep for yourselves:* This was not a sad day for Jesus but for those who had rejected Him, because the judgment of the nation would come.

Matthew 27:31-34 (cont.)	Mark 15:20-23 (cont.)	Luke 23:26-33a (cont.)	John 19:16b-17 (cont.)
		they will say, 'Blessed are the childless, the wombs that never bore, and the breasts that never nursed!' ³⁰ Then they will begin **to say to the mountains, 'Fall on us!' and to the hills, 'Cover us!'**ᵃ ³¹ For if they do these things when the wood is green, what will happen when it is dry?" ³² Two others—criminals—were also led away	
³³ When they came to a place called *Golgotha* (which means Skull Place), ³⁴ they gave Him wineᵃ mixed with gall to drink. But when He tasted it, He would not drink it.	²² And they brought Jesus to the place called *Golgotha* (which means Skull Place). ²³ They tried to give Him wine mixed with myrrh, but He did not take it.	to be executed with Him. ³³ When they arrived at the place called The Skull,	He went out to what is called Skull Place, which in Hebrew is called *Golgotha*.
		ᵃ**23:30** Hs 10:8	
ᵃ**27:34** Other mss read *sour wine*			

Mt 27:33 *Golgotha:* In Latin this was *Calvariae locum,* thus our familiar word Calvary.

Mt 27:34 *wine mixed with gall:* A narcotic sedative that drugged the victim. Jesus would not receive it; He faced the redemption of mankind with senses intact.

Lk 23:31 *what will happen when it is dry:* If green wood suffers in such a manner (referring to Himself as a crucifixion victim), then what will happen with dead wood (those who rejected Him, victims of Roman might in AD 70)?

Sec. 164   The Crucifixion

Matthew 27:35-44	Mark 15:24-32	Luke 23:33b-34,38,35-37, 39-43	John 19:18,23-24, 19-22,25-27
³⁵ After crucifying Him they divided His clothes by casting lots.ᵃ ³⁶ Then they sat down and were guarding Him there.	²⁴ Then they crucified Him and divided His clothes, casting lots for them to decide what each would get.	they crucified Him there, along with the criminals, one on the right and one on the left. [³⁴ Then Jesus said, "Father, forgive them, because they do not know what they are doing."]ᵃ And they divided His clothes and cast lots.	¹⁸ There they crucified Him and two others with Him, one on either side, with Jesus in the middle. ²³ When the soldiers crucified Jesus, they took His clothes and divided them into four parts, a part for each soldier. They also took the tunic, which was seamless, woven in one
ᵃ**27:35** Other mss add *that what was spoken by the prophet might be fulfilled: "They divided My clothes among them, and for My clothing they cast lots."*		ᵃ**23:34** Other mss omit bracketed text	

Mt 27:35 Mark 15:25 notes that Jesus was crucified about the third Jewish hour, nine in the morning; Matthew, Mark, and Luke tell that Jesus died on Passover Eve about the ninth Jewish hour, three in the afternoon, the hour Passover lambs were slaughtered. Most Jews from Galilee, along with many Pharisees, celebrated Passover on the 14th of Abib or Nisan. Most Jews from Jerusalem, along with the Sadducees, celebrated on the 15th. Evidently Jesus, a Galilean, celebrated Passover with His disciples the night before the Jerusalem Passover.

Mk 15:24 *they crucified Him:* Mark's Gospel does not focus attention on the physical suffering involved in Jesus' death but simply states, "They crucified Him."

Lk 23:34 *Father, forgive them:* Recalling His own words in Luke 6:28.

Matthew 27:35-44 (cont.)	Mark 15:24-32 (cont.)	Luke 23:33b-34,38, 35-37,39-43 (cont.)	John 19:18,23-24, 19-22,25-27 (cont.)
			piece from the top. ²⁴ So they said to one another, "Let's not tear it, but cast lots for it, to see who gets it." ⌊They did this⌋ to fulfill the Scripture that says: **They divided My clothes among themselves, and they cast lots for My clothing.**ᵃ And this is what the soldiers did.
³⁷ Above His head they put up the charge against Him in writing:	²⁵ Now it was nine in the morningᵃ when they crucified Him. ²⁶ The inscription of the charge written against Him was:	³⁸ An inscription was above Him:ᵃ	¹⁹ Pilate also had a sign lettered and put on the cross. The inscription was:
THIS IS JESUS THE KING OF THE JEWS	THE KING OF THE JEWS	THIS IS THE KING OF THE JEWS	JESUS THE NAZARENE THE KING OF THE JEWS
³⁸ Then two criminalsᵃ were crucified with Him, one on the right and one on the left.	²⁷ They crucified two criminalsᵇ with Him, one on His right and one on His left. [²⁸ So the Scripture was fulfilled that says: **And He was counted among outlaws.**]ᶜ ᵈ		²⁰ Many of the Jews read this sign, because the place where Jesus was crucified was near the city, and it was written in Hebrew,ᵇ Latin, and Greek. ²¹ So the chief priests of the Jews said to Pilate, "Don't write, 'The King of the Jews,' but that He said, 'I am the King of the Jews.' " ²² Pilate replied, "What I have written, I have written."
³⁹ Those who passed by were yelling insults atᵇ Him, shaking their heads ⁴⁰ and saying,	²⁹ Those who passed by were yelling insults atᵉ Him, shaking their heads, and saying, "Ha! The	³⁵ The people stood watching,	ᵃ**19:24** Ps 22:18 ᵇ**19:20** Or *Aramaic*

ᵃ**27:38** Or *revolutionaries*
ᵇ**27:39** Lit *passed by blasphemed* or *were blaspheming*

ᵃ**15:25** Lit *was the third hour*
ᵇ**15:27** Or *revolutionaries*
ᶜ**15:28** Other mss omit bracketed text ᵈ**15:28** Is 53:12 ᵉ**15:29** Lit *passed by blasphemed*

ᵃ**23:38** Other mss add *written in Greek, Latin, and Hebrew letters*

Mt 27:37 The irony is that the sign proclaimed truth, though it was meant derisively.
Mt 27:38 *two criminals: Rebel* or *insurrectionist* is probably a better translation than "robber." The nature of their crimes likely involved terrorism and assassination.
Mk 15:29 *shaking their heads:* People shook their heads as a sign of contempt, often toward someone facing disastrous suffering (2 Kg 19:21; Jb 16:4; Ps 22:7; 109:25; Jr 18:16; Lm 2:15). Psalm 22 is particularly relevant since it describes a righteous sufferer mocked by people who sneer (Ps 22:7).
Jn 19:19-22 Pilate put up a trilingual inscription on Jesus' cross saying that Jesus of the Nazareth was the King of the Jews. This inscription, was written in Aramaic, Latin and Greek. Aramaic was the local indigenous language, Latin, the official language of the Empire, and Greek the language for communication throughout the Empire.
Jn 19:24 John saw Psalm 22:18 regarding dividing and casting lots for one's clothing as fulfilled in how the soldiers dispensed with Jesus' garments.

Matthew 27:35-44 (cont.)	Mark 15:24-32 (cont.)	Luke 23:33b-34,38, 35-37,39-43 (cont.)	John 19:18,23-24, 19-22,25-27 (cont.)
"The One who would demolish the sanctuary and rebuild it in three days, save Yourself! If You are the Son of God, come down from the cross!" ⁴¹ In the same way the chief priests, with the •scribes and elders,^a mocked Him and said, ⁴² "He saved others, but He cannot save Himself! He is the King of Israel! Let Him^b come down now from the cross, and we will believe in Him. ⁴³ He has put His trust in God; let God rescue Him now—if He wants Him!^c For He said, 'I am God's Son.'" ⁴⁴ In the same way even the criminals who were crucified with Him kept taunting Him.	One who would demolish the sanctuary and build it in three days, ³⁰ save Yourself by coming down from the cross!" ³¹ In the same way, the chief priests with the scribes were mocking Him to one another and saying, "He saved others; He cannot save Himself! ³² Let the •Messiah, the King of Israel, come down now from the cross, so that we may see and believe." Even those who were crucified with Him were taunting Him.	and even the leaders kept scoffing: "He saved others; let Him save Himself if this is God's Messiah, the Chosen One!" ³⁶ The soldiers also mocked Him. They came offering Him sour wine ³⁷ and said, "If You are the King of the Jews, save Yourself!" ³⁹ Then one of the criminals hanging there began to yell insults at^a Him: "Aren't You the Messiah? Save Yourself and us!" ⁴⁰ But the other answered, rebuking him: "Don't you even fear God, since you are undergoing the same punishment? ⁴¹ We are punished justly, because we're getting back what we deserve for the things we did, but this man has done nothing wrong." ⁴² Then he said, "Jesus, remember me^b when You come into Your kingdom!" ⁴³ And He said to him, "•I assure you: Today you will be with Me in paradise."	

^a**27:41** Other mss add *and Pharisees*   ^b**27:42** Other mss read *If He . . . Israel, let Him*   ^c**27:43** Or *if He takes pleasure in Him*; Ps 22:8

^a**23:39** Or *began to blaspheme*   ^b**23:42** Other mss add *Lord*

Lk 23:37 *King of the Jews:* This inscription makes it clear why Rome crucified Jesus. They found Him guilty of being King of the Jews. Jesus died for something that was true.

Lk 23:43 *Today you will be with Me in paradise:* Jesus assured the thief that blessing will not need to wait for the full coming of the kingdom, but will start this very day.

John 19:18,23-24,
19-22,25-27 (cont.)

²⁵ Standing by the cross of Jesus were His mother, His mother's sister, Mary the wife of Clopas, and •Mary Magdalene. ²⁶ When Jesus saw His mother and the disciple He loved standing there, He said to His mother, "•Woman, here is your son." ²⁷ Then He said to the disciple, "Here is your mother." And from that hour the disciple took her into his home.

Jn 19:26-27 *Woman, here is your son:* At the crucifixion, besides the officials and soldiers, members of Jesus' family and friends were standing as well. Jesus addressed His mother and the disciple He loved, entrusting the care of His mother to the disciple.

Sec. 165 The Death of Jesus

Matthew 27:45-50	Mark 15:33-37	Luke 23:44-45a,46	John 19:28-30

⁴⁵ From noon until three in the afternoonᵃ darkness came over the whole land.ᵇ ⁴⁶ About three in the afternoon Jesus cried out with a loud voice, *"Elí, Elí, lemá sabachtháni?"* that is, **"My God, My God, why have You forsaken**ᶜ **Me?"**ᵈ ⁴⁷ When some of those standing there heard this, they said, "He's calling for Elijah!"

ᵃ**27:45** Lit *From the sixth hour to the ninth hour* ᵇ**27:45** Or *whole earth* ᶜ**27:46** Or *abandoned* ᵈ**27:46** Ps 22:1

³³ When it was noon,ᵃ darkness came over the whole landᵇ until three in the afternoon.ᶜ ³⁴ And at threeᶜ Jesus cried out with a loud voice, *"Eloi, Eloi, lemá*ᵈ *sabachtháni?"* which is translated, **"My God, My God, why have You forsaken Me?"**ᵉ ³⁵ When some of those standing there heard this, they said, "Look, He's calling for Elijah!"

ᵃ**15:33** Lit *the sixth hour* ᵇ**15:33** Or *whole earth* ᶜ**15:33,34** Lit *the ninth hour* ᵈ**15:34** Other mss read *lama*; other mss read *lima* ᵉ**15:34** Ps 22:1

⁴⁴ It was now about noon,ᵃ and darkness came over the whole landᵇ until three,ᶜ ⁴⁵ because the sun's light failed.ᵈ

ᵃ**23:44** Lit *about the sixth hour* ᵇ**23:44** Or *whole earth* ᶜ**23:44** Lit *the ninth hour* ᵈ**23:45** Other mss read *three, and the sun was darkened*

Mt 27:45 *darkness:* The darkness mentioned here was supernatural. It could not have been an eclipse, because the Passover season was at the full moon. It was God's way of veiling the cross while His Son bore the sins of the world and tasted the wrath of God.

Mt 27:46 *Elí, Elí:* Considerable variations exist in the spelling in the manuscripts at this verse, but the Hebrew *Eli* and the Aramaic *Eloi* both mean *My God.* Jesus apparently sensed an abrupt loss of the communion with the Father.

Mk 15:34 Psalm 22 has many connections with Jesus' passion, referring to the insults against a righteous sufferer (Ps 22:7-8), piercing of His hands and feet (Ps 22:16), and gambling for His clothes (Ps 22:18).

Matthew 27:45-50 (cont.)   Mark 15:33-37 (cont.)   Luke 23:44-45a,46 (cont.)   John 19:28-30 (cont.)

Matthew 27:45-50 (cont.)	Mark 15:33-37 (cont.)	Luke 23:44-45a,46 (cont.)	John 19:28-30 (cont.)
48 Immediately one of them ran and got a sponge, filled it with sour wine, fixed it on a reed, and offered Him a drink. 49 But the rest said, "Let's see if Elijah comes to save Him!"	36 Someone ran and filled a sponge with sour wine, fixed it on a reed, offered Him a drink, and said, "Let's see if Elijah comes to take Him down!"		28 After this, when Jesus knew that everything was now accomplished that the Scripture might be fulfilled, He said, "I'm thirsty!" 29 A jar full of sour wine was sitting there; so they fixed a sponge full of sour wine on hyssopª and held it up to His mouth.
50 Jesus shouted again with a loud voice and gave up His spirit.	37 But Jesus let out a loud cry and breathed His last.	46 And Jesus called out with a loud voice, "Father, **into Your hands I entrust My spirit.**"ª Saying this, He breathed His last.	30 When Jesus had received the sour wine, He said, "It is finished!" Then bowing His head, He gave up His spirit.
		ª**23:46** Ps 31:5	ª**19:29** Or *with hyssop*

Mk 15:36 *sour wine:* A common, thirst-quenching drink among ordinary people. Therefore, giving Jesus sour wine was an act of kindness. However, the purpose was apparently to help sustain Him long enough to see how foolish it was to call on Elijah for help.

Lk 23:46 *Father, into Your hands I entrust My Spirit:* With these words of trust from Psalm 31:5, Jesus died.

Sec. 166   Events that Accompanied the Death of Jesus

Matthew 27:51-56   Mark 15:38-41   Luke 23:45b,47-49

Matthew 27:51-56	Mark 15:38-41	Luke 23:45b,47-49
51 Suddenly, the curtain of the sanctuaryª was split in two from top to bottom; the earth quaked and the rocks were split. 52 The tombs also were opened and many bodies of the saints who had gone to their restᵇ were raised. 53 And they came out of the tombs after His resurrection, entered the holy city, and appeared to many.	38 Then the curtain of the sanctuaryª was split in two from top to bottom.	The curtain of the sanctuary was split down the middle.
54 When the •centurion and those with him, who were guarding Jesus, saw the earthquake and the things that had happened, they were terrified and said, "This man really was God's Son!"ᶜ	39 When the •centurion, who was standing opposite Him, saw the way Heᵇ breathed His last, he said, "This man really was God's Son!"ᶜ	47 When the •centurion saw what happened, he began to glorify God, saying, "This man really was righteous!"
ª**27:51** A heavy curtain separated the inner room of the temple from the outer. ᵇ**27:52** Lit *saints having fallen asleep*; that is, they had died ᶜ**27:54** Or *the Son of God*	ª**15:38** A heavy curtain separated the inner room of the temple from the outer. ᵇ**15:39** Other mss read *saw that He cried out like this and* ᶜ**15:39** Or *the Son of God*; Mk 1:1	

Mt 27:51-54 The veil was torn because His blood opened a new and living way to God (Heb 10:19-25). The tombs opened because His death conquered death (Heb 2:14-18). Judas and Pilate confessed His innocence, as did the Roman soldier (v. 54), showing that the death of Christ is for Jew and Gentile alike.

Mk 15:38 According to Josephus, the veil was a handbreadth thick. Thus, the event was remarkable.

Mk 15:39 *the centurion:* In Mark, the centurion is the only human character (other than Jesus Himself in 14:61-62) to confess Jesus as God's Son. He foreshadowed the devotion of countless Gentiles to Jesus, including Mark's earliest readers who were likely Gentiles.

Lk 23:47 *Righteous:* This remark is unique to Luke. In the parallels, Jesus is said to be the Son of God. Of course, if Jesus was righteous, then He was who He claimed to be.

Matthew 27:51-56 (cont.)	Mark 15:38-41 (cont.)	Luke 23:45b,47-49 (cont.)
55 Many women who had followed Jesus from Galilee and ministered to Him were there, looking on from a distance. 56 Among them were •Mary Magdalene, Mary the mother of James and Joseph, and the mother of Zebedee's sons.	40 There were also women looking on from a distance. Among them were •Mary Magdalene, Mary the mother of James the younger and of Joses, and Salome. 41 When He was in Galilee, they would follow Him and help Him. Many other women had come up with Him to Jerusalem.	48 All the crowds that had gathered for this spectacle, when they saw what had taken place, went home, striking their chests.ᵃ 49 But all who knew Him, including the women who had followed Him from Galilee, stood at a distance, watching these things. ᵃ**23:48** Mourning

Sec. 167   Jesus' Burial

Matthew 27:57-60	Mark 15:42-46	Luke 23:50-54	John 19:31-42
			31 Since it was the preparation day, the Jews did not want the bodies to remain on the cross on the Sabbath (for that Sabbath was a specialᵃ day). They requested that Pilate have the men's legs broken and that ⌊their bodies⌋ be taken away. 32 So the soldiers came and broke the legs of the first man and of the other one who had been crucified with Him. 33 When they came to Jesus, they did not break His legs since they saw that He was already dead. 34 But one of the soldiers pierced His side with a spear, and at once blood and water came out. 35 He who saw this has testified so that you also may believe. His testimony is true, and he knows he is telling the truth. 36 For these things happened so that the Scripture would ᵃ**19:31** Lit *great*

Jn 19:33-37 To ensure that all of three of the crucified men were dead before the Sabbath, the soldiers were breaking their legs. However, when they came to Jesus they noted He was already dead. Instead, they pierced his side with a spear. Both events fulfilled Scripture. Passover passages spoke of not breaking the bones of the sacrificial animal (Ex 12:46; Nm 9:12) and Zechariah 12:10 noted the piercing of the Messiah.

Matthew 27:57-60 (cont.)	Mark 15:42-46 (cont.)	Luke 23:50-54 (cont.)	John 19:31-42 (cont.)
			be fulfilled: **Not one of His bones will be broken.**[a] [37] Also, another Scripture says: **They will look at the One they pierced.**[b]
[57] When it was evening,	[42] When it was already evening, because it was preparation day (that is, the day before the Sabbath), [43] Joseph of Arimathea, a prominent member of the Sanhedrin	[50] There was a good and righteous man named Joseph, a member of the •Sanhedrin, [51] who had not agreed with their plan and action. He was	[38] After this, Joseph of Arimathea,
a rich man from Arimathea named Joseph came,			
who himself had also become a disciple of Jesus.	who was himself looking forward to the kingdom of God,	from Arimathea, a Judean town, and was looking forward to the kingdom of God.	who was a disciple of Jesus—but secretly because of his fear of the Jews—asked Pilate that he might remove Jesus' body.
[58] He approached Pilate and asked for Jesus' body.	came and boldly went in to Pilate and asked for Jesus' body. [44] Pilate was surprised that He was already dead. Summoning the centurion, he asked him whether He had already died. [45] When he found out from the centurion, he gave the corpse to Joseph.	[52] He approached Pilate and asked for Jesus' body.	
Then Pilate ordered that it[a] be released.			Pilate gave him permission, so he came and took His body away. [39] Nicodemus (who had previously come to Him at night) also came, bringing a mixture of about 75 pounds[c] of myrrh and aloes. [40] Then they took Jesus' body and wrapped it in linen cloths with the aromatic spices, according to the burial custom of the Jews.
[59] So Joseph took the body, wrapped it in •clean, fine linen,	[46] After he bought some fine linen, he took Him down and wrapped Him in the linen.	[53] Taking it down, he wrapped it in fine linen	

[a]**27:58** Other mss read *that the body*

[a]**19:36** Ex 12:46; Nm 9:12; Ps 34:20   [b]**19:37** Zch 12:10 [c]**19:39** Lit *100 litrai*; a Roman *litrai* = 12 ounces

Mk 15:43 *a prominent member of the Sanhedrin:* Mark created tension by presenting the Sanhedrin as condemning Jesus (14:55,64; 15:1) and then positively portraying one of its members, Joseph of Arimathea, as caring for the burial of Jesus. Compare this to Jesus' general condemnation of the scribes (12:38-40) after His positive evaluation of a scribe who showed insight (12:28-34). Mark allowed general statements about groups that rejected Jesus to stand, while also noting exceptions.
Lk 23:51 *was looking forward to the kingdom of God:* Joseph believed the message of the kingdom Jesus gave.
Jn 19:38 Joseph of Arimathea is mentioned as a secret disciple of Jesus who feared the Jewish leaders.
Jn 19:39 Nicodemus, first seen in John 3, participated in the burial of Jesus.

Matthew 27:57-60 (cont.)   Mark 15:42-46 (cont.)   Luke 23:50-54 (cont.)   John 19:31-42 (cont.)

60 and placed it in his new tomb, which he had cut into the rock. He left after rolling a great stone against the entrance of the tomb.	Then he placed Him in a tomb cut out of the rock, and rolled a stone against the entrance to the tomb.	and placed it in a tomb cut into the rock, where no one had ever been placed.ᵃ 54 It was preparation day, and the Sabbath was about to begin.ᵇ	41 There was a garden in the place where He was crucified. A new tomb was in the garden; no one had yet been placed in it. 42 They placed Jesus there because of the Jewish preparation and since the tomb was nearby.

ᵃ23:53 Or *interred*, or *laid* **ᵇ23:54** Lit *was dawning*; not in the morning but at sundown Friday

Sec. 168   The Closely Guarded Tomb

Matthew 27:61-66	Mark 15:47	Luke 23:55-56
61 Mary Magdalene and the other Mary were seated there, facing the tomb.	47 Now Mary Magdalene and Mary the mother of Joses were watching where He was placed.	55 The women who had come with Him from Galilee followed along and observed the tomb and how His body was placed.
62 The next day, which followed the preparation day, the chief priests and the •Pharisees gathered before Pilate 63 and said, "Sir, we remember that while this deceiver was still alive, He said, 'After three days I will rise again.' 64 Therefore give orders that the tomb be made secure until the third day. Otherwise, His disciples may come, steal Him, and tell the people, 'He has been raised from the dead.' Then the last deception will be worse than the first." 65 "You haveᵃ a guard ⌊of soldiers⌋,"ᵇ Pilate told them. "Go and make it as secure as you know how." 66 Then they went and made the tomb secure by sealing the stone and setting the guard.ᶜ		56 Then they returned and prepared spices and perfumes. And they rested on the Sabbath according to the commandment.

ᵃ27:65 Or *"Take* **ᵇ27:65** It is uncertain whether this guard consisted of temple police or Roman soldiers. **ᶜ27:66** Lit *stone with the guard*

Mt 27:61 *Mary Magdalene:* A devoted disciple from whom Jesus had cast seven demons. She is identified by tradition with the woman who anointed Him in Luke 7.

Lk 23:55 *The women . . . observed:* These women knew where Jesus was buried and function as eyewitnesses to His burial.

PART XIV

THE RESURRECTION, APPEARANCES, AND ASCENSION OF JESUS

Sec. 169   The Women Prepare to Visit Jesus' Tomb

Matthew 28:1	Mark 16:1
[1] After the Sabbath, as the first day of the week was dawning, •Mary Magdalene and the other Mary went to view the tomb.	[1] When the Sabbath was over, •Mary Magdalene, Mary the mother of James, and Salome bought spices, so they could go and anoint Him.

Mt 28:1 *After the Sabbath:* A general indication of time. The women could not walk far *during* the Sabbath, so they waited until *after* the Sabbath. But by then Saturday night was becoming Sunday morning, so early on the *first day of the week* they went to the tomb.

Sec. 170   An Angel of the Lord Rolls Back the Stone

Matthew 28:2-4

[2] Suddenly there was a violent earthquake, because an angel of the Lord descended from heaven and approached ⌊the tomb⌋. He rolled back the stone and was sitting on it. [3] His appearance was like lightning, and his robe was as white as snow. [4] The guards were so shaken from fear of him that they became like dead men.

Mt 28:2 *He rolled back the stone:* The stone was rolled back, the seal broken, and the soldiers rendered helpless not to let the risen Jesus out, but to let the first witnesses in.

Sec. 171   Early Sunday Morning

Matthew 28:5-8	Mark 16:2-8	Luke 24:1-8	John 20:1
	[2] Very early in the morning, on the first day of the week, they went to the tomb at sunrise. [3] They were saying to one another, "Who will roll away the stone from the entrance to the tomb for us?" [4] Looking up, they observed that the stone—which was very large—had been rolled away.	[1] On the first day of the week, very early in the morning, they[a] came to the tomb, bringing the spices they had prepared. [2] They found the stone rolled away from the tomb. [a]**24:1** Other mss add *and other women with them*	[1] On the first day of the week •Mary Magdalene came to the tomb early, while it was still dark. She saw that the stone had been removed[a] from the tomb. [a]**20:1** Lit *She saw the stone removed*

Lk 24:1 *very early in the morning:* The women, named in verse 10, came first thing in the morning to the tomb, not expecting anything unusual, but in order to anoint the dead body with spices to protect against the odor and to honor Jesus. The parallels make it clear they started for the tomb as soon as it was dawn. The fact that they were perplexed (v. 3) on entering the tomb indicates their surprise that the body was gone.

Matthew 28:5-8 (cont.)	Mark 16:2-8 (cont.)	Luke 24:1-8 (cont.)
5 But the angel told the women, "Don't be afraid, because I know you are looking for Jesus who was crucified. 6 He is not here! For He has been resurrected, just as He said. Come and see the place where He lay. 7 Then go quickly and tell His disciples, 'He has been raised from the dead. In fact, He is going ahead of you to Galilee; you will see Him there.' Listen, I have told you." 8 So, departing quickly from the tomb with fear and great joy, they ran to tell His disciples the news.	5 When they entered the tomb, they saw a young manª dressed in a long white robe sitting on the right side; they were amazed and alarmed.ᵇ 6 "Don't be alarmed," he told them. "You are looking for Jesus the •Nazarene, who was crucified. He has been resurrected! He is not here! See the place where they put Him. 7 But go, tell His disciples and Peter, 'He is going ahead of you to Galilee; you will see Him there just as He told you.'" 8 So they went out and started running from the tomb, because trembling and astonishment overwhelmed them. And they said nothing to anyone, since they were afraid. ª**16:5** In Mt 28:2, the young man = an angel ᵇ**16:5** *Amazed and alarmed* translate the idea of one Gk word.	3 They went in but did not find the body of the Lord Jesus. 4 While they were perplexed about this, suddenly two men stood by them in dazzling clothes. 5 So the women were terrified and bowed down to the ground.ª "Why are you looking for the living among the dead?" asked the men. 6 "He is not here, but He has been resurrected! Remember how He spoke to you when He was still in Galilee, 7 saying, 'The •Son of Man must be betrayed into the hands of sinful men, be crucified, and rise on the third day'?" 8 And they remembered His words. ª**24:5** Lit *and inclined their faces to the ground*

Mt 28:6 There are three important things to believe about the resurrection of Jesus according to the Church Fathers. One is numerical identity: the same body that went into the tomb came out three days later. Two is materiality: it was a material, fleshly body that was raised from the dead. Three is historicity: it really happened in history.

Mk 16:5 *a young man.* Mark was reporting the scene from the perspective of the women. The messenger looked to them like a young man. That the messenger was an angel is indicated by his long white robe and his supernatural knowledge.

Mk 16:8 *since they were afraid:* In the oldest manuscripts of Mark, the narrative stops with the phrase in verse 8 "since they were afraid." Verses 9-20 are not in the oldest manuscripts, and some scholars maintain that these verses are a later attempt by someone other than Mark himself to smooth out what would otherwise be a rather abrupt ending. If verses 9-20 are a later addition, then basically three options are open to interpreters for why Mark's Gospel ends so abruptly: 1) the real ending of Mark's Gospel was lost; 2) Mark was unable to finish writing his Gospel and although he stopped at 16:8 it was not his intended ending; or 3) Mark intentionally ended his Gospel abruptly to cause people to think and reflect on his message. English Bibles normally include verses 9-20, since these verses appear in most Greek manuscripts of Mark's Gospel, but recent translations also communicate that they may be a later addition.

Lk 24:4 *dazzling clothes:* This description of shiny clothes is how one describes the presence of angels, which explains why the women were terrified (see v. 23).

Lk 24:5 *Why are you looking for the living among the dead?:* Only Luke records this remark. It makes the key point that Jesus is now alive, resurrected.

Lk 24:7 *The Son of Man must be betrayed into the hands of sinful men, be crucified, and rise on the third day:* This recollection of Jesus' prediction underscores that what took place was according to the divine plan.

Sec. 172   The Empty Tomb

Luke 24:9-12

9 Returning from the tomb, they reported all these things to the Eleven and to all the rest. 10 •Mary Magdalene, Joanna, Mary the mother of James, and the other women with them were telling the apostles these things. 11 But these words seemed like nonsense to them, and they did not believe the women. 12 Peter, however, got up and ran to the tomb. When he stooped to look in, he saw only the linen cloths.a So he went home, amazed at what had happened.

a24:12 Other mss add *lying there*

John 20:2-10

2 So she ran to Simon Peter and to the other disciple, the one Jesus loved, and said to them, "They have taken the Lord out of the tomb, and we don't know where they have put Him!"
3 At that, Peter and the other disciple went out, heading for the tomb. 4 The two were running together, but the other disciple outran Peter and got to the tomb first. 5 Stooping down, he saw the linen cloths lying there, yet he did not go in. 6 Then, following him, Simon Peter came also. He entered the tomb and saw the linen cloths lying there. 7 The wrapping that had been on His head was not lying with the linen cloths but was folded up in a separate place by itself. 8 The other disciple, who had reached the tomb first, then entered the tomb, saw, and believed. 9 For they still did not understand the Scripture that He must rise from the dead. 10 Then the disciples went home again.

Lk 24:11 *nonsense:* The reaction of the apostles and others to the women's announcement of an empty tomb is honest. They did not expect or believe this report. They reacted much as a modern person might. That women were the first witnesses to the empty tomb is important. It affirms their value to God. But more importantly shows that this story was not made up. In ancient cultures, a woman could not be a courtroom witness, so if one were to make up such a story, one would not use women as the first witnesses. The women are recorded as having this role because they had this role in real history.

Lk 24:12 *amazed:* An enigmatic term. Did Peter believe at that point that Jesus had been raised or was he simply amazed at the empty tomb, contemplating its possibility? Luke 24:24 shows the Emmaus disciples also expressing some uncertainty at this point.

John 20:2 Mary's first suspicion, a natural one in the light of human experience, was that someone had come and stolen Jesus' body.

John 20:4-8 The implication was that this was not simply a grave robbery, since the body was unwrapped and the cloths neatly left in the tomb. Suddenly much of what Jesus had said regarding His death came clear to the other disciple.

John 20:9 The disciples, although they may now have understood about Jesus' death, did not fully appreciate what was involved in His rising from the dead.

Sec. 173   Mary Magdalene Sees the Risen Lord

Mark 16:9-11

John 20:11-18

11 But Mary stood outside facing the tomb, crying. As she was crying, she stooped to look into the tomb. 12 She saw two angels in white sitting there, one at the head and one at the feet, where Jesus' body had been lying. 13 They said to her, "•Woman, why are you crying?"

Jn 20:11 Mary Magdalene had not yet entered the tomb, but was standing outside crying. Her world had now collapsed. Mary Magdalene is not mentioned much in John's Gospel, her first appearance being at the cross (19:25). However, what we do know is that she was a repentant sinner whose Redeemer had died on the cross.

Jn 20:12-13 Either the disciples did not see the angels, or they appeared especially for Mary, perhaps because of her emotionally devastated condition. All she asked of the angels was that they tell her where thieves put the body. The angels made no reply, nor was one needed.

Mark 16:9-11 (cont.)

[⁹ Early on the first day of the week, after He had risen, He appeared first to Mary Magdalene, out of whom He had driven seven demons.

¹⁰ She went and reported to those who had been with Him, as they were mourning and weeping. ¹¹ Yet, when they heard that He was alive and had been seen by her, they did not believe it.

John 20:11-18 (cont.)

"Because they've taken away my Lord," she told them, "and I don't know where they've put Him." ¹⁴ Having said this, she turned around and saw Jesus standing there, though she did not know it was Jesus.

¹⁵ "Woman," Jesus said to her, "why are you crying? Who is it you are looking for?"

Supposing He was the gardener, she replied, "Sir, if you've removed Him, tell me where you've put Him, and I will take Him away."

¹⁶ Jesus said, "Mary."

Turning around, she said to Him in Hebrew, *"Rabbouni!"*ᵃ —which means "Teacher."

¹⁷ "Don't cling to Me," Jesus told her, "for I have not yet ascended to the Father. But go to My brothers and tell them that I am ascending to My Father and your Father—to My God and your God."

¹⁸ Mary Magdalene went and announced to the disciples, "I have seen the Lord!" And she told them whatᵇ He had said to her.

ᵃ**20:16** *Rabbouni* is also used in Mk 10:51 ᵇ**20:18** Lit *these things*

Jn 20:14-16 Mary did not recognize Jesus, because she was not expecting to see a living being. The use of her name, and no doubt the inflection with which it was used, suddenly made her realize that it was Jesus.

Jn 20:17 *Don't cling to Me*: Some scholars think that Jesus was in the process of ascending, and that after He left Mary He ascended (briefly) before seeing the disciples in the upper room. More likely Jesus was telling Mary to not keep on hanging on Him. He wanted her to go to the disciples and tell them that He would ascend, but that for now He wanted to see them.

Sec. 174   Jesus Appears to the Other Women

Matthew 28:9-10

⁹ Just thenᵃ Jesus met them and said, "Good morning!" They came up, took hold of His feet, and worshiped Him. ¹⁰ Then Jesus told them, "Do not be afraid. Go and tell My brothers to leave for Galilee, and they will see Me there."

ᵃ**28:9** Other mss add *as they were on their way to tell the news to His disciples*

Mt 28:10 *My brothers:* Probably refers not only to the eleven apostles but also to all who had become His followers and were still in Jerusalem, most of whom had accompanied Him from Galilee.

Sec. 175   The Soldiers Are Bribed to Lie

Matthew 28:11-15

¹¹ As they were on their way, some of the guards came into the city and reported to the •chief priests everything that had happened. ¹² After the priestsᵃ had assembled with the elders and agreed on a plan, they gave the soldiers a large sum of money ¹³ and told them, "Say this, 'His disciples came during the night and stole

ᵃ**28:12** Lit *After they*

Mt 28:13 *stole Him while we were sleeping:* It is difficult to believe that Pilate's soldiers would admit to falling asleep since that could result in a penalty of death.

Matthew 28:11-15 (cont.)

Him while we were sleeping.' ¹⁴ If this reaches the governor's ears,ᵃ we will deal withᵇ him and keep you out of trouble." ¹⁵ So they took the money and did as they were instructed. And this story has been spread among Jewish people to this day.

ᵃ28:14 Lit *this is heard by the governor* **ᵇ28:14** Lit *will persuade*

Mt 28:15 *this story has been spread among Jewish people to this day:* To the very day that Matthew was writing these words this rumor was being circulated. Even today nonbelievers propagate this indefensible theory.

Sec. 176   The Emmaus Disciples

Mark 16:12-13	Luke 24:13-32

¹² Then after this, He appeared in a different form to two of them walking on their way into the country. ¹³ And they went and reported it to the rest, who did not believe them either.

¹³ Now that same day two of them were on their way to a village calledᵃ Emmaus, which was about seven milesᵇ from Jerusalem. ¹⁴ Together they were discussing everything that had taken place. ¹⁵ And while they were discussing and arguing, Jesus Himself came near and began to walk along with them. ¹⁶ But theyᶜ were prevented from recognizing Him. ¹⁷ Then He asked them, "What is this dispute that you're havingᵈ with each other as you are walking?" And they stopped ⌊walking and looked⌋ discouraged.

¹⁸ The one named Cleopas answered Him, "Are You the only visitor in Jerusalem who doesn't know the things that happened there in these days?"

¹⁹ "What things?" He asked them.

So they said to Him, "The things concerning Jesus the •Nazarene, who was a Prophet powerful in action and speech before God and all the people, ²⁰ and how our •chief priests and leaders handed Him over to be sentenced to death, and they crucified Him. ²¹ But we were hoping that He was the One who was about to •redeem Israel. Besides all this, it's the third day since these things happened. ²² Moreover, some women from our group astounded us. They arrived early at the tomb, ²³ and when they didn't find His body, they came and reported that they had seen a vision of angels who said He was alive. ²⁴ Some of those who were with us went to the tomb and found it just as the women had said, but they didn't see Him."

²⁵ He said to them, "How unwise and slow you are to believe in your hearts all that the prophets have spoken! ²⁶ Didn't the •Messiah have to suffer these things and enter into His glory?" ²⁷ Then beginning with Moses and all the Prophets, He interpreted for them the things concerning Himself in all the Scriptures.

ᵃ24:13 Lit *village, which name is* **ᵇ24:13** Lit *about 60 stadia; 1 stadion = 600 feet* **ᶜ24:16** Lit *their eyes* **ᵈ24:17** Lit *What are these words that you are exchanging*

Lk 24:16 *they were prevented from recognizing Him:* The text does not tell us how this worked. It sets up a scene where the reader knows more about what is happening than the two Emmaus disciples.

Lk 24:18 *who doesn't know the things that happened there in these days:* In one of the great ironic remarks of Scripture, the disciples ask Jesus how He could have missed these unusual events.

Lk 24:19 *Prophet powerful in action and speech:* The Emmaus disciples summarized their expectation, beginning with the prophetic quality of Jesus deeds and sayings. Those who heard His words and saw His deeds would acknowledge this.

Lk 24:21 *we were hoping that He was the One who was about to redeem Israel:* Here is the declaration of messianic hope for Israel.

Lk 24:23 *reported that they had seen a vision of angels who said He was alive:* The women's report is handled with a level of neutrality about its truth.

Lk 24:24 *but they didn't see Him:* The doubt lingered because there was no confirmation at the tomb for those who went to the tomb to check it out. There was no body and nothing else. The matter of fact with which the account reports the hesitation to believe the resurrection speaks to the account's truthfulness.

Lk 24:25 *unwise and slow you are to believe in your hearts all that the prophets have spoken:* Jesus rebuked their hesitation to believe what the prophets taught.

Lk 24:26 *Didn't the Messiah have to suffer these things and enter into His glory?:* Here is what the prophets taught. Messiah must suffer and enter into glory with God, an allusion to resurrection and where Jesus was as a result.

Lk 24:27 *beginning with Moses and all the prophets, He interpreted for them in all the Scriptures the things concerning Himself:* Likely many of the passages cited in Acts are among the specific texts intended here. Jesus showed how Scripture revealed a divine plan about Messiah.

Luke 24:13-32 (cont.)

28 They came near the village where they were going, and He gave the impression that He was going far-ther. 29 But they urged Him: "Stay with us, because it's almost evening, and now the day is almost over." So He went in to stay with them.

30 It was as He reclined at the table with them that He took the bread, blessed and broke it, and gave it to them. 31 Then their eyes were opened, and they recognized Him, but He disappeared from their sight. 32 So they said to each other, "Weren't our hearts ablaze within us while He was talking with us on the road and explaining the Scriptures to us?"

Lk 24:31 *their eyes were opened, and they recognized Him:* Now God granted them an understanding that Jesus was among them and had been raised.

Sec. 177   Jesus Appears to Simon Peter

Luke 24:33-35	1 Corinthians 15:5a
33 That very hour they got up and returned to Jeru-salem. They found the Eleven and those with them gathered together, 34 who said,a "The Lord has cer-tainly been raised, and has appeared to Simon!" 35 Then they began to describe what had happened on the road and how He was made known to them in the breaking of the bread.	5 and that He appeared to •Cephas,

ª**24:34** Gk is specific that this refers to the Eleven and those with them.

Lk 24:34 *The Lord has certainly been raised, and has appeared to Simon:* The disciples headed to Jerusalem to tell the group, only to arrive and hear that the Lord has also appeared to Simon Peter. The Lord was appearing in a variety of places to a variety of people.

Sec. 178   The Reality of the Risen Jesus

Mark 16:14	Luke 24:36-43	John 20:19-25
14 Later, He appeared to the Eleven themselves as they were re-clining at the table.	36 And as they were saying these things, He Himself stood among them. He said to them, "Peace to you!" 37 But they were startled and terrified and thought they were see-ing a ghost.	19 In the evening of that first day of the week, the disciples were ⌊gathered together⌋ with the doors locked because of their fear of the •Jews. Then Jesus came, stood among them, and said to them, "Peace to you!"
He rebuked their unbelief and hardness of heart, because they did not believe those who saw Him after He had been resurrected.		
	38 "Why are you trou-bled?" He asked them. "And why do doubts arise in your hearts?	

Lk 24:38 *why do doubts arise in your hearts?:* Jesus again assured them of the resurrection and called on them to believe.

Luke 24:36-43 (cont.)	John 20:19-25 (cont.)

³⁹ Look at My hands and My feet, that it is I Myself! Touch Me and see, because a ghost does not have flesh and bones as you can see I have." ⁴⁰ Having said this, He showed them His hands and feet. ⁴¹ But while they still were amazed and unbelieving because of ⌊their⌋ joy, He asked them, "Do you have anything here to eat?" ⁴² So they gave Him a piece of a broiled fish,ᵃ ⁴³ and He took it and ate in their presence.

ᵃ24:42 Other mss add *and some honeycomb*

²⁰ Having said this, He showed them His hands and His side.

So the disciples rejoiced when they saw the Lord.

²¹ Jesus said to them again, "Peace to you! As the Father has sent Me, I also send you." ²² After saying this, He breathed on them and said,ᵃ "Receive the Holy Spirit. ²³ If you forgive the sins of any, they are forgiven them; if you retain ⌊the sins of⌋ any, they are retained."

²⁴ But one of the Twelve, Thomas (called "Twin"), was not with them when Jesus came. ²⁵ So the other disciples kept telling him, "We have seen the Lord!"

But he said to them, "If I don't see the mark of the nails in His hands, put my finger into the mark of the nails, and put my hand into His side, I will never believe!"

ᵃ20:22 Lit *He breathed and said to them*

Lk 24:39 *Touch Me and see:* Jesus assured them that this was no vision, and that He had been raised physically from the grave in a spiritual body, something 1 Corinthians 15 describes. His eating of the fish confirmed this as well (v. 42).

Sec. 179   Jesus Appears to Thomas and the Other Disciples

John 20:26-31	1 Corinthians 15:5b

²⁶ After eight days His disciples were indoors again, and Thomas was with them. Even though the doors were locked, Jesus came and stood among them. He said, "Peace to you!"

then to the Twelve.

²⁷ Then He said to Thomas, "Put your finger here and observe My hands. Reach out your hand and put it into My side. Don't be an unbeliever, but a believer."

²⁸ Thomas responded to Him, "My Lord and my God!"

²⁹ Jesus said, "Because you have seen Me, you have believed.ᵃ Those who believe without seeing are blessed."

³⁰ Jesus performed many other signs in the presence of His disciples that are not written in this book. ³¹ But these are written so that you may believe Jesus is the •Messiah, the Son of God,ᵇ and by believing you may have life in His name.

ᵃ20:29 Or *have you believed?* (as a question)   **ᵇ20:31** Or *that the Messiah, the Son of God, is Jesus*

Jn 20:28 Thomas's confession of Jesus as His "Lord" and "God" provides a literary inclusion with the references to Jesus as God in the prologue (1:1,18).
Jn 20:29 After Thomas realized Jesus was alive (v. 28), Jesus commended those who believe without needing physical, empirical proof.
Jn 20:30-31 The purpose statement of the Gospel tells us several things about John's account. One is that there were many more things that Jesus did that are not recorded in this one book. The ones that are given, however, were included for two reasons. First is that those who read them may be convinced that Jesus is God's anointed Messiah and the Son of God. The second reason is so that those who believe that Jesus is Messiah, the Son of God, may have eternal life.

Sec. 180 Jesus' Third Appearance to the Disciples

John 21:1-25

[1] After this, Jesus revealed Himself again to His disciples by the Sea of Tiberias.[a] He revealed Himself in this way:

[2] Simon Peter, Thomas (called "Twin"), Nathanael from Cana of Galilee, Zebedee's sons, and two others of His disciples were together.

[3] "I'm going fishing," Simon Peter said to them.

"We're coming with you," they told him. They went out and got into the boat, but that night they caught nothing.

[4] When daybreak came, Jesus stood on the shore. However, the disciples did not know it was Jesus.

[5] "Men,"[b] Jesus called to them, "you don't have any fish, do you?"

"No," they answered.

[6] "Cast the net on the right side of the boat," He told them, "and you'll find some." So they did,[c] and they were unable to haul it in because of the large number of fish. [7] Therefore the disciple, the one Jesus loved, said to Peter, "It is the Lord!"

When Simon Peter heard that it was the Lord, he tied his outer garment around him[d] (for he was stripped) and plunged into the sea. [8] But since they were not far from land (about 100 yards[e] away), the other disciples came in the boat, dragging the net full of fish. [9] When they got out on land, they saw a charcoal fire there, with fish lying on it, and bread.

[10] "Bring some of the fish you've just caught," Jesus told them. [11] So Simon Peter got up and hauled the net ashore, full of large fish—153 of them. Even though there were so many, the net was not torn.

[12] "Come and have breakfast," Jesus told them. None of the disciples dared ask Him, "Who are You?" because they knew it was the Lord. [13] Jesus came, took the bread, and gave it to them. He did the same with the fish.

[14] This was now the third time[f] Jesus appeared[g] to the disciples after He was raised from the dead.

[15] When they had eaten breakfast, Jesus asked Simon Peter, "Simon, son of John,[h] do you love[i] Me more than these?"

"Yes, Lord," he said to Him, "You know that I love You."

"Feed My lambs," He told him.

[16] A second time He asked him, "Simon, son of John, do you love Me?"

"Yes, Lord," he said to Him, "You know that I love You."

"Shepherd My sheep," He told him.

[17] He asked him the third time, "Simon, son of John, do you love Me?"

Peter was grieved that He asked him the third time, "Do you love Me?" He said, "Lord, You know everything! You know that I love You."

"Feed My sheep," Jesus said. [18] "•I assure you: When you were young, you would tie your belt and walk wherever you wanted. But when you grow old, you will stretch out your hands and someone else will tie you

a21:1 The Sea of Galilee; *Sea of Tiberias* is used only in John; Jn 6:1,23 **b21:5** Lit *Children* **c21:6** Lit *they cast* **d21:7** Lit *he girded his garment* **e21:8** Lit *about 200 cubits* **f21:14** The other two are in Jn 20:19-29. **g21:14** Lit *was revealed* (see v. 1) **h21:15-17** Other mss read *Simon, son of Jonah*; Mt 16:17; Jn 1:42 **i21:15-17** Two synonyms are translated *love* in this conversation: *agapao*, the first 2 times by Jesus (vv. 15-16); and *phileo*, the last time by Jesus (v. 17) and all 3 times by Peter (vv. 15-17). Peter's threefold confession of love for Jesus corresponds to his earlier threefold denial of Jesus; Jn 18:15-18,25-27.

Jn 21:1 This episode is a subsequent revelation of Jesus to His disciples, but this time not in Jerusalem but by the Sea of Tiberias (Galilee).

Jn 21:4 The lack of recognition may relate to the distance (although v. 8 says they were only 100 yards from shore), or it may be that they were still not expecting to see the living Jesus.

Jn 21:6-7 The miracle prompted the disciple whom Jesus loved to recognize Jesus. The relationship between a physical sign and recognition persisted even after the resurrection.

Jn 21:14 This was the third time in John that Jesus had appeared after the resurrection, the first before the disciples in the upper room (20:19-20) and the second eight days later with Thomas present (20:26).

Jn 21:15-17 Peter became frustrated with Jesus' persistence in repeatedly asking him the same question. Some scholars think that there is no difference between the words for "love" used. Others think that the meaning of the episode hinges on these words, with a distinction being made between a particularly close kind of love and friendship love. Still others see Jesus leading Peter to make three affirmations of love as corresponding to (and in a sense undoing) his earlier three denials.

John 21:1-25 (cont.)

and carry you where you don't want to go." [19] He said this to signify by what kind of death he would glorify God.[a] After saying this, He told him, "Follow Me!"

[20] So Peter turned around and saw the disciple Jesus loved following them. ⌊That disciple⌋ was the one who had leaned back against Jesus at the supper and asked, "Lord, who is the one that's going to betray You?" [21] When Peter saw him, he said to Jesus, "Lord—what about him?"

[22] "If I want him to remain until I come," Jesus answered, "what is that to you? As for you, follow Me."

[23] So this report[b] spread to the brothers[c] that this disciple would not die. Yet Jesus did not tell him that he would not die, but, "If I want him to remain until I come, what is that to you?"

[24] This is the disciple who testifies to these things and who wrote them down. We know that his testimony is true.

[25] And there are also many other things that Jesus did, which, if they were written one by one, I suppose not even the world itself could contain the books[d] that would be written.

a21:19 Jesus predicts that Peter would be martyred. Church tradition says that Peter was crucified upside down. **b21:23** Lit *this word*
c21:23 The word *brothers* refers to the whole Christian community. **d21:25** Lit *scroll*

Jn 21:19 The reference "to signify by what kind of death he [Peter] would glorify God" in the present passage echoes the similar reference "to signify what kind of death He [Jesus] was about to die" in 12:33. The present instance, therefore, establishes a connection between the deaths of Jesus and Peter.
Jn 21:21 Peter inquired regarding the kind of death the beloved disciple (the one who had asked Jesus about his betrayer; v. 20) would suffer.
Jn 21:22-23 Jesus responded to Peter with a conditional question: *"If I want him to remain until I come . . ."* Some mistook the conditional question for an assertive statement, when what Jesus was saying was not that he would not die but that if Jesus were to want that for him, it was none of their business.
Jn 21:24 In the closing epilogue, the disciple whom Jesus loved lays claim to being the one who wrote the Gospel, and that his testimony is true. The notion of true testimony is fundamental to the entire Gospel.
Jn 21:25 The final statement of the Gospel is that Jesus did other things that could have been recorded but that were not (see 20:30-31). Authors continue to write about just the incidents that we know of, which itself is a threat to the number of books that the world can contain!

Sec. 181   Jesus Appears to 500 in Galilee and Gives the Great Commission

Matthew 28:16-20	Mark 16:15-18	1 Corinthians 15:6
[16] The 11 disciples traveled to Galilee, to the mountain where Jesus had directed them. [17] When they saw Him, they worshiped,[a] but some doubted. [18] Then Jesus came near and said to them, "All authority has been given to Me in heaven and on earth. [19] Go, therefore, and make disciples of[b] all nations, baptizing them in the name	[15] Then He said to them, "Go into all the world and preach the gospel to the whole creation. [16] Whoever believes and is baptized will be	[6] Then He appeared to over 500 brothers at one time, most of whom remain to the present, but some have fallen •asleep.

a28:17 Other mss add *Him* **b28:19** Lit *and instruct*, or *and disciple* (as a verb)

Mt 28:16 *traveled to Galilee, to the mountain:* These eleven went to Galilee, for that is where Jesus had promised to meet them. Jesus had called His disciples on a mountain; it was also on a mountain that He departed from them.
Mt 28:19-20 These are the marching orders of the church. The one imperative in these verses is "make disciples." But we are to go into the entire world to do it. We are to witness and win to Christ people from every nation. We are to baptize them and then disciple or teach them all that Jesus taught us to do. Conversion is prerequisite to discipleship. Baptism is the link between conversion and discipleship. Baptism does not save, but it is the first thing Jesus asks for Christian life, growth, and witness.

Matthew 28:16-20 (cont.)	Mark 16:15-18 (cont.)
of the Father and of the Son and of the Holy Spirit, [20] teaching them to observe everything I have commanded you. And remember,[a] I am with you always,[b] to the end of the age."	saved, but whoever does not believe will be condemned. [17] And these signs will accompany those who believe: In My name they will drive out demons; they will speak in new languages; [18] they will pick up snakes;[a] if they should drink anything deadly, it will never harm them; they will lay hands on the sick, and they will get well."
a28:20 Lit *look* **b28:20** Lit *all the days*	**a16:18** Other mss add *with their hands*

Mk 16:17 *these signs will accompany:* Jesus' statement concerning signs is a *prediction* of what will happen, not a *promise* of what must always happen. Mark 16:20 is a report that in fact Jesus' prediction came true when the disciples went out to preach and God confirmed their word through accompanying signs.

Sec. 182   Jesus Appears to James

1 Corinthians 15:7

[7] Then He appeared to James, then to all the apostles.

Sec. 183   Jesus Appears to His Disciples in Jerusalem

Luke 24:44-49	Acts 1:3-8
[44] Then He told them, "These are My words that I spoke to you while I was still with you—that everything written about Me in the Law of Moses, the Prophets, and the Psalms must be fulfilled." [45] Then He opened their minds to understand the Scriptures. [46] He also said to them, "This is what is written:[a] the Messiah would suffer and rise from the dead the third day, [47] and repentance for[b] forgiveness of sins would be proclaimed in His name to all the nations, beginning at Jerusalem. [48] You are witnesses of these things. [49] And look, I am sending you[c] what My Father promised. As for you, stay in the city[d] until you are empowered[e] from on high."	[3] After He had suffered, He also presented Himself alive to them by many convincing proofs, appearing to them during 40 days and speaking about the kingdom of God. [4] While He was together with them,[a] He commanded them not to leave Jerusalem, but to wait for the Father's promise. "This," ⌊He said, "is what⌋ you heard from Me; [5] for John baptized with water, but you will be baptized with the Holy Spirit not many days from now." [6] So when they had come together, they asked Him, "Lord, at this time are You restoring the kingdom to Israel?"
a24:46 Other mss add *and thus it was necessary that* **b24:47** Other mss read *repentance and* **c24:49** Lit *upon you* **d24:49** Other mss add *of Jerusalem* **e24:49** Lit *clothed with power*	**a1:4** Or *He was eating with them,* or *He was lodging with them*

Lk 24:44 *everything written about Me in the Law of Moses, the Prophets, and the Psalms must be fulfilled:* Jesus again underscored that what took place was declared in the Scriptures. He then led then into an understanding of what Scripture taught.
Lk 24:46 Three ideas are key: 1) Messiah would suffer; 2) He would rise on the third day; and 3) repentance would be preached starting from Jerusalem (Ac 1-2).
Lk 24:48 *witnesses:* As Acts 1:8 also affirms, these who saw Jesus were called to give testimony about Him and that He was raised.
Lk 24:49 *I am sending you what my Father promised:* A reference to the Holy Spirit, as Luke 3:15-17 and Acts 1:5 and all of Acts 2 shows. *until you are empowered from on high:* The work of the Spirit is summarized as the giving of enablement for the task.

Acts 1:3-8 (cont.)

⁷ He said to them, "It is not for you to know times or periods that the Father has set by His own authority. ⁸ But you will receive power when the Holy Spirit has come upon you, and you will be My witnesses in Jerusalem, in all Judea and Samaria, and to the ends[a] of the earth."

a1:8 Lit *the end*

Sec. 184   Jesus' Last Appearance and His Ascension

Mark 16:19-20	Luke 24:50-53	Acts 1:9-12
¹⁹ Then after speaking to them, the Lord Jesus was taken up into heaven and sat down at the right hand of God.	⁵⁰ Then He led them out as far as Bethany, and lifting up His hands He blessed them. ⁵¹ And while He was blessing them, He left them and was carried up into heaven.	⁹ After He had said this, He was taken up as they were watching, and a cloud received Him out of their sight. ¹⁰ While He was going, they were gazing into heaven, and suddenly two men in white clothes stood by them. ¹¹ They said, "Men of Galilee, why do you stand looking up into heaven? This Jesus, who has been taken from you into heaven, will come in the same way that you have seen Him going into heaven."
²⁰ And they went out and preached everywhere, the Lord working with them and confirming the word by the accompanying signs.][a] **a16:9-20** Other mss omit bracketed text	⁵² After worshiping Him, they returned to Jerusalem with great joy. ⁵³ And they were continually in the •temple complex praising God.[a] **a24:53** Other mss read *praising and blessing God. Amen.*	¹² Then they returned to Jerusalem from the mount called Olive Grove, which is near Jerusalem—a Sabbath day's journey away.

Lk 24:51 *while He was blessing them, He left them:* Jesus departed to the side of the Father (Ac 2:30-36).
Lk 24:52 *with great joy:* Luke ends as it began with a note of joy about the things God had done. Luke likes the note of joy: Luke 1:14; 2:10; 10:20; 13:17; 15:5,32; 19:37; 24:41,52.
Lk 24:53 *praising God:* In obedience, the disciples stayed in Jerusalem thanking God and awaiting the enablement to come, a work described in Acts 2.

Holman CSB Bullet Notes for the Gospels

Bullet Notes are one of the unique features of the Holman Christian Standard Bible®. These notes explain frequently used biblical words or terms. These "bullet" words (for example: •abyss) are normally marked with a bullet only on their first occurrence in a chapter of the biblical text. However, certain important or easily misunderstood terms, such as •Jews or •slaves, will have more than one bullet per chapter.

Abba	The Aramaic word for "father"
abyss	The *bottomless pit* or *the depths* (of the sea); the prison for Satan and the demons
Amen	The transliteration of a Hebrew word signifying that something is certain, valid, truthful, or faithful; it is often used at the end of biblical songs, hymns, and prayers.
asleep	A term used in reference to those who have died
Beelzebul	A term of slander, which was variously interpreted "lord of flies," "lord of dung," or "ruler of demons"; 2 Kg 1:2; Mk 3:22
cause the downfall of/ causes to sin	The Greek word *skandalizo* has a root meaning of "snare" or "trap," but has no real English counterpart.
clean/unclean	When something is clean, it is holy or acceptable to God, and when it is unclean, it is unholy (such as an unclean spirit). The terms can be used in a ritual sense to apply to moral standards for living.
centurion	A Roman officer who commanded about 100 soldiers
Cephas	The Aramaic word for *rock*; it is parallel to the Greek word *petros* from which the English name Peter is derived; Jn 1:42; 1 Co 1:12.
chief priest(s)	A group of Jewish temple officers that included the high priest, captain of the temple, temple overseers, and treasurers
company	Or cohort, a Roman military unit that numbered as many as 600 men
Counselor	The Greek word *parakletos* means one called alongside to help, counsel, or protect; it is used of the Holy Spirit in Jn and in 1 Jn.
cubit	An OT measurement of distance that equaled about 18 inches
Decapolis	Originally a federation of 10 Gentile towns east of the Jordan River
denarius/denarii	A small silver Roman coin, which was equal to a day's wage for a common laborer
engaged	Jewish engagement was a binding agreement that could only be broken by divorce.
Hades	The Greek word for the place of the dead; it corresponds to the Hebrew word *Sheol*.
Hallelujah!	Or *Praise the Lord!*; it literally means *Praise Yah!* (a shortened form of Yahweh)
headquarters	The Latin word *Praetorium* was used by Greek writers for the residence of the Roman governor; it may also refer to military headquarters, the imperial court, or the emperor's guard.

hell/hellfire	Greek *Gehenna*; Aramaic for Valley of Hinnom on the south side of Jerusalem; it was formerly a place of human sacrifice and in NT times a place for the burning of garbage; the place of final judgment for those rejecting Christ.
Herod	The name of the Idumean family ruling Palestine from 37 B.C. to A.D. 95; the main rulers from this family mentioned in the four Gospels of the NT are:
Herod I	(37 B.C.–4 B.C.) also known as Herod the Great; built the great temple in Jerusalem and massacred the male babies in Bethlehem
Herod Antipas	(4 B.C.–A.D. 39) son of Herod the Great; ruled one-fourth of his father's kingdom (Galilee and Perea); killed John the Baptist and mocked Jesus
Herodians	Political supporters of Herod the Great and his family
horn	A symbol of power based on the strength of animal horns
Hosanna	A term of praise derived from the Hebrew word for *save*
I assure you	This is a phrase used only by Jesus to testify to the certainty and importance of His words; in Mt, Mk and Lk it is literally *Amen, I say to you*, and in Jn it is literally *Amen, amen, I say to you*.
Jew(s)	In Jn the term *Jews* usually indicates those in Israel who were opposed to Jesus, particularly the Jewish authorities in Jerusalem who led the nation.
life/soul	The Greek word *psyche* can be translated life or soul.
Mary Magdalene	Or *Mary of Magdala*; Magdala was probably on the western shore of the Sea of Galilee, north of Tiberias.
Messiah	Or *the Christ*; the Greek word *Christos* means "the anointed one".
Mount of Olives	A mountain east of Jerusalem, across the Kidron Valley
Nazarene	A person from Nazareth; growing up in Nazareth was an aspect of the Messiah's humble beginnings; Jn 1:46
offspring/seed	This term is used literally or metaphorically to refer to plants or grain, sowing or harvest, male reproductive seed, human children or physical descendants, and also to spiritual children or to Christ (Gl 3:16).
One and Only	Or *one of a kind*, or *incomparable*, or *only begotten*; the Greek word can refer to someone's only child such as in Lk 7:12; 8:42; 9:38. It can also refer to someone's special child as in Heb 11:17.
Passover	The Israelite festival celebrated on the fourteenth day of the first month in the early spring. It was a celebration of the deliverance of the Israelites from Egypt, commemorating the final plague on Egypt when the firstborn were killed.
Pharisee(s)	In Judaism a religious sect that followed the whole written and oral law
Pilate	Pontius Pilate was governor of the province of Judea A.D. 26–36.
proselyte	A person from another race or religion who went through a prescribed ritual to become a Jew
Rabbi	The Hebrew word *Rabbi* means *my great one*; it is used of a recognized teacher of the Scriptures.

sacred bread	Literally *bread of presentation*; 12 loaves, representing the 12 tribes of Israel, put on the table in the holy place in the tabernacle, and later in the temple. The priests ate the previous week's loaves; Ex 25:30; 29:32; Lv 24:5-9.
Sadducee(s)	In Judaism a religious sect that followed primarily the first 5 books of the OT (Torah or Pentateuch)
Samaritan(s)	People of mixed, Gentile/Jewish ancestry who lived between Galilee and Judea and were hated by the Jews
Sanhedrin	The supreme council of Judaism with 70 members, patterned after Moses' 70 elders
scribe(s)	A professional group in Judaism that copied the law of Moses and interpreted it, especially in legal cases
slave	The strong Greek word *doulos* cannot be accurately translated in English by "servant" or "bond servant"; the HCSB translates this word as "slave," not out of insensitivity to the legitimate concerns of modern English speakers, but out of a commitment to accurately convey the brutal reality of the Roman empire's inhumane institution as well as the ownership called for by Christ.
Son of Man	The most frequent title Jesus used for Himself; Dn 7:13
soul	(see "life/soul")
stumble	(see "cause the downfall of/cause to sin")
synagogue	A place where the Jewish people met for prayer, worship and teaching of the Scriptures
tabernacle	Or *tent*, or *shelter*; terms used for temporary housing
tassel	Fringe put on the clothing of devout Jews to remind them to keep the law; Nm 15:37-41
temple complex	In the Jerusalem temple, the complex included the sanctuary (the holy place and the holy of holies), at least 4 courtyards (for priests, Jewish men, Jewish women, and Gentiles), numerous gates, and several covered walkways.
Unleavened Bread	A seven-day festival celebrated in conjunction with the Passover; Ex 12:1-20
wise men	The Greek word is *magoi*; the English word "Magi" is based on a Persian word. They were eastern sages who observed the heavens for signs and omens.
woman	When used in direct address, "Woman" was not a term of disrespect but of honor.
world	The organized Satanic system that is opposed to God and hostile to Jesus and His followers. The non-Christian culture including governments, educational systems, and businesses

Textual Issues in the Gospels

Bill Warren

Since a Gospel harmony highlights some textual issues, understanding the textual background of the Gospels is foundational for the comparative studies so easily facilitated by a Gospel harmony. An awareness of the kinds of differences in the textual witnesses provides a starting point for this understanding.[1]

Due in large part to how the Gospels were copied and used in the early church, assorted types of textual differences appear in the witnesses that preserve the text, with most of the variants originating during the first three centuries. The majority of the variants have little impact on determining the original text, involving spelling differences, the addition or omission of the definite article, the use of *nomina sacra* (a shortened form for reverenced words like Jesus, God, Christ, Savior, Father, etc.), and the inclusion or omission of the moveable "nu" (a Greek letter included or omitted at the end of certain words). While most variants were inadvertent, likely caused by unprofessional copying practices, some originated due to conscious attempts to clarify, correct, strengthen, or preserve readings. When determining the nature of the variants, many can be identified as obvious unintentional changes or as clearly intentional ones. On the other hand, identifying the differences between intentional and unintentional variants is not always easy, for some are less distinguishable as to their cause, lying between the poles with possibly multiple causes for their origin. Actually, the types of differences are best understood as a continuum rather than only with the two concrete categories of intentional and unintentional variants. As a general rule, the variants that are further toward the "intentional change" pole of the spectrum have drawn the most attention for NT textual and exegetical studies.

Understanding why variants occurred requires some consideration of the factors surrounding the transmission of the texts, such as: 1) who was copying the texts; 2) how the texts were being copied; and 3) why the texts were being copied. Especially before Constantine's legalization of Christianity, scribes with various levels of expertise copied Christian texts. A few were probably expert scribes, the type generally employed or owned by the ruling class, who were trained to produce highly accurate copies of literary texts. The vast majority of the scribes involved in copying Christian texts surely came from lower social affiliations more associated with the selling of their services in the marketplace where a somewhat lower level of accuracy often resulted. For Christian texts, these scribes often came from within the church or were sought out due to an affiliation with a church member, as implied by some of the intentional changes to the text. Such scribes made good copies that were overall faithful but were more prone to variations than a high-level professional copy would have been.[2] In at least one place in Egypt, however, professional copying for the Gospels was in place around the year AD 200. The transmission processes behind manuscripts *p*4 and *p*75 from the late second to early third century and the fourth century manuscript Vaticanus attest to this, for

---

1. Introductions to the field of NT textual criticism give fuller discussions of the general issues and data associated with the field. See the following: Bruce Metzger and Bart Ehrman, *The Text of the New Testament: Its Transmission, Corruption, and Restoration*, 4th ed. (New York: Oxford University Press, 2005); Kurt and Barbara Aland, *The Text of the New Testament: an Introduction to the Critical Editions and to the Theory and Practice of Modern Textual Criticism*, 2nd rev. ed. (Grand Rapids: Eerdmans, 1995); Harold Greenlee, *Introduction to New Testament Textual Criticism*, rev. ed. (Peabody, MA: Hendrickson, 1995); and Bart Ehrman and Michael Holmes, eds., *The Text of the New Testament in Contemporary Research: Essays on the Status Quaestionis* (Grand Rapids: Eerdmans, 1995).
2. For more information on scribes and copying practices, see Harry Gamble, *Books and Readers in the Early Church: A History of Early Christian Texts* (New Haven: Yale University Press, 1995); and Kim Haines Eitzen, *Guardians of Letters: Literacy, Power, and the Transmission of Early Christian Literature* (New York: Oxford University Press, 2000).

these manuscripts demonstrate a highly similar text in spite of both the 150-year time span between the manuscripts and the fact that Vaticanus is not a direct copy of either of these papyri.

Regarding the copying of the texts, a norm would have been to read a phrase from the text out loud looking at the base text, then repeat the phrase while writing it in the copy. This process is likely the cause of so many vowel changes in the copy process since most of these changes sounded alike. A scribe could write the word correctly regarding sound even while misspelling it regarding the exact letters (as with "augment" and "augmint" in English). Confusion in the repetition of the phrase likely accounts for numerous other variants, with faulty memory as well as knowledge of the passage in another form being factors. If the passage was known in more than one Gospel, the scribe might either inadvertently write the more familiar, memorized wording rather than the actual wording or consciously conform the passage to the popular version (harmonization). For example, the wording of Matthew, the most used Gospel in the early church, often influenced the wording of similar phrases in the other Gospels, as is the case in Luke 11:2-4, where some scribes changed Luke's text to agree with the wording of the Lord's Prayer in Matthew 6:9-13.

The Gospels were being copied, not for the general public, but for those in the churches. As the eyewitnesses were passing away, Christians gained continued access to the story of Jesus through the circulation of oral traditions within the church and by means of the written Gospels. By the middle of the second century, however, accurate oral tradition was rapidly passing from the scene and the written Gospels became the standard for information about the teachings, actions, death, and resurrection of Jesus. Justin Martyr (*The First Apology of Justin*, LXVII), writing near the middle of the second century, noted that the churches were reading the "memoirs of the apostles" in their worship settings, thereby indicating that the church was now using the Gospels regularly in worship as a source of information and authority.

The desire to save some of the oral traditions and the effort to aid the liturgical use of the Gospels are behind some of the variants in the text. The church decided to canonize books, not independent sayings of Jesus or stories about Jesus. So when oral traditions that were especially esteemed in the church were not in one of the Gospels, such traditions either needed to be inserted into the text of one of the Gospels (most often in Luke or John) or fall by the wayside. Some of the longer additions to the Gospels fit into this category, like the story of the woman caught in adultery in John 7:53b–8:11.

At other times, small changes were made to the text to clarify the meaning so that those listening in the church would not misunderstand the text, as seen in Mark 9:29 where the phrase "and fasting" is added after "prayer" in order to explain fervent prayer like when fasting is meant, not just a casual type of prayer. This type of change could also be made to protect how a Christian teaching was understood, as in Mark 6:3. Some manuscripts read "the son of the carpenter and of Mary" here rather than the accepted reading of "the carpenter, the son of Mary." The addition of the reference to Jesus' father likely is a means of avoiding the stigma of Jesus not being identified with an earthly father (which is probably the cause of the remarks in verses 4-5 about the lack of a good reception in Nazareth, for the mention of only Jesus' mother would have been a social slap in the face, insinuating illegitimacy) as well as not being identified with the lowly role of a carpenter. The most obvious intentional changes to the text are normally made to help the church understand its texts better. These types of variant readings, even when not original, offer early commentaries on what the text may mean.

Textual Issues in Matthew

The variant found in Matthew 6:13 has thoroughly impacted the life of the church. The original ending of the Lord's Prayer is "deliver us from evil." As early as the late first century, however, a doxological ending was added to the prayer ("for Yours is the power and glory for ever and ever" is the form in *Didache* 8.2). While the various forms of the doxology are obviously later additions, they reflect how Christians in the early church came to use this passage not simply as a model of how to pray, but as a prayer itself.

In Matthew 24:35, many textual witnesses omit the phrase "nor the Son," a phrase well attested in some of the earliest Greek manuscripts. The phrase "neither the angels in heaven nor the Son" is undoubtedly original in Mark 13:32, which means that Matthew likely knew of the saying and included it in his Gospel. On the other hand, saying that Jesus did not know something in His incarnate state probably proved awkward for the church's high Christology, so in the copy process the phrase was removed so that the difficulty disappeared.

What was Barabbas's actual name? *Bar* means "son of" and normally, rather than serving as an actual name, forms part of a word that defines a person by family relationships or at times by means of a trait. In Matthew 27:16-17, the name "Jesus" is noted for Barabbas in some textual witnesses as his actual name. While "Jesus" was a common Jewish name (the Greek word "Jesus" is identical with "Joshua" from the OT, a name any Jew would have been pleased to bear), it became revered and fell out of use among most Christians except in reference to Jesus Christ. Even in Colossians 4:11, Justus apparently changed his name so as not to be called "Jesus." The suppression of the name "Jesus" for Barabbas in so many of the manuscripts may be due to this attitude. While the textual evidence is not at all decisive, most likely the name "Jesus Barabbas" was original to the text or minimally represents an authentic tradition.[3]

Textual Issues in Mark

Two major textual considerations in Mark involve the beginning and the ending of the Gospel. Mark begins with a phrase instead of a complete sentence ("The beginning of the gospel of Jesus Christ, the Son of God"), with several textual variants found in the second half of this phrase. Numerous manuscripts omit the words "the Son of God," one omits everything after "Jesus" in the verse, two church fathers (Irenaeus, late second century, and Epiphanius, late fourth century) omit everything after "gospel," and one manuscript reads "the Son of the Lord." Due to this large amount of variation in the first verse, which was a rare phenomenon in ancient writings since the beginning of a work normally had minimal variation, some scholars held that the beginning of Mark has been lost.[4] While this is possible, manuscripts do not omit or disagree about the first three words of the verse as would be expected if the beginning had been lost. Also, no church father mentions a lost beginning. On the other hand, whether or not "the son of God" is original to the text is an open question due to the conflicting textual evidence. The intrinsic evidence is likewise indecisive, for although the centurion affirms this title for Jesus with a positive emphasis in Mark 15:39 ("This man really was God's Son") in a way that nicely reinforces a thematic use of the phrase in Mark 1:1, this reasoning assumes the originality of the phrase and explains its importance rather than answering the question of whether the phrase is original at the beginning of the Gospel. Based primarily upon the nature of the manuscript evidence, however, the evidence tilts slightly toward an answer of "yes, the phrase is original."

The major textual issue in Mark involves the ending of the Gospel: should Mark end at 16:8 or 16:20? Additional text was appended to Mark 16:8 in many textual witnesses, whether a short

---

3. For the best available overview of the major textual variants in the Greek NT, see Bruce Metzger, *Textual Commentary on the Greek New Testament*, 2nd ed. (New York: United Bible Societies, 1994).
4. For a good overview of the textual issues related to both the ending and the beginning of Mark (especially the idea of these being lost), see N. Clayton Croy, *The Mutilation of Mark's Gospel* (Nashville: Abingdon, 2003).

text of two verses, the longer ending of 16:9-20, or an even longer version with an addition to verse 14. Nevertheless, the diversity of witnesses, their early dates, and the lack of agreement among the various endings highly favor verse 8 as the original ending, although the ending is still highly shocking since the women are not shown as overcoming their fear in order to bear witness to the resurrection. On the other hand, the Mark 16:8 ending depicts a dilemma quite in sync with the situation that Mark's readers were facing in Rome, if it was written during the Neronian persecutions. Christians there likewise lived in fear of sharing about the resurrected Christ with others due to their fear in the midst of a life-threatening situation.

But if 16:8 is the original ending, why did the other endings arise? When Mark 16:8 is put beside the other Gospels' reporting of the appearances of the risen Lord to the disciples, Mark pales in comparison and begs for more of an ending than 16:8 provides. The various endings after Mark 16:8 are likely early second century attempts to round out Mark in light of the other three Gospels.

Textual Issues in Luke

Few variants have drawn as much attention as the ones in Luke 22:43-44 and 23:34. The first involves the garden of Gethsemane scene in which an angel comes to strengthen Jesus because He was in such agony that He was sweating profusely "like drops of blood falling to the ground" (22:44). So many early manuscripts from a variety of textual traditions omit these verses that their originality is highly unlikely. On the other hand, this account was known as early as the middle of the second century (Justin Martyr, *Dialogue with Trypho,* CIII) as being part of a Gospel. Those supporting the originality of the passage often argue that the omission was due to the depiction of a too-human, weak Jesus who needed divine help amidst tremendous personal agony. The omission protected a high Christology of the divine nature of Jesus.[5] More likely, however, this is an oral tradition about Jesus that some wanted to preserve by inserting it into Luke. While the oral tradition may be accurate, the dilemma facing a textual critic is that of determining what was most likely original to the text, not what is authentic to the tradition.

A similar dilemma occurs with what may be the most troublesome textual variant in the entire NT, the statement of Jesus in Luke 23:34, "Then Jesus said, 'Father, forgive them, because they do not know what they are doing.'" Although the manuscript evidence is strongly against the originality of this passage in Luke, many consider this saying as authentic to Jesus whether or not it is original to Luke. Looking beyond the manuscript data to the reasons why this passage would have been omitted or added, a major argument in favor of the passage's originality is that it espouses such a blanket forgiveness that some in the church would have excised it to avoid the implications of easy forgiveness. The early church struggled with the offering of forgiveness, especially to Christians who bowed to the pressure of persecution or committed certain sins. This passage, which was known by the second half of the second century (Irenaeus, *Against Heresies*, XVIII), opens the door to forgiveness for virtually any sin since Jesus forgave those who sinned so horribly by crucifying Him. Perhaps even anti-Semitism could have caused the church to excise the passage. On the other hand, the early widespread evidence against the passage indicates that this is likely another case of oral tradition looking for a home in the text. So while this passage may be authentic tradition and even indicate the attitude of Jesus, the data indicate that it was not a part of the original text of Luke.

---

5. Raymond Brown offered one of the best defenses of the originality of both Luke 22:43-44 and 23:34. See Raymond Brown, *The Death of the Messiah*, 2 vols. (New York: Doubleday, 1994).

Textual Issues in John

Two passages in John follow the same pattern of oral tradition as those just discussed in Luke: the story of the angel moving the water in John 5:3-4 and the story of the woman caught in adultery in John 7:53b–8:11. The textual evidence decisively favors the omission of both of these passages. Although John 5:3-4 is probably oral tradition that has made its way into the text, the information explains why the people were trying to get into the pool, thereby offering an excellent early commentary on the text.

The powerful story in John 7:53b–8:11, besides being omitted entirely in a number of manuscripts, is sometimes found at the end of John, after John 8:36, or in Luke. While the idea of easy forgiveness for a cardinal sin could have caused difficulty with this passage in the early church, a more likely scenario is that this story was circulating outside of any book of the NT. The story ministered to those needing forgiveness and so was preserved as a story, but long term it would have fallen by the wayside if not included in one of the accepted Gospels. Gospels were canonized, not stories, so this oral tradition was inserted most often after John 7:52, although it was not original to John's Gospel (the "floating" nature of the story shows that it was "searching for a home" in the text).

Another textual dilemma in John involves Christology. In John 1:18, the oldest manuscripts read "the unique God" while most others read "the unique Son" (one reads "the unique Son of God," a clear way of combining the readings rather than choosing between them). Elsewhere, John has no qualms about calling Jesus the unique Son (he did so in John 3:16,18, and 1 John 4:9), but did he also call Him the unique God? Since "unique Son" was better known to the scribes, they would have been more prone to change to that reading rather than away from it. Positing a satisfactory explanation of why as early as the second half of the second century (based on the assumption that p^{66} and p^{75} used even earlier exemplars) the reading would have been changed from the perfectly acceptable "unique Son" to "unique God." Due to how different the reading of "unique God" is from other NT passages, its early manuscript support, and the symmetry of this high Christology at both the beginning and ending of the prologue (John 1:1, "the Word was God"), the reading "unique God" is to be favored as the original text.

The Geographical Setting of the Gospels

Sidney D. Dyer

The land of Israel, located on the eastern rim of the Mediterranean Sea, is approximately 150 miles long and 80 miles wide. This strip of land is both historically and theologically significant, a region the Lord promised to Abraham and his descendants, where the unfolding of the Abrahamic covenant took place. The global position of the promised land implies the fulfillment of one of the Lord's promises to Abraham—that in him and his seed all the nations of the earth would be blessed (Gn 12:3; 22:18). This would eventually be accomplished through the proclamation of the gospel to all the nations. The land served as a passageway to the three continents of the eastern hemisphere. Barry Beitzel points out that "the Promised Land represents the only intercontinental land bridge that connects Africa with Asia and Europe, and that links the Indian Ocean, via the Red Sea, with the Atlantic Ocean, through the corridor of the Mediterranean."[1] One medieval map represents each of these continents as one leaf of a three-leaf clover with Jerusalem in the center.[2] Thus, the global location of the promised land points to the final stage of redemptive history.

Overview of the Land from West to East

The topography of Palestine is best comprehended by moving from the west to the east. It begins with the coastline of the Mediterranean Sea and moves to the coastal area consisting of the Plain of Sharon in the north and the Plain of Philistia to the south. Further eastward are the rolling hills of the Shephelah. The land rises upward to the central mountains, a ridge running north and south for about 90 miles. The ridge reaches a height of 2,500 feet above sea level. The eastern slopes of this ridge drop quickly into the Jordan Valley. The Jordan River, which flows out of the Sea of Galilee into the Dead Sea, meanders through this valley for about 60 miles. The surface of the Sea of Galilee is 696 feet below sea level, and the surface of the Dead Sea is 1,296 below sea level, the lowest place on the planet. This difference in elevation gives one a sense of the rapid descent from one body of water to the other, which explains the river's name. *Jordan* means "the descender."[3] East of the Jordan Valley is a plateau known as the Transjordan that averages 3,000 feet above sea level. The western territory from the Mediterranean Sea to the Jordan River is the Cisjordan, with Galilee in the north, Judea in the south, and Samaria in the middle.

The Northern Portion of Palestine

The territory where Jesus was reared and conducted His ministry was Galilee, hence He was known as Jesus the Galilean (Mt 26:69). The region was called "Galilee of the Gentiles" (Mt 4:15), since many Gentiles had settled there. O. Palmer Robertson describes Galilee as a "territory of vast hordes of various nationalities representing all the peoples of the world."[4] Although Jesus declared that He was sent to the lost sheep of the house of Israel (Mt 15:24), He extended His ministry to Gentiles, even outside Galilee. Jesus was in the region of Tyre and Sidon when He met a woman of Canaan whose faith He praised. He granted her request that He deliver her daughter

---

1. Barry J. Beitzel, *The Moody Atlas of Bible Lands* (Chicago: Moody, 1985), 25–26.
2. Ibid., p. 203.
3. Chad Brand, Charles Draper, and Archie England, eds., *Holman Illustrated Bible Dictionary* (Nashville: Broadman & Holman, 2003), s.v., "Jordon River," by Philip Lee.
4. O. Palmer Robertson, *Understanding the Land of the Bible: A Biblical-Theological Guide* (Phillipsburg, NJ: Presbyterian and Reformed, 1996), 33.

from demon possession (Mt 15:21). Tyre and Sidon were in Phoenicia, which was along the coast to the north of Galilee and outside Jewish territory. Thus, Jesus' ministry in this region points to the inclusion of people from all nations into His kingdom.

The city of Capernaum, located on the northwest shore of the Sea of Galilee, was the center of our Lord's Galilean ministry. Matthew describes it as our Lord's "own town" (Mt 9:1). Located along a major trade route, it was a commercial center where Jews and Gentiles mingled. In Capernaum Jesus healed a Roman centurion's slave and was amazed at the centurion's great faith (Lk 7:1-10). Only one other occasion in the Gospels is it recorded that Jesus was amazed (Mk 6:6). The cosmopolitan nature of this city and the Lord's amazement at this Gentile's faith points to the geographical expansion of the kingdom.

Southeast of Galilee, beyond the Jordan Valley, was a region known then as Decapolis, a territory of 10 Greek cities that formed an alliance for commerce and protection. Harvey E. Dana described the inhabitants as "despised by the Jews as lawless intruders."[5] Jesus journeyed here, and in the region of the Gerasenes, about six miles southeast of the Sea of Galilee, a demon-possessed man met Him (Mk 5:1-20). Jesus allowed the demonic multitude possessing this man to enter a herd of pigs, which ran down a steep embankment and drowned, probably in the Sea of Galilee. The man went about Decapolis declaring what Jesus had done for him, and all who heard the report were amazed (Mk 5:20). The man Jesus delivered from demon possession was most likely a Gentile. Regardless of his ethnicity, however, Jesus' journey to this Greek territory and the resulting spread of His fame pointed to the fulfillment of the Lord's promise to Abraham regarding all the nations of the earth (Gn 22:18).

The Middle Portion of Palestine

South of Galilee is the territory known as Samaria. Its northern boundary then was marked by the southern edge of the Plain of Esdraelon, which begins westward at Mount Carmel and reaches eastward as far as Mount Gilboa, located in the central mountain range. The western border was the shore of the Mediterranean Sea and on the east was the Jordan River. The southern border fluctuated north and south a few times because it lacked any major geographical formations to mark it. The feature that generally marks the southern boundary is the valley of Aijalon, which descends to the west and the Wadi Makkuk, which descends eastward toward the Jordan Valley.

The population in biblical times was ethnically mixed. Israelites who escaped the Assyrian conquest intermarried with the foreigners the king of Assyria imported to repopulate the area. When the exiles returned from the Babylonian exile, they would not allow the Samaritans to assist in rebuilding the temple and this provoked Samaritan animosity toward them. The Jews despised the Samaritans because their race and religion were impure. The animosity between the Jews and Samaritans was so intense that the Jews in Galilee and Judea went out of their way when traveling from one region to the other. Rather than taking the shorter route through Samaria, they would go around along the Jordan Valley. On one occasion Jesus' Jewish opponents mocked Him by saying, "Aren't we right in saying that You're a Samaritan and have a demon?" (Jn 8:48).

Jesus did not share His countrymen's prejudice. Although He did instruct His disciples not to go into any city of Samaria (Mt 10:5), He demonstrated love for these people. Early in His ministry, He departed from Judea to journey to Galilee. John explains that it was necessary for Jesus to travel through Samaria (Jn 4:4). Taking the more direct route apparently was not merely a practical consideration. John 4:7-42 shows that Jesus spoke to a Samaritan woman at Jacob's well. The result was that she and many in her town, Sychar, believed in Jesus. They embraced Him as the Messiah

---

5. Harvey E. Dana, *The New Testament World*, 3rd ed. (Nashville: Broadman, 1937), 43.

and declared Him to be the Savior of the world. There are other accounts demonstrating Jesus' favorable view of the Samaritans (Lk 9:52-53; 10:30-37; 17:11-19), but this account especially points to the inclusion of all peoples, including despised Samaritans, into the church.

The Southern Portion of Palestine

South of Samaria is Judea. The western border, of course, was the shore of the Mediterranean Sea. The eastern border then consisted of the Jordan River and the Dead Sea, while the southern-most portions went as far as Beersheba.

The birthplace of Jesus, Bethlehem, is only six or seven miles south of Jerusalem (Mt 2:1). The location of His nativity points to His Davidic ancestry, and it fulfilled an ancient messianic prophecy (Mt 2:5-6). John the Baptist was born in Judea, specifically in the hill country (Lk 1:39). John conducted his ministry in the wilderness of Judea, a region in the east bordered by the Jordan River and the Dead Sea (Mk 1:4; Lk 3:2). Jesus came to this wilderness to be baptized by John and tempted by Satan for 40 days. The wilderness appears to represent the nation's former relationship to the Lord in the wilderness at the beginning of her relationship to Him. Jeremiah 2:2 relates that the Lord said to His people, "I remember the loyalty of your youth, your love as a bride—how you followed Me in the wilderness." John, calling the people to the wilderness to be baptized, indicated the beginning of a new relationship with God. Jesus' baptism, with the descent of the Spirit and the declaration of the Father, indicated His role in this new beginning. The wilderness of the exodus had become a place of testing. There is a definite parallel between Israel's 40 years of wandering and Jesus' 40 days of temptation. Jesus succeeded in a similar environment where Israel failed.

Jerusalem and Golgotha

Jerusalem is located in Judea within the central mountain range, about 34 miles from the Mediterranean and about 14 miles west of the Dead Sea. The city was surrounded by a wall and situated on a geographical formation that is somewhat like a right hand with the tip joints folded in and the thumb pointing south. The valley running west and south of the city was Gehenna, also known as the Valley of Hinnom. It represented the place of eternal punishment (Mt 5:22,29,30; 10:28; 18:9; 23:15,33; Mk 9:43,45,47; Lk 12:5; Jms 3:6.). Between the area's hand portion and the thumb is the Tyropoeon Valley. North of the thumb stood the higher temple area with its outer wall and inner courts. The pinnacle of the temple was actually the southeast corner of the outer wall. The eastern side of the city was bordered by the Kidron Valley, which runs from the tip of the thumb beyond the northern-most portion of the city. East of the valley is the Mount of Olives. During His triumphal entry Jesus descended the mount into the Kidron Valley and then ascended into the city. The garden of Gethsemane was on the western slope of the mount and opposite the temple area.

According to tradition, Golgotha was northwest of the city, but many evangelicals have accepted Gordon's Calvary to be the true place of the crucifixion, a site due north and further away from the city. Jerusalem was the required location for Christ's death. The general vicinity is mentioned first in Genesis 22:2, where the Lord commanded Abraham to go to the land of Moriah to sacrifice Isaac on one of the mountains. After the Lord stayed him from sacrificing Isaac and provided a ram as a substitute, Abraham named that place "The LORD Will Provide" (Gn 22:14a). Moses (as writer of Genesis) then added, "so today it is said: 'It will be provided on the LORD's mountain" (Gn 22:14b). This refers to God's provision of salvation in Jesus' crucifixion. Second Chronicles 3:1 explains that Solomon built the temple on Mount Moriah, "the rocky outcropping . . . located just north of the ancient city of David."[6] Thus, Jesus' death was on the same mount and points back to Abraham and the promise that in him and his seed all the nations of the earth would be blessed (Gn 12:3; 22:18; Gl 3:18).

Conclusion

Bible students should study the Gospels using various resources for gaining familiarity with NT geography. Increasing in knowledge of the geographical setting of the Gospels promotes love for God's word and increases one's appreciation for His redemptive plan for the earth. God has connected the geographical setting of the Gospels to the gospel message that went forth from that land. The function of the land as a bridge between three continents, the prominence of Jesus' ministry in Galilee of the Gentiles, His ministry to those of Samaria, and His crucifixion on Mount Moriah point to the inclusion of people from every nation into His church. A theological understanding of the geographical setting of the Gospels points to the geographical setting for the advance of the gospel itself—the entire world.

---

6. Chad Brand, Charles Draper, and Archie England, eds., *Holman Illustrated Bible Dictionary* (Nashville: Broadman & Holman, 2003), s.v., "Moriah."

The Religious Milieu in the Gospels

Mark E. Taylor

A basic understanding of the religious milieu from which Christianity emerged is essential for an informed reading of the Gospels. At the risk of oversimplification, scholars often discuss such a vast topic under general headings like "Judaism" and "Paganism."[1] The former seems to be more relevant for the purposes of this essay since it is in the Gospels that one particularly encounters the religious matrix of Judaism: the religious sects (Pharisees, Sadducees), the focal points of religious life (temple, synagogue), the festivals (Passover, Tabernacles), and the symbols of Jewish national identity (Sabbath observance, dietary laws, circumcision). However, since the earliest followers of Jesus encountered a wide assortment of pagan philosophies and religious options as they carried the good news throughout the Mediterranean world, the latter category, "Paganism," is not entirely beyond the scope of our inquiry. Therefore, what follows is a description of the religious environment of the Greco-Roman world more generally as the context in which Christianity emerged and spread and then, more specifically, the shape of Judaism in first-century Palestine.[2]

Hellenistic Religions of the Greco-Roman World[3]

In the ancient Greco-Roman world, religion was inseparable from other areas of life, intricately woven into the fabric of society; it was the air that people breathed. By the time of the NT, traditional mythology was on the decline, new belief systems were emerging, and, much like our own world, a staggering amount of religious diversity pervaded the culture.[4] For centuries philosophy had influenced religious ideas and practice, and several strands of philosophical thought, most indebted to the legacy of Socrates and Plato, exerted wide influence. The most important were stoicism, Epicureanism, and cynicism.[5]

---

1. For representative examples of this approach, see David A. deSilva, *An Introduction to the New Testament: Contexts, Methods & Ministry Formation* (Downers Grove, IL: InterVarsity, 2004), 73–100; Craig L. Blomberg, *Jesus and the Gospels* (Nashville: Broadman & Holman, 1997), 28–53; Raymond E. Brown, *An Introduction to the New Testament*, in *Anchor Bible Reference Library* (New York: Doubleday, 1997), 74–96; Bruce M. Metzger, *The New Testament: Its Background, Growth, and Content*, 3rd ed. (Nashville: Abingdon, 2003), 48–86; Chris Church, "Religious Background of the New Testament," in *Foundations for Biblical Interpretation* (Nashville: Broadman & Holman, 1994), 509–24.

2. Obviously, space only allows for a summary treatment here. Furthermore, the reader should be aware of the inherent subjectivity of all historical reconstructions. Our sources are limited and scholars continue to debate various aspects of the religious world of the NT. Nevertheless, there are broad areas of consensus and the knowledge gleaned from those who work in the field are enormously helpful to our understanding of Scripture. For perhaps the best up-to-date comprehensive resource for the study of NT backgrounds, the reader should consult Craig A. Evans and Stanley E. Porter, eds., *Dictionary of New Testament Background: A Compendium of Contemporary Biblical Scholarship* (Downers Grove, IL.: InterVarsity, 2000). See also Joel B. Green, Scot McKnight, and I. Howard Marshall, eds., *Dictionary of Jesus and the Gospels* (Downers Grove, IL: InterVarsity, 1992) and David Noel Freedman, ed., *The Anchor Bible Dictionary* (New York: Doubleday, 1992). For an excellent resource targeting a lay readership see Albert A. Bell, *Exploring the New Testament World* (Nashville: Thomas Nelson, 1998).

3. For primary sources for the study of ancient Greco-Roman religions, see David G. Rice and John E. Stambaugh, eds., *Sources for the Study of Greek Religion* (Missoula, MT: Scholars Press, 1980) and Howard Clark Kee, *The New Testament in Context: Sources and Documents* (Englewood Cliffs, NJ: Prentice-Hall, 1984).

4. Blomberg noted that, "Intriguingly, almost every religious option of the first century has its counterpart in today's world; only the names have changed." Blomberg, *Jesus and the Gospels*, 28.

5. See R. W. Sharples, *Stoics, Epicureans, and Skeptics: An Introduction to Hellenistic Philosophy* (New York: Routledge, 1996). In Acts 17:16-34, Luke records Paul's encounter with Epicurean and stoic philosophers in Athens.

Stoicism,[6] arguably the most influential philosophical tradition in NT times, taught that all matter is infused with a "world soul" called *logos*, or "reason."[7] Stoics were pantheistic, that is, they believed God permeates everything. Thus, since everything in life is providentially ordered for the good of the whole, one finds contentment by living in harmony with nature according to reason and by exercising self-control in all circumstances.

Epicureanism, on the other hand, emphasized long-term peace and happiness attained through the cultivation of friendships, the enjoyment of cultural activities, and withdrawal from public life.[8] Anything stressful should be avoided, particularly the fear of death, the gods, and punishment in the afterlife. Thus, Epicureans held that God was unknowable and death ended one's conscious existence. This philosophy generated the famous slogan, "Eat, drink, and be merry, for tomorrow we die" (see Lk 12:19).

Finally, cynicism was counter cultural, promoting a simple, unconventional lifestyle and disdain for social conventions. Cynics objected to wealth and limited their traveling possessions. Similarities between this movement and the teaching of Jesus (Lk 10:4) have led some to identify Jesus as a cynic,[9] but the differences outweigh the similarities.[10]

In addition to Greco-Roman philosophy, there were other important religious movements that roughly coincided with the NT period. The most important were Gnosticism and what has been termed the "mystery religions."

Gnosticism[11] strongly emphasized an antithesis between the spiritual and material world; the material world is inherently evil and only "spirit" is good. This developed into two opposite ethical systems. Some were hedonists and sought only to gratify the desires of the flesh, while others resorted to asceticism, a complete denial of bodily appetites. For gnostics, salvation was the liberation of the soul imprisoned in the body that was attained through a secret knowledge (*gnosis*) as revealed in the cult.

Finally, scholars have classified yet another form of religion that flourished during the Greco-Roman period under the heading "mystery religions," a wide variety of secret organizations often unrelated yet with common belief systems. These cults were exotic and experiential in nature, emphasizing the dying and rising again of the god or goddess and promising the worshiper eternal life in communion with the deity. Because of their elaborate rituals and various forms of baptism and sacred meals, scholars continue to debate their relationship to Christianity.[12]

---

6. Stoicism was founded by Zeno of Citium (335–263 BC) who taught on the outdoor porches (Greek, *stoa*) in Athens.

7. Stoic ideas proved attractive to Christianity because of its emphasis on divine providence and the similarities between the stoic "*logos*" and the "*logos*" of John 1:1-18, translated "Word" with reference to Jesus.

8. See J. M. Rist, *Epicurus: An Introduction* (Cambridge: Cambridge University Press, 1972).

9. J. D. Crossan, *The Historical Jesus: The Life of a Mediterranean Jewish Peasant* (San Francisco: Harper, 1991); and F. G. Downing, *Cynics and Christian Origins* (Edinburgh: T. & T. Clark, 1992).

10. Gregory A. Boyd, *Cynic, Sage, or Son of God?* (Wheaton: Victor, 1995).

11. The term "Gnosticism" refers to a variety of religious movements that stressed salvation through "knowledge" (Gk, *gnôsis*). Scholars continue to inquire into the origins of Gnosticism and its relationship to the Christian era, debating whether or not the movement should be understood as a Christian heresy or an altogether independent religion that assimilated Christian ideas. Prior to the twentieth century, most of our information came from early Christian writers such as Irenaeus, Tertullian, and Hyppolytus, who viewed Gnosticism as a heretical movement, a distortion of true Christianity. But our knowledge of the movement increased greatly with the discovery of the Nag Hammadi Library in Egypt in 1945; see J. D. Turner and A. McGuire, eds., *The Nag Hammadi Library After Fifty Years* (Leiden: E. J. Brill, 1997). The most significant find for NT studies was the *Gospel of Thomas*, a document containing 114 sayings attributed to Jesus. Chronologically, these sources are likely no earlier than the second century, but few doubt that gnostic ideas were present well before then. Thus, scholars often use the terms "proto-Gnosticism" and "incipient Gnosticism." See M. A. Williams, *Rethinking "Gnosticism:" An Argument for Dismantling a Dubious Category* (Princeton, NJ: Princeton University Press, 1996).

12. For a brief overview of the mystery cults see Metzger, *New Testament*, 78–86. For a more detailed treatment the reader should consult Joscelyn Godwin, *Mystery Religions in the Ancient World* (San Francisco: Harper & Row, 1981); Robert Turcan, *The Cults of the Roman Empire* (Oxford: Blackwells, 1996); John B. Noss, *Man's Religions*, rev. ed. (New York & London: Macmillan, 1980).

Judaism

Pre-AD 70 Judaism was more diverse than the rabbinic movement that emerged after the destruction of the temple, yet there were common focal points and unifying principles, such as the centrality of Torah (law), temple worship, and Jewish tradition. Israel's national identity as the "people of God" was shaped through important practices such as Sabbath keeping, dietary laws, and circumcision.[13] In the Gospels, Jesus often challenged these focal points and presented Himself as their fulfillment (see Jn 2:13-22; Mt 5:17-48).[14]

The fundamental expression and unifying principle of Judaism was the keeping of Torah. Jews would daily recite the *Shema* (see Dt 6:4-9; 11:13-21; Nm 15:37-41) as an expression of their belief and commitment to the one God. This Jesus affirmed when questioned about the greatest commandment, to which He added Leviticus 19:18; taken together, these two commandments, love of God and neighbor, summarize the intent of the Law and Prophets (Mt 22:34-40).

The Jewish temple was inseparable from the commitment to Torah. It was an impressive and magnificent complex (see Mk 13:1) dedicated to worship and sacrifice[15] and maintained by the priests and Levites.[16] While Jesus affirmed the temple as the locus of God's presence (Mt 12:4; Lk 6:4), He also exercised His authority over it (Mk 11:15-18 and parallels), promised to replace it (Jn 2:14-22), and predicted its demise (Mk 13:1-3 and parallels).

But since participation in the temple was a rare privilege for most Jews, daily religious life revolved more around the synagogue, which served as the local place of judicial decision, worship, and instruction in the law. The origins of the synagogue are unknown, but it is likely that it emerged in the aftermath of the destruction of the temple by Nebuchadnezzar in 586 BC. The term synagogue appears more than 50 times in the Gospels; it was a customary locus of Jesus' teaching (see Lk 4:15-30).

The festivals also served as a unifying force within Judaism.[17] Three major celebrations occurred annually, each linked to the agricultural cycle and requiring all male Israelites to appear in Jerusalem (see Lv 23). Passover marked the beginning of the wheat and barley harvest, Pentecost the grain harvest, and Tabernacles the end of the olive and grape harvest. By the time of the NT, however, the religious significance was more dominant. Passover celebrated the Israelites deliverance from Egypt; Pentecost was associated with the giving of the Law; and Tabernacles (also called the festival of "Booths") commemorated God's provision for Israel during the wilderness wanderings.[18] Jesus as the fulfillment of the festivals is particularly strong in the Gospel of John. For example, in the context of the Festivals of Tabernacles (see Jn 7–8), with its elaborate water-pouring and lamp-lighting rituals, Jesus proclaimed, "If anyone is thirsty, he should come to Me and drink!" (Jn 7:37-39) and "I am the light of the world" (Jn 8:12). And, of course, Jesus fulfilled Passover as "the Lamb of God, who takes away the sin of the world!" (Jn 1:29,36).

Despite this unifying core within Judaism, there were diverse interpretations regarding how best to express one's commitment to the essentials. The Jewish historian Flavius Josephus (AD 37–100)

---

13. See N. T. Wright, *The New Testament and the People of God* (Minneapolis: Augsburg Fortress, 1989), 224–32. For a comprehensive treatment of Judaism during the time of Jesus, see E. P. Sanders, *Judaism: Practice and Belief, 63 BC–AD 66* (Philadelphia: Trinity Press International, 1992).

14. Blomberg, *Jesus and the Gospels*, 46.

15. The temple in the NT is the Herodian temple, renovated and expanded by Herod the Great (37 BC–4 AD) in order to replace the Solomonic temple after the exile.

16. Throughout its history the temple was vulnerable to foreign hostile powers; it was destroyed by Nebuchadnezzar in 586 BC, desecrated by Antiochus IV (167–66 BC) and Pompey (63 BC), and demolished once again by the Roman armies under Titus (AD 70).

17. H. Schauss, *The Jewish Festivals: History and Observance* (New York: Schocken, 1962).

18. deSilva, *Introduction*, 79.

mentioned three chief religious sects in Palestine: the Pharisees, Sadducees, and Essenes.[19] Only the Pharisees and Sadducees are mentioned in the Gospels. Other religious/political movements include the Zealots and the Herodians. Most Palestinian Jews were unaffiliated with any sect or group and are referred to as the *Am-ha-Aretz,* the "people of the land."[20]

There is no record of the origin of the Pharisees, but it is commonly assumed that they were the successors of the *Hasidim,* pious Jews of the second century BC who vigorously opposed the influence of Greek ideology on Jewish religious life. The exact meaning of the name "Pharisee" is also the subject of debate, but most interpret it to mean "the separated ones." In the Gospels the Pharisees are often mentioned with the scribes—the professional teachers and interpreters of Scripture, the experts in the law.

Modern Christians often assume that the Pharisees were nothing but self-righteous hypocrites, but scholars now rightly caution against such an unqualified conclusion. To be sure, John the Baptist called both the Pharisees and Sadducees a "brood of vipers" (Mt 3:7), and in Matthew, Jesus consistently denounced the Pharisees for their hypocrisy in relation to the Mosaic Law (Mt 6:6,11-12; 23:1-39; see also Mk 3:6; Jn 11:47-57).[21] But Luke presents the Pharisees in a favorable light on a number of occasions (Lk 7:36-37; 13:31), and in John, Nicodemus, a Pharisee, demonstrated a favorable attitude toward Jesus.

The Pharisees were composed primarily of laymen who sought to apply the Torah to every area of life (eating, tithing, Sabbath legislation, and vows). Subsequently, they developed a large body of oral law, the "traditions of the elders" (Mk 7:3,5; Mt 15:2)[22] that often brought them into conflict with Jesus. They believed in a combination of predestination and freewill, the immortality of the soul, a bodily resurrection, future punishments and rewards, angels and demons, and the supreme authority of both Scripture and oral tradition.

By contrast, the Sadducees, a small group composed of the well-to-do elite of priestly heritage, denied immortality, the resurrection, angels, and demons. They emphasized the freedom of the human will and affirmed only that doctrine demonstrably based upon the books of Moses. Jesus opposed them by demonstrating the truth of resurrection, citing Exodus 3:6 (see Mt 12:18-27). Although small in numbers, the Sadducees exerted significant influence politically and religiously. They were educated men of prominent status and wealthy landowners centered in Jerusalem. Unlike the Pharisees, they had no following among the masses. And due to their strong priestly connections, they disappeared from the scene after the destruction of the temple in AD 70.

The third major sect, the Essenes, is not mentioned in the NT, although it is likely that Jesus and His disciples interacted with them. Interest in this sect increased significantly with the discovery of the Dead Sea Scrolls at Qumran. Described by Josephus alongside the Pharisees and Sadducees, most Essenes were withdrawn from society, intensely devoted to the law, and apocalyptic in their outlook. They were highly deterministic in their theology and rigidly structured in practice. Prospective members were subjected to extensive and formal initiation procedures, a process

---

19. See Josephus, *Antiquities of the Jews, 18.1.2-4, 13.10.6* and *Jewish War 1.5.2, 2.8.14.* See also G. Stemberger, *Jewish Contemporaries of Jesus: Pharisees, Sadducees, Essenes* (Minneapolis: Fortress, 1995).

20. According to Metzger, the term *"Am-ha-Aretz"* referred in NT times to those who failed to observe the Mosaic law and its ramifications. Thus, the common people were regarded as immoral and irreligious by the Pharisees who avoided all contact with them as far as possible. However, Jesus was friendly with this class and freely associated with them, making Him the object of animosity by the religious leaders of His day. See Metzger, *New Testament,* 56–57.

21. Many modern day scholars assume that this consistent negative assessment represents the later bias of the predominantly Gentile church against the Jews. However, as Blomberg pointed out, "One must be alert to the diversity within ancient Judaism so that one neither dismisses the accounts of Jesus' disputes with certain Jews as historically improbable nor assumes that all Jews would have believed or acted the way those specific individuals and groups did." Blomberg, *Jesus and the Gospels,* 43.

22. This oral tradition was later codified in the Mishnah.

lasting three years. There was diversity of expression to the Essene way of life. While the Qumran community was monastic, some Essenes lived in small towns and raised families.[23]

Josephus also mentioned a "fourth sect of the Jewish philosophy,"[24] the Zealots, a revolutionary group that formally organized shortly before the Jewish revolt against Rome in the mid to late 60s. Whether or not one of Jesus' followers was an actual member of the precursors of this movement is unclear (cp. Lk 6:15). One also encounters the "Herodians" in the Gospels (cf. Mk 3:6; 12:13; Mt 22:16) as the enemies of Jesus. The origins of the Herodians are unknown; the term may simply refer to Jews of standing who supported the Herodian rule.[25]

The religious milieu of the NT era was varied and complex, but it is within this diverse religious culture that "the Word became flesh and took up residence among us" (Jn 1:14) and Jesus proclaimed Himself to be "the way, the truth, and the life" (Jn 14:6). Religious pluralism is nothing new. The challenges that confront contemporary Christians are, in fact, the same kinds of challenges that the first followers of Jesus encountered, whether in the mysterious belief systems of paganism or aberrations within our own Judeo-Christian heritage.

---

23. See Josephus *Jewish War, 2.8.2-13, Antiquities 18.1.2-5.*
24. *Jewish War, 2.8.1.*
25. Metzger, *New Testament,* 54.

Jewish Sects of the New Testament Era

Steven L. Cox

The Judaism to which Jesus and the apostles were born was composed of a rich and often conflicted diversity. Some of these groups like the Pharisees, Sadducees, and Zealots are found on the pages of the Gospels. We have become aware of other sects from historical documents discovered in the 20th century. Understanding these diverse groups within Judaism makes possible a more accurate interpretation of the Gospels.

The Jewish Sects

Pharisees

The Pharisees were the largest Jewish sect and had little association with Rome. They were the only sect to survive the Jewish War AD 66–73. There were approximately 6,000 Pharisees in the days of Herod the Great. The two great Pharisee teachers (rabbis) during the last days of Herod (c. 10 BC) were the strict and legalistic Shammai and Hillel—a more moderate man who sought to make the law bearable.

The Pharisees were probably the descendants of the Hasidim (the pious ones). They were concerned with remaining in a state of ritual purity before God and they took seriously their relationship with God. They viewed ritual purity as being of great importance in one's relationship with God. They were ritually clean to the point where they debated over how long an object was defiled and how long it would be before it was clean again.

The Pharisees had a deep concern about the law of God, for they deemed it a joy to keep the law and did not consider it a burden. The Pharisees considered the Ten Commandments, the Pentateuch, and other legal requirements of God in the Old Testament as components of the law. The common people (see *Am ha arets* below) respected the Pharisees for the latter tried to make the law applicable.

The Pharisees interpreted the law by oral traditions, which were interpretations and sayings that were passed on over generations, and in time the law and oral tradition became equally binding. In some instances, tradition was used to get around the intention of the law. An example is Mark 7:11 where *corban* is mentioned. Corban was a legal maneuver in which a Jewish male could get out of the duty of taking care of aged parents (as referred to by Leviticus 1:2 and Numbers 7:13). A person could declare a part of his income as *corban*. The person could dedicate property as given to the glory of God and yet retain possession of that property and the crops of the field that were offered as *corban*.

By the time of Jesus, the Pharisees had developed loopholes in their interpretation of the law. These loopholes were what Jesus attacked in many of the conflicts with the Pharisees. These loopholes were designed to prevent people from breaking the law. They put safeguards around the law so that they could legally break the law without facing the penalty.

The Pharisees had no regard for politics, except when their religious liberty was threatened. They would approve of war only when their religious liberty was in question; however, when they attained religious freedom, they would return to life as normal.

The beliefs of the Pharisees consist of the following: 1) a bodily resurrection at the end of the world; 2) a judgment day for both good and evil people; 3) the existence of angels and demons;

4) a belief that they were the true Israel, God's people; 5) a belief that the Messiah would be kingly (as David); and 6) worship centered in the synagogue, not the temple.

The Scribes (a sub-sect of the Pharisees) studied and sought to understand and interpret the law. The Scribes had three responsibilities: the preservation of the law; instruction of pupils; and the administrators of the law (judges). A small number of Scribes and Pharisees were members of the Sanhedrin.

Sadducees

The Sadducees were an aristocratic and priestly sect that numbered only a few hundred. They were an exclusive social group who did not welcome the poor or middle class among their ranks. As a result, the Sadducees were very unpopular with common folk. They were not concerned with remaining in a state of ritual purity, except in ceremonial exercises. The Pharisees accepted the authority of all of the Old Testament with the exception of the book of Esther; however, the Sadducees accepted only the Pentateuch as authoritative and this was only halfhearted.

The Sadducees were political to the core. They maintained a *status quo* perspective and they aligned themselves to the political/military powers that were in control in order to protect their existence and role in society. High priests came out of this sect. Unlike the Pharisees, the Sadducees refused to make oral tradition binding. The Sadducees dominated the Sanhedrin in number; however, they often voted with the Pharisees because of the latter's popularity with the common people. This sect died out with the destruction of the temple, AD 70.

Most Jews were devout and would do without basic necessities in order to be able to pay this tax. Peasant Jews (*am ha arets*) were faithful in paying a temple tax that was equivalent to two days wages. The Sadducees' lifestyle was supported by the poverty of such people.

The primary center of activity of the Sadducees was the temple. The temple was the bank, depository, and place of commerce (the money-changing and the selling of sacrificial animals at an inflated price) for the Sadducees. The Sadducees did not care that Jesus challenged their interpretation of the law, but they were highly concerned when Jesus became a threat to their commerce and political position.

The beliefs of the Sadducees consisted of the following: 1) a rejection of a bodily resurrection. 2) an acceptance of only the Pentateuch as authoritative; therefore, it was the only Scripture they used; 3) a concern with the things of this world only; therefore, they were materialistic; 4) a rejection of the afterlife; and 5) an acceptance of free-will.

Essenes

The Essenes were a sect that numbered about 4,000[1] at their peak and existed from the second century BC till the end of the first century AD. This Jewish sect is not mentioned in the New Testament. They rejected Herod's temple and priesthood as corruption. Although Essenes generally lived in small communes, some Essenes lived in Jerusalem. In 1947 some of the Dead Sea Scrolls were discovered in a cave (at Qumran) and are linked with the Essene sect. The significance of this discovery is that the Dead Sea Scrolls contained a whole copy of the book of Isaiah, which has been dated approximately one thousand years older than any other existing manuscript of Isaiah, as well as several other canonical and non-canonical writings.

---

1. See Josephus, *Jewish Antiquities*, (*LCL*, vol. 9, trans. by Louis H. Feldman, Cambridge, MA: Harvard University Press and London: William Heinemann, Ltd., 1981), 18.20-1 and Philo, *Every Good Man is Free*, vol. 9, (trans. by F. H. Colson: *Loeb Classical Library*; Cambridge: Harvard University Press and London: William Heinemann, LTD., 1985), 75.

The beliefs of the Essenes were: 1) a rigorous observance of the law, even more so than the Pharisees; 2) an acceptance of all of the OT as well as some apocalyptic writings as authoritative; 3) a nationalistic belief that they were the "true Israel;" 4) a belief in the after life in the manner of the "immortality of the soul"[2]; 5) an expectation of two Messiahs, a kingly one (Davidic) and a priestly one (Aaron); and 6) withdrawal from Jerusalem and the rest of society. They believed that the temple was corrupt. The Essenes spiritualized the concept of the temple. The temple became the people and not a building; therefore, the law keepers were the people of God.

The Zealots

The Zealot movement began in AD 6 by Judas the Galilean, who opposed the payment of taxes by Jews to Caesar which was viewed as treason against Yahweh, the true king. The original Zealot movement was crushed, but the spirit lived and was expressed in occasional raids and attacks on Romans. A rebirth of Zealotism led to the revolt of AD 66–73 and was briefly revived by the bar Kokhba rebellion in AD 132–135.

The Zealots were revolutionaries who desired the independence of the Jewish nation, both politically and religiously. The Zealots were very nationalistic and in order to gain the backing of other Jewish groups they were religious to the point when it would be beneficial for political independence, just as the Pharisees were politically oriented only when they were seeking religious freedom. Although the Zealots did have limited organization, they were not an autonomous political party, but they were an underground organization. A person could be a Zealot and also be affiliated with any other Jewish sect except the Sadducees.

The Zealots sought to upset the *status quo,* and they were pragmatic in their methods. First-century Palestine was like a powder keg and with their Messianic fervor, Zealots were all too ready to instigate a revolt against the Romans.

Therapeutae

This group took their name from the Greek word *therapeuo,* which means "to heal." The Therapeutae (Therapeutrides for the female members) were mentioned by Philo and were a group of Jews who lived near Alexandria, Egypt.[3] They were concerned with the intellectual and philosophical aspects of the law.

Baptist Sects

These were groups of Jews who had various forms of baptismal rites, primarily immersion. They obeyed the law in a similar fashion as the Pharisees. They stressed the spiritual aspect of baptism. It is important to note that most religions had some sort of baptism.

The entire six sects, above, make up less than 10% of the population of Palestine.

Am ha Arets

The *am ha arets* were common people who were not bothered by legalism, for they were more concerned with death, disease, paying taxes, and making a living. They paid the temple tax without question, for they were moralists who respected religious leaders, although the religious leaders

---

2. Immortality of the soul is not a Christian or Jewish doctrine. It comes from the Greek belief that a person has a soul, and when a person dies the soul goes on to its maker. A person is a duality in Greek philosophy. See Phil Logan, "Immortality," in *Holman Illustrated Bible Dictionary*, edited by Chad Brand, Charles Draper, and Archie England (Nashville: Broadman & Holman, 2003, 810.
3. Philo, *The Special Laws* (trans. F. H. Colson: *LCL*; Cambridge, MA: Harvard University Press and London: William Heinemann, Ltd., 1999 rpt.), 4.191; Philo, *On the Contemplative Life or Suppliants*, vol. 9, 1-90.

did not care for them. The *am ha arets* found Jesus to be their friend. Many of this group followed Jesus, and Jesus was criticized by the religious authorities because He associated Himself with them. Peter and John were of the *am ha arets*. The *am ha arets* had the reputation of being ignorant and unlearned (Acts 4:13).

A Unity in Judaism

Although there was much diversity in first century Judaism, there existed a unity in Judaism. The basic beliefs in which all Jews shared: 1) a belief in only one God; 2) a sense of nationalism; and 3) an emphasis on the importance of the law. The law was central to all sects, for it was given by God. The law was a means of expressing one's relationship with God.

The activities in which all Jews participated: 1) an understanding of the temple as God's house, abode, pavilion, and place of sacrifice; 2) circumcision was practiced by all Jewish males; 3) prayer; 4) Sabbath laws; and 5) an observance of dietary regulations (they refused to eat pork).

The Gospels in the Light of Qumran and the Dead Sea Scrolls

This article examines the Gospels of Matthew, Mark, and Luke in light of the documents from the Qumran area of Israel. These documents are commonly known as the "Dead Sea Scrolls" (DSS). An analysis will be made of any connections between the NT Gospels and the Qumran scrolls. Also, an attempt will be made to draw conclusions from these possible connections. One difficulty in this study relates to the fact that the Gospels and the scrolls share a common heritage—the Jewish Scriptures and culture. Therefore, it is logical to assume that an overlap would exist in vocabulary and themes. This common ground would occur although the Gospel content and the scroll content may have no direct or verifiable connection. Also, the fragmentary nature of many of the scroll documents makes it difficult to draw definitive conclusions.

The Nature of the Qumran Materials

(a) Geographic Background

The region of Qumran (Khirbet Qumran) has remains that date back to the eighth century BC. The beginnings of a water system date to this period, though originally the Qumran water system was more of a cistern than the later aqueducts and reservoir system. The area of Qumran may be identified with the biblical "*Ir ha Melah*" or "City of Salt" around 130 BC. After this time Qumran experienced extensive and systematic growth in infrastructure. The manuscripts discovered in the Qumran area caves possibly belonged to the community of this time.[1]

During the war for Jewish independence from the control of Rome, the Qumran area was apparently stormed by Roman legionnaires and ruined. Though much of the area was laid waste, a Roman garrison occupied the area for almost twenty years. Jewish soldiers under Bar-Kokhba occupied the ruins from about AD 132 to 135.

The main building on the Qumran site was constructed of large undressed stones with a strong tower in the northwestern corner. On the west side was a long room used apparently as a dining facility. Near this room over a thousand ceramic vessels were found. These vessels may have been manufactured on the site, showing one of the trades practiced within the Qumran community.

One room in the main Qumran building was evidently furnished as a writing or document copying room. Flour mills, a stable, a laundry, and various workshops were also uncovered. The occupants apparently aimed to be as self-sufficient as possible. There were apparently no sleeping quarters; tents or caves may have served the occupants for shelter. Near the settlement and separated from it by a wall is a large cemetery.[2]

(b) The Qumran Documents

The scrolls and scroll fragments found at Qumran represent a large library dating from the third century BC to AD 68. This library contained numerous copies of certain works, while other documents were found only in fragmentary form. Tens of thousands of these scroll fragments were

---

1. Jodi Magness, *The Archaeology of Qumran and the Dead Sea Scrolls* (Grand Rapids: Eerdmans, 2002), 24–28.
2. Cecil Roth, ed., *Encyclopedia Judaica*, vol. 13 (Jerusalem: Encyclopedia Judaica, 1972), s.v., "Qumran," by Frederick Fyvie Bruce.

written in three different languages: Hebrew, Aramaic, and Greek. Though this body of materials is now commonly referred to as the Dead Sea Scrolls, less agreement remains on the specifics of what the Qumran library contains. The chief categories represented among the Dead Sea Scrolls are: 1) works contained in the Hebrew Bible—all of the books of the Bible are represented in the DSS collection except Esther; 2) *apocryphal* or *pseudepigraphal works*—those works commonly omitted from the Bible; and 3) *sectarian works*—scrolls related to a monastic community. These works include ordinances, biblical commentaries, apocalyptic visions, and liturgical works.[3]

While the group producing the sectarian scrolls is believed by many to be the Essenes, other scholars state that too little evidence remains to support the view that one sect produced all of the sectarian material. Perhaps a fourth category of scroll materials should be recognized. This material is neither biblical, apocryphal, nor "sectarian." In the view of these scholars, such scrolls, which may include "Songs of the Sabbath Sacrifice," should be designated simply as contemporary Jewish writing.[4]

The Gospels of Matthew and Luke and the Qumran Materials

Although scholars disagree on the level of connection between the Qumran materials and the NT documents, some interesting parallels exist between the Dead Sea Scrolls and the NT Gospels. One connection appears to tie Matthew 11:4-6, Luke 7:22, and Qumran document 4Q521. (Materials found in cave four of Qumran are designated "4Q." This document is number 521 from Qumran cave four.) A comparison of the Gospel passages and the Qumran document shows several apparent connections.

Matthew 11:4-6

Jesus replied to them, "Go and report to John what you hear and see: the blind see, the lame walk, those with skin diseases are healed, the deaf hear, the dead are raised, and the poor are told the good news. And if anyone is not offended because of Me, he is blessed."

Luke 7:22

He replied to them, "Go and report to John the things you have seen and heard: The blind receive their sight, the lame walk, those with skin diseases are healed, the deaf hear, the dead are raised, and the poor have the good news preached to them."

Qumran 4Q521:

[The hea]vens and the earth will listen to His Messiah, and none therein will stray from the commandments of the holy ones. Seekers of the L-rd, strengthen yourselves in His service! All you hopeful in (your) heart, will you not find the L-rd in this? For the L-rd will consider the pious (hasidim) and call the righteous by name. Over the poor His spirit will hover and will renew the faithful with His power. And He will glorify the pious on the throne of the eternal Kingdom. He who liberates the captives,

---

3. James H., Charlesworth, ed., *The Dead Sea Scrolls: Hebrew, Aramaic, and Greek Texts with English Translations*, vol. 6B. *Pesharim, Other Commentaries, and Related Documents* (Tübingen: Mohr Siebeck, 2002). (See the indices in Charlesworth.)
4. *Encyclopedia Judaica*, vol. 13, s.v., "Qumran," by Bruce.

restores sight to the blind, straightens the b[ent] And f[or] ever I will clea[ve to the h]opeful and in His mercy, . . .

And the fr[uit . . .] will not be delayed for anyone. And the L-rd will accomplish glorious things which have never been as [He . . .] For He will heal the wounded, and revive the dead and bring good news to the poor. . . He will lead the uprooted and knowledge . . . and smoke (?).

James Trimm stated of this seeming connection:

The existence of so many common phrases both in the Dead Sea Scrolls and in the New Testament is of the utmost importance. Some of these phrases may be idioms of first-century Hebrew and Aramaic. Other phrases may be technical theological terms used in discussing Jewish religion and mysticism in the first century. We cannot, of course, be certain if any or all of these terms were Essene terms, or if they were common to Judaism in general. What we can be certain of is that the presence of these terms in the New Testament proves its first century Jewish origin.Moreover, the presence of these terms in non-New Testament Jewish literature of the same time period will help us to better understand what these terms meant to the first-century Semitic mind.[5]

While several common phrases do exist, this Qumran fragment could be connected to yet another source. This source would be biblical, but it would not be from the NT. A comparison to the writings of the prophet Isaiah shows many of the same similarities that the Matthew and Luke passages showed.

Isaiah 62:1-2

I will not keep silent because of Zion, and I will not keep still because of Jerusalem until her righteousness shines like a bright light, and her salvation like a flaming torch. Nations will see your righteousness, and all kings your glory. You will be called by a new name that the LORD's mouth will announce.

The evidence is at best inconclusive. 4Q521 could be one of three things. It could be a fragment of a copy of Matthew's (or Luke's) Gospel. It could be a fragment of the book of Isaiah. And finally, 4Q521 could be a commentary of some form. If it is indeed a commentary, it would be hard to determine whether it is commenting on the text of one of the Gospels or the text of the book of Isaiah. Due to the overwhelming Jewish scriptural materials at Qumran, the weight of evidence would seem to connect this fragment to Isaiah before it would be connected to a NT Gospel.

The Gospel of Mark and the Qumran Materials

For decades suggestions have been made that the Qumran fragment 7Q5 may be the Gospel passage Mark 6:52-53. The debate on this issue is complicated by the limited nature of the material in question. Only one clear word exists in the fragment—*kai*. Only six other letters are undisputed: *tw* (line 2), *t* (line 3, immediately after the *kai*), *nh* (line 4), *h* (line 5).

Daniel Wallace said:

---

5. James Scott Trimm, "Nazarenes, Qumran and the Essenes," *The Society for the Advancement of Nazarene Judaism (Netzari Yehudim) (N.d.): 1.*

(1) To build a case on such slender evidence would seem almost impossible. . . . But to identify this as Mark 6:52-53 requires two significant textual emendations (*tau* for *delta* in a manner which is unparalleled; and the dropping of *ejpiV thVn gh'n* even though no other MSS omit this phrase); and (2) unlikely reconstructions of several other letters. Add to this that the MS is from a *Qumran* cave and that it is to be dated no later than 50 CE and the case *against* the Marcan proposal seems overwhelming. If it were not for the fact that José O'Callaghan is a reputable papyrologist and that C. P. Thiede is a German scholar, one has to wonder whether this hypothesis would ever have gotten more than an amused glance from the scholarly community.[6]

Though much scholarly debate centers around this minute fragment, 7Q5 does hold out the distinct possibility that some NT documents are contained within the DSS corpus. No definite conclusion can be drawn from this small fragment but the possibility of 7Q5 being Mark 6:52-53 exists.

Conclusion

The concluding matters related to this subject revolve around two key points: how the DSS materials impact the NT and how the NT impacts the DSS and Qumran. Definitive conclusions are difficult to draw because of the paucity of evidence.

Even before examining the DSS and Qumran's impact on the corpus of the NT, it should be understood that no expectations exist that new Gospel information will be brought to light. In other words, since the NT canon is closed, materials from the DSS would not add to the body of the NT. However, NT documents discovered at Qumran would shed light on the accuracy of the transmission process and help in the evaluation of the accuracy of later copies of NT documents.

If DSS materials do turn out to be biblical in nature, this would have a major impact on the study of the Qumran community. Links between Qumran and biblical figures such as John the Baptist have long been theorized, but a definite connection would force a reinterpretation of Qumran by many contemporary scholars.

Again the major difficulty lies in the fact that the DSS materials and the NT Gospels share a common heritage and literature: the Jewish Scriptures. These common traits show the interrelationship of the NT and the DSS. The jury, however, is still out as to whether the Gospels are a part of the Qumran library.

---

6. Daniel Wallace, "7Q5: The Earliest NT Papyrus?" *Biblical Studies* (2000): 1. See also Carston Peter Thiede, *The Earliest Gospel Manuscript? The Qumran Fragment 7Q5 and Its Significance for New Testament Studies* (London: Paternoster Studies, 1992), 40–41, n. 31.

The Synoptic Problem/Question

Daniel L. Akin

The question of the relationship between the Gospels is often discussed but not easily answered. This is especially true when attention is focused on the Gospels of Matthew, Mark, and Luke—the popularly designated "Synoptic Gospels."

The term *synoptic* means to see together or to view from a common perspective. The first three Gospels are so designated because they present the life and ministry of Jesus from a common point of view that is different from that of the Gospel of John, whose content is 92% unique. Further, John's Gospel, written between AD 80 and 95, is usually dated later than the Synoptics, and no extensive literary dependence is readily discerned. In contrast, the Synoptics often use similar vocabulary and word order, tend to follow the same outline, and record similar material from the life and teachings of Jesus. Sometimes their accounts are almost identical. However, at other times important differences are clearly evident. This phenomena has given rise, especially in the modern era, to what is called the "Synoptic Problem" or "Synoptic Question."

How then are we to understand and explain what appears to be an unmistakable literary relationship among the first three Gospels? Several theories have surfaced that attempt to explain these similarities. Four stand out as the most prominent.

Primitive Gospel Theory

Also known as the Ur-gospel theory, this position was first posited by Gotthold E. Lessing in 1778 and suggests that the three biblical or canonical Gospels drew their material from an earlier, more primitive gospel written in Aramaic. Johann G. Eichhorn elaborated on Lessing's theory in 1794, suggesting AD 35 as the date of origin for this primitive—though no longer extant—gospel.

There have been unfruitful and untenable ramifications of this model. Eichorn eliminated eyewitness authority for the existing Synoptic Gospels, claiming that the "primitive" gospel was written by a student of one of the apostles. This work was used as the basis for other gospel accounts prior to the writing of the Gospels as we know them today. Matthew, Mark, and Luke then used these gospels as the sources for their respective works, thus explaining the similarities seen within the Synoptics.

That an early gospel existed is certainly possible. However, such a theory has little if any historical support and, further, it both begins and concludes with extensive speculation. The idea originally postulated by Lessing had in and of itself one main flaw: if Matthew, Mark, and Luke drew from the same source (the Ur-gospel), why then do their Gospels differ as they do? Lessing's theory is therefore unsatisfactory.

Eichhorn's notion of multiple gospels succeeding the Ur-gospel creates additional problems as well. While it seems to solve the above flaw, Eichhorn's claim that the extant Gospels are simply translations of non-existent, third-hand accounts undermines the authority historically given to the authors of the Synoptics. They are relegated to mere scribes void of any eyewitness credibility. Such a ramification leads to further logical conclusions that both compromise the integrity of the Gospels and are inadequate to account for the historical data.

Oral Tradition Theory

J. G. von Herder (1744–1803) advanced the theory that an "oral gospel" or tradition of material was behind the Synoptic Gospels—that the Gospel material was passed along by word of mouth before being written down. This oral gospel would have originated with the disciples, passed along throughout Palestine between AD 35 and 40 before spreading to other parts of the Roman Empire. Finally, several decades after its inception, the need for a permanent, written gospel arose. This led to the writing of the Synoptic Gospels.

The necessity for a concrete gospel was two-fold. First, the disciples were aging, and there was a need to secure an accurate, eyewitness account of Jesus' teachings. Second, a unified and definitive set of teachings was needed to combat early church heresy and to serve as the foundational basis of Christian doctrine. The result was the oral tradition finally being transcribed into written form and subsequently published. The new, written material was then used by Matthew, Mark, and Luke in the writing of their Gospels, thus explaining, according to Herder and other oral traditionalists, the similarities among them.

That an early, orally transmitted form of Jesus' teachings existed is not debated. There most certainly is some plausibility in this theory. However, in and of itself, this theory is unable to account for the existence of early written accounts (see Luke 1:1-3), the different order of events discovered in the Synoptics, and the variations in form, content, vocabulary, grammar, and word order that are present in the Synoptic Gospels. Thus, while not wanting to minimize the influence of a common oral tradition upon the writers of the Synoptics, the phenomena of Synoptic Gospels seems to require more than a common oral tradition.

Markan Priority

The Markan priority theory was not advocated until the nineteenth century. However, due in large to the rise of historical criticism (especially the works of H. J. Holtzmann in 1863 and B. H. Streeter in 1924), it has become without question the most popular hypothesis among contemporary New Testament scholars. This model initially began as a two-source theory, though it is now usually expanded into a four-source theory.

Here Mark is viewed as the first Gospel written and is the foundation for Matthew and Luke, both of whom incorporated much of Mark. Matthew and Luke also utilized another source (usually assumed to have been written) commonly called Q, from the German word *Quelle,* meaning *source.* This second source is said to account for about 250 verses of mostly Jesus' teaching material that is common to Matthew and Luke but not in Mark. Expanding the two-source theory, a supposed M-source is thought to account for material unique to Matthew, and an L-source is hypothetically set forth to account for material peculiar to Luke, thus explaining the additional material in their respective Gospels.

The case for Markan priority primarily stems from the vast amount of material seen in both Matthew and Luke that is together repeated in Mark's Gospel. However, there are other reasons Markan priority is commonly affirmed. First, many scholars insist Mark contains harder readings than Matthew and Luke, as the theological content of Mark is said to be more difficult. Rather than Mark taking the less complex passages in Matthew and Mark and making them more difficult, many scholars now suggest that Matthew and/or Luke edited Mark to make the readings easier.

Second, Mark is said to have the poorer Greek. Mark contains frequent redundancies, which are speculated to have been eliminated in the Gospels written by Matthew and Luke. Similar to above, it is easier to envision Matthew and Luke improving upon Mark's Greek than to think Mark used Matthew and/or Luke and made the Greek more difficult and cumbersome.

Third, Mark's theology is less developed than the other two Synoptics. One example of this is the occurrence of the term "Lord" (*kyrios*). Mark uses this term only six times. Matthew uses *kyrios* not only in those *same* six instances but also an additional twenty-four times. Moreover, Luke uses this title for Jesus even more frequently than did Matthew. Supporters of Markan priority argue that it is easier to understand Matthew and Luke adding this term to their accounts than for Mark to omit it so frequently.

Finally, Mark is the shortest Gospel. While Mark contains 661 verses, Luke contains 1,149 and Matthew has 1,068. It is maintained that this can be explained easier by assuming Matthew and Luke chose to add additional information to Mark's account than to hold that Mark omitted so much material.

Though Markan priority is the most popular theory today, this model does face a number of difficulties. Two such problems stand out as major obstacles that tend to weaken the argument that Mark was the first Gospel written. First, the early church tradition is quite unanimous that Matthew was the primary Gospel (i.e., Clement of Alexandria, Irenaeus, Eusebius, and Augustine). Virtually no early support can be found to favor Mark as the initial Gospel writer. Furthermore, much of the support for Markan priority rests on the shoulders of the completely conjectured and unsubstantiated sources of Q, L, and M. There is currently no firm, historical evidence to support their existence. These two objections alone are enough for a number of scholars to remain skeptical of the Markan priority theory.

Matthean Priority

Matthean priority was the dominant position within the church from the first century until the Enlightenment. Matthew was seen as the first Synoptic, usually Luke, who utilized Matthew, as the second, and Mark as the third. Mark was viewed as an abbreviated combination or conflation of Matthew and Luke. The preaching of Peter was also seen as a significant influence on Mark's Gospel, though this is true for most New Testament scholars regardless of how they resolve the Synoptic Problem.

Though the Matthean priority theory was first proposed by H. Owen in 1764, it received the more popular name, "The Griesbach Hypothesis," from its main advocate, Johann J. Griesbach (1783). It has since received a considerable revival of interest due to the influence of William R. Farmer's publication of *The Synoptic Problem* in 1976.

Like the Markan priority model, significant support exists for the argument that Matthew was the initial Gospel. First, that Matthew was written first was virtually the unanimous view of the early church. The opinion of most church fathers, such as Irenaeus and Origen, was that Matthew initially wrote a Gospel in Hebrew or Aramaic that was later translated into Greek. This was the view of Jerome and Augustine. Further, Clement of Alexandria stated that the first Gospel written was the one containing the genealogies. There is no ancient evidence that concludes Mark was written before Matthew. Any such theory must overcome the overwhelming witness of the early Christian fathers.

Second, this theory can account for the literary relationship that exists among the Synoptic Gospels without postulating hypothetical documents that have little or no historical support (e.g., a Q source). The phenomenon of agreement among Matthew, Mark, and Luke is explained as follows: Matthew and Luke agreements against Mark occur when Luke follows Matthew and Mark deviates from both sources. Matthew and Mark agreements against Luke occur when Luke deviates from Matthew but Mark does not. Likewise, the agreements seen in Luke and Mark result when

Luke departs from his Matthean source, but Mark follows Luke. No hypothetical documents are needed.

Still, there are reasons why many modern New Testament scholars find the Griesbach Hypothesis problematic. For example, there are certain Gospel agreements that appear to be better explained by the priority of Mark. Most of these examples are found when Matthew and Mark deviate from Luke's account and with Mark-Luke agreements against Matthew. However, most of these conflicts are resolved when Luke is assumed as the second Gospel written. Further, Mark contains redundancies that can be explained by assuming the two-document hypothesis.

While many scholars believe the Synoptic Problem has been resolved by the Markan priority hypothesis, this judgment may need to be reevaluated. The fact remains that all of our different theories may put more weight on the historical data than is fairly warranted. The early church position, though not definitive, may deserve a renewed hearing. Nevertheless, while we do not know for sure how the first three Gospel writers possibly interacted with one another or what sources may have influenced their work, we can be confident that the result of their work has given us three inspired, truthful, and authoritative portraits of the Lord Jesus Christ. They write from different perspectives and with different theological emphases, but as a whole they present a complementary portrait of God's Messiah/King and the Savior of the world, the Lord Jesus Christ. In this, all students of Scripture can confidently rest.

Critical Methodologies: Source Criticism, Form Criticism, Redaction Criticism

Gerald Cowen

Matthew, Mark, and Luke are called the Synoptic Gospels because of the similar accounts they present of the life of the Lord Jesus. The extensive agreement between the three causes many to conclude that there is direct literary dependence among the three Gospels. The primary argument for this dependence is that this similar wording is in Greek, which was certainly not the original language. The matter is complicated by the considerable number of differences between the accounts. The difficulty of explaining both the similarities and differences between the accounts has been called the Synoptic Problem.

Source Criticism

The early church believed that the Gospel writers depended on their personal memories and eye-witness accounts, and for most of the history of the church that was the accepted view, at least until modern times. The most popular theory today concerning the origin of the Synoptics is the two-source theory. This view concludes against tradition that Mark was written first. Matthew and Luke then relied on Mark and another source called Q (from the German *Quelle*), which has now been lost.

Some of the arguments used to support this view are these: 1) Most of the material in Mark is found in Matthew (about 90%) and Luke (about 50%). It is argued that it is more likely that Matthew and Luke would have expanded Mark rather than Mark abbreviating the others. 2) Matthew and Luke do not agree with each other when they diverge from Mark. 3) The order of the events in Mark is original because when Matthew departs from Mark, Luke supports Mark's order, and when Luke departs from Mark's order, Matthew supports Mark. 4) Mark is more primitive than the others. The inclusion of eight Aramaic words to Matthew's one is used to support this conclusion. 5) The distribution of Markan and non-Markan material in Matthew and Luke shows their dependence on Mark. Matthew uses Mark as his framework and Luke alternates his material in Markan and non-Markan blocks.

Although the two-source theory has been popular for almost a century, there are several arguments that work against it. The first problem concerns the sections where Matthew and Luke argue against Mark. There are approximately 230 of these. While this number is less than the number of agreements between Matthew and Mark against Luke, and the number of arguments of Luke and Mark against Matthew, they are sufficient to make one question the two-source theory.

A second problem is what has been called the "great omission." If Luke used Mark as a source, there is no good explanation as to why he omitted all of the material from Mark 6:45–8:26. While one may suppose reasons why Luke omitted this important material, it is just as easy to suppose that he did not have it in front of him.

A third problem is related to the existence and the content of Q. There is no objective evidence that Q ever existed as a single written source, and, if it did, how does one explain the changes made by Matthew and Luke?

A fourth consideration is the testimony of the early church, which clearly says that Matthew the apostle wrote the first Gospel. To accept the priority of Mark is to reject the testimony of many of the church fathers. A greater problem is to conclude that Matthew, an eyewitness, depended on

Mark who was not an eyewitness. It seems to deny the fact that an eyewitness could tell the story without any help.

This theory also ignores the probability that Matthew and Mark must have spent time together in Jerusalem after Pentecost, since the church met in Mark's mother's house.[1] Luke also spent time with Mark in his travels with Paul (Col 4:10,14; Phm 24). This could surely explain some of the similarities. Other issues that should be considered are the fact that at least some of Jesus' disciples took notes on His teaching, and that Jesus had His disciples commit these teachings to memory.

While most today support the two-source theory, there are many able scholars who support the priority of Matthew. Since there are so many uncertain factors, the issue should remain an open question.

The Four-Source Hypothesis

```
        Mark                          Q

M*                                              L*



        Matthew                    Luke
```

*omit M and L and the two-source theory remains

Form Criticism

This variety of Gospel criticism came into existence in the early twentieth century with the works of Rudolf Bultman (1921), Martin Debelius (1919), and K. L. Schmidt (1919). Form criticism rests upon several assumptions. 1) It accepts the conclusions of source criticism that there are at least two written sources for the Gospels: Mark, Q, and possibly more such as M and L. 2) It assumes that the chronological and geographical framework of the Synoptics is not historically accurate. 3) A third assumption is that the different units in the traditions (pericopes) circulated separately during a 40- to 60-year period of oral tradition, from the ascension of Christ to the writings of the Gospels. 4) The practical interest of the Christian community is the guiding factor that led to the production and presentation of these forms. 5) The Gospel material can be classified according to form. 6) The original form of individual pericopes can be recovered by applying the laws of tradition.

The object of form criticism is to study these individual units of the tradition before they were collected and included in the Gospels. Form critics classify the pericopes into categories of oral tradition such as: 1) paradigms or pronouncement stories, 2) tales or miracle stories, 3) sayings and parables, 4) legends or stories about Jesus, and 5) myths.[2] Then, it attempts to discover the historical situation (*Sitz im Leben*) in the early church that formed the background to each form. It tries to push the investigation of the origins of the Gospels beyond the written period to the oral

---

1. Robert L. Thomas and Stanley N. Gundry, eds., *The NIV Harmony of the Gospels* (San Francisco: Harper and Row, 1988), 265.
2. See Darrell L. Bock, "Form Criticism," in David Alan Black and David S. Dockery, eds., *New Testament Criticism and Interpretation* (Grand Rapids: Zondervan, 1991).

period. The more radical critics conclude that the pericopes were produced by the early Christian community, and thus reflect the life of the early church rather than the life of Christ. The forms are clues to their relative historical value.

Radical critics believe the church not only passed on the tradition, but formed the tradition to meet its own needs. It even created some stories about Jesus as needed, and the Gospel writers then used this tradition in an artificial context to serve their own purposes.

Problems Concerning Form Criticism

The greatest roadblock to the acceptance of the tenets of form criticism is the presence of eyewitnesses. The oral period probably lasted only 20 to 30 years rather than 50 to 60. For form criticism to be true, eyewitnesses must be totally ignored and others allowed to invent traditions to their own advantage. This could not happen if eyewitnesses were present. This theory assumes that none of Jesus' disciples ever wrote down His teachings.

The second problem is it presumes that the church was lacking in honesty, so that what really happened and what Jesus actually said are not vital. On the contrary, they should have wanted to preserve the accuracy of the tradition. Paul (1 Co 7:10) claims to be very familiar with the exact words of Jesus. Luke says he received reports from eyewitnesses (Lk 1:1-2). Other references by Luke to eyewitnesses are found in Acts 2:32; 3:15; and 10:41.

A third problem is that form criticism assumes that the early church created and formed its own traditions. For this to happen, Jesus had to have been a weak or remote figure who exercised little influence on the emerging church. The church it seems was not created by Jesus, but created itself. There is no answer, however, to the question, who or what created the church if it did not begin firmly based on the tradition passed down from Jesus Himself. Evidence that demonstrates the weakness of this claim is the presence of major emphases in the Gospels which are seldom used by the church. One example is Jesus' title for Himself: Son of Man. It is bypassed by the church in favor of other titles such as "Lord." The truth is, Christ is greater than the community He founded. It originated with Him and it is His teaching that has been passed down.

Finally, form criticism ignores evidence that the context of the Gospels is rooted in history. Close examination of the sequence of Mark, including the chronological and geographical information, are not artificial. In addition, some parts of the tradition such as the passion narrative circulated as a long, continuous narrative.

In conclusion, the value of form criticism for an evangelical student is not great. Any discipline that causes us to look at Scripture will add some insight, but the results of form criticism have not been spectacular, nor have they advanced the understanding of the gospel to any great degree.[3]

Redaction Criticism

Redaction criticism is an outgrowth of form criticism. Its primary focus is to uncover the theological focus of the Gospel writers. Redaction critics generally do not accept the traditional conclusions concerning authorship of the Gospels. They assume that the names Matthew, Mark, and Luke were pseudonyms used to give the works authenticity. Redaction critics further assume that the theological views of the writers were not necessarily the views of the Christian community as a whole nor do they necessarily represent the specific teachings of Jesus.

---

3. Donald Guthrie, *New Testament Introduction*, rev. ed. (Downers Grove, IL and Leicester, England: Apollos, 1990), 213.

Redaction criticism arose as a separate discipline in the mid-twentieth century. The early formulators were Gunther Bornkamm in his work on Matthew, Willi Marxsen on Mark, and Hans Conzelmann on Luke.

The starting point for redaction criticism is the acceptance of the priority of Mark. It is difficult to analyze any editorial changes Mark may have made because his sources are not available for comparison. However, Marxsen tried to distinguish between the *Sitz im Leben* of Jesus Himself, that of the early church, and that of the Gospel writers. He concluded that Mark "joins, edits, and expands isolated units of tradition in accordance with four guidelines."[4] Marxsen claims that Mark: 1) added the predictions of Christ's death to his narrative, 2) invented the idea of the Messianic secret, 3) coined the term "gospel," and 4) included a geographical preference for Galilee where he expected the *parousia* to happen.

Bornkamm assumed that Matthew was based on the two sources: Mark and Q (which is reconstructed artificially). He assumed the date to be somewhere between AD 80–90 and the place between Syria and Palestine. He saw a conflict between Jewish and Gentile Christianity. Matthew represents Jesus as a teacher who has captured the true essence of the law that was missed by the Pharisees. This new system is given its own title of "church." So Matthew's theology is expanded from Mark's to include the concept of the church, and also takes into account the *parousia* might not be as soon as previously thought.

Conzelmann believed that Luke was written shortly after Matthew. He held that Luke has three periods of time: the time of Israel, the time of Jesus (middle time), and the time of the church. Luke is concerned with middle time. Strangely, he argued that Luke says Satan was not active during the time of Jesus. Luke differs from the other Gospel writers in that he was trying to prepare Christians for a longer wait for the coming of Christ. Therefore, he sets forth ethical standards for Christian living and calls for perseverance.

Each of the Gospel writers took the individual units of the tradition and reshaped them for their own purposes. They were in effect theologians, not historians. In adapting these units of tradition, the Gospel writers connect them in a way that seemed best to them. They attribute to Jesus the teaching that the church needed at that time in order to give their own ideas credibility. They create what is called the realm of faith. Whatever is thought subjectively to be true is counted as true whether it actually happened or not. In other words, the early Christians were motivated by their faith, whatever they strongly believed to be true, such as the resurrection, rather than what actually happened in time, space, and history. It is not then necessary to prove the resurrection if you already *believe* it. To write an actual life of Jesus with historical accuracy is then not important. Redaction critics conclude that the theology in the Gospels is that of the individual writers, not of Jesus.

While evangelicals cannot accept the presuppositions of redaction criticism as a whole, there are some things to be observed by using some of its methodology. If one looks at the Gospels both vertically and horizontally (comparing the wording of each), distinct emphases of writers may become evident. If one studies the seams between stories in the Gospels, makes note of the summary passages and editorial comments, and identifies favorite words and phrases, the purpose of the author may become clearer. However, one should not turn distinctives into contradictions.

---

4. Thomas and Gundry, *The NIV Harmony of the Gospels*, 276.

A Brief History of Hermeneutical Methods Used in the Quest of the Historical Jesus

Robert Stewart

One encounters certain key thinkers and moments in the history of Jesus research. Many of those key moments result from the critical methods significant scholars pioneered or applied.

The Hermeneutics of the Original Quest

Most scholars follow Albert Schweitzer in dating the beginning of the quest of the historical Jesus to 1778, when G. E. Lessing's edition of German scholar Hermann Samuel Reimarus's essay, "On the Aims of Jesus and His Disciples" was published. Prior to Reimarus many harmonies of the Gospels existed, but no scholarly attempt to study the Gospels as historical documents had been made. All that changed with Lessing's posthumous publication of Reimarus's work in a series Lessing named *Fragmente eines Ungenannten* (Fragments from an Unnamed Author), commonly referred to today as the *Wolfenbüttel* Fragments.

Deism's influence upon Reimarus may be seen in his attempt to ground understanding of the historical Jesus in deistic reason (*Vernunft*). Reimarus is consumed with answering one basic question: "What sort of purpose did Jesus himself see in his teachings and deeds?" Reimarus argued that Jesus: 1) was a pious Jew; 2) called Israel to repent; 3) did not intend to teach new truth, found a new religion, or establish new rituals; 4) became sidetracked by embracing a political position; 5) sought to force God's hand; and 6) died alone, deserted by his disciples. What began as a call for repentance ended up as a misguided attempt to usher in an earthly, political kingdom of God.

Reimarus argued that the disciples stole Jesus' body and claimed his resurrection in order to obscure his failed ministry and ensure themselves some standing. Historian Peter Gay wrote that this sort of conspiracy theory is typical of Deism: "Even the sane among the deists had a paranoid view of history and politics: they saw conspiracies everywhere."[1]

In typical deistic fashion, Reimarus concluded that there are "no mysteries" or "new articles of faith" in the teachings of Jesus, but rather, it was the apostles who authored the uniquely Christian doctrines of the New Testament. Reimarus maintained that Jesus' mindset was eschatological in nature and essentially Jewish, but Reimarus wrongly saw Christianity as discontinuous with Judaism.

Reimarus' rejection of miracles and prophecy, the twin pillars of traditional Christian apologetics concerning the deity of Jesus, is a dismissal of the supernatural based on his prior commitment to the deistic worldview, not the influence of literary criticism. In this sense Reimarus can rightly be called *pre-critical.*

In *The Life of Jesus Critically Examined* David Friedrich Strauss employed Georg Wilhelm Friedrich Hegel's historical dialectic to understanding Jesus as well as applying the concept of myth to the Gospels, something his teacher, F. C. Baur, had already done in Old Testament studies. Jesus understood mythically is the synthesis of the thesis of supernaturalism and the antithesis of rationalism. As a committed Hegelian, Strauss maintained that the inner nucleus of Christian faith

---

1. Peter Gay, *Deism: An Anthology* (Princeton: Princeton University Press, 1968), 10.

is not touched by the mythical approach. Strauss intended to critique the Gospels historically and not to destroy the Christian faith.

Although Strauss is not methodologically "critical" in the sense of questioning the order or authorship of the Gospels, his emphasis on the literary nature of the Gospels represents a paradigm shift in Gospel studies. Whereas Reimarus read the Gospels through the lens of natural or supernatural, Strauss proposed two different categories for interpreting the Gospels: mythic or historical. Unlike Reimarus, Strauss believed the apostles were not intentionally deceitful, just subject to their own unconscious mythic imagination and therefore produced poetic, rather than historical or philosophical myth. Historically, Strauss maintained that the biblical narratives were written long after the event and embellished by years of oral retelling and religious reflection.[2]

Strauss's *Life of Jesus* was of such immediate and intense controversy that it cost him his position as a teacher of theology. In his revision, *Das Leben Jesu: für das deutsche Volk*, Strauss abandoned Hegelian categories for moral categories. Eventually Strauss repudiated entirely any attachment to Christianity and died a committed materialist.

Neither Reimarus nor Strauss were concerned about what became the most consuming question for a generation of Jesus scholars to follow: in what order were the Gospels written?

Karl Lachmann was the first to propose, in 1835, that Mark was the earliest of the canonical Gospels. But it was Heinrich Julius Hotzmann who took upon himself the task of approaching the matter systematically. Contra Strauss, Holtzmann insisted that the single most significant task of the historical quest is that of determining the correct order of sources. In *Die Synoptischen Evangelien: Ihr Ursprung und geschichtlicher Charakter* Holtzmann proposed that the evangelists had two written sources available to them, what he calls *Urmarcus* and *Urmatthäus*.

Holtzmann shared a key presupposition of nineteenth-century German liberalism—that the theological elements of the Gospels were later accretions of the early church and that stripping these elements away would reveal Jesus the moral teacher and preacher of a timeless ethic. It can be said that the first quest, the liberal quest, was based largely on an unwarranted optimism concerning the amount of historical knowledge that could be gleaned from the proper application of source criticism.

Albrecht Ritschl and Adolf Harnack understood Jesus primarily in ethical terms. Ritschl taught that Jesus is the bearer of God's ethical Lordship over humanity and that God's kingdom and Jesus' message are ethical in nature. For Harnack Jesus' message of the kingdom emphasized: 1) the kingdom of God and its coming; 2) God the Father and the infinite value of the human soul; and 3) the higher righteousness and the commandment of love.

Ben Meyer held that most Jesus scholars of that day coupled the liberal emphasis upon ethics with an equally liberal "hermeneutic of empathy."[3] The host of imaginative theses that were put forward attempted to trace out the psychological development of Jesus' messianic awareness, allowing the authors to write something akin to a *biography* of Jesus that unfortunately was more dependent upon imagination than historical method.

In 1901 William Wrede published *The Messianic Secret in the Gospels: Forming a Contribution also to the Understanding of Mark,* debunking the psychological theories of 19th century life of Jesus work and maintaining that the Gospels were not to be understood as biographies. In order to explain the presence of the messianic theme in the Gospels, Wrede proposed that Mark was attempting to harmonize history with the beliefs of the post-Easter church which, he said, understood

---

2. This statement is the author's summary of Strauss' position as laid out in pages 39–92 of David Friedrich Strauss, *The Life of Jesus Critically Examined*, ed. Peter C. Hodgson (Life of Jesus Series, ed. Leander E. Keck; trans. George Eliot; Philadelphia: Fortress, 1972).

3. Ben Meyer, *The Aims of Jesus* (London: SCM, 1979), 40.

that Jesus *was made* Messiah at His resurrection, not that He *was revealed* as Messiah through the resurrection.[4] While Wrede allowed that some of Jesus' actions and sayings may have led to speculation of His messiahship prior to the resurrection, Jesus never claimed it for Himself.

Wrede appealed to messianic passages as support for his hypothesis while, at the same time, jettisoning problematic texts by favoring literary-critical questions over historical ones. Predictably, truncated Gospels result in a truncated Jesus, who lacks both messianic consciousness and theological creativity. Consistent with the school of thought that Wrede represented, the *Religionsgeschichtliche Schule,* the focus shifted from Jesus to the communities and traditions behind the text.

The very day in 1901 that Wrede's *Messianic Secret* was published also marked the publication of Albert Schweitzer's *The Mystery of the Kingdom of God: The Secret of Jesus' Messiahship and Passion.* In contrast to Wrede, Schweitzer's Jesus was a heroic figure, along the lines of Nietzsche's cult of the hero (*Übermensch*), who is thoroughly conscious of his messianic role and seeks to usher in the kingdom through his decisive self-sacrifice. Schweitzer saw the messianic themes, which Wrede understood to be later creations, as central to any understanding of Jesus. Tragically, although the idea of resurrection is clearly in the mind of Schweitzer's Jesus, his summary concluded, "On the afternoon of the fourteenth of Nisan, as they ate the Paschal lamb at even, he uttered a loud cry and died."[5]

Schweitzer's first offering was not overly well received, prompting him to write *The Quest of the Historical Jesus: A Critical Study of Its Progress from Reimarus to Wrede* in 1906. Eventually this work became the standard by which all other histories of life of Jesus research would be measured.

Schweitzer did not wish to end historical Jesus research, but instead to redirect it. He valued historical research because of its ability to destroy fictional platforms erected by ecclesiastical dogma and/or enlightenment historicism, including the most monstrous one of all—Jesus as a modern man. For Schweitzer, Jesus was the product of first-century Jewish apocalyptic expectation, not enlightenment rationalism. Historical knowledge of Jesus, according to Schweitzer, results in the recognition of one's inability to know Him through investigation. Instead, Jesus is known most fully in decisive individual commitment.

From the standpoint of biblical criticism and interpretive method, Schweitzer's work is fairly simplistic. In light of his concern with critical history, his lack of concern with source-critical questions is surprisingly non-critical. He accepted the general synoptic narrative as historical and interpreted the Gospels in light of his one guiding principle: thoroughgoing eschatology.

The Hermeneutics behind the Abandonment of the Quest

It is often assumed that Schweitzer's *Quest* ended the first phase of historical Jesus research, but such a position is simplistic. While it is true that Schweitzer offered up a devastating critique of the liberal quest, it was left to others to provide the positive diversion that actually affected its demise.

In 1896 Martin Kähler published *The So-Called Historical Jesus and the Historic Biblical Christ,* in which he maintains that the certainty of faith could not rest on the uncertain and provisional finds of historical research that are subject to new information. Instead of searching for the *historical* Jesus, one should seek the *historic* Jesus, the one who has molded history and contributed to it.

---

4. William Wrede, *The Messianic Secret*, trans. J. C. G. Greig (Cambridge: James Clarke, 1971), 216–19.

5. Albert Schweitzer, *The Mystery of the Kingdom of God: The Secret of Jesus' Messiahship and Passion*, trans. Walter Lowrie (New York: Macmillan Company, 1950), 173.

Influential also in halting the first quest was the *Religionsgeschichtliche Schule,* the history of religions school, and prominent representatives such as Ernst Troeltsch and Wilhelm Bousset.

Troeltsch insisted that, like all religions, Christianity was a historical phenomenon in its own time, with Jesus being no different than other historical figures. He considered Kähler's assertion that faith in Jesus is exempt from historical critique to be naïve. The historian's role is to explain the origin of Christianity in terms of causal events, not to answer theological or metaphysical questions concerning Jesus. As a result, the hermeneutical question changed from "Who was Jesus?" to "How did the early church come to think of Jesus in this way?"

Bousset's answer in *Kyrios Christos* was that the church came to deify Jesus through a historical process of transformation due to its encounter with Hellenism, an encounter in which alien ideas were grafted into Christianity. He maintained that the earliest traditions concerning Jesus contained nothing miraculous and did not proclaim Jesus to be divine.

The shadow of Rudolf Bultmann fell over any attempt to understand twentieth century New Testament theology. As a pioneer of New Testament form criticism, Bultmann saw the Gospels as fragmentary pieces woven together to address particular needs of the early church. This thesis is the driving force behind his search for the oral tradition that lay behind the written pericopae of the Gospels. In *Jesus and the Word* he declared, "I do indeed think that we can now know almost nothing concerning the life and personality of Jesus, since the early Christian sources show no interest in either, are moreover fragmentary and often legendary; and other sources about Jesus do not exist."[6]

Bultmann posited that the origin of certain sayings of Jesus emanated from in-fighting between the Hellenistic and Palestinian Jewish believers and makes our knowledge of Christianity's origins suspect. The result was not only that form criticism, like the history of religions school, focused on something other than Jesus, namely the *Sitz im Leben* of the early church, but also that its foremost proponent announced that historical Jesus research could not succeed.

Bultmann's objections to historical Jesus research were not only methodological, but also philosophical and theological. Influenced as he was by Kierkegaard and Heidegger, as well as the early Karl Barth, Bultmann thought that historical knowledge of Jesus' personhood (*Persönlichkeit*) was secondary in importance to existential knowledge of his word. Bultmann's approach involves first, recognizing the mythological nature of the New Testament and second, demythologizing the myths. Bultmann openly draws upon Heidegger's categories of existence and being to interpret the New Testament. A point often missed is that Bultmann's adoption of these categories stems from his belief that the New Testament demands to be demythologized—that such was the intention of the authors.

Bultmann thus contributed to a decline in historical Jesus research. 1) His form critical method shifted the emphasis from Jesus onto the early Christian communities. 2) His form critical conclusions led to a sense of pessimism concerning historical Jesus research in general. 3) His demythologization shifted the emphasis from history to anthropology. 4) His commitment to existentialism assigned historical knowledge of Jesus to a secondary status, and thus undermined the entire project in general.

Many factors influenced the abandonment of the original quest of the historical Jesus, including: 1) Wrede and Schweitzer's critiques of nineteenth-century liberal views of Jesus; 2) the influence of Martin Kähler; 3) the influence of the history of religions school; 4) the rise of form criticism; and 5) Bultmann's demythologizing hermeneutic.

---

6. Rudolf Bultmann, *Jesus and the Word*, trans. Louise Pettibone Smith and Erminie Huntress Lantero (New York: Scribner's, 1958), 8.

The Hermeneutics of the New Quest of the Historical Jesus

The "New Quest of the Historical Jesus" began with a 1953 address by Ernst Käsemann in which he voiced agreement with Bultmann that the earlier quest was largely impossible and at least partially irrelevant. Käsemann insisted that the primitive church was primarily interested in proclaiming the *kerygma* rather than verifying historical facts concerning Jesus, and that for the early church, as well as Christians today, the reality of their present experience of Jesus as Lord establishes Jesus as a historical figure. He thus argued for a new type of historical inquiry concerning Jesus, one that considers the hermeneutical significance of historical events. Käsemann's solution to the difficult task of historical inquiry was to apply the criterion of dissimilarity to Jesus' preaching in order to separate the authentic from the inauthentic.

Although Käsemann was the initiator of the new quest, James M. Robinson popularized the movement. His 1959 book, *A New Quest of the Historical Jesus,* gave the phrase "new quest" intelligibility in the vocabulary of contemporary historical Jesus research. Robinson focused on the question of how Jesus the proclaimer became Jesus Christ the proclaimed. Along with Käsemann and Robinson, other participants in the new quest include Günther Bornkamm, Norman Perrin, Hans Conzelmann, Ernst Fuchs, and Gerhard Ebeling.

Redaction criticism as developed by Bornkamm and Conzelmann attempted to read the gospel as a whole, stressed the role of the evangelist before that of community or tradition, and sought to answer the question: "What is the theology of this gospel?" The hermeneutical result of redaction criticism was a renewed interest in theology that focused upon the theology of the gospel editors, rather than upon Jesus.

The effect of the new quest of the historical Jesus was a focus upon the message of Jesus and the theological intentions of those who edited his message for later readers. Through it all the new quest still maintained Bultmann's existential concerns and was relatively short-lived because it was perceived to be much the same in nature as the Bultmannian "no quest."

The Present State of the Quest

In the last part of his *Quest* Schweitzer concluded that there were only two live options for those wishing to find the historical Jesus: Wrede's thoroughgoing skepticism or his own thoroughgoing eschatology. Wrede's approach led to historical skepticism and non-Jewish, modernist conclusions concerning Jesus, based in large part upon his willingness to treat messianic texts as inventions of the evangelists. Schweitzer's approach, on the other hand, led to wholly eschatological, Jewish conclusions concerning Jesus, due in large part to his refusal to assign messianic statements to the early church.

N. T. Wright held that Schweitzer's words, written at the beginning of the century, have clearly proven prophetic in that most who are seeking the historical Jesus may be grouped into two camps: those who have followed Wrede (thoroughgoing skepticism) and those who have followed Schweitzer (thoroughgoing eschatology). In recognizing these two distinct groups, Wright distinguished between the Third Quest and the Renewed New Quest. The Renewed New Quest has adopted the thoroughgoing skepticism of Wrede concerning the Gospels as sources and has sought to discover a non-Jewish Jesus. The Third Quest has sought to ground Jesus within the Judaism of the first century, and has been far less skeptical than the Renewed New Quest concerning the value of the canonical Gospels as sources for the life of Jesus. The most obvious expression of the Renewed New Quest is the Jesus Seminar of Robert Funk. Some prominent advocates of the Third Quest include Wright, E. P. Sanders, John P. Meier, Ben Witherington, and Ben F. Meyer. This does not mean, of course, that all contemporary parties in historical Jesus research fit neatly into one of these two categories. But recognition that these two overarching categories are not perfect does not render them useless.

Two other critical approaches must be noted in any survey of the quest today: narrative criticism and social-scientific criticism. Narrative criticism builds on the observations of form and redaction criticism, but goes a step beyond. Whereas redaction criticism understood the Gospels as pieced-together collections of theology, narrative criticism seeks to study the overall story of the Gospels in much the same way that a literary scholar studies any story. There have been a number of significant studies of the Gospels as narratives in the last quarter century.

Social-scientific criticism seeks to understand the Gospels in light of their social setting. It seeks to uncover the social world of the text through application of the methods of cultural anthropology. Gerd Theissen prepared the way for social-scientific criticism to be used in historical Jesus research. Latin American Liberation theologians and feminist theologians have approached historical Jesus research from their own social-scientific perspective. Contemporary scholars often combine these diverse methods in an effort to provide interdisciplinary insights.

In summary the quest of the Historical Jesus has been impacted not only by various philosophical presuppositions but also by different critical methods throughout its history. The conclusions of significant thinkers have consistently been impacted by their philosophical presuppositions and hermeneutical/critical methodology. There has never been more activity and variety in the field of historical Jesus research than there is today, in large part because of the variety of interpretive methods and interdisciplinary approaches used in today's New Testament scholarship.

Harmonization in the Patristic Period

Daryl Cornett

The first harmonization that concerned the early church was that between the Jewish Scriptures and Christian writings. The first generation of Christians emerging from a Jewish context perceived God's revelation in Jesus as a continuation of His dealings with Israel. Therefore, the Scriptures (later labeled Old Testament) were maintained. Early Christians particularly focused on the writings of the Prophets as they now clearly saw Jesus as their subject. Corporate reading of the Prophets and the apostles hallmarked early Christian worship.

The apostles had taught the unity of God's revelation in Jesus and the Jewish Scriptures, albeit progressive in nature. Augustine declared that in the old the new had been concealed, but in the new the old was now revealed. Most early Christians assumed the harmony of the older Scriptures with the newer revelation in Christ and expounded by the apostles. There were exceptions, however, like Marcionite Christians who blended gnostic dualism with their Christian dogma and reached the opposite conclusion. They created an irreconcilable division between the old and the new.

To demonstrate the harmony between the covenants, or testaments, the early church fathers depended on typology and allegory to prove their case, in addition to certain prophetic writings. Typology included Christ symbols and foreshadowing, such as Abraham's offering of Isaac, as crucial markers of the harmony between the revelations. However, typology did not diminish the importance of the historicity of the Old Testament text. Those who employed allegorical exegesis became much more imaginative. The literal sense of the text was considered the least important level of the Scripture and treated at times as irrelevant. The allegorical sense was the obscured yet intended meaning of the text for those who had the proper spiritual discernment. This method helped many of the more philosophically inclined church fathers downplay the historicity of the more "unfavorable" narratives in the Jewish Scriptures that made God appear capricious, harsh, or unfair—the same narratives that led Marcion and others to reject them. Theologians in the West, such as Clement of Alexandria, Origen, and Augustine used allegory, by modern exegetical standards, to the point of incredulity. But their view of Scripture was a much more mystical view than the modern mind typically allows. In the East during the patristic period, however, some did consider this method as an unreliable way to interpret the Scriptures.

Gospel harmony became a concern for Christians as early as the second century. As the adherents to Christianity increased, so did the number of its critics. Among the varieties of criticisms with which early apologists contended was the charge of inconsistency within Christian writings. Outsiders easily observed the apparent chronological variances within the four canonical Gospels as well as differences in the details among the accounts. The consensus among the early Christian community, however, was an early acceptance of the witness of the four evangelists despite these apparent inconsistencies.

The earliest extant harmony of the canonical Gospels is attributed to the apologist Tatian, a Syrian, who traveled west and settled in Rome where he became a Christian and a student of Justin Martyr. After his teacher's death in 165, Tatian returned to Mesopotamia about 172. Scholars disagree on the date and place of the writing, but one can declare with certainty that he compiled the *Diatessaron* sometime between AD 170 and 180, probably in Syriac. It remains the earliest and most extensive collection of second-century Gospel texts. The title *Diatessaron* means "through four." There is evidence that no earlier than the eighth century was the name

Diatessaron affixed to the work. In Syrian Christianity it first bore the name "the Gospel of the Mixed." No direct copy of Tatian's *Diatessaron* exists, but numerous translations, fragments, and commentaries have survived as witnesses to the original. The work was translated into Arabic, Persian, Greek, Latin, and Armenian.

Tatian wove together the four Gospels into one continuous, harmonized account. Until the fifth century it remained the favored text of the Gospel accounts in the East. During this time it was the preferred Gospel account because it had eliminated textual inconsistencies, repetitions, and incompatibilities that existed among the four separate accounts. This popularity and subsequent influence was mainly confined to the Orient.

While under the tutelage of Justin, Tatian's faith was orthodox; however, after his teacher's death, Tatian incorporated some of the gnostic teachings of Marcion. Although the *Diatessaron* witnesses the early acceptance of the four canonical Gospels, Tatian, as the harmonizer, took liberty to alter certain texts to conform to his more gnostic understandings. These alterations give evidence for his more severe asceticism, including his rejection of marriage, and his dualism so characteristic of gnostic groups. His views helped to fuel, if not found, the Encratite movement that held marriage in contempt and abstained from eating meat.

Although it was present in certain Christian circles, the *Diatessaron* never won widespread favor in the Latin West. Since Tatian had been dubbed a heretic in the West because of his gnostic tendencies, his *Diatessaron* was naturally rejected. It was rejected not just for its biases, but also because the idea of a fourfold Gospel had gained acceptance. Irenaeus in *Against Heresies* branded Tatian a heretic for denying the salvation of Adam and inculcating gnostic beliefs attributed to Valentinus, Marcion, and Saturninus.[1] Although not explicitly stated, Irenaeus invalidated the *Diatessaron* by claiming that "It is not possible that the Gospels can be either more or fewer in number than they are [four]."[2] He believed there was a naturally divine order that accentuated the quantity of four. Since there are four zones of the world, four winds, and four living creatures in Revelation (that correspond to the four evangelists), then it is reasonable that the church has the four pillars of the Gospels. Although not a convincing argument to modern minds, Irenaeus' reasoning resonated with the orthodox-minded of his day.

The first mention of the *Diatessaron* in the West is found in Eusebius' *Ecclesiastical History*. He repeated Irenaeus' accusations of heresy but also added that Tatian "formed a certain body and collection of the gospels, I know not how, has given this the title, *Diatessaron*, that is the gospel by the four, or the gospel formed of the four; which is in the possession of some even now."[3]

In the third century Ammonius of Alexandria, a teacher of Origen, produced a harmony. The work was produced around AD 220 but has been lost. His work took Matthew as the basis and harmonized the other Gospels with it. In the fourth century Eusebius of Caesarea produced *Ten Evangelical Canons,* building upon the work of Ammonius. Where Ammonius had used Matthew as his standard, Eusebius devised ten categories by which to harmonize the evangelists. In this table of canons he categorized sections of each Gospel under the following headings: 1) passages common to all four Gospels; 2) those common to Matthew, Mark, and Luke; 3) those common to Matthew, Luke, and John; 4) those common to Matthew, Mark, and John; 5) those common to Mathew and Luke; 6) those common to Matthew and Mark; 7) those common to Matthew and John;

1. Irenaeus, *Against Heresies*, *Ante-Nicene Fathers*, vol. 1, edited by Alexander Roberts and James Donaldson (United States: Christian Literature Publishing Co., 1885; reprint, Peabody, MA: Hendrickson, 1994), 353 (citations are to the reprint edition).
2. Ibid., 428.
3. Eusebius, *Ecclesiastical History*, *Nicene and Post-Nicene Fathers*, second series, vol. 1, edited by Philip Schaff and Henry Wace (United States: Christian Literature Publishing Co., 1890; reprint, Peabody, MA: Hendrickson, 1994), 4.29.6 (citations are to the reprint edition).

8) those common to Luke and Mark; 9) those common to Luke and John; and 10) those peculiar to each Gospel.

In *Ecclesiastical History,* Eusebius discussed the written order of the Gospels. He declared that the four evangelists are not at any variance with one another, as some suggest, but stand in perfect harmony in spite of their differences. He noted particularly the uniqueness of John's account. John's purpose seems at least twofold. First he wanted to communicate the happenings of Jesus' ministry before the imprisonment of John the Baptist. Second, he wanted to accentuate the divine nature of Jesus. He stated that the "doctrine of divinity" had been "reserved for him, as their [other evangelists] superior, by the divine Spirit."[4]

About AD 400 Augustine of Hippo produced a treatise, *Harmony of the Evangelists.* The work is not a harmonizing of the texts side by side, or combining them into one narrative as Tatian had done. Augustine's work is primarily apologetic prose. Not all of the material deals with purely harmonization issues because at times he does digress. Its purpose is to exonerate the Gospel writers from the criticisms of pagans, those dealing with harmonization issues as well as others. Pagans had long been charging that there existed incongruity between the OT and the NT. In addition, critics accused the Gospel writers of contradictions in their different histories of Jesus. In *The Retractions* Augustine mentioned that during the years he was composing *On the Trinity,* he took periodic breaks from that work to pen others. Among these side ventures were four books entitled *Harmony of the Evangelists.* He desired to answer those who falsely accused the evangelists of lacking agreement because he considered this their most potent argument against the Christian faith. He also stated that he desired to help believers, who may be genuinely concerned about such apparent contradictions in the Gospels, personally to understand their nature and be ready to give an answer to critics.[5]

In the first book Augustine defended the authority of the four canonical Gospels as the Christian community had received them. He believed that the accounts were produced in the following order: Matthew (originally in Hebrew), Mark, Luke, and then John. Augustine explained that each evangelist employed a different emphasis for his record. For example, Matthew and Mark emphasized the kingly nature of Jesus, Luke the priestly, and John the divinity of Jesus. According to some outside critics, like the emperor Julian (the Apostate), it was John who had introduced the perversion of the worship of Jesus as God. Augustine countered such notions by asserting that John simply had Jesus' divinity more in view in his writing than the others because God had uniquely given him greater insight. Augustine concluded, "For he [John] is like one who has drunk in the secret of His divinity more richly and somehow more familiarly than others, as if he drew it from the very bosom of his Lord on which it was his wont to recline when He sat at meat."[6]

In the second book he dealt with the fact that Matthew and Luke presented different genealogies for Jesus, particularly the apparent contradiction concerning the father of Joseph. Matthew recorded that Jacob begat Joseph, whereas Luke stated that Joseph was the son of Heli (Eli). Augustine harmonized this apparent contradiction by claiming that Jacob biologically fathered Joseph and Heli was his adoptive father. Augustine asserted that Matthew and Luke's accounts could be harmonized easily, and he proceeded to blend their accounts together into one narrative, covering Christ's nativity, infancy, and childhood. He went on to harmonize numerous other parts of the

4. Ibid., 2.24.13.

5. Augustine, *The Retractions, The Fathers of the Church,* vol. 60, translated by Mary Inez Bogan (Washington, D.C.: The Catholic University of America Press, 1968), 150–51.

6. Augustine, *Harmony of the Evangelists, Nicene and Post-Nicene Fathers,* first series, vol. 6, edited by Philip Schaff (United States: Christian Literature Publishing Co., 1888; reprint, Peabody, MA: Hendrickson, 1994), 80 (citations are to the reprint edition).

Gospel narratives. He meticulously tackled one account after another up to the supper, showing how the other three evangelists in no substantive way contradict any of Matthew's narrative.

Augustine devoted the third book to an explanation of the evangelists' accounts from the supper to their ends. He discussed the differences concerning the betrayal of Judas at the supper to the differences in the post resurrection appearances reported by the evangelists, such as the difference Mark has with Matthew concerning the angelic appearance at the tomb. Matthew recorded that an angel was sitting on the rolled-away stone, whereas Mark reported that the women saw the angel after entering the tomb. Augustine harmonized this by suggesting that it is perfectly reasonable to assume that there were two angels, one inside the tomb and one outside.[7] And in the fourth book, Augustine examined passages in Mark, Luke, and John that have no parallels in Matthew. The majority of this shortest book is dedicated to giving explanation to the unique nature of John's Gospel. Augustine concluded, "Like an eagle, he abides among Christ's sayings of the sublimer order, and in no way descends to earth but on rare occasions."[8]

Throughout his work Augustine enumerated supposed contradictions among the evangelists and then demonstrated how the inconsistency is only apparent or that there is a reasonable explanation for the difference, whether it is an issue of chronology or detail. Therefore, the testimonies of the evangelists are completely trustworthy and no real evidence for the critics' charges of error can be found.

---

7. Ibid., 209.
8. Ibid., 232.

Christology in the Gospels

David G. Shackelford

A study of Christology in the Gospels is appropriately a study of how the Gospels present Jesus as the Christ, the anointed of God. This is the Messiah of whom the prophets spoke and who was the expected hope of Israel. He is also the hope of all the world.

There are several ways to approach such a study. One of the most common and effective would be to examine the Synoptic Gospels as a corpus, and then complement that study with the Christology of the Gospel of John.[1] There are good reasons for such an approach. On the other hand, since this is a harmony of all four Gospels, I shall explore their Christologies in concert. God gave four Gospels that present one Christ with one Christology.[2]

Christology involves the person and work of Jesus Christ. The two are inseparably linked and mutually dependent. Jesus Christ was who He was and came as He came that He might do what He did. If any part of this trilogy of truths is taken away, the gospel message is the gospel no longer.

The Person of Christ

The Full Deity of Jesus

The Gospels are clear that Jesus is God incarnate. John 1:1-3 says: "In the beginning was the Word, and the Word was with God, and the Word was God. He was with God in the beginning. All things were created through Him, and apart from Him not one thing was created that has been created."

These verses provide clear statements regarding the eternality of Jesus Christ, His full deity, and His agency in creation of the universe. There are others as well. One of the most concise statements of the deity of Jesus Christ is in John 8:58, where Jesus claims to be the "I am" of the OT. Then there are also the well-known "I am" statements in John's Gospel. In those passages, Jesus claims to be the bread of life (Jn 6:35,41,48,51), the light of the world (8:12), the door (10:7,9), the good shepherd (10:11,14), the resurrection and the life (11:25), the way, the truth, and the life (14:6), and the true vine (15:1,5).

One of Jesus' strongest claims came in conversation with Jewish leaders (Jn 8:48-59). Jesus told them that their father Abraham foresaw Jesus' day and rejoiced in it. The Jewish leaders asked how Jesus could know so much about Abraham since Jesus was less than fifty years old. In response to the skeptics, Jesus made one of His strongest and most profound claims: "I assure you: Before Abraham was, I am."

I Am is God's name that He revealed to Moses at the burning bush (Ex 3:14). Jesus' claim to be God in no way conflicted with Israel's foundational confession of faith: "Listen, Israel: the LORD our God, the LORD is One" (Dt 6:4). A number of OT passages take on a fuller and more complete meaning in light of the events of Jesus' life, death, and resurrection.

---

1. See Chad Brand, Charles Draper, and Archie England, in the *Holman Illustrated Bible Dictionary* (Nashville: Broadman & Holman, 2003), s.v., "Christology," by Daniel Akin, Ralph Martin, and Charlie Draper.

2. Many theological studies employ philosophy as an aid in the pursuit of theological clarity. There is a place for such a methodology; however, given the nature of a harmony of the Gospels, the desire herein is to draw a Christology specifically from statements of Scripture.

In John 1:23 John the Baptist, when asked of his own identity, confessed and said, "I am a voice of one crying out in the wilderness: Make straight the way of the Lord—just as Isaiah the prophet said." John was quoting Isaiah 40:3. In the OT passage, the Hebrew word for "Lord" is *hw"+hy* (*YHWH*).[3] Yet, when John was fulfilling Isaiah's prophecy, he was preparing the way for Jesus Christ. The only viable conclusion is that the Christ of the NT is Yahweh of the OT.

Another passage is Isaiah 43:11: "I, I *am* the LORD; and there is no other Savior but Me." In Luke 1:46-47, Mary confirmed that Yahweh is her Savior: "And Mary said: My soul proclaims the greatness of the Lord, and my spirit has rejoiced in God my Savior."[4] John 14:6 likewise says that the only way to the Father is through Jesus. Of course, since the Scriptures are clear that only Yahweh is the one true Savior, this means that if Jesus is not Yahweh, He is not the Savior either.

Again the Scriptures are clear. In Luke 2:11 the angel of the Lord told the shepherds, "Today a Savior, who is Messiah the Lord, was born for you in the city of David." In Luke 19:10 Jesus said, "For the Son of Man has come to seek and to save the lost."[5] In John 4:42 many of the Samaritan men said to the Samaritan woman, "We no longer believe because of what you said, for we have heard for ourselves and know that this really is the Savior of the world." Once again, one must conclude that Jesus and Yahweh are one and the same person, yet distinct personalities.

An often overlooked equation that the Scriptures make between Yahweh and Jesus has to do with the Sabbath day. The OT Scriptures associate the Sabbath day with the Lord. In every one of those verses where the words "Lord" and "Sabbath" are used in the same verse and associated with one another, the word for "Lord" is actually "Yahweh."[6] Clearly Yahweh is the Creator and Lord of the Sabbath Day: *it's His Sabbath.* But this is also the designation that Jesus claimed for Himself as Lord of the Sabbath.[7]

Not only do the Gospels equate Jesus with Yahweh, but they also teach that Jesus is the Son of Yahweh.[8] Mark 1:1 clearly says that Jesus is the Son of God.

In Matthew 2:15, when Joseph received the vision from the angel of the Lord to take Jesus and Mary to Egypt, verse 15 quotes Hosea 11:1 that says it was a fulfillment "so that what was spoken by the Lord through the prophet might be fulfilled: Out of Egypt I called My Son." In the context of Hosea 11:1, Yahweh Himself is the One calling His Son out of Egypt.[9] Matthew 2:15 specifically states that the sending of Joseph, Mary, and Jesus to Egypt and calling them back was a fulfillment of Hosea 11:1 where Yahweh is calling His son out of Egypt. Since the fulfillment of that Scripture is specifically applied to Jesus in Matthew 2:15, Jesus is not only equated with the Yahweh of the OT, but is also the Son of the Yahweh of the OT.

Jesus as the Son of Yahweh is also revealed at the baptism of Jesus[10] and at His transfiguration.[11] In both instances, when Jesus came out of the water, a voice from heaven said, "This is My beloved Son. I take delight in Him."[12]

---

3. Isaiah 40:3—"A voice of one crying out: Prepare the way of the LORD [*hw"+hy>*] in the wilderness; make a straight highway for our God in the desert."

4. Outside the Gospels, the Bible clearly refers to Jesus Christ as the only Savior (Ti 2:3; et al.).

5. There are passages outside the Gospels were Jesus is specifically referred to as "our Lord and Savior" (for example: Ti 2:13; 2Pt 1:11; 2:20; 3:2,18).

6. Exodus 16:23,25,29; 20:1-11; 31:13,15; 35:2; Leviticus 19:3,30; 23:3,11,16,18,38; 24:8; 25:2,4; 26:2; Deuteronomy 5:12,14,15; 1 Chronicles 23:31; 2 Chronicles 2:4; 31:3; 36:21; Isaiah 56:4,6; Isaiah 58:13; 66:23; Jeremiah 17:21,24; Lamentations 2:6; Ezekiel 20:12,20; 46:1,3,4,12.

7. Matthew 12:8; Mark 2:28; Luke 6:5.

8. Matthew 16:16-17; Mark 1:1; Luke 1:32,35; John 1:18,34; 3:16,18,36; 5:25; 10:36; 11:34; 20:31.

9. Hosea 11:1—"the LORD's declaration" [*hw"+hy*].

10. Matthew 3:17; Mark 1:11; Luke 3:22.

11. Matthew 17:5; Mark 9:7; Luke 9:35.

12. In fact, even the demons recognized Jesus to be the Son of God (Mt 8:29; Mk 3:11; 5:7; Lk 4:41; 8:28).

To Judaism, claiming to be the Son of Yahweh was itself a claim to deity. This is why the Jews sought to kill Jesus when He claimed to be the Son of God (Mk 14:61-62). Clearly, two distinct, yet equal, persons of the Triune Godhead are in view.

The Full Humanity of Jesus

The deity of Jesus, His eternity, and His Sonship are all significant to the person of Jesus Christ and the fulfillment of His mission on earth. But essential to the fulfillment of His messianic mission is His full humanity. It will be evident presently that Jesus could not have fulfilled His primary mission on earth apart from His full humanity. With this in mind, one finds that the Gospels are as clear concerning Jesus' humanity as they are His deity.

Perhaps the most clear and important statements underscoring the humanity of Jesus are found in the genealogies of Matthew and Luke. Matthew presents Jesus' human lineage through David and Abraham and ultimately through Joseph, who is identified as the husband of Mary. Luke, on the other hand, presents Jesus' human lineage through Adam. Both are unique in that Matthew's genealogy has a distinctively Jewish flavor that Luke's does not. But both are parallel and are very significant in that they provide a fully human lineage, especially through David, Abraham, and Adam; and both provide testimony to the virgin birth of Christ. Jesus' lineage through David and Abraham espouses clear fulfillments of prophecy.[13] But they also reveal that Jesus has a literal and legitimate human ancestry. No one would question that the people listed in the genealogies were real, literal individuals whose progeny consisted of real, literal offspring. This requires that Adam was likewise a real, literal person who was the first individual from whom all others are descended.[14]

The Work of Jesus Christ

All aspects of the person of Christ—His full deity, His Sonship, and His full humanity—are essential to the accomplishment of His primary messianic mission. That work of His mission is multi-faceted. It involved the establishment of His kingdom, the building of His church, the judgment of the world, and making provision for the coming of the Holy Spirit. But these things and others do not comprise the main purpose for which Jesus entered the world.

The main purpose of Christ—the purpose that He stated—was to seek and to save the lost. The provision of man's substitute as the Lamb who takes away the sins of the world (Jn 1:29) is the only aspect of Jesus' messianic mission that required an incarnate Messiah. When one ponders all the things Jesus did—the teachings, the healings, the miracles—one realizes that all these things could have been accomplished without Jesus taking human flesh. Indeed, similar events to all of these occurred in the OT. Even the establishment of Jesus' kingdom did not require that Jesus become incarnate. Jesus told Pilate, "My kingdom is not of this world" (Jn 18:35-36). But for Jesus to become sin—"who did not know sin to be sin for us, so that we might become the righteousness of God in Him (2 Co 5:21)—this required the Yahweh of the OT to take on full humanity in the person of Jesus.

In this atonement for the sins of all mankind, Jesus Christ fulfilled a dual prophetic role. On the one hand, He fulfilled His high priestly role. The high priest was the one who made intercession for the people. He offered the sacrifice for the sins of the people on the Day of Atonement. Jesus surely

---

13. Genesis 22:18; Isaiah 9:6-7; Psalm 110:1; Matthew 22:44; Luke 20:42.

14. Many theologians have long considered Adam and Eve, the first couple in Genesis, *not* to be literal individuals, but to be figurative and representative of mankind. Such a position is incompatible in the light of the genealogies. Adam is presented as the first of a long line of literal people, including Abraham and David. It is ludicrous to think that a figurative, metaphorical Adam could father real, literal descendants.

fulfilled this OT high priestly picture (Heb 4:14-15). Hebrews 9:11-12 reveal that in His sacrifice, Jesus entered into the true tabernacle "not made with hands" and offered His own blood in the holy place, "having obtained eternal redemption" for us.

But Jesus was not only the high priest who offered the Lamb; He also fulfilled the role of the paschal Lamb who was offered. That is, as the Lamb who takes away the sins of the world, Jesus was also the offering. God would later inspire Paul to write in 1 Corinthians 5:7, "For Christ our Passover has been sacrificed." Jesus is our great high priest who made the ultimate offering for sin; as the Lamb who takes away the sins of the world, this great high priest made an offering that no other priest before Him could make: He offered Himself. In so doing, all the thousands of lambs slain from the days of Moses—all the thousands of gallons of blood shed and sprinkled on the mercy seat in the holy of holies—all find their fulfillment in the great God and our Savior, Jesus Christ.

Christology in the Gospels finds its capstone in the resurrection of Jesus Christ. The payment of sin and the conquering of death require the bodily resurrection of Jesus Christ. The necessity of this resurrection of the Lamb slain is clearly emphasized in the Gospels. There are three passages in the Gospels (Mk 8:31; Lk 24:7; Jn 20:9) that state Jesus *must* rise the third day. The word for "must" (*dei*) is a word that bespeaks a necessity. In the NT it is regularly used to describe a *divine* necessity.[15]

There are those who question whether the Bible teaches a literal bodily resurrection, whether of Jesus or men. But the Scriptures are clear. The prophecies of the OT teach without equivocation a literal bodily resurrection. There are numerous passages, but one of the most clear is Job 19:26 which says, "Even after my skin has been destroyed, yet I will see God in my flesh."

Likewise, one cannot give an honest reading to the NT without conceding a bodily resurrection of Jesus Christ. When the disciples first went to the garden tomb on resurrection Sunday, what did they find? They found an empty tomb; they found grave clothes neatly folded; they found an angel. But they did not find a body. The Bible teaches that Mary took spices to the tomb site to anoint the body (Mk 16:1; Lk 23:56–24:1). But Mary did not find the body she sought.

Besides, it is the body that needs to be resurrected. The Bible teaches that "we are . . . satisfied to be out of the body and at home with the Lord" (2 Co 5:8). Jesus told the dying thief on the cross, "Today you will be with Me in paradise" (Lk 23:43). The soul of Jesus went to the Father that day. It was His body that died and was buried, and it was His body that had to be resurrected.

The importance of the bodily resurrection of Jesus Christ cannot be overstated. God's word is clear: "For if the dead are not raised, Christ has not been raised. And if Christ has not been raised, your faith is worthless; you are still in your sins" (1 Co 15:16-17). Truly, all the other works of Christ, including the substitutionary atonement of our Lord, find their validity and vindication in the bodily resurrection of Jesus. It is through the resurrection that Jesus "was established as the powerful Son of God" (Rm 1:4).

As to the person of Jesus Christ, He is, without equivocation, God. As to the work of Jesus Christ, He is our Lord and Savior. There is none other, "for there is no other name under heaven given to people by which we must be saved" (Ac 4:12).

---

15. This is also the word Jesus used when He said that He *must* go through Samaria. There He had a divine appointment with the woman at the well.

A Chronology of the Life of Christ

Harold W. Hoehner

A chronology of Christ's life gives a framework for His ministry on earth.

The Birth of Christ

The year and the time of the year of Jesus' birth can only be approximate because the early Christians were not as concerned with the date as the fact of Jesus' birth. In order to pinpoint the birth of Christ, there are three areas to be considered: 1) the year of the death of Herod, 2) the census of Quirinius, and 3) the star of the wise men.

The Date of Herod's Death

Jesus was born before Herod the Great died (Mt 2:15-16,19-20). Shortly before his death, there was an eclipse of the moon. This is the only eclipse mentioned by Josephus and it occurred on March 12/13, 4 BC. After Herod's death Josephus wrote that the Passover was celebrated, the first day of which would have occurred on April 11, 4 BC. His death, therefore, would have been between March 12th and April 11th, setting Jesus' birth at no later than March/April 4 BC.

The Census of Quirinius

According to Luke 2:1-5 Augustus decreed a worldwide census, the first census during the time Quirinius was governor of Syria and occurring prior to Jesus' birth. As a result it was necessary for Joseph and Mary to travel to their hometown, Bethlehem, to register. It is difficult to pinpoint the date of this census. Although no Roman historian specifically mentions this particular one, periodic censuses were taken in different provinces. The census of Luke 2 is not the same as the one organized by Quirinius in AD 6, because this latter one occurred immediately after the deposition of Herod's son Archelaus, whereas the census of Luke 2 is in the context of the birth narrative of Jesus in the days of Herod the Great. The troublesome issue is the meaning of the adjective "first" census in Luke 2:2. There have been several attempts to resolve this dilemma. Some have suggested that Quirinius was governor of Syria twice: once from 11–10 to 8–7 BC, the time of the "first" census, and later in AD 6–7 or 6–9, the time of the second census. But there is no solid evidence that Quirinius was governor of Syria before AD 6. Others think the adjective "first" should be a comparative meaning "former" and thus would be rendered, "this census was earlier than [the census] when Quirinius was governor of Syria," which at best is cumbersome. Possibly the most acceptable way to resolve this is to see the adjective adverbially as "before" rendering it "this census occurred before Quirinius was governor." Although the time of the "first" census is difficult to ascertain, it might possibly have been when Herod the Great was weak politically and in health, sometime around 6 to 4 BC.

The Star of the Wise Men

According to Matthew 2:1-12, the wise men (astrologers) from the east had come to Jerusalem searching for Jesus because they had seen a star at its rising and had come to worship Him. Astronomers note that there was an alignment of the planets Jupiter and Saturn with Mars (occurs every 805 years) that occurred early in February of 6 BC and would have alerted the wise men that something significant was about to occur. Then in March/April of 5 BC, the wise men observed the star mentioned in Matthew 2:2, traveled to Israel and upon arriving in Bethlehem saw again the star they had seen in the east. It stood over where Jesus was, namely, Bethlehem (Mt 2:9). This star was not the above-mentioned alignment of planets, because this phenomenon was not close enough to earth to have led the wise men and to have stood precisely over Bethlehem. On the other hand, a comet would have been clearly visible to the naked eye for a prolonged period of time. Records show that a tailed comet was visible for 70 days and had first been seen in the east in March/April of 5 BC and would again have been visible in Bethlehem in April/May.

With the census of Quirinius having occurred somewhere between 6 and 4 BC and Herod's death having occurred in the spring of 4 BC, it is likely that Jesus was born in the spring of 5 BC.

The Ministry of Jesus

To discover the time of the beginning of Jesus' ministry, it is necessary to consider three chronological markers: the commencement of John the Baptist's ministry, the commencement of Jesus' ministry, and the first Passover of Jesus' ministry.

The Commencement of John the Baptist's Ministry

Luke 3:1-3 specifically states that John the Baptist's ministry began in the fifteenth year of Tiberius. There is debate on which calendar Luke would have used. The fifteenth year in the Roman Julian calendar would have been January 1 to December 31, AD 29, but Luke may have reckoned it from the beginning of Tiberius' reign, the normal Roman method, making it from August 19, AD 28 to August 18, AD 29. Using either one of these calendars, the fifteenth year of Tiberius would have occurred sometime between August 19, AD 28 and December 31, AD 29. Consequently, John the Baptist's ministry began sometime during this period.

The Commencement of Jesus' Ministry

The impression from the Gospels is that not long after the beginning of John the Baptist's ministry, Jesus was baptized and began His ministry. Luke states that at the commencement of His ministry, Jesus was "about 30 years old" (Lk 3:23). If Jesus had been born in the spring of 5 BC and had been baptized in the summer or autumn of AD 29, He would have been 33 years of age. This fits well with Luke's statement that Jesus was "about" 30 years of age when He began His ministry.

The First Passover of Jesus' Ministry

Shortly after His baptism, the first recorded visit of Jesus to Jerusalem (Jn 2:13–3:21) marks the first Passover of His ministry. This was the occasion when the Jews stated that the Herodian temple had been constructed 46 years ago (Jn 2:20). Josephus stated that the temple construction began in Herod's eighteenth year,[1] which coincides with the arrival of Augustus in Syria,[2] and, according to Dio Cassius, that event occurred in spring or summer of 20 BC.[3] The temple was built in two parts: the first was the inner sanctuary called the *naos,* located within the priests' court and completed by the priests in one year and six months.[4] The second included the whole temple area including the three courts, called the *hieron,* which was completed in AD 63, a distinction maintained by both Josephus and the NT. The Jews had been referring to the *naos* as having stood for 46 years.

1. Josephus, *The Jewish Antiquities,* trans. Ralph Marcus: *Loeb Classical Library* 8 (Cambridge, MA: Harvard University Press and London: William Heinemann, Ltd., 1980), 15.11.1.
2. Ibid., 15.10.3.
3. *Dio Cassius,* Roman History, trans. Earnest Cary and Herbert B. Foster: *LCL* 6 (Cambridge, MA: Harvard University Press and London: William Heinemann, Ltd., 1917), 54.7.4–6.
4. Josephus, *Antiquities*, 15.11.6.

Therefore, if the construction of the *naos* had begun in 20–19 BC and had been completed in one and a half years (18–17 BC), 46 years later would bring the date to the year AD 29–30. This means then that Jesus' first Passover was the spring of AD 30.

In conclusion, the fifteenth year of Tiberius, AD 28–29, marked the commencement of John the Baptist's ministry. If John began his ministry in the early part of AD 29 and Jesus was baptized in the summer or autumn of that same year, He would have been 33 years of age. His first Passover in AD 30 would have been four to nine months after He began His ministry, which was 46 years after the *naos* had been completed. Therefore, Jesus began His ministry sometime in the summer or autumn of AD 29.

The Duration of Jesus' Ministry

The mention of three Passovers in the Gospel of John (2:13; 6:4; 11:55) suggests that Jesus' ministry was at least two years in addition to the time between His baptism and the first Passover of His ministry in AD 30 as mentioned above. There are, however, reasonable grounds to suggest that there was an additional year of ministry between the Passovers of John 2:13 and 6:4. The Passover of John 6:4 is around the time Jesus fed the 5,000, the only miracle mentioned in all four Gospels. Previous to this feeding, the Synoptic Gospels mention the disciples plucking grain in Galilee (Mt 12:1; Mk 2:23; Lk 6:1). This must have been after the Passover of John 2:13 because this occurred shortly after His baptism, at which time the locale of His ministry was in Judea; whereas the plucking of the grain occurred a considerable time after Jesus' baptism when the locale of His ministry was in Galilee. The plucking of the grain, therefore, would fit well around the Passover that occurred between the Passovers of John 2:13 and 6:4.

Furthermore, there are two other time notes in John that indicate there was an additional year between these two Passovers. First, after the Passover of John 2:13 Jesus ministered in Judea and then went to Samaria where He stated that there were four months until harvest (Jn 4:35), which would indicate the following January/February. The second time note is in John 5:1 where there is mention of another feast. Although not specified, some would make it another Passover, but more likely it was the Festival of Tabernacles. Thus, these two time notes would substantiate that there was another Passover between the Passovers of John 2:13 and 6:4. In conclusion, the above calculations would suggest a total of four Passovers during Jesus' public ministry making it a duration of three-and-one-half or three-and-three-quarter years.

The Death of Jesus

In determining the date of the death of Jesus, the day of His death as well as the year of His death must be taken into account.

The Day of Jesus' Death

Traditionally, Jesus died on the Friday of the Passion week. Because Jesus states in Matthew 12:40: "For as Jonah was in the belly of the huge fish three days and three nights, so the Son of Man will be in the heart of the earth three days and three nights," some say Jesus could not have died on Friday. They propose that Jesus died either on Wednesday or Thursday allowing for the three days and three nights. It is important, however, to understand that the Jews reckoned a part of a day as a whole day. This fact removes the problem of Jesus' death having occurred on Friday.

Furthermore, the NT repeatedly refers to Jesus' resurrection as having occurred on the third day (not on the fourth day) (e.g., Mt 16:21; 17:23; Lk 9:22; 18:33; Ac 10:40; 1 Co 15:4). Moreover, the Gospels specifically mention the day before the Sabbath as the day of His death (Mt 27:62;

Mk 15:42; Lk 23:54; Jn 19:14,31,42). Both scripturally and traditionally, however, it seems best to accept Friday as the day of the week that Jesus died. The Passion week can be charted as follows:

Day	Event	Scripture
Saturday	Arrived at Bethany Jesus anointed Crowd came to see Jesus	John 12:1 John 12:3-8 John 12:9-11
Sunday	Triumphal entry Jesus wept over Jerusalem Jesus viewed the temple Return to Bethany	Matthew 21:1-9; Mark 11:1-10; Luke 19:28-44; John 12:12-13 Luke 19:41 Mark 11:11 Mark 11:11

Monday	Cursed fig tree
	Cleansed temple
	
	Some Greeks seek to see Jesus
	Jesus responds to the crowd's
	    unbelief
	Return to Bethany
		Matthew 21:18-19; Mark 11:12-14
		Matthew 21:12-13; Mark 11:15-17;
		    Luke 19:45-46
		John 12:20-36
		John 12:37-50
		
		Mark 11:19

Tuesday	The disciples see the withered fig
	    tree
	Temple controversy
	
	Olivet Discourse
		Matthew 21:20-22; Mark 11:20-26
		
		Matthew 21:23–23:39; Mark 11:27–
		    12:44; Luke 20:1–21:4
		Matthew 24:1–25:46; Mark 13:1-37;
		    Luke 21:5-36

Wednesday	The Sanhedrin plots to kill Jesus
	
	Judas agrees to betray Jesus
		Matthew 26:1-5; Mark 14:1-2;
		    Luke 22:1-2
		Matthew 26:14-26; Mark 14:10-11;
		    Luke 22:3-6

Thursday	Last Supper
	
	Betrayed and arrested
	
	Tried by Annas and Caiaphas
		Matthew 26:20-30; Mark 14:17-26;
		    Luke 22:14-30
		Matthew 26:47-56; Mark 14:43-52;
		    Luke 22:47-53; John 18:2-12
		Matthew 26:57-75; Mark 14:53-72;
		    Luke 22:54-65; John 18:13-27

Friday	Tried by Sanhedrin
	Tried by Pilate, Herod, Pilate
	
	Crucified and buried
		Matthew 27:1; Mark 15:1; Luke 22:66
		Matthew 27:2-30; Mark 15:2-19;
		    Luke 23:1-25; John 18:28–19:16
		Matthew 27:31-60; Mark 15:20-46;
		    Luke 23:26-54; John 19:16-42

Saturday	Dead in tomb	
Sunday	Resurrected	Matthew 28:1-15; Mark 16:1-8; Luke 24:1-35

All the Gospels state that Jesus ate the Last Supper the day before His crucifixion (Mt 26:20; Mk 14:17; Lk 22:14; Jn 13:2; see also 1 Co 11:23). The Synoptic Gospels (Mt 26:17; Mk 14:12; Lk 22:7-8) delineate that the Last Supper was the Passover meal celebrated on Thursday evening, Nisan 14, and that Jesus was crucified the following day, namely, Friday, Nisan 15. On the other hand, John states that the Jews who took Jesus to the Praetorium did not enter it "otherwise they would be defiled and unable to eat the Passover" (Jn 18:28) and that Jesus' trial was on the "preparation day for the Passover," not after the eating of the Passover (Jn 19:14). Hence, it appears that Jesus' Last Supper (which occurred on Thursday night, Nisan 13) was not a Passover and that Jesus was tried and crucified on Friday, Nisan 14, just before the eating of the Passover.

In the attempt to reconcile the Synoptics and John, several theories have been proposed. According to some the Last Supper was not a Passover meal but a meal the night before the Passover (Jn 13:1,29), but the Synoptic Gospels explicitly state that the Last Supper was a Passover (Mt 26:2,17-19; Mk 14:1,12,14,16; Lk 22:1,7-8,13,15). Others have proposed that Jesus and His disciples had a private Passover. The Passover lamb, however, had to be slaughtered within the temple precincts, and the priest would not have allowed the slaughter of the paschal lamb for a private Passover. Yet others think that they celebrated it according to the Qumran calendar, but there is no evidence that Jesus and His disciples followed the Qumran calendar. There are those who suggest that the Passover was celebrated on two consecutive days since it would have been impossible to slay all the Passover lambs on one day. In the final analysis, it is most likely that different calendars were used. On the one hand, the Synoptic Gospels followed the method of the Galileans and the Pharisees in reckoning the day from sunrise to sunrise, thus Jesus and His disciples had the paschal lamb slaughtered in the late afternoon of Thursday, Nisan 14, and later that evening they ate the Passover with the unleavened bread. On the other hand, John's Gospel seems to have followed the method of the Judeans by reckoning the day from sunset to sunset allowing the Judean Jews to have the paschal lamb slaughtered in the late afternoon of Friday, Nisan 14, which they ate for Passover with the unleavened bread that night, Nisan 15. This would explain why Jesus had eaten the Passover meal when His enemies, who had not as yet had the Passover, arrested Him.

The Year of Jesus' Death

The year of Jesus' death can be narrowed down by several considerations.

a. The Officials of the Trial

Three officials involved in the trial of Jesus were Caiaphas, the high priest (Mt 26:3,57; Jn 11:49-53; 18:13-14) who began his office in AD 18 and was deposed at the Passover of AD 37;[5] Pilate, prefect of Judea (Mt 27:2-26; Mk 15:1-15; Lk 23:1-25; Jn 18:28–19:16; Ac 3:13; 4:27; 13:28; 1 Tm 6:13) from AD 26 to 36;[6] and Herod Antipas, tetrarch of Galilee and Perea (Lk 23:6-12) from 4 BC until AD 39.[7] According to these dates, Christ's crucifixion must have occurred between AD 26 and 36.

b. The Contribution of Astronomy

Having concluded that Jesus was crucified on Friday, Nisan 14, one needs to determine when Nisan 14 fell on Friday within AD 26–36. Studies indicate the only possible times that this was the case were in the years of AD 27, 30, 33, and 36. Of these, AD 27 is the least likely astronomically,

5. Josephus, *The Jewish Antiquities,* trans. Louis H. Feldman: *LCL* 9 (Cambridge, MA: Harvard University Press and London: William Heinemann, Ltd., 1981), 18.2.2; 4.3.

6. Ibid., 18.2.2; 4.2.

7. Josephus, *Antiquities,* 17.11.4; 18.7.2; 19.8.2.

and it is questionable as to whether or not Nisan 14 fell on Friday in AD 30 and 36. The AD 33 date has the least problems astronomically.

c. The Ministry of Jesus

In discussing the ministry of Jesus earlier, it was concluded that neither an AD 27 or 36 crucifixion fit within the framework of His ministry. The year AD 30 for Jesus' death is accepted by many, but it has real difficulty if one accepts that the commencement of John the Baptist's ministry occurred in the fifteenth year of Tiberius, AD 29 (Lk 3:1-3), for this would mean that Jesus' ministry could not have lasted more than one year. As already stated, the AD 33 seems to fit the evidence best.

The Confirmation of History

Pilate is portrayed by his contemporary Philo[8] and later by Josephus[9] as one who is greedy, inflexible, and cruel and who resorted to robbery and oppression, much like his portrayal in Luke 13:1 where he mixed the blood of the Galileans with their sacrifices. When he tried Jesus, however, Pilate is portrayed as one who was readily submissive to the pressures of the religious leaders who were demanding that Jesus be handed over to them.

How does one explain such a change of attitude? It must be understood that Pilate was probably appointed prefect of Judea through the intervention of the equestrian Lucius Aelius Sejanus, a trusted friend of Tiberius, the prefect of the Praetorian Guard, and a dedicated anti-Semite who wanted to exterminate the Jewish race.[10] When Pilate caused any problems with the Jews in Israel, Sejanus accepted this behavior and did not report it to Tiberius who resided on the island of Capri. When, however, Sejanus was deposed and executed by Tiberius on October 18, AD 31, Pilate no longer had protection in Rome. In fact, it is highly probable that Herod Antipas had reported the incident where Pilate brought shields to Jerusalem, probably at the Festival of Tabernacles in AD 32, causing problems with the Jews.[11] Now that Herod Antipas "had one" on Pilate, it is understandable that in the midst of the trial of Jesus when there was mention that Jesus had stirred up trouble in Judea and Galilee (Lk 23:5), Pilate became eager to allow Herod Antipas to try Jesus (Lk 23:6-12). In light of these factors, the AD 33 date for the trial makes good sense for three reasons: 1) the move by Pilate when he handed Jesus over to Antipas was not required by Roman law but by doing so he ingratiated himself to Antipas so that Antipas would not have another negative report to relate to the emperor; 2) the trial's seeming lack of progress in Luke 23:6-12 makes sense because Antipas' refusal to make a judgment would have prevented Pilate from making a bad report about him; and 3) the fact that Luke 23:12 states that Pilate and Antipas were friends from that day onward, which would be inaccurate if the crucifixion were in AD 30 because they were at odds with each other in AD 32. Consequently, the AD 33 date fits best historically.

---

8. Philo, *The Embassy to Gaius,* trans. F. H. Colson: *LCL* 10 (Cambridge, MA: Harvard University Press and London: William Heinemann, Ltd., 1971), 299–305.

9. Josephus, *Antiquities,* 18.3.1 and Josephus, *The Jewish War,* trans. H. St. J. Thackeray: *LCL* 2 (Cambridge, MA: Harvard University Press and London: William Heinemann, Ltd., 1976), 2.9.2-4.

10. Philo, *Flaccus,* trans. F. H. Colson: *LCL* 9 (Cambridge, MA: Harvard University Press and London: William Heinemann, Ltd., 1985), 1 and Philo, *The Embassy to Gaius,* 159–61.

11. Philo, *The Embassy to Gaius,* 299–305.

Conclusion

Having examined the data regarding the day of the week and month as well as the year of His death, it is concluded that the evidence points to Jesus' death having occurred on Friday, Nisan 14, April 3, AD 33.[12]

Summary of the Dates

The birth, life, and death of Jesus can be charted as follows:

Jesus' birth	spring 5/4 BC
Death of Herod the Great	March/April BC
Jesus at the temple when 12	Passover, April 29, AD 8
Commencement of John the Baptist's ministry	AD 29
Commencement of Jesus' ministry	summer/autumn AD 29
Jesus' first Passover (Jn 2:13)	April 7, AD 30
Jesus' second Passover	April 25, AD 31
Jesus at the Festival of Tabernacles (Jn 5:1)	October 21–28, AD 31
Jesus' third Passover (Jn 6:4)	April 13–14, AD 32
Jesus at the Festival of Tabernacles (Jn 7:2,10)	September 10–17, AD 32
Jesus at the Festival of Dedication (Jn 10:22-39)	December 18, AD 32
Jesus' death	Friday, April 3, AD 33
Jesus' resurrection	Sunday, April 5, AD 33
Jesus' ascension (Ac 1)	Thursday, May 14, AD 33
Day of Pentecost (Ac 2)	Sunday, May 24, AD 33

---

12. This account of the year of the resurrection is different from other articles in this Harmony of the Gospels. The editors hold to an earlier year with regard to the resurrection. These dates, however, are debated by scholars.

The Two Genealogies of Jesus Christ in Matthew and Luke

Stanley E. Porter

Both Matthew and Luke have a genealogy of Jesus Christ. That there are differences between these two genealogies has long been recognized, and this fact has generated a number of different proposals as to their respective functions (see Bacon; Carson; Fitzmyer; Johnson; Huffman for alternatives and descriptions). This article will first describe the differences between the two genealogies and the major features that require comment, and then survey and assess the major proposals that have been offered in explanation.

Matthew's genealogy of Jesus Christ occurs at the very beginning of his Gospel (1:1-17) and is introduced almost as part of the title of the book: "The historical record of Jesus Christ, the Son of David, the Son of Abraham" (1:1). The names of David and Abraham are important to the overall structure and shape of Matthew's genealogy (although the third dividing name, Jechoniah, is not). The genealogy proceeds from Abraham through David (1:6) and the deportation to Babylon (1:11-12) to Joseph and Mary (1:16). Thus, the genealogy proceeds from earliest to latest, as far back as Abraham, and appears to trace the line of Joseph. The author further states that this genealogy is structured around fourteen generations, and he counts fourteen generations from Abraham to David, fourteen from David to the deportation, and fourteen from the deportation to the birth of the Messiah (1:17). Once this recounting is complete, Matthew then begins the description of the birth of Jesus Christ (1:18).

Luke's genealogy does not occur at the beginning of the Gospel but occurs after the events surrounding the background and birth of Jesus Christ (1:5–2:38), his childhood (2:39-52), and the ministry of John the Baptist (3:1-20). The baptism of Jesus by John marks the beginning of Jesus' public ministry (3:21-22), and Luke's genealogy is given in the context of Jesus beginning His ministry at about 30 years old (3:23-38). Luke's genealogy works back from Joseph, who was thought to be His father (3:23), all the way back to Adam and then God (3:38), a total of 77 names if one counts God.

A number of factors have been noted in the genealogies that have led to much speculation regarding their purpose.[1] Some of these factors are the following:

- The genealogies are placed in different literary and historical contexts, with Matthew's at the beginning of the book and Luke's at the beginning of Jesus' ministry.
- They proceed in opposite chronological order.
- Luke's genealogy goes all the way back to God (with the early names found in Genesis 5 and 11), while Matthew's begins at Abraham.
- They are structured along different principles of organization, with Matthew following three groups of 14[2] but Luke not forming any groupings. Some have speculated that he is following a plan of 11 x 7.
- The literary structure is different, with Matthew using the phrasing "x fathered y," while Luke simply says "x of y."

---

1. J. A. Fitzmyer, *The Gospel According to Luke I–IX* (Anchor Bible 28; New York: Doubleday, 1981), 495–96.
2. See D. A. Hagner, *Matthew 1–13* (Word Biblical Commentary 33A; Dallas: Word, 1993), 5–7 on issues surrounding the four-teens.

- They contain essentially the same names from Abraham to David (with most of them found in 1 Ch 1–2) but very few names in common after that (although Matthew's names are found in 1 Ch 1–3).
    * Matthew contains a group of unknown people (though the names sound biblical) from Abiud to Jacob.
    * Luke contains a list of 18 otherwise unknown descendants of David's son Nathan between Heli and Rhesa (it has been posited by Hervey that many of the names in this list derive from Nathan and indicate that David's line through Nathan is being followed;[3] others such as Kuhn have thought that Luke 3:26-29 and 29-31 are two parallel lists).[4]
- Matthew's genealogy includes the names of four women—Tamar, Rahab, Ruth, and the wife of Uriah, besides some other titles and designations.

As a result of weighing these and other factors, there have been a number of proposals that have been made regarding the genealogies.

Theological not Historical

Many scholars have despaired of finding any reconciliation of the difficulties and historical basis for the genealogies, since they differ so widely and include names not known in other sources.[5] Instead, they argued that the genealogies serve a theological rather than a historical purpose. Johnson, for example, argued that Matthew's genealogy is a midrash, designed to "comfort, exhort, and edify."[6] He noted that other genealogies had a midrashic character as they speculated about the origins of various figures, including the Messiah. Johnson cites two major bodies of evidence in support of the midrashic view. The first is evidence from within the text. Matthew's genealogy opens with wording that links it to the OT, but includes the additional feature of mentioning the four women. Various proposals have been made for including these disenfranchised and humble women. For example, some see the women as types of Mary. Their inclusion on this view could deflect questions about Jesus' birth by pointing to questionable births in the lineage.[7] But Johnson concluded that when the genealogy was written post AD 70 the women were already prominent, and thus Matthew was showing that Jesus fulfilled the Pharisaic expectations regarding the Davidic Messiah.[8] The structure of the Matthean genealogy also reveals midrashic elements, according to Johnson. These include the structuring around 14 and the emphasis upon Abraham and David. There have been various proposals regarding the use of 14—such as OT examples, *gematria* (a form of numerology in which letters were assigned numerical value), and various other notions of the value of numbers, such as association of the Messiah with 14 epochs.[9] The midrashic character of the genealogy is seen by Johnson to be appropriate to Matthew's Gospel, which is structured around discrete units, utilizes the Greek OT as does the genealogy, and puts forth theological ideas found throughout the Gospel, such as Jesus as Son of David and Son of Abraham, and a messianic eschatology.

---

3. A. Hervey, *The Genealogies of Our Lord and Saviour Jesus Christ, as Contained in the Gospels of St. Matthew and St. Luke* (Cambridge: Bell, 1853), 36–37, 88.
4. K. G. Kuhn, "Die Geschlechtsregister Jesu bei Lukas und Matthäus, nach ihrer Herkunft untersucht," *ZNW* 22 (1923), 208–209.
5. See M. D. Johnson, *The Purpose of the Biblical Genealogies, with Special Reference to the Setting of the Genealogies of Jesus* (Cambridge: Cambridge University Press, 1969), 144–45 and Fitzmyer, *The Gospel According to Luke I–IX*, 496.
6. Johnson, *The Purpose of the Biblical Genealogies*, 145.
7. Ibid., 152–79.
8. Ibid., 178.
9. Ibid., 190–208.

There have been a number of different proposals regarding Luke's genealogy and its theological rather than historical significance. Since there are fewer structuring elements and variances in presentation (such as not including the women), these proposals often put more emphasis upon the placement of the genealogy. These three proposals are worth mentioning.

Jesus as the Second Adam

Jeremias[10] believed that the typology of Adam and Christ stands behind Luke's genealogy that goes back to Adam. According to Jeremias, there is midrashic evidence that Adam was honored by the wild animals in paradise,[11] just as Jesus was with the animals after His temptation, and thus brings in the last days, which will be filled with peace. This view has not been widely accepted because the second-Adam motif is not found elsewhere in Luke or Acts, the parallel with the Jewish literature is not found in Luke's account of the temptation but only Mark's (see 1:13), and the genealogy actually begins with God, not Adam.[12]

Apocalyptic Viewpoint

This position argues that Luke's genealogy consists of 77 names, or 11 x 7 names, and that Jesus comes as the Messiah to inaugurate the messianic period, the twelfth; a common division of world history in a number of apocalyptic texts. This view has been criticized on the grounds that the notion of the number of periods in history varies. With 14 a common number (see above), the text of the Lukan genealogy is subject to question at a number of places and hence may not have 77 names. Perhaps most importantly, many scholars do not see in Luke a sense of messianic expectation but eschatological fulfillment.[13]

Jesus as the Son of God and Prophet

After toying with the idea that Luke's Gospel originally began at 3:1, Johnson argued that the placement of the genealogy after the baptism of Jesus by John reinforces the idea, not that Jesus is the Son of David, but that He is the Son of God. The baptism ends with this affirmation (3:22), which is then reinforced by the genealogy. The genealogy also, however, promotes the idea of Jesus as prophet. The genealogy proceeds from God to Abraham to David, but then through his son Nathan, who was seen in a variety of literature as the one continuing the line of David and even identified with the prophet Nathan and that the Messiah would come from this line. Luke throughout the Gospel sees Jesus' ministry in terms of its being validated as a prophetic ministry in the line of the OT prophets.[14] Johnson's proposal, however, falls down in light of the Gospel actually beginning with the first two chapters, whose excise cannot be substantiated and that emphasize the virginal conception of Jesus.

No doubt the genealogies of the Gospels have theological significance, but the use of ancient genealogies, including those in the Bible, though they may have had other purposes, often was for the historical purpose of substantiating and indicating the origins of a figure. The same is true of the genealogies of Matthew and Luke, even if they vary in significant details for which they are the only witnesses (such as the inclusion of certain names). There have been, therefore, a number of proposals related to the historical purposes of the genealogies.

10. J. Jeremias, "Adam," (*TDNT* 1; Grand Rapids: Eerdmans, 1964, 1983), 141.
11. See *The Apocalypse of Moses*, 16:1–5.
12. Johnson, *The Purpose of the Biblical Genealogies*, 234–35.
13. Ibid., 231–33.
14. Ibid., 240–52.

Luke Has the Genealogy of Mary and Matthew of Joseph

One of the common explanations of the two differing genealogies is that Luke's is the genealogy of Mary and Matthew's is of Joseph. A number of well-known earlier scholars held to this position, including Annius of Viterbo (fifteenth century), Luther, and Bengel, among others. This explanation directly addresses the issue of why the two lines have different names in them, since Joseph and Mary would have come through different descendants of David. Presumably Luke does not mention Mary here in order to avoid mentioning a woman,[15] something that only Matthew does. This requires that the wording of Luke 3:23 be interpreted as follows: Jesus was "son, as was supposed of Joseph, but (actually) of Heli ..." in which Heli is the father of Mary. Some have objected that there is no evidence that Mary came from the line of David,[16] although some have responded that there is in fact some evidence.[17] It is also unlikely that the genealogy would have followed the mother's line.[18] Most problematic, however, is the understanding of the Greek. Most scholars assume that the Greek either would have been written differently or would have required some form of punctuation (not found in the earliest manuscripts) to make it clear. The lack of an article in front of Joseph, rather than aiding this interpretation, seems to be consistent with Luke's style of reference to Joseph and is consistent with the beginning of a genealogy.[19]

Both Are Genealogies of Joseph but One Is Biological and the Other Legal

There have been two forms of this proposal.

Luke's Genealogy Is Legal and Matthew's Is Biological

This theory dates back to the third century and Julius Africanus[20] and appears to have been the most popular explanation until the fifteenth century. Julius contended that the legal line of Jesus was recorded by Luke and passed through David and Nathan to Melchi and Heli and then Joseph, while the biological or physical line was recorded by Matthew and passed through David and Solomon to Matthan and Jacob and then Joseph. Counting back three generations from Jesus, Julius contends, one finds Matthan in Matthew's line and Melchi in Luke's line. Julius contended that Matthan married Estha and gave birth to Jacob, but that Matthan then died and Estha married Melchi, and they gave birth to Heli. Jacob and Heli were therefore half brothers of the same mother. When Heli died without having any children, Jacob took his wife according to the laws of levirate marriage and gave birth to Joseph. Thus the legal line of Heli was fulfilled by the physical line of Jacob. Luke records this in 3:23 by stating that it "was thought" that Jesus was the son of Joseph and of Heli. Regardless of the fact that Julius appears not to have had Matthat and Levi in his genealogy, many scholars question this solution.[21] The Lukan genealogy does have Matthat and Levi, with Matthat often thought to be the same person as Matthew's Matthan. There is question whether levirate marriage was practiced at the time, and if it was why it would have been important to record the legal lineage since it had been superseded.

---

15. D. A. Carson, *Matthew* (The Expositor's Bible Commentary 8; ed. F. E. Gaebelein; Grand Rapids: Zondervan, 1984), 64.
16. Fitzmyer, *The Gospel According to Luke I–IX*, 497.
17. Carson, "Matthew," 64, citing Luke 1:32.
18. B. W. Bacon, "Genealogy of Jesus Christ," (*A Dictionary of the Bible* 2; ed. J. Hastings; Edinburgh: T. & T. Clark, 1899), 139.
19. Johnson, *The Purpose of the Biblical Genealogies*, 143–44.
20. Eusebius, *Ecclesiastical History, Books 1–5*, trans. Kirsop Lake: *Loeb Classical Library* 1 (Cambridge, MA: Harvard University Press and London: William Heinemann, Ltd., 1976), 1.7.1–17.
21. See R. E. Brown, *The Birth of the Messiah* (New York: Doubleday, 1977), 503–504.

Matthew's Genealogy Is Legal and Luke's Is Biological

Some more recent scholars have reversed the above position and argue that Matthew's genealogy is legal and Luke's biological. Hence Luke traces Jesus' actual succession back through Nathan to David, while Matthew traces the legal and hence royal succession back through Solomon to David. Some forms of this theory require that Matthew then records a secret line of royal descent from Zerubbabel to Joseph, since these people were never kings of Israel. There have been variations upon this position regarding how they converge on Joseph as the next in line before Jesus. Some contend that there was a levirate marriage involved. Carson believed that levirate marriage was being practiced at the time, as witness the inquiry from the Sadducees in Matthew 22:24-28, but is also highly problematic, as he points out.[22] According to this view, Jacob and Heli were full brothers, but that when Jacob died Heli married Jacob's wife. However, if Jacob and Heli were full brothers, then Matthat in Luke and Matthan in Matthew are the same person, but their fathers are different. If they are half brothers, then it means that their mother married two men, Matthan and Matthat, with surprisingly similar names. As a result, others contend that one need not posit a levirate marriage, but that, like Jeconiah had done in appointing Shealtiel as his son (1 Ch 3:17), one can appoint another as one's heir. In fact, some have argued that the verb translated "begat" can be translated as "adopted." Thus Jacob did as Jeconiah had done and appointed Heli's son Joseph as his heir when Jacob failed to have children.[23]

In conclusion, it appears that we need to affirm both a historical and a theological understanding of the genealogies. There is no point in affirming the theological significance of the genealogies if they are not grounded in historical events, and there is good reason to believe that they were.[24] That is not to say that the various problems regarding the genealogies have been convincingly solved. We still lack definitive knowledge of a number of different factors, such as the identity of people mentioned, the purpose of the organizing principles, and how the two genealogies can be harmonized, among others. It appears, however, that in the two different genealogies there is a convergence around them both indicating the descent to Joseph, whether by levirate law or, more likely, through a designated heir, such that the two lines converge in the single man. The genealogies are also placed within their respective Gospels to help to reinforce the theology of each Gospel. Matthew's genealogy, like the Gospel itself, is clearly structured around significant numbers to show the significance of sayings and events, while Luke's genealogy places the events of Jesus' birth within their historical context, working from the present back to the past. Both genealogies help to reinforce the theme that the events surrounding the birth of Jesus Christ were pre-ordained and divinely superintended, so that the birth of Jesus occurred as it did and when it did in the fullness of a time that could be traced to that moment.

---

22. Carson, *Matthew*, 64.
23. This view is supported by J. G. Machen, *The Virgin Birth of Christ* (London: Marshall, Morgan & Scott, 1930), 207–209; Carson, *Matthew*, 65; and Johnson, *The Purpose of the Biblical Genealogies*, 142.
24. J. Jeremias, *Jerusalem in the Time of Jesus* (Philadelphia: Fortress, 1969), 284–97.

The Time of Jesus' Birth

John B. Polhill

On the basis of current Christmas celebrations, one might assume that Jesus was born on the night of December 24/25 at the outset of the first millennium. This assumption would be wrong on two accounts, both as to the year and the time of year of Jesus' birth. What is the NT evidence for the date of Jesus' birth?

The Death of Herod

That Jesus was born during the reign of Herod the Great (37–4 BC) is attested by both Matthew 2:1-20 and Luke 1:5. Matthew relates the wise men's questioning of Herod (2:1-8), Herod's slaughter of the babies (2:16), and the death of Herod (2:15,19-20). The Jewish historian Josephus recounts the death of Herod at some length, noting that it occurred in the thirty-fourth year of his reign and that it was followed shortly thereafter by an eclipse of the moon[1] and prior to the Passover.[2] An eclipse of the moon was visible in Palestine on the night of March 12/13, 4 BC, and the Passover that year occurred in March/April. Thus, Herod died most likely sometime in March of 4 BC. Jesus was probably born a year or two before the death of Herod, since Herod ordered his soldiers to kill all the boys in Bethlehem two years old or younger. A date of 6 BC would not be far off for the birth of Jesus. Such a date is supported by Luke 3:1, which dates the beginning of Jesus' ministry during the fifteenth year of Tiberius (AD 27/28) and notes that Jesus was approximately 30 years old at that time.

If our calendar is based on the time of Jesus' birth, why is it 4 to 6 years off? The answer is that it is based on an erroneous calculation of AD 533 by Dionysius Exiguus, who wished to establish a calendar based on Jesus' birth rather than the then-current calendar based on the establishment of Rome.[3] He chose the year 754 of the Roman calendar for Jesus' birth rather than 750, the year of Herod's death. In any event, the death of Herod is the most reliable line of evidence we have for establishing Jesus' date of birth.

The Star

Attempts have often been made to establish Jesus' birthday by the star that guided the wise men. Three types of astral phenomena have been suggested.[4] The first is a comet. Chinese records mention the appearance of a comet (the one later designated as Halley's) in 12 BC. The problem with this view is that a comet is not a star and does not have a star's appearance. Also, the date of 12 BC is too early for Jesus' birth.

A second view maintains that the star of the wise men was a planetary conjunction. In 1606 the astronomer Johannes Kepler noted that a conjunction of Jupiter and Saturn occurred in May/June, September/October, and December of 7 BC, with Mars aligning with the conjunction shortly

---

1. Josephus, *Jewish Antiquities,* translated by Ralph Marcus: *Loeb Classical Library* 8 (Cambridge, MA: Harvard University Press and London: William Heinemann, Ltd., 1980), 17.167.
2. Ibid., 17.213.
3. Raymond E. Brown, *The Birth of the Messiah* (Garden City, NY: Doubleday, 1977), 167.
4. For further treatment, see Brown, 171–172; Karl Donfried, "Chronology" in *The Anchor Bible Dictionary*, ed. David N. Freedman (Garden City, NY: Doubleday, 1992), I:1013; Ben Witherington III, "Birth of Jesus," in *Dictionary of Jesus and the Gospels*, eds. Joel B. Green and Scot McKnight (Downers Grove, IL: InterVarsity, 1992), 68–69.

thereafter. This date of 7 BC is less of a problem than the comet view, but the problem of appearance to the naked eye remains. Though such a conjunction produces a brighter light than that of single planets, the conjunction is not a perfect alignment and the outlines of the individual planets are clearly visible.

Kepler himself advocated a third view—that the Christmas star was a supernova, which occurs when a star explodes and gives off an unusually bright light. The problem with this view is that we have no record of a supernova that was visible to the naked eye in the period close to Jesus' birth date (as determined by the death of Herod).

Such attempts to pin down the star of the wise men continue but so far have yielded nothing definite. Further, one should bear in mind the caveat of John Broadus, who noted that the Christmas star was anything but a natural astronomical phenomenon. A normal star would continue to appear as moving in the sky and not come to a standstill over the place where Jesus was (Mt 2:9). This was an exceptional, miraculous star.[5]

A further chronological observation is also in order regarding the wise men. It is likely that their visit did not occur on the night of Jesus' birth. Mary and Joseph appear to have moved into a house (Mt 2:11), and Herod slaughtered not just the newborns of Bethlehem but all male children two years of age and younger (Mt 2:16). The wise men's visit may thus have taken place when Jesus was a year or two old.[6] Our celebration of Jesus' birth on December 25 and the coming of the kings at a later time (Jan 6) is thus appropriate.

The Census

The third piece of NT evidence that might help in determining the date of Jesus' birth is Luke's dating of the birth at the time of Caesar Augustus during the census conducted by the governor of Syria, Quirinius (Lk 2:1-2). In connection with this census, Joseph traveled with Mary from Nazareth to "his own town," at which time Jesus was born (Lk 2:3-7).

Actually Luke's chronological note about the census proves to be more of a problem than a help. We simply have no record of such a census at the time of Jesus' birth, if one assumes the birth took place before the death of Herod. Long ago the historian Emil Schürer pointed to five problems with Luke's reference to the census.[7] First, no historical record exists for a general imperial census in the time of Augustus. Second, under Roman census practice, enrollment was by place of residence or where one owned property, not by ancestral domain, but Luke has Joseph going *from* his place of residence to that of his ancestral domain. Third, it is unlikely a Roman census would have been carried out in Palestine during the time of Herod's reign.

All three of these first objections of Schürer present no insuperable problems. As for the first, though Augustus may not have issued a general census to be conducted simultaneously throughout the empire, ample evidence exists that he endorsed the *principle* of censuses, and many were conducted at separate times throughout the provinces. The second problem also can easily be answered. Either Joseph may have held property in Bethlehem,[8] or the Romans may have followed Jewish census practice, which was by tribes (2 Sm 24:1-2). As for the third problem, the Romans indeed would not likely have carried out a census (for taxation purposes) in defiance of Herod.

5. John A. Broadus, *Commentary on the Gospel of Matthew* (An American Commentary on the New Testament: Philadelphia: American Baptist Publication Society, 1886), 17.

6. Craig L. Blomberg, *Matthew,* ed. David S. Dockery; *New American Commentary,* vol. 22 (Nashville: Broadman, 1992), 62.

7. Emil Schürer, "The Census of Quirinius, Luke 2:1-5," in *The History of the Jewish People in the Age of Jesus Christ (175 BC–AD 135),* new English version revised and edited by Geza Vermes and Fergus Millar (Edinburgh: T. & T. Clark, 1973), I:399–427 (originally published in 1890). See also Darrell L. Bock, *Luke 1:1–9:50* (Baker Exegetical Commentary: Grand Rapids: Baker, 1994), 903.

8. I. Howard Marshall, *The Gospel of Luke* (New International Greek Testament Commentary: Grand Rapids: Eerdmans, 1978), 101.

As a client King Herod had the power to tax his subjects, and his heavy taxes are legendary. It is possible, however, that he could have enlisted Roman assistance in the enrollment and conducting of the process.

Schürer's final two problems are more difficult. The fourth is his observation that Josephus recorded only one census under Quirinius.[9] It took place when Herod's son Archelaus was deposed as the ruler over Judea and replaced by a Roman procurator Coponius. At the same time Quirinius was appointed governor of Syria and directed to conduct a census of Judea. This census provoked a revolt led by one Judas the Galilean, a revolt also referred to in Acts 5:37. All of this is wholly plausible. As Judea was now under direct Roman administration, the power of taxation belonged to them, and a census was necessary for such purposes. That a census and its accompanying taxes would provoke rebellion on the part of the occupied Jews comes as no surprise. Josephus placed this census in the thirty-seventh year after Augustus's defeat of Antony at Actium (31 BC), which would be AD 6/7.[10] Obviously this date is too late for the birth of Jesus.

Schürer's fifth problem is closely related to the fourth: no record exists for Quirinius serving as governor of Syria prior to his assuming that role in AD 6. Quirinius was indeed in Asia Minor between 12 BC and 6 BC. The Roman historian Tacitus[11] related that during this period he defeated the Homodanensians along the Cilician border. After 4 BC he served as adviser to the adopted son of Augustus, Gaius, who served in the eastern provinces and was later made legate of Syria (1 BC–AD 4). Quirinius himself served as legate of Syria from AD 6–9. Thus, though he was present in the near east and held prominent roles there during the period when Jesus was born, no evidence exists for his having served as legate (governor) prior to AD 6. In fact, according to Josephus, the legates during this period were Sentius Saturninus (9–6 BC) and Quinctilius Varus (6–4 BC or later). The next one mentioned is Gaius Caesar (1 BC–AD 4).[12] At most, the only dates where the governorship is uncertain during this period are 4–1 BC. Attempts have been made to place a prior tenure as governor during this period,[13] but even if such could be proved, the date would still be too late for the birth of Jesus.

Solutions to these last two of Schürer's problems generally follow along four lines. First is a grammatical consideration. Luke 2:2 is usually translated along the following lines: "This first (*prote*) registration took place while Quirinius was governing Syria," or "this first census was taken." Some have suggested that the Greek word *prote* should not be translated "first" but "before," or "prior to." This verse is then rendered "this census occurred *before* Quirinius was governor of Syria," or "this census was *prior to* (that of) Quirinius."[14] This is not an impossible translation, but it is unlikely, given the fact that *prote* is followed by a genitive absolute.

A second solution was proposed by the British archaeologist Sir William Ramsay, who sought to prove that Quirinius had two terms as governor of Syria. He based this on a damaged inscription from Tivoli, known as the *titulus tiburtinus*. Ramsay argued that the inscription referred to a man who served as the legate of Syria and Phoenicia twice, whom Ramsay identified with Quirinius.

9. Josephus, *The Jewish Antiquities,* trans. Louis H. Feldman: *LCL* 9 (Cambridge, MA: Harvard University Press and London: William Heinemann, Ltd., 1981), 18.1–10.

10. Ibid., 18.26. See also Joseph A. Fitzmyer, *The Gospel According to Luke (I–IX)* (The Anchor Bible: Garden City, NY: Doubleday, 1981), 402.

11. Tacitus, *The Annals,* trans. John Jackson: *LCL* 3 (Cambridge, MA: Harvard University Press and London: William Heinemann, Ltd., 1992), 3:48.

12. Brown, 550.

13. A view attributed to Mommsen by A. N. Sherwin-White, *Roman Society and Roman Law in the New Testament* (Oxford: Clarendon, 1963), 163.

14. Rene Laurentin, *The Truth of Christmas,* trans. Michael J. Wrenn (Petersham, MA: St. Bede's Publications, 1986), 329. See also Marshall, 104.

The inscription would thus solve the problem by allowing for an earlier service of Quirinius at the time of Jesus' birth. Ramsay's view, however, seems to be based on a mistranslation. The inscription should read that a (unnamed) man served Augustus twice as legate, the second time serving in Syria and Phoenicia. No other evidence exists for an imperial legate serving twice in the *same* province, though some did serve as legates more than once but in *different* provinces.[15]

A third solution calls for an emendation of the text of Luke. It is based on the following text from Tertullian: "There is historical proof that at this very time a census had been taken in Judea by Sentius Saturninus."[16] Tertullian was arguing that Jesus' birth should be well documented, since a census was held at the time of this birth. Obviously, Tertullian was not depending on our text of Luke, where the census is attributed to Quirinius. Tertullian's reference to Saturninus' census fits the chronology of Jesus' birth, since Saturninus served as legate between 9 and 6 BC. So, some have argued that our text of Luke 2:2 is corrupt and "Quirinius" should instead read "Saturninus." Unfortunately, no textual evidence whatever exists in support of this view.[17]

The Tertullian reference is also sometimes employed in support of a fourth line of solution that maintains that Quirinius took a census under imperial commission during the administration of Saturninus. This would be the census referred to in Luke 2:2, not the subsequent census of AD 6/7.[18] A number of variations of this solution exist—namely, a two-step census under Quirinius, with an initial registration (not as governor but under special imperial commission) during the period of Jesus' birth and the actual conduct of the taxation process during his tenure as governor in AD 6/7.

The fact that so many solutions exist points to the difficulty of the problem. Nevertheless, they remind us of the limitations of our sources and offer reasonable alternatives to the unacceptable view that the text of Luke is inaccurate. As for the date of Jesus' birth, the census offers little help, and the death of Herod remains the most certain point of reference. So, if we can determine the *year* of Jesus' birth as being around 6 BC, can we know the *day* of His birth?

The Day of Jesus' Birth[19]

Determining the day of Jesus' birth is basically futile. The closest thing to biblical evidence is the reference to the shepherds watching over their flocks at night in the open fields (Lk 2:8). This would indicate a nighttime birth (hence our Christmas Eve traditions). It would also seem to indicate a birth between March and November, since the sheep were usually kept in folds rather than in open fields during the winter months, making our December date of the observance suspect.

Early Christian tradition is not very helpful either. Our earliest reference is probably that of Clement of Alexandria (about AD 200), who mentions two dates suggested in his time, May 20 and April 20–21.[20] Various speculations of the third century likewise date the birth in the spring, among these being April 2, March 25, and March 28. These datings seem to have been related to the spring equinox and the assumption that the earth was created at a time when day and night were of equal length and that Jesus' birth must have followed the same creation pattern.

---

15. Donfried, I:1012.
16. Tertullian, *Against Marcion* (Alexander Roberts, James Donaldson, and A. Cleveland Coxe: The Ante-Nicene Fathers 3: Translations of the writings of the Fathers down to AD 325: Grand Rapids: Eerdmans and Edinburgh: T. & T. Clark, 1978), 378.
17. Brown, 553.
18. Donfried, I:1013.
19. For an excellent discussion, see Oscar Cullmann, "The Origin of Christmas" in *The Early Church: Studies in Early Christian History and Theology*, abridged edition, edited by A. J. B. Higgins (Philadelphia: Westminster, 1966), 21–36.
20. Clement of Alexander, *Stromata* (Alexander Roberts, James Donaldson, and A. Cleveland Coxe: ANF 2: Translations of the writings of the Fathers down to AD 325: Grand Rapids: Eerdmans and Edinburgh: T. & T. Clark, 1978), 333.

The earliest Christians do not seem to have celebrated Jesus' birth. The earliest celebration of anything even approximating His birth was that of "Epiphany" on January 6 in the eastern churches. Epiphany was primarily a celebration of the incarnation, of the coming of Christ to earth rather than of His birth. The choice of January 6 may have come from pagan celebrations, such as the feast of Dionysus held on that day. The Roman church seems to have begun celebrating Jesus' birth in the fourth century, particularly under the influence of Constantine. A major holiday for the Romans was in honor of the sun god, held on December 25 around the time of the winter solstice. During Constantine's reign this holiday was Christianized, with Christ rather than the sun celebrated as the true light of the world.

Perhaps the questionable origin of the date of our Christmas celebration should remind us of what is *primary* about the holiday. It is not just the celebration of a birthday. Origen (early third century) was right in observing that birthday celebrations are not distinctly Christian. He noted that in the Bible only pagans are depicted observing their birthdays—Pharaoh and Herod.[21] What should be central about Christmas for us is what was central in the early Epiphany celebrations—not the birth so much as the *coming* of Christ as the incarnate Son of God, the word made flesh, the light of the world.[22]

---

21. Origen, *Commentary on Matthew* (Alexander Roberts, James Donaldson, and A. Cleveland Coxe: ANF 10: Translations of the writings of the Fathers down to AD 325: Grand Rapids: Eerdmans and Edinburgh: T. & T. Clark, 1978), X.22.
22. *The Teaching of the Apostles* (Alexander Roberts, James Donaldson, and A. Cleveland Coxe: ANF 10: Translations of the writings of the Fathers down to AD 325: Grand Rapids: Eerdmans and Edinburgh: T. & T. Clark, 1978), 6.

The Language Jesus Spoke

Rick Melick

At the crucifixion of Jesus, Pilate placed a *titulus* above the cross as an official explanation of Jesus' death. It was written in three languages: Latin, Greek, and Hebrew (or Aramaic) (Jn 19:19-20). Presumably Pilate wanted to communicate to persons of all local dialects. All three languages were common in first-century Palestine. How many of the three would Jesus likely have used?

The earliest texts of the NT are all in koine Greek, the common language of the world at that time. Yet for most of the NT writers, Greek was an acquired language. Jews generally spoke Aramaic, as they had done for centuries, both in Palestine and Persia, though their Scriptures were originally written in Hebrew. In Rome, the capital of the Roman Empire, they spoke Latin, and that was the preferred language of all official communication with Rome. In addition, many people spoke one or more of the various dialects that still prevailed around the Mediterranean world. In Jewish Palestine that would mean Aramaic or Hebrew.

What language did Jesus speak? Perhaps more to the central NT question, did Jesus ever teach in Greek? An affirmative answer may even suggest we do have the exact words of Jesus recorded in the NT, since the writers could have quoted Him verbatim. Even in the remote places of the Roman world, most people knew multiple languages.

The Languages of Palestine

Ostensibly a small and relatively unimportant area like Palestine would be monolingual. Yet its strategic location as the gateway between three continents brought it a disproportionate contact with the world and its languages. At most times multiple languages were spoken.

Hebrew

The classic Jewish language is Hebrew. In the earliest days of Israel's nationhood, it was the national language. As such, it was also the language of most of the OT whose writings spanned 1,500 years. Hebrew has remained the preferred Jewish language and is now the official language of Israel.

Aramaic

Near the end of the OT era the political situation changed drastically. First Assyria, then Babylon captured portions of Palestine and instituted mass deportations to places of other languages. In particular, the Babylonian captivity of 586 BC brought lasting change. The Jews of the Diaspora learned foreign languages in order to survive. Because of the political influence, Aramaic also became the preferred language of Palestine. Thus Aramaic replaced Hebrew as the common language of the Middle East. It remained the popular language until after Jesus' death.

Greek

In 332 BC Alexander the Great conquered the known world. Among his policies, he attempted to teach everyone a common version of Classical Greek, called *koine*. Because Palestine lay in the main route to Egypt, the Greeks occupied Palestine for approximately 150 years. These were years of radical change. The Greeks established the *polis* everywhere they went. Roughly equivalent to a modern city, the *polis* was a place that perpetuated Greek civilization with its philosophy and language. Jerusalem was declared a *polis,* and many Jews acculturated to Greek thought. In Alexandria the Hebrew Bible was translated into Greek. Called the Septuagint (LXX), this was the Bible of most Jews as succeeding generations lost their fluency in Hebrew.

Beyond Jerusalem, in Galilee and eastern Palestine, the Greeks built the Decapolis, a region consisting of 10 Greek cities patterned after cities in Greece. These *poloi* influenced most of Palestine, but particularly Galilee, where Jesus was raised. When the Romans conquered Greece, they kept Greek as the language of commerce and society world-wide. Without doubt Greek was frequently spoken in Palestine.

Latin

Rome occupied Palestine from approximately 63 BC. For the most part Rome allowed Greek as the *lingua franca* for pragmatic reasons. The Romans, however, spoke Latin. It was the preferred language of government and literature. Latin did not spread widely until approximately AD 400, when it replaced Greek as the *lingua franca* of the western world.

Few in Palestine spoke Latin. Nevertheless the Roman officials certainly preferred it and probably required it for matters of state. Some of the inscriptions in Palestine and general knowledge of customs of the day suggest that Latin was familiar in Jesus' world.

The Common Languages of Jesus' Day

In the AD first century, Palestine enjoyed much more cultural and linguistic variety than is often assumed. Sacred languages die slowly; national languages transcend cultural changes; and the language of occupying nations is usually resisted. Both the religious and social institutions bear witness to a variety of language options.

Religion

Classical Jewish faith intertwined with Hebrew. As noted, it was the language of the OT writers because it was the language of national Israel. Frequently other languages vied for acceptance in Palestine primarily through the worship of foreign or Canaanite deities, but they were never accepted since they represented idolatrous institutions. In the first- or second-centuries BC, the rabbis began the process of oral interpretation that became the Mishnah. By far the majority of the tractates of the Mishnah were in Hebrew, although it was somewhat different from biblical Hebrew.

Other indications of Hebrew include the Dead Sea Scrolls (and other such writings), from approximately 200 BC, and the letters of Bar Kochba, approximately AD 130. The Dead Sea Scrolls intentionally attempted to recapture the glory days of Israel, including its language. The letters of Bar Kochba reflect the same intent with a religious and political rebellion after the fall of Jerusalem. While some of Bar Kochba's letters are in Greek out of necessity in communicating with the masses, clearly some Jews could still speak Hebrew. Surprisingly, there are few inscriptions from the period in Hebrew.

Religious language broadened to incorporate Aramaic and Greek in the centuries immediately preceding the birth of Jesus. Because of the Dispersion (586 BC), both Aramaic and Greek became the vernacular.

When the Hebrew Bible was translated into Greek in the second-century BC, Greek became increasingly the language of the synagogues. Apparently many Hellenistic Jews found their way back to Jerusalem (Ac 6:1). The Greek translation became the standard Bible of Greek speaking Jews and Christians. Other religious literature was produced in Greek. This includes many of the

OT Apocrypha and Pseudepigrapha, Philo's writings, Jewish Apocalyptic writings, and some of Josephus's works.

Aramaic naturally assumed prominence through political movements. Some of the OT shows Aramaic influence. Portions of Daniel were written in Aramaic, and there are traces of Aramaic influence (Aramaisms) in the Pentateuch, Chronicles, and the Prophets.

Early on, the synagogue services were in Aramaic. Although the biblical texts were always read in Hebrew, Aramaic paraphrases accompanied the readings. These eventually became the Talmuds.

Thus the religious language of the first century demonstrated variety. Spiritual truth had to be communicated in the vernacular.

Society

Palestinian society was also multi-cultural and multi-lingual. For the most part, Aramaic replaced Hebrew. Inasmuch as the political systems often correlated with the religious systems, Hebrew was maintained in some matters of Jewish politics. In the first century, however, many Jews were unable to communicate in Hebrew. Increasingly, Aramaic gained prominence.

Recent archaeological sites reveal a well-developed Roman structure around lower Galilee in particular. The combination of the Greco-Roman cities, extensive commercial interests, military presence, and strategic location of Palestine, made it imperative to speak Greek. This evidence suggests that most Galileans could speak Greek, learning it quite early. The major Roman city of Sepphoris was only four air miles from Nazareth, and Capernaum was the commercial center of northern Palestine. Without doubt, Greek permeated the entire areas of Jesus' boyhood and primary ministry. This is evidenced by coins with Greek inscriptions, some minted by Herod the Great, the king at Jesus' birth.

Latin was the official language of the occupying nation. No doubt Roman officials preferred it—the language of Rome and Italy. There is some evidence that judicial verdicts had to be communicated officially with a sensitivity to Latin. Practically, however, Rome was content to use the linguistic infrastructure established by Greece, keeping Greek as the *lingua franca*.

Language Evidences from the Gospels

Ultimately knowledge of the language Jesus spoke must be reflected in the Gospels. This is at once the most compelling and most elusive evidence. Knowing with certainty involves extensive linguistic criteria to distinguish between the original words of Jesus and those of the interpreters. Nevertheless, the evidence is significant.

The primary text suggesting Jesus spoke Hebrew is Luke 4:16-19. There Jesus read from the Isaiah scroll in the synagogue. No doubt the scroll was written in Hebrew, indicating Jesus' ability to read, if not speak, the classic religious language.

Several texts involve Aramaic. Most come from the Gospel of Mark, written to Romans. Mark intended to interpret for a Latin speaking community. He preserved and interpreted the following Aramaic sayings: Mark 5:41, *"Talitha koum"*; Mark 14:36, *"Abba"; and Mark 15:34, "Eloi, Eloi, lemá sabachtháni."* Mark chose to leave these in the original and translated them into Greek for his readers.

The case for Jesus speaking Greek rests on logical assumptions. Since all the extant copies of the Gospels are in Greek, it would be difficult to determine when the authors were translating instead of quoting Jesus. The assumptions arise from the situations reflected in the Gospels where it is most likely that Jesus interacted in Greek.

Jesus spoke with many Greek-speaking persons. The most extensive, and official, is in the trial before Pilate (Mk 15:2-5; Mt 27:11-14; Lk 23:2-5; Jn 18:29-38). Two aspects of the account suggest a Greek dialogue. First, it is unlikely that a politician in a short-term appointment would learn the local language. Pilate probably did not learn Aramaic. Second, the discourses between Jesus and Pilate, and Pilate and the crowd, are reported in a way that suggests no translator was present. It seems most natural to assume that Jesus and the crowds could speak Greek with Pilate.

Other encounters with Greek speakers support this hypothesis. Jesus spoke with the Syrophoenician woman, recorded in Mark 7:25-30. Mark seems intent on clarifying that she was a Greek-speaking woman. Another case is John 12:20-28, where the Greeks sought Philip as an intermediary to bring them to Jesus. Additionally, Jesus met with a Roman centurion in Capernaum (Mt 8:5-13; Lk 7:2-10), and a similar encounter occurred in John 4:46-53. Doubtless these persons spoke Greek. If so, Jesus would have had to speak with them in their language.

The confession of Peter also supports Jesus' ability to speak in Greek (Mt 16:13-20, especially; Mk 8:27-30; Lk 9:18-21). Primarily, Jesus' play on words with Peter's name makes more sense in Greek than in Aramaic. The contrast between *petros,* the stone, and *petra,* the cliff, is clear in Greek but loses its dynamic in Aramaic.

Conclusions

Two questions guided this discussion. What language did Jesus speak? What was the preferred language in which Jesus taught? The discussion illuminates the situation of both Jesus and His environment.

Regarding Jesus' language, several summary statements may be made. Jesus was, doubtless, multi-lingual. He could move among at least three languages with some comfort. First, growing up He would have had significant exposure to Greek both from the non-Jews in Palestine and from the Jews who had to speak Greek to engage in the international aspects of life in Palestine. Second, His deep spiritual interests growing up in a synagogue would likely have led Him to a deep appreciation of Hebrew. After all, He could engage in deep spiritual discussions at an early age with learned rabbis (Lk 2:46-47). Third, His daily life in an Aramaic speaking community doubtless facilitated ability in the common language.

Some conclusions may be made regarding Jesus' teaching. First, it seems quite unlikely that Jesus would have, or could have, drawn the large crowds of interested listeners if He had spoken in a second language. Further, Greek was the language of the occupying nation, always hated because their presence implied the triumph of heathen nations over God's people. Aramaic was the language of the heart. Second, the earliest account of the origins of the Gospels state that Matthew wrote first in Hebrew, or possibly Aramaic (Papias, AD 112). That the Gospel accounts were first in Hebrew or Aramaic finds some support from scholars who have translated the Greek texts into Aramaic, discovering an Aramaic rhythm and style to most of the accounts. Third, the varieties of wording in the parallel accounts of the Synoptic Gospels suggest that the three are translations/interpretations of Jesus' words.

At the present state of evidence, strong conclusions are impossible. The best conclusion is that Jesus ministered in the language of the heart. For most that was Aramaic; for others that was Greek. At the same time, Jesus was capable of speaking multiple languages—the languages prevalent in first-century Palestine. It may be that some of the words of Scripture are actual quotations from Jesus in Greek. Most likely, however, by far the majority of the Gospels are interpretations into Greek.

The Apostles: Four Lists

Matthew 10:2-4; Mark 3:16-19; Luke 6:13-16; Acts 1:13,26

David G. Shackelford

Matthew 10:2-4	Mark 3:16-19	Luke 6:13-16	Acts 1:13,26
Simon called Peter	Simon Peter	Simon (Peter)	Peter
Andrew, Peter's brother	James, son of Zebedee	Andrew, Peter's brother	John
James, son of Zebedee	John, brother of James	James	James
John, brother of James	Jesus surnamed them Boanerges (Sons of Thunder)	John	Andrew
Philip	Andrew	Philip	Philip
Bartholomew	Philip	Bartholomew	Thomas
Thomas	Bartholomew	Matthew	Bartholomew
Matthew (Levi)	Matthew	Thomas	Matthew
James, son of Alphaeus	Thomas	James, son of Alphaeus	James, son of Alphaeus
Thaddaeus	James, son of Alphaeus	Simon called Zealot	
Simon the Zealot	Thaddaeus	Judas, son of James	Simon the Zealot
Judas Iscariot, the betrayer	Simon the Zealot	Judas Iscariot, the traitor	Judas, son of James
	Judas Iscariot, the betrayer		Matthias

The NT provides four lists of the names of the original 12 apostles. Occasionally a name is accompanied by another marker, for example, Matthew, the tax collector (Mt 10:3). At other times, it is not. One might ask, "Why four lists?" While the Bible does not say specifically, we might safely assume that God would only repeat Himself for good reason. Instead of saying that Jesus called 12 apostles, God names them—not once, but four times. It is reasonable that their identities are therefore significant, and that certain conclusions may be drawn from this observation. Consideration might be given to two related possibilities. First, their names and additional identifying markers help us understand them personally and, in several instances, politically and geographically. One was a Zealot, one a tax collector, several were fishermen. Second, these observations indicate the variety of their divine choosing and maybe something of their places in the strategy of Jesus and His mission.

The Meaning of "Apostle." The Greek *apostolos* has an interesting history. The word serves as an example of how the NT usage developed the meaning of the term beyond its previous signification. Originally a nautical term in classical Greek, it did not contain any of the authoritative connotation that is usually associated with the term.[1] But in its NT use, the word indicates not only the one who is sent, but emphasizes the full authority attached to his commission by the sender. He is given the wherewithal to act as the full representative in the "cause of another."[2]

In the NT, the term was first applied to the original 12 apostles, including Matthias, Judas' replacement in Acts 1:26. But we find the term apostle also applied to Paul, (Rm 1:1; 1 Co 1:1) as one "abnormally born" (1 Co 15:8), to Jesus (Heb 3:1), and to Andronicus and Junia (Rm 16:7).[3] In each case the idea is that full authority is extended to the one sent. This authority is vital to the mission of Jesus as well as the Twelve. Jesus was sent by His Father (Lk 4:18; Jn 5:24,30,36); He is described as an apostle with the full authority of His Father who sent Him. If the Twelve were to carry on the same mission as Jesus, subsequent to His atonement for our sins, they had to be fully trained and authorized to do so.

The Calling of the Twelve. Jesus knew that He had only three years to call, commission, and train those who would carry on a mission He had designed from eternity. At first glance, the individuals Jesus chose seemed to belie the seriousness of His choices. But Jesus did not underestimate the task before Him. When we look at the whole, we find a rather colorful and unimpressive group—some fishermen, a tax collector, a Zealot. First Corinthians 1:26-29 immediately comes to mind:

> Brothers, consider your calling: not many are wise from a human perspective, not many powerful, not many of noble birth. Instead, God has chosen the world's foolish things to shame the wise, and God has chosen the world's weak things to shame the strong. God has chosen the world's insignificant and despised things—the things viewed as nothing—so He might bring to nothing the things that are viewed as something, so that no one can boast in His presence.

Their unimpressive credentials notwithstanding, with the directive Jesus received from His Father the night before in prayer, we observe that Jesus knew these men better than they knew themselves. We find that Jesus is the One who is able to make the weak mighty and the ignoble noble. He can transform those who are not into those who are.

The choosing of 12 is undoubtedly a reference to the 12 tribes of Israel, over whom they will judge (Mt 19:28; Lk 22:30). There are no qualifications given in Scripture until Acts 1:21-22 where Judas Iscariot's replacement had to have companied with Jesus and the apostles from the time of John's baptism to the ascension. Apparently, Jesus determined His selections solely upon the basis of His prayer the night before. We therefore find that their individual enlistment was upon the simplest of terms. On some occasions, Jesus simply called whom He wanted to follow Him: Simon and Andrew (Mt 4:19); James and John, sons of Zebedee (Mt 4:21); Matthew (Mt 9:9); Philip (Jn 1:43). With Nathanael, Jesus did not even make the initial contact. Philip introduced Nathanael (also known as Bartholomew) to Jesus (Jn 1:45). From that point, Nathanael became convinced of the person of Jesus, but there is not even a formal invitation to follow Christ. Nonetheless, there was no misunderstanding. When Jesus told him, "You will see greater things than this" (Jn 1:50), Nathanael knew that he would follow the Master. The witness of Scripture is that the event constituted a legitimate "call" (Mk 3:13-19).

Between the lists and related passages, the Bible identifies the original Twelve with other names. Matthew is also the one known as Levi (see Mk 2:14; Mt 9:9; Lk 5:27). Simon Peter is also called

1. Gerhard Kittel and Gerhard Friedrich, eds., *Theological Dictionary of the New Testament* (Grand Rapids: Eerdmans, 1964), s.v., "*apostolos*," by Rengstorf.
2. Ibid.
3. Romans 16:7 says that Andronicus and Junia are "outstanding among the apostles" (*en tois apostolois*).

Cephas (Jn 1:42) and Simon (son of) Jonah (Mt 16:17). Thomas is sometimes identified as Twin (Jn 11:16; 20:24; 21:2). Jude is distinguished from Judas Iscariot by the phrase "not Iscariot," that he might not be confused with the betrayer. From a comparison with Luke 6:16 and Acts 1:13, most conclude that this Jude, Thaddaeus, and Lebbaeus are the same. Bartholomew is named as such in all four lists. But in John 21:2, Nathanael is listed with several of the apostles at one of the post-resurrection appearances of Jesus. Upon further examination we find that Bartholomew is listed as one of the apostles in all places except John's Gospel (Matthew, Mark, Luke, Acts). Bartholomew is not found in John's Gospel at all. Instead, Nathanael is named. Most consider Bartholomew and Nathanael to be the same individual. Why John refers to him as Nathanael instead of Bartholomew is not explained.

The Training and Mission of the Twelve. The training of the apostles is vitally linked to their call. When the Bible indicates that they left everything and followed Jesus (Mk 10:28; Lk 5:28), they literally did that very thing. They not only left all to follow Him, they left all and lived with Him. We find that from the time of their enlistment, the lives of Jesus and His apostles are not identical, but they are inseparable. We observe their training to be personal and individualistic. Jesus empowered them to have authority over demonic spirits (Lk 10:19), but He also empowered them to understand spiritual truths and parables (Mk 4:11). They heard His teachings, witnessed His miracles, and sometimes performed miracles themselves. Sometimes they failed. In the course of it all, they were convinced that Jesus was the promised Messiah, the Christ of God, and God in the flesh. Scripture is clear that they did not understand much that Jesus tried to teach them until after the ascension. This is particularly the case concerning His death and resurrection. But the task for which they were called and trained they fulfilled faithfully. Jesus depended upon them to be available that, through them, He might continue the establishment and building of His church.

The Deaths of the Twelve. We know little about the deaths of the apostles. For most details we must rely upon church tradition. Scripture indicates that **Peter** was crucified (Jn 21:18-19). According to Origen, Peter did not consider himself worthy to be crucified as Christ was, so at his request, he was crucified upside down. **Andrew** was commanded to renounce his preaching and sacrifice to the pagan gods. When he refused, he was scourged and crucified on a cross that was in the shape of an X. This came to be known as St. Andrew's cross. He hung for three days encouraging the onlookers to come to Christ.[4] This tradition also says he died on November 30, but we do not know the year. **James**, the son of Zebedee, was slain with the sword by Herod (Ac 12:2). **John** was allegedly thrown into a caldron of boiling oil. When it did not cause his death, he lived in Ephesus. He is the only one of the original Twelve to die of natural causes. **Philip** was imprisoned, scourged, and eventually crucified. **Bartholomew** took the responsibility for Philip's body, but for doing so, he himself was nearly martyred. There are conflicting traditions concerning Bartholomew's death. Some say he was beaten with clubs, others that he died at the edge of the sword. Still another tradition says that he was skinned alive with knives and then crucified upside down. **Thomas** was thrust through with a spear because he angered the priests of pagan idols. **Matthew** was martyred with a sword. Nothing is known about the death of **James**, the son of Alphaeus. **Judas Thaddaeus** was crucified. **Simon the Zealot** was crucified. **Judas Iscariot** hanged himself (Mt 27:5).

As we look upon the original Twelve, we see that they were not chosen because of special abilities, social standing, or political or economic influence. Neither were they perfect men. But they were God's perfect choices. In truth, their call and usefulness is the same as all disciples today. Our Lord does not look upon us for who we are, but for who we can be through His Spirit.

---

4. John Foxe, *Foxe's Christian Martyrs of the World,* reprint ed. (San Antonio, TX: Mantle Ministries, n.d.), 30.

Sermon on the Mount

Charles Quarles

Importance

No sermon ever preached has been more significant to the Christian church than the Sermon on the Mount (SM). Tragically, the sermon has been largely ignored by contemporary America. A recent Gallup poll indicated that only one-third of adult Americans are familiar enough with the sermon to identify Jesus as its source. Many Americans think that the sermon was a famous homily by Billy Graham.

In sharp contrast to the current neglect of the SM, the early church prized Matthew 5–7 as one of the most important sections of the Scriptures. Probable allusions to the Sermon on the Mount appear in other NT books including Romans, James, and 1 Peter. Some of these allusions predate the composition of the Gospel of Matthew and suggest that the sermon was emphasized in apostolic teaching in the earliest history of the church. Christian writings from the close of the NT up to the council of Nicaea in AD 325 quote Matthew 5 more frequently and extensively than any single chapter of the Bible and quote Matthew 5–7 more frequently and extensively than any three chapters of the entire Bible.[1]

The lofty ethic of the Sermon on the Mount has inspired many people who do not embrace evangelical Christianity. Many Jewish, Islamic, and Hindu readers have expressed admiration for Jesus because of His consummate teaching in this sermon. On the other hand, many critics of the Christian church frequently point to the disparity between Jesus' teachings in the sermon and the actual conduct of those who claim to follow Him. Rediscovering the ethical and theological truths of the Sermon on the Mount is necessary to the revitalization of the church and the effectiveness of the church's mission.

History of Interpretation

The earliest sample of interpretation of the SM after the close of the NT appears in the *Didache,* a church manual probably written some time between AD 60 and 80.[2] The *Didache* opens with a discussion of the "two ways," the way of life and the way of death. These two ways are comparable to the two ways described in Matthew 7:13-14. At the conclusion of the description of the two ways, the author advised: "See that no one leads you astray from this way of the teaching, for such a person teaches you without regard for God. For if you are able to bear the whole yoke of the Lord, you will be perfect. But if you are not able, then do what you can."[3] The "way" of teaching is the way of life drawn largely from the SM. The words "you will be perfect" appear to be an allusion to Matthew 5:48. The author of the *Didache* thus viewed the SM as a description of the true righteousness that characterizes the ideal Christian disciple. Inability to live up to the standards of the SM fully at the present should not dissuade the Christian disciple from aspiring

---

1. Warren S. Kissinger, *The Sermon on the Mount: A History of Interpretation and Bibliography* (Metuchen, N.J.: Scarecrow, 1975), 6.
2. Michael W. Holmes, ed., *The Apostolic Fathers* (Grand Rapids: Baker, 1989), 146–47.
3. Ibid., 152.

to do so more and more. He should constantly strive to "be perfect, therefore, as your heavenly Father is perfect" knowing that God will grant righteousness to those who hunger and thirst for it.

Most early Christian interpreters of the SM believed that the SM was applicable to all Christians and that every believer should seek to live by its precepts here and now. Although these early believers recognized that fulfilling the SM was difficult, they denied that such was impossible for those who had and were experiencing God's transforming grace. After Chrysostom urged his audience to seek to live by the SM more and more each day, he pointed out that some believers, from the apostolic age to his own time, had been characterized by such righteousness. He counseled believers to begin with the easier precepts of the SM and to seek to advance to the more difficult precepts until they had progressed to true holiness. In this fashion, believers "may arrive at the very summit of all good things; unto which may we all attain, by the grace and love towards man of our Lord Jesus Christ, to whom be glory and dominion for ever and ever."[4] Divine grace would empower those who sought such righteousness to attain it.

Augustine, who wrote the first commentary on the sermon and who appears to have been the first to refer to this sermon as the "Sermon on the Mount" (*De Sermone Domini in Monte*), viewed the sermon as "a perfect standard of the Christian life" and "perfect in all the precepts by which the Christian life is formed."[5] This interpretation of the SM prevailed in the early church until the time of Thomas Aquinas.

During the middle ages, Aquinas introduced the notion that not all of the SM was applicable to every believer. Aquinas distinguished between "precepts" and "evangelical counsels." Precepts were commands that all followers of Christ were obligated to keep. "Counsels" were guides to Christlike perfection that were not obligatory but might be voluntarily adopted by those who wished to attain true holiness. Aquinas's teaching resulted in a "double-standard view" that became basic in Catholic moral theology.

The Protestant reformers rejected the Thomist interpretation of the SM. Martin Luther argued that the sermon addressed those who were already Christians and that divine grace produced the life described in the sermon. The righteous life that the SM described was a product of the Spirit's transforming work rather than mere human effort and was the result of salvation rather than the requirement for it. John Calvin taught that the purpose of the SM was to rescue the law from the erroneous teaching of the Pharisees who saw the law as related only to external acts and not internal attitudes.[6] The SM was intended to demonstrate the law's true purpose that had been obscured in the teaching of the Jews.[7] Against objections that the precepts were too difficult for believers to fulfill, Calvin replied:

> To our weakness, indeed, everything, even to the minutest tittle of the Law, is arduous and difficult. In the Lord we have strength. . . . That Christians are under the law of grace, means not that they are to wander unrestrained without law, but that they are engrafted into Christ, by whose grace they have the Law written in their hearts.[8]

The Anabaptists stressed that the SM should be obeyed by all Christians in the most radical way. Consequently, they prohibited the use of oaths even in a court of law, personal acts of violence

---

4. Philip Schaff, ed., *Saint Chrysostom: Homilies on the Gospel of Matthew,* vol. 10 of Nicene and Post-Nicene Fathers of the Christian Church (Grand Rapids: Eerdmans, 1983), 21.6.

5. Philip Schaff, ed., *Saint Augustine: Sermon on the Mount, Harmony of the Gospels, Homilies on the Gospels,* vol. 6 of Nicene and Post-Nicene Fathers of the Christian Church (Grand Rapids: Eerdmans, 1979), 3.

6. John Calvin, *Institutes of the Christian Religion* (Philadelphia: Westminster, 1964), 8.7.

7. John Calvin, *Matthew, Mark, Luke: Harmony of the Gospels,* vol. 1, translated by A. W. Morrison (Grand Rapids: Eerdmans, 1972), 1.183.

8. Calvin, *Institutes,* 8.52.

including self-defense, military force, legal judgments, and sometimes even the possession of personal property.

Dispensationalists championed a view of the SM that is the polar opposite of the Anabaptist view. They argued that the SM is not applicable to believers today. They insist that the SM expresses the standards of Christ's millennial reign. Lewis Sperry Chafer argued that difficulties in interpreting and applying the SM to contemporary believers resulted from a failure to discern the intended audience of the discourse. He stated, "As a rule of life, it is addressed to the Jew before the cross and to the Jew in the coming kingdom, and is therefore not now in effect."[9] For Chafer, whereas the law of Moses governed the behavior of Jews before the dispensation of grace, the teachings of the kingdom, particularly the SM, would govern the behavior of God's people in the eschatological kingdom. Their application requires "the binding of Satan, a purified earth, the restoration of Israel, and the personal reign of the King."[10]

Perhaps the prevailing interpretive approach to the SM among modern evangelical scholars is the "inaugurated eschatology" approach. This approach insists that the kingdom of God was inaugurated on earth through the ministry of Jesus. However, His kingdom will not be consummated until Jesus' return. The SM does indeed express a kingdom ethic. Since Jesus' kingdom has already been inaugurated, the ethic of the SM is the goal and ideal of Christian disciples here and now. However, disciples will not be fully characterized by the righteousness that the sermon describes until the kingdom is consummated at the time of the second coming. This approach takes seriously the unwavering conviction of the church during the first millennium of its history that the SM is applicable to all believers. However, it also recognizes that the promise that "those who hunger and thirst for righteous . . . will be filled" is being progressively fulfilled here and now but will only be finally and completely fulfilled in the final redemption when believers are resurrected and glorified.

Relation to the Sermon on the Plain

The Sermon on the Mount (Mt 5–7) and the Sermon on the Plain (Lk 6:17-49) have remarkable similarities. Most of the material that appears in the SM is either included in the Sermon on the Plain (SP) or appears elsewhere in Luke's Gospel. Material from the SM that has no parallel in Luke (Mt 5:33-37; 6:1-6,16-18; 7:6) had special importance to Matthew's Jewish-Christian audience but was less applicable to Luke's primarily Gentile-Christian audience. Consequently, several important figures in the early church, including Origen and Chrysostom, believed that the SM and the SP were two different accounts of the same sermon. This opinion is possible since the "level place" from which Jesus preached the SP may have been a mountain plateau. Augustine argued that the SM and the SP were two different sermons preached on two different occasions. His view became the dominant view of the church until the Protestant Reformation. John Calvin suggested that the SM was "a short summary of the teaching of Christ gathered from many and various discourses."[11] He felt that Luke presented Jesus' teaching in a chronological format but that Matthew's arrangement was topical.

The interpretation that best accounts for all the data and appreciates the historical reliability of both Matthew and Luke suggests that the SM and the SP are two accounts of the same sermon. The material in SM, which is similar to material appearing outside of the SP in Luke's Gospel, was

9. Lewis Sperry Chafer, *Christology,* vol. 5 of *Systematic Theology* (Dallas: Dallas Theological Seminary, 1948), 97.
10. Chafer, *Ecclesiology-Eschatology*, vol. 4 of *Systematic Theology* (Dallas: Dallas Theological Seminary, 1948), 207.
11. Calvin, *Matthew, Mark, Luke*, 1.168

preached on more than one occasion. That Jesus preached similar material on multiple occasions is evident from a comparison of Matthew 5:31-32 and 19:8-9.

Structure

The Beatitudes serve as the introduction to the SM. The salt and light sayings in Matthew 5:13-16 have a very similar form since both introductory statements begin with "You are the . . . " and end with a universal focus ("of the earth" and "of the world"). This section completes the introduction. The central section of the SM begins in 5:17 and extends to 7:12. The references to "Law and the Prophets" at the beginning and end of the section serve as a literary bracket for the material. The material in Matthew 7:13-27 serves as a conclusion for the sermon.

Theological Emphases

The SM has enormous implications for understanding the identity of Christ and the nature of salvation. The introduction and content of the SM show that Jesus is the new Moses who will deliver God's people from their slavery to sin much like the OT Moses delivered God's people from their slavery to Pharaoh (Dt 18:15-19; Ac 3:17-24). The words in Matthew 5:1, "He went up on the mountain," are an exact verbal parallel to the description of Moses ascending Mount Sinai to receive the Law in Exodus 19:3. The reference is part of a series of parallels between Jesus and Moses that Matthew has highlighted in his Gospel in order to show that Jesus is the fulfillment of the Deuteronomy 18 prophecy. Matthew 7:21-23 confirms Jesus' identity as both Savior (Mt 1:21) and Deity (Mt 1:23) by showing that Jesus is the eschatological judge to whom people appeal for entrance into the kingdom of heaven.

The Beatitudes express God's grace to undeserving and repentant sinners. God's gracious character is emphasized repeatedly in the sermon (Mt 5:45; 6:7-11). The SM insists, however, that one must not devalue divine grace by appealing to it as an excuse for a sinful lifestyle. True disciples will be characterized by a remarkable righteousness that exceeds even that of the scribes and Pharisees. Those who have become sons and daughters of the heavenly Father will resemble Him in their character and behavior (Mt 5:9,44-48; 6:7-12). As a result, personal holiness is an important indication of whether or not one who professes to follow Christ is truly His disciple (Mt 7:15-23). The disciple's righteousness is not a product of his self-effort. He expresses his repentance by hungering and thirsting "for righteousness" and God graciously begins to fill him with that righteousness here and now and will finally and completely fill him with that righteousness when Christ returns and consummates His kingdom.

Women in the Gospels

Nancy M. Easley

"Perhaps it is no wonder that the women were first at the Cradle and the last at the Cross. They had never known a man like this man—there has never been such another."[1]

To appreciate Jesus' perspective on women one must understand the status of women during the era of the NT and compare His actions with those of the culture at large. Barker held that the role of women verged on slavery, even in the Israelite culture.[2] Females were viewed as property and seen as useful for keeping the home, caring for the children, and supporting those who traveled. At best, the more sophisticated societies, such as those that were Hellenized, viewed women as inferior.

So how did Jesus view women in the Gospels? Were they treated as invisible stewards or were they given access to full stature of the image of God and allowed to be active participants in the fulfillment of the kingdom? Are there evidences of Jesus' interactions that give women today spiritual guidance and an idea of the importance of their place in God's kingdom? Reviewing the interactions between Jesus and women in the Gospels clearly shows that Jesus actively included and involved women in His ministry in surprising and substantive ways.[3]

Birth and Early Years

The genealogy of Christ appears both in Matthew and Luke. In this case, the genealogy functioned as proof of Jesus' right to be Messiah by tracing His ancestry back to David. Perhaps the surprising element is the broad scope of women, both Jewish and Gentile, both religious and scandalous. We will also consider Mary and others involved in Jesus' birth.

Ancestry

Matthew includes the names of women in Jesus' genealogy. These are unexpected characters for ancestors in the line of the prophesied Messiah. They did not all start out as pillars of great righteousness. After she was widowed, Tamar, a Canaanite, tricked her father-in-law into an incestuous liaison that bore a son in the ancestry of David (Gn 38:6-30). After hiding Hebrew spies, Rahab, a prostitute, bore a son in the ancestry of David (Jos 2; Mt 1:5). In Hebrews 11:31 and in James 2:25 she was commended for her faith. Ruth, a Moabite, left her own country to care for her mother-in-law and bore a son in David's ancestry. Despite their early religious affiliations, God brought these women to faith. Even women of faith can fall. Certainly "Uriah's wife" (Mt 1:6) knew better than to sleep with David, yet she bore a son in Messiah's ancestry (2 Sm 11).

Mary is the last woman mentioned in the genealogy. She was a poor, young village maiden betrothed to Joseph. An angel appeared to Mary and declared what was conceived in her to be of the Holy Spirit (Lk 1:35). Although Jesus was not the physical son of Joseph, He was the legal son and therefore also a descendant of David. Mary's response was one of praise and obedience (Lk 1:38,46).

Customarily women would not be included in a genealogy. Their inclusion by Matthew foreshadows at the outset of his Gospel that God's activity is not limited to only the righteous men of Israel. These women represent both pagan women and women of faith who performed both extraordinary acts of

---

1. As cited in W. Barker, *Women and the Liberator* (Old Tappan: N.J. Fleming H. Revell, 1972), 12.
2. Ibid., 9.
3. Herbert Lockyer, *The Women of the Bible,* 11th ed. (Grand Rapids: Zondervan, 1974), 14.

evil and uncommon acts of faith. What can we deduce from their presence in Christ's line? God chose these women from unexpected circumstances to be part of bringing Messiah to the world. Outside their physical role, what does this tell us? Women, both Jew and Gentile, played an important part in the expansion of the kingdom of God. Women from any ethnic background could be converted, live lives of faith, and act on that faith in dangerous or socially unacceptable situations. Except for Mary, they had no clue about their importance in the line of Christ.

Elizabeth

After Mary learned the news of her special assignment, she hurried to be with Elizabeth, a relative. When Elizabeth saw her, she was filled with the Holy Spirit and declared, "You are the most blessed of women, and your child will be blessed! How could this happen to me, that the mother of my Lord should come to me?" (Lk 1:42-43). Elizabeth was perhaps the first person given special insight and faith to understand and acknowledge Jesus as the promised Messiah and Lord.[4]

Mary

Mary proved to be a character of unusual courage and strength as well. Near the time of Jesus' delivery, she traveled to the city of David to register (Lk 2:5). While they were there, Jesus was delivered in a stable and she received a variety of unusual visitors. Of all these things Scripture says: "But Mary was treasuring up all these things in her heart and meditating on them" (Lk 2:19). On the day of the child's presentation (Lk 2:22), Mary received word that her child would be honored but also be the cause of much pain. Later she exercised her faith again as she followed Joseph to Egypt in order to preserve the life of God's special gift.

As time passed and Jesus grew, Mary continued to grow in her understanding of her special charge and His mission. During a yearly trip to Jerusalem for the festival of Passover, Jesus left His parents and began teaching. When they found Him three days later, Jesus asked her: "Why were you searching for Me? . . . Didn't you know that I had to be in My Father's house?" (Lk 2:49). Again she did not understand what Jesus was saying to them. Once more, Mary treasured all these things in her heart.

Anna

Anna is the last woman in Jesus' early years noteworthy for her response of worship to Jesus. After serving in the temple and waiting years for the fulfillment of the promise God had given her of seeing the Messiah, Anna saw the Christ and worshiped: "At that very moment, she came up and began to thank God and to speak about Him to all who were looking forward to the redemption of Jerusalem" (Lk 2:38).

Ministry

Jesus and His disciples did not provide for their needs by miracles but were supported by the service and means of women. Contrary to the custom of that day, women traveled with Jesus and the disciples to help care for their physical needs.[5] As Luke described them, they were no ordinary group of camp followers: "And also some women who had been healed of evil spirits and sicknesses: Mary, called Magdalene (seven demons had come out of her); Joanna the wife of Chuza, Herod's steward; Susanna; and many others who were supporting them from their possessions" (Lk 8:2-3).

This group was unique because Jesus accepted the ministry of a sinful woman, a woman of some authority from a Roman household, and others of unknown backgrounds. Jesus met their needs for

---

4. Ibid., 51.

5. Elisabeth Moltmann-Wendel, *The Women around Jesus* (New York: Crossroad, 1988), 131.

healing and their spiritual needs. These grateful women responded to His teachings with faith and spiritual insight. Thus, Jesus and His disciples did not provide for themselves by miracles but were supported by the service and means of women recognized as a vital part of His ministry. A glance around the foot of the cross shows these women were still with Him.

Cana

The Gospels continue to give insight into the influence women had on Jesus' ministry. In Cana, Jesus' mother influenced Him to intervene in a wedding feast and turn water into wine so the host would not be embarrassed. Her faith in Him and the resulting miracle began a new phase of His ministry. The significance of the beginning of His public ministry was, of course, more than doing a favor for His mother (Jn 2:1-4).

Samaria

Later while traveling with His disciples through the unfriendly territory of Samaria, Jesus encountered a woman at a well. Overlooking cultural taboos, Jesus asked the astonished woman for a drink (Jn 4:7-8). Even more amazing, Jesus offered her living water, letting her in on the "way to salvation" despite her current sin and her ethnicity. Her faith gave her rights far above her social station; the right to bring other Samaritans to the source of "living water".

Compassion on Women

Luke tells of a time Jesus expressed compassion for a widow whose only son had died. According to the culture, the widow had no way to care for herself without her son. Luke reported that, "When the Lord saw her, He had compassion on her and said, 'Don't cry'" (Lk 7:13). Jesus spoke, raised the boy from the dead and restored him to his mother (Lk 7:14-15). This caused those who saw to rejoice greatly and increased the crowds that followed Christ expecting miracles.

Healing

Jesus healed both men and women. Mark reports the healing of Peter's mother-in-law. "Simon's mother-in-law was lying in bed with a fever, and they told Him about her at once. So He went to her, took her by the hand, and raised her up. The fever left her, and she began to serve them" (Mk 1:30-31). Some may believe Jesus did this for Peter, but what about the place of the woman in the household and her useful service?

Jesus called out seven evil spirits from Mary Magdalene (Lk 8:2). A woman with an issue of blood touched the tassel of Christ's robe with faith. Immediately she was healed and Jesus commended her great faith. In the same setting, the daughter of Jairus, a synagogue leader, was raised (Lk 8:40-56). What was their response to Jesus? We know from Luke that Mary Magdalene helped support Jesus and care for His material needs. The woman with the issue of blood showed great faith and was commended rather than condemned (Lk 8:43-48). The raising of Jairus' daughter served to increase the faith of others throughout the region. Jesus did not ignore the plight of women in His day as others did. He responded to their needs and they had a part in building the kingdom of heaven.

Woman in Adultery

Often Jesus came face to face with women who were outcasts of society. He did not scorn them or push them aside as the religious men of the day would have done. When confronted by the Pharisees with a woman caught in adultery, instead of Jesus stoning her, He called for those without sin to step forward and stone her; thus pointing out their own guilt was as great as hers. As the guilty men crept away, the woman stayed and received forgiveness and the charge to go and sin no more (Jn 8:9-11).[6] Even women can be forgiven their sins.

Mary and Martha

Jesus made friends with women outside His immediate circle. The Gospels give us the picture of Martha as a landowner, a "lady of the house."[7] Mary and Martha were sisters who provided a place for Jesus to stay in their home in Bethany (Jn 12:1). He taught both women along with their brother Lazarus things of the kingdom, and He knew each of their natures well (Lk 10:38-39). How unusual for a traveling rabbi to teach women of that time.[8]

On the day He arrived and went to the tomb of Lazarus, Martha approached Him with great faith. Martha greeted Him with the assurance, "Even now I know that whatever You ask from God, God will give You" (Jn 11:22). She also received the same insight into His relationship with God that was given to Peter.[9] "Yes, Lord," she told Him, "I believe You are the Messiah, the Son of God, who was to come into the world" (Jn 11:27). When Mary arrived, her entreaties moved Jesus to act and call Lazarus forth from the grave.

Before the final Passover, this same Mary startled the onlookers by anointing Jesus' feet with costly perfume and wiping them with her hair (Jn 12:1-8). Respectable women did not let down their hair in public; neither did they perform the duty of a servant to wash a guest's feet. This act of deep devotion was an unprecedented act of love and worship. A woman's worship of Jesus overturned cultural and religious traditions.[10]

The Woman from Tyre

Jesus was weary from ministry when a pagan woman from Tyre cried out to Him to deliver her daughter from demon possession. At first Jesus did not respond to her pleas. Then:

> She came, knelt before Him, and said, "Lord, help me!" He answered, "It isn't right to take the children's bread and throw it to their dogs." "Yes, Lord," she said, "yet even the dogs eat the crumbs that fall from their masters' table!" Then Jesus replied to her, "Woman, your faith is great. Let it be done for you as you want." And from that moment her daughter was cured (Mt 15:25-28).

Undaunted, the woman knelt before Him and expressed a faith so great that it gave insight into the nature of His salvation that was not meant only for Jews. The salvation Jesus offered superseded all religious traditions of the day.[11]

Two Mites

Lockyer held that even in the temple, Jesus did not ignore the acts of worship of women.[12] He observed a poor widow giving all she had as an offering. He used the occasion to teach the men:

---

6. The textual problem concerning this passage is well known.
7. Moltmann-Wendel, *The Women around Jesus*, 23.
8. Barker, *Women and the Liberator*, 105.
9. Moltmann-Wendel, *The Women around Jesus*, 25.
10. Barker, *Women and the Liberator*, 44.
11. Jane Kopas, "Jesus and Women in Matthew," n.p. (cited 13 September 2005). Online: *http://theologytoday.ptsem.edu/apr1990/ v47-1-article2.htm.*
12. Lockyer, *The Women of the Bible*, 227–28.

Summoning His disciples, He said to them, "I assure you: This poor widow has put in more than all those giving to the temple treasury. For they all gave out of their surplus, but she out of her poverty has put in everything she possessed—all she had to live on" (Mk 12:43-44).

The Crucifixion and Resurrection

We can gain no greater insight into Jesus' equal treatment of women than through their role in His death and resurrection. From the cross Jesus noticed His mother Mary with John the apostle. Not wanting to leave His mother without support, "He said to His mother, 'Woman, here is your son.' Then He said to the disciple, 'Here is your mother.' And from that hour the disciple took her into his home" (Jn 19:26-27).

Luke tells us that the same women that supported Jesus through His ministry watched His death on the cross from a distance (Lk 23:49). Then they followed and saw the tomb where the body was laid. Still seeking to serve, they left to prepare spices for His burial after the Sabbath. They were also the first ones to arrive at the tomb on the third day. Although frightened by the scene at the tomb, they heard the news of Jesus' resurrection from the angels and ran to tell the disciples:

> But the angel told the women, "Don't be afraid, because I know you are looking for Jesus who was crucified. He is not here! For He has been resurrected, just as He said. Come and see the place where He lay. Then go quickly and tell His disciples, 'He has been raised from the dead. In fact, He is going ahead of you to Galilee; you will see Him there.' Listen, I have told you" (Mt 28:5-7).

What an important job for women, considered by their culture to be insignificant and inept. As if this were not enough to give women significance, Jesus appeared to Mary Magdalene (Jn 20:14-18). In those days, women were not allowed to be witnesses in a legal proceeding. Why would Jesus use them as the first witnesses to the resurrection? He valued them as partners with men in the kingdom.

Conclusion

Even in a day of women's liberation, society nor the church has never caught up with Jesus in making women equal with men.[13] Reviewing the text of the Gospels clearly demonstrates that Jesus considered women equal with men, even those beyond the bounds of Israel. He demonstrated His regard for them by healing their physical and spiritual needs.[14] He acted upon their faith to heal, bring salvation, and deliver from demons.

He overturned cultural taboos to state women's human worth and dignity. He cared deeply about their emotions and life's hurts. He unconditionally accepted their worship and confirmed their beliefs about Him. By sharing life's experiences with women, He showed them how to live lives that please God. In those same experiences, Christ showed males that the sin in their own hearts could be cured by the same salvation.

Is there a time in the life of a woman today that is not represented in His interactions with women in the Gospels? No. In every way, we can follow the example of the women in the Gospels in our relationships with Jesus. Women today need to remember that Jesus is still the "most dynamically liberating force" in our lives.[15] He is the one who came "to proclaim freedom to the captives and . . . to set free the oppressed" (Lk 4:18).

---

13. Barker, *Women and the Liberator*, 11.
14. Jane Kopas, "Jesus and Women: Luke's Gospel." n.p. (cited 13 September 2005). Online: *http://theologytoday.ptsem.edu/jul1986/v43-2-article4.htm.*
15. Barker, *Women and the Liberator*, 27.

The Kingdom of God

David S. Dockery

Just before Jesus ascended to heaven, His disciples asked, "At this time are You restoring the kingdom to Israel?" (Ac 1:6). They were seeking to put together some pieces that didn't quite seem to fit. What they were asking is this, "Is it time yet to complete what You came to do?"

They had heard Jesus proclaim, "The kingdom of heaven has come near" (Mt 4:17). He had announced in the synagogue in Nazareth:

> The Spirit of the Lord is on Me,
> because He has anointed Me
> to preach good news to the poor.
> He has sent Me
> to proclaim freedom to the captives
> and recovery of sight to the blind,
> to set free the oppressed,
> to proclaim the year of the Lord's favor. (Lk 4:18-19)

As they reflected on these words they thought, "Under Your ministry the blind received sight, the lame walked, those with leprosy were cured, the deaf heard, the dead were raised and the poor had good news preached to them." They wanted to ask the Lord, "When are You going to finish what You started?"

When He proclaimed, "The kingdom of heaven has come near," He was announcing a new order in which His miracles served as symbols of what is to come. It will be a new order of life in which the gentle will inherit the earth (Mt 5:5), where the wolf will lie down with the lamb (Is 11:6-9), and the pure in heart will see God (Mt 5:7). The disciples had observed signs and wonders, but their questions went deeper, "When will You fix this broken world?" The expectations regarding the kingdom preceded the time of Jesus. The questions and longings of the disciples have continued for almost two thousand years.

Old Testament Expectations

The promise of the coming kingdom is embedded in the three major covenants of the OT. These three covenants are the Abrahamic covenant (Gn 12:1-3), the Davidic covenant (2 Sm 7:12-16), and the new covenant (Jr 31:31-34), each filled with promise and hope.

The Abrahamic Covenant

The Abrahamic covenant is the beginning announcement of the coming of the kingdom. The declarations made by God in this covenant represent promises that He will surely bring to pass. These kingdom promises will accrue only to those individuals who manifest a true and living faith, expecting their fulfillment in the manifestation of God's kingdom. Thus the first aspect is found in this covenant to Abraham. God promised him a land, a seed, to make of him a great blessing, and to make his name great.

Paul teaches us that this covenant finds its fulfillment in Jesus Christ and those who have placed faith in Him:

> Now the promises were spoken to Abraham and to his seed. He does not say "and to seeds," as though referring to many, but and to your seed, referring to one, who is Christ . . . For if the inheritance is from the law, it is no longer from the promise; but God granted it to Abraham through the promise. . . . And if you are Christ's, then you are Abraham's seed, heirs according to the promise (Gl 3:16,18,29).

Thus God's kingdom plan, ultimately focused in Christ, is set forth from the beginning; nothing shall frustrate it. Yet, participation in the promise is restricted to those who manifest the faith and obedience of Abraham (see Ex 19:5). God will see to it that His kingdom plan will be carried out in history, but He will also see to it that none partake of the covenant in violation of the demands of holiness. No person who finally presents to God a faithless and insincere heart will participate in kingdom blessings. Thus, faith in and expectation of the coming kingdom is to be commended and desired.

The Davidic Covenant

The promises to Abraham are expanded in God's covenant to David:

> When your time comes and you rest with your fathers, I will raise up after you your descendant, who will come from your body, and I will establish his kingdom. He will build a house for My name, and I will establish the throne of his kingdom forever . . . . Your house and kingdom will endure before Me forever, and your throne will be established forever (2 Sm 7:12-13,16).

The main themes of the covenant, namely the King and the kingdom, are vital to understanding God's plan for the ages. All the promises of the Davidic covenant have been fulfilled by and in Christ.

God promised three things to David: 1) he would have a son; 2) David's throne would be established; and 3) David's kingdom was to be established forever. During Jesus' day the people expected to see the Messiah come as a fulfillment of the promise to David. The genealogies of Jesus, found in Matthew 1 and Luke 3, are significant because they establish Christ's descent from David and thus support the claim of Jesus of Nazareth to be the OT's promised Messiah. Like the Abrahamic covenant, the Davidic covenant is timeless, in that it looks ahead to a day when God will keep His promise and Jesus Christ will rule all as King.

The New Covenant

The purposes of God in the Abrahamic and Davidic covenants and the accompanying expectations regarding the establishment of the kingdom are expanded further through the prophet's words:

> "Look, the days are coming"—this is the LORD's declaration—"when I will make a new covenant with the house of Israel and with the house of Judah. This one will not be like the covenant I made with their ancestors when I took them by the hand to bring them out of the land of Egypt—a covenant they broke even though I had married them"—the LORD's declaration. "Instead, this is the covenant I will make with the house of Israel after those days"—the LORD's declaration. "I will place My law within them and write it on their hearts. I will be their God, and they will be My people. No longer will one teach his neighbor or his brother, saying: Know the LORD, for they will all know Me,

from the least to the greatest of them"—the LORD's declaration. "For I will forgive their wrongdoing and never again remember their sin" (Jr 31:31-34).

The new covenant was not instituted in Jeremiah's day. Jeremiah only foresaw it. The new covenant was sealed by the incarnation, death, and resurrection of Jesus Christ (see Mt 26:28; Lk 22:20). The death of Christ was a culmination of the imagery present in the covenant of blood, that most solemn way of guaranteeing an ancient oath. God's promise of forgiveness, which is inherent in and at the heart of the kingdom, was sealed with the shed blood of His Son. The covenant blessings can be summarized as follows:

Covenant Name	Purpose	Blessing
Abrahamic	To bless Abraham with a land, a seed, and to make Abraham and his descendants a blessing to all people	The promise is fulfilled in the coming of Christ and has benefit for those who believe in Christ (Gl 3:16,29).
Davidic	To provide a divine King and Savior from David's family line	Jesus Christ was born as a descendant of David, and by faith we enter the kingdom of God's Son (Rm 1:3; Col 1:13).
New	To forgive sins and transform the people of God	All who believe in Christ receive all the benefits promised under the new covenant (Heb 10:10-18).

The OT expectations regarding the kingdom thus include two key aspects, sometimes distinct and other times commingled. One aspect claims that the Messiah would be a Redeemer who would restore humankind to a right relationship with God (best exemplified in Is 52:13–53:12). Here the Messiah is pictured as One who would provide a sacrifice for the sins of men and women. The other aspect is focused on the Messiah as coming King. The promises point to a time characterized by righteousness, peace, and joy (see Rm 14:17).

New Testament Expectations

Kingdom teachings can be seen in the covenant promises and the prophetic pictures, though the details of the completion of these teachings remained somewhat unclear. The NT, however, interprets the OT and announces that the promised Messiah came in Jesus of Nazareth. Through His ministry, teachings, sacrificial death, and resurrection, Jesus fulfilled the messianic promises, accomplished the messianic mission, and provided for the salvation of a lost world. The NT also declares that Jesus will come again and will reign as King, bringing peace and joy and righteousness.

The more clearly focused expectations regarding the kingdom have their basis in Jesus' own teachings. As noted above, the establishment of the kingdom under a descendant of David was central to these expectations. Jesus spoke of a day when this kingdom would arrive in all its glory (Mk 9:1; Lk 19:11; 22:18).

In biblical thought a kingdom is not primarily a particular geographical area but a people governed by the will of a king. Thus when Jesus began to announce that the "kingdom of God has come near" (Mk 1:15; Mt 4:17), He did not primarily have a physical kingdom in mind. He called on

His listeners to enter, or receive, God's kingdom (Mt 12:28). Jesus taught that God's sovereign authority over all things is to be experienced as well as affirmed. He also taught that God's kingdom is a present reality for His people as well as a future promise. Those who establish their lives according to the will of God in this present world will experience the sovereignty of God working in the events and circumstances of life.

Jesus warned that no one could experience this kingdom without being born again (Jn 3:3-5). To experience the kingdom demands an inner renewal, which is possible only through the spiritual transformation Jesus came to provide. While this kingdom has a present aspect to it, it also has a future expectation. This future expectation is tied to the second coming of Christ (Mt 19:28; 24:1-51; Mk 13:24-37; Lk 12:35-48; 21:25-28). What is announced by Jesus is clearly taught by the apostles as well (1 Co 15:51-58; 1 Th 4:13-18; 2 Th 1:7-10, 2Pt 3:10-12; Rv 19:11-21). While the events associated with the establishment of the kingdom are clearly affirmed, the sequence of events and time span involved is less clear. Jesus Himself said,

> "Now concerning that day and hour no one knows—neither the angels in heaven, nor the Son—except the Father only" (Mt 24:36).

Since we cannot pinpoint the time or season, the year, decade, or even century, Christians are told to "keep watch." Jesus said, "Therefore be alert, since you don't know what day your Lord is coming" (Mt 24:42). Thus Jesus did not simply affirm His coming to establish the kingdom, but also He emphasized the appropriate preparation in light of this fact. Many of Jesus' parables were associated with this great fact. His followers were urged to wait, watch, and work (Mt 25:1-30), for the kingdom has come near.

Hell and Heaven

David S. Dockery

Judgment is of great significance in Holy Scripture. The OT message is that God is holy and righteous and demands holiness and righteousness from His creatures. Sometimes God's judgments are seen in the present life, but most often it is the future judgment that is in mind. The psalmist wrote, "For He is coming to judge the earth. He will judge the world with righteousness and the peoples with His faithfulness" (Ps 96:13). All people, not just Israel, will answer to Him.

The Biblical Picture of Judgment

The NT expands the OT pictures of judgment. God's judgment is connected with the cross of Christ. Jesus Himself in looking forward to the cross said: "Now is the judgment of this world. Now the ruler of this world will be cast out" (Jn 12:31). The concept of judgment in connection with the defeat of Satan and sin is important.

Judgment is inevitable. It is as inescapable as death (Heb 9:27; 12:23). While believers may not face judgment regarding their eternal destiny, they nevertheless will face judgment for their deeds (Rm 2:16). Indeed judgment begins with the family of God (1Pt 4:17). This judgment will be on the basis of works. Jesus declared, "For the Son of Man is going to come with His angels in the glory of His Father, and then He will reward each according to what he has done" (Mt 16:27).

The place of eternal punishment and separation represents the infinite gulf between the righteous and the wicked, between God and the realm of Satan. In the concluding words of the Sermon on the Mount, Jesus pronounced:

> Enter through the narrow gate. For the gate is wide and the road is broad that leads to destruction, and there are many who go through it. How narrow is the gate and difficult the road that leads to life, and few find it. . . . Not everyone who says to Me, "Lord, Lord!" will enter the kingdom of heaven, but only the one who does the will of My Father in heaven. On that day many will say to me, "Lord, Lord, didn't we prophesy in Your name, drive out demons in Your name, and do many miracles in Your name?" Then I will announce to them, "I never knew you! Depart from Me, you lawbreakers!" (Mt 7:13-14,21-23).

In His parable of the last judgment, Jesus clearly distinguishes the two abodes, "And they will go away into eternal punishment, but the righteous into eternal life" (Mt 25:46).

Those who go away into eternal punishment experience the withdrawal of God's grace and goodness. This eternal separation from God is called hell. The separation is tragic because it is avoidable. What makes hell in part is the recognition that positive response to God's grace would have made all the difference. The separation is tragic because hell is a place "where their worm does not die, and the fire is not quenched" (Mk 9:48). For believers the reality of this picture serves as a motivator to evangelism (2 Co 5:11-20).

The separation is painful. Hell is associated with thirst and fire. It is godless because hell is separation from God. The images of the horrors of hell are graphic ways of describing the absence of God and eternal condemnation. Those who die without faith in Jesus Christ face an eternal state of condemnation. Again, the words from the Gospels are straightforward:

For God did not send His Son into the world that He might condemn the world, but that the world might be saved through Him. Anyone who believes in Him is not condemned, but anyone who does not believe is already condemned, because he has not believed in the name of the One and Only Son of God. This, then, is the judgment: the light has come into the world, and people loved darkness rather than the light because their deeds were evil (Jn 3:17-19).

As painful as the separation of hell is, its most tragic feature is that it is irreversible. In Jesus' account of the rich man and Lazarus (Lk 16:19-31), He gave no indicator that the rich man could endure the torment for a while and then be granted another chance. Thus the author of Hebrews warns of impending doom to those who persist in unbelief with this question, "How will we escape if we neglect such a great salvation?" (Heb 2:3).

Only God's grace granted to those who have a faith relationship with Him will inherit salvation. It is not ritual or religiosity by which one escapes condemnation. Some think maybe if we get religion we can escape hell. Remember the scribes and Pharisees? They were the most religious people around the time Jesus lived on earth. For all who think ritual or religious works will help, the words of Jesus are stinging: "Snakes! Brood of vipers! How can you escape being condemned to hell?" (Mt 23:33).

Living a good life, being baptized, obeying the law, being a good citizen, or sharing one's goods with those in need cannot form the basis for relationship with God. God requires perfect righteousness, not human goodness. All of these things are expected of those who are Christ's followers, but they are not the criteria by which one becomes a Christ follower. God requires perfect righteousness, the kind of righteousness that comes only as a gift of God to those who confess by faith that Jesus is Lord and Savior (see Rm 3:21-26; 10:9). Righteousness that fits us for eternal life comes only through the Lord Jesus Christ.

While it is appropriate to speak of hell as the eternal abode of the lost, technically the ultimate abode is the lake of fire (Rv 20:11-15). We must remember that heaven and hell do not have equal status in the purpose of God. The kingdom has always been God's goal for His people (Mt 25:34). Hell, on the other hand, was prepared for the Devil and his angels (Mt 25:41). If people go there, it is because they have rejected God's gift of salvation and His best for their lives.

We can rest assured that those in hell are in the hands of a God who is both righteous and merciful, and we can trust that His mercy as well as His justice will be manifest among them, though in no way does this mean final universal salvation.

Those in hell are there because of their sins, because of their continued rejection of the grace of God. Hell is not a human creation but is the creation of a just, yet loving, God for those who refuse the grace and mercy offered to them in Christ. Only God, not we, can righteously know who will be banished to hell. But we do know that none will be lost and separated from God for all eternity except for those who to the end obstinately refuse God and His gift of salvation in Christ.

All believers will be judged in the presence of God. The destiny of unbelievers will be the eternal fire of hell (see Mt 25:41). Unbelievers, Satan and his demons, the false prophet, and the beast will all be cast into the lake of fire.

Heaven

The NT mentions heaven with considerable frequency. Yet, even with this frequency, detailed description of this abode is missing. Perhaps God has intentionally revealed or covered it in mystery, for it is more important for us to focus on the God of heaven than the description of it. It is more important to know the *why* than the *what*. The NT focuses on the *purpose* of heaven more so than telling us what it is *like*. We have seen that hell is for separation and punishment. Heaven, on the other hand, is for fellowship and worship.

The two-fold destiny of humankind is strongly affirmed throughout the NT. These realities are not merely states of mind but spatial dimensions beyond our space and time. These abodes are both a state and a place. Jesus said:

> In My Father's house are many dwelling places; if not, I would have told you. I am going away to prepare a place for you. If I go away and prepare a place for you, I will come back and receive you to Myself, so that where I am you may be also. You know the way where I am going (Jn 14:2-4).

Eternity is not simply the same as the future; it signifies the absolute future beyond the temporal or historical future, beyond this life, beyond the intermediate state, and beyond the millennial kingdom.

The distinction between those who possess eternal life and those who do not ultimately will be made known at the final judgment. Believers in the Lord Jesus Christ will enter into God's presence for all eternity. The Bible describes heaven as the place where God is. Jesus taught His disciples to address God in prayer, "Our Father in heaven" (Mt 6:9). Heaven is where Christ has ascended. The author of Hebrews writes, "Therefore since we have a great high priest who has passed through the heavens—Jesus the Son of God—let us hold fast to the confession" (Heb 4:14). By implication then heaven is where believers go at death since they are with Christ in the presence of God. Paul said that if he died, he would "be with Christ" (Php 1:23). Jesus promised the dying thief on the cross, "I assure you: Today you will be with Me in paradise" (Lk 23:43).

Heaven is the place where the life of the living God is experienced in its fullness. Its most beautiful characteristics are worship and fellowship. We are with God without the hindrance of any distraction, sin, or imperfection. Heaven is life with the living, creative, and redemptive God.

Life with God on earth in the here and now is clouded by sin, circumstances, and other distractions. We do not experience the fullness of love, fellowship, or worship of God in this life because the things of the world get in the way. In this life the world, the flesh, the Devil and personal struggle keep us from all we were meant to be.

The fellowship and worship of God is permanent. The heavenly beings will constantly proclaim: "Holy, holy, holy, Lord God, the Almighty, who was, who is, and who is coming . . . You are worthy to receive glory and honor and power, because You have created all things, and because of Your will they exist and were created" (Rv 4:8,11). Once we are invited into God's presence in heaven we can never be separated from Him. We will be with Him for all eternity. His presence, His life will sustain us eternally. God has called us to live with Him, to be refreshed by Him and renewed by Him. Christians have a blessed hope indeed!

Demons in the Gospels

David G. Shackelford

Introduction

Within systematic theology, the study of demons (demonology) is properly a subset of angelology. In this article, the focus will be on aspects of demonology that are revealed specifically within the Gospels. The Scriptures provide only a modest amount of information regarding the origin of demons and their leader, Satan. Hebrews 2:7 indicates that they are created beings of a higher order than man. They are considered to be fallen angels (Lk 10:18). This fall from heaven was apparently precipitated by the rise of pride within the heart of Lucifer and his subsequent rebellion (Ezk 28:13-17; Rv 12:7-9). Satan is the head or ruler over all the other demons in that he is ruler over his own kingdom (Mt 12:26; Lk 11:18). In 2 Corinthians 4:4, he is referred to as the "god of this age" and in Ephesians 2:2, he is called the "ruler of the atmospheric domain."

Demons, or evil spirits, are mentioned more often in the Gospels than in any other section of Scripture. Of particular interest is the fact that the existence of Satan and demons is never rationalized in the Gospels, but is assumed. The first four books of the NT are filled with examples of their activities that reveal a number of things about the nature of Satan and his demons.

Elements of Personality

An entity reflecting personality possesses self-awareness, self-determination, intellect, sensibility, will, and moral responsibility. Clearly the Gospels demonstrate that demons possess these traits. As early as Matthew 4 (the temptations of Jesus in the wilderness), one finds Jesus in confrontation with the devil. There are several truths that are immediately self-evident. First, there are no contextual markers to suggest figurative language. The only conclusion viable here is that this event is historically and literally true. Second, Jesus and the devil are engaged in a conversation. Those who would consider Satan to be nothing more than an evil influence must explain how one could have a conversation with an influence. It is this same conversation that proves that Satan has self-awareness ["I"], self-determination, ["will give"], awareness of others, ["You"], and even personal ambition ["all these things if you will fall down and worship me"] (Mt 4:9). Likewise, Satan's subordinates, the demons, demonstrate these same characteristics.

Demonic Possession

One of the most well known activities of demon spirits is that they can enter into a person and create havoc within. The Gospels abound with examples of those individuals possessed by evil spirits. From the perspective of the evil spirit, the purpose of such possession appears to be two-fold. Foremost is the disruption, even the destruction, of human life. Subsequent to, perhaps even coincidental, is finding rest. Jesus said in Matthew 12:43, "When an unclean spirit comes out of a man, it roams through waterless places looking for rest but doesn't find any."

The Gospels only describe the outward manifestations of demonic possession. One such possessed individual was blind and unable to speak (Mt 12:22-23). The Gadarene demoniacs were so ferocious that they made travel through their area extremely dangerous (Mt 8:28-34). Another man was unable to speak due to the demon within (Mt 9:32). On another occasion a child was given to seizures and threw himself into a fire at the prompting of the demonic spirit possessing him (Mt 17:14-21). This particular possession is especially interesting because the possession was of such a nature that the disciples were ineffective against the spirit. Upon Jesus casting out the demon, He explained to them that this demon was so strong that it could only be cast out by prayer coupled with fasting. This also attests to the nature of the spiritual warfare in which believers are engaged.

These demonic entries into an individual are considered distinct from physical illness (Mk 1:32). Mark 1:34 says, "and He healed many who were sick with various diseases, and drove out many demons . . ." These verses establish that the causes of physical illness and disabilities are not necessarily caused by demonic activity. Matthew 4:24 goes even further in that it distinguishes demon possession from physical illness and mental illness. The Bible is equally clear that demonic activity may be responsible for physical problems such as the man who could not speak (Mt 9:32) or the woman whose body was bowed over as a result of being "disabled by a spirit" (Lk 13:11). The conclusion is that, whereas demons certainly *may* be the cause of physical impairment and illness, such is not a foregone conclusion.

Dealing with demonic activity was not just a part of Jesus' ministry. When Jesus was accused by the Pharisees of casting out demons by the prince of demons, Jesus asked them, "And if I drive out demons by Beelzebul, who is it your sons drive them out by?" (Mt 12:27). Thus, there were Jewish exorcists and others who dealt with demonic issues. But the difference in the processes is very revealing. The exorcists of Jesus day "usually tried to subdue demons by incantations invoking higher spirits, by using smelly roots or by pain-compliance techniques."[1] By contrast and regardless of the perceived power of the demon and the intensity of the possession, each time a demon was exorcised by Jesus, the only efficacious means was associated with His Name. The same was true of the disciples. When the seventy returned from their mission, they returned with great joy saying, "Lord, even the demons submit to us in Your name" (Lk 10:17).

Whereas the Gospels provide numerous examples of demon possession, the Bible is also clear that a Christian cannot be possessed by an evil spirit. Upon conversion, the Spirit of Christ takes up permanent residence within that individual. 1 John 4:4 assures all the saved that "the One who is in you is greater than the one who is in the world." Likewise, the presence of the divine nature in any individual is a certain guarantee that no demon can enter.[2]

Extent of Knowledge

Through the years those who reject Christianity and the authority of the Bible have done so for a vast array of reasons, but there are three areas of denial that seem to be common among most of them: the existence of the devil as a personal entity, the full deity of Jesus Christ, and the veracity of the Scriptures themselves. Neither Satan nor his demons are omniscient, but the Gospels reveal that they have extensive knowledge in certain areas – particularly in these three that are commonly denied by unbelievers. The Bible clearly teaches the existence of a personal Devil, and it is equally clear that Satan and his minions are fully self-aware – they do not have an identity crisis. Since this area has already been touched upon, there is no need to rehearse those points again. The remaining two: the recognition of Jesus and Satan's belief in the truthfulness of Scripture, are of great importance since these two areas are attacked more than any other areas of theology.

---

1. C. S. Keener, *The IVP Bible Background Commentary: New Testament* (Downers Grove, IL: InterVarsity, 1993), 159.
2. Lewis Sperry Chafer, "Eternal Security: Part 2." *Bibliotheca Sacra*. Vol. 106 (Dallas: Dallas Theological Seminary, 1949; 2002), 398–399.

Recognition of Jesus

Neither Satan nor his demons had any doubts about Jesus' identity. In Matthew 4, the Scriptures are clear that Satan knew precisely who Jesus was. In verse 3, Satan told Jesus, "If You are the Son of God, tell these stones to become bread." The protasis (the "if" clause) of this sentence is known among Greek grammarians as a first class condition. This simply means that Satan is not asking a question of doubt, but rather, is stating, "*Since* You are the Son of God . . . " The same construction is used in verse 6 with the meaning, "*Since* You are the Son of God, throw yourself down."

The demons were also certain of Jesus' full deity. Mark 1:23-24 reports, "Just then a man with an unclean spirit was in their synagogue. He cried out, 'What do You have to do with us, Jesus—Nazarene? Have You come to destroy us? I know who You are—the Holy One of God!'" The presence of the definite article in the phrase "the Holy One of God" leaves no doubt. The demons knew that Jesus is fully God.

Acknowledgment of the Veracity of Scripture

One amazing concession of Satan had to do with the inspiration of Scripture itself. Going back to the Matthew 4 passage, Jesus was led by the Holy Spirit for the specific purpose of being tempted by the Devil. There were three specific tests advanced by Satan: 1) to make stones into bread; 2) to cast Himself down from the pinnacle of the temple; and 3) to receive the kingdoms of the world in exchange for worshiping the devil. In all three instances, Jesus responded with Scripture introduced by the formula, "It is written." (Mt 4:4, 7, and 10). These events are well known and a general exposition of the passage is not necessary here.

What is not usually observed has to do with the phrase, "It is written." The English phrase translates one Geek word: *gegraptai*. While the word simply means, "to write," the tense Jesus employed makes the significant point. This particular use, known as the intensive perfect, refers to a past action with the focus on the present result. That is, the act has been completed at a particular point in time, but the results of that action continue indefinitely up to the present time. Jesus acknowledged the permanence and veracity of Scripture – that it had been written and that it still stands as Scripture. This is why the translation, "It stands written" is so appropriate for this phrase. This is the same observation that Scripture makes for itself (Is 40:8; 1Pt 1:23-25) and that Jesus makes elsewhere (Mt 5:18; Lk 21:33).

One might argue that the use of the perfect is coincidental to Jesus' statement; that He never intended such a connotation. However, if no such meaning was intended, the Greek aorist tense would be the expected form, and is, in fact, much more common than the perfect tense.[3] That Scripture claims inerrancy and permanency for itself, that Jesus affirmed that claim, and that He consistently used the perfect tense in all three statements in Matthew 4 cannot be construed to be anything less than deliberate. Jesus knew what He was saying.

When one considers that Satan and his demons believe the truthfulness of the most significant Christian teachings, there are two observations immediately manifest themselves. First, ironic indeed is the fact that the most malevolent and evil of all created beings gives the proverbial nod to truths that most unbelievers deny. The second observation comes in the form of a question: "If Satan believes the truthfulness of the most essential Christian teachings, why is he not saved?" The answer is surprisingly simple. Believing the right doctrine is important, but the missing ingredient is the one thing that Scripture says is required: repentance toward God and faith toward the Lord Jesus Christ (Ac 20:21). Jesus told those who reported to Him that Pilate had mixed the blood of

---

3. For all possible grammatical constructions in the Greek New Testament in which tense is used (verbs, participles, and infinitives), there are 7,052 uses of the aorist tense, but only 1,444 instances of the perfect.

some Galileans with their sacrifices, ". . . I tell you, but unless you repent, you will all perish as well!" (Lk 13:3,5). Satan and his demons are consumed with a malevolent, passionate hatred of all things having to do with Yahweh and His Son, Jesus. Revelation 12:12 says, ". . . for the Devil has come down to you with great fury, because he knows he has a short time." Though Jesus' atoning death is not applicable to demonic beings, Satan's malevolence toward God and his refusal to repent would by themselves insure his condemnation.

Ultimate Defeat

Satan and his demon subordinates also know that they are ultimately defeated. In Matthew 8:28-29, Jesus encountered two demon-possessed men coming out of the tombs. There, the Bible says:

> When He had come to the other side, to the region of the Gadarenes, two demon-possessed men met Him as they came out of the tombs. They were so violent that no one could pass that way. Suddenly they shouted, "What do You have to do with us, Son of God? Have You come here to torment us before the time?"

The phraseology in verse 29 indicates that the demons recognized that there is an appointed and inescapable date with God. At that time their final judgment and subsequent eternal torment will become a reality.

In acknowledging the ultimate defeat of Satan and his demons, one must realize that the battle between Satan and the Lord Jesus Christ is ultimately no contest. There is no question of the outcome. The Scriptures are clear that the defeat of Satan is not a challenge for the Lord God. Jesus Himself said in Luke 11:20: "If I drive out demons by the finger of God, then the kingdom of God has come to you." This parallels Revelation 20:1-3 where only one angel is required to bind Satan and cat him into the bottomless pit for 1,000 years. When Satan is ultimately cast into the lake of fire and brimstone in v. 10, it is safe to assume that only one angel is needed to accomplish the task.

All this is to say that the power Satan and his subordinates possess is only allowed at the behest of God for the accomplishment of His sovereign will and purposes. He who makes even the wrath of man to praise Him is the God of the universe who has already defeated Satan at the Cross.

The Arrest and Trials of Jesus

Darrell Bock

Jesus' arrest was the result of a combination of factors. First, there was the opposition of the Jewish leadership. They did not like Jesus' self claims, the way He handled issues of the Law like the Sabbath, the manner in which He engaged sinners, and especially His cleansing of the temple. They were looking for a way to trap Him. They also knew that if this were to be done legally, it would have to involve the Romans, who alone possessed the right to execute someone. In addition, if Rome were to do it, then they would have ultimate responsibility for Jesus' death. The leadership would have merely done their duty as Roman citizens. Second, the arrest and subsequent examination of Jesus before Rome played off of the key Roman concern in Judea, that the peace be kept and no one be placed in a position to challenge Caesar. Third, with Judas' betrayal, the leadership became protected at the start of the process as well. They could always make the case that one of Jesus' own had "turned Him in." So Jesus' arrest in Gethsemane one Thursday night took place as the result of an alignment of these three factors.

The subsequent trials of Jesus are better thought of as legal examinations rather than formal trials. The only meetings that had any legal relevance were the two before Pilate and Herod. Other meetings were more like pre-trial hearings or information gatherings like in a grand jury. This includes the key examination by the Jewish leadership, because their goal was not to issue a verdict they could execute, but to gather evidence to take to Rome. There were five examinations and trials combined. The most important of these were the examinations by the Jewish leadership, the visit with Herod, and the examinations by Pilate. We will take the meetings in their likely order.

Meeting with Annas (Jn 18:13-28)

This seems to have been a preliminary hearing before the patriarch of the high priestly family, as Caiaphas, the high priest was Annas' son-in-law. In addition, many of the high priests from AD 6 to 36 came from this family, including Annas himself at the start. Nothing decisive came of this meeting. Annas examined Jesus about His disciples and teachings. This line of questioning was unproductive as Jesus responded that He had taught openly, making the point that witnesses were available for His teachings. In John, this was the time when Peter denied Jesus.

Jesus Examined before the Jewish Council
(Mt 26:57-75; Mk 14:53-72; Lk 22:54-71; Jn 18:13-28)

This was a crucial examination. It involved the Jewish leadership and led to Jesus being taken to the Romans. It is often said that the Jews violated their own Mishnaic rules for trials here (*M Sanhedrin* 4.1; 11.2; and especially 7.5). However, this was not a trial but a gathering of evidence to take to Pilate. This is why Mark's account begins with the temple destruction issue. Had this been proved, then a charge of disrupting the peace as a political activist could have been made to Rome. However, the evidence was not strong enough to make the case, something even the Jewish leadership recognized. The Jews needed a political charge to take to Rome, although their own objections to Jesus were largely religious.

The key part of this examination came when Jesus was asked if He was the Christ. Jesus' reply uses language from Daniel 7:9-14 about the Son of Man coming on the clouds and from

Psalm 110:1 about being at the right hand of God. Luke's version simplifies the reply to the Son of Man and the right hand of God, because this is the core of the reply. Jesus was claiming that God would vindicate Him and give Him a place at God's side in heaven. In fact, He would be given a place at God's side as the Son of Man, the judge of the end. To Jewish ears, who believed in the unique glory of God, this claim struck them as the height of arrogance, even as blasphemous. No one could sit in God's presence. Just look at the temple. The holy of holies was the only place for the unique presence of God. No one else was allowed in except for the high priest once a year to offer a sacrifice. And that holy place was only a picture of the presence of God. So what Jesus was claiming was worse than claiming that He would live in the holy of holies. The Jewish leadership labeled this as blasphemy, a religious violation Judaism saw as worthy of death, and confirmed that Jesus was claiming to be Israel's king, a political charge they could take to Rome.

Of course, if Jesus is who He claimed to be and God did vindicate Him, then the Jewish judgment is wrong. This is one reason the resurrection is so important to Christianity. The resurrection was God's vote in this dispute, showing that Jesus' claim was vindicated. In the Synoptics, Peter's denials come here. It is likely that this examination came directly after Annas' interview with Jesus. The irony of this scene is that the charge that the Jewish leadership wanted so badly to get, they could not get with their witnesses. It was Jesus who supplied the testimony that led to His death. In a sense, Jesus took Himself to the cross by testifying to the truth.

Jesus before Pilate
(Mt 27:11-14; Mk 15:2-5; Lk 23:2-5; Jn 18:29-38)

This initial examination by Pilate attempted to bring a political charge. The charge was that Jesus subverted Israel, forbade the paying of taxes to Rome, and claimed to be a Christ, a king. All the charges could have been challenged. Jesus did dispute with the leadership about Israel's customs, especially as interpreted by the Jewish leadership. However, the charge that He forbade the paying of taxes was an outright lie. The claim that He was the Christ was true, but not in the politically subversive sense the leadership intended. These charges were important because Pilate's responsibility in Judea was to keep the peace, to collect taxes, and to make sure no rival to Caesar arose. Pilate declared Jesus innocent and then sent Him to Herod. John's Gospel gives us some of their dialogue. Pilate examined whether Jesus claimed to be King of the Jews and what was truth. Jesus made it clear that His kingdom was not of this world, so Jesus' kingship did not mean what Pilate thought when he asked about it. Pilate's sense that Jesus was innocent caused him to send Jesus to Herod, who, being partially Jewish, might be able to help him sort things out.

Jesus before Herod Antipas
(Lk 23:6-12)

This interrogation is not in the other Gospels because it was basically inconsequential. Herod was more interested in being entertained and Jesus was silent when examined. Jesus was mocked during this time. Herod returned Jesus to Pilate with a note that in his view Jesus was not guilty.

Jesus before Pilate and the People
(Mt 27:15-26; Mk 15:6-15; Lk 23:13-25; Jn 18:39-40)

In this scene the final decision was made. Pilate tried to get Jesus scourged and released, but the leadership insisted on Jesus being crucified. Then he offered a choice of amnesty between Jesus and Barabbas, a dangerous murderer, thinking that Barabbas would be chosen by the people to die. But this also turned out to be wrong as the crowd present insisted that Jesus be crucified. In Matthew, Pilate gave Jesus over to be crucified and washed his hands to signify his innocence from the matter. However, he was in part responsible because he could have stopped everything, and it was his authority that allowed Jesus to be crucified. Also in Matthew, the Jewish crowd took responsibility for Jesus' death, invoking their responsibility for His blood before God. They believed they were right and were willing to be made accountable for it. With Pilate's acceptance of the Jewish leadership's pressure and that of the crowd, Jesus was led to His death.

Conclusion

So who was responsible for Jesus' death? Historically, the answer to that question is complex. First, the Jewish leadership was responsible, for they drove the process and pressured Pilate. Even Josephus, a Jewish historian from the late first century, testified that the leadership had a role in Jesus' death. So it is not only the Bible that gives us such historical evidence (*Ant* 18.63-64). Second, Pilate was also responsible, making Rome responsible, for as judge, he believed Jesus to be innocent but allowed Him to be crucified. Third, Judas was responsible, for he enabled the leadership to get Jesus. Finally, some Jews in Jerusalem were responsible, for their cries were heard by Pilate when the choice was Jesus or Barabbas.

However, to answer the query historically is to fail to appreciate why Jesus chose to go to the cross. Theologically, it was sin in all of humanity that took Jesus to the cross (Rm 3:9-26). Jesus died for all of us as sinners. No one is immune from responsibility for the cross, for it was the presence of sin in all of us that motivated Jesus' love to go to the cross for us (Rm 5:6-11). This is why the message of the church to every human being is to be reconciled to God, for God in His love has made reconciliation with Him possible through the death of Jesus (2 Co 5:19-21).

The Day, Hour, and Year of Jesus' Crucifixion

Brad Arnett and James Flanagan

Christ's crucifixion occurred in a time when, and a place where, systems of time reckoning were neither uniform nor consistent according to modern standards. Hence, the answer to the question "When did Jesus die?" requires the interlocutor to transpose dates and times into modern equivalents. This effort is usually neither precise nor simple. In the following analysis, an effort will be made to identify the day, hour, and year of Jesus' death.

The canonical Gospels do not reflect a major concern with the time of Jesus' death and hence do not answer the question satisfactorily to the contemporary inquirer. The evidence they do provide creates some complexity. This is primarily due to the significantly different means of measuring time today as compared to measuring time in antiquity. As a consequence, scholars continue to debate all four aspects of the time of Jesus' death: the time of day, the day of the week, the day of the month, and the year.

The Time of Day

Each evangelist records a "check of the clock" at or near the time of Jesus' death. In Mark's account, we find that "It was nine in the morning when they crucified him" (Mark 15:25) and that "When it was noon, darkness came over the whole land until three in the afternoon. And at three Jesus cried out with a loud voice" (Mark 15:33-34a).

The other Synoptics appear to agree with Mark's time markers for the hour of darkness and the hour of expiration (Matt 27:45-46; Luke 23:44). They also agree on the time of Jesus' interrogation before the Jewish council in the very early morning (Matt 27:1; Mark 15:1; see also Matt 26:74; Luke 22:66). Neither Matthew nor Luke, however, repeat the "nine in the morning" reference of Mark 15:25.

An apparent difficulty in reconciling the time of Jesus' death occurs only when one compares Mark's "nine in the morning" reference with the Gospel of John. The only reference to the hour of the day that John gives in his account of the crucifixion is 19:14. It was "about six in the morning" when Pilate sat in judgment of Jesus.

Since Mark's nine in the morning for the crucifixion cannot precede John's six in the morning of judgment, an apparent dilemma exists. To remove the dilemma some have suggested that Mark 15:25 is the result of a copyist's interpolation.[1] Removing the verse removes the difficulty. Pilate's judgment (or lack thereof) and the crucifixion would have occurred closely together at or around six in the morning. Darkness would have followed immediately thereafter, and Jesus would have died about three hours later, at nine in the morning. Such a solution seems simple enough, yet it is based on conjecture and scriptural emendation with little textual support. (A few manuscripts do have the "sixth hour" instead of the "third hour.")[2]

Others have argued that John's account reflects a theological desire to position Jesus' death at a later time of day. The result has Jesus' crucifixion occurring about the same time the paschal

---

1. Jack Finegan, *Handbook of Biblical Chronology: Principles of Time Reckoning in the Ancient World and Problems of Chronology in the Bible,* rev. (Peabody, MA: Hendrickson, 1964, 1998), 359.

2. See Bruce M. Metzger, *A Textual Commentary on the Greek New Testament,* 2d ed. (New York: United Bible Societies, 1971, 2002), 99, see also 216.

lambs were being slaughtered in the temple[3] and presents Jesus as "our Passover" lamb. (See 1 Co 5:7.) The paschal lamb theme, however, was probably not a major issue for the evangelist. Indeed, if John intended for his readers to draw the suggested inference regarding the connection between the slaughter of Jesus and the slaughter of the lambs, he could have been at least a little more explicit without adding much to his account.[4] This view is further complicated if the Passover meal occurred on Thursday evening rather than Friday evening. (See "The Day of the Month" below.)

Perhaps the best solution is to regard the discrepancy as merely apparent. Several notable scholars have argued that the modern precision of marking time of day should not be read back into the Gospel accounts. At a time when there was no standardization of hours or modern timepieces dividing the days into minutes, the hour of day may be judged differently by various observers. It has been suggested that the day was frequently divided into three-hour periods of time (third, sixth, ninth hours) because of the lack of precision (today one needs only to visit rural areas of the world to discover that measuring time is not always accurate to the hour). The observer in the synoptic tradition, therefore, judged the time to be closer to midmorning whereas the observer in John's tradition considered the time to be closer to midday.[5]

The Day of the Week

The day of the week is the least disputed aspect of the time of Christ's crucifixion, but it too has had its challengers. All four Gospels indicate that Jesus was crucified the day before the Sabbath and was raised the day after the Sabbath, the first day of the week (Matt 27:62; 28:1; Mark 15:42; 16:1-2,9; Luke 23:54,56–24:1; John 19:14,31,42; 20:1). Yet, some see a sequential conflict with Matthew 12:40, "For as Jonah was in the belly of the huge fish three days and three nights, so the Son of Man will be in the heart of the earth three days and three nights," and have suggested that Jesus was actually crucified and buried on either Wednesday or Thursday rather than Friday.

Two problems attend this challenge to the Friday view. One, the Jewish reckoning of a day counted a portion of a day as a whole. Since the overwhelming evidence suggests Jesus was raised "on the third day," the argument loses its force; nowhere do we find evidence that Jesus was raised on the fourth day. Two, the verse itself does not require such a strict interpretation, which would demand a 72 hour interment and thus result in a resurrection on Saturday evening or Sunday evening rather than Sunday morning. Hoehner has correctly suggested that "three days and three nights" is an idiomatic expression equal to "the third day."[6]

The Day of the Month

The day of the month is perhaps the most debated aspect of the time of Christ's crucifixion. The Gospel evidence again appears to be a contradiction of a more serious nature. The choice is between two days: Nisan 14 or Nisan 15. If Jesus died on Nisan 14, the Last Supper was not a Passover meal, but if he died on Nisan 15, it was. One's view of the date will dramatically impact one's interpretation of the Last Supper and, consequently, the continual celebration of the Lord's Supper.

---

3. Craig A. Evans, *Mark 8:27-16:20,* The Word Biblical Commentary 34B: eds. Bruce M. Metzger, David A. Hubbard, and Glen W. Barker (Nashville: Thomas Nelson, 2001), 503.

4. Eugen Ruckstuhl, *Chronology of the Last Days of Jesus: A Critical Study,* trans. Victor J. Drapela (New York: Desclee, 1965), 6 and John Hamilton, "The Chronology of the Crucifixion and the Passover," *Churchman* 106 (1992): 324.

5. Craig L. Blomberg, *The Historical Reliability of the Gospels* (Downer's Grove: InterVarsity, 1987), 180 and idem, *Historical Reliability of John's Gospel: Issues and Commentary* (Downer's Grove: InterVarsity, 2001), 247.

6. Harold W. Hoehner, *Chronological Aspects of the Life of Christ* (Grand Rapids: Zondervan, 1977), 66.

The Synoptic Gospels indicate that the Last Supper of Jesus and his disciples occurred during the feast of the Passover (Matt 26:17; Mark 14:12; Luke 22:7-8). Although no lamb is mentioned in their accounts, several statements lead the reader to conclude the meal was the Passover. On the other hand, John's Gospel seems to place the Passover meal on the evening after Jesus was crucified, not the evening before. Two statements are the primary evidence. The first, John 18:28, records that those who delivered Jesus to Pilate did not enter the Praetorium so they would not become ceremonially unclean and "unable to eat the Passover." This seems to indicate that the Passover would be eaten on the evening following Jesus' execution. The second statement, John 19:14, appears to be in accord with this timing, stating that Jesus was crucified on "the preparation day for the Passover." If this means that the next day, which began at nightfall, would be Passover, Nisan 15, the Last Supper held the night before Jesus' death was not the official Passover meal.

Joachim Jeremias argued that the meal Jesus shared with His disciples the night before He died, was indeed a Passover meal in both the Synoptic and Johannine accounts (41-61). While his fourteen evidences do not prove the meal was Paschal, they are certainly suggestive despite the misgivings that some have leveled against them.[7] The evidences are as follows: 1) the meal was held in Jerusalem (a requirement of the Passover), 2) the upper room was made available for the meal, 3) the meal was held at night, which was not a common practice, 4) the Twelve were present, 5) they reclined; again, an uncommon practice for regular meals, 6) levitical purity was maintained, indicating a special meal, 7) Jesus broke bread during the course of the meal, 8) they drank wine, 9) the wine was probably red wine, 10) Jesus dismissed Judas, other disciples assumed he was going to make last minute purchases, 11) others thought Judas was going to give alms to the poor, a common practice on Passover, 12) the participants sang a hymn, 13) Jesus and His band remained within Jerusalem limits, rather than returning to Bethany, and 14) Jesus gives an interpretation of the meal's elements, common to the Passover. In the end, Jeremias concluded that in his time the attempts to reconcile the two traditions were insufficient, but he argued strongly that both traditions spoke of the same meal which was replete with Paschal characteristics.

Scholarly opinions on the apparent discrepancy fall into three categories. Some argue that the Synoptics are correct and John is incorrect. Others declare that John is accurate and the Synoptics are inaccurate. A third group represents those who attempt to harmonize the two divergent traditions. This third group is of our main concern here, but the proponents hold widely varying views, none of which has gained widespread consensus.[8]

Perhaps the most popular means of harmonizing the two accounts is to argue that two different rituals were followed and that the Synoptics record one while John records the other. Paul Billerbeck argued that the Pharisees and Sadducees followed two different calendars and had a controversy which resulted in celebrating sequential Passovers in the year Jesus died.[9] Jaubert strongly suggested that Jesus and early Christians followed essentially the same type of calendar found in the *Book of Jubilees;* they celebrated the Passover on Tuesday evening, and the crucifixion occurred several days later on Friday rather than on the next day, as the Gospels seem to imply.[10] Hoehner deduced that the Pharisees and Sadducees differed on the start of day to an extent that the days overlapped and allowed for the paschal lambs to be slaughtered on two consecutive days for Passover.[11] Shepherd suggested that the Diaspora Jews in that year celebrated the Passover

7. George Ogg, "The Chronology of the Last Supper" in *Historicity and Chronology in the New Testament,* ed. D. E. Nineham (London: SPCK Press, 1965), 84–85.

8. Hamilton, "The Chronology," 326.

9. Hermann L. Strack and Paul Billerbeck, *Kommentar zum Neuen Testament* (vol. 2: Müchen, 1924), 812–53.

10. Annie Jaubert, *The Date of the Last Supper* (trans. Isaac Rafferty: Staten Island, NY: Alba House, 1965), 64–66, 97–101.

11. Hoehner, *"Chronological Aspects,"* 86–90.

on Thursday evening and the Palestinian Jews did so on Friday.[12] The Synoptics date the event by Diaspora tradition while John records the correct Palestinian chronology. By Shepherd's own admission, however, very little is known about calendars of dispersion Jews.[13] These solutions, which are noble attempts at harmonization, all falter on the same point: a lack of hard evidence.

Other proposed solutions tend to minimize the apparent discrepancies between the two accounts. Story[14] and Hamilton[15] have suggested that the Passover meals were *prepared* the night before the crucifixion, but those who escorted Jesus to Pilate had not yet *eaten* their meal (John 18:28). Though this is a possibility, the suggestion probably introduces too much technicality into John's terminology.

Mark 14:1 and 12 appear to coalesce the two feasts into one. Casey held that Mark 14:12 occurs in the Temple, and the disciples ask Jesus where to prepare the feast after He has just offered the sacrifice.[16]

Perhaps a solution is best found in Craig Blomberg's studies,[17] which follow the line of thinking best exemplified by Norval Geldenhuys.[18] There is really no contradiction in the two traditions!

The Year

While the time of day and day of the week and day of the month of Christ's death show some interest to the four evangelists, the question of the year Christ died is not an issue to them. None of the evangelists indicates the year Christ died. In order to answer the question of the year, one must reconstruct the historical situation and make an attempt at guessing which year was most probable.

Two suggestions among a number of proposed solutions have risen to the top of the list. A fair consensus exists among biblical scholars and historians that Christ either died on April 7, AD 30 or April 3, AD 33.

We can know with certainty a few facts about the year Christ died. First, we know from the evangelists that Pontius Pilate was *praefectus Iudaeae* who oversaw Jesus' execution. According to ancient historians, Pilate held this position from AD 26 to 36. Second, we know that Caiaphas was high priest the year that Christ died. He held that post from AD 18 to 37. Thus, Jesus' death could have occurred only within the ten year window of AD 26 to 36. This is a firm conclusion.

Other biblical evidence may be used to support one year or another. We know from the Gospels that John the Baptist's death occurred prior to the crucifixion of Jesus (Matt 14:1-12; Mark 6:14-16; Luke 9:7-9) and that John's ministry began in the fifteenth year of Tiberius (Luke 3:1-3). The fifteenth year of Tiberius would be dated AD 28 to 29. Since Jesus' ministry began after John's, we can safely limit the death of Jesus to after AD 29, and thus limit the range even further to AD 29 to 36.

---

12. Massey H. Shepherd, Jr. "Are Both the Synoptics and John Correct about the Date of Jesus' Death?," *Journal of Biblical Literature* 80 (1961): 125.

13. Ibid., 131.

14. Cullen I. K. Story, "The Bearing of Old Testament Terminology on the Johannine Chronology of the Final Passover of Jesus," *Novum Testamentum* 31 (1989): 322.

15. Hamilton, "The Chronology," 333.

16. Maurice Casey, *Aramaic Sources of Mark's Gospel* (Society for New Testament Studies Monograph Series 102: ed. Richard Bauckham: New York: Cambridge University Press, 1998), 223.

17. Blomberg, *The Historical Reliability of John's Gospel*, 254, 258; idem. *The Historical Reliability of the Gospels*, 175–78; and idem. *Jesus and the Gospels: An Introduction and Survey* (Nashville: Broadman and Holman, 1997), 190.

18. Norval Geldenhuys, *Commentary on the Gospel of Luke: The English Text with Introduction, Exposition and Notes* (Grand Rapids: Eerdmans, 1979), 649–70.

In John 2:20, "the Jews" reply to Jesus that the Temple had taken forty-six years to build. Sometimes this evidence is used to calculate the time of Jesus' first Passover, when the discussion about the Temple occurred.

Then there is the evidence from Paul. In Galatians 1:13–2:1, Paul recounts his conversion experience and includes two different periods in his life following that event. For three years he remained in Arabia and Damascus, after which he went up to Jerusalem. Then, fourteen years later, he made a second trip to Jerusalem. If we count backwards from the Jerusalem visits, it is assumed that we can know about when Paul was converted and make a guess as to how much time stood between Christ's death and Paul's conversion. There is just one problem. Scholars do not agree how to interpret this information from Paul. For one thing, does Paul use the time periods in succession or do they overlap? In other words, does the fourteen year period begin following the three year period or does the counting begin at the original spot, his conversion? Also, scholars cannot come to a consensus regarding which visit to Jerusalem was the first and second. There is wide disagreement over whether Luke records all of Paul's visits to Jerusalem. Suffice it to say that the evidence from Paul's life does not significantly add any hard evidence to the discussion over the year of Christ's death and resurrection. The most it can do is push for an earlier date rather than a later one, within our already defined parameters (AD 29 to 36).

Some also bring into the discussion of the year historical information regarding the tenure of Christ's ministry, the defeat of Herod Antipas by his former father-in-law, Aretas, in AD 36 (Josephus mentions that the defeat was considered by Jews as vengeance for the beheading of John the Baptist), the actions of Pilate (why did he give in so easily to the Jews at the trial of Jesus?), and astronomy.

Nearly all discussions of the year of Christ's crucifixion in some way incorporate evidence from astronomy. The most popular method is to trace the new moon occurrences back to this range of years in an effort to determine which years the Passover (which occurred fourteen days after the new moon) was likely to have occurred on a Thursday or Friday. Roger Beckwith cited several reasons that a firm date cannot be established using astronomical calculation, and any conclusions, he argues, are "at best probable."[19] Unfortunately, writers on New Testament chronology are impervious to the irregularities such a method would produce.[20] Astronomy cannot narrow down the possible years, fix a date in those years, or exclude the Synoptic chronology.[21] The Jewish calendar was based on observation rather than scientific calculation since astronomy was not studied in Palestine.[22] Beckwith concluded that any year within 30 to 36, except 34, is a possible year in which Christ was crucified.[23] With this we concur.

---

19. Roger T. Beckwith, *Calendar and Chronology, Jewish and Christian,* trans. of "Arbeiten zur Geschichte des Antiken Judentums und des Urchristentums": *Biblical, Intertestamental and Patristic Studies* 33, ed. Martin Hengel (Leiden: E. J. Brill, 1996), 184.

20. Ibid., 188.

21. Ibid., 189.

22. Ibid., 190.

23. Ibid., 195.

The Amount of Time Between the Crucifixion and the Resurrection of Christ

R. Kirk Kilpatrick

Frequently around Easter questions arise in the minds of those celebrating the anniversary of Christ's death and resurrection. Did Jesus Christ rise from the dead "on the third day" or "after three days" according to the New Testament? Did He eat the Passover meal or was the Last Supper held before Passover? On what day of the week was the crucifixion of Jesus? All of these questions, and others as well, are related to the issue at hand.

Statements of the Time Factor

Twenty-one passages in the NT deal with the amount of time between the crucifixion and the resurrection of Jesus Christ. The Gospel writers employed four different phrases to express this interval of time:

1. "on the third day" as in Matthew 16:21; 17:23; 20:19; 27:64; Luke 9:22; 18:33, 24:7,21,46; Acts 10:40; and 1 Corinthians 15:4.
2. "in three days" (with *en* or *dia*) as in Matthew 26:61; 27:40; Mark 14:58; 15:29; and John 2:19-20.
3. "after three days" (with *meta*) as in Matthew 27:63; and Mark 8:31; 9:31; and 10:34.
4. "three days and three nights" as in Matthew 12:40.

The formula occurring most frequently in the NT indicates clearly that Jesus rose from the dead on the third day ("on the third day" or "in three days" as in numbers 1 and 2 above). Sixteen of the twenty-one passages contain this formula pointing to the traditional understanding of Jesus' crucifixion occurring on Friday of Passion week. However, due to the phrases "after three days" and "three days and three nights" (as in 3 and 4 above), some have argued that the crucifixion should be placed earlier in the week.

Matthew, Mark and *Meta*

Of the twenty-one passages in the NT that deal with the time factor between the crucifixion and the resurrection, four of them use the Greek preposition *meta* with the accusative that is normally translated "after three days" (see 3 under "Statements of the Time Factor"). In Bauer, there is an interesting entry under *meta* with the accusative:

Meta treis hēmeras . . . Matt 27:63; Mark 8:31; 10:34; Luke 2:46; cp. Matt 26:2; Mark 14:1 (cp. Caesar, Bell. Gall. 4,9,1 *post tertiam diem* = on the third day).[1]

The equivalent in Latin of the Greek phrase normally translated "after three days" (*meta* with the accusative) was *post tertiam diem*. While Mark uses *meta* with the accusative in 8:31; 9:31; and 10:34 in reference to the time factor between the crucifixion and the resurrection, the only other place that it is so used is in Matthew 27:63. Since the traditional audience of Mark's Gospel

1. William F. Arndt and F. Wilbur Gingrich, *A Greek-English Lexicon of the New Testament and Other Early Christian Literature: A Translation and Adaptation of the Fourth Revised and Augmented Edition of Walter Bauer's "Griechisch-Deutsches Worterbuch zu den Schriften des Neun Testaments und der ubrigen urchristlichen Literatur,"* 2d ed. revised by F. Wilbur Gingrich and Frederick W. Danker (Chicago: University of Chicago Press, 1979), s.v. "*meta.*" See page 510.

was Roman and the audience in Matthew 27:63 was Pilate, the above reference to the Latin phrase from a time very near that of the NT should be seriously considered.

In D'ooge and Eastman's treatment of the Gallic Wars, they gave both a note and a grammatical explanation for understanding this prepositional phrase. In the note to the passage, they wrote:

"**108** 6 [line] Chap. 9. *post diem tertium:* i.e. the next day but one. The first and last days are usually included in the Roman reckoning (227.g)."

In their note they referred to 227.g in their grammatical section that treated this phenomenon with Latin dates:

227.g The dates intervening between any two points were counted as so many days *before* the second point. The Romans, however, in reckoning a series, counted both extremes; for example, the eleventh day of April was counted as the *third* day before the Ides (that is, the thirteenth), the tenth of April as the *fourth* day before the Ides.

The example of the eleventh day of April being counted as the third day before the thirteenth harmonizes beautifully with the traditional view of a Friday crucifixion. The above was not always considered when translating Latin, much less when considering Greek equivalents of Latin thought concerning time.

Though he does not allow that this was the usage in NT times, according to A. T. Robertson, the use of *meta* with the accusative should yield "into the midst" or "among."[2] However, this classic, root idea behind *meta* helps to make sense out of Matthew 27:62-64. Had the rulers of the Jews understood Jesus to mean "after three days," then they would have asked for a guard until the fourth day. But the text clearly indicates their request was limited "until the third day."

Instead of the later Greek idea of meta meaning "after," the context clearly calls for understanding the earlier idea of "within" behind the use of the preposition. Since the traditional audience of Mark's Gospel was Roman and the audience in Matthew 27:63 was Pilate (a Roman), it seems that the Gospel writers were using *meta* for a Roman audience whose first language was Latin, knowing that they would equate the usage to Latin "*post diem tertium.*"

The Sign of Jonah

The "three days and three nights" statement by Jesus in Matthew 12 is a quotation from the book of Jonah. Some interpret this to mean that Jesus was in the tomb a full seventy-two hours. Not only is this untenable due to the many references that emphasize the truth that Jesus rose on the third day, it is also impossible considering the simple understanding of the prophecy of the preservation of Jesus' body from decay (cp. Ac 2:27 and Jn 11:39).

The Jewish Talmud held that "any part of a day is as the whole."[3] The OT, in parallel or similar Hebrew usage, clearly presents the teaching that "part of a day" is to be looked upon as comprising the whole of that day (see Gn 40:13,20; 1 Sm 30:12,13; 2 Ch 10:5,12; Est 4:16 and 5:1). Hence the Friday of Passion week began, according to Jewish reckoning, on Thursday at sunset (see Gn 1:5, the first day began in the evening). So, day one consisted of Thursday night and Friday during the daylight hours. Day two was Friday from sunset until Saturday at sunset. Day three began as the sun set on the Sabbath.

In Matthew 12, Jesus said "as Jonah **was** ... so the Son of Man will **be**." In Greek the use of the verb "to be" was not required; but in this passage Jesus' emphasis is clear by its presence in

---

2. A. T. Robertson, *A Grammar of the Greek New Testament in the Light of Historical Research*, 4th ed. (Nashville: Broadman, 1934), 609-12. "*With the Accusative.* At first it seems to present more difficulty. But the accusative-idea added to the root-idea 'midst' with verbs of motion would mean 'into the midst' or 'among.' But this idiom does not appear in the N.T." See page 612.

3. *Nazir* 5b.

both places. Jesus said, "as Jonah was" using the imperfect form of the verb "to be." For those considering the chronology of Passion week, the focus is generally upon the statement of time. Yet, since the phrase relating the amount of time here differs from the other six mentions of it in Matthew, the actual emphasis here appears to be upon the state of Jonah in the huge fish and the state of Jesus in the tomb.

Most Christians learn from an early age that Jonah was preserved in the huge fish by a miracle of God; and they understand the language of Jonah's second chapter as figurative with regard to death. Rare, "urban-legend," type examples of men swallowed by sharks or other large fish are drawn upon from far and wide to prove the possibility of such. While nothing is impossible for God, was Jesus alive in the tomb?

The followers of Islam are quick to pick up on this widespread, Christian approach to the book of Jonah (stressing Jonah's preservation) to argue for the "Swoon Theory."[4] In a debate between Ahmed Deedat and Josh McDowell in South Africa, Deedat called out to his followers in the crowd about Jonah's state in the whale, and they answered, "Alive!" Then he asked about Jesus' state in the tomb, and they again responded, "Alive!"[5]

Jonah 2 indicates that Jonah cried out the name of the Lord as he lost consciousness in the fish (Jnh 2:7). A greater miracle than preservation is taught by way of the "sign of Jonah." Resurrection was the debate of Jesus' time. Even the language of resurrection is used by God in Jonah 3:1-2 (cp. the Hebrew command "*Cum* ..."—"Arise" with Jesus' words when He raised the little girl in Mk 5:41). Ultimately only two people knew the state of Jonah in the belly of the huge fish: Jonah and God. Jesus, who is God incarnate, knew the state of Jonah during his ordeal in the fish.

While some might balk at the possibility of Jonah actually having been raised from the dead by God on the shore, his would not have been the first resurrection in the OT. The miracles of resurrection that God wrought in the days of Elijah and Elisha would predate the resurrection of Jonah. While some prefer to consider the text of Jonah presenting a miracle of preservation and merely figurative language referring to a death-like state, the mystery of the state of Jonah in the huge fish is merely hinted at in the poetry of Jonah's second chapter. The "sign of Jonah" alluded to in Matthew 12 pointed literally to Jesus' death and resurrection.

According to this reckoning, Jesus arrived at Bethany on Friday before sunset, six days before the Passover (Jn 12:1), which was Nisan 8, in keeping with the Jewish custom of arriving in the vicinity of Jerusalem six days before the feast.[6] He entered Jerusalem on Palm Sunday, Nisan 10 (see Ex 12:3) as many lambs were being set apart for inspection at Jerusalem. The disciples came to Jesus and inquired where they should prepare to celebrate the Passover together on Thursday, Nisan 14, the day when the feast lambs must be slain (see Mt 26:17; Mk 14:12; and Lk 22:7-8). Jesus was crucified on Friday, Nisan 15, the anniversary of their freedom from Egypt, at the time the law of Moses called for sacrifice and solemn assembly (see Ex 23:14-15; Lv 23:5-8; Nm 28:16-25; and Dt 16:1-8).

Jesus arose on Sunday, Nisan 17, the anniversary of the ark of Noah coming to rest (see Gn 8:4 and Ex 12:1-2). Peter used the ark of Noah as a type of Christ (1Pt 3:20). The ark kept those eight passengers safe "through" the waters of death. The ark came to rest on Mount Ararat many centuries before Jesus' resurrection. However, Genesis 8:4 says that it came to rest in the seventh month, the seventeenth day of the month. The seventh month of Genesis is the first month of Exodus 12.

---

4. The "Swoon Theory," which is popular among modern Muslim apologists, is the theory that Jesus did not actually die on the cross but swooned and awakened in the tomb.

5. Josh McDowell and John Gilchrist, *The Islam Debate* (San Bernardino, CA: Here's Life, 1983), 153.

6. J. B. Segal, *The Hebrew Passover: From the Earliest Times to A.D. 70* (London: Oxford, 1963), 256.

The Synoptics and John's Gospel

Jesus ate the Passover, not at an earlier time than the law stipulated, but at the only time the law allowed. Matthew and Mark recorded the initiative of the disciples to come to Jesus. Their initiative demonstrated that Jesus did not eat the Passover early. Luke's version does not explicitly replace the disciples' initiative with Jesus' initiative; instead, he recorded the names of the two that Jesus sent to make preparations. The Greek construction with "must" that Luke added is noteworthy. This was the day when the feast lambs "must" be slain. Since the Exodus, this day had been the close of Nisan 14. The lambs for the memorial supper were slain just before evening when the fifteenth of Nisan began.

Jesus was crucified, therefore, on Friday morning, Nisan 15. Though the Synoptics give clear testimony to this, John's Gospel has been interpreted by some to indicate that the crucifixion occurred on Nisan 14. John used the term "Passover" several ways to indicate either: 1) the Passover meal, 2) the feast lamb itself, or 3) the "Festival of Unleavened Bread." This varied usage is the source of the confusion (see Jn 13:1; 18:28; and 19:14).[7]

Conclusion

Sixteen of the twenty-one statements that mention the time factor between the death and resurrection of Jesus pointed to His resurrection on "the third day" (see points 1-2 under "Statements of the Time Factor"). Three of the statements (normally translated as "after three days") should be understood in light of the traditional Roman audience of Mark's Gospel with one like this kind occurring in Matthew's Gospel when a Roman audience is obvious in the context of the passage (see point 3 under "Statements of the Time Factor"). An accurate translation for these phrases would be "within three days." All four of these passages (listed under 3 above) indicated the same interval of time expressed through the other phrases, namely, on the third day or within three days. The fourth phrase used to express the time factor between the death and resurrection of Jesus (see point 4 under "Statements of the Time Factor") was cited as a quotation from the book of Jonah and was an idiom understood by the ancient audience in line with the other phrases. Thus, the NT is consistent when it comes to the expression of the amount of time that elapsed between the crucifixion and the resurrection of Jesus Christ.

---

7. A. T. Robertson, *A Harmony of the Gospels for Students of the Life of Christ* (Chicago: W. P. Blessing, 1922), 283.

The Resurrection of Jesus Christ

Norman L. Geisler

The Apostle Paul listed seven disastrous consequences of denying Jesus' resurrection in one passage. If He did not rise, then: 1) our preaching is without foundation; 2) our faith is in vain; 3) the apostles are false witnesses; 4) our faith is worthless; 5) we are still in our sins; 6) dead believers have perished; and 7) we should be pitied more than anyone (1 Co 15:14-19). To these others may be added: 8) Jesus was a deceiver because He said He rose bodily (Lk 24:39), and 9) the Devil won by bringing death that God never reversed (Heb 2:14).

There is no salvation apart from Christ's resurrection (Rm 4:25). As Paul said, "And if Christ has not been raised, your faith is worthless; you are still in your sins" (1 Co 15:17). The resurrection of Christ is a *sine qua non* of salvation. Not only is salvation not achievable without it, but one cannot be saved without believing in it. For the Bible declares that salvation comes only "if you confess with your mouth, 'Jesus is Lord,' and believe in your heart that God raised Him from the dead, you will be saved" (Rm 10:9). Hence, the resurrection is truly one of the great fundamentals of the Christian faith.

Various Views of Jesus' Resurrection

There are three basic views on the resurrection. These are held respectively by orthodox, liberal, and neoorthodox scholars. Regarding the dead body of Jesus placed in the tomb, the orthodox view holds that **God raised it**. The liberal view contends that **someone removed it** to another location. The neoorthodox view believes that **God destroyed it** by transforming its state.

As for Christ's "appearances," orthodox theologians hold that they were **physical**. Liberals believe they were merely **mental**. And many neoorthodox insist that they were **spiritual** manifestations like a theophany. As will be shown below, the evidence supports the orthodox view.

The Nature of Jesus' Resurrection

The nature of the resurrection of Jesus is that He was raised immortal in the same physical body in which He died. His resurrection body was both material and imperishable.

It Was Physical

This physical nature of the resurrection is evidenced by several factors: 1) the empty tomb reveals that His physical body was raised and vacated the tomb (Mt 28:6); 2) the empty grave clothes indicate the physical body was raised and the head cloth was deliberately folded (Jn 20:7); 3) the crucifixion scars showed it was the same body that was crucified (Lk 24:40; Jn 20:27); 4) there were many tangible, visible appearances in which He was seen and heard with the natural senses (see below); 5) the fact that Jesus was touched and performed physical actions (Mt 28:9; Lk 24:30; Jn 20:17,27); 6) the fact that He handled or ate physical food on at least three occasions (Lk 24:30,43; Jn 21:12); and 7) the fact that He said it was a body of "flesh and bones," not a spirit (Lk 24:39).

It Was Immortal

Jesus' resurrection body was physical but it was also immortal. Luke said it did not see "decay" (Ac 2:31). John described our resurrection bodies as being like Jesus' resurrection body (1 Jn 3:2-

3). The believer's resurrected body will be immortal, incorruptible, and imperishable (1 Co 15:43-44,53-54). It is also described as a "glorious body" (Php 3:21) or one "raised in glory" (1 Co 15:43).

The Evidence for Jesus' Resurrection

Given the overwhelming evidence that Jesus died on the cross (see below), there are two lines of proof for His resurrection: direct and indirect.

Direct Evidence of the Resurrection

The direct proof of the resurrection of Christ is His 12 appearances over a period of 40-plus days to over 500 people in which He was seen, heard, and touched with the natural senses. These include in order of appearances to: 1) Mary Magdalene (Jn 20:11-18); 2) Mary Magdalene and the other Mary (Mt 28:1-10); 3) Peter (1 Co 15:5; see Jn 20:3-9); 4) two disciples going to Emmaus (Lk 24:13-35); 5) 11 apostles (Lk 24:36-49; Jn 20:19-23); 6) 11 apostles (Jn 20:24-31); 7) seven apostles (Jn 21); 8) all the apostles (Mt 28:16-20; Mk 16:14-18); 9) 500 disciples (1 Co 15:6); 10) James the brother of Jesus (1 Co 15:7); 11) all the apostles at His ascension (Ac 1:3-8); 12) Paul after His ascension (1 Co 15:8; Ac 9:1-9). During all the appearances He was seen and heard by the natural senses. Four times He was touched or offered to be touched (numbers 1, 2, 5, 6). Three times Jesus ate physical food (numbers 4, 5, 7). Four times they saw the empty tomb (numbers 1, 2, 3, plus John [Jn 20:6-8]). Two people, Peter and John, saw His empty grave clothes (Jn 20:2-8). Twice they witnessed His crucifixion scars (numbers 5, 6). The sum total of this evidence places the event beyond all reasonable doubt. There are literally no other ways one could prove that He had risen from the dead in the same physical body in which He died.

As for why Jesus was not always immediately recognized when He appeared, there are several reasons: 1) Sometimes it was the disciples' **dullness** (Lk 24:25-26). 2) At other times it was their **disbelief** (Jn 20:24-25). 3) Once their **dismay** played a factor (Lk 24:21). 4) On another occasion it was their **dread** (Lk 24:36-37). 5) Once **distance** appeared to be a factor (Jn 21:1-4). 6) On another occasion **dimness** of light may have contributed to it (Jn 20:14-15).

What is important to note, however, is that on every such occasion the lack of recognition was only temporary. Before the appearance was over, they had no doubt that it was the same Jesus in the same body they had known for over three years before the resurrection. Indeed, so sure were they that they willingly died for their conviction.

Indirect Evidence of the Resurrection

Indirect evidence for the resurrection comes from many sources. First, there is **the immediate transformation of the apostles** from cowards to courageous witnesses; from doubters to martyrs. Second, there was **the conversion of Saul of Tarsus** from persecutor to proclaimer of Christ (Ac 9). Third, there was **the unlikely conversion of many Jewish priests** in the same city in which Jesus' death and resurrection occurred (Ac 6:7). Fourth, **the fearless preaching of early Christians** is best explained by the life-changing event of the resurrection. Finally, **the unlikely overnight conversion of devout tradition-ridden Jews** from a law-keeping, Sabbath-observing, sacrifice-offering religion to one that repudiated all these as followers of Christ is best explained by their encounters with the resurrected Christ.

Objection to Jesus' Resurrection Based on Biblical Texts

Several counter arguments from the Bible are offered in support of the denial that Jesus was raised immortal in the same physical body in which He died. All of them are based on a misunderstanding of the text offered.

Paul Speaks of a "Spiritual Body" (1 Co 15:44)

First of all, "spiritual" means immortal, not immaterial. A "spiritual" body denotes an immortal one, not an immaterial one. A "spiritual" body is one dominated by the spirit, not one devoid of matter. The Greek word *pneumatikos* (translated "spiritual" here) means a body directed by the spirit, as opposed to one under the dominion of the flesh. It is not ruled by flesh that perishes but by the spirit that endures (vv. 50-58).

Second, "spiritual" denotes the **source** of the body, not its **substance**. It has a spiritual or supernatural source, but it is a real physical body in its substance. Further, this same Greek word *pneumatikos* can be understood as "supernatural" in 1 Corinthians 10:4 when it speaks of the "spiritual rock that followed them." Paul spoke of the "spiritual rock" that followed Israel in the wilderness from which they got "spiritual drink" (1 Co 10:4). But the OT story (Ex 17; Nm 20) reveals that it was a physical rock from which they got literal water to drink. What is more, "spiritual" (*pneumatikos*) is used to describe physical objects elsewhere in 1 Corinthians. Further, when Paul spoke about a "spiritual person" (1 Co 2:15), he obviously did not mean an invisible, immaterial man with no corporeal body. He was, as a matter of fact, speaking of a flesh and blood human being whose life was lived by the supernatural power of God. He was referring to a literal person whose life had spiritual direction. A spiritual man is one who is "taught by the Spirit" unlike the natural man who "does not welcome what comes from God's Spirit" (1 Co 2:13-14). The resurrection body can be called a "spiritual body" in much the same way we speak of the Bible as a "spiritual book." Regardless of their spiritual source and power, both the resurrection body and the Bible are material objects.

"Flesh and Blood Cannot Inherit the Kingdom" (1 Co 15:50)

As early as the second century Irenaeus noted that this passage was used by heretics in support of their "very great error."[1] But to conclude from this phrase that the resurrection body will not be a body of physical flesh is without scriptural justification. First, the very next phrase omitted from the above quotation indicates clearly that Paul is speaking not of flesh as such but of **corruptible** flesh. For he adds, "and corruption cannot inherit incorruption" (v. 50). So Paul is not affirming that the resurrection body will not have flesh, but that it will not have **perishable** flesh. Second, Jesus emphatically told them that His resurrection body had flesh. He declared: "Look at My hands and My feet, that it is I Myself! Touch Me and see, because a ghost does not have flesh and bones as you can see I have" (Lk 24:39). Peter said directly that the resurrection body would be the same body of **flesh** that went into the tomb and never saw corruption (Ac 2:31; see 13:35). And John implies that it is against Christ to deny that He remains "in the flesh" even after His resurrection (1 Jn 4:2; 2 Jn 7). Third, the phrase "flesh and blood" in this context apparently means **mortal** flesh and blood, that is, a mere human being. This is supported by parallel uses in the NT. When Jesus said to Peter, "Flesh and blood did not reveal this to you" (Mt 16:17), He could not have been referring to the mere substance of the body as such, which obviously could not reveal that He was the Son of God.[2]

---

1. Irenaeus, *Against Heresies,* Alexander Roberts, James Donaldson, and A. Cleveland Coxe: The ANF: Translations of the writings of the Fathers down to AD 325 1 (Grand Rapids: Eerdmans and Edinburgh: T. & T. Clark, 1978), 357.
2. See John A. Schep, *The Nature of the Resurrection Body: A Study of the Biblical Data* (Grand Rapids: Eerdmans, 1964), 204.

Jesus Could Pass Through Closed Doors (John 20:19,26)

It is inferred by some that since the resurrected Christ could appear in a room with closed doors (Jn 20:19,26), this proves that His body must have been essentially immaterial. Others suggest that He dematerialized on this occasion. But these conclusions are not warranted. First, the text does not actually say Jesus passed through a closed door. It simply says that "the disciples were gathered together with the doors locked because of their fear of the Jews. Then Jesus came, stood among them" (Jn 20:19). The text does not affirm how He got into the room. Like the angel who used his special powers to unlock prison doors (Ac 12:7-10), the supernatural Christ certainly possessed this same power. Second, if He chose to do so, Jesus could have performed this same feat before His resurrection with His physical body. Third, even before His resurrection Jesus performed miracles with His physical body that transcended natural laws, such as walking on water (Jn 6:16-20). But walking on water did not prove that His pre-resurrection body was not physical (Mt 14:29). Fourth, although physical, the resurrection body is by its very nature a supernatural body. Hence, it should be expected that it can do supernatural things like appearing in a room with closed doors. Finally, according to modern physics it is not an impossibility for a material object to pass through a door. It is only statistically improbable. Physical objects are mostly empty space. All that is necessary for one physical object to pass through another is for the right alignment of the particles in the two physical objects. This is no problem for the One who created the body to begin with.

Jesus Was Raised "in the Spiritual Realm" (1 Peter 3:18)

According to 1 Peter 3:18, Jesus was "put to death in the fleshly realm but made alive in the spiritual realm." Some have used this to prove that the resurrection body was not flesh but was in "spirit" or immaterial. This interpretation, however, is neither necessary nor consistent with the context of this passage and the rest of Scripture. First of all, the passage can be translated "having been put to death in the flesh, but made alive in the spirit" (NIV; see NKJV). Second, the parallel between death and being made alive normally refer to the resurrection of the body in the NT. For example, Paul declared that "Christ died and came to life" (Rm 14:9) and "He was crucified in weakness, but He lives by God's power" (2 Co 13:4). Third, the context refers to the event as "the resurrection of Jesus Christ" (1Pt 3:21). But this is everywhere understood as a bodily resurrection in the NT. Fourth, even if "spirit" refers to Jesus' human spirit (not to the Holy Spirit), it cannot mean He had no resurrection body. Otherwise, the reference to His "body" (flesh) before the resurrection would mean He had no human spirit then. It seems better to take "flesh" in this context as a reference to His whole condition of humiliation before the resurrection and "spirit" to refer to His unlimited power and imperishable life after the resurrection.[3]

Christ Was "Life-Giving Spirit" after the Resurrection (1 Corinthians 15:45)

According to 1 Corinthians 15:45 Christ was made a "life-giving Spirit" after His resurrection. Some have also used this passage to prove that Jesus had no physical resurrection body. But this does not follow for reasons similar to those just given to the previous argument.

First, "life-giving spirit" does not speak of the **nature** of the resurrection body but of the divine **origin** of the resurrection. Jesus' physical body came back to life only by the power of God (see Rm 1:4). So Paul is speaking about its spiritual **source**, not its physical **substance** as a material body. Second, if "spirit" describes the nature of Christ's resurrection body, then Adam (with whom He is contrasted) must not have had a soul since he is described as "was from the earth and made of dust"

---

3. Ibid., 77.

(1 Co 15:47). But the Bible says clearly that Adam was "a living being [soul]" (Gn 2:7). Third, Christ's resurrection body is called "spiritual body" (1 Co 15:44), which, as we have seen, is the same word used by Paul to describe material food and a literal rock (1 Co 10:4). Fourth, it is called a "body" *soma,* which always means a physical body when referring to an individual human being.[4]

Other Objections to Jesus' Resurrection

Many other objections have been offered to Jesus' resurrection, all of which are contrary to the above evidence. Some are based on a denial of Jesus' death and others on alternate interpretations to His appearances.

Those theories, like the swoon theory and the replacement theory (that someone else, like Judas, died in Jesus' place) are all contrary to the overwhelming evidence that Jesus died, which includes the following:

1. His death was predicted in the OT (Ps 16:10; Is 53; Dn 9:26);
2. It is verified, eyewitness accounts in the NT (Mt 27; Mk 15; Lk 23; Jn 19);
3. Jesus announced it many times (Mt 12:40; 17:22-23; Jn 2:19-21; 10:10-11);
4. The nature of His crucifixion guaranteed His death;
5. The nature of His wounds and many hours of bleeding assured death;
6. The piercing of Jesus' side with the spear proved it (Jn 19:34);
7. Jesus' death cry indicates it (Lk 23:46-49; see Jn 19:30) was heard by those who stood by (Lk 23:47-49);
8. the Roman executioners pronounced Jesus dead (Jn 19:33);
9. Pilate double-checked to make sure Jesus was dead before he released the corpse (Mk 15:44-45);
10. Being wrapped in about 100 pounds of cloth and spices in a sealed and guarded tomb confirmed it (Mt 27:60; Jn 19:39-40);
11. Non-Christian historians and writers from the first and second centuries recorded the death of Christ. For example, the Jewish historian in the time of Christ, Josephus, believed that Jesus died on the cross. He wrote, "Pilate, at the suggestion of the principal men among us, had **condemned him to the cross**."[5] Likewise, the Roman historian, Cornelius Tacitus (AD 55?–117), wrote: "a wise man who was called Jesus . . . **Pilate condemned Him to be condemned and to die**"[6] and that Jesus' disciples "reported that He had appeared to them three days after **His crucifixion** and that He was alive."[7] According to Julius Africanus (AD 221), the first-century Samaritan born historian, Thallus (AD 52), "when discussing the darkness which fell upon the land **during the crucifixion of Christ**," spoke of it as an eclipse.[8]
12. The earliest Christian writers after the time of Christ affirmed His death on the cross by crucifixion. Polycarp, a disciple of the Apostle John, repeatedly affirmed the death of Christ,

4. Robert Gundry, *Soma in Biblical Theology with Emphasis on Pauline Anthropology* (Society for New Testament Studies 29: Cambridge and New York: Cambridge University Press, 1976), 168.

5. Josephus, *The Jewish Antiquities,* trans. Louis H. Feldman: *Loeb Classical Library* 9 (Cambridge, MA: Harvard University Press and London: William Heinemann, Ltd., 1981), 18.3, emphasis added.

6. Tacitus, *The Annals,* trans. John Jackson: *LCL* 5 (Cambridge, MA: Harvard University Press and London: William Heinemann, Ltd., 1992), 15.44.

7. Ibid.

8. F. F. Bruce, *Jesus and Christian Origins Outside the New Testament* (Grand Rapids: Eerdmans, 1974), 113, emphasis added.

speaking, for example, of "our Lord Jesus Christ, who for our sins suffered even unto death."[9] Ignatius (AD 30–107) was a friend of Polycarp. He clearly affirmed the suffering and death of Christ, saying, "[He] was truly crucified and died in the sight of those in heaven and on earth and under the earth; who also was truly raised from the dead."[10] Otherwise, he added, "As in the same manner his Father shall raise up in Christ Jesus us who believe in him, without whom we have no true life."[11] In his *Dialogue With Trypho,* Justin Martyr noted that Jews of his day believed that "Jesus [was] a Galilean deceiver, whom we crucified."[12]

13. Medical authorities who have examined the circumstances and nature of Christ's death have concluded that He actually died on the cross. W. D. Edwards, W. J. Gabel, and F. E. Hosmer concluded:

Clearly, the weight of historical and medical evidence indicates that Jesus was dead before the wound to his side was inflicted and supports the traditional view. . . . Accordingly, interpretations based on the assumption that Jesus did not die on the cross appear to be at odds with modern medical knowledge.[13]

Other medical authorities have come to the same conclusion beginning with Dr. William Stroud[14] and Pierre Barbet.[15]

Most other theories admit Jesus died and even that the tomb was empty, but deny that His physical body was supernaturally raised from the dead. This they do by either claiming someone (like the disciples, Joseph of Arimathea, Roman authorities, or thieves) removed the body from its tomb. Some theories propose that the "appearances" of Christ were cases of mistaken identity, hallucination, telepathy, or even a theophany. All of these cases are contrary to the overwhelming evidence (presented above) that Jesus was raised in the same physical body of flesh and bones in which He died. This was supported by 12 appearances in the same crucifixion-scarred body, which they saw, heard, and touched with their natural senses and which ate food on several occasions.

9. Polycarp, *To the Philippians, Apostolic Fathers,* trans. Kirsopp Lake: *LCL* 1 (Cambridge, MA: Harvard University Press and London: William Heinemann, Ltd., 1994), 1.33.

10. Ignatius, *Ignatius to the Trallians,* trans. Kirsopp Lake: *LCL* 1 (Cambridge, MA: Harvard University Press and London: William Heinemann, Ltd., 1994), 9.1-2.

11. Ibid., 9.2.

12. Justin Martyr, *Dialogue of Justin, Philosopher and Martyr, with Trypho, a Jew,* Alexander Roberts, James Donaldson, and A. Cleveland Coxe: ANF 1: Translations of the writings of the Fathers down to AD 325 (Grand Rapids: Eerdmans and Edinburgh: T. & T. Clark, 1978), 253.

13. W. D. Edwards, W. J. Gabel, and F. E. Hosmer, "On the physical death of Jesus Christ," *Journal of the American Medical Association* 255.11 (March 21, 1986): 1463.

14. William Stroud, *The Physiological Cause of the Death of Christ* (New York: D. Appleton, 1874).

15. Pierre Barbet, *A Doctor at Calvary: the Passion of Our Lord Jesus Christ as Described by a Surgeon* (New York: P. J. Kenedy & Sons, 1953).

The Resurrection Appearances of Jesus

Gary R. Habermas

Critical scholars regularly charge that the Gospels are full of contradictions and inconsistencies. Reginald Fuller contends that one way to discredit an account is to discover various inconsistencies.[1] Among the most common examples from the Gospels are questions regarding the nature and sequence of particular events after Jesus' death.

Yet most recent scholars are largely unconcerned with these presumed problems and agree that harmonies are unnecessary. Generally, they think that the underlying outline of events is clear enough in spite of such problems. For example, in spite of his concerns about the texts, Fuller clearly agrees that these issues do not keep us from knowing the original apostolic preaching.[2]

In this essay, we will look at three of the most common examples of claimed post-death discrepancies in the Gospel accounts: the number and identity of the women who went to Jesus' burial tomb, the number of angels they reportedly saw there, and a listing of Jesus' appearances. It is my contention that none of these issues has any merit as a Gospel contradiction. Further, the central point must be repeated clearly: this sort of issue is insufficient to question the accounts of Jesus' resurrection appearances.

The Women Who Visited the Tomb

All four Gospels report that, after Jesus' death, one or more women came to His tomb, presumably to anoint Jesus' dead body (Mk 16:1; Lk 24:1). Matthew names Mary Magdalene and "the other Mary" (Mt 28:1). In addition to the two Marys, Mark adds Salome (16:1), while Luke adds Joanna (24:10). But John names specifically only Mary Magdalene (20:1).

Before even looking further at these texts, the seriousness of the overall difficulty must be assessed. The two Marys seem to be the central characters. In the four Gospel accounts, these two names were mentioned possibly eight times. They definitely appear seven times, only one short of the maximum. Only two other names are mentioned in any of the texts, one each in Mark and Luke. As we have seen, John mentions explicitly only Mary Magdalene. Given four books written over a few decades by four different authors, the agreement on this issue actually seems remarkable.

From the outset, then, we are not dealing with wildly divergent lists of names. But given the number of times critics employ this example, one might expect far more diversity. This is not what we find. Moreover, none of the authors says that there was "only" a certain number of women present; in fact, the opposite is the case.

Looking in more detail, there are other indications that the writers never intended to provide a full list of names. When Luke identified the women, he immediately added that other unidentified women were also present (24:10). For Mark, the women who found the tomb empty (16:1) were the same women who were at the cross (15:40-41), as reported just a few verses earlier. There, Mark clearly added that other unnamed women were also present, who had made the trip to Jerusalem.

So Luke explicitly stated that other unnamed women were present at the tomb besides those whose names he included, while Mark stated that this was at least the case at the crucifixion. So

---

1. Reginald H. Fuller, *The Formation of the Resurrection Narratives*, 2nd ed. (New York: Macmillan, 1980), 2.
2. Ibid., 46–49.

it is clear that neither author intended to give an exhaustive list of the females who were present at these events.

But John explicitly mentioned only Mary Magdalene (20:1). However, in the very next verse (20:2), Mary told two of the disciples that "*we* do not know" the whereabouts of Jesus' body. This could very well be a hint that other women were present at the tomb. At the very least, it surely guards against the comment that John thought that only one woman was present.

In conclusion, we simply do not know how many women visited Jesus' empty tomb. As Luke's explicit comment makes clear, buttressed by Mark's and John's implications, it simply was not the Gospel writer's intention to name all the women who were present that weekend. Even today, we regularly cite two or three names while failing to report that others were also part of our conversation. Similarly, for at least three of the four Gospel authors, it cannot be said that they intended to name every woman. To make them say otherwise is simply unfair to the texts.

The Angels at the Tomb

Another common charge is that the number of angels at the tomb differs in the Gospels. Matthew mentions one angel (28:2-5), while Mark states that the women saw "a young man" in a white robe (16:5). Luke records the presence of two men in shining clothes (24:4), while John states that two angels dressed in white were present (20:12). So it is regularly charged that the first two Gospels report one angel, while the last two increase the number to two angels.

However, it is commonly missed that there was more than one trip to the tomb. Luke has a trip by the women and, depending on a textual variation, a second trip by Peter (24:12). John has three trips to the tomb—by Mary Magdalene (and probably other women, 20:1-2), by Peter and John (20:3-9), followed by Mary's return (20:10-18). Actually, no angels are listed in the trip by John and/or Peter, or even in John's initial trip. Only on Mary's return does John mention the angels.

This is a curious situation. Sometimes one angel is mentioned, sometimes two are present, and more than once, the writer does not answer the question. What should we conclude when none is mentioned? If we count Luke's report about Peter, no angels are mentioned in almost half—three out of seven—of the total trips to the tomb.

We have a choice here regarding these three trips. We can conclude that angels were present on at least one of these occasions, but that, for whatever reason, their presence simply was unreported by Luke and John. Or perhaps no angels were present during any of the other three trips. But since we do have these additional scenarios, it is no longer possible to speak of a contrast in the Gospels.

If angels were present but unreported in at least one of these other trips, this raises the strong possibility that other angels likewise could have been present at any time but were similarly unreported. On this possibility, differences in the angelic count can be explained the same way as with the women—providing exact numbers was not the writer's purpose.

But if angels were not present on any of the other three trips, this indicates that for Luke and/or John, for whom there were two or three visits to Jesus' tomb within hours, angels can come and go, or even appear and disappear. On this scenario, once again, there is likewise no problem with varying numbers of angels being reported.

Thus, the extra two or three trips to the tomb are the key to the number of angels. Whatever option is chosen, these cases reveal that there is no need to require that an exact count be given. The Gospel writers themselves provide the ammunition for this conclusion.

Jesus' Appearances

Some scholars have asserted that there is little or no overlap between Paul's early list of resurrection appearances in 1 Corinthians 15:3-8 and the later Gospel narratives.[3] This seems to be a rather incredible claim, implying at least that the various Christian communities were unaware of what the others were teaching. We will consider this specific charge that there is almost a total lack of correlation. In the process, we will be making general comments regarding various details of Jesus' appearances.

Paul's list begins with an appearance to Peter (1 Co 15:5a). Not only is this event clearly mirrored in Luke 24:34, but just like the early, pre-Pauline report, Luke's mention is also regarded as another early, pre-Gospel creedal comment.[4]

Paul's next-listed appearance is to "the 12" (15:5b). The overlap here with Jesus' appearance to the disciples on Easter Sunday (Lk 24:36-49; Jn 20:19-23) is difficult to miss. This is especially the case when, in Luke, the order from Peter to the disciples is precisely the same as for Paul.

Next, the pre-Pauline creed states that Jesus appeared to more than 500 persons at one time (15:6). While there is no direct correlation with this particular number, Matthew relates Jesus' appearance on a mountain in Galilee (28:16-20), and Mark predicts such an event (16:7). Such a rural setting at least makes sense of such an occurrence, although we cannot be sure.

The appearance to James (1 Co 15:7a) clearly has no correlation in the Gospels or Acts. All we know from these latter texts is that James had been a skeptic (Mk 3:20-21; Jn 7:1-5) but later was a leader in the Jerusalem church (Ac 15; Gl 1–2).

Next, we are told that Jesus appeared "to all the apostles" (1 Co 15:7b). Probable candidates for correlation include several of Jesus' Gospel appearances (Mt 28:16-20/Mk 16:7; Jn 20:24-29; Ac 1:6-11).

If we were to include Paul's addition of his own appearance (1 Co 15:8), we have three clear, parallel stories in Acts (9:1-8; 22:6-11; 26:12-18). Like the appearance to Peter, here we are on the strongest grounds.

In conclusion, comparing the Pauline list of six post-resurrection appearances with those in the Gospels and Acts, we have three clearly positive correlations (to Peter, the 12, and to Paul), one probable account (to all the apostles), one possible account (to the 500), and one without confirmation (to James). Although this is by no means a direct match, the partial correlation is difficult to miss. Given that these reports come from very different sources, different literary styles, from various locations, decades apart, and were written by several different authors, this amount of correlation seems actually rather remarkable. This is especially the case when it is remembered that each community would most likely have preserved those appearances from its own locale. By no means, then, should it be said that there is little or no overlap between the early report in 1 Corinthians 15:3-8 and the later Gospels and Acts.

Conclusion

At least two final lessons need to be gleaned from this study. First, we have briefly examined three of the most frequently mentioned cases of alleged contradictions in the Gospel accounts of the empty tomb and resurrection appearances of Jesus. Far from establishing the presence of contradictions, each question can be answered in terms of normal, everyday language. Additional

3. John E. Alsup, *The Post-Resurrection Appearance Stories of the Gospel Tradition: A History-of-Tradition Analysis with Text-Synopsis,* Calwer Theologische Monographien 5 (Stuttgart, Germany: Calwer Verlag, 1975), 57.

4. John Kloppenborg, "An Analysis of the Pre-Pauline Formula in 1 Cor 15:3b-5 in Light of Some Recent Literature," *Catholic Biblical Quarterly* 40 (1978): 358.

charges against this material would have to be examined similarly. But given that these are among the most frequently cited examples, we may be hopeful of similar results.[5]

A few excellent reminders here have been voiced by Eleonore Stump, who argues that many NT scholars are overly zealous in finding problems in the Gospel texts. But their methods are frequently unsupported by either historical or philosophical considerations, and say more about the researcher's own misconceptions. More particularly, their examples regularly fail to demonstrate the presence of true contradictions. Further, while eschewing textual harmonizations, their own methodologies amount to a type of harmony.[6]

Second, as mentioned from the outset, scholars almost always agree that these sorts of textual issues are insufficient to annul the basic report regarding Jesus' appearances, like the very early pre-Pauline report in 1 Corinthians 15:3-8.[7] It is clear, in spite of such differences, that Jesus' earliest followers were absolutely convinced that they had seen the risen Jesus. The chief reason for this conclusion is that if we concentrate on the data that are established on the very strongest grounds, we have a firm basis on which to draw conclusions regarding Jesus' resurrection appearances.[8] In other words, we must emphasize the unquestioned material rather than the questions, since the former is sufficient for the most crucial details. As Raymond Brown explains, we can "get behind the divergences and construct a sequence of appearances."[9]

---

5. John Wenham, *Easter Enigma: Are the Resurrection Accounts in Conflict?* (Grand Rapids: Zondervan, 1984). See the section on "resurrection."

6. Eleonore Stump, "Visits to the Sepulcher and Biblical Exegesis," *Faith and Philosophy* 6 (1989): 353, 366–371.

7. Gary Habermas, *The Risen Jesus and Future Hope* (Lanham, MD: Rowman and Littlefield Publishers, 2003). See chapter 1.

8. Gary Habermas and Michael R. Licona, *The Case for the Resurrection of Jesus* (Grand Rapids: Kregel, 2004). See chapters 3–4.

9. Raymond E. Brown, *The Gospel According to John (13-21),* in *The Anchor Bible Commentary* (Garden City: Doubleday, 1970), 971–972.

Messianic Prophecies Fulfilled in the Gospels

Craig Marlowe

All the canonical Gospels agree that the OT provides evidence that Jesus of Nazareth is the long-awaited Jewish Messiah/Christ. How Jesus is the ultimate understanding of many of these texts differs within a Gospel or between the Gospels, and among modern Bible students and scholars (for example, directly or indirectly, exegetically, or analogically). Which passages "predict" or prefigure the person and passion of the coming Savior are not always the same among the Gospels. That, however, He is in some way foreseen or foreshadowed by the OT is assumed by the NT. Popular preaching and teaching will name approximately sixty-seven OT passages as fulfilled in the life of Christ. But of these only about thirty-three or so are actually quoted or cited or both by a Gospel author.[1] Of these, about twenty-four OT texts, references are quoted/paraphrased and cited as Scripture or named by the OT prophet or book that is assumed or acclaimed to be fulfilled by a NT messianic event. Of these, about ten are from Psalms and ten from Isaiah. The distant runner-up is Zechariah with four, with one of these being combined with a chapter from Jeremiah and cited as the latter rather than the former.[2] Four other OT "quotations" used by the Gospels are neither cited as Scripture in any manner nor employ a fulfillment formula.[3] Five times (of ten) the Gospels both cite the OT and use a fulfillment formula; eight times (of ten) for Isaiah; and three times (of four) for Zechariah. For the purposes and parameters of this study, with a few exceptions (for example, Ps 22:1),[4] those OT texts directly cited as OT Scriptures in some way by one or more of the four Evangelists, and applied to Jesus or an event related to His ministry, will be considered for characterizing the "fulfillment" of messianic prophecy in the Gospels.

Psalms in the Gospels

Synoptics' Use of Psalms as Messianic Prophecy. Matthew alone uses Psalm 8:2 (Mt 21:16) and 78:2 (Mt 13:34-35). For Luke alone there is only Psalm 31:5 (Lk 23:46). Mark employs, with Matthew, Psalm 22:1 (Mt 27:46; Mk 15:34). Matthew, Luke, and Mark use Psalm 110:1 (Mt 22:41-45; Mk 12:35-37; Lk 20:41-44), Psalm 118:22-23 (Mt 21:42-44; Mk 12:10; Lk 20:17-19), and Psalm 118:25-26 (Mt 21:9; Mk 11:9; Lk 19:38). Neither Psalm 22:1, 31:5, nor 118:25-26 appear with any fulfillment formulas or are directly connected to the OT by the Synoptic author.

John's Use of Psalms as Messianic Prophecy. John alone uses Psalm 22:18 (Jn 19:24); 34:20b and/or Ex 12:46; Nm 9:12 (Jn 19:36); 35:19 and/or 69:4(5) (Jn 15:25); 41:9 (Jn 13:18); and 69:9(10) (Jn 2:14-22). In addition he quotes, with the Synoptics, Psalm 118:26 (Jn 12:13), making this the only passage in the Psalms quoted by all four Gospels; yet only John (12:16) describes it as something in OT Scripture relating to Jesus.

---

1. See Gleason L. Archer and G. C. Chirichigno, *Old Testament Quotations in the New Testament* (Chicago: Moody, 1983) for a listing of the OT references cited by the Gospels.
2. See Matthew 27:9-10, which cites Jeremiah but quotes more directly from Zechariah.
3. Psalms 22:1; 31:5; 118:26; Isaiah 35:5-6 (with 26:19; 42:18 and 61:1); A "fulfillment formula" is some statement that the OT source being used is "fulfilled" by the event or experience of the Messiah or of someone or something directly affecting the Messiah (that is, the Christ, or Jesus, from the viewpoint of his disciples and the authors of the four Gospels).
4. In such a case the OT text is quoted but not referenced in any way as coming from the OT, and not said explicitly to be a fulfillment of the OT. However, by the very way in which it is employed, little doubt exists that the one who quotes it (Jesus in this instance) assumes His audience knows the source and understands that He is implying some kind of valid connection and verity between that OT wording and what happens historically to this one who claims to be the Messiah.

Gospels' Use of Psalms as Messianic Prophecy. The use of passages from the OT Psalter as messianic indicators by the four NT Evangelists involves ten Psalms of which eight are Davidic according to the superscriptions. Psalms is the main messianic book for John. Of the two remaining, one is by Asaph (Ps 78) and the other is anonymous (Ps 118). This suggests the high degree of perception on the part of the NT community that David's life served as a type of the future Messiah. The true Messiah would be one whose experience paralleled King David's. From these ten Psalms, twelve or thirteen passages in whole or part are quoted by at least one of the four Gospels. Three are employed just once (8:2 and 78:2 by Matthew; and 31:5 by Luke). Ten passages are directly described as having some parallel or prescriptive value for identifying Jesus as their "fulfillment" or completion: 8:2; 22:18; 34:20b; 35:19 (and/or 69:4); 41:9; 69:9; 78:2; 110:1; 118:22-23; and 118:25-26. Of these, six are specified only by John as OT events with which Jesus can be interpretively identified: 22:18; 34:20b; 35:19 (= 69:4); 41:9b; 69:9a; 118:25-26a (compare with the Synoptics with just two each). In the case of Psalm 22:1a and 31:5, no fulfillment formula is employed to introduce the OT quotation. Jesus on the cross recites these phrases from two Davidic Psalms with no reference to the OT; but this still indicates that he intended his audience to make some kind of connection between his life and that of David in Psalms 22 and 31.

Isaiah in the Gospels

Synoptics' Use of Isaiah as Messianic Prophecy. Isaiah has four Messianic passages which only Matthew employs: Isaiah 7:14 (Mt 1:22-23); 9:1-2 (Mt 4:13-16); 42:1-4 (Mt 12:15-21); and 53:4a (Mt 8:17b). Only Luke uses Isaiah 53:12 (Lk 22:37) and Isaiah 61:1-2 (Lk 4:18-19). Isaiah 6:9-10 and 40:3 are consulted by all three Synoptics (Mt 3:3; 13:14-15; Mk 1:3; 4:12; Lk 3:4; 8:10). Matthew 11:4-6 and Luke 7:22 make use of Isaiah 35:5-6.

John's Use of Isaiah as Messianic Prophecy. John alone cites Isaiah 53:1 (Jn 12:38). He shares two other passages from Isaiah with Matthew, Mark, and Luke (Is 6:9-10 in Jn 12:39-41 and Is 40:3 in Jn 1:23); but the former is not employed in the same manner as the Synoptics.

Gospels' Use of Isaiah for Messianic Prophecy. The Gospels' messianic use of texts from the Book of Isaiah incorporates material from eight chapters. Isaiah is the main messianic book for Matthew. Based on the major thematic content of these contexts, one can conclude that the four NT Evangelists understood that the true Messiah's life would be characterized by events prophesied by Isaiah, which parallel certain experiences of Israel as God's chosen servant: the arrival of Divine revelation, spiritual healing, and social justice in the context of unbelief.

Zechariah in the Gospels

Synoptics' Use of Zechariah as Messianic Prophecy. Just Matthew seems to appropriate Zechariah 11:12-13 but in connection clearly with Jeremiah 19:1-13 (Mt 27:9b-10), because Matthew cites only Jeremiah (27:9a). Yet the quotation fits best with the verses from Zechariah. The text in Jeremiah shares similar ideas but not the wording. Also only Matthew, of the Synoptics, quotes from Zechariah 9:9 (Mt 21:5), although Mark (11:1-10) and Luke (19:28-38) have the same story. For some reason they are not compelled to make reference back to Zechariah as anticipatory of this event, as did Matthew. Matthew (26:31; compare 26:56) and Mark (14:27; compare 14:49) use Zechariah 13:7. Zechariah 11:12-13 is apparently the text referenced by Matthew (27:9-10) but Matthew attributes it to Jeremiah. Thematic links exist in Jeremiah 9:1-13. Likely, Matthew was quoting (paraphrasing) from memory and combined these two passages in his thinking and his application to the events surrounding Judas' betrayal of Jesus and repentance over the blood money. Matthew wanted to show that another part of Jesus' life has very similar, and at times exact, parallels with Israelite history and prophecy. Such a blending of two prophetic texts also occurs in Mark 1:2-3, where Isaiah is named but Malachi 3:1 and Exodus 23:20 are closer to the wording Mark quotes. In each case the Gospel writer seems to defer to the major or better-known prophet when naming his source. For Matthew also the Jeremiah passage would have carried more prophetic and predictive punch. Therefore his "quotation" had Jeremiah in mind principally but also incorporated terminology and phraseology from Zechariah.

John's Use of Zechariah as Messianic Prophecy. The Apostle John is unique among the Gospels in using one verse from Zechariah (12:10 in Jn 19:37). With Matthew he also quotes from Zechariah 9:9 (Jn 12:15) but only indirectly cites "what has been written" (12:14,16) as the source, as compared with Matthew who only a bit more directly cites the source as the "prophet."

Gospels' Use of Zechariah for Messianic Prophecy. All uses of the Book of Zechariah come from the second major section (chapters 9–14), which contains two prophetical and eschatological oracles (9–11, 12–14), often considered intentionally messianic. Matthew and John almost exclusively see Zechariah as containing passages fulfilled by Jesus (with one exception in Mark) to support the claim that Jesus is the true and coming OT "Messiah," or, more precisely, Savior or King. Two passages concern a coming righteous king of Jerusalem (9:9), who will be maligned and then mourned by the House of David (12:10).

Conclusion

According to the four Gospels and their use of fulfillment formulas, the OT foretells or foreshadows the Christ, who would receive the praise of children (Ps 8:2); have His garments gambled over (Ps 22:18); have no bones broken (Ps 34:20); be hated by the Jews for no valid reason (Ps 35:19; 69:4); be betrayed by a close friend (Ps 41:9); be zealous to defend the sanctity of the Temple (Ps 69:9); teach in parables (Ps 78:2 and Is 6:9-10); be David's Lord (Ps 110:1); be the rejected ruler of God's people (Ps 118:22); arrive in Jerusalem in God's name bringing salvation (Ps 118:25-26); speak to an audience with hard hearts (Is 6:9-10); be born of a virgin (Is 7:14); bring the light of revelation to Galilee (Is 9:1-2); be preceded by a desert preacher (Is 40:3); minister quietly not ostentatiously by God's Spirit (Is 42:1-4); be disbelieved in spite of miraculous works (Is 53:1); heal many physical infirmities (Is 53:4); be treated as a transgressor of the law, although innocent (Is 53:12); proclaim good news (Is 61:1-2); enter Jerusalem riding on a young donkey (Zch 9:9); be betrayed with blood money of thirty silver coins (Zch 11:12-13); be pierced in public view (Zch 12:10); and finally be deserted by His disciples when He is arrested (Zch 13:7).

In only about seven or eight of these twenty-three (that is, one third of the time) can it be said that the OT context directly shows intention on the part of the author to speak about the Messiah. Sixteen[5] (about 70%) of these may be said to be typological or other analogical or applicational uses of the OT by the NT authors, while the remaining seven[6] (about 30%) are exegetical and contextual completions of the OT texts as predicted and perceived by the OT author. In one case Matthew's and John's use of the same OT verses (Is 6:9-10) is contrasted between the former's typological and the latter's exegetical treatment. This same distinction is found as well when Matthew uses fulfillment formulas with four Psalms (8:2; 78:2; 110:1; and 118:22-23), while John chooses six others (22:18; 34:20; 35:19; 41:9; 69:9; and 118:25-26). In general Mark and Luke follow Matthew's style rather than John's (that is, more typological than exegetical); except in the seven instances where the OT context reads as an intentional messianic prediction (see note 6 on

---

5. Psalm 8:2; 22:18; 34:20; 35:19; 41:9; 69:9; 78:2; 118:22-23; 118:25-26; Isaiah 6:9-10; 7:14; 40:3; Zechariah 9:9; 11:12-13; 12:10; 13:7.

6. Psalm 110:1; Isaiah 9:1-2; 42:1-4; 53:1; 53:4; 53:12; 61:1-2.

p. 343; six of which are from Isaiah). Among these twenty-three OT texts used with fulfillment formulas in the Gospels, Jesus (the Christ) is the anti-type of David once (Ps 8:2); of Asaph once (Ps 78:2); of an anonymous Israelite leader once (Ps 118:22-23); of Isaiah's Immanuel child once (Is 7:14); and of Isaiah twice (Is 6:9-10 per Matthew; and 61:1-2). The Messiah's predecessor and promoter (John the Baptist) is an anti-type of Isaiah once (Is 40:3). David speaks directly of Him once (Ps 110:1);[7] and Isaiah does this six times (Is 9:1-2; 6:9-10 per John; 42:1-4; 53:1; 53:4; 53:12). Jesus completes an OT event, directly or indirectly, six times (Ps 22:18; 34:20; 118:25-26; Zch 9:9; 12:10; 13:7). Judas, Jesus' betrayer, completes an OT passage two times (Ps 41:9; Zch 11:12-13). The Jews and Jesus' disciples complete an OT text related to the life of Christ once each (Ps 35:19/69:4; and 69:9[10], respectively). Mere coincidence, however, cannot explain how so many events in the life of Jesus were predicted by OT prophets, or parallel OT events in the life of Israel or David as types of the Messiah.

---

7. Here the fulfillment formula in Matthew and Mark adds the rare comment that David spoke by the (Holy) Spirit (only Mark says "holy"). Of course all the OT authors (via the doctrine of inspiration; 2 Timothy 3:16) were led by the Holy Spirit and clearly at times did and other times did not speak directly and intentionally (per the context) about Messiah, while at the same time all of these OT passages qualify interpretively or applicationally as direct forth-telling or indirect foreshadowing of Jesus the Christ. So a comment like "He spoke by the Holy Spirit" does not guarantee that a particular OT statement was a messianic prediction in the strict sense.

Missiological Concepts in the Gospels

Stan May

Missions is a collage of images etched upon the heart. The OT provides the canvas for this montage, while the NT provides the brushstrokes that capture God's missionary zeal. Many of the major NT missionary commands and practices, moreover, emanate from the four Gospels. The Lord Jesus Himself is the master artist, painting on the heart of every one of His servants a portrait of a world lost without Him. Missions is the heartbeat of the Gospels, because missions is the heartbeat of God. Father, Son, and Holy Spirit all are involved in the missionary endeavor: the Father's love compels missions, the Son's ministry exemplifies missions, and the Spirit's power and illumination guide missionary activity. Missions in the Gospels flows from three foundational presuppositions and pulsates with a plan, a passion, and a purpose that reveal the eternal love of the triune God.

Three Presuppositions

First, the Gospels are missionary tracts written by missionaries. These four life pictures of the Lord Jesus are not written primarily as treatises to be studied by scholars, but as accurate records of the message that the Lord Jesus commands to be proclaimed to all the nations. Each author travels as a missionary, each Gospel is written to a different people so that the message will be understood with that culture in mind (e.g., Matthew to the Jews, Mark to the Romans), and each Gospel's purpose is to point people to faith in Christ as Lord (Jn 20:30-31). The Gospel writers contextualize the message so that the people to whom they write can receive and understand this unique message in a culturally relevant manner.

Second, these Gospels were presented essentially to an oral society. As primary oral learners, first-century believers received news verbally, retained it by memory, and passed it along orally to others without benefit of written materials. Many could not read; these nonliterates, however, were able to remember voluminous amounts of material with an accuracy that modern literate people cannot understand. Thus, when Luke says that he is writing to give Theophilus a document "so that [he might] know the certainty of the things about which [he has] been instructed" (Lk 1:4), his written account buttresses and verifies the current oral gospel. Contemporary missionaries minister largely among primary oral learners (most of the people of the world are functional nonliterates). The Gospels present a methodology of communicating divine truth in stories and parables. Informed missionaries learn from the Lord Jesus ways to present the message so that nonliterates can retain and pass along His glorious truth.

Third, Jesus' ministry is a missionary ministry. Jesus is the primary missionary. Matthew includes three Gentile women in Christ's genealogy (Mt 1:3,5). His incarnation stands as the peerless model for the modern missionary who goes to another culture, learns the language and culture of that people, and seeks to reveal the one true and living God to them. Jesus, the Word who is God, becomes flesh and lives in humanity's midst (Jn 1:1,14). The Christmas event prepares for this universal message; the angel declares to the shepherds the "good news [of His birth] of great joy that will be for all the people" (Lk 2:10). Simeon's blessing on the child speaks of a salvation prepared "in the presence of all peoples—a light for revelation to the Gentiles" (Lk 2:31-32). The visit of the "wise men from the east" (Mt 2:1) signals the intention of the Father to draw others from the nations to Himself through the King.

The Lord Jesus lives with missionary passion and purpose in every area of His life. He sees Himself as the One sent by the Father. As He spoke with His disciples in Samaria, He reminded them of His purpose, "My food is to do the will of Him who sent Me and to finish His work" (Jn 4:34). When faced with the temptation to continue preaching to those who had already heard, He responded, "I must proclaim the good news about the kingdom of God to the other towns also, because I was sent for this purpose" (Lk 4:43). From a heart filled with compassion for the multitudes that He saw as sheep without shepherds, He commanded His disciples to "pray to the Lord of the harvest to send out workers into His harvest" (Mt 9:38). This was His single specific order in prayer. He stated plainly to His disciples that He must bring in "other sheep that are not of this fold," so that there would be "one flock, one shepherd" (Jn 10:16). He marveled at the Gentile centurion's faith (Mt 8:10-11) and used him to prophesy of the entry of the Gentiles into the kingdom. His missionary passion spills over into all that He does; His eye is ever on the nations.

Plan

The Gospels exhibit a clear missionary strategy. Two facets of this strategy emerge. The first facet is the "sentness" of the followers of Jesus. Jesus said, "As the Father has sent Me, I also send you" (Jn 20:21). Throughout His earthly ministry, the Lord Jesus regularly sent forth His disciples; their forays into the Judean and Galilean countryside demonstrated a clear plan of action. His followers were sent before Him "in pairs" with detailed mission instructions (Lk 10:5-6) to prepare the way for His message and ministry. While Jesus Himself confined the activity of His earthly ministry almost exclusively to the "lost sheep of the house of Israel," the Gospel writers foreshadow the larger Gentile ministry at several phases of His life (Mt 12:21; Jn 4:4). In fact, John unconsciously shows the Lord's passion in the simple statement, "He had to travel through Samaria" (Jn 4:4).

Jesus further reflected this "sentness" by the name He gave to His chosen disciples—"apostles" (Mk 3:14). Apostle means "one sent forth with authority and commission." This term reveals His heart to send His followers forth to proclaim His word. These men must win and train future disciples. The organic union all believers share comes through believing the words of these apostles (Jn 17:20). When Peter told Him that they had left all to follow Him, Jesus promised, "I assure you, ... there is no one who has left house, brothers or sisters, mother or father, children, or fields because of Me and the gospel, who will not receive 100 times more, now at this time—houses, brothers and sisters, mothers and children, and fields, with persecutions—and eternal life in the age to come" (Mk 10:29-30). Missionaries, according to Jesus, are defined by what they leave, not by where they go; they leave houses, family, and occupations to go "because of Him and His Gospel" to wherever He will send them.

The second facet of His missionary strategy is revealed in the commissions at the conclusions of the Gospels (and in Ac 1:8, the continuation of Luke's Gospel). In each of these climactic messages, Jesus ordered His followers to take His name to the ends of the earth. Jesus' plan is striking in its simplicity. He entrusted the evangelization of the nations to a band of about 120, commanding them to go everywhere and preach His word. Evangelizing means to "make disciples," those who will be both followers and learners of His truth. He commanded them to mark these disciples by believer's baptism and to mature these disciples by teaching them to obey all things He Himself commanded (Mt 28:19-20). Mark says that He commanded them to preach the gospel to the whole creation, and Luke says that His followers are to preach repentance and forgiveness in His name to all the nations, beginning at Jerusalem. He left to the succeeding generations of followers the mighty task of making Him known to all people everywhere.

Jesus called them to make disciples of *panta ta ethnē,* "all the nations." This phrase means not the modern convention of nations, but rather individual sociolinguistic ethnic groups (*ethnē*). Though the Jewish people were the primary focus of His earthly work, His ministry touched differing people groups as He evangelized the village of the Samaritans (Jn 4), healed the Roman centurion's son (Mt 8), and ministered to the Syro-Phoenician woman (Mk 7:26). He commissioned His followers to go to all tribes, peoples, and languages, and make known to them His reconciling love and forgiveness. Christ's followers can neglect neither the ripe harvest fields nor the resistant hardest fields. "All nations" means the whole world. This emphasis appears not only at the commissioning statements but is actually foreshadowed by Him at various times. During His Olivet discourse, He insinuated that the worldwide preaching of the gospel prepares the way for the end to come (Mt 24:14). When the woman anointed Him and washed His feet with her hair, He said, "I assure you: Wherever the gospel is proclaimed in the whole world, what this woman has done will also be told in memory of her" (Mk 14:9).

Passion

John's Gospel announces the clearest declaration of God's missionary passion. As Jesus spoke to Nicodemus, He uttered the most famous verse in the Bible, "For God loved the world in this way" (Jn 3:16). Though this verse often is used to teach personal salvation (and rightly so), the Father's heart for the world takes center stage. No one country, people group, or language is elevated; the whole world is the object of the Father's love. The Father, Son, and Spirit together exhibit mighty passion for the lost of the world. Jesus said that the field is the world (Mt 13:38) and that the fields are ripe already for the harvest (Jn 4:36). As the true harvester of all nations at the end of the age (Mt 13:39-41), He sent forth His servants into this world to sow and to reap in preparation for His coming.

He sent them forth with authority and power. Since all authority is given to Him (Mt 28:18), no political, military, or spiritual foe can stand in the way of those who go and make disciples of all the nations. He empowers them by granting the Holy Spirit (Jn 20:22) and by commanding them to wait for the promise of the Father (Lk 24:49). He further promised His presence with those who go in His name (Mt 28:20). He even promised that their persecution on account of Him would be a witness to the nations (Mt 10:18). To see His passion realized, however, requires an unyielding sacrifice on the part of His servants; He demands that they take up their cross and follow Him without reservation, willing to lose their lives for Him and His gospel (Mk 8:34-35).

Purpose

The heart of all this missionary activity and passion is seeing people come into the kingdom of God. Jesus begins and ends His ministry speaking of the kingdom. God's kingdom is a missionary kingdom, for His missionary purpose is to fulfill Abraham's blessing to all nations. Jesus, as the seed of Abraham, sends His emissaries out to proclaim "forgiveness of sins … in His name to all the nations" (Lk 24:47). But His purpose is much greater than proclamation alone; He sends out His servants to "make disciples." The gospel message does not produce mere decisions, but rather disciples who confess Christ, unite with one of His local churches, follow Him in believer's baptism, and grow into maturity by obeying all that He says. His purpose is to convert people from the nations into passionate followers who love Him with all their heart, mind, soul, and strength. He draws these to Himself to produce worshipers, because the Father seeks true worshipers to worship Him in spirit and in truth (Jn 4:23-24). Matthew's quote from the Prophet Isaiah sums up Jesus' missionary ministry, "Here is My Servant whom I have chosen, My beloved in whom My soul delights; I will put My Spirit on Him, and He will proclaim justice to the nations . . . The nations will put their hope in His name" (Mt 12:18-21). God's missionary purpose brings justice to the nations and hope to all people.

A List of the Parables of Jesus in the Gospels[1]

Steven L. Cox

Parable Name	Text	Theme
A. Recorded only in Matthew		
1. The wheat and the weeds	Matt 13:24-30	The climax of the kingdom
2. The hidden treasure and priceless pearl	Matt 13:44-46	The immense value of the kingdom
3. The net	Matt 13:47-50	The climax of the kingdom
4. The storehouse of truth	Matt 13:52	The centrality of the kingdom
5. The unforgiving slave	Matt 18:23-35	The cost of the kingdom
6. The vineyard workers	Matt 20:1-16	The gift of the kingdom
7. The two sons	Matt 21:28-32	The universality of the kingdom
8. The wedding banquet	Matt 22:1-14	The challenge of the kingdom
9. The 10 virgins	Matt 25:1-13	The challenge of the kingdom
10. The talents	Matt 25:14-30	The nearness of the kingdom
11. The sheep and the goats	Matt 25:31-46	The cost of the kingdom
B. Recorded only in Mark		
1. The seed growing secretly	Mark 4:26-29	The certainty of the kingdom
2. The suddenness of His coming	Mark 13:34-37	The nearness of the kingdom
C. Recorded only in Luke		
1. The two debtors	Luke 7:41-43	The universality of the kingdom
2. The good Samaritan	Luke 10:30-37	The cost of the kingdom
3. The friend at midnight	Luke 11:5-8	The universality of the kingdom
4. The rich fool	Luke 12:16-21	The nearness of the kingdom
5. The watchful servants	Luke 12:35-40	The nearness of the kingdom
6. The wise steward	Luke 12:42-48	The nearness of the kingdom
7. The barren fig tree	Luke 13:6-9	The nearness of the kingdom
8. The lowest seats at a feast	Luke 14:7-14	The universality of the kingdom
9. The large banquet	Luke 14:16-24	The universality of the kingdom
10. The cost of following Jesus	Luke 14:28-33	The cost of the kingdom
11. The lost coin	Luke 15:8-9	The universality of the kingdom

---

1. One should note that there are no parables in the Gospel of John.

Parable Name	Text	Theme
C. Recorded only in Luke (cont.)		
12. The lost son	Luke 15:11-32	The universality of the kingdom
13. The dishonest manager	Luke 16:1-13	The challenge of the kingdom
14. The rich man and Lazarus	Luke 16:19-31	The challenge of the kingdom
15. The master and slave	Luke 17:7-10	The gift of the kingdom
16. The persistent widow	Luke 18:2-5	The universality of the kingdom
17. The Pharisee and the tax collector	Luke 18:10-14	The universality of the kingdom
18. The ten minas	Luke 19:12-27	The nearness of the kingdom
D. Reported by Matthew and Luke		
1. The speck and the log	Matt 7:3-5 Luke 6:41-42	The nearness of the kingdom
2. The two foundations	Matt 7:24-27 Luke 6:46-49	The challenge of the kingdom
3. The yeast	Matt 13:33 Luke 13:20-21	The centrality of the kingdom
4. The lost sheep	Matt 18:10-14 Luke 15:4-6	The universality of the kingdom
E. Reported by Matthew, Mark, and Luke		
1. The lamp and the basket	Matt 5:14-15 Mark 4:21-25 Luke 8:16-18	The nearness of the kingdom
2. Concerning fasting	Matt 9:14-17 Mark 2:18-20 Luke 5:33-35	The nearness of the kingdom
3. The sower	Matt 13:3-9,19-23 Mark 4:3-9,14-20 Luke 8:5-8,11-15	The centrality of the kingdom
4. The mustard seed	Matt 13:31-32 Mark 4:30-32 Luke 13:18-19	The centrality of the kingdom
5. The wicked vineyard owner	Matt 21:33-41 Mark 12:1-9 Luke 20:9-16	The universality of the kingdom
6. The fig tree	Matt 24:32-35 Mark 13:28-31 Luke 21:29-33	The nearness of the kingdom

A List of the Miracles of Jesus in the Gospels

Steven L. Cox

A. Recorded only in Matthew

1. Healing of the Blind	Matt 9:27-31
2. Driving out a Demon	Matt 9:32-33
3. Paying the Temple Tax–Money Taken from a Fish's Mouth	Matt 17:24-27

B. Recorded only in Mark

1. Jesus Does Everything Well–Deaf and Mute Man Healed	Mark 7:31-37
2. Healing a Blind Man	Mark 8:22-26

C. Recorded only in Luke

1. The First Disciples–Draught of Fishes	Luke 5:1-11
2. A Widow's Son Raised to Life	Luke 7:11-17
3. Healing a Daughter of Abraham–Woman's Infirmity Healed	Luke 13:11-17
4. A Sabbath Controversy–A Man with Dropsy Healed	Luke 14:1-6
5. Ten Lepers Cleansed/Healed	Luke 17:11-19

D. Recorded only in John

1. Turning Water into Wine at Cana	John 2:1-12
2. Healing an Official's Son	John 4:46-54
3. The Healing of a Lame/Paralyzed Man, at Jerusalem	John 5:1-15
4. The Healing of a Man Born Blind, at Jerusalem	John 9:1-7
5. Raising Lazarus from the Dead	John 11:38-44
6. Jesus' Third Appearance to the Disciples–The Catch of 153 Fish	John 21:1-14

E. Reported by Matthew and Mark

1. A Gentile Mother's Faith–Her daughter is Healed	Matt 15:21-28; Mark 7:24-30
2. Feeding Four Thousand	Matt 15:32-39; Mark 8:1-10
3. The Barren Fig Tree	Matt 21:18-22; Mark 11:12-14

F. Reported by Matthew and Luke

1. A Centurion's Faith–His Paralyzed Servant Healed	Matt 8:5-13; Luke 7:1-10
2. A House Divided–A Blind and Mute Demoniac Healed	Matt 12:22-32; Luke 11:14-23

G. Reported by Mark and Luke

1. Driving out an Unclean Spirit–Demoniac in Synagogue Healed	Mark 1:21-28; Luke 4:31-37

H. Reported by Matthew, Mark, and Luke

1. A Man Cleansed
   Matt 8:1-4
   Mark 1:40-45
   Luke 5:12-16

2. Healings at Capernaum
   Matt 8:14-17
   Mark 1:29-34
   Luke 4:38-41

3. Wind and Wave Obey the Master–The Calming of a Storm
   Matt 8:23-27
   Mark 4:35-41
   Luke 8:22-25

4. Demons Driven Out by the Master
   Matt 8:28-34
   Mark 5:1-20
   Luke 8:26-39

5. The Son of Man Forgives and Heals–A Paralytic Healed
   Matt 9:1-8
   Mark 2:1-12
   Luke 5:17-26

6. Jairus' Daughter Raised
   Matt 9:18-19, 23-26
   Mark 5:21-23,35-43
   Luke 8:40-42a, 49-56

7. Woman's Issue of Blood Healed
   Matt 9:20-22
   Mark 5:24-34
   Luke 8:42b-48

8. The Man with the Paralyzed Hand
   Matt 12:9-14
   Mark 3:1-6
   Luke 6:6-11

9. The Power of Faith over a Demon–Demon Cast out of Boy
   Matt 17:14-21
   Mark 9:14-29
   Luke 9:37-43a

10. Two Blind Men Healed
    Matt 20:30-34
    Mark 10:46-52
    Luke 18:35-43

I. Reported by Matthew, Mark, and John

1. Jesus Walks on the Water
   Matt 14:22-33
   Mark 6:45-52
   John 6:16-21

J. Reported by All the Gospels

1. The Feeding of Five Thousand
   Matt 14:13-21
   Mark 6:30-43
   Luke 9:10-17
   John 6:1-15

2. The Slave of the High Priest Healed
   Luke 22:49-51

Old Testament Quotations in New Testament

H. David Philipps

<table>
<tr><td colspan="3" align="center">Matthew</td></tr>
<tr><td>Text</td><td>Source</td><td>Reference/Quote</td></tr>
<tr><td>1:23</td><td>Isaiah 7:14</td><td>Quote</td></tr>
<tr><td>2:6</td><td>Micah 5:2</td><td>Quote</td></tr>
<tr><td>2:6</td><td>2 Samuel 5:2</td><td>Quote</td></tr>
<tr><td>2:15</td><td>Hosea 11:1</td><td>Quote</td></tr>
<tr><td>2:18</td><td>Jeremiah 31:15</td><td>Quote</td></tr>
<tr><td>2:23</td><td>Isaiah 11:1</td><td>Loose Reference</td></tr>
<tr><td>3:3</td><td>Isaiah 40:3</td><td>Quote</td></tr>
<tr><td>4:4</td><td>Deuteronomy 8:3</td><td>Quote</td></tr>
<tr><td>4:6</td><td>Psalm 91:11-12</td><td>Quote</td></tr>
<tr><td>4:7</td><td>Deuteronomy 6:16</td><td>Quote</td></tr>
<tr><td>4:10</td><td>Deuteronomy 6:13</td><td>Quote</td></tr>
<tr><td>4:15-16</td><td>Isaiah 9:1-2</td><td>Quote</td></tr>
<tr><td>5:21</td><td>Exodus 20:13; Deuteronomy 5:17</td><td>Quote</td></tr>
<tr><td>5:27</td><td>Exodus 20:14; Deuteronomy 5:18</td><td>Quote</td></tr>
<tr><td>5:31</td><td>Deuteronomy 24:1</td><td>Quote</td></tr>
<tr><td>5:33</td><td>Leviticus 19:12; Numbers 30:2; Deuteronomy 23:21</td><td>Quote</td></tr>
<tr><td>5:38</td><td>Exodus 21:24; Leviticus 24:20; Deuteronomy 19:21</td><td>Quote</td></tr>
<tr><td>5:43</td><td>Leviticus 19:18</td><td>Quote</td></tr>
<tr><td>7:23</td><td>Psalm 6:8</td><td>Reference</td></tr>
<tr><td>8:17</td><td>Isaiah 53:4</td><td>Quote</td></tr>
<tr><td>9:13</td><td>Hosea 6:6</td><td>Quote</td></tr>
<tr><td>10:35-36</td><td>Micah 7:6</td><td>Quote</td></tr>
<tr><td>11:10</td><td>Malachi 3:1</td><td>Quote</td></tr>
<tr><td>12:7</td><td>Hosea 6:6</td><td>Quote</td></tr>
<tr><td>12:18-21</td><td>Isaiah 42:1-4</td><td>Quote</td></tr>
<tr><td>13:14-15</td><td>Isaiah 6:9-10</td><td>Quote</td></tr>
<tr><td>13:35</td><td>Psalm 78:2</td><td>Quote</td></tr>
</table>

Matthew (cont.)		
Text	**Source**	**Reference/Quote**
15:4	Exodus 20:12; Deuteronomy 5:16	Quote
15:4	Exodus 21:17; Leviticus 20:9	Quote
15:8-9	Isaiah 29:13	Quote
18:16	Deuteronomy 19:15	Quote
19:4	Genesis 1:27; 5:2	Quote
19:5	Genesis 2:24	Quote
19:18-19	Exodus 20:12-16; Leviticus 19:18; Deuteronomy 5:16-20	Quote
21:5	Isaiah 62:11	Loose Reference
	Zechariah 9:9	Quote
21:9	Psalm 118:25-26	Quote
21:13	Isaiah 56:7	Quote
21:13	Jeremiah 7:11	Quote
21:16	Psalm 8:3	Quote
21:42	Psalm 118:22-23	Quote
22:24	Deuteronomy 25:5	Quote
22:32	Exodus 3:6,15-16	Quote
22:37	Deuteronomy 6:5	Quote
22:39	Leviticus 19:18	Quote
22:44	Psalm 110:1	Quote
23:39	Psalm 118:26	Quote
24:15	Daniel 9:27	Quote
	Daniel 12:11	Loose Reference
24:29	Isaiah 13:10; 34:4	Loose Reference
26:31	Zechariah 13:7	Quote
26:64	Psalm 110:1	Loose Reference
27:9-10	Jeremiah 19:1-13; 32:6-9	Loose Reference
	Zechariah 11:12-13	Quote
27:35	Psalm 22:18	Loose Reference
27:46	Psalm 22:1	Quote

Mark		
Text	**Source**	**Reference/Quote**
1:2	Malachi 3:1	Quote
1:3	Isaiah 40:3	Quote
1:44	Leviticus 13:49; 14:2-4,10	Reference
4:12	Isaiah 6:9-10	Quote
7:6-7	Isaiah 29:13	Quote
7:10	Exodus 20:12; Deuteronomy 5:16	Quote
7:10	Exodus 21:17; Leviticus 20:9	Quote
8:18	Jeremiah 5:21; Ezekiel 12:2	Quote
9:48	Isaiah 66:24	Quote
10:6	Genesis 1:27; 5:2	Quote
10:7-8	Genesis 2:24	Quote
10:19	Exodus 20:12-16; Deuteronomy 5:16-20	Quote
11:9-10	Psalm 118:25-26	Quote
11:17	Isaiah 56:7	Quote
11:17	Jeremiah 7:11	Quote
12:10-11	Psalm 118:22-23	Quote
12:19	Genesis 38:8; Deuteronomy 25:5-10	Quote
12:26	Exodus 3:6,15-16	Quote
12:29	Deuteronomy 6:4	Quote
12:30	Deuteronomy 6:5	Quote
12:31	Leviticus 19:18	Quote
12:36	Psalm 110:1	Quote
13:14	Daniel 9:27	Quote
13:24-25	Isaiah 13:10; 34:4	Loose Reference
14:27	Zechariah 13:7	Quote
14:62	Psalm 110:1; Daniel 7:13	Quote
15:28	Isaiah 53:12	Quote
15:34	Psalm 22:1	Quote

Luke		
Text	**Source**	**Reference/Quote**
2:23	Exodus 13:2,12	Quote
2:24	Leviticus 5:11; 12:8	Quote
3:4-6	Isaiah 40:3-5	Quote
4:4	Deuteronomy 8:3	Quote
4:8	Deuteronomy 6:13	Quote
4:10-11	Psalm 91:11-12	Quote
4:12	Deuteronomy 6:16	Quote
4:18-19	Isaiah 61:1-2	Quote
7:27	Malachi 3:1	Quote
8:10	Isaiah 6:9	Reference
10:27	Leviticus 19:18; Deuteronomy 6:5	Quote
12:53	Micah 7:6	Quote
13:35	Psalm 118:26	Quote
18:20	Exodus 20:12-16; Deuteronomy 5:16-20	Quote
19:38	Psalm 118:26	Quote
19:46	Isaiah 56:7; Jeremiah 7:11	Quote
20:17	Psalm 118:22	Quote
20:28	Deuteronomy 25:5	Quote
20:37	Exodus 3:6,15	Quote
20:42-43	Psalm 110:1	Quote
21:27	Daniel 7:13	Quote
22:37	Isaiah 53:12	Quote
22:69	Psalm 110:1	Quote
23:30	Hosea 10:8	Quote
23:46	Psalm 31:5	Quote

John		
Text	**Source**	**Reference/Quote**
2:17	Psalm 69:9	Quote
6:31	Exodus 16:15; Nehemiah 9:15; Psalm 78:24	Quote
6:45	Isaiah 54:13	Quote
10:34	Psalm 82:6	Quote
12:13	Psalm 118:25-26	Quote
12:15	Isaiah 62:11; Zechariah 9:9	Quote
12:38	Isaiah 53:1	Quote
12:40	Isaiah 6:10	Quote
13:18	Psalm 41:9	Quote
15:25	Psalm 35:19; 69:4	Quote
19:24	Psalm 22:18	Quote
19:36	Exodus 12:46; Numbers 9:12; Psalm 34:20	Quote
19:37	Zechariah 12:10	Quote

SELECTED BIBLIOGRAPHY

Aharoni, Yohanan. *The Land of the Bible: A Historical Geography*. Trans. A.F. Rainey. Philadelphia: Westminster, 1967.

Aland, Kurt. *Synopsis of the Four Gospels*. 9th ed. Stuttgart, Germany: German Bible Society, 1989.

———, and Barbara Aland. *The Text of the New Testament: An Introduction to the Critical Editions and to the Theory and Practice of Modern Textual Criticism*. 2nd rev. ed. Grand Rapids: Eerdmans, 1995.

Allen, Clifton J., et al. eds. *Broadman Bible Commentary*. 12 vols. Nashville: Broadman, 1969.

Alsup, John E. *The Post-Resurrection Appearance Stories of the Gospel Tradition: A History-of-Tradition Analysis with Text-Synopsis*. Calwer Theologische Monographien 5. Stuttgart, Germany: Calwer Verlag, 1975.

Apostolic Fathers. Trans. Kirsopp Lake. 2 vols. *Loeb Classical Library*. Cambridge, MA: Harvard University Press and London: William Heinemann, Ltd., 1994.

Aquinas, Thomas. *On the Truth of the Catholic Faith: Summa Contra Gentiles*. Trans. Anton C. Pegis, James F. Anderson, Vernon J. Bourke, and Charles J. O'Neil. 5 vols. New York: Doubleday, 1955-57. Repr. as *Summa Contra Gentiles,* Notre Dame, IN: University of Notre Dame Press, 1975.

Archer, Gleason L., and G. C. Chirichigno. *Old Testament Quotations in the New Testament: A Complete Survey*. Chicago: Moody, 1983.

Arndt, William F., and F. Wilbur Gingrich. *A Greek-English Lexicon of the New Testament and Other Early Christian Literature: A Translation and Adaptation of the Fourth Revised and Augmented Edition of Walter Bauer's Griechisch-Deutsches Worterbuch zu den Schriften des Neun Testaments und der ubrigen urchristlichen Literatur*. 2nd ed. Revised by F. Wilbur Gingrich and Frederick W. Danker. Chicago: University of Chicago Press, 1979.

Athenagoras. *Embassy for the Christians; The Resurrection of the Dead*. Ancient Christian Writers: The Works of the Fathers in Translation, vol. 23. New York: Newman Press, 1955.

Bacon, B. W. "Genealogy of Jesus Christ." *A Dictionary of the Bible*, ed. J. Hastings. Edinburgh: T. & T. Clark, 1899.

Bailey, Denis. *The Geography of the Bible: A Study in Historical Geography*. New York: Harper & Brothers, 1957.

Barbet, Pierre. *A Doctor at Calvary: The Passion of Our Lord Jesus Christ as Described by a Surgeon*. New York: P. J. Kenedy & Sons, 1953.

Barclay, William. *Introduction to the First Three Gospels*. Philadelphia: Westminster, 1975.

Barker, William Pierson. *Women and the Liberator*. Old Tappan, N.J.: Fleming H. Revell, 1972.

Barrett, C. K. *The New Testament Background: Selected Documents*. New York: Harper & Row, 1961.

Beckwith, Roger T. *Calendar and Chronology, Jewish and Christian: Biblical, Intertestamental and Patristic Studies*. Arbeiten zur Geschichte des Antiken Judentums und des Urchristentums 33. Ed. Martin Hengel et al. Leiden: E. J. Brill, 1996.

Beitzel, Barry J. *The Moody Atlas of Bible Lands*. Chicago: Moody, 1985.

Bell, Albert A. *Exploring the New Testament World*. Nashville: Thomas Nelson, 1998.

Black, David Alan, and David S. Dockery, eds. *New Testament Criticism and Interpretation*. Grand Rapids: Zondervan, 1991.

Blomberg, Craig L. *The Historical Reliability of the Gospels*. Downer's Grove, IL: InterVarsity, 1987.

———. *The Historical Reliability of John's Gospel: Issues and Commentary*. Downer's Grove, IL: InterVarsity, 2001.

———. *Jesus and the Gospels*. Nashville: Broadman & Holman, 1997.

———. "The Legitimacy and Limits of Harmonization." In *Hermeneutics, Authority, and Canon*, ed. D. A. Carson and John D. Woodbridge, 139–74. Grand Rapids: Baker, 1995.

———. *Matthew*. The New American Commentary, vol. 22. Ed. David S. Dockery. Nashville: Broadman & Holman, 1992.

Bock, Darrell L. *Luke 1:1–9:50, Baker Exegetical Commentary*. Grand Rapids: Baker, 1994.

Boyd, Gregory A. *Cynic, Sage, or Son of God?* Wheaton: Victor, 1995.

Brand, Chad, Charles Draper, and Archie England, eds. *Holman Illustrated Bible Dictionary.* Nashville: Broadman & Holman, 2003.

Bratcher, Robert G., ed. *Old Testament Quotations in the New Testament.* Helps for Translators Series. Rev. ed. London: United Bible Societies, 1961.

Broadus, John A. *Commentary on the Gospel of Matthew.* An American Commentary on the New Testament. Philadelphia: American Baptist Publication Society, 1886.

Bromiley, Geoffrey W., ed. *New International Standard Bible Encyclopedia.* 4 vols. Grand Rapids: Eerdmans, 1979.

Brown, Raymond E. *The Birth of the Messiah.* Garden City, NY: Doubleday, 1977.

———. *The Death of the Messiah.* 2 vols. New York: Doubleday, 1994.

———. *The Gospel According to John (13–21).* Anchor Bible Commentary. Garden City: Doubleday, 1970.

———. *An Introduction to the New Testament.* New York: Doubleday, 1997.

Bruce, F. F. *Jesus and Christian Origins Outside the New Testament.* Grand Rapids: Eerdmans, 1974.

———. *New Testament History.* New York: Doubleday, 1971.

Bultmann, Rudolf. *Jesus and the Word.* Trans. Louise Pettibone Smith and Erminie Huntress Lantero. New York: Scribner's, 1958.

Burridge, Richard. *Four Gospels, One Jesus?* London: SPCK, 1994.

Burrows, Millar. *The Dead Sea Scrolls, with Translations by the Author.* New York: Gramercy Publishing Company, 1955.

Burton, Ernest de Witt, and Edgar Johnson Goodspeed. *A Harmony of the Synoptic Gospels in Greek.* Chicago: University of Chicago Press, 1920.

Butler, Trent C., ed. *Holman Bible Dictionary.* Nashville: Broadman and Holman, 1991.

Calvin, John. *Institutes of the Christian Religion.* Philadelphia: Westminster, 1964.

———. *Matthew, Mark, Luke: Harmony of the Gospels.* Trans. A. W. Morrison. Grand Rapids: Eerdmans, 1972.

Carson, D. A. *Matthew.* The Expositor's Bible Commentary, vol. 8. Ed. F. E. Gaebelein. Grand Rapids: Zondervan, 1984.

Carson, D. A., Douglas J. Moo, and Leon Morris. *An Introduction to the New Testament.* Grand Rapids: Zondervan, 1992.

Casey, Maurice. *Aramaic Sources of Mark's Gospel.* Society for New Testament Studies Monograph Series 102. Ed. Richard Bauckham. New York: Cambridge University Press, 1998.

Chafer, Lewis Sperry. "Eternal Security: Part 2." *Bibliotheca Sacra* 106 (1949): 392–419.

———. *Systematic Theology.* 8 vols. Dallas: Dallas Theological Seminary, 1948.

Charlesworth, James H., ed. *Pesharim, Other Commentaries, and Related Documents.* The Dead Sea Scrolls: Hebrew, Aramaic, and Greek Texts with English Translations, vol. 6B. Tübingen: Mohr Siebeck, 2002.

Church, Chris. "Religious Background of the New Testament." In *Foundations for Biblical Interpretation,* ed. David S. Dockery, Kenneth A. Matthews, Robert B. Sloan, 509–24. Nashville: Broadman & Holman, 1994.

Collins, Raymond F. *Introduction to the New Testament.* Garden City: Doubleday, 1983.

Cox, Steven L. *A History and Critique of Scholarship Concerning the Markan Endings.* New York and San Francisco: Mellen, 1993.

Craig, William Lane. *Knowing the Truth about the Resurrection: Our Response to the Empty Tomb.* Knowing the Truth series. Ann Arbor, MI: Servant Books, 1988.

———. *The Son Rises.* Chicago: Moody, 1981. Repr. Wipf and Stock, Publishers, 2001.

Crossan, John Dominic. *The Historical Jesus: The Life of a Mediterranean Jewish Peasant.* San Francisco: Harper San Francisco, 1991.

Croy, N. Clayton. *The Mutilation of Mark's Gospel.* Nashville: Abingdon, 2003.

Dana, Harvey E. *The New Testament World.* 3d ed., rev. Nashville: Broadman, 1937.

deSilva, David A. *An Introduction to the New Testament: Contexts, Methods and Ministry Formation.* Downers Grove, IL: InterVarsity, 2004.

Dio Cassius, Roman History. Trans. Earnest Cary and Herbert B. Foster. 9 vols. *Loeb Classical Library.* Cambridge, MA: Harvard University Press and London: William Heinemann, Ltd., 1917.

Donfried, Karl P. "Chronology: New Testament." *The Anchor Bible Dictionary,* vol. 1, ed. David Noel Freedman et al. 6 vols, 1011–12. New York: Doubleday, 1992.

Downing, F. G. *Cynics and Christian Origins.* Edinburgh: T. & T. Clark, 1992.

Dungan, David L. "Synopses of the Future." *The Interrelations of the Gospels*, ed. David L. Dungan. Macon, GA: Mercer University Press, 1990.

———. "Theory of Synopsis Construction." *Biblica* 61 (1980): 330–42.

Edwards, W. D., W. J. Gabel, and F. E. Hosmer. "On the physical death of Jesus Christ." *Journal of the American Medical Association* 255.11 (March 21, 1986): 1455–63.

Ehrman, Bart, and Michael Holmes, eds. *The Text of the New Testament in Contemporary Research: Essays on the Status Quaestionis.* Grand Rapids: Eerdmans, 1995.

Ellis, E. Earle. "Jesus' Use of the Old Testament and the Genesis of New Testament Theology." *Bulletin for Biblical Research* 3 (1993): 59–75.

———. *The Old Testament in Early Christianity.* Tübingen: J. C. B. Mohr, 1991.

Elwell, Walter, ed. *Baker Encyclopedia of the Bible.* 2 vols. Grand Rapids: Baker, 1988.

Eusebius. *Ecclesiastical History.* Trans. Kirsopp Lake and J. E. L. Oolton. 2 vols. *Loeb Classical Library.* Cambridge, MA: Harvard University Press and London: William Heinemann, Ltd., 1976.

Evans, Craig A. *Mark 8:27–16:20.* The Word Biblical Commentary, vol. 34B. Nashville: Thomas Nelson, 2001.

———, and Stanley E. Porter, eds. *Dictionary of New Testament Background*: *A Compendium of Contemporary Biblical Scholarship.* Downers Grove, IL: InterVarsity, 2000.

Farmer, William Reuben. *The Synoptic Problem: A Critical Analysis.* New York: Macmillan, 1964.

Fee, Gordon D., and Douglas Stuart. *How to Read the Bible for All Its Worth.* 3rd ed. Grand Rapids: Zondervan: 2003.

———. "Some Dissenting Notes on 7Q5 = Mark 6:52-53." *Journal of Biblical Literature* 92 (1973): 109–112.

Ferguson, Everett. *Backgrounds of Early Christianity.* 3rd. ed. Grand Rapids: Eerdmans, 2003.

Finegan, Jack. *Handbook of Biblical Chronology: Principles of Time Reckoning in the Ancient World and Problems of Chronology in the Bible.* Rev. ed. Peabody, MA: Hendrickson, 1964, 1998.

Fitzmyer, Joseph A. *The Gospel According to Luke (I–IX).* The Anchor Bible. Garden City, NY: Doubleday, 1981.

Fotheringham, J. K. "Astronomical Evidence for the Date of the Crucifixion." *Journal of Theological Studies* 12 (October 1910): 120–27.

Foxe, John. *Foxe's Christian Martyrs of the World.* Rept. ed. San Antonio, TX: Mantle Ministries, n.d.

France, R. T. "Chronological Aspects of 'Gospel Harmony.'" *Vox Evangelica* 16 (1986): 33–59.

Freedman, David Noel, ed. *The Anchor Bible Dictionary.* 6 vols. New York: Doubleday, 1992.

Fuller, Reginald H. *The Formation of the Resurrection Narratives.* 2d ed. New York: Macmillan, 1980.

Gaebelein, F. E., ed. *The Expositor's Bible Commentary.* Grand Rapids: Zondervan, 1984.

Gamble, Harry. *Books and Readers in the Early Church: A History of Early Christian Texts.* New Haven: Yale University Press, 1995.

Geisler, Norman. *The Battle for the Resurrection.* Nashville: Nelson Publishers, 1989.

———. *In Defense of the Resurrection.* Lynchburg, VA: Quest Publications, 1991.

———, and William Nix. *General Introduction to the Bible.* Chicago: Moody, 1968.

Geldenhuys, Norval. *Commentary on the Gospel of Luke: The English Text with Introduction, Exposition and Notes.* Grand Rapids: Eerdmans, 1979.

Godwin, Joscelyn. *Mystery Religions in the Ancient World.* San Francisco: Harper & Row, 1981.

Green, Joel B., Scot McKnight, and I. Howard Marshall, eds. *Dictionary of Jesus and the Gospels.* Downers Grove, IL: InterVarsity, 1992.

Greenlee, Harold. *Introduction to New Testament Textual Criticism.* Rev. ed. Peabody, MA: Hendrickson, 1995.

Greeven, Heinrich. "The Gospel Synopsis from 1776 to the Present Day." Trans. Robert Althann. In *J. J. Griesbach: Synoptic and Text-Critical Studies 1776–1976,* ed. Bernard Orchard. Cambridge: Cambridge University Press, 1978.

Gundry, Robert H. *Soma in Biblical Theology with Emphasis on Pauline Anthropology.* Society for New Testament Studies 29. Cambridge and New York: Cambridge University Press, 1976.

———. *A Survey of the New Testament.* 3rd ed. Grand Rapids: Zondervan, 1994.

Guthrie, Donald. *New Testament Introduction.* Rev. ed. Downers Grove, IL: InterVarsity and Leicester, England: Apollos, 1990.

Habermas, Gary. *The Historical Jesus: Ancient Evidence for the Life of Christ.* Joplin, MO: College Press, 1996.

———. *The Resurrection of Jesus.* Grand Rapids: Baker, 1980.

———. *The Risen Jesus and Future Hope.* Lanham, MD: Rowman and Littlefield Publishers, 2003.

———, and Michael R. Licona. *The Case for the Resurrection of Jesus.* Grand Rapids: Kregel, 2004.

Hagner, D. A. *Matthew 1–13.* Word Biblical Commentary, vol. 33A. Dallas: Word, 1993.

Haines Eitzen, Kim. *Guardians of Letters: Literacy, Power, and the Transmission of Early Christian Literature.* New York: Oxford University Press, 2000.

Hamilton, John. "The Chronology of the Crucifixion and the Passover." *Churchman* 106 (1992): 323–338.

Harris, Murray J. *From Grave to Glory: Resurrection in the New Testament.* Grand Rapids: Zondervan, 1990.

Hastings J., ed. *A Dictionary of the Bible.* 5 vols. Edinburgh: T. & T. Clark, 1899.

Held, Heinz Joachim. "Matthew as Interpreter of the Miracle Stories." In *Tradition and Interpretation in Matthew,* ed. Günther Bornkamm, Gerhard Barth, and Heinz Joachim Held. Philadelphia: Westminster, 1963, pp. 165–300.

Hervey, A. *The Genealogies of Our Lord and Saviour Jesus Christ, as Contained in the Gospels of St. Matthew and St. Luke.* Cambridge: Bell, 1853.

Hiebert, Paul G. "Spiritual Warfare and Worldview." *Evangelical Review of Theology.* Carlisle, Cumbria, UK: Paternoster Periodicals. 24.3 (July 2000): 114–24.

Higgins, A. J. B., ed. *The Early Church: Studies in Early Christian History and Theology,* abr. ed. Philadelphia: Westminster, 1966.

Hoehner, Harold W. *Chronological Aspects of the Life of Christ.* Grand Rapids: Zondervan, 1977.

Holmes, Michael W., ed. *The Apostolic Fathers.* Grand Rapids: Baker, 1989.

Huck, Albert. *Synopsis of the First Three Gospels.* 9th ed. Revised by Hans Lietzmann. English ed. by F. L. Cross. New York: American Bible Society, 1935.

Humphreys, Colin J. "The Star of Bethlehem, a Comet in 5 BC and the Date of Christ's Birth." *Tyndale Bulletin* 43.1 (May 1992): 31–56.

———, and W. G. Waddington. "The Jewish Calendar, a Lunar Eclipse and the Date of Christ's Crucifixion." *Tyndale Bulletin* 43.2 (November 1992): 331–51.

Honeycutt, Roy L., ed. *The Review and Expositor* 84 (Spring 1987): 177–321.

Instone-Brewer, David. "Jesus' Last Passover: The Synoptics and John." *Expository Times* 112 (January 2001): 122–23.

Jaubert, Annie. *The Date of the Last Supper.* Trans. Isaac Rafferty. Staten Island, NY: Alba House, 1965.

Jeffers, James S. *The Greco-Roman World of the New Testament Era: Exploring the Background of Early Christianity.* Downers Grove, IL: InterVarsity, 1999.

Jeremias, Joachim. *The Eucharistic Words of Jesus.* Trans. Norman Perrin. 3rd ed. New Testament Library, ed. Alan Richardson, C. F. D. Moule, and Floyd V. Filson. London: SCM Press, 1966.

———. *Jerusalem in the Time of Jesus.* Philadelphia: Fortress, 1969.

Johnson, M. D. *The Purpose of the Biblical Genealogies, with Special Reference to the Setting of the Genealogies of Jesus*. Cambridge: Cambridge University Press, 1969.

Josephus. *Josephus*. Trans. H. St. J. Thackeray, Ralph Marcus, Allen Wikgren, Louis H. Feldman. 13 vols. *Loeb Classical Library*. Cambridge, MA: Harvard University Press and London: William Heinemann, Ltd., 1926–1976.

Kee, Howard Clark. *The New Testament in Context: Sources and Documents*. Englewood Cliffs, NJ: Prentice-Hall, 1984.

Keener, C. S. *The IVP Bible Background Commentary: New Testament*. Downers Grove, IL: InterVarsity, 1993.

Kissinger, Warren S. *The Sermon on the Mount: A History of Interpretation and Bibliography*. Metuchen, NJ: Scarecrow, 1975.

Kittel, Gerhard, and G. Friedrich, eds. *Theological Dictionary of the New Testament*. Trans. Geoffrey W. Bromiley. 10 vols. Grand Rapids: Eerdmans, 1964–1976.

Klauck, Hans-Josef. *Magic and Paganism in Early Christianity*. Edinburgh: T. & T. Clark, 2000.

Kloppenborg, John. "An Analysis of the Pre-Pauline Formula in 1 Cor 15:3b-5 in Light of Some Recent Literature." *Catholic Biblical Quarterly* 40 (1978): 351–67.

Kopas, Jane. "Jesus and Women in Matthew," n.p. (cited 13 September 2005). *http://theologytoday. ptsem.edu/apr1990/v47-1-article2.htm*.

Knight, George W. *A Simplified Harmony of the Gospels*. Nashville: Broadman & Holman, 2001.

Kraft, Robert A., and W. E. Nickelsburg, eds. *Early Judaism and Its Modern Interpreters*. The Bible and Its Modern Interpreters. Series ed. Douglas A. McKnight. Atlanta: Scholars Press, 1986.

Kuhn, K. G. "Die Geschlechtsregister Jesu bei Lukas und Matthäus, nach ihrer Herkunft untersucht." *Zeitschrift für die neutestamentliche Wissenschaft und die Kunde der älteren Kirche* 22 (1923): 206–28.

Ladd, George. *I Believe in the Resurrection of Jesus*. Grand Rapids: Eerdmans, 1975.

Laurentin, Rene. *The Truth of Christmas*. Trans. Michael J. Wrenn. Petersham, MA: St. Bede's Publications, 1986.

Lea, Thomas D. *The New Testament: Its Background and Message*. Nashville: Broadman & Holman, 1996.

———, and David Alan Black. *The New Testament: Its Background and Message*. 2nd ed. Nashville: Broadman and Holman, 2003.

Lewis, C. S. *An Experiment in Criticism*. Cambridge: Cambridge University Press, 1961.

Lockyer, Herbert. *The Women of the Bible*. 11th ed. Grand Rapids: Zondervan, 1974.

Long, Anthony A. *Stoic Studies*. Cambridge: Cambridge University Press, 1996.

Longenecker, Richard. *Biblical Exegesis in the Apostolic Period*. Grand Rapids: Eerdmans, 1975.

Machen, J. G. *The Virgin Birth of Christ*. London: Marshall, Morgan & Scott, 1930.

Magness, Jodi. *The Archaeology of Qumran and the Dead Sea Scrolls*. Grand Rapids: Eerdmans, 2002.

Maier, Paul L. *In the Fulness of Time: A Historian Looks at Christmas, Easter, and the Early Church*. San Francisco: Harper, 1991.

———. "Sejanus, Pilate, and the Date of the Crucifixion." *Church History* 37 (March 1968): 3–13.

Marshall, I. Howard. *The Gospel of Luke*. New International Greek Testament Commentary. Grand Rapids: Eerdmans, 1978.

———, ed. *New Testament Interpretation: Essays on Principles and Methods*. Repr. ed. Grand Rapids: Eerdmans, 1985.

Martin, Luther H. *Hellenistic Religions: An Introduction*. Oxford: Oxford University Press, 1987.

May, Herbert G., ed. *Oxford Bible Atlas*. 2nd ed. London: Oxford University Press, 1974.

Mayhue, Richard L. "Rediscovering Pastoral Ministry." In *Rediscovering Pastoral Ministry: Shaping Contemporary Ministry with Biblical Mandates*, ed. John MacArthur, Jr., 3–18. Dallas: Word, 1995.

McArthur, Harvey K. *The Quest through the Centuries: The Search for the Historical Jesus.* Philadelphia: Fortress, 1966.

McDowell, Josh, and John Gilchrist. *The Islam Debate.* San Bernardino, CA: Here's Life, 1983.

Melick, Richard R., Jr. "Literary Criticism of the New Testament." In *Foundations for Biblical Interpretation,* ed. David S. Dockery, Kenneth A. Matthews, Robert B. Sloan, 434–53. Nashville: Broadman and Holman, 1994.

Metzger, Bruce M. *The Early Versions of the New Testament: Their Origin, Transmission, and Limitations.* Oxford: Clarendon Press, 1977.

———. *The New Testament: Its Background, Growth, and Content.* 3rd ed. Nashville: Abingdon, 2003.

———. *A Textual Commentary on the Greek New Testament.* 2nd ed. New York: United Bible Societies, 1994.

———, and Bart Ehrman. *The Text of the New Testament: Its Transmission, Corruption, and Restoration,* 4th ed. New York: Oxford University Press, 2005.

Meyer, Ben. *The Aims of Jesus.* London: SCM, 1979.

Moltmann-Wendel, Elisabeth. *The Women around Jesus.* New York: Crossroad, 1988.

Montgomery, John. *History and Christianity.* Downer's Grove, IL: InterVarsity, 1970.

Nash, Ronald H. *Christianity and the Hellenistic World.* Grand Rapids: Zondervan, 1984.

New, David S. *Old Testament Quotations in the Synoptic Gospels, and the Two-Document Hypothesis.* Septuagint and Cognate Studies 37, ed. Leonard J. Greenspoon. Atlanta: Scholars Press, 1993.

Nineham, D. E., ed. *Historicity and Chronology in the New Testament.* London: SCM Press, 1965.

Noss, John B. *Man's Religions.* Rev. ed. New York & London: Macmillan, 1980.

Ogg, George. "The Chronology of the Last Supper." In *Historicity and Chronology in the New Testament,* ed. D. E. Nineham, et al., 92–96. London: SPCK Press, 1965.

———. *The Chronology of the Public Ministry of Jesus.* Cambridge: Cambridge University Press, 1940.

Orchard, John Bernard, O. S. B. *A Synopsis of the Four Gospels in Greek.* Edinburgh: T. & T. Clark, 1983.

Orr, James, ed. *The International Standard Bible Encyclopedia.* 5 vols. Grand Rapids: Eerdmans, 1949.

———. *The Resurrection of Jesus.* London: Hodder and Stoughton, nd.

Perrin, Norman. *What Is Redaction Criticism?* Guides to Biblical Scholarship. Ed. Dan O. Via. Philadelphia: Fortress, 1969.

Pfeiffer, Charles F. *Baker's Bible Atlas.* Grand Rapids: Baker, 1961.

Philo. *Every Good Man Is Free.* Trans. F. H. Colson, G. H. Whitaker, Ralph Marcus. *Loeb Classical Library.* 10 vols and 2 suppl. vols. Cambridge, MA: Harvard University Press and London: William Heinemann, Ltd., 1929–1971.

Rice, David G., and John E. Stambaugh, eds. *Sources for the Study of Greek Religion.* Missoula, MT: Scholars Press, 1980.

Rist, J. M. *Epicurus: An Introduction.* Cambridge: Cambridge University Press, 1972.

Roberts, Alexander, and James Donaldson, eds. *The Ante-Nicene Fathers.* 10 vols. Repr ed. Grand Rapids: Eerdmans, 1979.

———, James Donaldson, and A. Cleveland Coxe. *The Ante-Nicene Fathers: Translations of the Writings of the Fathers down to A.D. 325.* 10 vols. Grand Rapids: Eerdmans and Edinburgh: T. & T. Clark, 1978.

Robertson, A. T. *A Grammar of the Greek New Testament in the Light of Historical Research.* 4th ed. Nashville: Broadman, 1934.

———. *A Harmony of the Gospels for Students of the Life of Christ.* New York: Harper & Row, 1922.

Robertson, O. Palmer. *Understanding the Land of the Bible: A Biblical-Theological Guide.* Phillipsburg, NJ: Presbyterian and Reformed, 1996.

Robinson. Haddon W. "Busting Out of Sermon Block." In *Making a Difference in Preaching*, ed. Haddon W. Robinson and Scott M. Gibson, 96–106. Grand Rapids: Baker, 1999.

Roetzel, Calvin J. *The World That Shaped the New Testament*. Rev. ed. Louisville, KY: Westminster/ John Knox, 2002.

Roth, Cecil, et al. eds. *Encyclopedia Judaica*. 26 vols. Jerusalem: Encyclopedia Judaica, 1972.

Ruckstuhl, Eugen. *Chronology of the Last Days of Jesus: A Critical Study*. Trans. Victor J. Drapela. New York: Desclee, 1965.

Saldarini, A. J. *Pharisees, Scribes and Sadducees in Palestinian Society: A Sociological Approach*. Wilmington, DE: Michael Glazier, 1988.

Sanders, E. P. *The Historical Figure of Jesus*. London: Penguin, 1993.

———. *Judaism: Practice and Belief, 63 B.C.–A.D. 66*. Philadelphia: Trinity Press International, 1992.

Schaff, Philip. *New Schaff-Herzog Encyclopedia of Religious Knowledge,* ed. Samuel Macauley Jackson. 13 vols. New York: Funk and Wagnalls, 1908–1912. Repr., Grand Rapids: Baker, 1949–1950.

———, and Henry Wace, eds. *A Select Library of Nicene and Post-Nicene Fathers of the Christian Church*. 28 vols. Repr. ed. Grand Rapids: Eerdmans, 1979.

Schauss, H. *The Jewish Festivals: History and Observance*. New York: Schocken, 1962.

Schep, John A. *The Nature of the Resurrection Body: A Study of the Biblical Data*. Grand Rapids: Eerdmans, 1964.

Schürer, Emil. *The History of the Jewish People in the Age of Jesus Christ*. 5 vols. Ed. Geza Vermes, Fergus Miller, and Matthew Black. Edinburgh: T. & T. Clark, 1979.

Scott, J. Julius. "Crisis and Reaction: Roots of Diversity in Intertestamental Judaism." *The Evangelical Quarterly* 64 (1992): 197–213.

Sedley, D. N. *The Hellenistic Philosophers*. 2 vols. Cambridge: Cambridge University Press, 1987.

Segal, J. B. *The Hebrew Passover: From the Earliest Times to A.D. 70*. London: Oxford, 1963.

Sharples, R. W. *Stoics, Epicureans, and Skeptics: An Introduction to Hellenistic Philosophy*. New York: Routledge, 1996.

Sherwin-White, A. N. *Roman Society and Roman Law in the New Testament*. Oxford: Clarendon, 1963.

———. "The Trial of Christ." In *Historicity and Chronology in the New Testament*, ed. D. E. Nineham. London: SPCK Press, 1965.

Shepherd, Massey H., Jr. "Are Both the Synoptics and John Correct about the Date of Jesus' Death?" *Journal of Biblical Literature* 80 (1961): 123–32.

Simon, Marcel. *Jewish Sects at the Time of Jesus*. Philadelphia: Fortress, 1980.

Sloane, Robert B. "Canonical Theology of the New Testament." In *Foundations for Biblical Interpretation*, ed. David S. Dockery, Kenneth A. Matthews, Robert B. Sloan, 565–94. Nashville: Broadman and Holman Publishers, 1994.

Smith, Adam. *The Historical Geography of the Holy Land Especially in Relation to the History of Israel and of the Early Church*. London: Hodder and Stoughton, 1894.

Smith, Barry D. "The Chronology of the Last Supper." *Westminster Theological Journal* 53 (1991): 29–45.

Snider, P. Joel. "Harmony of the Gospels." In *The Holman Illustrated Bible Dictionary*, ed. Chad Brand, Charles Draper, and Archie England, 716–19. Nashville: Broadman and Holman, 2003.

Stein, Robert H. *The Synoptic Problem: An Introduction*. Grand Rapids: Baker, 1987.

Stemberger, G. *Jewish Contemporaries of Jesus: Pharisees, Sadducees, Essenes*. Minneapolis: Fortress, 1995.

Story, Cullen I. K. "The Bearing of Old Testament Terminology on the Johannine Chronology of the Final Passover of Jesus." *Novum Testamentum* 31 (1989): 316–24.

Strack, Hermann L., and Paul Billerbeck. *Kommentar zum Neuen Testament*. Vol. 2. Müchen: 1924.

Strauss, David Friedrich. *The Life of Jesus Critically Examined.* Ed. Peter C. Hodgson. Trans. George Eliot. *Life of Jesus Series.* Series ed. Leander E. Keck. Philadelphia: Fortress, 1972.

Stroud, William. *The Physiological Cause of the Death of Christ.* New York: D. Appleton, 1874.

Stump, Eleonore. "Visits to the Sepulcher and Biblical Exegesis." *Faith and Philosophy.* 6 (1989): 355–77.

Tacitus. *The Histories and the Annals.* Trans. M. Hutton, W. Peterson, Clifford H. Moore, and John Jackson. 5 vols. *Loeb Classical Library.* Cambridge, MA: Harvard University Press and London: William Heinemann, Ltd., 1986–1996.

Tenney, Merrill C. *The Reality of the Resurrection.* Chicago: Moody, 1963, 1972.

———, ed. *The Zondervan Pictorial Encyclopedia of the Bible.* 5 vols. Grand Rapids: Zondervan, 1976.

Thiede, Carston Peter. *The Earliest Gospel Manuscript? The Qumran Fragment 7Q5 and Its Significance for New Testament Studies.* London: Paternoster Studies, 1992.

Thomas, Robert L., ed. *A Harmony of the Gospels.* Chicago: Moody, 1986.

———, and Stanley N. Gundry. *A Harmony of the Gospels.* San Francisco: Harper, 1978.

Throckmorton, Burton H., Jr. *Gospel Parallels: A Synopsis of the First Three Gospels.* New York: Thomas Nelson & Sons, 1949.

Trimm, James Scott. "Nazarenes, Qumran and the Essenes." *The Society for the Advancement of Nazarene Judaism* (*Netzari Yehudim*). (N.d.). www.nazarene.net/Essenes.htm?

Turcan, Robert. *The Cults of the Roman Empire.* Oxford: Blackwells, 1996.

Turner, George A. *Historical Geography of the Holy Land.* Washington, DC: Canon Press, 1973.

Turner, J. D., and A. McGuire, eds. *The Nag Hammadi Library after Fifty Years.* Leiden: E. J. Brill, 1997.

Vardaman, Jerry, and Edwin Yamauchi, eds. *Chronos, Kairos, Christos.* Winona Lake, MN: Eisenbrauns, 1989.

Vermes, Geza. *The Complete Dead Sea Scrolls in English.* London: Penguin, 1997.

———. *The Dead Sea Scrolls in English: Revised and Extended.* 4th ed. London: Penguin, 1995.

Wallace, Daniel. "7Q5: The Earliest NT Papyrus?" *Biblical Studies* (2000). *http://www.bible.org/page.asp?page_id=1196.*

Wenham, John. *Easter Enigma: Are the Resurrection Accounts in Conflict?* Academie Books. Grand Rapids: Zondervan, 1984.

———. *Redating Matthew, Mark, and Luke.* Downer's Grove, IL: InterVarsity, 1992.

Williams, M. A. *Rethinking "Gnosticism:" An Argument for Dismantling a Dubious Category.* Princeton, NJ: Princeton University Press, 1996. Wrede, William. *The Messianic Secret.* Trans. J. C. G. Greig. Cambridge: James Clarke, 1971.

Wright, N. T. *The New Testament and the People of God.* Minneapolis: Augsburg Fortress, 1989.

Zarley, Kermit. *The Gospels Interwoven.* Wheaton: Victor, 1987.

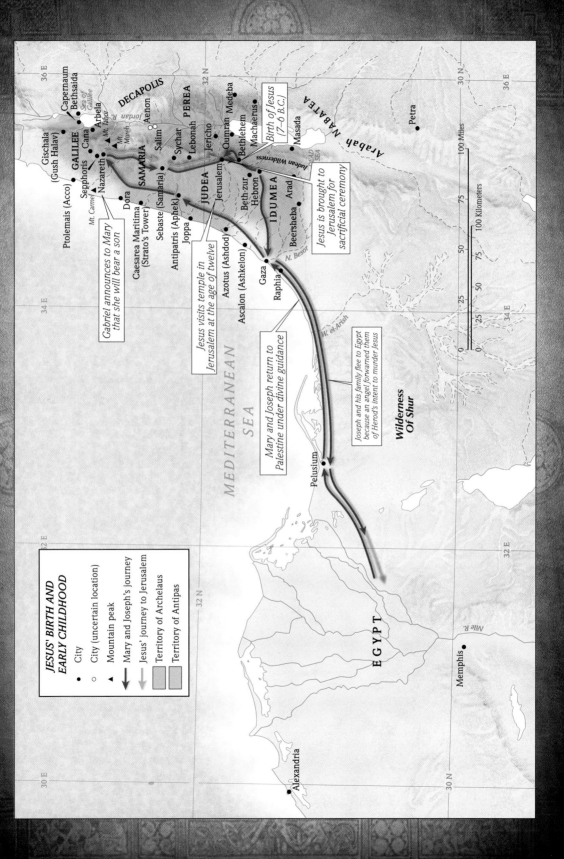

JESUS' BIRTH AND
EARLY CHILDHOOD

• City
○ City (uncertain location)
▲ Mountain peak
→ Mary and Joseph's journey
→ Jesus' journey to Jerusalem
◻ Territory of Archelaus
◻ Territory of Antipas

Gabriel announces to Mary
that she will bear a son

Jesus visits temple in
Jerusalem at the age of twelve

Mary and Joseph return to
Palestine under divine guidance

Joseph and his family flee to Egypt
because an angel forewarned them
of Herod's intent to murder Jesus

Jesus is brought to
Jerusalem for
sacrificial ceremony

Birth of Jesus
(7–6 B.C.)

DECAPOLIS
PEREA
GALILEE
SAMARIA
JUDEA
IDUMEA
NABATEA
Arabah
EGYPT
MEDITERRANEAN SEA
Wilderness
Of Shur

Capernaum
Bethsaida
Sea of Galilee
Arbela
Mt. Tabor
Cana
Aenon
Salim
Gischala
(Gush Halav)
Sepphoris
Nazareth
Mt. Carmel
Dora
Caesarea Maritima
(Strato's Tower)
Sebaste (Samaria)
Antipatris (Aphek)
Joppa
Ptolemais (Acco)
Mt. Moreh
Sychar
Lebonah
Jerusalem
Jericho
Qumran
Bethlehem
Beth-zur
Hebron
Arad
Beersheba
Medeba
Machaerus
Masada
Petra
Azotus (Ashdod)
Ascalon (Ashkelon)
Gaza
Raphia
N. Besor
Pelusium
Alexandria
Memphis
Nile R.
Jordan R.
Judean Wilderness
DEAD SEA
W. el-Arish

100 Miles
100 Kilometers
0 25 50 75
0 25 50 75 100

36 E
34 E
30 E
32 N
30 N
32 E
36 E

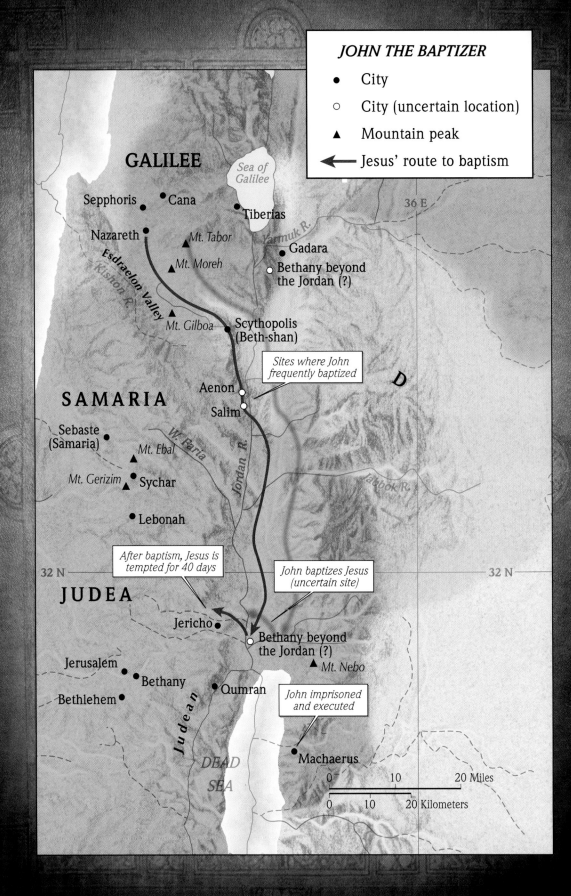

JOHN THE BAPTIZER

- • City
- ○ City (uncertain location)
- ▲ Mountain peak
- ← Jesus' route to baptism

GALILEE

Sea of Galilee

Sepphoris •Cana

36 E

•Tiberias

Nazareth ▲ Mt. Tabor

Gadara

Esdraelon Valley

▲ Mt. Moreh

Bethany beyond the Jordan (?)

Kishon R.

Yarmuk R.

▲ Mt. Gilboa

Scythopolis (Beth-shan)

Sites where John frequently baptized

Aenon

D

Salim

SAMARIA

Sebaste (Samaria)

▲ Mt. Ebal

W. Faria

Mt. Gerizim ▲ •Sychar

Jordan R.

Jabbok R.

•Lebonah

After baptism, Jesus is tempted for 40 days

32 N

John baptizes Jesus (uncertain site)

32 N

JUDEA

Jericho

Bethany beyond the Jordan (?)

Jerusalem

▲ Mt. Nebo

•Bethany

Bethlehem

•Qumran

Judean

John imprisoned and executed

DEAD

SEA

0   10   20 Miles

•Machaerus

0   10   20 Kilometers

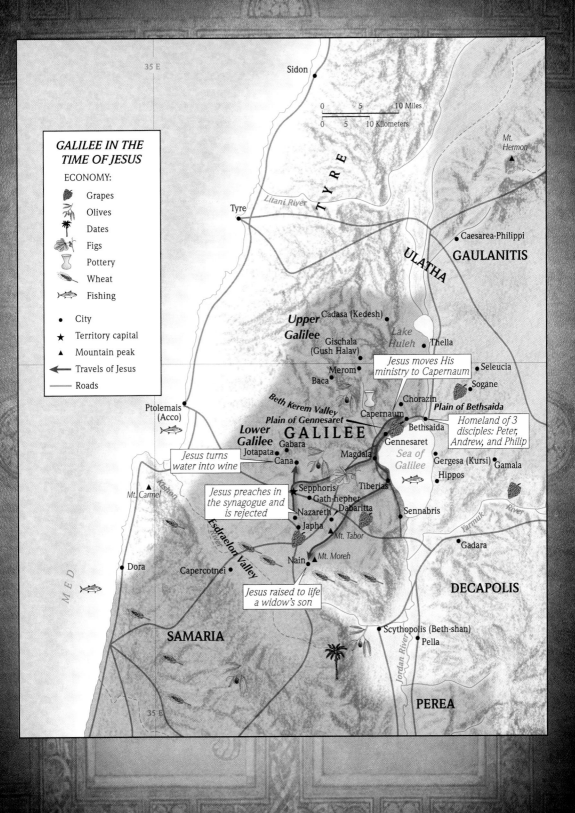

GALILEE IN THE TIME OF JESUS

ECONOMY:

- Grapes
- Olives
- Dates
- Figs
- Pottery
- Wheat
- Fishing

- City
- ★ Territory capital
- ▲ Mountain peak
- ← Travels of Jesus
- Roads

35 E

Sidon

0   5   10 Miles
0   5   10 Kilometers

Mt. Hermon

TYRE

Litani River

Tyre

Caesarea-Philippi

ULATHA   GAULANITIS

Upper Galilee

Cadasa (Kedesh)

Lake Huleh   Thella

Gischala (Gush Halav)

Merom

Baca

Jesus moves His ministry to Capernaum

Chorazin

Plain of Bethsaida

Seleucia

Sogane

Beth Kerem Valley

Capernaum

Ptolemais (Acco)

Plain of Gennesaret

Lower Galilee   **GALILEE**

Gabara

Bethsaida

Homeland of 3 disciples: Peter, Andrew, and Philip

Jotapata

Gennesaret

Cana

Magdala

Sea of Galilee

Gergesa (Kursi)   Gamala

Hippos

Jesus turns water into wine

Mt. Carmel

Kishon

Sepphoris   Gath-hepher

Tiberias

Jesus preaches in the synagogue and is rejected

Nazareth   Dabaritta

Esdraelon Valley

Japha

Mt. Tabor

Sennabris

Varmuk River

Nain   Mt. Moreh

Gadara

MED

Dora

Capercotnei

DECAPOLIS

Jesus raised to life a widow's son

Scythopolis (Beth-shan)

Pella

SAMARIA

Jordan River

PEREA

35 E

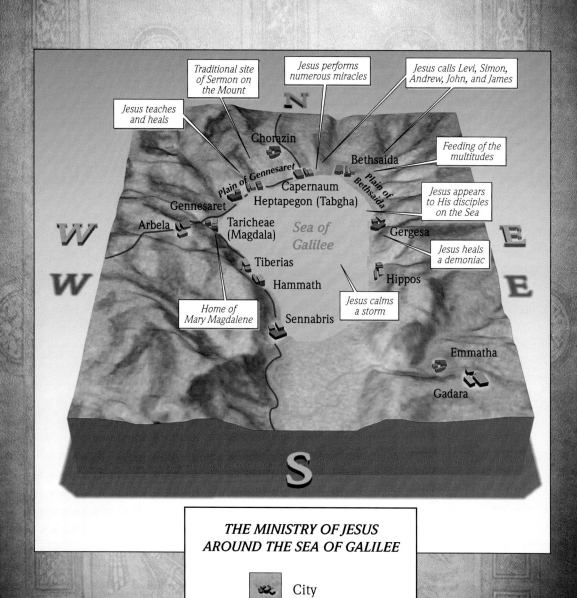

Traditional site
of Sermon on
the Mount

Jesus performs
numerous miracles

Jesus calls Levi, Simon,
Andrew, John, and James

Jesus teaches
and heals

Feeding of the
multitudes

N

Chorazin

Bethsaida

Plain of
Bethsaida

Plain of Gennesaret

Capernaum
Heptapegon (Tabgha)

Jesus appears
to His disciples
on the Sea

Gennesaret

Arbela

Taricheae
(Magdala)

W

Sea of
Galilee

Gergesa

Jesus heals
a demoniac

E

Tiberias

W

Hammath

Hippos

E

Home of
Mary Magdalene

Jesus calms
a storm

Sennabris

Emmatha

Gadara

S

THE MINISTRY OF JESUS
AROUND THE SEA OF GALILEE

City

Road

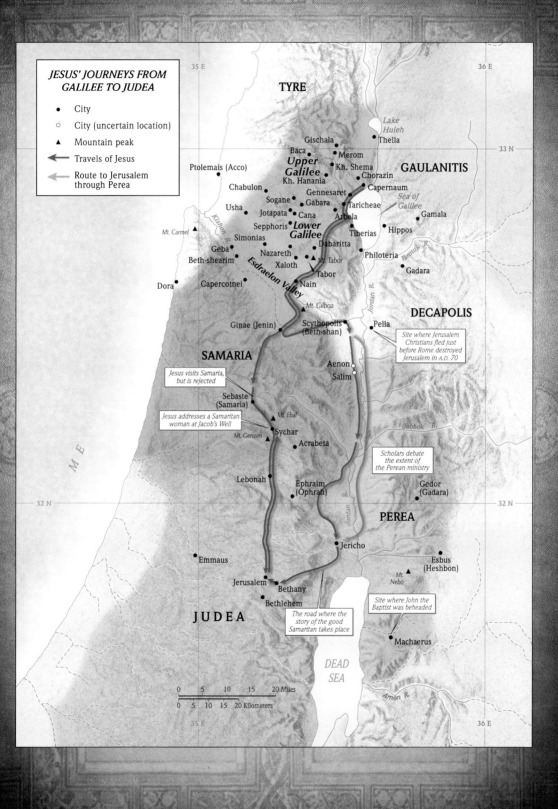

JESUS' JOURNEYS FROM
GALILEE TO JUDEA

- ● City
- ○ City (uncertain location)
- ▲ Mountain peak
- → Travels of Jesus
- → Route to Jerusalem through Perea

TYRE

Lake Huleh

Gischala
Baca
Merom
Kh. Shema
Chorazin
Thella

Ptolemais (Acco)

Upper Galilee

GAULANITIS

Chabulon
Kh. Hanania
Capernaum

Sea of Galilee

Gennesaret
Sogane
Gabara
Taricheae
Gamala

Usha
Jotapata
Cana
Arbela

Sepphoris
Lower Galilee
Tiberias
Hippos

Mt. Carmel
Simonias
Dabaritta

Geba
Nazareth
Mt. Tabor
Philoteria

Beth-shearim
Xaloth
Tabor
Gadara

Dora
Capercotnei
Esdraelon Valley
Nain

DECAPOLIS

Mt. Gilboa

Ginae (Jenin)
Scythopolis (Beth-shan)
Pella

Site where Jerusalem Christians fled just before Rome destroyed Jerusalem in A.D. 70

SAMARIA

Aenon
Salim

Jesus visits Samaria, but is rejected

Sebaste (Samaria)

Jesus addresses a Samaritan woman at Jacob's Well

Mt. Ebal
Sychar
Mt. Gerizim
Acrabeta

Scholars debate the extent of the Perean ministry

Lebonah
Ephraim (Ophrah)
Gedor (Gadara)

PEREA

Emmaus
Jericho
Esbus (Heshbon)
Mt. Nebo

Jerusalem
Bethany
Bethlehem

Site where John the Baptist was beheaded

JUDEA

The road where the story of the good Samaritan takes place

Machaerus

DEAD SEA

0   5   10   15   20 Miles
0 5 10 15   20 Kilometers

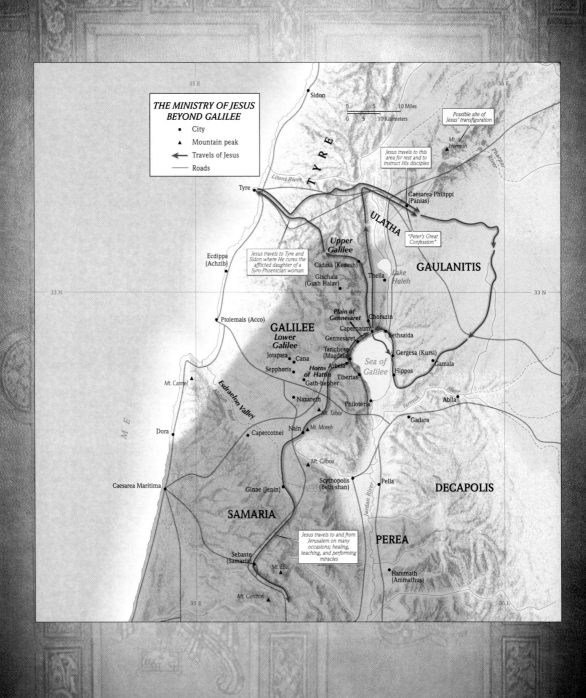

THE MINISTRY OF JESUS
BEYOND GALILEE

• City
▲ Mountain peak
← Travels of Jesus
— Roads

Possible site of
Jesus' transfiguration

Jesus travels to this
area for rest and to
instruct His disciples

Jesus travels to Tyre and
Sidon where He cures the
afflicted daughter of a
Syro-Phoenician woman

"Peter's Great
Confession"

Jesus travels to and from
Jerusalem on many
occasions; healing,
teaching, and performing
miracles

Sidon

TYRE
Litani River
Tyre
Ecdippa
(Achzib)

Upper
Galilee
Cadasa (Kedesh)
Glschala
(Gush Halav)

ULATHA
Caesarea-Philippi
(Panias)

Mt.
Hermon
PharPar
River

GAULANITIS

Thella
Lake
Huleh

Ptolemais (Acco)

GALILEE
Lower
Galilee

Jotapata
Sepphoris
Cana

Horns
of Hattin
Gath-hepher

Mt. Carmel

Esdraelon Valley

Dora

Nazareth

Capercotnei

Caesarea Maritima

Ginae (Jenin)

SAMARIA

Sebaste
(Samaria)

Mt. Ebal

Mt. Gerizim

Plain of
Gennesaret
Capernaum
Gennesaret
Taricheae
(Magdala)
Arbela
Tiberias

Sea of
Galilee

Chorazin

Bethsaida
Gergesa (Kursi)
Hippos
Gamala

Abila

Philoteria

Nain
Mt. Moreh
Mt. Tabor

Mt. Gilboa

Scythopolis
(Beth-shan)

Gadara

Yarmuk
River

Pella

Jordan River

DECAPOLIS

PEREA

Hammath
(Ammathus)

M E

35 E
36 E
33 N

0   5   10 Miles
0   5   10 Kilometers

35 E

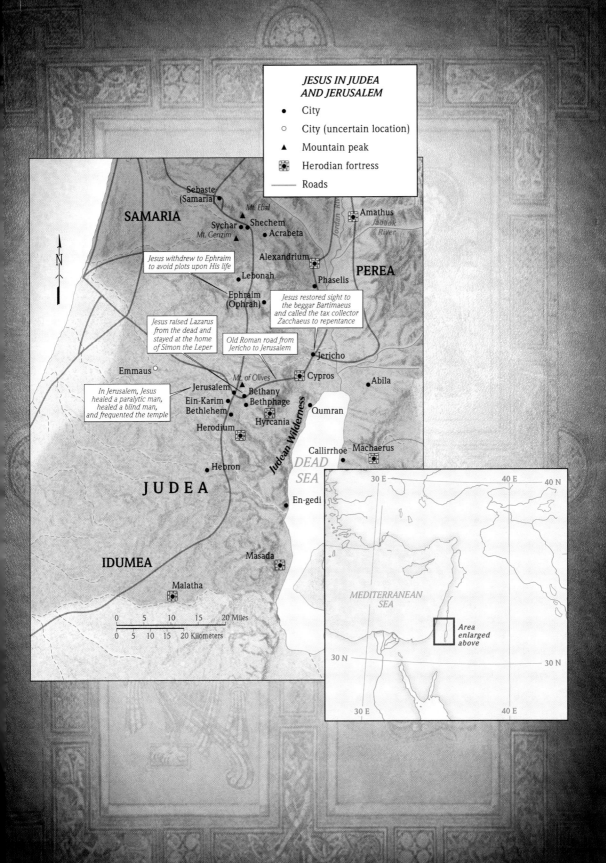

JESUS IN JUDEA AND JERUSALEM

- ● City
- ○ City (uncertain location)
- ▲ Mountain peak
- ⊞ Herodian fortress
- — Roads

SAMARIA

Sebaste (Samaria)

Mt. Ebal

Sychar
Mt. Gerizim

Shechem

Acrabeta

Amathus

Jabbok River

Jordan River

Jesus withdrew to Ephraim to avoid plots upon His life

Alexandrium

PEREA

Lebonah

Phaselis

Ephraim (Ophrah)

Jesus restored sight to the beggar Bartimaeus and called the tax collector Zacchaeus to repentance

Jesus raised Lazarus from the dead and stayed at the home of Simon the Leper

Old Roman road from Jericho to Jerusalem

Jericho

Emmaus

Mt. of Olives

Cypros

Abila

In Jerusalem, Jesus healed a paralytic man, healed a blind man, and frequented the temple

Jerusalem

Bethany

Ein-Karim

Bethphage

Bethlehem

Qumran

Herodium

Hyrcania

Callirrhoe

Machaerus

Judean Wilderness

DEAD SEA

JUDEA

Hebron

En-gedi

IDUMEA

Masada

Malatha

0   5   10   15   20 Miles

0   5   10   15   20 Kilometers

30 E   40 E   40 N

MEDITERRANEAN SEA

Area enlarged above

30 N   30 N

30 E   40 E

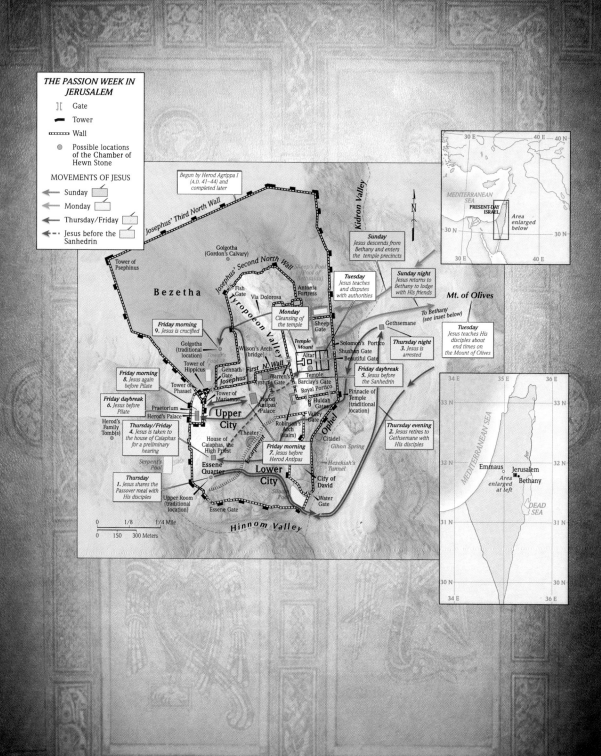

THE PASSION WEEK IN
JERUSALEM

][Gate

Tower

········· Wall

● Possible locations
of the Chamber of
Hewn Stone

MOVEMENTS OF JESUS

← Sunday

← Monday

← Thursday/Friday

⇠ Jesus before the
Sanhedrin

Begun by Herod Agrippa I
(A.D. 41–44) and
completed later

Josephus' Third North Wall

Golgotha
(Gordon's Calvary)

Sheep's Pool
(Pool of
Bethesda)

Bezetha

Josephus' Second North Wall

Fish
Gate

Via Dolorosa

Antonia
Fortress

Tower
of Psephinus

Kidron Valley

Sunday
Jesus descends from
Bethany and enters
the temple precincts

N

Tuesday
Jesus teaches
and disputes
with authorities

Sunday night
Jesus returns to
Bethany to lodge
with His friends

Mt. of Olives

Tyropoeon Valley

Monday
Cleansing of
the temple

Sheep
Gate

Temple
Mount

Altar

Gethsemane

To Bethany
(see inset below)

Tuesday
Jesus teaches His
disciples about
end times on
the Mount of Olives

Friday morning
9. Jesus is crucified

Golgotha
(traditional
location)

Wilson's Arch
(bridge)

Solomon's Portico
Shushan Gate
Beautiful Gate

Thursday night
3. Jesus is
arrested

Tower of
Hippicus

Gennath
Gate

First N. Wall

Josephus

Xystus

Warren's
Gate
Barclay's Gate
Royal Portico

Temple

Friday daybreak
5. Jesus before
the Sanhedrin

Friday morning
8. Jesus again
before Pilate

Tower
of Phasael

Tower of
Mariamne

Herod
Antipas'
Palace

Huldah
Gates

Pinnacle of
Temple
(traditional
location)

Friday daybreak
6. Jesus before
Pilate

Praetorium
Herod's Palace

Upper
City

Robinson's
Arch
(stairs)

Valley
Gate

Ophel

Thursday evening
2. Jesus retires to
Gethsemane with
His disciples

Herod's
Family
Tomb(s)

Thursday/Friday
4. Jesus is taken to
the house of Caiaphas
for a preliminary
hearing

House of
Caiaphas, the
High Priest

Theater

Escarpment

Friday morning
7. Jesus before
Herod Antipas

Citadel

Gihon Spring

Hezekiah's
Tunnel

Serpent's
Pool

Thursday
1. Jesus shares the
Passover meal with
His disciples

Essene
Quarter

Lower
City

City of
David

Water
Gate

Siloam
Pool

Upper Room
(traditional
location)

Essene Gate

Hinnom Valley

0   1/8   1/4 Mile

0   150   300 Meters

MEDITERRANEAN
SEA

30 E   40 E   40 N

PRESENT-DAY
ISRAEL

Area
enlarged
below

30 N   30 N

30 E   40 E

34 E   35 E   36 E

33 N   33 N

MEDITERRANEAN
SEA

32 N   32 N

Emmaus   Jerusalem
Bethany

Area
enlarged
at left

31 N   31 N

DEAD
SEA

34 E   36 E